The Myths of Plato

The Myths of Plato

Originally translated
and introduced by
J. A. STEWART, M.A.,
late tutor of Christ Church
and White's Professor of
Moral Philosophy in the
University of Oxford; Hon.
Ll.D., Edinburgh; and
now edited and newly
introduced by

G. R. LEVY, M.A., F.S.A.

BARNES AND NOBLE INC.

1970

First published 1905

Editor's introduction and translations
© Centaur Press Ltd., 1960

Reprinted 1970

SBN 389–01057–X

*This edition, edited and introduced
by G. R. Levy, was first published
1960 by the Centaur Press Ltd.,
now of Fontwell, Sussex.*

*Printed in Great Britain by
Stephen Austin and Sons Ltd., Hertford*

PREFACE TO THE FIRST EDITION

The object of this volume is to furnish the reader with material for estimating the characteristics and influence of Plato the Mythologist, or Prophet, as distinguished from Plato the Dialectician, or Reasoner.

In order to effect this special object within a reasonable space, it was necessary to extract the Myths from the Dialogues in which they occur, with only the shortest possible indication of the Context in each case, and to confine the Observations to the Myths as individual pieces and as a series. The reader, therefore, must not expect to find in the Observations on, say, the *Phaedo* Myth or the *Phaedrus* Myth a Study of the *Phaedo* or the *Phaedrus*.

The Greek text printed opposite the Translations and followed by them throughout, except in a few places where preferred readings are given in footnotes, is that of Stallbaum's *All Plato's Works contained in one Volume* (1867).*

I owe a large debt of gratitude to two friends for help received.

Professor J. S. Phillimore read all the Translations through in proof with the most friendly care; and errors which may be detected in these Translations will, I feel sure, turn out to be in places where, from some cause or other, I may have failed to make proper use of his suggestions.

---

* Editor's Note.—The text upon which the translations are founded, is omitted from the present edition, for the reason given on p. 5 below.

The other friend who helped me, Frederick York Powell, is gone. A few weeks before his last illness began to cause serious anxiety to his friends, he read through all the Translations in manuscript up to the *Phaedrus* Myth, inclusive, and I read to him nearly the whole of the Introduction, and also other parts, especially those relating to the Theory of Poetry. The help he then gave me by his suggestive and sympathetic discussion of various points closed a long series of acts of friendship on which I shall always look back with a feeling of deep gratitude.

J. A. STEWART.

Oxford, *December* 1904.

ACKNOWLEDGMENTS

The Editor would like to thank Mrs. H. Groenewegen-Frankfort for sound criticism and advice, and Professor Leon Roth for permission to quote from his letter about Stewart as a teacher.

For permission to produce this new edition, the Publishers wish to thank Miss M. E. Stewart, Miss H. M. Stewart, A. H. A. Stewart, Esq., and Mrs. A. M. R. Wilson.

INTRODUCTION TO THE SECOND EDITION

It is more than fifty years since the publication of this book first recalled the attention of English scholars to the organic importance of Plato's Myths, as a unit in that upsurge of discovery which was just then opening a vista of the emotional and spiritual aspects of Greek religion, long buried under the pressure of Olympian orthodoxy. This was a result of the recent archaeological discoveries of a prehellenic civilization.

Jane Harrison, writing to Gilbert Murray of *The Doctrine of Ideas*, which was Stewart's successor to *The Myths of Plato*, shows immediate recognition of his part in a movement of which she was the centre: "It explains why thinking is no good unless one feels and is excited. It gives me the psychology of ecstasy." This was what Stewart calls 'Transcendental Feeling'.

The researches of half a century since then, especially in anthropology and psychology, have broadened and deepened the general understanding of Myths, and in doing so they show Stewart's introduction to be a little restricted, a little too closely confined to the literary analogies which he understood so well. But he was the first Englishman of his time to recognize their universal nature in contrast to Allegory, which is the illustration of a particular theme, and also their importance in Plato's method of imparting knowledge: "A Myth cannot deceive, as a doctrine can." True, he is more concerned with establishing poetic affinities than religious ones, but if they matter to him first as literature, it is a literature sacred for its beauty.

It had, indeed, taken many centuries after Plato's death before the religious significance of the Myths was accepted

and studied, and through Neoplatonism enriched Christian
and Moslem philosophy, and helped to create the Renaissance.

Since Stewart's time, the religious aspect of Platonism,
in which the Myths play so vital a part, has received increasing attention, especially from French scholars, who
have upheld the unity which Stewart perceived aesthetically.

At the present time there are sources in use, which he
left untapped, for reasons which will become clear in the
course of this summary. These will show how true an
instinct caused him to publish the Myths together, and apart
from their settings in Plato's dialogues, to form a body whose
structure can now be made available to a much wider
public than he could ever have had in mind. With this
object in view, the Greek text has been removed from the
new edition, leaving intact Stewart's translations which
formerly faced the Greek page by page. In his introduction
and intermediate commentaries, the many quotations from
Greek and Latin literature and from Dante, together with
the notes of a few French and German scholars, have been
replaced by translations for which the Editor is responsible,
the originals being allowed to remain in two cases only,
where the argument depends upon their style. The illustra-
tions from English poetry, and from folklore, have been
retained in their sometimes excessive length, for to interfere
with these would weaken the book's character.

Again, the Greek technical terms formerly interspersed
through the text, have been replaced by their nearest
English equivalents, thereby inevitably losing some of their
metaphysical reverberations.

THE PLACE OF MYTH IN THE PLATONIC DIALOGUES

Plato's whole plan for the dissemination of philosophy
in writing was a continuation of personal relationships, not
the perpetuation of a doctrine. This attitude kept it always
on the level of fluid enquiry, so that it remains alive today,
receiving its spiritual nourishment from the prophetic
personality of Socrates. Such a method already existed in
the relationship of Pythagoras to his school, which attributed

to the Founder all its individual discoveries. Because of the practice of Socrates also, Plato's written philosophy was kept at the level of conversation, or, as Stewart acutely observes, his researches took the form of drama in which the arguments themselves were characters. Here again, Plato's youthful study of dramatic art, before he burnt his plays on the altar of discipleship, was reborn in the art of dialectic. Into this setting the Myths were fitted without awkwardness, like the choric songs of the older drama, and sometimes even like the *deus ex machina*, the God from the Machine, to introduce a new dimension into the sphere of action.

The pupil and teacher relationship (which has its closest parallels in Hinduism and Buddhism), is briefly described in the *Phaedrus* and *The Republic*, but Stewart was unable to use the richest material now available, which shows once and for all the place of philosophy in Plato's regard, as a preparatory mental discipline, before that flash of light is suddenly kindled, which lifts teacher and pupil on to a new level of mutual understanding, whose test of authority lies in the place (he calls it a garden in the *Phaedrus*) where thoughts begin to nourish themselves.

This is the Seventh Letter, in which the aged Plato explains to the people of Syracuse his failure to convert their former ruler, the younger Dionysius, to the practice of philosophy. In Stewart's days the authenticity of the Letters, which have come down to us under Plato's name, was strongly doubted, but in the light of present linguistic analysis, most scholars now consider some of them at least, and in particular the seventh, to be genuine. In this letter he argues that the highest truths can never be written down, and that any such dissertation, if it existed, would fail to express its author's deepest knowledge. This bears some analogy to the methods, unknown to Stewart, of Ch'an and Zen in the Far East, and the "ear-whispered teaching" of the "beyond" in Tibet.[1] It simply explains the place of Myth in Plato's philosophy, which calls upon

---

[1] See, for instance, A. David-Neel & Lama Yongden, *The Secret Oral Teachings of the Buddhist Sects*, 1959, *passim*.

the kind of consciousness that is outside logic. Revelation is sudden, however long, arduous and necessary that preparation may have been, which the self-indulgent Dionysius would not endure. But it only opens the way to further research, for teacher and pupil alike.

A passage in *The Laws* shows the Myth as indisputable agent of such an unforced conversion:

Athenian stranger: "The true city will be named after God, who is the real ruler of men of enlightenment."

Cleinias: "But who is this God?"

Athenian stranger: "Ah, there for a little we must make use of Myth."

There follows the story of the Golden Age, in which men were governed, not by earthly rulers, but by a race of divinities, "since oxen are not set above oxen". So cities can be governed by Law in obedience to the Immortal who still survives within us,[1] and that Law will not become a dead letter.

But for every Myth he is accustomed to use a different means of introducing the break in the dramatic dialogue, and of disclaiming it as his own creation. "I am not good at inventing stories", says his spokesman Socrates. Stewart has gathered a bunch of these impersonal openings, whose diversity may hide a subjective, and therefore, perhaps, a universal, origin. Plato may attribute it to "The Wise" (under which name he sometimes refers to the Pythagoreans) or, as in the *Meno*, to "those priests and priestesses whose continual study it is", or "the Stranger from Mantinea", who is the initiatory priestess of the *Symposium*. In *The Laws* it is simply "a tale that we have received", in *The Republic*, "the tale will preserve us from perishing. Let us believe it, that we may be loving and beloved in both worlds." In *The Statesman*, "Be a child and listen." At the hour of desperate need in the *Phaedo*, "we must sing the tale over to ourselves like an incantation", and earlier in the same dialogue, "It may well be that those to whom we owe the Mysteries have long ago hinted at the truth. I shall find good friends and teachers there as here."

---

[1] In the *Phaedo*, 'To be our Guide through life and death'.

In the *Phaedrus* it runs: "Only a God could say what the soul is. We can merely tell what it is like." But here, in the exaltation of the ultimate vision, he does say: "For a man must speak truly when speaking of the truth."

It can now be demonstrated that this obliquity of approach to the incommunicable mystery does open the way to a common if mobile system beneath the self-existence of every myth, even if the system itself is regarded as a myth. As in other very original products of genius, none of it is simply new, but the principle of its coherence has received new life.

Bemused by the richness of this variety, Stewart treats each myth as a thing apart (to the reader's great enjoyment), without endeavouring to reach a central theme. Yet his very action in publishing them together, and separated from their dialogues, implies the recognition of a unity of kind, though not of purpose.

THE BASIS OF THE GREAT MYTHS

The fall and redemption of the soul is a conception which can be traced right back to the descent of the divine ancestors of primitive totemic clans, and becomes visible in historic Greece in the "disappearances and new births and sufferings and wanderings" of Dionysus, as a doctrine of Orphism, drawn into philosophy by Empedocles and Pythagoras.

It is the pivotal theme which holds together all the great Myths, whether they treat of earthly life, as in the tale of men chained in an underground cavern, which opens the seventh book of *The Republic*, or its related existence between lives, as in the *Gorgias*, the *Phaedo*, *Phaedrus* and the Vision of Er.

Stewart calls these last, *eschatological*, that is, to do with last things, because he has not recognised the law of cycles which is their connecting link, and Perceval Frutiger, writing his *Mythes de Platon* twenty-five years after the publication of Stewart's book, still retains that title, though he has made a table showing twelve constant features of the series, and chief among them the following:

1. The divine origin of the soul.

2. Fall of the soul.
3. Expiation in the cycle of births and deaths.
4. Reminiscence as the instrument of salvation.
5. Judgment.
6. Liberation of the Blessed.

To each of these, and others of less importance, he attaches three parallels, or sources, of Plato's symbolism. These three are Pindar, Empedocles, and the well-known gold tablets found in graves among the Greek colonies of Southern Italy and Sicily, and more rarely in Crete, Attica, and once in Rome. They are usually called Orphic, and have appeared chiefly in regions of Pythagorean influence. Some of these belong to Plato's own time, and all appear to be fragments of a single poem, part of which is quoted by Stewart in connection with the Vision of Er.

The poem takes the form of a Guide for the newly discarnate soul, in the form of question and answer, from which it appears that the successful accomplishment of the journey depends upon an affirmation of the soul's divine origin, of its payment for past sin, its rebirth in the bosom of the "pure Queen of those below", and escape by this means from "the sorrowful wheel" of earthly existence. The soul must show in word and action its memory of certain rites, and in this it resembles those of many primitive peoples, such as the inhabitants of some of the islands in the New Hebrides, whose newly-dead are required to complete diagrams half-effaced in the sand, to prove that they have passed through the required initiations in their lifetime (which were a rehearsal for this journey), before they can enter the cave of the dead, and reach the immortality which lies beyond it.[1]

We do, indeed, possess two complete documents which fulfil or have fulfilled, in civilized nations, the functions of such a passport and guide. These are the Egyptian and Tibetan Books of the Dead. The latter in particular, which is still in general use, contains a description of life between the worlds, which its philosophical commentators treat as

[1] J. Layard, *The Stone Men of Malekula, Vao*, 1942, p. 255.

mythical, that is, as subjective, and which resembles in many particulars Plato's Vision of Er. Both, for instance, lay great stress on Memory, which governs the soul's choice of its rebirth.[1]

Stewart's introduction is, as we saw, more directly concerned with the literary than the metaphysical position of these Myths—an attitude which rouses Frutiger's indignation (he calls it superficial). It seems right and natural, however, in one to whom poetry stands for the whole *theoria*, or imaginative reason (what Wordsworth calls the feeling intellect) which Plato himself, like the Pythagoreans before him, regarded as his aim. But Stewart, following Dieterich in his *Nekyia*, does place a supposed Orphic *Descent into Hades* as a source of the Vision of Er, and suggests that Pindar, during his Sicilian sojourn, may have been influenced by its teaching, or we should say more correctly perhaps, by a body of teaching of which these tablets are the only written testimony. And Frutiger, no more than Stewart, carries his very significant analogies to the wider world of Eastern religion which F. M. Cornford had opened to English students of early Greek philosophy in the years which followed the publication of Stewart's books.

Here the body of analogy is almost equally striking, and extends to a use of symbols and metaphors, some of which seem only explicable in the light of a common source, whether they are considered as developments out of an earlier psychological meeting ground, or of isolated contacts which may have heralded those missionary labours known to have existed in the centuries that followed Plato's death, after Alexander had torn down the curtain between Greek and 'Barbarian'.[2]

The testimony of the Myths shows the division to lie between a body of belief shared in general with the Greek mystical philosophy already formulated before Socrates and analogous with much of the cyclic cosmology of the con-

---

[1] W. Y. Evans-Wentz, *The Tibetan Book of the Dead*. Third edition, 1957, p. 183, and note 2.

See also p. 99 (endeavour to maintain an unbroken continuity of consciousness), and p. 100 (the soul's wanderings because it cannot retain its memory of the Clear Light).

[2] See W. W. Tarn, *The Greeks in Bactria and India*, 1951. A. K. Narain, *The Indo-Greeks*, 1957.

temporary Indian schools, and the linear Semitic faiths of prophecy and historic drama, and somewhere between them, Zoroaster.

A mind so uniquely original as Plato's can afford to make full use of the researches of other minds, but since it also brings fresh life into everything that it touches, the possibility of a reciprocal movement cannot be ignored, with a caution not to regard it as a one-way passage of influence.

In this connection, a glance at two of Plato's metaphors may prove instructive. The Soul-chariot of the *Phaedrus* already appears in the Upanishads, and in the *Bhagavad Gita* is the symbolic basis of the whole poem. But it is found later in the *Questions of Milinda*, where a Greek king (Menander) is instructed in Buddhism during the brief period of Hellenistic political influence.[1] Here it may have penetrated from the West.

The Tree of Man, with roots above and branches below, which appears in the *Timaeus*, also opens one of the cantos of the *Bhagavad Gita*, where the banyan tree is a natural image, but one which Plato could not have known. Therefore he seems likely to have borrowed it from an Eastern source.

THE SOUL IN ITS CYCLE OF LIFE AND DEATH

If these myths are to be regarded as parts of an organic whole, the question may well be asked, what is it that makes the descent and return?

The answer is by no means easy, for it varies with every dialogue, beginning with the *Gorgias*, which treats solely of the judgment of the naked soul by its semi-divine predecessors. In the early *Phaedo*, the soul is simply *nous*, the imaginative reason, and the way home is assimilation with God (*homoiosis*). In the final myth of the dialogue it is a human entity under the charge of a divinity, its individual daemon, through life and death. This is the self-chosen daemon of the end of *The Republic*, where the discarnate souls again appear as single beings, bearing beneath the

---

[1] *Milindapanha*, trans. T. W. Rhys-Davids, S.B.E. 35, 36.

throne of Necessity the records of past deeds, though in the body of the dialogue the soul has been analysed as tripartite, composed of the qualities of reason, activity and desire, like the Hindu *gunas*. Presumably the lower selves are not shed at death. They might rather be considered as absorbed, since their memory is carried on, to determine the fate and character of future lives. Absorbed, that is, into the integrated souls. For the rest, their choice is "pitiable and laughable and wonderful". But the *Cratylus* describes the philosopher's hunger for truth in the realm where alone it can be satisfied: "The God of the Dead knows all beauty, and holds his people in willing chains, for his fetters are the desire which in disembodied souls is stronger than necessity, the desire for wisdom."[1]

But then the philosopher will soon be free (in three lives only) from the "sorrowful, weary wheel".

When, in the *Phaedrus*, Plato says that All-Soul has care of the inanimate as Zeus cares for all things, he implies (as Hackforth points out)[2] the identity of the Soul with God. Within the myth the soul is seen as a struggling triplicity, united only when the Charioteer, following the cyclic procession of the Gods ("for envy has no place in the heavenly Choir"), drives his horses above the sky. Its fall into birth is due to forgetfulness of the Forms beyond the Heavens, in the frantic disunion of the steeds.

In the *Meno*, on the authority of Pindar, the soul in its cyclic journey is said to pay the penalty of ancient woe; Plato's single reference to the Orphic fall of the Titan ancestors of mankind who dismembered and devoured the child Dionysus, except for one mention of "our titanic nature", as we should say "the old Adam".

In the *Timaeus* the seed of divinity, fallen from the stars, is attached to a lower soul in which are terrible and indispensable passions, tethered to the divine Genius like a wild beast. But in this cosmological setting the fall is not the result of sin, whether of forgetfulness or loss of control, but occurs by divine foresight, in accordance with the Creator's plan for making the world "as like himself as possible".

---

[1] Plato, *Cratylus*, 403-4.
[2] R. Hackforth, *Phaedrus*, 1952.

In *The Laws* again, where "the ideas are melting into God",[1] Plato attributes to the World-Soul, and therefore to the individual soul in its true nature, much beside the God-like *nous*, for that which incarnates, by a law of spiritual gravitation resembling that of the Hindu *karma* (here treated psychologically where it was cosmic in the *Timaeus*) takes along with it the results of its past.

The problem of combining all these conceptions did not arise for Stewart, for whom the Myths were intrinsically separated from each other. But if a common basis exists, the contradictions may be no different in nature from the modes of approach, such contradictions being inherent in the images of mythical thinking, which can represent more than one conception at once.

THE SYSTEM. ITS RELATION WITH REALITY

Does this fluid system, to which each Myth contributed a different approach, represent Plato's own religion? Stewart is undoubtedly right in regarding it as poetry, but even the orthodox religion of the Greeks was, after all, a legacy from Homer and Hesiod. There was no Book of the Law. The seventh Letter describes how such a book would have shut mankind, in Plato's view. from living religious experience.

As poetry, on the contrary, the Olympian magic was so much alive that it has continued to inspire the poets and painters of the West down to modern times. But Plato, like his predecessors in Italy and Ionia, chose, as we saw, the older, more universal, body of beliefs, a revival from the prehellenic world (upon whose degenerate manifestations he constantly poured scorn), to reclothe his own vision of reality, his certainty of the wholeness of the divine order. The doubts of the atheist in *The Laws* arise, as Solmsen[2] has pointed out, because he does not see himself as part of the whole. The sin of the two lovers who lose their wings in the *Phaedrus*, is of the same nature.

The relation of the One to the Many is the distinguishing characteristic of this philosophy, which had a long history

---

[1] Rudolf Otto's phrase.
[2] F. Solmsen, *Plato's Theology*, Cornell, 1942.

before Plato, both in India and among the first scientific thinkers of Ionia and Italy, and the divine origin and return of the soul to God is its natural religious correlative there as here. What is peculiar to Plato is the method of salvation by imaginative participation in the world of Forms, or Ideas; the method at work in all the great Myths except the Vision of Er, which is more directly concerned with Fate and Freewill. Its earthly instrument is Memory.

This is where the cleavage appears between the Platonic and Indian systems whose conceptions of world-order so closely resemble it. Because of its permeation by the world of Forms the physical world is no mere illusion. The two great Myths of *The Republic* show the contemplation of reality, whether in life or death, as man's preparation for self conquest in the world of action, either in the midst of hostility which his glimpse of the Ideas provokes on his return to the Cave (as its memory provokes scorn after his rebirth in the *Phaedrus*) or in the reconciliation of death and rebirth at the dialogue's close, "that we may be friends with ourselves and with the Gods".

Stewart passes lightly over the Myth of the Cave, and does not even translate it, because he, with certain other scholars, regards it as an Allegory—surely with insufficient reason. He rightly points out that the greatest mythographers such as Plato and Dante, use allegory only as incidental material (Plato repudiates it in the *Phaedrus* as a substitute for myth), but the universal application of this tale is made quite clear in the opening scene: "Strange prisoners!" exclaims Glaucon. "They resemble ourselves," is Socrates' reply.

The soul's imprisonment and release to the light is indeed the subject of all those visions which Stewart classifies as eschatological, but are themselves no more than incidents in the single tremendous myth of the soul's cyclic journey. Those, therefore, which deal with earthly life cannot be detached from the scenes of discarnate existence.

"This roofed-in Cave" appears already as a source of the psychological nostalgia of the Sicilian poet-philosopher Empedocles, though he found no saviour to rescue his

exiled Daemon, the divinity within him, from its imprisonment in the flesh. But in several works of Plato the Daemon
himself is guardian and saviour of humanity "to his great
joy and our own". Stewart justly stresses the importance
of these intermediaries in Plato's imaginative world. But
in the omitted Myth of the Cave the rescuer is a human
being, a kind of Socrates, who is painfully forced up the
steep ascent out of the bondage of illusion, into the fellowship of sunlit existences of which he has hitherto watched
the shadows, only to return yet more painfully to set his
fellow prisoners free.

This is most important as the first recorded association
in the West, of liberation through enlightenment followed
by its renunciation, which was to become the central object
of faith to Northern Buddhism. It should therefore not be
cast aside.

"You do not seem aware," is the rebuke to the young
infidel in *The Laws*, "that every creation is for the sake of
the whole." That awareness, the logical corollary of Plato's
vision of the universe as a living creature, "only begotten"
of God, is of sharing (*methexis*) as both a natural and a
moral law. For this Myth of the Cave is introduced into
The Republic to make clear the vocation of the Guardians
of the earthly city, who must leave their contemplation of
the world of transcendent light to assume the burden of
government.

Psychologically associated with escape from the Cave is
the True Earth of the Phaedo, from whose hollows men
rise up like fishes out of the sea, to look upon as much of
the truth as they can endure. In contrast with the Tibetan
Book of the Dead, where the forms seen between the worlds
must be recognized as the stuff of dream, they must be
held to in the *Phaedrus* as the saving reality. In the *Timaeus*
the Creator fashions the Universe itself, the Only-Begotten,
on the pattern of that which is not begotten.

The two expositions of illumination by Beauty, which
appear to be most clearly Plato's own, and to have fewest
links with Eastern mysticism, are the two which make
direct reference to the Mysteries of Eleusis—the *Phaedrus*

recalling the image of the divine Child in his winged chariot
and *The Symposium* that of the Sacred Marriage. The
stages of transformation in *The Symposium* from earthly to
heavenly love, foreshadow those described by St. Teresa
and St. John of the Cross, and analysed by the mediaeval
Moslem philosophers. Stewart did not use these com-
parisons in the present book, but he had found them when
he wrote *The Doctrine of Ideas*, which was published four
years later. Indeed the discourse of Diotima in *The
Symposium*, which begins with an allegory of Love as the
daemonic child of Plenty and Poverty, does not develop
into a Myth in the full meaning of the term, but into a
description of mystical experience, and before the debate
of which it is the culmination, Socrates, its narrator, had
stood entranced in a neighbouring portico. So also, the
complex exposition of the *Phaedrus*, which passes through
the stages of scientific definition, allegory, myth, and the
Mysteries, is introduced by a warning from the daemon, or
inner voice, of Socrates, who is also encouraged by the
unseen presences of trees and water, to break away from
the artificial argument of the earlier dialogue, into the pure
and happy realm of imaginative comprehension. Then he
prays: "May the inward and outward man be at one."

Thus Plato, so intensely aware of invisible existence
"comprehensible to the Mind which is the only true Lord
of the soul," is a man "to whom the physical world exists,"
as Pater said of him. It exists because the apprehension of
beauty can be carried intellectually to the very brink of
enlightenment: "For sight is the keenest of our bodily
senses, but not by that is Wisdom seen."

Stewart's preoccupation, therefore, throughout his introduction to the Myths, with the poet in the philosopher,
and his constant reference to literary analogies, here receives
its final justification.

As there can be few now who remember him personally,
it might serve a useful purpose to end these notes with a
passage from a letter recently received from Prof. Leon
Roth: " . . . The other class was in Plotinus, and was a
very different affair. It was held in J. A. Stewart's private
house. There was no weighing of parallel passages and

alternative readings, only a cameo-like head silhouetted against the window, and a voice speaking almost to itself about the eternal truths of the spiritual life as they were reflected, partially and inadequately, on the page before us . . . We started with four, and then there were three, then two, then (alas) one. But *tres faciunt collegium*, and with Stewart talking I always felt we were not alone."

G. R. LEVY.

CONTENTS

Pages

PREFACE TO THE FIRST EDITION

1-2

ACKNOWLEDGMENTS FOR THE SECOND EDITION

3

INTRODUCTION TO THE SECOND EDITION

4-17

INTRODUCTION TO THE FIRST EDITION

1. The Platonic Drama—Two elements to be distinguished in it : Argumentative Conversation and Myth   24-27
2. General remarks on Story-telling—Primitive Story-telling described as Stories, or Myths, are (1) Simply Anthropological and Zoological; (2) Aetiological; (3) Eschatological— A Myth, as distinguished from an Allegory, has no Moral or Other-meaning   27-44
3. Plato's Myths distinguished from Allegories—To what experience, to what "Part of the Soul", does the Platonic Myth appeal? To that part which expresses itself, not in "theoretic judgments", but in "value-judgments", or rather "value-feelings"—The effect produced in us by the Platonic Myth is essentially that produced by Poetry; "Transcendental Feeling," the sense of the overshadowing presence of "That which was, and is, and ever shall be", is awakened in us— Passages from the Poets, quoted to exemplify the production of this effect   44-64
4. "Transcendental Feeling" explained genetically as the reflection in Consciousness of the Life of the "Vegetative Part of the Soul", the fundamental principle in us, and in all living creatures, which silently, in timeless sleep, makes the assumption on which the whole rational life of Conduct and Science rests, the assumption that "Life is worth living", that there is a Cosmos, in which, and of which, it is good to be— "Transcendental Feeling" is thus Solemn Sense of Timeless Being, and Conviction that Life is good, and is the beginning and end of Metaphysics—It is with the production of the first of these two phases of "Transcendental Feeling" that the Platonic Myth, and Poetry generally, are chiefly concerned—The Platonic Myth rouses and regulates this mode of "Transcendental Feeling" for the use of Conduct and Science   64-67

CONTENTS

19

Pages

5. The Platonic Myth rouses and regulates "Transcendental Feeling" by (1) Imaginative Representation of Ideas of Reason, and (2) Imaginative Deduction of "Categories of the Understanding" and "Moral Virtues"—Distinction between "Ideas" and "Categories" implicit in Plato—Kant's distinction explained—Why does Plato employ Myth when he "represents" Ideas of Reason, Soul, Cosmos, God, and when he "deduces" Categories of the Understanding and Moral Virtues?   67-76

6. Plato's treatment of the "Idea of God"   76-85

7. Plato's treatment of the "Idea of Soul"—Agnosticism of Plato's day with regard to the Immortality of the Soul—Influence of Orphic Belief as felt by Pindar and Plato—Plato's Eschatological Myths plainly reproduce the matter of Orphic teaching   85-97

8. Summary of Introductory Observations in the form of a defence of Plato against a charge brought against him by Kant, *Critique of Pure Reason*, Introduction, §3—Plato's Myths (roughly distinguished as (1) representing Ideas of Reason, or Ideals, and (2) deducing Categories, Faculties, Virtues, *i.e.* tracing them back to their origins) will be taken in the following order: (*a*) as representing Ideas of Reason, the *Phaedo* Myth, the *Gorgias* Myth, the Myth of Er (the three Eschatological Myths *par excellence*), the *Politicus* Myth together with the Myth of the Golden Age, the *Protagoras* Myth (Aetiological Myths), and the Discourse of Timaeus; (*b*) as chiefly concerned with the deduction of Categories or Virtues, the *Phaedrus* Myth, the *Meno* Myth, and the Myth told by Aristophanes and Discourse of Diotima in the *Symposium;* (*c*) the Atlantis Myth and the Myth of the Earth-born, which respectively represent the Ideals and deduce the Categories of the Nation, as distinguished from the Individual   97-102

THE *PHAEDO* MYTH

Context of the Myth   103
Translation   104-111

OBSERVATIONS ON THE *PHAEDO* MYTH

1. Plato's method of giving verisimilitude to Myth, by bringing it into conformity with the "Modern Science" of his day, illustrated from the *Phaedo*, and paralleled from Henry More   112-119

2. The subject of the last section further illustrated by reference to the parallel between Plato's Geography of Tartarus and the "True Surface of the Earth" and Dante's Geography of Hell, Purgatory, and the Earthly Paradise—The parallelism between Plato and Dante dwelt on chiefly with the view of suggesting the method by which we may best understand the function of Myth in the Platonic Philosophy, the method of sealing the impression made on us by the Myth of one great master by the study of the Myth of another with whom we may happen to be in closer sympathy   119-131

Pages

3. The distinction between Dogma and Myth insisted upon by
Socrates, *Phaedo*, 114 D—"Moral Responsibility" the *motif*
of the *Phaedo* Myth   131-132

THE *GORGIAS* MYTH

Context   133
Translation   134-138

OBSERVATIONS ON THE *GORGIAS* MYTH

1. "Moral Responsibility" is the *motif* of the *Gorgias* Myth, as it is
of the *Phaedo* Myth—The *Gorgias* Myth sets forth, in a Vision
of Judgment, Penance, and Purification, the continuity and
sameness of the Active, as distinguished from the Passive,
Self, the Self as actively developing its native power under
the discipline of correction, not as being the mere victim of
vengeance—Death as Philosopher   139-141
2. The mystery of the infinite difference between Vice with Large
Opportunity and Vice with Narrow Opportunity   142-143
3. Observations on Tablets affixed to the Judged Souls, on the
Meadow of Judgment, and on the Three Ways   143-145

THE MYTH OF ER

Context   146
Translation   147-156

OBSERVATIONS ON THE MYTH OF ER

1. Cosmography and Geography of the Myth   157-160
2. Dante's Lethe and Eunoè taken in connection with the Orphic
Ritual and Mythology, to which Plato is largely indebted
for his account of the Soul's Purification as a Process of
Forgetting and Remembering   160-168
3. More about the Cosmography and Geography of the Myth—
The Pillar of Light, the Spindle of Necessity, the Model of
the Cosmos in the lap of Necessity   168-175
4. The great philosophical question raised and solved in the Myth,
How to reconcile "Free Will" with the "Reign of Law"   175-178

THE *POLITICUS* MYTH

Introductory Remarks   179-181
Context   181
Translation   182-189
Translation of the Myth of the Golden Age   190-191

CONTENTS

Pages

OBSERVATIONS ON THE *POLITICUS* MYTH

1. Relation of the *Politicus* Myth to the "Science" of Plato's day   192-193

2. Is Plato "in earnest" in supposing that God, from time to time, withdraws from the government of the World?   193-194

3. Resurrection and Metempsychosis   194-196

4. "The Problem of Evil" raised in the *Politicus* Myth—How does Plato suppose the solution of this problem to be furthered by an Aetiological Myth like that of the *Politicus?*—The value of Aetiological Myth as helping us to "solve" a "universal difficulty" as distinguished from a "particular difficulty"—It helps us to "put by" the former kind of difficulty—The *Kalewala* quoted to illustrate the function of Aetiological Myth—The Story of the Birth of Iron—Transition from the *Politicus* Myth to the "Creation Myths" strictly so called, the *Protagoras* Myth, and the Discourse of Timaeus   196-207

THE *PROTAGORAS* MYTH

Context of the Myth   208
Translation   209-211

OBSERVATIONS ON THE *PROTAGORAS* MYTH

1. Is it a "Platonic Myth", or only a "Sophistic Apologue"?—It is a true Myth, as setting forth *a priori* elements in man's experience   212-214

2. It sets forth the distinction between the "mechanical" and the "teleological" explanation of the World and its parts—It raises the question discussed in Kant's *Critique of Judgment*   214-218

3. Account given in the Myth of the Origin of Virtue as distinguished from Art   218-221

4. A Sculptured Myth, the Prometheus Sarcophagus in the Capitoline Museum   221-222

5. The difference between Myth and Allegory—Sketch of the History of Allegorical Interpretation—The interpreters of Homer and of Greek Mythology—Philo—The Christian Fathers—The Neo-Platonists—Dante—Plato's Allegory of the Cave (which is a Myth as well as an Allegory)—His Allegory of the Disorderly Crew—Allegory and Myth compared with Ritual   222-251

THE *TIMAEUS*

Context   252
Translation   253-272

OBSERVATIONS ON THE *TIMAEUS*

1. General observations on its scope   273-277

2. Purification and Metempsychosis   277-279

3. On the Creation of Souls   279-280

Pages

THE *PHAEDRUS* MYTH

Context of the Myth   281
Translation   282-296

OBSERVATIONS ON THE *PHAEDRUS* MYTH

1. Preliminary   297
2. The *Phaedrus* Myth as giving a "Deduction" of the Categories of
   the Understanding—But it also sets forth the Ideas of Reason 298-300
3. The doctrines of Recollection, Love, Immortality—The *Meno*
   Myth translated, and compared with the *Phaedrus* Myth—
   In what sense is the "Doctrine of Ideas" "mythical"?   300-310
4. The Number 729   310-311
5. The celestial, or astronomical, *mise en scène* of the "History of
   the Soul" in the *Phaedrus* Myth, and the importance of that
   mise en scène for subsequent philosophical and religious
   thought down to Dante   311-343
6. Poetic Inspiration   344-357

THE TWO *SYMPOSIUM* MYTHS

Context of the Myths   358

I.—THE MYTH TOLD BY ARISTOPHANES

Translation   359-363

GENERAL OBSERVATIONS ON THE MYTH

and comparison with the Zagreus Myth and with Rabelais   364-369

II.—THE DISCOURSE OF DIOTIMA

Translation   370-377

OBSERVATIONS ON THE DISCOURSE OF DIOTIMA

1. The Discourse at once an Allegory and a Myth—May be taken
   as a study of the Prophetic Temperament—The nature of
   Prophecy   378-384
2. The History of the Doctrine of Daemons   384-401

GENERAL OBSERVATIONS ON MYTHS

WHICH SET FORTH THE NATION'S, AS DISTINGUISHED FROM
THE INDIVIDUAL'S, IDEALS AND CATEGORIES

Myths in which we have the spectacle of a Nation's life, (*a*) led on
  by a Vision of its Future, (*b*) conditioned by its Past. These
  are (*a*) the Atlantis Myth in the *Timaeus* and *Critias*, which,
  taken in connection with the account of the Ideal State in
  the *Republic*, sets forth the Vision of an Hellenic Empire; (*b*)
  the Myth of the Earth-born in the *Republic*   402-407

Pages

THE ATLANTIS MYTH

Abbreviated translation, or rendering   408-415

OBSERVATIONS ON THE ATLANTIS MYTH

The Geology and Geography of the Myth   416-420

THE MYTH OF THE EARTH-BORN

Translation   421-422

Note on the Myth of the Earth-born   422

CONCLUSION—THE MYTHOLOGY AND METAPHYSICS OF THE CAMBRIDGE PLATONISTS

The "Cambridge Platonists" represent Plato the Mythologist, or
   Prophet, rather than Plato the Dialectician, or Reasoner,
   and in this respect are important for the understanding of
   our modern English "Idealists", who, it is contended, are
   "Platonists" of the same kind as Cudworth and his associates 423-468

INDEX

469-481

INTRODUCTION TO THE FIRST EDITION

1. THE PLATONIC DRAMA

The Platonic Dialogue may be broadly described as a Drama in which speech is the action,[1] and Socrates and his companions are the actors. The speech in which the action consists is mainly that of argumentative conversation in which, although Socrates or another may take a leading part, yet everybody has his say. The conversation or argument is always about matters which can be profitably discussed—that is, matters on which men form workaday opinions which discussion may show to be right or wrong, wholly or in part.

But it is only mainly that the Platonic Drama consists in argumentative conversation. It contains another element, the Myth, which, though not ostensibly present in some Dialogues, is so striking in others, some of them the greatest, that we are compelled to regard it, equally with the argumentative conversation, as essential to Plato's philosophical style.

The Myth is a fanciful tale, sometimes traditional, sometimes newly invented, with which Socrates or some other interlocutor interrupts or concludes the argumentative conversation in which the movement of the Drama mainly consists.

The object of this work is to examine the examples of the Platonic Myth in order to discover its function in the organism of the Platonic Drama. That Myth is an organic part of the Platonic Drama, not an added ornament, is a

---

[1] Cf. *Cratylus*, 387B, "Speech is one form of action".

point about which the experienced reader of Plato can have no doubt. The Sophists probably ornamented their discourses and made them more interesting by the insertion of illustrative fables or allegories like the Choice of Hercules;[1] but the Platonic Myth is not illustrative—it is not Allegory rendering pictorially results already obtained by argument. Of this the experienced reader of Plato is well aware. He feels when the brisk debate is silenced for a while, and Socrates or another great interlocutor opens his mouth in Myth, that the movement of the Philosophic Drama is not arrested, but is being sustained, at a crisis, on another plane. The Myth bursts in upon the Dialogue with a revelation of something new and strange; the narrow, matter-of-fact, workaday experience, which the argumentative conversation puts in evidence, is suddenly flooded, as it were, and transfused by the inrush of a vast experience, as from another world—"Put off thy shoes from off thy feet, for the place whereon thou standest is holy ground."

It is in the mouth of the dramatic Socrates that Plato puts those Myths best fitted to fill us with wondering surmise and make us think—the so-called Eschatological Myths. It may be that here Plato represents a trait of the real Socrates. Socrates' method of argumentative conversation, it is fully recognised, determined the dialogue-form of the Platonic writings. It may be that also the introduction of Myths, at least of the Eschatological Myths—Myths distinguished by great impressiveness of matter and style— was suggested to Plato by something in the real Socrates. The personal influence of Socrates worked as a vital principle in Plato's mind, and bodied itself forth in Socratic dramas— plays in which, as I have said, Socrates and his companions are the actors, and philosophical discourse is the action. Any element, then, in the Platonic writings which the experienced reader finds of great dramatic moment—and the Myth is such—is likely to represent some striking trait in the person and influence of the real Socrates. In the Myths put into his mouth Socrates *prophesies*—sets forth, by the aid of imaginative language, the fundamental conditions of conduct and knowledge. He "prophesies", and his

---

[1] See Grote's *Plato*, ii, 38, note *e*.

hearers listen spellbound. That Socrates possessed what is
now called mesmeric influence is very likely. The comparison of his influence (in ordinary debate) with that of
the electric fish,[1] may be thought to imply as much; while
his familiar spirit must be taken as evidence of "abnor-
mality".[2] I venture to offer the suggestion, for what it may
be worth, that the Platonic Myths, in manner if not always
in matter, represent (directly as spoken by "Socrates"
himself, indirectly as spoken by "Timaeus", "Critias",
"Protagoras", "the Eleatic Stranger") certain impressive
passages in the conversation of the real Socrates, when he
held his hearers spellbound by the magnetism of his face
and speech. Be this as it may, Myth distinguished once for
all by weight and ring from Allegory[3] is an essential element
of Plato's philosophical style; and his philosophy cannot be
understood apart from it.[4]

The main plan of this work is to append to the English
translation of each of the Platonic Myths observations and
notes relating specially to that Myth itself. Each Myth is a
unique work of art, and must be dealt with individually in
its own context. But I hope that the general effect of these
special observations will be to leave the reader, at the end,

[1] *Meno*, 80 A.

[2] Hegel (*Gesch. d. Philos.* ii. 94-101) regards the divine sign as a "magnetic"
phenomenon, physiologically explicable. C. R. Volquardsen (*Das Dämonium
des Socrates und seine Interpreten*, Kiel, 1862) holds (pp. 58 and 71) that it
cannot be explained by any *law* of anthropology or physiology, but is a
"singular" phenomenon. Zeller (*Socrates and the Socratic Schools*, pp. 72-79,
Eng. Transl.) concludes that it is "a vague apprehension of some good or
ill result following on certain actions."

F. W. H. Myers (*Human Personality*, ii. 95 ff.) cites the divine sign of
Socrates "as an example of *wise automatism*; of the possibility that the
messages which are conveyed to the supraliminal mind from subliminal strata
of the personality—whether as sounds, as sights, or as movements—may
sometimes come from far beneath the realm of dream and confusion—from
some self whose monitions convey to us a wisdom profounder than we know"
(p. 100). Against L. F. Lélut (*On the daemon of Socrates*, 1856), who argues
from the records of the divine sign in Xenophon and Plato that Socrates was
insane, Myers contends (p. 95) that "it is now possible to give a truer explanation; to place these old records in juxtaposition with more instructive
parallels; and to show that the messages which Socrates received were only
advanced examples of a process which, if supernormal, is not abnormal, and
which characterises that form of intelligence which we describe as *genius*."
Dr. H. Jackson's article on "the divine sign of Socrates" in the *Journal of
Philology* (vol. x. pp. 232 ff.) may also be referred to, and Kühner's
Prolegomena (v. *on the divine sign of Socrates*) to his edition of Xen. *Mem.*

[3] See *infra*, p. 39 and pp. 222 ff.

[4] Zeller's *Plato*, pp. 159-163 (Eng. Transl.), may be read in connection
with this and preceding paragraphs.

with an adequate impression of the significance of Myth, first in Plato's philosophy, and then in present-day thought.

Before beginning, however, to carry out the main plan of this work, I will offer some preliminary remarks on *mythologia*, or story-telling in general, in the course of which I hope to indicate what I conceive to be the ground of Plato's methodical employment of it in philosophy.

2. GENERAL REMARKS ON *MYTHOLOGIA*, OR STORY-TELLING. MYTH DISTINGUISHED FROM ALLEGORY

It is a profound remark that Imagination rather than Reason makes the primary difference between man and brute.[1]

The brute lives mainly among the immediate impressions of sense. The after-images of these impressions are evidently of little account in his life, being feeble and evanescent.[2]

But man lives a double life—not only, with the brute, in the narrow world of present sensations, but also in a wide world of his own, where his mind is continually visited and re-visited by crowds of vivid, though often grotesque and grotesquely combined, images of past sense-impressions. It is in this wide wonder-world of waking dream, which encompasses the narrow familiar world of his present sense-impressions, that man begins his human career. It is here that the savage and the child begin to acquire what the brute has no such opportunity of beginning to acquire, and never does acquire—a sense of vast environment and of the

---

[1] "In the lower stages of civilisation, Imagination, more than Reason, distinguishes men from the animals; and to banish art would be to banish thought, to banish language, to banish the expression of all truth."—Jowett, *Dialogues of Plato*, Introduction to the Republic, p. clxiv.

[2] "At the proper season these birds (swallows) seem all day long to be impressed with the desire to migrate; their habits change; they become restless, are noisy, and congregate in flocks. Whilst the mother-bird is feeding, or brooding over her nestlings, the maternal instinct is probably stronger than the migratory; but the instinct which is the more persistent gains the victory, and at last, at a moment when her young ones are not in sight, she takes flight and deserts them. When arrived at the end of her long journey, and the migratory instinct has ceased to act, what an agony of remorse the bird would feel if, from being endowed with great mental activity, she could not prevent the image constantly passing through her mind of her young ones perishing in the bleak north from cold and hunger" (Darwin, *The Descent of Man*, part i. chap. iv. p. 173, ed. 1901).

long course of time. This waking dream, which constitutes
so great a part of man's childish experience, probably owes
much of its content to the dreams of sleep. Some of the
lower animals, as well as man, seem to have dreams in
sleep. But man, we may suppose, differs from the lower
animals in remembering his dreams. And he can tell them,
and improve upon them in the telling, whether they be
dreams of sleep or waking dreams—indeed, he must tell
them. They are so vivid that they will out; he cannot keep
them to himself; and, besides, the telling of them gives what
may be called secondary expression and relief to certain
emotions and feelings, which in the case of the brute find
only primary expression in acts within the world of sense-
impressions. In the case of man, fear, confidence, anger,
love, hate, curiosity, wonder, find not only primary expression in acts within the world of sense-experience, but
also secondary and, as it were, dramatic expression in the
adventures and doings of the dream-world, all circumstantially told. It is impossible to over-estimate the early
debt which man owes to his love of story-telling thus
inspired and supplied with material. In telling and listening
to stories about the dream-world, man, in short, learns to
think. The dream-world of the primitive story-teller and
his audience is a large, easy world, in which they can move
about freely as they like—in which they are rid of the hard
facts of the world of sense-experience, and can practise their
powers without hindrance on tractable material, calling up
images and combining them at will, as the story goes on,
and thus educating, in play, the capacity which, afterwards
applied to the explanation of the world of sense-experience,
appears as the faculty of constructive thought. The first
essays of this faculty are the so-called Aetiological Myths,
which attempt to construct a connection between the world
of sense-experience and the dream-world—which take the
dream-world as the context which explains the world of
sense-experience. Judged by the standard of positive science
the matter of the context supplied from the dream-world by
the mythopœic fancy is in itself, of course, worthless; but
the mind is enlarged by the mere contemplation of it; the
habit of looking for a context in which to read the sense-

given is acquired, and matter satisfactory to science is easily received when it afterwards presents itself. The conceptual context of science thus gradually comes to occupy the place once filled by the fantastical context of the dream-world. But this is not the only respect in which the mythopœic fancy serves the development of man. If it prepares the way for the exercise of the scientific understanding, it also indicates limits within which that exercise must be confined. This it does by supplying an emotional context, if the phrase may be used, along with the fantastical context. The visions of the mythopœic fancy are received by the Self of ordinary consciousness with a strange surmise of the existence, in another world, of another Self which, while it reveals itself in these visions, has a deep secret which it will not disclose. It is good that a man should thus be made to feel in his heart how small a part of him his head is—that the Scientific Understanding should be reminded that it is not the Reason —the Part, that it is not the Whole Man. Herein chiefly lies the present value of Myth (or of its equivalent, Poetry, Music, or whatever else) for civilised man.

The stories which the primitive inhabitants of the dream-world love to tell one another are always about the wonderful adventures and doings of people and animals. *Anthropologia* and *Zoologia*[1] may be taken as a full description of these stories. The adventures and doings happened "Once upon a time"—"Long ago"—"Somewhere, not here"—that is preface enough for the most improbable story—it receives belief or make-believe simply because it is *very interesting*—because the animals speak and behave like people, and everything else happens topsy-turvy in a wonderful manner, and there is no lack of bloodshed and indecency. If the story is not "very interesting", *i.e.* not marvellous, gruesome, indecent, it does not carry belief or make-believe, and is not interesting at all. The attitude of make-believe, which I have mentioned, is worth the careful attention of the psychologist. This is not the

---

[1] I hope that I may be pardoned for introducing two words which are not in *Liddell and Scott*, but seem to be justified, in the sense in which I use them, by Aristotle's *anthropologos* (*E. N.* iv. 3. 31)="fond of personal talk".

place to analyse it.[1] I will only say that it seems to me likely that it is very often the attitude of the primitive story-teller and his audience. The story may be very interesting to its teller and audience without being believed. This is as true, I take it, of a grotesque Zulu tale as of a modern novel written with due regard to probability or a *jeu d'esprit* like *Alice in Wonderland*. But if the story is very interesting, there will always be make-believe at least, and often serious, deliberate make-believe. It is in the spirit of this serious make-believe that not only the little girl talks about her dolls, but we ourselves read our Dante, or make pilgrimages to places associated with the events of great fiction. The adventures of Robinson Crusoe and the journey of Dr. Johnson are followed with little difference in our sense of actuality. The topography of the *Inferno* and that of the Roman Forum are approached in much the same spirit by the interested student in each case. These instances from civilised experience may serve to show how vague the line must be dividing belief from make-believe in the mind of primitive man with his turbulent feelings and vivid imagination controlled by no uniform standard of ascertained fact.[2] His tendency is to believe whatever he tells and is told. That he sometimes stops short of belief at make-believe is, after all, a small matter. At any rate, we may be sure that Nature in this case, as in all other cases, does nothing that is superfluous. If make-believe serve Nature's "purpose" as well as belief, which is more difficult, she will take care that her protégé stops at make-believe. Certain stories, we assume, have to be wonderful or horrid up to a certain pitch, in order to give full expression and relief to feeling and imagination at a certain stage of development; and the belief without which these necessary stories could not maintain themselves at all, we further assume, will be that which comes easiest, *i.e.* make-believe.

It is plain that in proportion as stories are more extravagantly wonderful or horrid, the more likely is make-

[1] Coleridge, referring to *Lyrical Ballads*, speaks of "that willing suspension of disbelief for the moment, which constitutes poetic faith".

[2] Professor Tylor (*Primitive Culture*, i. 284) describes "a usual state of the imagination among ancient and savage peoples" as "intermediate between the conditions of a healthy prosaic modern citizen and a raving fanatic or a patient in a fever-ward."

believe to be the attitude of tellers and hearers; and that, where this is the attitude, stories are likely to go on becoming more and more extravagantly wonderful or horrid.

This is one tendency which, however, is met by another. When a wonderful story is often told and becomes very familiar, it comes to be believed more seriously; and, in proportion as it is believed more seriously, it tends to disembarrass itself more and more of the wilder improbabilities which pleased when the attitude towards it was still that of make-believe. An impromptu story full of extravagant improbability and, it may be, of revolting indecency is told about some one. When and if that some one afterwards comes to be regarded, it may be on the sole authority of this story itself, as a hero or god of the race, those who revere him become ashamed of the old story about him. They rationalise and moralise it, either leaving out the improbabilities and indecencies, and retaining the parts that are probable and proper; or allegorising it, *i.e.* showing that the improbabilities and indecencies are not to be regarded as historical facts, but to be interpreted as figures of some philosophic or scientific or religious doctrine favoured by the interpreters. Thus make-believe accumulates material for the "higher criticism".

"About people and animals" is a sufficient account of what story-telling always is and why it is interesting.

1. Sometimes the story is about adventures and doings which happened once upon a time, and left no results to enhance the interest which belongs to it intrinsically as a story about people and animals. Such a story may be called "Simply Anthropological and Zoological".

A very large elephant came and said, "Whose are those remarkably beautiful children?" The child replied, "Unanana-bosele's." The elephant asked a second time, "Whose are those remarkably beautiful children?" The child replied, "Unanana-bosele's." The elephant said, "She built in the road on purpose, trusting to self-confidence and superior power." He swallowed them both, and left the little child. The elephant then went away.

In the afternoon the mother came and said, "Where are the children?" The little girl said, "They have been taken away by an elephant with one tusk." Unanana-bosele said, "Where did he put them?" The little girl replied, "He ate them." Unanana-bosele said, "Are they dead?" The little girl replied, "No, I do not know."

They retired to rest. In the morning she ground much maize, and put it into a large pot with amasi, and set out, carrying a knife in her hand. She came to the place where there was an antelope; she said, "Mother, mother, point out for me the elephant which has eaten my children; she has one tusk." The antelope said, "You will go till you come to a place where the trees are very high and where the stones are white." She went on.

She came to the place where was the leopard; she said "Mother, mother, point out for me the elephant which has eaten my children." The leopard replied, "You will go on and on, and come to the place where the trees are high and where the stones are white."

She went on, passing all animals, all saying the same. When she was still at a great distance she saw some very high trees, and white stones below them. She saw the elephant lying under the trees. She went on; when she came to the elephant she stood still and said, "Mother, mother, point out for me the elephant which has eaten my children." The elephant replied, "You will go on and on, and come to where the trees are high and where the stones are white." The woman merely stood still, and asked again saying, "Mother, mother, point out for me the elephant which has eaten my children." The elephant again told her just to pass onward. But the woman, seeing that it was the very elephant she was seeking, and that she was deceiving her by telling her to go forward, said a third time, "Mother, mother, point out for me the elephant which has eaten my children."

The elephant seized her and swallowed her too. When she reached the elephant's stomach, she saw large forests, and great rivers, and many high lands; on one side there were many rocks; and there were many people who had built their villages there; and many dogs and many cattle; all was there inside the elephant; she saw, too, her own children sitting there. She gave them amasi, and asked them what they ate before she came. They said, "We have eaten nothing, we merely lay down." She said, "Why did you not roast this flesh?" They said, "If we eat this beast, will it not kill us?" She said, "No; it will itself die; you will not die." She kindled a great fire. She cut the liver, and roasted it and ate with her children. They cut also the flesh and roasted and ate.

All the people which were there wondered, saying, "Oh, forsooth, are they eating, whilst we have remained without eating anything?" The woman said, "Yes, yes. The elephant can be eaten." All the people cut and ate.

And the elephant told the other beasts, saying, "From the time I swallowed the woman I have been ill; there has been a pain in my stomach." The other animals said, "It may be, O chief, it arises because there are now so many people in your stomach." And it came to pass after a long time that the elephant died. The woman divided the elephant with a knife, cutting through a rib with an axe. A cow came out and said, "Moo, moo, we at length see the country." A goat came out and said, "Mey, mey, at length we see the country." A dog came out and said, "At length we see the country." And the people came out laughing and saying, "At length we see the country." They made the woman presents; some gave her cattle, some goats, and some sheep. She set out with her children, being very rich. She went home rejoicing because she had come back with her children. On her arrival her little girl was there; she rejoiced, because she was thinking that her mother was dead.[1]

2. Sometimes the story is about doings and adventures which produced interesting results which remain, and are explained by means of these doings and adventures—as when the shape of a hill is explained by the action of some giant or wizard—"He cleft the Eildon Hills in three." This is the Aetiological Story. It is not only interesting as a piece of simple anthropology—every story must have that intrinsic interest—but it satisfies what may be called the "scientific curiosity"—the desire to know the causes of things. It sets forth the cause.

To the class of Aetiological Stories belong those myths in which the creation of the heavens and earth as one whole is set forth—the so-called Cosmological Myths; also myths which set forth the creation of man, and the origin of his faculties and virtues; also Foundation Myths describing the origin of society and of particular nations and cities, as well as myths describing the invention of the arts and their instruments; and myths—a large and important section—explaining the origin of ritual practices—the so-called Cultus Myths; and lastly, myths explaining topographical features and the peculiarities of animals and plants.

The "scientific" curiosity which inspires these Aetiological Stories is not idle. Curiosity, indeed, is never idle.

[1] *Nursery Tales, Traditions, and Histories of the Zulus*, Callaway, 1868, vol. i. pp. 332 ff.

"To know the cause" is matter of much practical concern to the savage as well as to the civilised man. If one knows the cause one can control the effect. For example, to heal a wound made by iron one must know the story of the origin of iron. That story duly recited becomes the charm which will heal the wound.[1] Many Aetiological Myths doubtless have their rise in the practice of magic.

Let me illustrate the Aetiological Myth by giving examples of its principal varieties, beginning with a Cosmological Myth—the "Story of the Children of Heaven and Earth," written down by Sir George Grey among the Maoris.[2]

> From Rangi, the Heaven, and Papa, the Earth, it is said, sprang all men and things; but sky and earth clave together, and darkness rested upon them and the beings they had begotten, till at last their children took counsel whether they should rend apart their parents or slay them. Then Tane-mahuta, father of forests, said to his five great brethren, "It is better to rend them apart, and let the heaven stand far above us, and the earth lie under our feet. Let the sky become as a stranger to us, but the earth remain close to us as our nursing mother." So Rongo-ma-tane, god and father of the cultivated food of man, rose and strove to separate the heaven and the earth; he struggled, but in vain; and vain, too, were the efforts of Tangaroa, father of fish and reptiles, and of Haumia-tikitiki, father of wild-growing food, and of Tu-matauenga, god and father of fierce men. Then slow uprises Tane-mahuta, god and father of forests, and wrestles with his parents, striving to part them with his hands and arms. "Lo, he pauses; his head is now firmly planted on his mother the earth, his feet he raises up and rests against his father the skies, he strains his back and limbs with mighty effort. Now are rent apart Rangi and Papa, and with cries and groans of woe they shriek aloud. . . . But Tane-mahuta pauses not; far, far beneath him he presses down the earth; far, far above him he thrusts up the sky." But Tawhiri-ma-tea, father of winds and storms, had never consented that his mother should be torn from her lord, and now there arose in his breast a fierce desire to war against his brethren. So the Storm-god rose

---

[1] See *infra*, pp. 200 ff., where the Finnish Story of the Origin of Iron is given.

[2] I give this myth as it is quoted from Grey's *Polynesian Mythology* (p. 1, ff.) by Prof. Tylor (*Prim. Cult.* i. 290 ff.). Mr. A. Lang compares this myth, and others like it found in India and China, with the Greek myth of the mutilation of Uranus by Cronus (*Custom and Myth*, "The Myth of Cronus").

and followed his father to the realms above, hurrying to the
sheltered hollows of the boundless skies, to hide and cling
and nestle there. Then came forth his progeny, the mighty
winds, the fierce squalls, the clouds dense, dark, fiery, wildly
drifting, wildly bursting; and in the midst their father rushed
upon his foe. Tane-mahuta and his giant forests stood
unconscious and unsuspecting when the raging hurricane
burst on them, snapping the mighty trees across, leaving
trunks and branches rent and torn upon the ground for the
insect and the grub to prey on. Then the father of storms
swooped down to lash the waters into billows whose summits
rose like cliffs, till Tangaroa, god of ocean and father of all
that dwell therein, fled affrighted through his seas. His
children, Ika-tere, the father of fish, and Tu-te-wehiwehi,
the father of reptiles, sought where they might escape for
safety; the father of fish cried, "Ho, ho, let us all escape to
the sea;" but the father of reptiles shouted in answer, "Nay,
nay, let us rather fly inland," and so these creatures separated, for while the fish fled into the sea, the reptiles sought
safety in the forests and scrubs. But the sea-god Tangaroa,
furious that his children the reptiles should have deserted
him, has ever since waged war on his brother Tane, who
gave them shelter in his woods. Tane attacks him in return,
supplying the offspring of his brother Tu-matauenga, father
of fierce men, with canoes and spears and fish-hooks made
from his trees, and with nets woven from his fibrous plants,
that they may destroy withal the fish, the Sea-god's children;
and the Sea-god turns in wrath upon the Forest-god, over-
whelms his canoes with the surges of the sea, sweeps with
floods his trees and houses into the boundless ocean. Next
the god of storms pushed on to attack his brothers, the gods
and progenitors of the tilled field and the wild; but Papa,
the Earth, caught them up and hid them, and so safely were
these her children concealed by their mother that the Storm-
god sought for them in vain. So he fell upon the last of his
brothers, the father of fierce men, but him he could not even
shake, though he put forth all his strength. What cared
Tu-matauenga for his brother's wrath? He it was who had
planned the destruction of their parents, and had shown
himself brave and fierce in war; his brethren had yielded
before the tremendous onset of the Storm-god and his
progeny; the Forest-god and his offspring had been broken
and torn in pieces; the Sea-god and his children had fled
to the depths of the ocean or the recesses of the shore; the
gods of food had been in safe hiding; but man still stood
erect and unshaken upon the bosom of his mother Earth,
and at last the hearts of the Heaven and the Storm became
tranquil, and their passion was assuaged.

But now Tu-matauenga, father of fierce men, took thought how he might be avenged upon his brethren who had left him unaided to stand against the god of storms. He twisted nooses of the leaves of the whanake tree, and the birds and beasts, children of Tane the Forest-god, fell before him; he netted nets from the flax-plant, and dragged ashore the fish, the children of Tangaroa the Sea-god; he found in their hiding-place underground the children of Rongo-ma-tane, the sweet potato and all cultivated food, and the children of Haumia-tikitiki, the fern-root and all wild-growing food; he dug them up and let them wither in the sun. Yet, though he overcame his four brothers, and they became his food, over the fifth he could not prevail, and Tawhiri-ma-tea, the Storm-god, still ever attacks him in tempest and hurricane, striving to destroy him both by sea and land. It was the bursting forth of the Storm-god's wrath against his brethren that caused the dry land to disappear beneath the waters: the beings of ancient days who thus submerged the land were Terrible-rain, Long-continued-rain, Fierce-hailstorms, and their progeny were Mist, and Heavy-dew, and Light-dew; and thus but little of the dry land was left standing above the sea. Then clear light increased in the world, and the beings who had been hidden between Rangi and Papa before they were parted now multiplied upon the earth. "Up to this time the vast Heaven has still ever remained separated from his spouse the Earth. Yet their mutual love still continues: the soft warm sighs of her loving bosom still ever rise up to him ascending from the woody mountains and valleys, and men call these mists; and the vast Heaven, as he mourns through the long nights his separation from his beloved, drops frequent tears upon her bosom, and men seeing these term them dewdrops."

Another important variety of the Aetiological Myth— the Cultus Myth—is well illustrated by Grote in the following passage:[1]—

It was the practice to offer to the gods in sacrifice the bones of the victim only, enclosed in fat; how did this practice arise? The author of the Hesiodic Theogony has a story which explains it.[2] Prometheus tricked Zeus into an imprudent choice, at the period when the gods and mortal men first came to an arrangement about privileges and duties (in Mekônê). Prometheus, the tutelary representative of man, divided a large steer into two portions; on the

[1] Grote's *History of Greece*, part i. chap. i.
[2] Hesiod, *Theog.* 550-557.

one side he placed the flesh and guts, folded up in the
omentum and covered over with the skin; on the other he
put the bones enveloped in fat. He then invited Zeus to
determine which of the two portions the gods would prefer
to receive from mankind. Zeus "with both hands" decided
for and took the white fat, but was highly incensed on finding
that he had got nothing at the bottom except the bones.
Nevertheless the choice of the gods was now irrevocably
made; they were not entitled to any portion of the sacrificed
animal beyond the bones and the white fat; and the standing
practice is thus plausibly explained. I select this as one
amongst a thousand instances to illustrate the genesis of
legend out of religious practices. In the belief of the people,
the event narrated in the legend was the real producing
cause of the practice; but when we come to apply a sound
criticism, we are compelled to treat the event as existing
only in its narrative legend, and the legend itself as having
been, in the greater number of cases, engendered by the
practice—thus reversing the supposed order of production.[1]

Let me complete my illustration of the Aetiological Myth
by giving the pretty Japanese story which accounts for the
physiological effect produced by tea:—

It is Daruma whom legend credits with the origin of tea.
Before he went off into his present trance he made another
effort at permanent contemplation, and had failed through
falling asleep at the end of the ninth year. When he awoke
he was so vexed at his eyelids for their drooping that he cut
them off. No sooner had they fallen to the ground than, lo!
they took root, sprouted, and sent forth leaves. As the old
monk looked in wonder, a disciple of Buddha appeared and
told him to brew the leaves of the new shrub and then drink
thereof. Daruma plucked the leaves, which now all the
world knows as tea, did as the vision commanded him to
do, and has not slept a minute since.[2]

3. From the Simply Anthropological Story and from the

---

[1] The reader who wishes to pursue the subject of the Cultus Myth may
consult Miss Harrison's *Mythology and Monuments of Ancient Athens*, pp. xxvi.
ff., where he will find a very interesting treatment of the story of the birth
of Erichthonios "as an instance of aetiological myth-making of a special kind,
of a legend that has arisen out of a ritual practice, the original meaning of
which had become obscured"; also Robertson Smith's *Religion of the Semites*,
pp. 20 ff., where the rule is laid down that "in the study of ancient religions
we must begin, not with Myth but with ritual and traditional usage"; cf.
p. 16—"The antique religions had for the most part no creed; they consisted
entirely of institutions and practices."

[2] *The Heart of Japan*, by C. L. Brownell (1902), p. 197. The spelling of
Daruma's name has been restored. Ed.

Aetiological Story it is convenient to distinguish a third kind of story, the Eschatological Story. Here the teller and his audience are not concerned with the adventures and doings of people once upon a time, long ago, but with adventures and doings which they themselves must take part in after death, like all who have gone before them. It is not to mere love of "personal talk" or to mere "scientific curiosity" that the Eschatological Story appeals, but to man's wonder, and fear, and hope with regard to death. This seems to make a great difference, and to justify us in putting the Eschatological Myths in a class by themselves. Where men fear and hope, they tend to believe strongly; and if ritual practice is associated with their fear and hope, more strongly. Hence we find that Eschatological Myths as a class have more actuality, more consistency and sobriety, and more dignity, than other myths, in proportion as the belief given is, for these reasons, stronger. If make-believe is enough for other myths, Eschatological Myths demand genuine belief, and easily get it from primitive man. It is in no spirit of make-believe that he performs the rites for the departed, which he knows will be performed one day for himself, when he shall have gone to the other world of which the stories tell.

It is not always easy to assign a story to its class. The cause of something that attracts notice may be found in something done by somebody in the course of adventures which have already been recounted as being in themselves interesting. A story which started as "Simply Anthropological", being told from pure love of the study of man, may be annexed by the scientific imagination and become Aetiological. And, again, a story which started as Aetiological may easily forget its original scientific inspiration and become a simple tale about man. Lastly, the interest of Eschatology—of talk about man's latter end—is so peculiar and engrossing that it tends to compel into its service Simply Anthropological and Aetiological Stories already in existence. The *Phaedrus* Myth may be mentioned as showing this tendency at work.

We have seen that in form every story of the dream-world, to whichever of the three classes it belongs, is anthropological and zoological; that it is about the adventures and

doings of people and animals—men and men-like beasts and
gods; and that it is intrinsically interesting as a story, and
receives belief, or, at any rate, make-believe. We must now
add that it has no moral—*i.e.* the teller and his hearers do
not think of anything but the story itself. This is the criterion
of Myth as distinguished from Allegory or Parable: Myth
has no moral or other meaning in the minds of those who
make it, and of those for whom it is made. It is a later age
which reads other meaning into it, when the improbability
and indecency of stories told by savage men provoke the
rationalising work of those who are unwilling to give up the
stories entirely, but cannot receive them as they stand. The
stories which seem to need this work most, and on which it is
most effectually done, are apt to perish under the treatment
which they receive. Becoming transparent allegories or fulfilled prophecies, they cease to be interesting, and are soon
forgotten. But there stand out among the myths of the world
some which rationalism has not been able to destroy or even
impair. These, we may be sure, were the creations, not of
ordinary story-tellers, but of "divine poets" and "inspired
prophets"—of genius, using, indeed, material supplied by
ordinary story-tellers, but transforming it in the use.[1] Such
myths—chiefly Eschatological Myths, created and originally
received in the spirit of genuine belief, not of make-believe—
yield precious fruit to interpretation. But the interpretation
of a masterpiece of imagination, to be fruitful, must be
"psychological". The revival, in any shape, must be
eschewed of that now formally discredited method which
treated a masterpiece of creative imagination as an allegory
by which the accepted dogma of the day might be supported,
or as a prediction to be fulfilled, if not already fulfilled, in
some particular event of history. Fruitful interpretation of
a masterpiece of creative imagination will consist in showing
the mind of its maker, and in so placing his creation before
our own minds by means of some accompaniment or
rendering—some parallel corroborative appeal to imagina-

---

[1] "We must not be astonished if we come across myths which surprise
us by their ingenious direction, or even by their profound philosophy. This
is often the character of spontaneous products of the human mind. . . . The
human mind, when it works thus spontaneously, is a philosopher just as the
bee is a mathematician."—Reville, *Prolégomènes de l'Histoire des Religions*,
Eng. Transl. by Squire, p. 112.

tion and feeling—that it does for us in our age what it did for him in his age, making us pause in the midst of our workaday life, as he paused in the midst of his, filled

> With admiration and deep muse, to hear
> Of things so high and strange.

The allegorical interpretation of old myths (which were made, it is hardly necessary to say, without thought of the doctrine got out of them by the interpretation) doubtless suggested the deliberate making of allegorical tales and parables. When their makers are men of genius, these tales are often myths as well as allegories and parables. Such are Plato's *Cave* and Bunyan's *Pilgrim's Progress*, which I shall consider later with reference to this point.[1]

Aesop's Fables, again, though retaining much of the "anthropological and zoological" interest which belongs to the African Beast-tale on which they were modelled, were doubtless, for the most part, deliberately composed for the sake of their morals or applications.

As the Beast-tale is rewritten "with a purpose" in Aesop's Fables, so in the moral zoology of *Physiologus* even "The Natural History of Animals" is rewritten and turned into allegory.[2] The following, *about the Lion*, based on *Physiologus*, occurs in a British Museum Bestiary (Codd. Reg. 2 C. xii.) quoted by Mann in his instructive work, *der Bestiaire Divin des Guillaume le Clerc* (p. 37):—

"*Concerning the nature of the Lion, king of beasts or living creatures.* For Jacob in blessing his son Judah said (Gen. 49. 9): 'Judah my son is a lion's whelp, who shall lift him up?'"

---

[1] See *infra*, "Excursus on Allegory," pp. 222 ff.

[2] *Physiologus* is a work, in its original Greek form, compiled at Alexandria towards the end of the second century, consisting of chapters, in each of which an animal, real or fabulous, (or a precious stone) is first described in the manner of natural history (or rather, *as if* in that manner), and then presented as a type of Christian doctrine and life. After being translated into Latin, *Physiologus* spread over the whole West, and versions of it were made everywhere in the vulgar tongues—in Anglo-Saxon, Old English, Old High German, Flemish, Icelandic, Provençal, Old French, and Italian. In the East, too, it appeared in Syrian, Armenian, Arabic, Ethiopic, and Slavonic versions. After the Bible it was probably the most popular book throughout the Middle Age. Examples of it—the so-called Bestiaries—are to be found in all the libraries of Europe. See *der Bestiaire Divin des Guillaume le Clerc* (*Französische Studien*, 1888), by Max Friedr. Mann, pp. 17 ff.; Pitra, *Spicilegium Solesmense*, 1855, t. iii. pp. xlvii. ff.; Carus, *Gesch. d. Zoologie*, pp. 108 ff.; and article, *Physiologus*, by Prof. J. P. N. Land, in *Encycl. Brit.*

"The *Physiologus* says that the lion has three natures: First: He walks among the hills, and if it happens that he is sought by the hunters, their scent reaches him, and with his tail he wipes out his footprints behind him, so that the pursuing huntsman may not discover his den through his tracks, and so capture him. So also our Saviour, 'the spiritual Lion of the tribe of Judah, the root of Jesse, son of David' (Rev. 5. 5) sent by the Father above, has hidden from the wise the marks of his divinity. That is: He was created among angels an angel, among archangels an archangel, among thrones a throne, among powers a power, until he descended to the Virgin's womb, that he might save this human race which had gone astray. Therefore those who did not know that he had ascended to the Father, they who were angels on high, said to those who were ascending with the Lord (Ps. 24. 8. f): 'Who is the King of Glory?' And they replied: 'The Lord strong and mighty, He is the King of Glory.'

"*Second characteristic:* When he would sleep, his eyes keep watch, for they are open, as in the Song of Songs the bridegroom bears witness saying (5. 2): 'I sleep and my heart keeps watch.' For in the body my Lord is sleeping on the Cross and in the tomb, but his deity keeps watch. 'Behold he shall not sleep who guards Israel' (Ps. 121. 4).

"*Third characteristic:* When a lioness gives birth to her young, she bears him dead, and watches over his body for three days, until his father comes on the third day, and breathes into his face, and revives him. So the omnipotent father restored from the dead his Son our Lord Jesus Christ on the third day, as Jacob says (Num. 24. 9): 'He couched as a lion, and as a lion's cub. Who shall stir him up?' "

In *Physiologus* "The Natural History of Animals" has a double character: it is not only a narrative of "facts", but, at the same time, a divinely appointed, as it were dramatic, representation of doctrine for the benefit of man.

Similarly, "Old Testament History" is regarded by Philo and his school as at once a chronicle of actual events, and a great allegorical representation of doctrine in which events are figures or symbols of philosophic truths—and that, in the intention of God, not merely in the mind of the inter-

preter. I shall have occasion to return to this strange school
of allegory; meanwhile the purpose of this introductory
reference to the subject will be sufficiently served if I quote
in passing, without comment, a classical passage in which
one of the great masters of Myth distinguishes between the
literal and the allegorical or mystical truth of events recorded
in history.

In the letter to Kan Grande,[1] which is really a preface
to the *Commedia*, Dante writes as follows, §§ 7, 8:—

"On the evidence of those who speak in this manner, it
should be known that in this work (the *Commedia*) there is
not one simple meaning, but it can be said to have many
meanings, for it is to be interpreted according to the letter,
and also according to the sense. The first is called *literal*,
the second *allegorical* or *mystic*. In order that this distinction
may be clarified, let us consider it in these verses: 'In the
departure of Israel from Egypt, the house of Jacob from a
strange people, Jacob became his sanctuary and Israel his
dominion.' For if we only look at the *letter*, it signifies to us
the departure of the children of Israel from Egypt, in the
time of Moses. If we see it as an *allegory*, it signifies our
redemption through Christ; if *in a moral sense*, it signifies the
conversion of the soul from the grief and sorrow of the
sinner to a state of grace; if in an anagogic sense, it signifies
the escape of the holy soul from the slavery of this corruption
to the freedom of eternal Glory. And although these hidden
meanings are called by various names, they can all in
general be called allegorical, because they are other than
literal or narrative . . . When we have seen that, it is obvious
that there must be a twofold *subject*, around which alternative
meanings may flow. And the subject of this work is to be
regarded in such a manner, according as it is taken literally,
and then in such a manner, according as it is perceived
allegorically. This, then, is the subject of the whole work,
in so far as it is understood literally: 'The condition of souls
after death, simply treated.' For the process of the whole

[1] Dean Church (*Dante and other Essays*, p. 103, ed. 1897) refers to this
letter as one "which, if in its present form of doubtful authenticity, without
any question represents Dante's sentiments, and the substance of which is
incorporated in one of the earliest writings on the poem, Boccaccio's commentary."

work is from that and round that. But if the poem is understood to be allegorical, the subject is 'man, according as he
is accountable, by what he has earned and deserved, to the
unfettered arbitration' of Justice who allots rewards and
punishments."[1]

In the *Convivio* (ii. 1 and 13) the four "senses" are distinguished exactly as in the *Letter*. Of the moral and
anagogic senses he says (ii. 1, p. 252, 1. 42, Oxf. ed.): "The
third sense is called *moral;* it is that which readers ought
attentively to note, as they go through writings, for their
own profit and that of their disciples; as it may be noted in
the Gospel, when Christ went up into the Mount to be
transfigured, that of the twelve apostles he took with him the
three; wherein morally we may understand, that in matters
of the greatest secrecy we ought to have few companions.

"The fourth sense is called *anagogic*, that is, above sense;
and this is when a writing is expounded spiritually which,
even in its literal sense, by the matters signified, sets forth
the high things of glory everlasting: as may be seen in that
Song of the Prophet which says that in the coming out of
the people of Israel from Egypt, Judah was made holy and
free. Which, although it is plainly true according to the
letter, is not less true as understood spiritually: that is, the
Soul, in coming out from sin, is made holy and free."

The rest of the chapter (*Conv.* ii. 1) dwells on the point,
which Dante evidently considers of great importance, that
the literal sense must always be understood before we go on
to seek out the other senses. The reversal of this order is,
indeed, *impossible*, for the other senses are contained in the
literal sense, which is their envelope; and besides, the

---

[1] Gebhart (*L'Italie Mystique*, pp. 318 ff.), referring to this *Letter*, remarks
that the literal interpretation of the *Divina Commedia* represents the traditional
belief of the mediæval church, the other interpretations represent Dante's
own personal religion. M. Gebhart's analysis of Dante's "personal religion"
is very instructive: "The final word of his faith, this 'religion of the heart'
which he has named in the *Convito*, is in the twenty-fourth Canto of the
Paradiso, and it is to St. Peter himself that he makes his confession. He has
come back to the very plain symbolism of St. Paul, faith, hope and charity; for
him as for the apostle, faith itself is, at bottom, nothing but hope, *faith is the
substance of things hoped for* . . . for him the supreme sin, which he punishes
with crushing scorn, is neither heresy nor incredulity, which he has shown,
by the very disdain and haughty countenance of the damned, to be superior
to Hell; it is pusillanimity, the timid renunciation of active duty, of one's
vocation in life, the slackness of Pope Celestino.
'Who made through cowardice the great refusal'."

literal sense is "better known to us", as the Philosopher says in the First Book of the *Physics;* and not to begin with it would be *irrational*—contrary to the natural order.

3. PLATO'S MYTHS DISTINGUISHED FROM ALLEGORIES. TO WHAT EXPERIENCE, OR "PART OF THE SOUL", DOES THE PLATONIC MYTH APPEAL?

Plato, we know from the *Republic*[1] and *Phaedrus,*[2] deprecated the allegorical interpretation of Myths, and his own Myths, we assume, are not to be taken as allegories; but rather as representing, in the action of the Platonic Drama, natural products of that dream-world consciousness which encompasses the field of ordinary wide-awake consciousness in educated minds as well as in the minds of children and primitive men.

In appealing to the dream-world consciousness of his readers by a brilliant literary representation of its natural products—those stories which primitive men cannot leave untold, and philosophers love to hear well told[3]—Plato appeals to an experience which is more solid than one might infer from the mere content of the mythology in which it finds expression. He appeals to that major part of man's nature which is not articulate and logical, but feels, and wills, and acts—to that part which cannot explain what a thing is, or how it happens, but feels that the thing is good or bad, and expresses itself, not scientifically in "existential" or "theoretic judgments," but practically in "value-judgments"—or rather "value-feelings". Man was, with the brute, practical, and had struck the roots of his being deep into the world of reality, ages before he began to be scientific, and to think about the "values" which he felt. And long before he began to think about the "values" which he felt, feeling had taken into its service his imagination with its whole apparatus of phantasms—waking dreams and sleep-dreams—and made them its exponents. In

---

[1] *Rep.* 378 D.
[2] *Phaedrus,* 229 B-E, and see *infra,* pp. 223 ff.
[3] "The man who likes stories is a kind of philosopher".—Arist. *Met.* xi 2, 982 b. 18.

appealing, through the recital of dreams, to that major part
of us which feels "values," which wills and acts, Plato
indeed goes down to the bedrock of human nature. At that
depth man is more at one with Universal Nature—more in
her secret, as it were—than he is at the level of his "higher"
faculties, where he lives in a conceptual world of his own
making which he is always endeavouring to "think". And
after all, however high he may rise as "thinker", it is only
of "values" that he genuinely thinks; and the ground of all
"values"—*the Value of Life itself*—was apprehended before
the dawn of thinking, and is still apprehended independently
of thinking. It is good, Plato will have us believe, to appeal
sometimes from the world of the senses and scientific understanding which is "too much with us", to this deep-lying
part of human nature, as to an oracle. The responses of
the oracle are not given in articulate language which the
scientific understanding can interpret; they come as dreams,
and must be received as dreams, without thought of doctrinal
interpretation. Their ultimate meaning is the "feeling"
which fills us in beholding them; and when we wake from
them, we see our daily concerns and all things temporal
with purged eyes.

This effect which Plato produces by the Myth in the
Dialogue is, it is hardly necessary to say, produced, in various
degrees, by Nature herself, without the aid of literary or
other art. The sense of "might, majesty and dominion"
which comes over us as we look into the depths of the starry
sky,[1] the sense of our own short time passing, passing, with
which we see the lilacs bloom again—these, and many like
them, are natural experiences which closely resemble the
effect produced in the reader's mind by Plato's art. When
these natural moods are experienced, we feel "That which
was, and is, and ever shall be" overshadowing us; and
familiar things—the stars, and the lilac bloom—become
suddenly strange and wonderful, for our eyes are opened to
see that they declare its presence. It is such moods of feeling
in his cultivated reader that Plato induces, satisfies, and

---

[1] Coleridge says (*Anima Poetae*, from unpublished note-books of S. T.
Coleridge, edited by E. H. Coleridge, 1895; p. 125), "Deep sky is, of all
visual impressions, the nearest akin to a feeling. It is more a feeling than a
sight, or rather, it is the melting away and entire union of feeling and sight!"

regulates, by Myths which set forth God, Soul, and Cosmos, in vision.

The essential charm of these Myths is that of Poetry generally, whether the theme of a poem be expressly eschatological and religious, like that of the *Divina Commedia*, or of some other kind, for example, like that of the *Fairy Queen*, or like that of a love song. The essential charm of all Poetry, for the sake of which in the last resort it exists, lies in its power of inducing, satisfying, and regulating what may be called Transcendental Feeling, especially that form of Transcendental Feeling which manifests itself as solemn sense of Timeless Being—of "That which was, and is, and ever shall be," overshadowing us with its presence. Where this power is absent from a piece—be it an epic, or a lyric, or a play, or a poem of observation and reflection—there is no *Poetry;* only, at best, readable verse—an exhibition of wit and worldly wisdom, of interesting "anthropology", of pleasing sound—all either helpful or necessary, in their several places, for the production of the *milieu* in which poetic effect is felt, but none of them forming part of that effect itself. Sometimes the power of calling up Transcendental Feeling seems to be exercised at no point or points which can be definitely indicated in the course of a poem; this is notably the case where the form of the poem is dramatic, *i.e.* where all turns on our grasping "one complete action". Sometimes "a lonely word" makes the great difference. At any rate, elaborate dream-consciousness apparatus, such as we find employed in the Platonic Myths, in the *Divina Commedia*, and in poems like *Endymion* and *Hyperion*, is not essential to the full exercise of the power of Poetry. Some common scene is simply pictured for the mind's eye; some place haunted by memories and emotions is pictured for the heart; a face declaring some mood is framed in circumstances which match it and its mood; some fantasia of sound or colour fills eye or ear; some sudden stroke of personification amazes us; there is perhaps nothing more than the turn of a phrase or the use of a word or the falling of a cadence—and straightway all is done that the most elaborate and sustained employment of mythological apparatus could do—we are away in the dream-world; and

when we presently return, we are haunted by the feeling that
we have "seen the mysteries"—by that Transcendental
Feeling which Dante finds language to express in the twenty-
fifth sonnet of the *Vita Nuova*,[1] and in the last canto of the
Paradiso :—

> O grace abounding, in which I presumed to fix my
> regard upon the eternal light, for so long that I wore away
> my sight in it. Within its depths I saw, gathered and bound
> by love into one volume, that which is scattered throughout
> the universe.
>   Substance and accidents and their relations, as though
> fused together in such a manner that what I describe is a
> single flame.
>   The universal form of this complexity I think that I
> beheld, because in saying this I feel myself the more largely
> to rejoice. A single moment brings me deeper stillness than
> five and twenty centuries have laid upon the quest, which
> gave Neptune such astonishment at the Argo's shadow.[2]

Let me give some examples from the Poets of their
employment of the means which I have just now mentioned.

A common scene is simply pictured for the mind's eye:—

> Sole listener, Duddon! to the breeze that played
> With thy clear voice, I caught the fitful sound
> Wafted o'er sullen moss and craggy mound—
> Unfruitful solitudes, that seem'd to upbraid
> The sun in heaven!—but now, to form a shade
> For thee, green alders have together wound
> Their foliage; ashes flung their arms around;
> And birch-trees risen in silver colonnade.
> And thou hast also tempted here to rise,
> Mid sheltering pines, this cottage rude and grey;
> Whose ruddy children, by the mother's eyes
> Carelessly watched, sport through the summer day,
> Thy pleased associates:—light as endless May
> On infant bosoms lonely Nature lies.

Sometimes, again, *the scene is pictured for the heart rather
than for the eye*—we look upon a place haunted, for the Poet,
and after him for ourselves, by memories and emotions:—

---

[1] See *infra*, p. 63, where this sonnet is quoted.
[2] *Paradiso*, xxxiii. 82-9.

Row us out from Desenzano, to your Sirmione row!
So they row'd and there we landed—"O venusta Sirmio!"
There to me thro' all the groves of olive in the summer glow,
There beneath the Roman ruin where the purple flowers
   grow,
Came that "Ave atque Vale" of the Poet's hopeless woe,
Tenderest of Roman poets nineteen hundred years ago,
"Frater Ave atque Vale"—as we wander'd to and fro
Gazing at the Lydian laughter of the Garda Lake below
Sweet Catullus's all-but-island, olive-silvery Sirmio!

Again, *it is a face that we see declaring some mood, and framed in circumstances which match it and its mood:*—

At eve a dry cicala sung,
   There came a sound as of the sea;
Backward the lattice-blind she flung,
   And lean'd upon the balcony.
There all in spaces rosy-bright
   Large Hesper glitter'd on her tears,
   And deepening thro' the silent spheres
Heaven over Heaven rose the night.

Again, *some fantasia of sound or light fills ear or eye—of sound, like this:*—

Sometimes a-dropping from the sky
I heard the skylark sing;
Sometimes all little birds that are,
How they seemed to fill the sea and air
With their sweet jargoning!
And now 'twas like all instruments,
Now like a lonely flute;
And now it is an angel's song,
That makes the heavens be mute.

Or like this:—

The silver sounding instruments did meet
With the base murmur of the Water's fall:
The Water's fall with difference discrete,
Now soft, now loud, unto the Wind did call:
The gentle warbling Wind low answerèd to all.

Of sound and light together, like this:—

A sunny shaft did I behold,
   From sky to earth it slanted:

And poised therein a bird so bold—
　Sweet bird, thou wert enchanted!
He sank, he rose, he twinkled, he trolled
　Within that shaft of sunny mist;
His eyes of fire, his beak of gold,
　All else of amethyst!

And thus he sang: "Adieu! adieu!
Love's dreams prove seldom true.
The blossoms, they make no delay:
The sparkling dewdrops will not stay.
　　Sweet month of May,
　　We must away;
　　Far, far away!
　　To-day! to-day!"

Again, *it is some stroke of personification that fills us with amazement*—where we thought that Nature was most solitary, see! some one is present!

　　The nightingale, up-perched high,
And cloister'd among cool and bunched leaves—
She sings but to her love, nor e'er conceives
How tiptoe Night holds back her dark-grey hood.

Or, it may be, the presence is that of Great Nature herself— and she feels what we feel, and knows what we know:—

O fair is Love's first hope to gentle mind!
As Eve's first star thro' fleecy cloudlet peeping;
And sweeter than the gentle south-west wind,
O'er willowy meads and shadowed waters creeping,
And Ceres' golden fields;—the sultry hind
Meets it with brow uplift, and stays his reaping.

Lastly, *it is perhaps but the turn of a phrase or the fall of a cadence that touches the heart:*—

　　I heard a linnet courting
　　　His lady in the spring;
　　His mates were idly sporting,
　　　Nor stayed to hear him sing
　　　　His song of love:—
　　I fear my speech distorting
　　　His tender love.

So much by way of illustrating poetic effect produced, as only the inspired poet knows how to produce it, by very simple means. I venture to ask the student of Plato to believe with me that the effect produced, in the passages just quoted, by these simple means, does not differ in kind from that produced by the use of elaborate apparatus in the Myths with which this work is concerned. The effect is always the induction of the dream-consciousness, with its atmosphere of solemn feeling spreading out into the waking consciousness which follows.

It will be well, however, not to confine ourselves to the examples given, but to quote some other examples from Poetry, in which this effect is produced in a way more closely parallel to that in which it is produced in the Platonic Myths. I will therefore ask the reader to submit himself to an experiment: first, to take the three following passages— all relating to Death—and carefully reading and re-reading them, allow the effect of them to grow upon him; and then, turning to Plato's Eschatological Myths in the *Phaedo*, *Gorgias*, and *Republic*, and reading them in the same way, to ask himself whether or no he has had a foretaste of their effect in the effect produced by these other pieces. I venture to think that the more we habituate ourselves to the influence of the Poets the better we are likely to receive the message of the Prophets.

> Deh peregrini, che pensosi andate
>   Forse di cosa che non v' è presente,
>   Venite voi di sì lontana gente,
>   Come alla vista voi ne dimostrate?
> Che non piangete, quando voi passate
>   Per lo suo mezzo la città dolente,
>   Come quelle persone, che neente
>   Par che intendesser la sua gravitate.
> Se voi restate, per volerla udire,
>   Certo lo core ne' sospir mi dice,
>   Che lagrimando n' uscirete pui.
> Ella ha perduta la sua Beatrice;
>   E le parole, ch' uom di lei può dire,
>   Hanno virtù di far piangere altrui.[1]

[1] Ah pilgrims, who go lost in thought, perhaps of a thing that is not present with you, do you come from a people so far off, as by your aspect you show?

For you do not mourn, when you pass through the midst of the sorrowing city, like men who understand nothing of her burden. If you pause from desire to hear it, my sighing heart tells me truly, that you will then depart in tears.

She has lost her Beatrice, and the words which a man can say of her, have power to make another weep.

La Vita Nuova, § 41, Sonetto 24.

To that high Capital,[1] where Kingly Death
Keeps his pale court in beauty and decay,
He came: and bought, with price of purest breath,
A grave among the eternal.—Come away!
Haste, while the vault of blue Italian day
Is yet his fitting charnel-roof! while still
He lies, as if in dewy sleep he lay;
Awake him not! surely he takes his fill
Of deep and liquid rest, forgetful of all ill.

He will awake no more—oh, never more!
Within the twilight chamber spreads apace
The shadow of white Death, and at the door
Invisible Corruption waits to trace
His extreme way to her dim dwelling-place;
The eternal Hunger sits, but pity and awe
Soothe her pale rage, nor dares she to deface
So fair a prey, till darkness and the law
Of change shall o'er his sleep the mortal curtain draw.

Oh, weep for Adonais!—The quick Dreams,
The passion-wingèd Ministers of thought,
Who were his flocks, whom near the living streams
Of his young spirit he fed, and whom he taught
The love which was its music, wander not,—
Wander no more from kindling brain to brain,
But droop there, whence they sprung; and mourn their lot
Round the cold heart, where, after their sweet pain,
They ne'er will gather strength, nor find a home again.

And one with trembling hand clasps his cold head,
And fans him with her moonlight wings, and cries:
"Our love, our hope, our sorrow, is not dead;
See, on the silken fringe of his faint eyes,
Like dew upon a sleeping flower, there lies
A tear some Dream has loosened from his brain."
Lost Angel of a ruined Paradise!
She knew not 'twas her own; as with no stain
She faded, like a cloud which had outwept its rain.

One from a lucid urn of starry dew
Washed his light limbs, as if embalming them;
Another clipt her profuse locks, and threw
The wreath upon him, like an anadem,
Which frozen tears instead of pearls begem;

[1] Shelley, *Adonais*.

Another in her wilful grief would break
Her bow and winged reeds, as if to stem
A greater loss with one which was more weak;
And dull the barbèd fire against his frozen cheek.

Another Splendour on his mouth alit,
That mouth whence it was wont to draw the breath
Which gave it strength to pierce the guarded wit,
And pass into the panting heart beneath
With lightning and with music: the damp death
Quenched its caress upon his icy lips;
And, as a dying meteor stains a wreath
Of moonlight vapour, which the cold night clips,
It flushed through his pale limbs, and passed to its eclipse.

And others came,—Desires and Adorations,
Winged Persuasions, and veiled Destinies,
Splendours, and Glooms, and glimmering Incarnations
Of hopes and fears, and twilight Phantasies;
And Sorrow, with her family of Sighs,
And Pleasure, blind with tears, led by the gleam
Of her own dying smile instead of eyes,
Came in slow pomp;—the moving pomp might seem
Like pageantry of mist on an autumnal stream.

All he had loved and moulded into thought
From shape, and hue, and odour, and sweet sound,
Lamented Adonais. Morning sought
Her eastern watch-tower, and her hair unbound,
Wet with the tears which should adorn the ground,
Dimmed the aerial eyes that kindle day;
Afar the melancholy thunder moaned,
Pale Ocean in unquiet slumber lay,
And the wild winds flew around, sobbing in their dismay.

Lost Echo sits amid the voiceless mountains,
And feeds her grief with his remembered lay,
And will no more reply to winds or fountains,
Or amorous birds perched on the young green spray,
Or herdsman's horn, or bell at closing day;
Since she can mimic not his lips, more dear
Than those for whose disdain she pined away
Into a shadow of all sounds:—a drear
Murmur, between their songs, is all the woodmen hear.

* * * * * *

* * * * * *

Alas! that all we loved of him should be,
But for our grief, as if it had not been,
And grief itself be mortal! Woe is me!
Whence are we, and why are we? of what scene
The actors or spectators? Great and mean
Meet massed in death, who lends what life must borrow.
As long as skies are blue, and fields are green,
Evening must usher night, night urge the morrow,
Month follow month with woe, and year wake year to sorrow.

       *   *   *   *   *   *
       *   *   *   *   *   *

Peace, peace! he is not dead, he doth not sleep—
He hath awakened from the dream of life—
'Tis we, who, lost in stormy visions, keep
With phantoms an unprofitable strife,
And in mad trance strike with our spirit's knife
Invulnerable nothings—*We* decay
Like corpses in a charnel; fear and grief
Convulse us and consume us day by day,
And cold hopes swarm like worms within our living clay.

He has outsoared the shadow of our night;
Envy and calumny, and hate and pain,
And that unrest which men miscall delight,
Can touch him not and torture not again;
From the contagion of the world's slow stain
He is secure, and now can never mourn
A heart grown cold, a head grown grey in vain;
Nor, when the spirit's self has ceased to burn,
With sparkless ashes load an unlamented urn.

       *   *   *   *   *   *
       *   *   *   *   *   *

He is made one with Nature: there is heard
His voice in all her music, from the moan
Of thunder to the song of night's sweet bird;
He is a presence to be felt and known
In darkness and in light, from herb and stone,
Spreading itself where'er that Power may move
Which has withdrawn his being to its own;
Which wields the world with never-wearied love,
Sustains it from beneath, and kindles it above.

He is a portion of the loveliness
Which once he made more lovely: he doth bear
His part, while the one Spirit's plastic stress

Sweeps through the dull dense world, compelling there
All new successions to the forms they wear;
Torturing the unwilling dross that checks its flight
To its own likeness, as each mass may bear;
And bursting in its beauty and its might
From trees and beasts and men into the Heaven's light.

The splendours of the firmament of time
May be eclipsed, but are extinguished not;
Like stars to their appointed height they climb,
And death is a low mist which cannot blot
The brightness it may veil. When lofty thought
Lifts a young heart above its mortal lair,
And love and life contend in it, for what
Shall be its earthly doom, the dead live there,
And move like winds of light on dark and stormy air.

The inheritors of unfulfilled renown
Rose from their thrones, built beyond mortal thought,
Far in the Unapparent. Chatterton
Rose pale, his solemn agony had not
Yet faded from him; Sidney, as he fought,
And as he fell, and as he lived and loved,
Sublimely mild, a Spirit without spot,
Arose; and Lucan, by his death approved:
Oblivion, as they rose, shrank like a thing reproved.

And many more, whose names on Earth are dark,
But whose transmitted effluence cannot die
So long as fire outlives the parent spark,
Rose, robed in dazzling immortality.
"Thou art become as one of us," they cry;
"It was for thee yon kingless sphere has long
Swung blind in unascended majesty,
Silent alone amid a Heaven of Song.
Assume thy wingèd throne, thou Vesper of our throng!"

When lilacs last in the dooryard bloom'd,[1]
And the great star early droop'd in the western sky in the
     night,
I mourn'd, and yet shall mourn with ever-returning spring.
Ever-returning spring, trinity sure to me you bring,
Lilac blooming perennial, and drooping star in the west,
And thought of him I love.

[1] Walt Whitman, *Leaves of Grass* (*Memories of President Lincoln*).

*   *   *   *   *   *
*   *   *   *   *   *

From this bush in the dooryard,
With delicate-colour'd blossoms and heart-shaped leaves of
    rich green,
A sprig with its flower I break.

In the swamp in secluded recesses,
A shy and hidden bird is warbling a song—

*   *   *   *   *   *
*   *   *   *   *   *

Song of the bleeding throat,
Death's outlet song of life.

Over the breast of the spring, the land, amid cities,
Amid lanes and through old woods, where lately the violets
    peep'd from the ground, spotting the grey débris,
Amid the grass in the fields each side of the lanes, passing
    the endless grass,
Passing the yellow-spear'd wheat, every grain from its shroud
    in the dark-brown fields uprisen,
Passing the apple-tree blows of white and pink in the orchards,
Carrying a corpse to where it shall rest in the grave,
Night and day journeys a coffin.

Coffin that passes through lanes and streets,
Through day and night with the great cloud darkening the
    land,
With the pomp of the inloop'd flags, with the cities drap'd
    in black,
With the show of the States themselves as of crape-veil'd
    women standing,

*   *   *   *   *   *
*   *   *   *   *   *

With the countless torches lit, with the silent sea of faces
    and the bared heads,

*   *   .   *   *   *   *
*   *   *   *   *   *

With the tolling tolling bells' perpetual clang,
Here, coffin that slowly passes,
I give you my sprig of lilac.

* * * * * *
* * * * * *

Sing on there in the swamp,
O singer bashful and tender, I hear your notes, I hear your
   call,
I hear, I come presently, I understand you,
But a moment I linger, for the lustrous star has detain'd me,
The star, my departing comrade, holds and detains me.

O how shall I warble myself for the dead one there I lov'd?
And how shall I deck my song for the large sweet soul that
   has gone?
And what shall my perfume be for the grave of him I love?
Sea-winds blown from East and West,
Blown from the Eastern sea and blown from the Western
   sea, . . . on the prairies meeting . . .—
With these and the breath of my chant,
I'll perfume the grave of him I love.

* * * * * *
* * * * * *

Sing on, sing on, you grey-brown bird,
Sing from the swamps, the recesses, pour your chant from the
   bushes,
Limitless out of the dusk, out of the cedars and pines.
Sing on, dearest brother, warble your reedy song,
Loud human song, with voice of uttermost woe.

O liquid and free and tender!
O wild and loose to my soul—O wondrous singer!
You only I hear—yet the star holds me (but will soon depart),
Yet the lilac with the mastering odour holds me.

* * * * * *
* * * * * *

With the knowledge of death as walking one side of me,
And the thought of death close-walking the other side of me,
And I in the middle as with companions, and as holding the
   hands of companions,
I fled forth to the hiding receiving night that talks not,
Down to the shores of the water, the path by the swamp in
   the dimness,
To the solemn shadowy cedars and ghostly pines so still.

And the singer so shy to the rest received me,
The grey-brown bird I know receiv'd us comrades three,
And he sang the carol of death, and a verse for him I love.

*   *   *   *   *   *

*   *   *   *   *   *

And the charm of the carol rapt me,
As I held as if by their hands my comrades in the night,
And the voice of my spirit tallied the song of the bird.

Come, lovely and soothing death,
Undulate round the world, serenely arriving, arriving,
In the day, in the night, to all, to each,
Sooner or later delicate death.

       *   *   *   *   *   *

       *   *   *   *   *   *

Dark mother always gliding near with soft feet,
Have none chanted for thee a chant of fullest welcome?
Then I chant it for thee, I glorify thee above all,
I bring thee a song that when thou must indeed come, come un-
    falteringly.

       *   *   *   *   *   *

       *   *   *   *   *   *

From me to thee glad serenades,
Dances for thee I propose saluting thee, adornments and feastings for
    thee,
And the sights of the open landscape and the high-spread sky are fitting,
And life and the fields, and the huge and thoughtful night—

The night in silence under many a star,
The ocean shore and the husky whispering wave whose voice I know,
And the soul turning to thee, O vast and well-veil'd death,
And the body gratefully nestling close to thee.

Over the tree-tops I float thee a song,
Over the rising and sinking waves, over the myriad fields and the
    prairies wide,
Over the dense-pack'd cities all and the teeming wharves and ways,
I float this carol with joy, with joy to thee, O death.

The conclusion which follows, as it seems to me, from examination of what one experiences in perusing great Poetry—of which the three widely dissimilar pieces which I have quoted at length are eminent examples—is that the essential charm of Poetry—that for the sake of which, in the last resort, it exists—lies in its power of inducing, in certain carefully chosen circumstances, that mode of Transcendental

Feeling which is experienced as solemn sense of the over-shadowing presence of "That which was, and is, and ever shall be". The Poet, always by means of Representations—images—products of the dream-consciousness in himself, and often with the aid of Rhythm and Melody which call up certain shadowy Feelings, strange, in their shadowy form, to ordinary consciousness, induces in his patient the dream-consciousness in which such Representations and Feelings are at home. But the dream-consciousness induced in the patient by the imagery and melody of the Poet lasts only for a moment. The effect of even the most sustained Poetry is a succession of occasional lapses into the state of dream-consciousness, each one of which occurs suddenly and lasts but for a moment, in the midst of an otherwise continuous waking consciousness which is concerned, in a matter-of-fact way, with "what the poem is about," and "how the poet manages his theme," and a hundred other things. It is at the moment of waking from one of these lapses into the dream-world that the solemn sense of the immediate presence of "That which was, and is, and ever shall be" is experienced —at the moment when one sees, in the world of wide-awake consciousness, the image, or hears the melody, which one saw or heard only a moment ago—or, was it not ages ago?—in the dream-world:—

> A single moment brings me a deeper stillness, than five and twenty centuries have laid upon the quest which brought Neptune such wonder at the shadow of Argo.[1]

It is thus, as these sudden lapses, each followed immediately by waking and amazement, succeed one another, it may be, at long intervals, in a poem, that the power of its Poetry grows upon us. It is essential to our experiencing the power of Poetry that there should be intervals, and intervals of considerable length, between the lapses. The sense of having seen or heard things belonging to a world in which "Time is not" needs for its immediate realisation the presence, in the world of waking consciousness, of things which shall "re-mind" us of the things of that other world in which "Time is not"—without such things to "remind" us, there would

[1] Dante, *Paradiso*, xxxiii, 94-96.

be no "recollection" of our visit to the world in which
"Time is not". The poet's image, therefore, which began
by throwing us into the dream-state, must persist in the
state of waking consciousness to which we are now returned,
and there, as we look at it in the light of common day,
amaze us by its "resemblance" to an archetype seen in the
world in which "Time is not". And its persistence in the
world of waking consciousness can be guaranteed only by a
more or less wide context addressed to our ordinary faculties
—to the senses and understanding—and to our ordinary
sentiments. Over this matter-of-fact context, however, the
amazement produced in us when we perceive that the image,
or other product of the Poet's dream-consciousness, which
just now set us, too, a-dreaming, is double—is something
both in the world without Time, and in this temporal
world—casts a glamour for a while. Then the glamour
fades away, and we find ourselves accompanying the Poet
through the every-day world; and it may be in accordance
with the secret scheme which he is carrying out that we are
kept in this every-day world for a long while, in order that
we may be taken the more by surprise when suddenly, as
we journey, the light from heaven shines round about us.
"Whatever specific import," says Coleridge,[1] "we attach to
the word poetry, there will be found involved in it, as a
necessary consequence, that a poem of any length neither
can be, nor ought to be, all poetry."

The chief end of Poetry, then, is to induce Transcendental Feeling—experienced as solemn sense of the
immediate presence of "That which was, and is, and ever
shall be"—in the Poet's patient, by throwing him suddenly,
for a moment, into the state of dream-consciousness, out of
a waking consciousness which the Poet supplies with objects
of interest; the sudden lapse being effected in the patient by
the communication to him of images and other products of
the Poet's dream-consciousness, through the medium of
language generally, but not always, distinguished from that
of ordinary communication by rhythm and melody.

But the same result—the induction of the same form of
Transcendental Feeling—is produced, not only by the means

[1] *Biog. Lit.* ch. xiv.

which the Poet employs—dream-imagery communicated by
language generally, but not necessarily, rhythmic and
melodious—but also by different artistic means—by the
means which the Painter and the Musician respectively
employ; indeed—and this seems to me to be a matter of
first-rate importance for the Theory of Poetry—it is sometimes produced by mere Nature herself without the aid of
any art, and by events as they happen in one's life, and,
above all, by scenes and situations and persons remembered
out of the days of childhood and youth. "We are always
dreaming," Renan (I think) says somewhere, "of faces we
knew when we were eighteen." In this connection let me
ask the reader to consider Wordsworth's lines beginning—

> There was a Boy; ye knew him well, ye cliffs
> And islands of Winander—

It seems to me that the mere scene described in these lines—
a scene to which it would not be difficult to find parallels in
any one's experience—is, entirely apart from the language
in which it is described, and simply as a picture in the mind
of the person who remembers it, and in the minds of those
to whom he describes it, the *milieu* in which true poetic
effect is experienced. As I write this, I can hardly recall a
line of Wordsworth's description; but the picture which the
reading of his description has left in my mind is distinct;
and it is in dwelling on the picture that I feel the poetic
effect—as it was, I am convinced, in dwelling on the
picture, before he composed a line of the poem, that
the poet himself experienced the feeling which he has
communicated to me.   And the re-reading of such a
poem is more likely to impair than to enhance the feeling
experienced by one who has once for all pictured the scene.
    The more I read and re-read the works of the great
poets, and the more I study the writings of those who have
some Theory of Poetry to set forth, the more am I convinced that the question *What is Poetry?* can be properly
answered only if we make *What it does* take precedence of
How it does it. The result produced by Poetry—identical, I
hold, with that produced by the other fine arts, and even
sometimes by the mere contemplation of Nature and

Human Life—is the one thing of prime importance to be kept always in view, but is too often lost sight of in the examination of the means by which Poetry produces it, as distinguished from those by which, say, Painting produces it. Much that is now being written on the Theory of Poetry leaves one with the impression that the writers regard the end of Poetry as something *sui generis*—in fact, something not to be distinguished from the employment of technique peculiar to Poetry among the fine arts.[1] I shall return to this point afterwards.

In making the essential charm of Poetry—that for the sake of which, in the last resort, it exists—lie in its power of inducing, in certain carefully chosen circumstances, and so of regulating, Transcendental Feeling experienced as solemn sense of "That which was, and is, and ever shall be" over-shadowing us with its presence, I must not be taken to mean that there is no Poetry where this sense is not induced as a distinct ecstatic experience. Great Poetry, just in those places where it is at its very greatest, indeed shows its peculiar power not otherwise than by inducing such distinct ecstatic experience; but generally, poetic effect—not the very greatest, but yet indisputably poetic effect—is produced by something less—by the presence of this form of Transcen-dental Feeling in a merely nascent state—just a little more, and it would be there distinctly; as it is, there is a "magic", as we say, in the picture called up, or the natural sentiment aroused, which fills us with wonderful surmise—of what, we know not. This "magic" may be illustrated perhaps most instructively from lyric poetry, and there, from the lightest variety of the kind, from the simple love song. The pictures and sentiments suggested in the love song, regarded in themselves, belong to an experience which seems to be, more than any other, realised fully in the present, without intrusion of past or future to overcast its blue day with shadow. But look at these natural pictures and sentiments not directly, but as reflected in the magic mirror of Poetry! They are still radiant in the light of their Present—for let

---

[1] Mr. Courthope (*Life in Poetry*, p. 78) says: "Poetry lies in the invention of the right metrical form—be it epic, dramatic, lyric, or satiric—for the expression of some idea universally interesting to the imagination." And cf. p. 63.

D

us think now only of the happy love song, not of the love
song which is an elegy—they are still in their happy Present;
but they are not of it—they have become something "rich
and strange". No words can describe the change which
they have suffered; it is only to be felt—as in such lines as
these:—

Das Mädchen.
Ich hab' ihn gesehen!
Wie ist mir geschehen?
O himmlischer Blick!
Er kommt mir entgegen:
Ich weiche verlegen,
Ich schwanke zurück.
Ich irre, ich träume!
Ihr Felsen, ihr Bäume,
Verbergt meine Freude,
Verberget mein Glück!

Der Jüngling.
Hier muss ich sie finden!
Ich sah sie verschwinden,
Ihr folgte mein Blick.
Sie kam mir entgegen;
Dann trat sie verlegen
Und schamroth zurück.
Ist's Hoffnung, sind's Träume?
Ihr Felsen, ihr Bäume,
Entdeckt mir die Liebste,
Entdeckt mir mein Glück!

The magic of such lines as these is due, I cannot doubt,
to the immediate presence of some great mass of feeling
which they rouse, and, at the same time, hold in check,
behind our mere understanding of their literal meaning.
The pictures and sentiments conjured up, simple and
familiar though they are, have yet that about them which
I can only compare with the mysterious quality of those
indifferent things which are so carefully noticed, and those
trifling thoughts which are so seriously dwelt upon, in an
hour of great trouble.

But the Transcendental Feeling which, being pent up
behind our understanding of their literal meaning, makes
the magic of such lines, may burst through the iridescent
film which contains it. We have an example of this in the

transfiguration of the Earthly into the Heavenly Beatrice. The Transcendental Feeling latent behind our understanding of the praise of Beatrice in the earlier sonnets and canzoni of the *Vita Nuova* emerges as a distinct experience when we assist at her praise in the *Paradiso*. Contrast the eleventh sonnet of the *Vita Nuova* with the twenty-fifth, which, with its commentary, is a prelude to the *Paradiso*. The eleventh sonnet of the *Vita Nuova* ends:—

> Aiutatemi, donne, a farle onore.
> Ogni dolcezza, ogni pensiero umile
>   Nasce nel core a chi parlar la sente;
>   Ond' è beato chi prima la vide.
> Quel ch' ella par quand' un poco sorride,
>   Non si può dicer, nè tener a mente,
>   Sì è nuovo miracolo gentile.[1]

Here it is the magic of the lines which is all in all. Now let us turn to the twenty-fifth, the last, sonnet of the *Vita Nuova*, and to the words after it ending the book with the promise of more worthy praise—more worthy, because offered with a deeper sense of the encompassing presence of "That which was, and is, and ever shall be":—

> Beyond the sphere that circles most widely, passes the sigh that issues from my heart: a new intelligence that weeping Love places within it, draws it ever upwards.
> When it is joined to that for which it longs, it beholds a lady who receives honour, and shines so brightly that the pilgrim spirit wonders at her splendour.
> It so looks upon her, that, when it recounts it to me, I cannot understand, so subtly does it talk to the sorrowing heart that forces it to speak.
> I know that it tells of that gentle one, for often it recalls Beatrice, and so I understand it well, my dear ladies.

"Straightway after this sonnet was writ, there appeared unto me a marvellous vision, wherein I beheld things which made me determine not to say more concerning this Blessed

---

[1] Help me, Ladies, to do her honour.
All sweetness, every humble thought is born in the heart of him who hears her speak; whence he is given praise who first beheld her.
What she appears when she smiles a little, cannot be told nor held in mind, so fresh and gentle a miracle is she.

One until I should be able to speak of her more worthily. To this end I studied with all diligence, as she knoweth well. Wherefore, if it shall be the pleasure of Him through Whom all things live that my life endure for some years, I hope to say of her that which never before hath been said of woman. And then may it please Him Who is Lord of Courtesy that my Soul may go to behold the glory of her Lady, to wit, of that Blessed Beatrice, who in glory doth gaze upon the face of Him Who is blessed for evermore."

4. TRANSCENDENTAL FEELING, THE EXPERIENCE TO WHICH THE PLATONIC MYTH AND ALL OTHER FORMS OF POETRY APPEAL, EXPLAINED GENETICALLY.

Transcendental Feeling I would explain genetically (as every mood, whatever its present value may be—that is another matter—ought to be explained) as an effect produced within consciousness (and, in the form in which Poetry is chiefly concerned with Transcendental Feeling, within the dream-consciousness) by the persistence in us of that primeval condition from which we are sprung, when Life was still as sound asleep as Death, and there was no Time yet. That we should fall for a while, now and then, from our waking, time-marking life, into the timeless slumber of this primeval life is easy to understand; for the principle solely operative in that primeval life is indeed the fundamental principle of our nature, being that "Vegetative Part of the Soul" which made from the first, and still silently makes, the assumption on which our whole rational life of conduct and science rests—the assumption that Life is worth living. No arguments which Reason can bring for, or against, this ultimate truth are relevant; for Reason cannot stir without assuming the very thing which these arguments seek to prove or to disprove. "Live thy life" is the Categorical Imperative addressed by Nature to each one of her creatures according to its kind.

At the bottom of the scale of Life the Imperative is obeyed silently, in timeless sleep, as by the trees of the tropical forest:—

The fair and stately things,
Impassive as departed kings,
All still in the wood's stillness stood,
And dumb. The rooted multitude
Nodded and brooded, bloomed and dreamed,
Unmeaning, undivined. It seemed
No other art, no hope, they knew,
Than clutch the earth and seek the blue.

   *   *   *   *   *   *
   *   *   *   *   *   *

      My eyes were touched with sight.
I saw the wood for what it was:
The lost and the victorious cause,
The deadly battle pitched in line,
Saw weapons cross and shine:
Silent defeat, silent assault,
A battle and a burial vault.

   *   *   *   *   *   *
   *   *   *   *   *   *

Green conquerors from overhead
Bestrode the bodies of their dead:
The Cæsars of the sylvan field,
Unused to fail, foredoomed to yield:
For in the groins of branches, lo!
The cancers of the orchid grow.[1]

When to the "Vegetative" the "Sensitive" Soul is first
added, the Imperative is obeyed by creatures which, experiencing only isolated feelings, and retaining no traces of
them in memory, still live a timeless life, without sense of
past or future, and consequently without sense of selfhood.

Then, with Memory, there comes, in the higher animals,
some dim sense of a Self dating back and prospecting forward. Time begins to be. But the sense of its passage
brings no melancholy; for its end in death is not yet anticipated by reflective thought.

Man's anticipation of death would oppress his life with
insupportable melancholy, were it not that current employ-
ments, especially those which are spoken of as duties, are so
engrossing—that is, I would explain, were it not that his
conscious life feels down with its roots into that "Part of the

---

[1] *Songs of Travel*, R. L. Stevenson: "The Woodman".

Soul" which, without sense of past or future or self, silently holds on to Life, in the implicit faith that it is worth living —that there is a Cosmos in which it is good to be. As it is, there is still room enough for melancholy in his hours of ease and leisure. If comfort comes to him in such hours, it is not from his thinking out some solution of his melancholy, but from his putting by thought, and sinking, alone, or led by some *initiator into life*, for a while into the sleep of that by some initiator into life, for a while into the sleep of that fundamental "Part of the Soul". When he wakes into daily life again, it is with the elementary faith of this Part of his Soul newly confirmed in his heart; and he is ready, in the strength of it, to defy all that seems to give it the lie in the world of the senses and scientific understanding. Sometimes the very melancholy, which overclouds him at the thought of death, is transfigured, in the glow of this faith, into an exultant resignation—"I shall pass, but He abideth for ever." Sometimes, and more often, the faith does not merely transfigure, but dispels, the melancholy, and fills his heart with sweet hope, which fancy renders into dreams of personal immortality.

To sum up in effect what I have said about Transcendental Feeling: it is feeling which indeed appears in our ordinary object-distinguishing, time-marking consciousness, but does not originate in it. It is to be traced to the influence on consciousness of the presence in us of that "Part of the Soul" which holds on, in timeless sleep, to Life as worth living. Hence Transcendental Feeling is at once the solemn sense of Timeless Being—of "That which was, and is, and ever shall be" overshadowing us—and the conviction that Life is good. In the first-mentioned phase Transcendental Feeling appears as an abnormal experience of our conscious life, as a well-marked ecstatic state;[1] in its other phase—as conviction that Life is good—Transcendental Feeling may be said to be a normal experience of our conscious life: it is not an experience occasionally cropping up alongside of other experiences, but a feeling which accompanies all the experiences of our conscious

---

[1] See *Paradiso*, xxxiii. 82-96, quoted *supra*, p. 47, and *Vita Nuova*, Sonnet xxv., quoted *supra*, p. 63.

life—that "sweet hope",[1] in the strength of which we take the trouble to seek after the particular achievements which make up the waking life of conduct and science. Such feeling, though normal, is rightly called Transcendental,[2] because it is not one of the effects, but the condition, of our entering upon and persevering in that course of endeavour which makes experience.

5. THE PLATONIC MYTH ROUSES AND REGULATES TRANSCENDENTAL FEELING BY (1) IMAGINATIVE REPRESENTATION OF IDEAS OR REASON, AND (2) IMAGINATIVE DEDUCTION OF CATEGORIES OF THE UNDERSTANDING AND MORAL VIRTUES.

I have offered these remarks about Transcendental Feeling in order to preface a general statement which I now venture to make about the Platonic Myths—that they are Dreams expressive of Transcendental Feeling, told in such a manner and such a context that the telling of them regulates, for the service of conduct and science, the feeling expressed.

How then are conduct and science served by such regulation of Transcendental Feeling?

In the wide-awake life of conduct and science, Understanding, left to itself, claims to be the measure of truth; Sense, to be the criterion of good and bad. Transcendental Feeling, welling up from another "Part of the Soul", whispers to Understanding and Sense that they are leaving out something. What? Nothing less than the secret plan of the Universe. And what is that secret plan? The other "Part of the Soul" indeed comprehends it in silence as it is,[3] but can explain it to the Understanding only in the symbolical language of the interpreter, Imagination—in Vision.[4] In the Platonic Myth we assist at a Vision in which the wide-awake life of our ordinary experiences and

---

[1] "Sweet Hope is his companion, cheering his heart, the nurse of age— Hope who, more than any other, steers the capricious will of mortal men."— Pindar, quoted *Rep.* 331 A.

[2] As distinguished from "Empirical Feeling"; see *infra*, p. 351.

[3] Plotinus, *Enn.* iii. 8. 4, and see *infra*, p. 70.

[4] *Tim.* 71 D, E. The liver, the organ of Imagination, was used in divination.

doings is seen as an act in a vast drama of the creation and consummation of all things. The habitudes and faculties of our moral and intellectual constitution, which determine *a priori* our experiences and doings in this wide-awake life, are themselves clearly seen to be determined by causes which, in turn, are clearly seen to be determined by the Plan of the Universe which the Vision reveals. And more than this—the Universe, planned as the Vision shows, is the work—albeit accomplished under difficulties—of a wise and good God; for see how mindful He is of the welfare of man's soul throughout all its wanderings from creation to final purification, as the Vision unfolds them! We ought, then, to be of good hope, and to use strenuously, in this present life, habitudes and faculties which are so manifestly in accordance with a universal plan so manifestly beneficent.

It is as producing this mood in us that the Platonic Myth, Aetiological and Eschatological, regulates Transcendental Feeling for the service of conduct and science. In Aetiological Myth the Categories of the Understanding and the Moral Virtues are deduced from a Plan of the Universe, of which they are represented as parts seen, together with the whole, in a former life, and "remembered" piecemeal in this; in Aetiological and Eschatological (but chiefly in Eschatological) Myth the "Ideas of Reason", Soul, Cosmos, as completed system of the Good, and God, are set forth for the justification of that "sweet hope which guides the wayward thought of mortal man"—the hope without which we should not take the trouble to enter upon, and persevere in, that struggle after ever fuller comprehension of conditions,[1] ever wider "correspondence with environment", which the habits and faculties of our moral and intellectual structure—the Categories of the Understanding and the Moral Virtues—enable us to carry on in detail.

At this point, before I go on further to explain Plato's handling of Transcendental Feeling, I will make bold to explain my own metaphysical position. A very few words will suffice.

---

[1] Kant makes "Reason" (*i.e.* the whole man in opposition to this or that part, *e.g.* "understanding") the source of "Transcendental Ideas", described as "conceptions of the unconditioned", "conceptions of the totality of the conditions of any thing that is given as conditioned".

I hold that it is in Transcendental Feeling, manifested normally as Faith in the Value of Life, and ecstatically as sense of Timeless Being, and not in Thought proceeding by way of speculative construction, that Consciousness comes nearest to the object of Metaphysics, Ultimate Reality. It is in Transcendental Feeling, not in Thought, that Consciousness comes nearest to Ultimate Reality, because without that Faith in the Value of Life, which is the normal manifestation of Transcendental Feeling, Thought could not stir. It is in Transcendental Feeling that Consciousness is aware of "The Good"—of the Universe as a place in which it is good to be. Transcendental Feeling is thus the *beginning* of Metaphysics, for Metaphysics cannot make a start without assuming "The Good, or the Universe as a place in which it is good to be"; but it is also the *end* of Metaphysics, for Speculative Thought does not really carry us further than the Feeling, which inspired it from the first, has already brought us: we end, as we began, with the Feeling that it is good to be here. To the question, "Why is it good to be here?" the answers elaborated by Thought are no more really answers than those supplied by the Mythopœic Fancy interpreting Transcendental Feeling. When the former have value (and they are sometimes not only without value, but mischievous) they are, like those supplied by the Mythopœic Fancy, valuable as impressive affirmations of the Faith in us, not at all as explanations of its ground. Conceptual solutions of the "problem of the Universe" carry us no further along the pathway to reality than imaginative solutions do. The reason why they are thought to carry us further is that they mimic those conceptual solutions of departmental problems which we are accustomed to accept, and do well to accept, from the positive sciences. Imaginative solutions of the "problem of the Universe" are thought to be as inferior to conceptual solutions as imaginative solutions of departmental problems are to conceptual. The fallacy involved in this analogy is that of supposing that there is a "problem of the Universe"—a difficulty presented which Thought may "solve". The "problem of the Universe" was first propounded, and straightway solved, at the moment when Life began on the earth—when a living being—as such, from the very first, lacking nothing which is essential to "selfhood" or "personality"—first appeared as Mode of the Universe. The "problem of the Universe" is not propounded to Consciousness, and Consciousness cannot solve it. Consciousness can *feel* that it has been propounded and solved elsewhere, but cannot genuinely *think* it. It is "propounded" to that on which Consciousness supervenes (and supervenes only because the problem has been already "solved")—it is propounded to what I would call "selfhood", or "personality", and is ever silently being "understood" and "solved" by that principle, in the continued "vegetative life" of individual and race. And the most trustworthy, or least misleading, report of what the "problem" is, and what its "solution" is, reaches Consciousness through Feeling. Feeling stands nearer than Thought does to that basal self or personality which is, indeed, at once the living "problem of the Universe" and its living "solution". The whole matter is summed up for me in the words of Plotinus, with which I will conclude this statement which I have ventured to make of my metaphysical position: "If a man were to inquire of Nature—'Wherefore dost thou bring forth creatures?' and she were willing to give ear and to answer, she would say—'Ask me not, but understand in silence, even as I am silent'."[1]

In suggesting that the Platonic Myth awakens and regulates Transcendental Feeling (1) by imaginative representation of Ideas of Reason, and (2) by imaginative deduction of Categories of the Understanding and Moral Virtues, I do not wish to maintain that the Kantian distinction between Categories of the Understanding and Ideas of Reason was explicit in Plato's mind. There is plenty of evidence in his writings to show that it was not explicit; but it is a distinction of vital importance for philosophical thought, and it need not surprise us to find it sometimes implicitly recognised by a thinker of Plato's calibre. At any rate, it is a distinction which the student of Plato's Myths will do well to have explicit in his own mind. Let us remind ourselves, then, of what Kant means by Categories of the Understanding and Ideas of Reason respectively.

Kant's Categories of the Understanding are certain *a priori* Conceptions, certain Characters of the Mental Struc-

[1] Plot. *Enn.* iiiB. 4.

ture, without which there could be no "experience"—no "knowledge" of that which alone is "known", the world of sensible phenomena. These Categories, however, if they are not to remain mere logical abstractions, must be regarded as *functions* of the Understanding—as active manifestations of the unifying principle of mind or consciousness. As functions, the Categories need for their actual manifestation the presence of "sensations". In the absence of sensations they are "empty". They are functions of the mental organism or structure which are called into operation by stimulation from "environment", and that only in *schemata* or "figurations" involving the "garment" or "vehicle" of Time.[1] Thus, the Category of Substance is realised in "the schema of the persistent in time"—Something present to sense is perceived as "Substance" persisting in change of "attributes"; the Category of Cause is realised in "the schema of succession in time"—two sensible phenomena, one of which is antecedent and the other consequent, are conceived as cause and effect—the latter is conceived as following necessarily from the former. "The schemata, then, are the true scientific categories."[2] This amounts to saying that the Understanding, if rightly conducted, will never make a transcendental use, but only an empirical use, of any of its *a priori* principles. These principles can apply only to objects of sense, as conforming to the universal conditions of a possible experience (*phenomena*), and never to things as such (*noumena*), or apart from the manner in which we are capable of perceiving them.[3]

In contrast to the Categories of the Understanding which are *immanent*—adequately realised in sense experience; we say, for instance, that this thing present to sense *is cause* of that other thing—the Ideas of Reason are *transcendent:* they overleap the limits of all experience—in experience no objects can be presented that are adequate to them. They are defined, generally, as "problematic conceptions of the totality of conditions of anything that is given as condi-

[1] See Wallace's *Kant*, p. 172.
[2] Wallace's *Kant*, p. 173.
[3] See *Kritik d. reinen Vern.* [2] pp. 297, 298, 303. A conception is employed transcendentally when it occurs in a proposition regarding things *as such* or *in themselves*; empirically, when the proposition relates merely to *phenomena*, or objects of a possible experience.

tioned"; or, since the unconditioned alone makes a totality of conditions possible, as "conceptions of the unconditioned, in so far as it contains a ground for the synthesis of the conditioned".[1] There are three Ideas of Reason, products of its activity in "carrying the fragmentary and detailed results of human experience to their rational issues in a postulated totality . . . . These three ideas are the Soul, as the supersensible substance from which the phenomena of Consciousness are derivative manifestations; the World [Cosmos, Universe], as ultimate totality of external phenomena; and God, as unity and final spring of all the diversities of existence. The ideas, strictly as ideal, have a legitimate and a necessary place in human thought. They express the unlimited obligation which thought feels laid upon itself to unify the details of observation; they indicate an anticipated and postulated convergence between the various lines indicated by observation, even though observation may show that the convergence will never visibly be reached; or they are standards and model types towards which experience may, and indeed must, if she is true to the cause of truth, conceive herself bound to approximate. Such is the function of ideas, as regulative; they govern and direct the action of intellect in the effort to systematise and centralise knowledge . . . . But the ideas naturally sink into another place in human knowledge. Instead of stimulating research, they become, as Kant once puts it, a cushion for the lazy intellect. Instead of being the ever-unattainable goals of investigation, they play a part in founding the edifice of science. Ceasing to be *regulative* of research, they come to be *constitutive* of a pretended knowledge."[2]

The Ideas of Reason, then, are aims, aspirations, ideals; but they have no adequate objects in a possible experience. The three "Sciences" which venture to define objects for them—Rational Psychology, Rational Cosmology, and Theology—are, according to Kant, sham sciences. The Idea of Soul, the absolute or unconditioned unity of the thinking subject, has no object in possible experience answering to it. We are making an illegitimate transcendental use of a

[1] *Kritik,*[2] pp. 379, 384 (Prof. Watson's Transl.).
[2] Wallace's *Kant,* pp. 182, 183.

Category when we conceive the subject of all knowledge as an object under the Category of Substance. Similarly, the ultimate totality of external phenomena—the Cosmos as absolute whole—is not an object of possible experience; it is not something given in sense, to be brought under Categories or scientific conceptions. Finally, the Idea of God is perverted from its regulative use, when it is made the foundation of a science—Dogmatic Theology—which applies the Categories of Substance, Cause, and the rest, to a Supreme Being, as if He were an object presented in sense experience.

To sum up:—The Categories of the Understanding are so many conditions of thought which Human Understanding, constituted as it is, expects to find, and does find, fully satisfied in the details of sensible experience. The Ideas of Reason indicate the presence of a condition of thought which is not satisfied in any particular item of experience. They are aspirations or ideals expressing that nisus after fuller and fuller comprehension of conditions, wider and wider correspondence with environment—in short, that nisus after Life, and faith in it as good, without which man would not will to pursue the experience rendered possible in detail by the Categories. But although there can be no *speculative science* of objects answering to the Ideas of Reason, we should come to naught if we did not *act as if* there were such objects; and any representation of objects answering to these Ideas which does not invite exposure by pretending to scientific rank is valuable as helping us to "*act as if*". The objects of these Ideas are objects, not for science, but for faith. When the scientific understanding "proves" that God exists, or that the Soul is immortal, refutation lies near at hand; but the "as if" of the moral agent rests on a sure foundation.[1]

---

[1] "We have three postulates of practical reason which are closely related to the three Ideas of theoretical reason. These Ideas reason in its theoretical use set before itself as problems to be solved; but it was unable to supply the solution. Thus, the attempt to prove theoretically the permanence of the thinking subject led only to paralogism; for it involved a confusion of the subject presupposed in all knowledge of objects, and only in that point of view permanent, with an object known under the Category of Substance. But now we find that a faith of reason in the endless existence of the self-conscious subject is bound up with the possibility of his fulfilling the moral law. Again, the attempt speculatively to determine the world as a system

To return now from Kant to Plato:—Plato's Myths
induce and regulate Transcendental Feeling for the service
of conduct and knowledge by setting forth the *a priori*
conditions of conduct and knowledge—that is, (1) by
representing certain ideals or presuppositions, in concrete
form—the presuppositions of an immortal Soul, of an
intelligible Cosmos, and of a wise and good God—all three
being natural expressions of the sweet hope in the faith of
which man lives and struggles on and on; and (2) by tracing
to their origin in the wisdom and goodness of God, and the
constitution of the Cosmos, certain habitudes or faculties
(categories and virtues), belonging to the make of man's
intellectual and moral nature, which prescribe the various
modes in which he must order in detail the life which his
faith or sweet hope impels him to maintain. Myth, not
argumentative conversation, is rightly chosen by Plato as
the vehicle of exposition when he deals with *a priori* conditions of conduct and knowledge, whether they be ideals or
faculties. When a man asks himself, as he must, for the
reason of the hope in which he struggles on in the ways
prescribed by his faculties, he is fain to answer—"Because I
am an immortal Soul, created with these faculties by a wise
and good God, under whose government I live in a Universe
which is His finished work." This answer, according to
Plato, as I read him, is the natural and legitimate expression of the "sweet hope which guides the wayward
thought of mortal man"; and the expression reacts on—
gives strength and steadiness to—that which it expresses.
It is a "true answer" in the sense that man's life would

complete in itself landed us in an antinomy which we were able to escape
only by the distinction of the phenomenal from the intelligible world—a
distinction which theoretic reason suggested, but which it could not verify.
But now, the moral law forces us to think ourselves as free, and therefore as
belonging to an intelligible world which we are further obliged to treat as
the reality of which the phenomenal world is the appearance. Lastly, the
Absolute Being was to theoretic reason a mere ideal which knowledge could
not realise; but now His existence is certified to us as the necessary condition
of the possibility of the object of a Will determined by the moral law. Thus,
through practical reason we gain a conviction of the reality of objects
corresponding to the three Ideas of Pure Reason. We do not, indeed,
acquire what is properly to be called knowledge of these objects. We only
change the problematic conception of them into an assertion of their real
existence; but, as we are not able to bring any perception under such Ideas,
so we are unable to make any synthetic judgment regarding the objects the
existence of which we assert."—Caird's *Critical Philosophy of Kant*, ii. 297.

come to naught if he did not act and think *as if* it were true. But Soul, Cosmos as completed system of the Good, and God are not particular objects presented, along with other particular objects, in sensible experience. This the Scientific Understanding fails to grasp. When it tries to deal with them—and it is ready enough to make the venture —it must needs envisage them, *more suo*, as though they were particular objects which could be brought under its Categories in sensible experience. Then the question arises, "Where are they?" And the answer comes sooner or later, "They are nowhere to be found." Thus "science" chills the "sweet hope" in which man lives, by bringing the natural expression of it into discredit.

This, I take it, is Plato's reason for employing Myth, rather than the language and method of "science", when he wishes to set forth the *a priori* as it expresses itself in Ideals. In the *mise en scène* of the *Timaeus* or Myth of Er, Soul, Cosmos, and God are presented concretely indeed, but in such visionary form that there is little danger of mistaking them for particulars of sense requiring "scientific explanation". Again, as for the *a priori* Habitudes or Faculties of man's moral and intellectual structure, whereby he corresponds with his invironment in detail—these, too, Plato holds, are to be set forth in Myth; for they are properly set forth when they are "deduced"—traced to their origin, which is that of the Cosmos—a matter beyond the reach of the Scientific Understanding. It is in a Myth of *Reminiscence*, therefore, such as that in the *Phaedrus*, that we must take account of the question of "the origin of knowledge"; in a Myth such as that of the *Golden Age* in the *Laws*, of the question of "the origin of society".[1]

These and other ultimate "questions of origin", carrying us back as they do to the nature of God and the constitution of the Cosmos, are not for "science". Plato found Myth invested in the minds of his contemporaries with the authority of old tradition and the new charm which Pindar and the tragedians had bestowed upon it; perhaps, too, if my

---

[1] The spirit, and much in the detail, of the *Cratylus* justify the view that Plato approached the question of the "origin of language" too through mythology.

suggestion[1] has any value, he found it associated, in his own mind and the minds of other Socratic men, with the personal influence of the Master where that influence was most impressive and mysterious—he found Myth thus ready to his hand, and he took it up, and used it in an original way for a philosophical purpose, and transformed it as the Genius of Sculpture transformed the wooden images of Daedalus.

Further remarks on the *a priori* in conduct and knowledge as set forth by means of the mythological deduction of Faculties will be best deferred till we come to the *Phaedrus* Myth; but some general observations on the *a priori* as set forth by means of the mythological representation of Ideals— "forms of hope,"[2] "objects of faith"—may be helpful at this introductory stage. Let us then consider broadly, first, Plato's handling of the "Idea of God", and then his handling of the "Idea of Soul". Consideration of his handling of the "Idea of Cosmos" may well be deferred till we come to the *Timaeus*.

6. PLATO'S TREATMENT OF THE IDEA OF GOD.

To the religious consciousness, whether showing itself in the faith which "non-religious people" sometimes find privately and cling to in time of trouble, or expressed to the world in the creeds and mythologies of the various religions, the Idea of God is the idea of a Personal God, or, it may be, of personal Gods. The God of the religious consciousness, whatever else he may be, is first of all a separate individual—one among other individuals, human and, it may be, superhuman, to whom he stands in relations by which he is determined or limited. He is Maker, King, Judge, Father, Friend. It may be true that attributes logically inconsistent with his being a finite individual person are ascribed to him in some of the creeds; but the inconsistency, when perceived, is always so dealt with that the all-important idea of his personality is left with undiminished power. The idea of the separate individuality or personality

[1] *Supra*, p. 26.
[2]   It never yet did hurt,
  To lay down likelihoods and forms of hope.
                    Henry IV. (Part ii.), i. 3.

of the Self is not more essential to the moral consciousness than the idea of the separate individuality or personality of God is to the religious consciousness; and in the religious consciousness, at any rate, both of these ideas are involved—an individual Self stands in a personal relation to another individual, God.[1]

But logical thinking—whether in natural science or in metaphysics—when it busies itself, as it is too fond of doing, with the "Idea of God", arrives at a conclusion—this cannot be too plainly stated—flatly opposed to the conviction of the religious consciousness. Aristotle's *energy without force* is not a Person; nor is Spinoza's *Infinite Substance;* nor is the Absolute of later systems, although its true logical character has sometimes been disguised; nor is the "Nature" of modern science. Logical or scientific thinking presupposes and makes explicit the idea of an orderly Universe, of an organic whole determining necessarily the behaviour of its parts, of a single system realising itself fully, at every moment and at every place, in events which, for the most part, recur, and recurring retain a uniform character, or only change their character gradually. We should not be here, science assures us—living beings, acting and thinking—if the changes in our environment were catastrophic, not orderly and gradual. But although the Universe must be orderly *if* we are to live, it does not follow that it is orderly *that* we may live. Logical or scientific thinking, as such, scouts teleology in that form in which it is cherished by the religious consciousness, belief in a Particular Providence—logical or scientific thinking, *as such*, that is, when it is not deflected from its path, as it sometimes is, by the attraction of religious conviction, just as the religious consciousness, on the other hand, is sometimes disturbed by science. Teleology, when taken up seriously, not merely played with, is a method which assumes the intentions of a Personal Ruler of the Universe, and explains the means which he employs in order to carry out his intentions.[2] Logical or scientific

---

[1] Cf. *Hegelianism and Personality*, A. S. Pringle-Pattison, pp. 217-218.

[2] In saying that "science" scouts the teleology which recommends itself to the "religious consciousness" I do not think that I contradict the view, so ably enforced by Prof. W. James, that "teleology is the essence of intelligence" —that the translation, in which "science" consists, of the perceptual into the conceptual order "always takes place for the sake of some subjective *interest,*

thinking, as such, finds it inconceivable that the Part—and a Personal God, an individual distinguished from other individuals, is a Part—should thus rule the Whole. If science and the religious consciousness try, as they sometimes do, to come to an understanding with each other on the basis of such a phrase as "Infinite Person" or "Universal Consciousness", the result is only to bring out more clearly, in the self-contradictory phrase, the incompatibility of their two points of view, and to make the breach, which it is attempted thus to heal, still wider. It is wise to recognise, once for all, that the scientific understanding, working within its own region, finds no place for a Personal God, and that the religious consciousness demands a Personal God—a Part which rules the Whole. The scientific conception of Whole ruling Parts is, indeed, so distasteful to the religious consciousness that it always leans to Polytheism rather than to Monotheism.

That the incompatibility of the scientific conception with the conviction of the religious consciousness was present to Plato's mind is proved, as it seems to me, by the circumstance that it is in Myth that he presents the idea of a Personal God and the correlate idea of a Personal Immortality of the Soul.

Lest it should be objected that it is "unhistorical" to ascribe to Plato any perception of the issue on which religion and "modern science" are at variance, it may be well to point out that Plato's pupil, Aristotle, was aware of the issue, and faced it with characteristic directness. Any one who reads the *Metaphysics*, *De Anima*, and *Ethics* in connection will be struck by the way in which the logician gives up, apparently without scruple, the idea of a Personal God, and the correlate idea of the Personal Immortality of the Soul.

It may help us to make out what Plato hopes for from presenting these correlate ideas, in Myth, to the adult readers of his Dialogue, if we recall what he lays down in the second book of the *Republic* about the religious instruction

. . . and the conception with which we handle a bit of sensible experience is really nothing but a teleological instrument. *This whole function of conceiving, of fixing, and holding-fast to meanings, has no significance apart from the fact that the conceiver is a creature with partial purposes and private ends.*"—*Princ. of Psych.* i. 482.

of young children, on which all mental and moral education, according to him, is to be founded.

The education of children, he tells us, is not to begin with instruction in "facts" or "truths". It is not to begin, as we might say, with the "elementary truths of science" and "facts of common life", as learned in the primer. Young children cannot yet understand what is true in fact. We must begin, then, with what is false in fact—with fictions, with stories. Their only faculty is that of being interested in stories. Hence it is all important to have good stories to tell them—to invent Myths with a good tendency. They are to be told what is *literally false,* in order that they may get hold of what is *spiritually true*—the great fundamental truth that God is "beneficent" and "truthful"—both adjectives applicable to a person; and a *finite* person, for they are to believe that he is the author only of what is good.

That God is such a finite person, then, is *true,* Plato would tell us; not, indeed, true in the sense in which the description of phenomena or data of experience may be *true,* but true, as being the only or best possible expression, at least for children, of the maxim or principle of guidance without which human life must come to naught. If children believe that God is the author, not of good only, but of evil, they will grow up to be discontented and without hope—without faith in the good providence which helps those who help themselves—ready always to blame God or bad luck, rather than themselves, for their troubles and failures. If they do not believe that he is truthful, they will grow up to be careless observers and abstract reasoners, neglecting, as insignificant and "due to accident", those so-called little things which the careful interpreter of nature recognises as important signs and symptoms. They will grow up without the principles on which Conduct and Science respectively depend. On the one hand, they will be without that "hope which guides the wayward thoughts of men"—the faith (which indeed all struggle for existence implies) that honest effort will, on the whole, succeed in attaining good; they will believe instead—so far as it is possible for a living being to believe this—that "life is not worth living"; and so far as they are not, and cannot be, consistent pessimists, they will be selfish, individualistic citizens. On the other hand, if they have not been taught in their childhood to believe that "God is truthful", they will grow up without the first postulate of science—faith in the order and interpretability of the world. In one sentence—"The Lie in the Soul"— the spirit of pessimism in conduct and scepticism in science— will bring to naught all those who have not believed, in their childhood, that God is a Person, good and true. *In their childhood:* May they, will they, give up afterwards the belief in his Personality when it has done its work?

Most of them, continuing to live in "sense and imagination"—albeit, under good guidance, useful lives—will have no difficulty in retaining the belief of their childhood; but a few will become so "logical" that they will hardly be able to retain it.

It is in relation to the needs of these latter that we ought to consider the Myths setting forth the idea of a Personal God and the correlate idea of Personal Immortality of the Soul, which Plato has put into his Dialogues. In these Myths they have *representations* of what they once believed *as fact* without questioning. .They see the world of childhood —that dream-world which was once so real—put on the stage for them by a great Maker of Mysteries and Miracles.

But why *represent* it? That the continuity of their lives may be brought home to them—that they may be led to sympathise with what they were, and, sympathising, to realise that what they now are—is due to what they were. It is because the continuity of life is lost sight of, that religious conviction and scientific thought are brought into opposition. The scientific thinker, looking back over his life, is apt to divide it sharply into the time during which he believed what is not true, and the time during which he has known the truth.

Thus to fail in sympathy with his own childhood, and with the happy condition of the majority of men and women, and with the feelings which may yet return to comfort him when the hour of his death draws near, betokens, Plato would say, a serious flaw in a man's "philosophy of life". The man abstracts "the present time" from its setting in his whole life. He plucks from its stem the "knowledge of

truth", and thinks that it still lives. The "knowledge of
truth", Plato would tell us, does not come except to the
man whose character has been formed and understanding
guided, in childhood and youth, by unquestioning faith
in the goodness and truthfulness of a Personal God. And
this faith he must reverence all his life through, looking
back to his childhood and forward to his death. To
speak of this faith as false, and a thing of the past, is
what no Thinker will care to do. The Thinker—"the
spectator of all time and all existence"—does not cut up the
organic unity of his life into the abstractions of Past, and
Present, and Future—Past which is non-existent, Present
which is a mere imaginary point, Future which is non-
existent. His life is all one Present, concrete, continuous,
indivisible.[1]

The man who cuts up life into Past, Present, and Future,
does so with the intent of appropriating something for his
own private use. The Thinker, who sees Life clearly and
sees it whole, will regard religious belief and scientific knowledge as both means for the sake of conduct, or corporate
action. He will show his devotion to this end by setting his
face steadily against individualism in the pursuit of knowledge and the holding of belief—against the scientific
specialist's ideal of the indefinite accumulation of knowledge
—against the priest's doctrine of the *opus operatum*, effectual
in securing the only true good, as it is thought, the private
profit of the individual—hardest of all, against the refined
form of individualism by which he is himself tempted, the
individualism of the schoolman, or doctrinaire, who withdraws himself within his logical faculty, and pleases himself
there with the construction of "a System"—"Words made
to resemble each other on purpose."

In the Allegory[2] of the *Cave*, Plato shows us the victory
of the Thinker over individualism. The Thinker has come
out at last into the daylight, and, when he might stay in it
always and enjoy it, he will not stay, but returns into the
Cave to pay for his upbringing—the debt which he owes for

---

[1] He realises in an eminent degree what seems to be the experience of
us all; for "our 'present' is always an extended time", not an indivisible
point: see Bosanquet's *Logic*, i. 351.
[2] —and Myth; see *infra*, p. 245.

the education which he has received—by carrying on, in the training of a new generation, the régime to which he owes it that he has seen the light. "We shall compel him to return," Plato says, and he adds, "We do him no injustice." The compulsion is moral, not external.[1] It is the *obligation* which the perfectly educated man feels laid upon him by his consciousness of his inherence in the continuous life of his city—the obligation of seeing to it that his own generation shall have worthy successors.

How important, then, to keep alive in the elders sympathy with the faith in which it is necessary they should bring up the young generation! Consciousness of what they owe as nurture, and earnest desire to pass the State on to worthy successors, will do most to keep alive this sympathy; but, on the other hand, the logical understanding will always be reminding them that "in truth" (though perhaps not "in practice") the doctrines of science and the convictions of the religious consciousness are "incompatible"; and it is here, I take it, with regard to this difficulty started by abstract thought, that Plato hopes for good from Myth, as from some great Ritual at which thinkers may assist and feel that there are mysteries which the scientific understanding cannot fathom.

That the scientific understanding, then, working within its own region, must reject the idea of a Personal God, was, I take it, as clear to Plato as it was to Aristotle.

Would Plato, then, say that the proposition "There is a Personal God" is *not true*? He would say that what children are to be taught to believe—"that once upon a time God or the Gods did this thing or that"—is not true as historical fact. Where historical or scientific *fact* is concerned, the scientific understanding is within its own region, and is competent to say "it is *true*" or "it is *not true*". But the scientific understanding cannot be allowed to criticise its own foundation—that which all the faculties of the living man, the scientific understanding itself included, take for granted—"that it is *good* to go on living the human life into which I have been born; and that it is worth while employing my faculties carefully in the conduct of my life, for they do

---

[1] *Rep.* 520.

not deceive me." This fundamental assumption of Life, "It is good to live, and my faculties are trustworthy," Plato throws into the proposition, "There is a Personal God, good and true, who keeps me in all my ways." He wishes children to take this proposition literally. He knows that abstract thinkers will say that "it is not true"; but he is satisfied if the men, whose parts and training have made them influential in their generation, read it to mean—things happen *as if* they were ordered by a Personal God, good and true. To this *as if*—this recognition of "Personal God" as "Regulative Principle"—they are helped—so I take Plato to think—by two agencies, of which Myth, breaking in upon the logic of the Dialogue with the *representation* of the religious experience of childhood, and of venerable old age like that of Cephalus, is one. The other agency is Ritual.[1] This is recognised by Plato as very important; and Myth may be taken to be its literary counterpart. One of the most significant things in the *Republic* is the deference paid to Delphi. Philosophy—that is, the Constitution of the Platonic State—indeed lays down "canons of orthodoxy",[2] and determines the religious dogma; but the ritual is to be determined from without, by Delphi.[3] Religion is to be at once rational and traditional—at once reformed, and conservative of catholic use. Plato was not in a position to realise the difficulty involved in this arrangement. It is a modern discovery, that ritual reacts on dogma, and in some cases even creates it. Plato seems to take for granted that the pure religious dogma of his State will not in time be

---

[1] "A rite is an assemblage of symbols, grouped round a religious idea or a religious act, intended to enhance its solemn character or develop its meaning—just as a myth is the grouping of mythic elements associated under a dramatic form. . . . Thus we have the rite of baptism, funeral rites, sacrificial rites." Réville, *Prolégomènes de l'Histoire des Religions* (Eng. Transl. by Squire), p. 110.

[2] *Rep.* 379 A.

[3] *Rep.* 427 B, "What then", he asked, "still remains for us as legislators to do?" And I replied, "For us, nothing, but for the Delphian Apollo there will remain the best and the most beautiful and highest acts of legislation." "What are these?" "The erection of temples, and sacrifices and other services of the Gods and daemons and heroes, and the methods of disposal of the dead, and all observances to be adopted to keep them happy. For such things we do not understand ourselves, and in founding a city we shall not, if we are wise, be persuaded by any other, nor obey any leader but our country's Guide. For this God, I think, instructs all men in such subjects, as national prophet, seated on the Omphalos at the world's centre."

affected by the priestly ritual. At any rate, he assumes that his State, as the civil head of a united Hellas,[1] and Delphi, as the ecclesiastical head, will, like Empire and Church in Dante's *De Monarchia*, be in sympathy with each other.

It is plain, then, from the place—if I have rightly indicated the place—which Plato assigns to Ritual in daily life, and to Myth in philosophical literature,[2] what place he assigns to the scientific understanding.

The scientific understanding, which is only a small part, and a late developed part, of the whole man, as related to his whole environment, is apt, chiefly because it has the gift of speech and can explain itself, while our deeper laid faculties are dumb, to flatter itself with the conceit that it is the measure of all things—that what is to it inconceivable is impossible. It cannot conceive the Part ruling the Whole: therefore it says that the proposition "the World is ruled by a Personal God" is *not true*.

Plato has, so far as I can gather, two answers to this pronouncement of the scientific understanding. The first is, "Life would come to naught if we acted *as if* the scientific understanding were right in denying the existence of a Personal God"; and he trusts to Ritual and Myth (among other agencies) to help men to feel this. His attitude here is very like Spinoza's:—

> That God seeks no other knowledge of himself from men through the prophets, than knowledge of his divine justice and love, that is to say, such attributes of God as men can imitate by a certain course of life, as Jeremiah teaches in exact words (xxii, 15, 16) . . . The evangelical doctrine contains nothing beyond simple faith; only to believe in God and to revere him, or, what is the same thing, to obey him . . . It follows lastly that faith requires not so much truths, as religious teachings, that is, such as move the mind

---

[1] See *infra*, pp. 403, 404, where it is argued that Plato's beautiful city is misunderstood (as in part by Aristotle) if its constitution is taken to be drawn for an isolated municipality, and not for an Empire-city (like the antediluvian Athens of the Atlantis Myth), under which, as civil head (Delphi being the ecclesiastical head), Hellas should be united against barbarians for the propagation of liberty and culture in the world.

[2] Or rather, in philosophical *conversation;* for the Platonic Dialogues, after all, with their written discussions and myths, are only offered as models to be followed in actual conversation—*actual* conversation being essential to the continued life of Philosophy.

to obedience. So the object of faith is not so much to exact
truth as piety.[1]

Plato's other answer goes deeper. It consists in showing
that the "Whole", or all-embracing Good, cannot be
grasped scientifically, but must be seen imperfectly in a
similitude.[2] The logical understanding, as represented by
Glaucon, not satisfied with knowing what the all-embracing
Good is *like*, wishes to know what it *is*—as if it were an
object presented to knowledge. But the Good is not an
object presented to knowledge. It is the condition of knowledge. It is like Light which is not one of the things seen,
but the condition of seeing. To suppose that the Whole,
or Good, is an object, among objects, of knowledge, is the
fault which Plato, as I read him, finds with the logical
understanding; and a Platonist might, I think, be allowed
to develop the Master's criticism as follows:—The conception of "Whole" or "Universe" which the logical understanding professes to have, and manipulates in its proof of
the non-existence of a Personal God, is not a "conception"
at all. The understanding *cannot* conceive the Universe as
finished Whole. Its "whole" is always also a "part" of
something indefinitely greater. The argument that "the
Ruler of the Universe is not a Personal God, because the
Part cannot rule the Whole," juggling, as it does, with this
sham conception—that of "Whole which is not also Part"—
is inconclusive.

7. PLATO'S TREATMENT OF THE IDEA OF SOUL.

Let us now turn to the "Idea of Soul". The Soul is
represented in the three strictly Eschatological Myths of the
Phaedo, *Gorgias*, and *Republic*, and in other Myths not strictly
Eschatological, as a Person created by God, and responsible
to him for acts in which it is a free agent within limits set by
Necessity—responsible to God throughout an existence which
began before its incarnation in this body, and will continue
for ever after the death of this body—an existence in which.

[1] Spinoza, *Tractatus Theologico-politicus*, chapters 13 and 14.
[2] *Rep.* 506.

it is subject to periodical re-incarnations, alternating with terms of disembodiment, during which it receives recompense for the deeds done in the flesh; till at last—if it is not incorrigible—it is thoroughly purified by penance, and enters into the peace of a never-ending disembodied state, like that which it enjoyed in its own peculiar star, before it began the cycle of incarnations.

Zeller,[1] while admitting that many details in Plato's doctrine of the pre-existence and future destiny of the immortal Soul are mythic, maintains that the doctrine itself, in its broad outlines, is held by him dogmatically, and propounded as scientific truth. Pre-existence, recollection, retribution, re-incarnation, final purification, and never-ending disembodied existence of the purified soul—these, Zeller thinks, are set forth by Plato as facts which are literally true. Hegel,[2] on the other hand, holds that the Platonic doctrine of the Soul is wholly mythic. I take it from a passage in the Introduction to the *Critique of Pure Reason*[3] that Kant would think with Zeller against Hegel. Where such authorities differ one might well remain neutral; but I cannot help saying that I incline to the view that the bare doctrine of immortality (not to mentioned the details of its setting) is conceived by Plato in Myth, and not dogmatically—or perhaps I ought to say, conceived *eminently* in Myth; for the dogmatic way of conceiving

---

[1] Zeller, *Plato*, Eng. Transl. pp. 397-413. Thiemann (*Die Platonische Eschatologie in ihrer genetischen Entwickelung*, 1892, p. 27) agrees with Zeller.

[2] Hegel, *Werke*, vol. xiv. pp. 207 ff. Couturat (*de Platonis Mythis*, Paris, 1896, pp. 84-88) agrees with Hegel. Grote (*Plato*, ii. 190, n. q.) expresses qualified agreement: "There is ingenuity," he says, "in this view of Hegel, and many separate expressions of Plato receive light from it; but it appears to me to refine away too much. Plato had in his own mind and belief both the Soul as a particular thing, and the Soul as an universal. His language implies sometimes the one, sometimes the other." That Coleridge would have endorsed Hegel's view is clear from the following passage in *Biogr. Lit.* ch. 22. Speaking of Wordsworth's Ode on the Intimations of Immortality from Recollections of Early Childhood, he says: "The Ode was intended for such readers only as had been accustomed to watch the flux and reflux of their inmost nature, to venture at times into the twilight realms of consciousness, and to feel a deep interest in modes of inmost being, to which they know that the attributes of time and space are inapplicable and alien, but which yet cannot be conveyed, save in symbols of time and space. For such readers the sense is sufficiently plain, and they will be as little disposed to charge Mr. Wordsworth with believing the platonic pre-existence in the ordinary interpretation of the words, as I am to believe that Plato himself ever meant or taught it."

[3] See *infra*, pp. 97, 98, where the passage is quoted.

immortality is not formally excluded on Platonic, as it is on Kantian, principles; although the mere circumstance that Plato has an alternative way of conceiving it—the mythological way, not to mention the great attraction which the mythological way plainly has for him—shows that he was dissatisfied with the scientific proof of immortality— entertained a doubt, to say the least, whether "the Soul is immortal" ought to be regarded as a scientific truth.

Nor need Plato's doubt surprise us, when we consider the state of opinion in the Athens of his day. Belief in personal immortality had become very feeble among a large number of educated and even half-educated people in Athens.[1] For the belief of the ordinary half-educated man, the Attic Orators, in their frequent references to the cult of the dead, are our best authorities. They seem to take for granted a belief very much like that which Aristotle makes the basis of his remarks in *Eth. Nic.* i. 10 and 11; and, like him, are concerned chiefly to avoid unkindness, statements likely to wound tender feeling. "The continued existence of the Soul after death," says Rohde,[2] "is not questioned by the orators; but its consciousness of what happens in this world is only affirmed with deliberate uncertainty. Such qualifications as "if any of the dead could feel in some way anything that is now being done" are frequent. Apart from the offerings of his relatives there is little more to bind the deceased to this world than his fame among survivors. Even in the exalted language of solemn funeral orations we miss, among the consolations offered to the mourners, any reference to a higher condition—to an eternal life of conscious blessedness attained to by the famous dead." Here the Orators are in agreement with that great master of the art of epitaph-writing, as Rohde[3] well describes Simonides, "who has never a word assigning the departed to a land of eternal blessedness," but places their im-

---

[1] See Jowett, *The Dialogues of Plato*, vol. i. 419 (Introduction to the *Phaedo*, § 12).

[2] *Psyche*, vol. ii. pp. 202, 203; and see his important footnotes to these pages, in which he gives references to H. Meuss (*über die Vorstellungen von Dasein nach dem Tode bei den attischen Rednern*, Jahrb. f. Philol., 1889, pp. 801 ff.), Westermann (on Demosth. *Lept.* 87), and Lehrs (*Popul. Aufs.* 329 ff.), for the views expressed by the Attic Orators concerning the state of the departed.

[3] *Psyche*, ii. 204.

mortality entirely in the memory of their deeds, which lasts, and will last, in this world:—

> "the dead have not died, but the valour which glorifies them raises them upwards from the house of Hades."[1]

Similarly Tyrtaeus[2] had identified immortality expressly with fame:—

> His high renown and his name are never lost,
> but even below the earth he becomes immortal.

His body is buried in peace, but his name liveth for evermore.

The Dramatists, too, did much to induce their public to look at the dead in the same way; for the dramatic interest required that prominence should be given to the posthumous influence of the dead here rather than to their personal condition in another world. When the Dramatists put the old national legends on the stage, attention was turned, as Rohde[3] points out, from the mere events of the story to the characters and motives of the hitherto shadowy legendary personages now presented, for the first time, clearly to sense. The plots were well known, and not so curiously attended to by the audience as the characters of the personages now moving before their eyes. Motives became more important than events. The Dramatist had to combine the traditional story of the legend with the motives of agents who must have the hearts of modern men, or else not be understood by the audience. Hence the tragic conflict between events and motives. It is fated that a good man shall do an evil deed. How can he be responsible for such a deed, and merit the retribution which the moral sense of the audience would resent if he did not merit it? This is the tragic difficulty which the Dramatists solved, I would suggest, by taking the Family, rather than the Individual, as the moral unit.[4] The descendant is free

---

[1] Simon. *Epigr.* 99, 3, 4, quoted by Rohde, *Psyche*, ii. 204, n. 1.
[2] Tyrtaeus, 12, 31 f., quoted by Rohde, *Psyche*, ii. 201, n. 3.
[3] *Psyche*, ii. 225.
[4] See Plutarch, *On the postponements of the Divine Vengeance*, 16, on the continuity of the Family, and the justice of punishing children for the sins of fathers.

because he is *conscious* of doing the ancestral, the fated, thing—a doctrine which Rohde,[1] in ascribing especially to Aeschylus, compares with the Stoic doctrine of assent.[2] The human interest of tragedy requires that the penalty for sin shall be paid here on earth rather than in Hades. This is why there is so little in the Greek Dramatists about the punishment of the wicked in the other world for their own sins. It is *in this world* that sin must be punished if the drama is to have any human interest. Since the Family, not the Individual, is the moral unit, it matters not that the sin punished here is ancestral. Nay, the tragic effect is heightened when the children suffer for the sins of their fathers. The dead fathers live in their children: that is, for aught we can ever know, the only life they have:—

> For if you wish to benefit those that have died
> Or to do them evil, it works both ways,
> For you will never rejoice nor grieve the dead.[3]

If the dead, then, are unconscious or barely conscious, the *living* must be punished for the sins of the dead, that the justice of the Gods may be satisfied.[4]   Aristotle did little

---

[1] *Psyche*, ii. 229.

[2] Cic. *de fato*, 18.

[3] Aeschylus, *frag.* 266, quoted by Rohde, *Psyche*, ii. 232.   "Under all circumstances," says Dr. Westcott (*Religious Thought in the West*, edit. 1891, pp. 91, 92), "the view of the condition of the Dead, which Aeschylus brings out into the clearest light in describing the condition of the Guilty, is consistent. The fulness of human life is on earth. The part of man, in all his energy and capacity for passion and action, is played out here; and when the curtain falls there remains unbroken rest, or a faint reflection of the past, or suffering wrought by the ministers of inexorable justice. The beauty and the power of life, the manifold ministers of sense, are gone. They can be regretted, but they cannot be replaced. Sorrow is possible, but not joy. "However different this teaching may be from that of the Myths of Plato, and the vague popular belief which they witnessed to and fostered; however different, again, even from that of Pindar, with which Aeschylus cannot have been unacquainted, it is pre-eminently Greek. Plato clothed in a Greek dress the common instincts of humanity; Aeschylus works out a characteristically Greek view of life. Thus it is that his doctrine is most clearly Homeric. As a Greek he feels, like Homer, the nobility of our present powers, the grandeur of strength and wealth, the manifold delights of our complex being; and what was 'the close-packed urn of ashes which survived the funeral pyre' compared with the heroes whom it represented?   That 'tear-stained dust' was the witness that man—the whole man—could not live again. The poet, then, was constrained to work out a scheme of divine justice upon earth, and this Aeschylus did, though its record is a strain of sorrow."

[4] On the necessity of satisfying the justice of the Gods, see Rohde, *Psyche*, ii. 232.

more than formulate the widely-prevalent opinion supported
by Orators and Dramatists, when he defined the Soul as
"the function of the body"—and Plato himself bears witness
to the prevalence of the opinion when he makes Glaucon
express surprise on hearing it suggested by Socrates that the
Soul is immortal.[1] It had never occurred to Glaucon that
the doctrine of the Soul's immortality could be taken
seriously.   Socrates then offers a "scientific" proof of its
immortality—a proof which he offers, I would suggest, only
or chiefly that he may supersede it by the Myth of Er.[2]

So much for considerations which make it reasonable to
suppose that Plato, like many others in the Athens of his
day, felt at least serious doubt as to whether anything could
be known scientifically about the conscious life of the Soul
after death, if he did not actually go the length of holding,
as his disciple Aristotle did, that, as conscious individual,
it perishes with the body whose function it is.   That, while
entertaining this serious doubt, Plato did not go so far as
Aristotle, seems to me to be shown by the manner in which
he allows himself to be affected by another class of opinions
opposed to the agnosticism of his time.   I refer to the opinions
associated with the Mysteries and the Orphic revival
throughout Greece, and especially in Athens. The Eleusinian
Mysteries were the great stronghold in Greece of the doctrine
of a future life;[3] and the same doctrine was taught, in
definite form, by the Orphic societies which appeared in
Italy and Sicily (in some cases in close connection with the
spread of Pythagoreanism) before the close of the latter half
of the sixth century. As Athens became more and more the
centre of Greek life, the Orphic cult gravitated thither. We
find it represented by Onomacritus at the Court of the
Pisistratids; and, meeting the need of "personal religion",
felt especially during the tribulation caused by the Peloponnesian War and the Great Plague,[4] it had, in Plato's day,
become firmly rooted in the city. The sure hope of salvation,
for themselves and those dear to them, in a future life, the

---

[1] *Rep.* 608 D, on which see Rohde, *Psyche*, ii. 264, 265, and Adam, *ad loc.*
[2] See *infra*, p. 99.
[3] See Gardner's *New Chapters in Greek History*, p. 397, and Gardner and
Jevons' *Manual of Greek Antiquities*, p. 275.
[4] See Rohde, *Psyche*, ii. 105, 106.

details of which were minutely described, was held before the anxious and afflicted who duly observed the prescribed Orphic rites.   The hope was all the surer because it was made to rest on the consciousness of having one's self done something; it was all the surer, too, because the comfort which it brought was offered, not to selfish, but to sympathetic feeling—for even ancestors long dead could be aided in their purgatorial state by the prayers and observances of their pious descendants.[1]

Now, what is Plato's attitude to this Orphic cult? This question can be answered, in part at least, without difficulty: —He derived the main doctrine, together with most of the details, of his Eschatological Myths—the doctrine of the pre-existence, penance, re-incarnation, and final purification of the Soul—directly, and through Pindar, from Orphic sources, the chief of which, if we accept the carefully formed view of Dieterich, was a popular Orphic Manual, the *Descent to Hades*, in which the vicissitudes endured by the immortal Soul, till it frees itself, by penance, from the Cycle of Births, were described—a work which lay at the foundation of Pindar's theology, was ridiculed by Aristophanes in the *Frogs*, was the ultimate source of the *Visits to the Dead*

---

[1] See important note (5), Rohde, *Psyche*, ii. 128, in which *Rep.* 364 B, C, E-365 A is cited—especially 365 A, "Persuading (not individuals only, but whole cities) that men may receive absolution and purification for their sins, both while they are alive and also after their death, by means of sacrifices and pleasant pastimes which they call Mysteries, which deliver us from those evils, but for those who do not perform those rites a dreadful doom remains."—as showing that deceased ancestors could be aided by the prayers and observances of descendants. Although the Orphic Fragm. 208 (cf. Mullach, *Fr. Ph. Gr.* i. 188) "They will perform the mystic rites which give release to their unrighteous ancestors, and you will release them from their heavy labours and endless sorrow," quoted by Rohde in the same note, seems to make it quite clear that dead ancestors could be aided by their descendants, I think that the passage quoted from *Rep.* 365 A leaves the matter in doubt; see Paul Tannery in *Rev. de Philol.* October 1901, on mysteries (*Orphica*, Fr. 221, 227, 228, 254), who explains the "they are alive, yet also dead" of *Rep.* 365 A to mean that the expiatory rites clear the initiated person, some of them for the time of his earthly life, some of them for his life after death. These latter are mysteries.   Mysteries cannot affect any one except the initiated person himself (to whom they supply directions as to his journey in the other world): they cannot clear an ancestor. According to this explanation, the reference in *Rep.* 364 C, "either the sins of himself or of his ancestors," is not to ancestors as affected by the observances of their descendants, but to sin inherited from an ancestor, which a man may cleanse himself of.   I do not think, however, that the reference in the "release from ancestral sins" of the Orphic fragment quoted by Mullach (i. 188) and Rohde can be to this.

of Plutarch and Virgil, and greatly influenced Neo-Platonic doctrine.[1]

Pindar, a poet and theologian after Plato's heart, whom he always quotes with deep respect, was, we may suppose, brought into contact with the Orphic cult in Sicily, where, along with the Pythagorean discipline, it had found a congenial home.[2]   The difference between Pindar's outlook, and that of the Athenian Orators and Dramatists and their agnostic public, is very striking.   In certain places he indeed speaks of the dead as gone, their earthly fame alone surviving. But this is not his dominant tone.   Not only have a favoured few—heroes like Amphiaraus—been translated, by a miracle, "body and soul," to immortal homes, but, when any ordinary man dies, his Soul survives his body, and that, not as a poor vanishing shade, but as a responsible person destined for immortal life.   The soul, as Pindar conceives it, is not the "totality of the bodily functions", as the philosophers and the agnostic Athenian public conceived it, but the Double which has its home in the body.   This Double comes from the Gods and is immortal:—

And the body of each man follows him to mighty death, but leaves behind a living image of its mortal existence, for this alone is from the Gods.[3]

Being of God, the Soul is necessarily immortal, but is immersed in the body because of ancient sin.

[1] See Dieterich, *Nekyia*, 116-158; and cf. Jevons, *Introduction to the History of Religion*, pp. 353, 354: Orpheus had descended into Hades; hence came to be regarded as the author of verses descriptive of Hades, which were current in *thiasi*, or disseminated by itinerant *agyrtae*.   In *Rep.* 364 E, "and they produce a pile of books written by Musaeus and Orpheus", the reference is, doubtless, to this and other Orphic guide-books for the use of the dead. These Orphic books may be compared with the Egyptian *Book of the Dead*, a guide for the use of the *Ka*, or "double" (on which see Budge's *Egyptian Ideas of the Future Life*, p. 163), which wanders from the body, and may lose its way; cf. Petrie's *Egyptian Tales*, second series, p. 124; see also *Eleusinia*, by le Comte Goblet d'Alviella (1903), pp. 73 ff., on the connection between Greek and Egyptian guide-books for the use of the dead.   To Dieterich's list of eschatological pieces in literature inspired by the Orphic teaching we ought perhaps to add the Voyage of Odysseus to Hades (*Od.* xi.); see v. Wilamowitz-Möllendorff, *Hom. Untersuch.* p. 199, who supposes that the passage was put in by Onomacritus, when Homer was being edited at Athens in the time of the Tyrants.

[2] See Rohde, *Psyche*, ii. 216, 217; and, for the spread of the Orphic Religion, Bury, *Hist. of Greece*, chap. vii. sec. 13.

[3] Pindar, *fr.* apud Plut. *Consol. ad Apoll.* 35.

At the death of its first body, the Soul goes to Hades, where it is judged and recompensed for the deeds, good or ill, done in the flesh. But its sin is not wholly purged. It reappears on earth in a second body, at the death of which it goes a second time to Hades, where its sin is further purged. Then it returns to animate a third body on earth (see Pindar, *Ol.* ii. 68 ff.). Then, if these three lives on earth, as well as the two periods of sojourn in Hades, have been spent without fault, and if, when it returns for the third time to Hades, it lives there without fault, Persephone, in the ninth year of this third sojourn in Hades, receives the full tale of satisfaction due for ancient sin, and sends it back to earth, to be born in the person of a Philosopher or King (see Pindar, quoted *Meno*, 81 B), who, at his death, becomes a holy Hero, or Daemon—a finally disembodied spirit: the Soul has at last got out of the cycle of births.[1] This is Pindar's doctrine—plainly Orphic doctrine, with beauty and distinction added to it by the genius of the great poet.

Plato's Eschatological Myths also, like Pindar's poems, plainly reproduce the matter of Orphic teaching. Is it going too far, when we consider Plato's reverence for the genius of Pindar, to suggest that it was Pindar's form which helped to recommend to Plato the matter which he reproduces in his Eschatological Myths—that the poet's refined treatment of the Orphic myth helped the philosopher,

---

[1] I am indebted to Rohde (*Psyche*, ii. 207-217) for the substance of this sketch of Pindar's Eschatology. In the last paragraph I have tried to combine the doctrine of *Ol.* ii. 68 ff. and the fragment, *Men.* 81 B. The life of Philosopher or King is indeed a bodily life on earth, but it is not one of the three bodily lives necessary (together with the three sojourns in Hades) to the final purification of the Soul. The Soul has been finally purified before it returns to this fourth and last bodily life which immediately precedes its final disembodiment. In the case of Souls which do not pass three faultless lives here and in Hades, the number of re-incarnations would be greater. Pindar's estimate seems to be that of the time required in the most favourable circumstances. We may take it that it is the time promised by the Orphic priests to those whose ritual observances were most regular. According to *Phaedrus*, 249 A, however, it would appear that a Soul must have been incarnate as a Philosopher in three successive lives before entering on the disembodied state: see Zeller, *Plato*, Eng. Tr. p. 393; and cf. *Phaedo*, 113 D ff., where five classes of men are distinguished with respect to their condition after death—on which see Rohde, *Psyche*, ii. 275, n. 1. "Thrice on either side," says Prof. Gildersleeve in his note on Pind. *Ol.* ii. 75, "would naturally mean six times. Thrice may mean three times in all. The Soul descends to Hades, then returns to earth, then descends again for a final probation." I do not think that this last interpretation can be accepted.

F

himself a poet, to see how that myth might be used to
express imaginatively what indeed demands expression of
some kind—man's hope of personal immortality—but
cannot, without risk of fatal injury, be expressed in the
language of science? It is Pindar, as chief among divine
seers who is quoted, in the *Meno* (81), for the pre-existence,
transmigrations, responsibility, and immortality of the
Soul; but the Platonic "Socrates" is careful to say that he
does not contend for the literal truth of the doctrine embodied in Pindar's myth, but insists on its practical value
in giving us hope and courage as seekers after knowledge
(*Meno*, 86 B). It is Pindar, again, who is quoted at the
beginning of the *Republic* (331 B) for that sweet hope, which
is visualised in Orphic outlines and colours at the close of
the Dialogue, in the greatest of Plato's Eschatological
Myths. Orphic doctrine, refined by poetic genius for
philosophic use, is the material of which Plato weaves his
Eschatological Myths. And he seems almost to go out of
his way to tell us this. Not only is the *Meno* Myth introduced
with special mention of the priestly source from which it is
derived (*Meno*, 81 B), but even brief allusions made elsewhere
to the doctrine contained in it are similarly introduced—as
in the *Phaedo*, 70 C, where the doctrine of the transmigrations
of the Soul is said to be derived from an ancient teaching;
in the *Phaedo*, 81 A, where it is connected with what is said
according to Initiates; and in the *Laws*, 872 E, where the
ancient priests are referred to for the doctrine that, if a man
kills his mother, he must be born again as a woman who is
killed by her son. But, after all, the most convincing evidence
for the great influence exercised by Orphic doctrine over
Plato is to be found in the way in which he loves to describe
Philosophy itself in terms borrowed from the Orphic cult
and the Mysteries.[1] Thus in the *Phaedo*, 69 C, "In my
opinion those who direct the Mysteries are not misguided,
but in fact they spoke truly in riddles long ago, when they
declared that when a man who is uninitiated and un-
transformed comes to Hades, he will lie in mud, but that
he who arrives there purified and enlightened will dwell
with the Gods. For those concerned with the Mysteries

---

[1] See Rohde, *Psyche*, ii. 279.

have a saying:—'Many are the wandbearers, but the God-inspired are few.' And those in my opinion are none other than the philosophers." Again, in the *Gorgias*, 493 A, borrowing an Orphic phrase, he likens the body, with its lusts, to a tomb—"our body (*sōma*) is a tomb (*sēma*)"—from which Wisdom alone can liberate the Soul (cf. also *Cratylus*, 400 B); and in the *Phaedrus*, 250 B, C, he describes Philosophy—the Soul's vision of the Eternal Forms—as a kind of Initiation: "But Beauty, shining in glory, it was granted us then to see, when in the happy choir we beheld that blessed and holy vision—we in the train of Zeus, and the rest following other Gods—and partook of that one among the Mysteries which is rightly called supremely blest. This we then celebrated, being whole and clean, and having no part in the sorrows which awaited us in the after-time, but chosen to participate in those visions, single and changeless and joyful, beholding them in pure light, pure ourselves, and without that which we now call the body and carry round with us, imprisoned like an oyster within its shell." Again, in the *Timaeus*, 44 c,[1] he speaks of the Soul which has neglected the right nurture which was a part of his upbringing as returning, "uninitiated" and "without knowledge of truth", into Hades—"he again returns to Hades uninitiated and without enlightenment"; and in the *Symposium*, 209 E, in Diotima's Discourse on love, the highest Philosophy is described as rites and visions, for the sake of which we seek initiation in the knowledge of love.[2]

Let us not think that this is "mysticism"—"the scholas-ticism of the heart"[3]—such as we find afterwards in the Neo-Platonic teaching. On the contrary, it is to be regarded as evidence of the non-scholastic, concrete view which Plato takes of Philosophy. Philosophy to Plato is not wisdom—a mere system of ascertained truth—but strictly love of wisdom—Love, child of Plenty and Poverty, as the parentage is set forth in Diotima's Myth in the *Symposium*: Philosophy is not what finally satisfies—or surfeits—the intellect: it is the organic play of all the human powers and functions—it

---

[1] See Archer-Hind's note on *Phaedo*, 69 c.
[2] See Couturat, *de Plat. Mythis*, p. 55.
[3] "Mysticism is the scholasticism of the heart, the dialectic of the feelings," Goethe, *Sprüche in Prosa: Maximen und Reflexionen:* third edition.

is Human Life, equipped for its continual struggle, eager
and hopeful, and successful in proportion to its hope—its
hope being naturally visualised in dreams of a future state.
These dreams the human race will never outgrow—so the
Platonist holds—will never ultimately cast aside as *untrue;*
for the young will believe in them in every generation, and
the weary and bereaved will cherish them, and men of
genius—poets, philosophers, saints—will always rise up to
represent them anew. The Philosophy of an epoch must be
largely judged by the way in which it "represents" them.
How much virtue Plato finds in "representation"—philosophical and poetical—may be gathered from the fact that,
while he attaches the highest value to the Orphic doctrine
which he himself borrows for philosophical use, he ascribes
the worst moral influence to the actual teaching of the
Orphic priests.[1]

I said that it is reasonable to suppose that Plato was
affected by the agnosticism which prevailed in Athens, and
felt, notwithstanding some "proofs" which he ventured to
offer, serious doubt as to whether even the bare fact of conscious immortality is matter of scientific knowledge.[2] It may
now be added, however, that his sympathy with the personal
religion, in which many took refuge from agnosticism, was
profound, and moved him to deal, in Myth openly borrowed
from the religious teachers, with subjects which Aristotle
left alone. Official (as distinct from personal) religion offers
no safe refuge from agnosticism. Recognising this, Plato
took the matter of his strictly Eschatological Myths almost
entirely from the Orphic teaching, which presented religion
as a way of salvation which all, without distinction of sex or

---

[1] *Republic*, 364 E. In Aristoph. *Ranae*, 159, and Demosth. *de Corona*, 259 ff.,
the practices of the *agyrtae*, or itinerant celebrants of initiatory rites, are held
up to ridicule.

[2] But see Zeller's *Plato*, p. 408 (Eng. Transl.). Zeller holds that the fact
of immortality and future retribution was regarded by Plato as established
beyond doubt; only details were uncertain. Couturat (*de Pl. Myth.* p. 112)
thinks that the whole doctrine of immortality in Plato is "mythic". Jowett
(Introduction to *Phaedo*) remarks that in proportion as Plato succeeds in
substituting a philosophical for a mythological treatment of the immortality
of the Soul, "the contemplation of ideas 'under the form of eternity' takes
the place of past and future states of existence." Mr. Adam (*Rep.* vol. ii. p.
456) says, "that soul is immortal, Plato is firmly convinced: transmigration
he regards as probable, to say the least."

civil status, simply as human beings, of their own free
choice, can enter upon and pursue.[1]

8. SUMMARY OF INTRODUCTORY OBSERVA-
TIONS IN THE FORM OF A DEFENCE OF
PLATO AGAINST A CHARGE BROUGHT
AGAINST HIM BY KANT.

Let me close this Introduction with a summing up of its
meaning, in the form of a defence of Plato against a charge
brought by Kant in a well-known passage.[2]

The light dove, in free flight cleaving the air and feeling
its resistance, might imagine that in airless space she would
fare better. Even so Plato left the world of sense, because

---

[1] See Gardner and Jevons' *Manual of Greek Antiquities*, Book iii. ch. iv.
"Orgiastic Cults," and Jevons' *Introduction to the History of Religion*, pp. 327-
374. "The leading characteristic," says Dr. Jevons (*o.c.* p. 339), "of the
revival in the sixth century B.C., both in the Semitic area, and as trans-
planted into Greece, is a reaction against the gift theory of sacrifice, and a
reversion to the older sacramental conception of the offering and the sacrificial
meal as affording actual communion with the God whose flesh and blood
were consumed by his worshippers. . . . The unifying efficacy (p. 331) of
the sacrificial meal made it possible to form a circle of worshippers. . . . We
have the principle of voluntary religious associations which were open to all.
Membership did not depend on birth, but was constituted by partaking in
the divine life and blood of the sacred animal." These voluntary associations
formed for religious purposes—*thiasi* or *erani*—"differed (p. 335) from the cult
of the national gods in that all—women, foreigners, slaves—were admitted,
not merely members of the State." In short, *initiatio* took the place of *civitas*
as the title of admission to religious privileges.
   Prof. Gardner closes the chapter on "Orgiastic Cults", referred to above,
with the following words:—"In several respects the thiasi were precursors of
Christianity, and opened the door by which it entered. If they belonged to a
lower intellectual level than the best religion of Greece, and were full of
vulgarity and imposture, they yet had in them certain elements of progress,
and had something in common with the future as well as the past history of
mankind. All properly Hellenic religion was a tribal thing, belonged to the
state and the race, did not proselytise, nor even admit foreign converts; and
so when the barriers which divided cities were pulled down it sank and
decayed. The cultus of Sabazius or of Cybele was, at least, not tribal: it
sought converts among all ranks, and having found them, placed them on a
level before the God. Slaves and women were admitted to membership and
to office. The idea of a common humanity, scarcely admitted by Greek philosophers before the age of the Stoics, found a hold among these despised
sectaries, who learned to believe that men of low birth and foreign extraction
might be in divine matters superior to the wealthy and the educated. In
return for this great lesson we may pardon them much folly and much
superstition." Prof. Gardner pursues this subject further in his *Exploratio
Evangelica*, pp. 325 ff., chapter on "Christianity and the thiasi"; see also
Grote's *History of Greece*, part i. ch. i. (vol. i. 19, 20, ed. 1862).
   [2] *Critique of Pure Reason*, Introduction, para. 3.

it sets so narrow limits to the understanding, and ventured beyond, on the wings of the Ideas, into the empty space of the pure understanding. He did not see that, with all his effort, he made no way.

Here Kant brings against Plato the charge of "transcendental use, or rather, misuse, of the Categories of the Understanding"[1]—of supposing super-sensible objects, Soul, Cosmos, God, answering to "Ideas" which have no adequate objects in a possible experience, and then determining these supposed objects by means of conceptions—the Categories—the application of which ought to be restricted to sensible objects.

In bringing this charge, Kant seems to me to ignore the function which Myth performs in the Platonic philosophy. I submit that the objects which Plato supposes for the "Transcendental Ideas"[2] are imaginatively constructed by him, not presented as objects capable of determination by scientific categories—that Plato, by means of the plainly non-scientific language of Myth, guards against the illusions which Kant guards against by means of "criticism"; or, to put it otherwise, that Plato's employment of Myth, when he deals with the ideals of Soul, Cosmos, and God—Kant's three Ideas of Reason—shows that his attitude is "critical", not dogmatic. The part which the Myth of Er plays in the philosophic action of the *Republic* may be taken as a specimen of the evidence for this view of Plato's attitude. There is nothing in the *Republic*, to my mind, so significant as the deep sympathy of its ending with the mood of its beginning. It begins with the Hope of the aged Cephalus—"The sweet hope which guides the wayward thought of mortal man"; it ends with the great Myth in which this Hope is visualised. As his Hope is sufficient for Cephalus, who retires to his devotions from the company of the debaters, so is the Representation of it—the Vision of Er—given as sufficient, in the end, for the debaters themselves. To attempt to rationalise here—to give speculative reasons for such a Hope, or against it, would be to forget that it is the foundation of all our special faculties, including the faculty of scientific explana-

---

[1] See *Critique of Pure Reason: the transcendent Dialectic*, Introduction 1.
[2] "Ideas" in Kant's sense, not the Platonic ideas.

tion; and that science can neither explain away, nor corroborate, its own foundation. The attempt which is made in the latter half of the Tenth Book of the *Republic* to place the natural expression of this Hope—man's belief in the immortality of the Soul—on a "scientific basis"—to determine "Soul" by means of "Categories of the Understanding"—I regard as intended by the great philosopher-artist to lead up to the Myth of Er, and heighten its effect by contrast—to give the reader of the *Republic* a vivid sense of the futility of rationalism in a region where Hope confirms itself by "vision splendid".[1]

Of course, I do not deny that passages may be found in which the Ideas of Soul, Cosmos, and God are treated by Plato, without Mythology, as having objects to be determined under the scientific categories of Cause and Substance—*e.g.* in *Phaedrus*, 245 E, and *Phaedo*, 105 C,[2] we seem to have serious scientific argument for the immortality of the Soul—indeed, it would be astonishing if there were no such passages, for the distinction between Category and Idea, as understood by Kant, is not explicit in Plato's mind; but I submit that such passages fade into insignificance by the side of the great Myths. We are safe in saying at least that, if sometimes Plato lapses into a logical treatment of these ideals, or "Ideas of Reason", he is well aware that there is another way of treating them—in Myth—and that he shows a marked preference for this latter way.

---

[1] "The argument about immortality (*Rep.* 608 c to 612 A)," says R. L. Nettleship (*Philosophical Lectures and Remains*, ii. 355), "does not seem to be in any organic connection either with what actually precedes or with what actually follows it. It would seem that Plato had two plans in his mind as to how to finish the *Republic*." I cannot think that Plato had two plans in his mind. The argument for the immortality of the Soul in *Rep.* 608 c-612 A is formally so inconclusive that it is impossible to suppose Plato to be serious with it. The equivocal use of the term *Death* in the argument could not have escaped a logician so acute as Plato. The argument is, that, as Injustice, the proper vice of the Soul, does not cause "Death", in the sense of the separation of Soul from body, nothing else can ever cause "Death", now, however, to be understood in the sense of the annihilation of the disembodied Soul itself.

[2] Grote (*Plato*, ii. 190) has an interesting note on *Phaedo*, 105 c—"Nemesius, the Christian bishop of Emesa, declares that the proofs given by Plato of the immortality of the Soul are knotty and difficult to understand, such as even adepts in philosophical study can hardly follow. His own belief in it rests upon the inspiration of the Christian Scriptures (Nemesius, *de Nat. Homin.* c. 2, p. 55, ed. 1565)."

The Platonic Myth, then, effects its purpose—the regulation of Transcendental Feeling for the service of conduct and science—in two ways which we may profitably distinguish, while admitting that the distinction between them was not explicit in Plato's mind: (1) by *representing ideals*, and (2) by *tracing faculties back to their origins*. In following either of these two ways the Platonic Myth carries us away to "Places" and "Times" which are, indeed, beyond the ken of sense or science, but yet are *felt* to be involved in the concrete "Here" and "Now" of ordinary experience.

The order in which I propose to take the Myths scarcely amounts to an arrangement of them in two classes according as the object is, either to represent ideals, or trace faculties to their origins, for most of them do both. I shall begin, however, with the Myths which are mainly concerned with ideals, and shall end with those which are mainly concerned with origins. The former, it may be remarked, answer roughly to the so-called Eschatological Myths—but only roughly, for some of them are more properly described as Aetiological; the latter answer to the Aetiological Myths.

I shall take first the Myths in the *Phaedo* and *Gorgias*, and the Myth of Er in the *Republic*—strictly "Eschatological" Myths—which present the Soul as immortal, free within limits set by necessity, and responsible, under God's government, throughout all its transmigrations.

Next I shall take the Myths—mainly "Aetiological"—in the *Politicus*, Fourth Book of the *Laws*, and *Protagoras*, where God's creative agency, and government of the Cosmos and Man, are broadly treated, and presented as consistent with the existence of evil.

Then I shall go on to the *Timaeus*,[1] in which the three ideals, or "Ideas of Reason"—Soul, Cosmos, and God—are represented in one vast composition.

Having examined these Myths—all *chiefly* interesting as representations of ideals, or "Ideas of Reason"—I shall examine three Myths which are *chiefly* concerned with the deduction of Categories or Virtues. These are the Myths in

---

[1] Couturat, *de Platonis Mythis* (Paris, 1896), p. 32, "the Timaeus itself is wholly mythical"; and Zeller, *Plato*, p. 160 (Eng. Transl.), "The whole investiture of the *Timaeus* is mythic—the Demiurgus, together with the subordinate gods, and all the history of the creation of the world."

the *Phaedrus, Meno,* and *Symposium.* They are mainly concerned with showing how man, as knowing subject and moral agent, is conditioned by his past. Although the "Eschatological" outlook, with its hope of future salvation, is by no means absent from these three Myths, their chief interest lies in the way in which, as "Aetiological" Myths, they exhibit the functions of the understanding and moral faculty as cases of recollection which, quickened by love, interprets the particular impressions, and recognises the particular duties, of the present life, in the light of the remembered vision of the Eternal Forms once seen in the Supercelestial Place.

Having examined the Myths which set forth the Ideals and Categories of the Individual, I shall end my review with an examination of two Myths which set forth respectively the Ideals and the Categories of a Nation—one of which gives us the spectacle of a Nation led on by a vision of its future, while the other shows us how the life of the "social organism" is conditioned by its past. These are the Atlantis Myth, introduced in the *Timaeus* and continued in the fragmentary *Critias,* and the Myth of the Earth-Born in the *Republic.* The Atlantis Myth (intended to complete the account of the Ideal State given in the *Republic*) is to be regarded as an Eschatological Myth; but it differs from the Eschatological Myths of the other class which have been examined in representing, not the future lot of the Individual Soul, but the ideal which a Nation has before it in this world—the ideal of a united Hellas, under a New Athens, maintaining civilisation against the assaults of outer barbarism.

After the Atlantis Myth I shall take the Myth of the Earth-Born in the *Republic,* which is an Aetiological Myth, differing from the Aetiological Myths of the other class which have been examined, in deducing, not the Categories —faculties and virtues—of the Individual, but the deep-cut characteristics of the "social organism". And yet, here again, while Categories are deduced, an Ideal—that of the orderly life of the Beautiful City—is represented. Indeed, this is more or less true of all the Platonic Myths. They all view man's present life *sub specie aeternitatis*—in God; exhibit it as part of the great plan of Providence—as one term of a continuous progress to be reviewed at once *a parte ante* and *a parte post*. Especially in the *Timaeus* do we see the "Genesis" and the "Apocalypse" of the Platonic Mythology blended in one Vision.

THE *PHAEDO* MYTH

CONTEXT OF THE MYTH

In the Phaedo, *the disciple from whom the Dialogue takes its name tells some Friends what was said and done in the Prison on the day of the Master's death.*

The conversation was concerning the Immortality of the Soul, and was continued up to the last hour.

Cebes and Simmias, the chief speakers, brought forward arguments tending to show that, even granted that the identity of Learning with Reminiscence is in favour of the Orphic doctrine of the pre-existence of the Soul, yet its after-existence, not to mention its immortality, is not proved.

Thereupon Socrates brought in the Doctrine of Eternal Ideas—a doctrine which the company were already prepared to accept—and showed, in accordance with it, that Life—*and the Soul is Life—excludes* Death.

Thus was the Immortality of the Soul proved.

Next came the practical question: How must a man live that it may be well with him both in this World and in the World Eternal?

It was then that Socrates, standing in the very presence of death, was filled with the spirit of prophecy, and made able to help his friends before he left them:—If, he said, they took to heart the Myth which he told them, they should know how to live, and it would be well with them both now and hereafter for ever.

When he had finished the telling of the Myth, and had warned his friends against a too literal interpretation of it, he gave directions about his family and some other private matters; then the Officer came in with the Cup.

PHAEDO 107 C—114 C

"It is meet, my friends, that we should take thought of this:—that the Soul, being immortal, standeth in need of care, not only in regard of the time of this present life, but in regard of the time without end, and that 'tis now, even to-day, that the jeopardy is great, if a man will still be careless of his Soul. Were death riddance of all, 'twould be good luck for the wicked man to die and be rid of body and soul and his wickedness; but inasmuch as the Soul is manifestly immortal, no other escape from evil hath she nor salvation save this—that she be perfected in righteousness and wisdom. For she taketh hence nothing with her to the House of Hades, save only her instruction and nurture—that, to wit, wherefrom they say the greatest profit cometh to the dead or greatest damage straightway at the beginning of their journey thither; for when a man dieth, his own Familiar Spirit, which had gotten him to keep whilst he lived, taketh and leadeth him to a certain place whither the dead must be gathered together; whence, after they have received their sentences, they must journey to the House of Hades with him who hath been appointed to guide thither those that are here; and when they have received there the things which are meet for them, and have sojourned the time determined, another Guide bringeth them again hither, after many long courses of time. The way, belike, is not as Aeschylus his Telephus telleth; for he saith that a single path leadeth to the House of Hades. But, methinks, if it were single and one, there would be no need of guides, for no man would go astray. Nay, that it hath many partings and windings I conclude from the offerings which men use to make unto the dead.

"The Soul which ordereth herself aright and hath wisdom, understandeth well her present case, and goeth with her Familiar. But the Soul which lusteth after the body, having fluttered about it and the Visible Place for a long while, and having withstood her appointed Familiar with great strife and pain, is by him at the last mastered and carried away; and when she is come to the place where the other Souls are assembled together, inasmuch as she is impure and hath wrought that which is impure, having shed innocent blood, or done like deeds which Souls that are her like use to do, her all flee and eschew, and none will be her companion or guide; wherefore she wandereth alone in great stress, until certain times have been accomplished; then is she constrained to go unto the habitation fit for her. But the Soul which hath lived all her days in purity and sobriety hath given unto her Gods to be her companions and guides, and she maketh her habitation in the place meet for her.

"The Earth hath many and wondrous places, and it is of a fashion and greatness whereof those who use to tell concerning the Earth have no true opinion. There is one who hath persuaded me of this."

"Socrates," quoth Simmias, "how sayest thou this? for I also have heard many things concerning the Earth, but not this of which thou art persuaded. Wherefore I would gladly hear it."

"Well, Simmias," quoth he, "methinks it needeth not the skill of Glaucus to set forth that which I have heard; but the truth thereof, which I wot it surpasseth the skill of Glaucus to find out, haply I should not be able to attain unto: nay, if I knew it, my life is too far spent, methinks, for the length of the discourse which should declare it: but my persuasion as touching the Earth and the places it hath nothing hindereth me from declaring unto thee."

"That is enough," said Simmias.

"I am persuaded, then," said he, "of this first—that if the Earth, being a globe, is in the middle of the Heaven, it hath no need of air or any other like constraint to keep it from falling, but 'tis sufficient to hold it that the Heaven is of one substance throughout, and that itself is equally balanced: for that which is itself equally balanced and set in the midst of that which hath one substance, will have no cause at all of inclining towards any side, but will continue the same and remain without inclination. Of this first I am persuaded."

"And rightly," said Simmias.

"Moreover, I am persuaded that the Earth is very great, and that we who inhabit unto the Pillars of Hercules from the river Phasis dwell in a small part thereof, like unto ants or frogs round about a pool, dwelling round this Sea; and that many other men dwell in many other like places; for in all parts of the Earth are hollows, many, various in shape and magnitude; into these flow water and thick clouds and air, and are therein gathered together; but the Earth itself is lifted up clear in the clear Heaven wherein are the stars. This Heaven is that which those who use to speak of these things call the *Aether*, whose sediment is that *colluvies* which is alway being gathered together into the hollows of the Earth. We, then, who dwell in the hollows, being ignorant, think that we dwell above on the Earth, even as he who had his dwelling down at the bottom of the sea would think that he was on the surface thereof, and beholding through the water the sun and the stars, would conceit the sea to be the heaven, inasmuch as, being sluggish and weak, he never mounted up to the surface of the sea, and put forth his head, and looked out at our place, and saw how far it excelleth the things of his own place in purity and beauty, neither had heard concerning it from another who had seen it. This is our case: for we, dwelling in a hollow of the Earth, think that we dwell upon the Earth itself; and the Air we call Heaven, and think that it is that Heaven wherein are the courses of the stars: whereas, by reason of weakness and sluggishness, we cannot go forth out of the Air: but if a man could journey to the edge thereof, or having gotten wings could fly up, it would come to pass that even as fishes here which rise out of the sea do behold the things here, he, looking out, would behold the things there, and if his strength could endure the sight thereof, would see that there are the True Heaven and the True Light and the True Earth. For the Earth here, with the stones thereof, and the whole place where we are, is corrupted and eaten away, after the manner of things in the sea by the salt wherein there is brought forth nothing either goodly or perfect at all, but only hollow rocks, and sand, and clay without measure, and miry sloughs wheresoever

there is also earth—things not worthy at all to be compared
with the things here that are fair, albeit the things beyond
do much more excel the things here in beauty.

"Wherefore, if ye desire of me a Tale, hearken to the
Tale of the Things that be beyond upon the Earth under
the Heaven."

"Indeed, Socrates," quoth he, "we would gladly hear
this Tale."

"The beginning of the Tale, then, is this, my friend,
that the Earth itself, if any one look down on it from the
Heaven, is like unto a ball which is fashioned with twelve
leathern stripes, whereof each hath his own colour. These
be the colours whereof the colours here which limners use
are as samples; but there the whole Earth is of such, yea of
far brighter than these and purer; for one part is purple
and of marvellous beauty, and another part is like gold,
and all that part which is white is whiter than chalk or
snow, and in like manner unto other parts are portioned
the other colours—yea, and colours besides more than all
those which we have seen here and fairer; for even these
hollows of the Earth, being full to the brim of water and
air, display a specific colour wherewith they glisten in the
midst of the variety of the other colours, so that the face of
the Earth seemeth, as it were, one picture of many colours
contiguous, without blot.

"According as the Earth is, so also are the things which
grow therein—her trees and flowers and fruits; and so also
are her mountains, and her stones, which are polished and
transparent and of exceeding fair colours; whereof the
precious stones here are fragments—sardian, jasper, smarag-
dus, and all such: but in that place there is no stone which
is not as these are and fairer. The reason whereof is this,
that the stones there are pure, and are not eaten away or
corrupted as are the stones here by the rot and salt of that
sediment which is gathered together here, whereof come,
unto stones, and earth, and likewise unto beasts and herbs,
deformities and diseases. Now, the True Earth hath these
things, and also gold and silver and other things like unto
them for her ornaments; for there they are not hidden but

manifest, and are in abundance, and of exceeding greatness, and in many places of that Earth; so that to behold it is a sight meet for the eyes of the blessed. And on that Earth there are beasts of many kinds, and men, whereof some dwell in the inland parts, and some round about the Air, as we about the Sea, and some in islands encompassed by the Air, hard by the mainland; for that which Water is and the Sea with us for our use, the Air is in that region, and that which the Air is with us, the Aether is with them. Moreover, their seasons are so tempered that disease smiteth them not at all, and they live far beyond the measure of our days, and as touching eyesight, and hearing, and wisdom, and all such parts, are distant from us even as Air is distant from Water, and Aether is distant from Air in purity. Also they have groves of the Gods and temples wherein Gods verily are dwellers; into whose very presence men come, hearing their voices and their prophecies and seeing them face to face. Moreover, the sun and moon and stars are seen there as they are truly; and likewise in all things else the state of these men is blessed.

"The Earth itself, then, and the parts that encompass the Earth are thus fashioned. But the Tale also telleth that in the Earth are many hollow places round about her whole girth, whereof some are deeper and more open than this place we dwell in, and some are deeper with a narrower mouth, and some are shallower and broader: all these are joined together, having channels bored under the Earth from one to another in many places, some narrow and some wide, whereby passage is given so that much water floweth from one into another, as into bowls, and measureless floods of perennial rivers run under the Earth, and streams hot and cold; also much fire floweth, and there are great rivers of fire, and many rivers of running mud, some clearer, some thicker, even as in Sicily there run before the fiery flood rivers of mud, and then cometh the fiery flood. With these floods, therefore, each place is filled according as at each time the stream floweth round unto each. Now, all these waters are moved upward and downward by that in the Earth which swayeth like a swing. And it swayeth after this wise. There is a cavern in the Earth, which is the greatest of them all, and, moreover, pierceth right through the whole Earth, whereof Homer maketh mention, saying, 'Afar off, where deepest underground the Pit is digged,' which he in other places, and many of the other poets, call Tartarus. Now, into this cavern all the rivers flow, and from it flow out again, and each one becometh such as is that part of the Earth it floweth through. The cause of all streams flowing out and flowing in is that this flood hath no bottom or foundation. Wherefore it swingeth and surgeth up and down, and the air and wind surge with it; for the wind goeth with it when it rusheth to the further side of the Earth, and with it returneth hitherward; and even as the breath of living creatures is driven forth and drawn in as a stream continually, so there also the wind, swinging with the flood, cometh in and goeth out, and causeth terrible, mighty tempests. Now, when the water rusheth back into the place "beneath", as men speak, coming unto the region of the streams which run through that part of the Earth, it floweth into them and filleth them, as men fill reservoirs with pumps; but when it ebbs again from thence and rusheth hither, it filleth again the streams here, which, being full, run through their conduits and through the Earth, coming severally to those places whither they are bound, and make seas and lakes and rivers and fountains. Thence they sink under the Earth again, and some, having fetched a longer compass and some a shorter, fall again into Tartarus, some far beneath the channel into which they were pumped up, and some a little way beneath; but all flow into Tartarus again beneath the places of their outflowing. Some waters there be that, coming forth out of the Earth at one side thereof, flow in at the contrary side; and some that go in and come out on the same side; and some there be that go round the whole Earth and are wound about it once—yea, perchance, many times, like serpents. These rivers pour their waters back into Tartarus as low down as water can fall. Now, it can fall as far as the centre in each way, but no further: each half of the Earth is a hill against the stream that floweth from the side of the other half.

G

"Now there are many great rivers of divers sorts, but amongst these there are four chiefest: whereof that one which is greatest, and floweth round the outermost, is that which is called Ocean, and over against him is Acheron, which floweth the contrary way, and flowing through desert places and also under the Earth, cometh to the Acherusian Lake, whither the Souls of the most part of the dead do come, and having sojourned there certain appointed times, some longer, some shorter, are again led forth to be born in the flesh. The third river issues forth betwixt these, and, near unto the part whence it issues forth, falleth into a great place burning with much fire, and maketh a lake greater than our Sea, seething with water and mud: thence it fetcheth a compass, and going thick and muddy, and winding round the Earth, cometh at last unto the coasts of the Acherusian Lake, mixing not with the water thereof. Then after many windings under the Earth it poureth itself into a lower part of Tartarus. This is the river which they name Pyriphlegethon, whereof also the fiery floods which boil up in divers places of the Earth are derivations. Over against him the fourth river issues forth, first into a fearful savage place, they tell, which hath wholly the colour of blue steel; and they call it the Stygian place, and the Lake which the river maketh with his flood they call Styx; whereinto this river falling conceiveth mighty virtues in his water, and afterward sinketh under the Earth, and windeth round, going contrary to Pyriphlegethon, and cometh to the Acherusian Lake from the contrary side: neither doth his water mix with any; but he also goeth round about, and falleth into Tartarus over against Pyriphlegethon. The name of this river, the poets tell, is Cocytus.

"When the dead are come unto the place whither his Familiar bringeth each, first are they judged, and according as they have lived righteous and godly lives, or lived unrighteously, are they divided. Thereafter all those who are deemed to have lived indifferently well journey unto Acheron, and go on board the vessels which are prepared for them, and so come to the Lake; and abiding there, get themselves cleansed, and paying the price of their evil deeds, are acquitted from the guilt thereof; and for their good deeds receive each the reward that is meet. But whoso are deemed incurable by reason of the greatness of their sins, robbers of temples, and those who have oftentimes shed blood unlawfully, or wrought other iniquities that are great, them the appointed Angel doth cast into Tartarus, and thence they come not out at all: and whoso are deemed to have committed sins great but curable, who in wrath have violently entreated father or mother and have repented them thereof all the days of their lives thereafter, or who in like manner are manslayers, they must needs fall into Tartarus, but when they have been there one year, the surge casts them forth, the manslayers by Cocytus, and the slayers of father or mother by Pyriphlegethon; and when they are carried down and are come to the Acherusian Lake, there they cry out aloud unto those whom they slew or used despitefully, and call upon them and beseech them with prayers that they will suffer them to come out into the Lake and will receive them; and if they prevail, they come out and cease from their torments; but if they prevail not, they are carried back into Tartarus, and thence again into the rivers, and they cease not from this torment till they have prevailed with those whom they have wronged; for this was the doom that was appointed of the Judges unto them. But whosoever are deemed to have been godly above others in their lives, they are released from these places in the Earth, and depart from them as from a prison-house, and come unto the Pure Mansions which are above, and dwell upon the Earth. And of these whoso have cleansed themselves throughly by Wisdom live without fleshly bodies for evermore, and come to yet fairer Mansions, whereof it is not easy to tell, nor doth the time now suffice for the telling. Nevertheless, by that which hath been told are we admonished to do all so that we may lay hold of Righteousness and Wisdom in this life; for the prize is fair and the hope is great."

Observations on the *PHAEDO* Myth

I

We may begin by noting that Plato here, as elsewhere, gives verisimilitude to Myth by making it explain facts, or what he accepts as facts, and bringing it, as far as possible, into conformity with the "modern science" of his day. The fact of the Earth's rotundity had already been ascertained—or guessed—in Plato's day;[1] and the geography of the Myth is made consistent with this fact, as well as with the supposed "fact" of the Earth's central position in the Cosmos—a position which it retains for a sufficient reason, which Plato sets forth "scientifically". The *Phaedo* Myth, starting with the "scientific truths" of the Earth's rotundity and central position, gives a consistent geography, which makes it easy for the reader to localise the "Earthly Paradise" and Tartarus, as real places continuous with the part of the world which men inhabit. Geography is treated in this Myth, as ancient history may, or must, be treated according to Plato—romantically: the general scheme is, as far as possible, true to facts; but blanks are filled in by myth-making.[2] The line between uncritical "science" and myth-making is difficult to draw, and Plato knows how to turn the difficulty to artistic, and more than that—to philosophic use. A sophistic use of the difficulty he happily has no temptation to make, because he holds no brief obliging him to contend for a large amount of literal truth in the traditional myths which he borrows.

Again, the *Phaedo* Myth recommends itself to the "scientific mind" by explaining the origin of hot and cold springs, volcanic action, winds, and, I think, the tides of the Atlantic Ocean. The suggestion, too, that gems—objects which have always been regarded with wonder, as possessing mysterious

---

[1] See Zeller's *Plato*, Engl. Transl. pp. 379, 380.
[2] See *Republic*, 382 D, "And in the legends of which we have just been talking, is it not because we are ignorant of the facts of ancient history that the lie becomes most useful to us, as the nearest likeness to the truth?" "Yes, indeed it is." Cf. *Legg.* 682 ff., where the early history of mankind appears as a myth, founded on fact, but embellished—"of many things which came into being according to the truth, but were each time touched up by the Graces and the Muses"; and cf. Campbell's *Politicus*, Introd. p. xxxi.

virtues—are fragments which have found their way down to this part of the world from the rocks of the "Earthly Paradise", is a touch of fine imagination which helps to bring the two regions—our part of the world and the "Earthly Paradise"—into physical connection.[1] Tartarus and the True Surface of the Earth, or Earthly Paradise, are indeed real places to which there are real approaches for the ghostly travellers from this inhabited world. The care, half playful, half earnest, which Plato takes to prove this scientifically from observed effects—volcanoes, tides, precious stones—has its parallel in the method of Dante and other great masters of Myth. Skilful use of "modern science" is indeed one of the marks of the great master. Before referring to Dante for this, let me first compare Plato's delicate handling of "science" in the *Phaedo* Myth with the work of one who is certainly not a great master of Myth—the Cambridge Platonist, Dr. Henry More; but let me preface his "Myth" with a few words explanatory of the "science" which serves as foundation to his "mythology".

The *Spirit of Nature*, according to More and his school, is an incorporeal substance, without sense, diffused through the whole universe, exercising *plastic power*, producing those phenomena which cannot be explained mechanically.[2] This plastic principle in nature explains "sympathetic cures", the "astral bodies" (the phrase More borrows from the Paracelsians) of witches, in which they appear as hares, cats, weasels (so that if the hare or other animal is wounded, the witch is found to be similarly wounded—More was a firm believer in all that, and could give "scientific" reasons for his belief), the growth of plants and embryos, and the instincts of animals, such as the nest-building instinct of birds, the cocoon-spinning instinct of silk-worms.[3] The Soul of man partakes in this plastic principle, and by means of it constructs for herself a body terrestrial, aerial, or aethereal (*i.e.* celestial), according as the stage of her development has brought her into vital relation with the vehicle of earth, air,

---

[1] Cf. *Conv.* iv, 20, p. 323, Oxf. Dante: "And so this our Good is defined, which in like manner descended to us from the highest and spiritual Worth, as the virtue in a precious stone from the most noble celestial body."

[2] More's *Immortality of the Soul*, book iii. ch. 12.

[3] More, *o.c.* iii. 13.

or aether. "As we see," he says,[1] "that the *perceptive* part of
the Soul is vitally affected with that which has no life in it,
so it is reasonable that the *plastick* part thereof may be so
too; that there may be an Harmony betwixt *matter* thus and
thus modified, and that Power that we call *plastick* that is
utterly devoid of all *perception*. And in this alone consists
that which we call *Vital Congruity* in the prepared matter
either to be organised or already shaped into the perfect
form of an Animal." He then lays it down as an "axiome"[2]
that "there is a Triple *Vital Congruity* in the Soul, namely,
Aethereal, Aerial, and *Terrestrial*"; and proceeds: "That this
is the common opinion of the *Platonists,* I have above
intimated (*Immortality of the Soul,* ii. 14). That this opinion
is also true in itself, appears from the foregoing axiome. Of
the *Terrestrial Congruity* there can be no doubt; and as little
can there be but that at least one of the other two is to be
granted, else the Soul would be released from all *vital union
with matter* after Death. Wherefore she has a *vital aptitude,* at
least, to unite with *Aire.* But *Aire* is a common receptacle
of bad and good spirits (as the *Earth* is of all sorts of men
and beasts), nay, indeed, rather of those that are in some
sort or other bad, than of good, as it is upon Earth. But the
Soul of man is capable of very high refinements, even to a
condition *purely angelical,* whence Reason will judge it fit,
and all Antiquity has voted it, that the souls of men arrived
to such a due pitch of purification must at least obtain
Celestial vehicles."

The Soul, by means of her plastic power, moulds the
vehicle—earth, air, or aether—to any form she pleases;
but having been first habituated to the human shape in the
terrestrial body, she naturally moulds the aerial and celestial
vehicles to the same shape. This is why ghosts (in whom
More is a firm believer),[3] being the Souls of the departed
in their aerial bodies, are easily recognised by their features,

---

[1] More, *o.c.* ii. 14.   [2] More, *o.c.* iii. 28.
[3] See *Immortality of the Soul,* ii. 16, for the wonderfully well-told story of
Marsilius Ficinus appearing (by arrangement) on the day of his death to his
friend Michael Mercatus. He rides up to Michael's window on a white
horse, saying, "Michael, Michael, those things are true." Michael sends to
Florence, and finds that Marsilius died the same hour his ghost appeared at
the window.

when they return to the scenes of their terrestrial life.[1] Now,
it may be asked what the effect of the Final Destruction of
the World by Fire at the Last Day will be on the human
souls which then have still only terrestrial bodies, and on
the human souls and souls of Daemons (or Angels) which
have still only aerial bodies. These bodies, unless saved by
a miracle, will be burnt up, and their souls, having no
vehicles, will cease to live the life of active consciousness.[2]
Therefore, More argues,[3] using Stoical terms, a restoration
and rebirth *after* the resurrection and burning would not
meet their case; for a soul whose body had been burnt
would have ceased to be conscious, and rebirth would only
bring it back to consciousness a different being. It will
require supernatural means to rescue the souls of good men
and Daemons (or Angels) at the time of the Final Conflagration, or even before that time, when the extinction of
the sun—presaged by his spots recently discovered by one

---

[1] Cf. More's *Philosophical Poems*, p. 260 (ed. 1647):—

> In shape they walk much like to what they bore
> Upon the Earth: for that light Orb of Air
> Which they inact must yielden evermore
> To Phansie's beck, so when the Souls appear
> To their own selves alive as once they were,
> So cloath'd and conversant in such a place,
> The inward eyes of Phansie thither stear
> Their gliding vehicle, that bears the face
> Of him that liv'd, that men may reade what Wight it was.

Similarly Dante (*Purg.* xxv. 91-99) explains the aerial bodies of the souls
in Purgatory:—

> And as the air, when it is quite filled, becomes adorned with varied
> colours through another ray which is reflected in it,
> So the neighbouring air sets itself into that shape which the soul that is
> stationed within it, stamps upon it by its power;
> And then like the small flame which follows the fire wherever it moves,
> the spirit is followed by its new form.

See also More's *Immortality of the Soul*, iii. 1, § 8, p. 149, where it is stated
that the Soul, although she has a marvellous power, by the *imperium* of her
will, of changing the temper and shape of her aerial vehicle, and of solidifying
it so that it reflects light and becomes visible, she has a much greater power
over her aethereal vehicle. The aethereally embodied soul can temper the
solidity of her vehicle (see *Immortality of the Soul*, p. 233), so as to ascend or
descend, and pass from one "vortex" to another. More looks forward
(*Defence of the Moral Cabbala*, ch. ii. p. 165) to the Millennium as the time
when, instead of occasional communications between souls terrestrially and
aethereally embodied, there will be close and constant intercourse.

[2] "The very nature of the Soul, as it is a Soul, is an *aptitude of informing
or actuating Body*."—More's *Defence of the Moral Cabbala*, ch. ii. p. 167, ed. 1662.

[3] More, *Immortality of the Soul*, iii. 18.

Shiner[1]—takes place. Neither terrestrial nor aerial bodies could, without the intervention of a miracle, survive such heat or such cold. But it is only in this lower part of the universe that such destructive agencies can operate. The aethereal region will not be affected by them; and souls which have reached the stage of aethereal or celestial embodiment will remain unharmed.

So much for the "science" which serves to give plausibility to the following Myth, as we may well call it:—

The greatest difficulty is to give a rational account whence the Bad *Genii* have their food, in their execrable Feasts, so formally made up into dishes. That the materials of it is a *vaporous Aire*, appears as well from the faintness and emptiness of them that have been entertained at those Feasts, as from their forbidding the use of Salt at them, it having a virtue of dissolving of all aqueous substances, as well as hindering their congelation. But how *Aire* is moulded up into that form and consistency, it is very hard to conceive: whether it be done by the mere power of Imagination upon their own Vehicles, first dabled in some humidities that are the fittest for their design, which they change into these forms of Viands, and then withdraw, when they have given them such a figure, colour, and consistency, with some small touch of such a sapour or tincture; or whether it be the priviledge of these *Aereal Creatures*, by a sharp Desire and keen Imagination, to pierce the *Spirit of Nature*, so as to awaken her activity, and engage her to the compleating in a moment, as it were, the full design of their own wishes, but in such matter as the Element they are in is capable of, which is this crude and vaporous Aire; whence their food must be very dilute and flashie, and rather a mockery than any solid satisfaction and pleasure.

But those Superiour *Daemons*, which inhabit that part of the Aire that no storm nor tempest can reach, need be put to no such shifts, though they may be as able in them as the other. For in the tranquillity of those upper Regions, that *Promus-Condus* of the *Universe, the Spirit of Nature*, may silently send forth whole Gardens and Orchards of most delectable fruits and flowers of an equilibrious ponderosity to the parts of the *Aire* they grow in, to whose shape and colours the transparency of these Plants may adde a particular lustre, as we see it is in precious stones. And the *Chymists* are never quiet till the heat of their Fancy have calcined and vitrified the Earth into a crystalline pellucidity, conceiting that it

---

[1] More, *Immortality of the Soul*, iii. 19.

will then be a very fine thing indeed, and all that then grows out of it: which desirable spectacle they may haply enjoy in a more perfect manner whenever they are admitted into those *higher regions* of the Aire. For the very Soile then under them shall be transparent, in which they may trace the very Roots of the Trees of this *Superiour Paradise* with their eyes, and if it may not offend them, see this opake Earth through it, bounding their sight with such a white faint splendour as is discovered in the Moon, with that difference of brightness that will arise from the distinction of Land and Water; and if they will recreate their palats, may taste of such Fruits as whose natural juice will vie with their noblest Extractions and Quintessences. For such certainly will they there find the blood of the Grape, the rubie-coloured Cherries, and Nectarines.

And if, for the compleating of the pleasantness of these habitations, that they may look less like a silent and dead solitude, they meet with Birds and Beasts of curious shapes and colours, the single accents of whose voices are very grateful to the Ear, and the varying of their notes perfect musical harmony; they would doe very kindly to bring us word back of the certainty of these things, and make this more than a *Philosophical Conjecture.*

But that there may be *Food* and *Feasting* in those higher Aereal Regions, is less doubted by the *Platonists;* which makes *Maximus Tyrius* call the Soul, when she has left the body, nursling of the sky; and the above-cited Oracle of *Apollo* describes the Felicity of that Chorus of immortal Lovers he mentions there, from feasting together with the blessed *Genii*—

With whom the Genius ever takes delight in festivities and good cheer.

So that the *Nectar* and *Ambrosia* of the Poets may not be a mere fable. For the *Spirit of Nature*, which is the immediate Instrument of God, may enrich the fruits of these *Aereal Paradises* with such liquors, as being received into the bodies of these purer *Daemons*, and diffusing it self through their Vehicles, may cause such grateful motions analogical to our *tast*, and excite such a more than ordinary quickness in their minds, and benign chearfulness, that it may far transcend the most delicate Refection that the greatest Epicures could ever invent upon Earth; and that without all satiety, burdensomeness, it filling them with nothing but Divine Love, Joy, and Devotion.[1]

---

[1] More's *Immortality of the Soul*, iii. 9, pp. 183, 184, ed. 1662. The indebtedness of More's "Myth" to the Platonic, and Stoic mythology of what encircles the earth, inhabited by daemons and human souls, is obvious. For further reference to that mythology see *infra*, pp. 387 ff.

It is very difficult to disentangle the motives which go to the production of a passage like this. We should say without hesitation that the writer wished to adorn his discourse with a myth, if we did not know how uncritical his "science" was, and how credulous he was in accepting, as literally true, things quite as visionary as those here described. In his *Antidote against Atheism* he shows how thoroughly he believes current stories about the doings of witches and ghosts (see especially Book iii. chap. vii. of that work, for the story of Anne Bodenham, a witch, who suffered at Salisbury in 1653), and how valuable he holds these stories to be as evidence for the immortality of the Soul; indeed, in the Preface to his *Philosophickal Poems* he goes the length of expressing the wish that stories of witchcraft and apparitions "were publicly recorded in every parish", for "that course continued would prove one of the best antidotes against that earthly and cold disease of Sadducisme and Atheisme which may easily grow upon us, if not prevented, to the hazard of all Religion and the best kinds of Philosophy." It is to be noted, however, that Cudworth and Smith are not so credulous as More. Cudworth may be said to be a cautious believer in apparitions, and dwells on the Scripture evidence for demoniacal possession, and not, like More, on that afforded by modern stories;[1] while Smith, in a sermon preached on an occasion when credulity seemed to be required,[2] expresses himself in a manner which makes one feel that he was in advance of his age.

There is just one general remark I should like to make in taking leave of More for the present:—That facility of scientific explanation is apt to make men indifferent about the substantiation of the facts, as facts. The facility of scientific explanation afforded by the hypothesis of "plastick power" doubtless made it more easy for More and other Cambridge Platonists to accept as sufficient the evidence forthcoming for the actual appearance of ghosts and Daemons. Facility of scientific explanation is a danger

[1] *Intellectual System*, vol. ii. p. 640 (ed. Mosheim).
[2] Discourse 10, *Of a Christian's Conflicts with and Conquests over Satan*, "delivered in publick at Huntingdon, where one of Queen's College, in every year on March 25, preached a Sermon against Witchcraft, Diabolical Contracts, etc."; see Worthington's Preface to Smith's *Select Discourses*.

which we have to be on our guard against at the present day too.

The true object of the *Phaedo* Myth is, indeed, moral and religious, not in any way scientific—its true object is to give expression to man's sense of responsibility, which it does in the form of a vivid history, or spectacle, of the connected life-stages of an immortal personality. This moral and religious object, however, is served best, if the history or spectacle, though carefully presented as a creation of fancy, is not made too fantastical, but is kept at least consistent with "modern science".[1] It is of the greatest importance that the student of the philosophy of Plato's Myths should learn to appreciate the terms of this alliance between Myth and Science;[2] and I do not know how the lesson can be better learnt than from parallel study of Dante's *Divina Commedia*, in which all the science—moral and physical—of the age is used to give verisimilitude to the great Myth of medieval Christianity. Fortunately, no better instances of the art with which Dante presses Science into the service of Myth could be found than in his treatment of a subject which has special interest for us here, in connection with the geography and geology of the *Phaedo* Myth. This brings me to the second head of observations which I have to offer on the *Phaedo* Myth.

II

In this section I wish to draw attention to the parallel between Plato's geography of Tartarus and the True Surface of the Earth, and Dante's geography of Hell and the Mount of Purgatory with the Earthly Paradise on its summit.

The parallel is close. On the one hand, the *Phaedo* Myth and the *Divina Commedia* stand entirely alone, so far as I know, among Eschatological Myths in making Tartarus or

[1] Aristotle's canon applies—"what is convincing though impossible should always be preferred to what is possible and unconvincing".—*Poet.* 1460 a 30.

[2] In this connection the reader should turn to Prof. Dill's illuminating remarks on the mixture of science with devotional allegory and myth in the Commentary of Macrobius on Cicero's *Dream of Scipio: Roman Society in the Last Century of the Western Empire*, Book i. ch. iv. pp. 88-90, ed. i.

Hell a chasm bored right through the globe of the Earth, *Phaedo*, 111 E; *Inferno*, xxxiv. *sub fin.*), with two antipodally placed openings.   On the other hand, while the *Phaedo* Myth stands alone among Plato's Eschatological Myths in describing a lofty terrestrial region raised, above the elements of water and air, up into the element of fire or aether, Dante also, in agreement with a common medieval belief, places the Earthly Paradise on the top of a mountain—his own Mount of Purgatory—which rises up into the element of fire.

The "Earthly Paradise" of the *Phaedo* Myth probably owes a good deal to the Homeric Olympus; and the Earthly Paradise of medieval belief and of the *Divina Commedia* may have derived at least its altitude from the same source.   But the description of Tartarus as bored right through the Earth, unique in Greek mythology, in no way countenanced by Virgil, and yet reappearing in the *Inferno*, which is so largely modelled on the Sixth Book of the *Aeneid*—this is surely a strange coincidence.   The *Timaeus* (in the version of Chalcidius) was, it would appear, the only work of Plato which Dante knew directly.[1]   There is no evidence whatever—unless this coincidence be regarded as evidence—that he was acquainted with the Latin version of the *Phaedo* which was made in the twelfth century.[2]   It is possible, however, but I hardly think likely, that the passage in the *Meteorologica* (ii. 2; 355 b, 32 ff.), in which the *Phaedo* description of Tartarus is referred to, may have given Dante the idea of an antipodal exit from Hell; although it is to be noted that Aristotle, in criticising the hydrostatics of the *Phaedo* Myth, curiously enough omits to quote, or paraphrase, Plato's emphatic piercing right through; and S. Thomas does not make good the omission in his commentary on the Aristotelian passage.   I do not think that any one reading the Aristotelian passage, without having read the *Phaedo*, would easily gather that the Tartarus of the *Phaedo* is bored right

---

[1] See Moore's *Studies in Dante*, first series, p. 156, and Toynbee's *Dante Dictionary*, s.v. "Platone".

[2] See Rashdall's *Universities of Europe in the Middle Ages*, i. 37, ii. 744, and Immisch, *Philologische Studien zu Plato*, pp. 33, 34.   Henricus Aristippus (Archdeacon of Catania) translated the *Phaedo* and *Meno* in 1156.   There is a MS. of his translation in Corpus Christi College, Oxford (243), written in 1423; see Coxe, ii. 100.

through the Earth. Aristotle is concerned to show that the theory of a central swing, or oscillation, gives a wrong explanation of the origin of seas and rivers; and, *more suo*, he is careless in his description of the theory to which he objects. Although the hydrostatics of the *Quaestio de Aqua et Terra*[1] agree in the main with those of the *Meteorologica*, the *Inferno* is not influenced by the *Meteorologica*. The *Inferno* follows the traditional mythology in supposing subterranean rivers, and, indeed, agrees with the account of these rivers given in the *Phaedo*, to the extent, at least, of regarding them as forming a single system of waters connected somehow with waters on the surface of the Earth. Dante may have been helped to this view by Brunetto Latini, who speaks, very much in the same way as Plato does, of waters circulating in channels through the Earth, like blood through the veins of the body, and coming out in springs.[2] But mark how the Poet uses these mere hydrostatics—how his genius transforms the physical relation between the living world and Tartarus into a moral relation! It is the *tears* of this world that flow in the rivers of Dante's Hell.[3]

Let me close this passage on Plato's Tartarus and Dante's Hell with the remark that an antipodal exit from Hell, near the Mount of Purgatory, is almost necessary to the movement of the *Commedia*. If such an exit—whether derived directly or indirectly from the *Phaedo*, or obtained from some other source—did not already exist among Dante's mythological data, he would practically have been obliged to invent it, and offer some explanation of it, such as that which he actually offers—the Fall of Lucifer (*Inf.* xxxiv.).

Now to pass on to the parallel between Plato's "True

---

[1] With regard to the authenticity of this treatise see Moore's *Studies in Dante*, second series, pp. 303 ff.

[2] See Schmidt, *über Dantes Stellung in der Geschichte der Kosmographie*, I. Teil, *de Aqua et Terra* (1876), p. 7.

[3] *Inferno*, xiv. Dante probably profited by the crude fancy of predecessors in the matter of the contents of the infernal rivers; see Cary on *Inf.* xii. It is perhaps worth noticing here that Dante's River of Blood (*Inf.* xii.) has its parallel in the Scottish ballad of Thomas the Rhymer:—

It was mirk mirk night and there was nae stern-light,
And they waded through red bluid to the knee;
For a' the bluid that's shed on earth
Rins through the springs o' that countrie (*i.e.* Elf-land).

Surface of the Earth" and Dante's Earthly Paradise on the top of the Mount of Purgatory:—Dante's Mount of Purgatory is definitely a part of this Earth. It is an island, antipodal to Jerusalem, in the middle of the ocean which covers the southern hemisphere. This island rises up, in a series of circular terraces, into one lofty height on which is situated the Earthly Paradise—where our first parents were created— where the souls which have been purified by penance during their ascent of the Mount are gathered together, before they drink the waters of Lethe and Eunoè, the twin streams of this Paradise, and are translated into the Heavenly Paradise. That Purgatory is a real place, on the surface of this globe, which an adventurous voyager from our hemisphere might possibly reach in a dark ship, is suggested with consummate art in the *Inferno*, Canto xxvi., where Ulysses describes his last voyage—how, with Ceuta on his left and Seville on his right, he sailed out through the Straits, and south over the ocean for five months, till the stars of the northern hemisphere sank beneath the horizon, and new stars appeared in the sky, and he sighted .

> A Mountain dim, loftiest, methought,
> Of all I e'er beheld[1]—

and then the storm burst which overwhelmed him.

Dante's Mount of Purgatory—for that was the land which Ulysses sighted—is identical with the lofty mountain on the top of which medieval belief placed the Earthly Paradise; but Dante apparently drew entirely on his own imagination when he localised Purgatory on its slopes.[2] This Mountain of the Earthly Paradise rises, according to the medieval belief, as high as the Lunar Sphere[3]—*i.e.* its upper parts are above the air, in the aether or fire, like Plato's True Surface of the Earth. Hence, as S. Thomas explains, the Earthly Paradise was not reached by the flood.[4]

---

[1] Cary's translation.
[2] See Scartazzini (*Companion to Dante*, Butler's Transl. p. 419). "Purgatory, so far as form and position go, is a creation quite of the poet's own." It may, I think, have relationship to the "steep hill of virtue" which the Stoics climbed; see Lucian, *Vera Hist.* ii. 18—no Stoics were to be seen in the Fortunate Island, because they were climbing this hill.
[3] See S. Thom. Aqui. *Summa*, i. 102, 2.
[4] Cf. Schmidt, *Cosmographie des Dante*, p. 23.

S. Thomas further remarks that Enoch and Elias are said to be now in it; also, that it is said to be *sub aequinoctiali circulo;* but he will not vouch for its exact position, only expressing his belief that it must be in a "temperate clime".[1] The Arabians, whose geographical treatises, and epitomes of the Greek geographers, Dante knew in Latin versions,[2] spoke of a great mountain in the far south. It is called Mons Caldicus by Albertus,[3] and Mons Malcus by Roger Bacon, who places it in India.[4] The view that this mountain, identified by the Christian Schoolmen with the seat of the Earthly Paradise, is an island antipodal to Jerusalem in the middle of the Southern Ocean (*Purg.* iv. 70), was due entirely, it would seem,[5] to Dante's own "scientific imagination" or "mythopœic faculty". According to the doctrine of Orosius, generally accepted in Dante's time, there is no land at all in the southern hemisphere. If there were land, its inhabitants would be cut off from those of the known world—the unity and continuity of the human race, postulated by the command, "Go ye into all the world and preach the gospel to every creature," would not exist. The

---

[1] *Summa*, i. 102, 2.
[2] See Lelewel, *Histoire de la Géographie*, i. lxxxv., and Toynbee's *Dante Dictionary* arts. "Alfergano" and "Tolommeo¹".
[3] *Meteor*, ii. 2. 7. Cf. Schmidt, *Cosm. d. Dante*, p. 23.
[4] *Op. Maj.* pp. 192, 195, ed. princ. Jebb, London.
[5] See Scartazzini's *Companion to Dante*, p. 419, Butler's Eng. Transl. It is, however, an *island* in the *Exeter Book* (an Anthology of Anglo-Saxon Poetry given to the Library of Exeter Cathedral by Leofric, first Bishop of Exeter, 1050-1071): see *Exeter Book*, edited by Israel Gollancz for the Early English Text Society, 1895, poem on the "Phœnix", pp. 200 ff.: "The Earthly Paradise is in eastern parts . . . it is all plain . . . is an island. . . . There the door of Heaven's Realm is oft-times opened. . . . It is green and flowery. There is no rain there, nor snow nor frost nor fire. It is neither too hot nor too cold. The plain (which is quite smooth) is higher than any mountain by 12 fathom measures. It escaped the flood. . . . It shall abide perennially blooming till the Day of Judgment. Water falls not there, but rises from the turf in the midst of the forest each month of the year, and irrigates the grove [we are reminded of Dante's Lethe and Eunoè]. The beautiful grove is inhabited by the Phœnix"—which the Poet then goes on to describe.
It ought to be mentioned that Claudian (*Idyll.* i. 1. *Phœnix*) makes "the Earthly Paradise" an island:—

There is a grove round which flow the deepest waters of Ocean,
Beyond the Indies and the East Wind it is green.

Mr. Toynbee, however, thinks it doubtful whether Dante had an acquaintance with Claudian (see *Dante Dict.* art. "Claudianus"). Benvenuto da Imola, in his Commentary on the *Divina Commedia*, quotes Claudian several times, describing him, erroneously, as a Florentine; see Mr. Toynbee's *Index of Authors quoted by Benv. de Imola in his Commentary on the D. C.* (Annual Report of the Dante Society, Cambridge, Mass., 1901).

ideal of *one* Church and *one* Empire (and one Aristotelian
Philosophy, as Dante adds in the *Banquet*, iv. 6) requires
the geographical condition of *one continuous inhabited world*.[1]
Dante's antipodal island, however, being people only by
the souls of the departed, is in no way inconsistent with the
teleological geography of Orosius—indeed, is made, with
consummate art, to corroborate it; for the cause which
produced the solitary island of Purgatory in the southern
hemisphere, simultaneously produced the one inhabited
region of the northern hemisphere.   Lucifer fell on the
southern hemisphere (*Inf.* xxxiv.), and the shock of his fall
submerged the land which originally existed there, and
caused an equivalent amount of land in the northern
hemisphere to bulge up above the sea; the Mount of Purgatory, the only land now in the southern hemisphere, having
been formed by the material extruded, as Lucifer, with the
force of his fall, bored a passage down to the centre of the
Earth. Thus does Dante give verisimilitude to his mythology
of "the abhorred worm that boreth through the world"
(*Inf.* xxxiv. 108), by making it explain a physical fact, or
what the science of his day accepted as a fact; and, at the
same time, by means of the explanation, be brings the fact—
so important for the doctrine of one Church and one
Empire—into clear connection with a vast system of belief
already accepted.   When the rebel angels—about a tenth
part of the original number created—were lost to Heaven,
the human race was created to make good the loss.[2]   The
descent of the Prince of these rebel angels produced, at one
blow, Hell, and Purgatory, and the One Continent which

---

[1] Orosius, *Hist. adv. paganos*, i. 2, §§ 87-89; vi. 22, § 1; vii. 1; vii. 3, 4;
and cf. Moore's *Studies in Dante*, first series, pp. 279 ff.

[2] See *Convivio*, ii. 6: "I say that of all these Orders, some were lost as
soon as they had been created, numbering perhaps a tenth part; to make
restoration for this, human nature was afterwards created." So also Spenser
(*An Hymn of Heavenly Love*):—

> But that eternal Fount of Love and Grace,
> Still showing forth his goodness unto all,
> Now seeing left a waste and empty place
> In his wide Palace, through those Angels' Fall,
> Cast to supply the same, and to enstall
>   A new unknowen Colonie therein,
>   Whose Root from Earth's base Ground-work should begin.

In this Hymn the whole drama worked out by Milton in *Paradise Lost* and
Paradise Regained is indicated in outline.

is the condition of the ecclesiastical and civil unity of the human race. All hangs together clearly. "Science" recommends Myth, and Myth "Science", in one consistent whole.

Again, in *Purg.* xxviii., the distribution of plants in our hemisphere, from a common centre of creation, is explained in such a way as to make the existence of an Earthly Paradise appear the only hypothesis consistent with "science". The wind which Dante notices with wonder among the trees of the Earthly Paradise is caused, he is told, by the rotation, from east to west, of the *first moving*, or crystalline sphere— the ninth sphere counted from that of the moon. The rotation of the *primum mobile* carries round with it the pure air or aether in which the Earthly Paradise is bathed; and this aether is impregnated with the seeds of the trees of the Earthly Paradise, and carries them round to our hemisphere, where they germinate according as they find soils and climates suitable to their various virtues. Here we have a "Myth", in which Faith, Fancy, and Science are blended in the true Platonic manner.

The close parallel between Plato's "True Surface of the Earth" and Dante's Earthly Paradise has been made evident, I trust, by what I have said about the latter. Plato's "True Surface of the Earth" is a real place in this world, physically connected with the region which we inhabit. It is distinguished from our region essentially by its altitude. With its foundation, like that of Dante's Island of Purgatory, bathed in the crass elements of water and air, it rises up into the region occupied by the element of fire or aether—a region which, we must remember, belonged as definitely to the domain of "science" for Plato and Dante as the regions of water and air, of which men have direct experience. Given a sufficient altitude, aether will take the place of air, and beneath aether, air will be as water. This is "scientifically" true. It is also in accordance with "science" to believe that the inhabitants of the aethereal altitudes live longer, more vigorously, and more happily, than we, poor frogs, do, down in the mists beside the waters of our hollow. A place has been found—or as good as found—by "science", where the souls of the virtuous may live in the enjoyment of the rewards of their virtue, and in preparation for an even more blessed

H

existence elsewhere. There can be no doubt, I think, that
the lofty terrestrial Paradise of the *Phaedo* Myth answers to
the "Islands of the Blessed" in the *Gorgias* Myth, to the
what surrounds the earth of the *Phaedrus* Myth,[1] and to the
"heaven" of the Myth of Er, from which the souls of the
virtuous, who have not yet completed their purgatorial
course, return, after a thousand years' sojourn, to the
"meadow", in order to journey thence to the plain of
Lethe, and drink the water of the river, and be born again
in terrestrial bodies. The "Islands of the Blessed" were
doubtless pictured by Hesiod and Pindar as islands in the
ordinary sense, surrounded by water, somewhere out in the
Western Ocean;[2] Plato, in the *Phaedo*, is singular in making
them aerial, not oceanic. With an art that is charming, he
not only gives direct "scientific" reasons for believing in the
existence of his aethereal altitudes of the Earth's surface
(the configuration of the Earth in its envelopes of air and
aether—deep hollows of its surface being compensated for
by lofty heights—naturally produces such blessed altitudes),
but he also knows how to add the authority of the poets to
the reasons of "science", by making his description of these
altitudes recall, not only the Homeric Olympus,[3] but the
Islands of the Blessed as described by Hesiod and Pindar.

The original conception, in Greek as in Celtic[4] mythology,
of Islands of the Blessed was that of an Elysium or Paradise,
somewhere on the surface of the Earth, inhabited by gods, in
which also certain elect heroes, who have been translated
thither, enjoy *in the flesh* eternal felicity. This is the conception which meets us in Homer,[5] Hesiod, Pindar, and the
Hymn to Harmodius and Aristogeiton. But in course of
time this original conception was modified in the interest of

---

[1] *Phaedrus*, 257 A; and cf. 248 E-249 A, where a region of the heaven
seems to answer to what is round the earth, as contrasted with what is under
the earth in 257 A.

[2] Hesiod, *O. et D.* 167:—

But to others Father Zeus the son of Cronos gave life and a habitation
apart from men, and established them at the world's end. And they live with
hearts untouched by sorrow in the Islands of the Blest, beside the deep-
eddying Ocean, happy heroes from whom the grain-giving soil bears honey-
sweet fruit which ripens three times yearly.

[3] See Thiemann, *die Platonische Eschatologie in ihrer genetischen Entwickelung*
(1892), p. 20.

[4] See Myer and Nutt's *Voyage of Bran*, i. 329.

[5] See Rohde, *Psyche*, i. 69.

morality and religion, especially the religion of the Orphic cult, and the Islands of the Blessed came to be regarded as the abode of the *souls* of the virtuous generally. This view is acquiesced in in the *Gorgias*, where Tartarus indeed appears as a Purgatory or place of temporary sojourn for the majority of the souls which go thither after judgment; but we are left to suppose that virtuous souls which go at once after judgment to the Islands of the Blessed remain there thenceforth for ever. In the *Phaedo*, however, the notion of progressive purification dominates the view taken of the Islands or "aethereal altitudes", as well as of Tartarus. For "Philosophers" mansions even fairer than the aethereal altitudes are indicated as the final abode. We are to think, perhaps, of the natal stars of the *Timaeus*. Finally, in the *Republic*, where the notion of re-incarnation, kept in the background in the *Gorgias* and the *Phaedo*,[1] is so prominent, the region to which virtuous souls go after judgment is, at any rate for many of them, only a place of temporary sojourn. They return from it, as other souls return from Tartarus, to be born again in the flesh. This view of Elysium as a place of pleasant sojourn from which souls, virtuous on the whole, but not yet completely purified, pass to the river of Lethe, and thence, after drinking of its water, proceed to enter into new terrestrial bodies, is that which we find in the Sixth Book of the *Aeneid*. The view of Elysium represented in the *Frogs* and the *Axiochus*, on the other hand, is rather that of a final abode of bliss, into which ceremonial observances secure a speedy entrance, immediately after death, to the soul of the mystic. With this substitution of the *opus operatum* for the personal struggle after purification, prolonged through this life and perhaps many other lives, Plato has no sympathy. The view of Elysium or Heaven as still a place of probation he would have us accept as that which, on the whole, will guide us best in the conduct of our earthly life.

Taking, then, the "Islands of the Blessed" in the *Gorgias* Myth, the Heaven in the Myth of Er, and the "True Surface of the Earth" in the *Phaedo* Myth, as names for the same region, we may perhaps venture to harmonise the

---

[1] In the *Phaedo* Myth; it appears in the Dialogue, 81 E-82 B.

accounts given of it in the three Myths, by saying that the souls of the virtuous, after judgment, go thither—some of them to sojourn for ever (*Gorgias*), some of them for a thousand years, till they return again to enter into the flesh (*Rep.*), and a few of them—Philosophers (*Phaedo*), till such time as they have been thoroughly purified, and are translated to still fairer mansions ("abodes that are yet more fair," *Phaedo*, 114 C) in the true Heaven, as the purified are taken up from Dante's Earthly Paradise into the Heavenly Paradise.

It is certainly important to note that the place to which the souls of the virtuous go in the three Platonic Myths—variously called "Islands of the Blessed", "True Surface of the Earth", and "Heaven"—is, for some of these souls at least, a temporary abode, a stage in their purgatorial course, just as Tartarus is a Purgatory for all except the utterly incorrigible.

In what part of the world are the Platonic "Islands of the Blessed" or "Altitudes of the True Surface of the Earth"? The *Phaedo* Myth does not say; but we are allowed to suppose that they are far away from our inhabited region, in another part of the world. Perhaps Plato, in writing the *Phaedo* Myth, did not even imagine a definite locality for them. We are bound to allow for this possibility, but, in doing so, we need not scruple to consider some evidence which may be thought to point to the conclusion that he did localise them—and that, in the antipodes, where Dante's Mount of Purgatory stands. The *Axiochus*, a pseudo-Platonic Dialogue,[1] identifies the world of the departed definitely with the antipodal hemisphere. The author of the *Axiochus* probably thought that the identification was in accordance with the geography and cosmography of Plato; at any rate, those who accepted the piece as written by Plato must have thought so. We may safely go the length of saying that the identification would not be impossible for Plato, so far as his view of the position and shape of the Earth is concerned.

---

[1] See Thiemann, *Plat. Eschat.* p. 26, and Rohde, *Psyche*, i. 314; ii. 247, n. 1, and 422. Rohde says that it can hardly be earlier than the third century B.C. It is a mythical discourse containing expressions which point to the direct influence of Orphic teaching and practice. Axiochus is described (371 D) as off-spring of the Gods—i.e. as initiated, and therefore as kinsman of the Gods by adoption, with which initiation is commonly identified.

He holds, with the writer of the *Axiochus*, that the Earth is a sphere in the centre of the Cosmos. The passage in the *Axiochus* is as follows (371 A ff.): "The subterranean dwelling, in which is Pluto's Queen, not less than that of the Hall of Zeus, for the earth keeps the middle part of the Universe, being spherical on its axis. Of this the heavenly Gods have as their portion one hemisphere, and those below, the other"—*i.e.* the "Palace of Pluto", in addition to its subterranean, or properly "infernal" parts, includes the whole antipodal hemisphere of the Earth, with its sky lighted by the sun, when it is night in our hemisphere (Pindar, *fragm.* 129)—"Son of Leto, you guard your children among the heroes, always traversing the region of the sanctified" (Kaibel, *ep. lap.* 228 b 7, 8).[1] To this "under world" the dead go to be judged. Some are sent into the subterranean parts, while others enjoy the light of day, in a land of flowers and streams, apparently still in the hemisphere of the antipodal gods, as we may call them. Among these blessed ones it is distinctly stated that the "initiated" take precedence, 371 D.

Now, we may safely say that there is nothing in the Platonic doctrine of the shape and position of the Earth inconsistent with this "under world" of the *Axiochus*. But can we say more? I venture to mention two points:—First, Plato's judgment-seat in the Myth of Er, between the openings of "Heaven" and Tartarus, is above ground, and so is the region across which the pilgrims travel towards the pillar of light; and so (as I believe in all Greek accounts) is the river of Lethe.[2] It is from the plain of Lethe, on the surface of the Earth, that the souls shoot up (*Rep.* 621 B) to be born again in terrestrial bodies—that is, I venture to suggest, up from the lower, antipodal hemisphere to our hemisphere. Secondly, the hollow or cave of Tartarus extends right through the globe of the Earth, as we have seen—(*Phaedo*, 111 E)—*i.e.* has an opening in the lower hemisphere as well as in this. Without going the length of supposing that Plato's unseen world is mapped out with the

---

[1] Quoted by Rohde, *Psyche*, ii. 210, n. 1.
[2] See Thiemann, *Plat. Esch.* p. 18. I shall return to this subject in my observations on the Myth of Er. Virgil's Lethe is of uncertain position; but Dante follows the universal Greek tradition in making Lethe a river of the surface of the Earth.

definiteness of Dante's, we may take it that Plato, with his poet's faculty of visualisation, must have formed a clear mental picture of the opening of Tartarus in the "lower" or antipodal hemisphere, and of the country into which one comes on issuing from it. The antipodal opening was not, we may assume, imagined by Plato in vain. Those souls which, after being judged (whether above or under ground does not appear in the *Phaedo*—but probably underground), go, not to the Islands of the Blessed, but down the river Acheron to the Acherusian Lake (which is certainly subterranean), have entered the infernal regions, we may fairly suppose, by the opening in our hemisphere, and will come out, after their penance, by the other—the antipodal—opening, and will start thence on their journey—always above ground—to the river of Lethe. That Plato actually thought of the souls as going into Tartarus, and coming out of it, by distinct openings, we know from the Myth of Er. But while the entrance and exit are antipodally placed in the *Phaedo* Myth, which takes careful account of cosmographical and geological conditions, in the Myth of Er the purpose of pictorial composition is served by placing them side by side, opposite the entrance and exit of "Heaven"; the "Meadow", at once the place of judgment and the starting-place for the plain of Lethe, lying between Tartarus and "Heaven". It would be easy to give examples, from Greek vase-painting, of similar compression in pictorial composition. I call attention to this discrepancy between the *Phaedo* Myth and the Myth of Er, to show how absurd it would be to attempt to construct one topographical scheme for Plato's Eschatological Myths, as rigid as the one scheme to which Dante is so faithful in the *Divina Commedia*. What I venture to suggest, however, is that, *in the Phaedo Myth*, Plato is possibly —or shall I say "probably"?—thinking of the world of the departed, so far as it is not subterranean, or celestial, as somewhere in the other hemisphere of the terrestrial globe —*somewhere*, but as in a dream, in which inconsistencies are accepted as natural; for the "True Surface of the Earth", though somewhere in the antipodal hemisphere, beneath us, is yet a region above us, whence gems have found their way down to our hollow!

I have dwelt on the parallel between the geography of the *Phaedo* Myth and that of the *Divina Commedia* with the view, not of clearing up particular difficulties in mythological geography, but of suggesting a method by which the function of Myth in the Platonic philosophy may be better understood—the method of sealing the impression made on us by the Myth of one great master by study of the Myth of another great master with whom we may happen to be in closer sympathy. The service which Myth, and poetical treatment generally, can render to the faith on which conduct and science ultimately rest is, I think, more easily and finely appreciated by us in Dante than in Plato; for we live, though in late days, in the same Christian epoch with the medieval poet.

III

Let me close these observations on the *Phaedo* Myth by calling attention to what Socrates says at the end of the narrative (114 D)—that, while it would not be sensible to maintain that all about the Soul and the next world contained in the Myth is absolutely true, yet, *since the Soul is plainly immortal*, one ought to hazard the pious belief that, if not absolutely true, this Myth, or some other like it, is not far from being true, and "sing it over oneself" as if it were an enchanter's song:—"That these are facts exactly as I have described them, no reasonable man would hold, but that either this or something of the kind is true of our souls and their future abodes—since it is clear that the soul is immortal—this seems to me a fitting argument and worth risking. For the risk is a fine one. One should sing such tales within one's self like an incantation. That is why I made so long a story." The distinction between Dogma and Myth is carefully insisted on here, and also the practical value of Myth as an expression of moral and religious feeling. Myth, it is suggested, may be put into such form that it will react favourably on the feeling expressed, and make it a surer guide to what is good. The reaction of expression on that which it expresses—of style on the man— is a matter about which Plato had reflected deeply, as is apparent from his whole scheme of education, mental, moral, and physical, in the *Republic*. If, then, the sense of responsibility, and the attendant sense of being a continuously existent Self, naturally express themselves, as Plato holds, in myth-making, pictorially, in visions of an immortal life, it follows from the general law of the reaction of expression on feeling, that, by refining and ennobling myth-making, we shall be able to refine and ennoble morals and faith. This is the "use" to which myth is put by Plato, not only in the education of young children, but in dialogues offered to mature readers as models on which they may mould their own conversations about the highest things. This is the "use" of great poetry, like Dante's *Commedia*, or of great painting, like the fresco on the left-hand wall of the Spanish Chapel—"the most noble piece of pictorial philosophy and divinity in Italy."[1]   As philosophy and pictorial composition are blended together in that fresco—the philosophy is *seen* as a whole, in all the beauty of its grandeur and order—so are philosophy and poetry blended together where Plato is at his highest—in his Myths. In the *Phaedo* Myth the poet-philosopher has taken moral responsibility as the *motif* of his piece. Moral responsibility cannot, he knows, be explained in scientific terms, as a phenomenon is explained by being put into its proper place among other phenomena; for moral responsibility attaches immediately to the subject of all phenomena—the continuously existing Self. But if it cannot be explained, moral responsibility may be pictured—pictured in a Myth representing the continuity of the responsible Self in terms of Pre-existence, Reminiscence, Judgment, Penance, Free Choice, Re-incarnation—a Myth not to be taken literally, but to be dwelt on ("it is necessary to sing this over to one's self"), till the charm of it touches one deeply—so deeply that, when the "uninitiated" say "it is not true", one is able to answer by acting as if it were true.

---

[1] Ruskin's *Mornings in Florence*, chap. iv., "The Vaulted Book"; cf. Renan, *Averroes et l'Averroïsme*, pp. 245, 246.

THE *GORGIAS* MYTH

CONTEXT

Gorgias, the famous teacher of Rhetoric, and his young disciple Polus, meet Socrates at the house of Callicles, an Athenian gentleman; and the conversation turns on the difference between Rhetoric and the Way of true Knowledge and the true Conduct of Life.

What is Rhetoric? Socrates asks. Neither Gorgias nor Polus can give an intelligible answer; and Socrates answers for them by describing it as the Simulation of Justice, the Art of getting people to believe what the Professor of the Art wishes them to believe, and they themselves wish to believe, without regard to Truth or Justice. It is the Art of Flattery. It ignores the distinction between Pleasure and the Good—a distinction to the reality of which human nature itself testifies—for all men, bad as well as good, wish the Good, and bad men, in doing what they think best for themselves, do what they do not wish to do. To seek after the Good is of the very essence of Life—it is better to suffer evil than to do evil; and if a man has done evil, it is better for him to be chastised than to escape chastisement.

Here Callicles, speaking as a man of the world, takes up the argument, and maintains that Statesmanship does not recognise this distinction drawn by Socrates between Pleasure and the Good. Pleasure is the Good. Might is Right.

After much talk Callicles is silenced, and Socrates points out that there are two kinds of Statesmanship—that which uses Rhetoric as its instrument, and flatters people, and deceives them, holding up Pleasure before them; and that which, keeping the Good always in view, makes them better.

At the Day of Judgment, which the Myth now told by Socrates declares, there will be no place for the Art of Flattery. Pretence will not avail. There will be no side issues then. The only issue will be: Is this man righteous or is he wicked?

With the Myth of the Day of Judgment the Gorgias ends.

Gorgias 523 A—527 C

Hearken now to an excellent True Story: a Fable, methinks, thou wilt deem it; but I deem it no Fable, for that the things are true, whereof I will now tell, I am fully persuaded. What Homer telleth, that will I now tell: That Zeus and Poseidon and Pluto divided amongst them the kingdom, when they had received it from their father Cronus. Now, in his time there was this law among the gods concerning men, which standeth fast unto this day as of old, that the man who hath gone through his life righteously in the fear of the Gods, after death goeth to the Isles of the Blessed, and dwelleth there in all felicity beyond the touch of ill; but the man who hath lived unrighteously without the fear of the Gods before his eyes, he goeth to the prison-house of just retribution, which men call Tartarus.

They who were Judges in the time of Cronus, and when Zeus was newly come to his kingdom, were living men; and they also were living men who were judged, each on that day on the which he should die. Now, judgments given thus were ill-given, and Pluto and the Overseers from the Isles of the Blessed came and spake unto Zeus, making complaint that many came unworthily unto either place. Wherefore Zeus said: Verily I will end this; for now are the judgments given ill, because they who are judged are judged with their raiment on, being judged alive. Many there be, he said, that have evil souls, and, for raiment, have fair bodies and noble birth and riches: when these are judged, many witnesses come to bear witness for them, that they have lived righteously. By these are the Judges confounded; and, moreover, they themselves sit in judgment with raiment on, having eyes and ears, yea, and the whole Body, as clothing wherewith their Soul is covered. All these things hinder them, to wit, their own raiment, and the raiment of those that are judged. First, then, he said, must they be stopped of their foreknowing the day of their death: for now have they foreknowledge. Wherefore Prometheus hath been charged to stop them of this. Then naked, stripped of all, must they be judged; for they must be judged dead. The Judge also must be naked, dead, with very Soul beholding the very

Soul of each, as soon as he is dead, bereft of all his kindred, having left upon the earth all the adornment he had there. So shall the judgment be just. I therefore, having considered all these things before that ye came unto me, have made my sons Judges—two from Asia, Minos and Rhadamanthys, and one from Europe, Aeacus. These, when they are dead, shall sit in judgment in the Meadow at the Parting of the Ways, whence the two Ways lead—the one unto the Isles of the Blessed, and the other unto Tartarus. And those of Asia shall Rhadamanthys judge, and those of Europe, Aeacus. But unto Minos will I appoint the chief place, that he may give judgment at the last, if the other two be in doubt as touching any matter. Thus shall the judgments concerning the Passage of Men be most just.

These are the things, O Callicles, which I have heard; and I believe that they are true; moreover, therefrom I conclude this, to wit:—Death is only the separation of two things, Soul and Body, from each other. When they have been separated from each other, the state of each of them is well nigh the same it was while the man lived. The Body keepeth the natural fashion it had, and the marks plain of all the care that was taken for it and of all that happened unto it. For if any man while he lived was great of body, by nature, or nurture, or both, his corpse also is great when he is dead; and if he was fat, his corpse also is fat when he is dead; also, if any man wore long hair, his corpse also hath long hair; and if any man was a whipped cur, and bore on his body the prints of his beatings—scars made by the whip, or scars of other wounds—while he lived, when he is dead thou mayest see his corpse with the same; and if any man had his limbs broken and disjoint while he lived, when he is dead also the same is plain. The sum of the whole matter is, that whatsoever conditions of Body a man hath while he liveth, these are plain when he is dead, all or most, for some while.

Now, O Callicles, that which happeneth unto the Body, happeneth, methinks, unto the Soul likewise, to wit, there are plain in the Soul, after she hath been stripped of the Body, her natural conditions and those affections which, through use in any matter, a man hath gotten in his Soul.

Wherefore, when they from Asia are come before the presence of Rhadamanthys their Judge, he causeth them to stand, and looketh at the Soul of each, not knowing whose Soul it is; but perchance having gotten hold of the Soul of the Great King, or of some other King or Ruler, perceiveth that it hath no soundness, but is seamed with the marks of many stripes, and full of the scars of perjuries and unrighteousness, according as the doings of each have stamped on his Soul their signs; and all therein is crooked by reason of falsehood and boasting, and nothing straight, because he hath been bred up without truth; and by reason of pride and luxury and wantonness and incontinency in his life, his Soul is altogether deformed and foul. This Soul then the Judge seeth, and having seen, sendeth with dishonour straightway unto the prison, whither it must go and endure the torments appointed for it. Now, it is appointed for every one who is punished, if he be punished righteously by another, either to become better and himself receive benefit, or to be set forth for an example unto others, that they, seeing his torments, may fear and become better. Now, they who are profited the while they pay unto Gods and Men the penalty of their sins, are they whose sins may be cured. Through afflictions and pains there cometh unto them profit both here and in the House of Hades; for otherwise can no man 'be rid of unrighteousness.

But they who have sinned to the utmost, and by reason of their great sins are beyond cure, they are the examples whereof I spake; for now they cannot themselves be benefited, inasmuch as they are beyond cure, but other men are benefited, when they see them by reason of their sins suffering torments exceeding great and terrible for evermore, being verily examples hung up in the House of Hades, in the prison-house, for a spectacle and admonition unto every sinner which cometh. ·

Of these that be set forth for examples I say that Archelaus will be, if Polus speaketh truly; and any other Prince that is like unto him. Most, methinks, were Princes and Kings and Rulers and Chief Men in their cities; for they, by reason of the power they have, do sin more heinously than other men. Whereof Homer is witness, in that he telleth that they which are tormented in the House of Hades for evermore are Kings and Rulers, to wit, Tantalus, and Sisyphus, and Tityus. But of Thersites, or any other Commoner which was an evildoer, no poet hath told that he is held in great torments as being beyond cure: nay, methinks, such an one had not the opportunity to sin greatly. Wherefore also he was happier than those who had opportunity. Verily, O Callicles, 'tis from among those who have power that the greatest sinners come, notwithstanding even among these may good men arise; whom, when they are found, it is most meet to reverence, for 'tis a hard thing, O Callicles, and worthy of all praise, for a man, who hath great opportunity to do injustice, to live justly all his days. Few such are found; yet are some found; for both here and elsewhere have there arisen, and, methinks, will arise again, men of a noble virtue and just conduct in those matters whereof charge at any time is given unto them: of whom was Aristides, the son of Lysimachus, a man famous throughout all Greece: but I tell thee, Sir, of them that have power in cities the most part are alway evil.

When one of these evil men, therefore, standeth, as I told, before Rhadamanthys the Judge, he knoweth nought else concerning him, neither who he is nor whose son, but only this, that he is one of the wicked; and perceiving this, sendeth him away unto Tartarus, having put a mark upon him to signify whether he can be cured or no: and he, coming to that place, there suffereth that which is due.

But perchance the Judge seeth a Soul that hath lived in holiness and truth; it may be, the Soul of a Common Man or of some other; but in most likelihood, say I, of a Philosopher, Callicles, who hath minded his own matters and been no busybody in his life. That Soul pleaseth the eye of Rhadamanthys, and he sendeth it away to the Islands of the Blessed.

In like manner Aeacus also judgeth. And each of these sitteth in judgment holding a rod in his hand. But Minos is seated as president over them; and he alone hath a golden sceptre, as Homer his Odysseus telleth, that he saw him "with a golden sceptre in his hand giving laws unto the Dead".

I am persuaded, O Callicles, that these things that are told are true. Wherefore I consider how I shall show my Soul most faultless before the Judge. I will take my farewell of the honours that are among men; and, considering Truth, will strive earnestly after Righteousness, both to live therein so far as I am able, and when I die, therein also to die. And I exhort all men, so far as I am able, and thee more especially do I exhort and entreat, to enter into this life and run this race, which, I say unto thee, is above all the races wherein men strive; and I tell thee, to thy shame, that thou shalt not be able to help thyself, when the Day of Judgment whereof I spake cometh unto thee, but when thou dost appear before the Judge, the son of Aegina, and he hath gotten hold of thee to take thee, thou shalt gape and become dizzy there, even as I do here; yea and perchance some one will smite thee on the cheek to dishonour thee, and will utterly put thee to despite.

Perchance this shall seem to thee as an old wife's fable, and thou wilt despise it: well mightest thou despise it, if by searching we could find out aught better and truer. But as the matter standeth, thou seest that ye are three, the wisest men of Greece living at this day, thou and Polus and Gorgias, and ye cannot show any other life that a man must live save this whereof I have spoken, which is plainly expedient also for that other life; nay, of all sayings this saying alone is not confuted, but abideth sure:—That a man must shun the doing of wrong more than the receiving, and study above all things not to seem, but to be, righteous in the doing of his own business and the business of the city; and that if any man be found evil in anything, he is to be corrected; and that the next good thing after being righteous is to become righteous through correction and just retribution; and that all flattery of himself and of other men, be they few or many, he must eschew; and that he must use Oratory and all other Instruments of Doing, for the sake of Justice alway.

Observations on the *GORGIAS* Myth

I

Here, again, as in the *Phaedo* Myth, it is *Responsibility* which Plato represents in a picture—a picture portraying the continuity of the Self through the series of its life-stages. It is in the consciousness of Responsibility—of being the cause of actions for which he takes praise and blame—that man first becomes conscious of Self as a constant in experience. Consciousness of an active—a responsible, or moral Self, is formally prior to consciousness of a passive, sensitive, Self realised as the one mirror in which sense-impressions are successively reflected. Thus, the *Gorgias* Myth gives a strictly natural representation of the Idea of Soul, when it sets forth, in a vision of Judgment, Penance, and Purification, the continuity and sameness of the active, as distinguished from the passive—of the responsible or moral, as distinguished from the sensitive Self. It is only in vision—in Myth—and not scientifically, that the Idea of Soul, or Subject, can be represented, or held up to contemplation as an Object at all; and it is best represented, that is, in the manner most suitable, not only to our consciousness of responsibility, but to our hope and fear, if it is represented in a vision of Judgment and Penance and Purification, where the departed are not the passive victims of vengeance, but actively develop their native powers under the discipline of correction.[1] In such a vision it is consciousness of wrong done and fear (that fear mentioned by Cephalus in the *Republic*)[2] which conjure up the spectacle of punishment; but hope, springing from the sense of personal endeavour after the good, speaks comfortably to the heart, and says, "If only a man will strive steadfastly to overcome evil passions in this life, and in future lives, all will be well with

---

[1]

> What we call sin
> I could believe a painful opening out
> Of paths for ampler virtue.
> > CLOUGH, *Dipsychus.*
> O happy sin, which earned
> such and so great a Redeemer.

Easter hymn quoted by Leibniz, *Théodicée*, p. 507, ed. Erdmann.

[2] 380 E.

him in the end. The very punishment which he fears will
be for his ultimate good, for punishment regards the future
which can still be modified, not the past which cannot be
undone." Pardon—for so we may bring home to ourselves
the deeper meaning of Plato's Purification—Pardon is thus
involved in Punishment. This is a thought which cannot be
set forth by the way of Science. Pardon is not found in the
realm of Nature which Science describes. It "comes of the
Grace of God". It is received under another dispensation
than that of Nature—a dispensation under which a man
comes by "Faith"—Faith which Science can only chill, but
Myth may confirm. "It is necessary to sing these words
over to one's self like an incantation."

Besides containing this notable theory of Punishment
and Pardon, the *Gorgias* Myth is remarkable for its powerful
imaginative rendering of the wonder with which man
regards death—a rendering which is best taken side by side
with another given in the *Cratylus*, 403, 4. Hades, the God
of Death, Socrates says in the *Cratylus*, is not called, as most
people in their fear suppose, "from the Formless" (Aeides)—
he is not the terrible Unseen One, who keeps the Dead in
Hell, against their will, bound in the fetters of necessity. He
is rather called "from the knowledge of all beauty"—he is
the All-wise, the Philosopher, who, indeed, holds the Dead
in fetters, but not against their will; for his fetters are those
of that desire which, in disembodied souls, is stronger than
necessity—the desire of knowledge. The Dead cleave to
Hades as disciples cleave to a great master of wisdom. The
wisest of men go to learn of him, and will not return from
his companionship. He charms the charmers themselves—
the Sirens[1]—so that they will not leave him. He is rightly

---

[1] The Sirens, although they became eventually simply Muses, were
originally Chthonian deities, and as such are sculptured on tombs and
painted on lekythi: see Miss Harrison's *Myths of the Odyssey*, pp. 156-166;
her *Mythology and Monuments of Ancient Athens*, pp. 582 ff.; and her article in
J.H.S. vol. vi. pp. 19 ff. ("Odysseus and the Sirens—Dionysiac Boat-races—
Cylix of Nicosthenes"), 1885. "As monuments on tombs, the Sirens," writes
Miss Harrison (*Myth. and Mon.* p. 584), "seem to have filled a double function;
they were sweet singers, fit to be set on the grave of poet or orator, and they
were mourners to lament for the beauty of youth and maiden. It is somewhat
curious that they are never sculptured on Attic tombs in the one function that
makes their relation to death clearly intelligible—*i.e.* that of death-angels.
The Siren of the Attic graves must surely be somehow connected with the
bird death-angels that appear on the Harpy tomb, but her function as such

called Pluto, because he has the true riches—wisdom. Here we have what is really a Myth offered in satisfaction of the deep wonder with which man regards that undiscovered country from whose bourn no traveller returns. Plato appeals openly to the "science of etymology" in support of his "myth", and, I would suggest, also appeals tacitly to traditional cultus:—Hades communicates true oracles to those who go down into his cave to sleep the sleep of death—truer oracles than those dreams which Trophonius sends to the living who sleep in his cave at Lebadia.[1] It is only with the disembodied soul that Hades will hold his dialectic, for only the disembodied soul, freed from the distractions of the bodily passions, can experience that invincible desire of knowledge, that love without which dialectic is vain, which makes the learner leave all and cleave to his Teacher. In this, that he will hold converse only with the disembodied soul, Hades declares himself the true Philosopher. It is at this point that the connection appears between the *Cratylus* Myth—for we may call it a Myth—and the *Gorgias* Myth. The judges in the *Gorgias* Myth are naked souls (the phrase "the soul bare of the body" occurs also in *Cratylus*, 403 B)—naked souls, without blindness or bias of the flesh, which see naked souls through and through, and pass true judgment upon them—

> There must be wisdom with Great Death:
> The dead shall look me thro' and thro'.

The wondering thought, that death may perhaps solve the enigma of life, has never been more impressively rendered than in these twin Myths of the Philosopher Death and the Dead Judges of the Dead.

seems to have been usurped for Attica by the male angels Death and Sleep."
Erinna's epitaph—

> Tombstones, and my Sirens, and mournful urns
> You who hold Hades as a small heap of ashes—

brings the Sirens and Hades into connection just as *Crat.* 403 D does—"Therefore let us say, Hermogenes, that no one over there has wished to leave it for here, not even the Sirens themselves, but he has summoned them with all the rest. Thus, as it seems, Hades knows the auspicious words to be spoken." According to Mr. J. P. Postgate (*Journal of Philology*, ix. pp. 109 ff., "A Philological Examination of the Myth of the Sirens"), they are singing birds = souls winged for flight hence.

[1] Cf. Rohde, *Psyche*, i. 115 ff.

I

II

Another point, and I have done with the "Philosophy" of the *Gorgias* Myth. I am anxious to have done with it, because I know that the "Philosophy of a Myth" too easily becomes "the dogmatic teaching which it covertly conveys"; but I trust that in the foregoing remarks I have avoided, and in the following remarks shall continue to avoid, the error of treating a Myth as if it were an Allegory. The point is this. The incurably wicked who suffer eternal punishment are mostly tyrants—men like Archelaus and Tantalus, who had the opportunity of committing the greatest crimes, and used it. All praise to the few who had the opportunity and did not use it. But Thersites, a mere private offender, no poet has ever condemned to eternal punishment. He had not the opportunity of committing the greatest crimes, and in this is happier than those offenders who had. Here a mystery is set forth. The man who has the opportunity of committing the greatest crimes, and yields to the special temptation to which he is exposed, is held worthy of eternal damnation, which is escaped by the offender who has it not in his power, and has never been effectively tempted, to commit such crimes. First, the greatness of the crime is estimated as if it were a mere quantity standing in no relation to the quality of the agent; and then the quality of the agent is determined by the quantity of the crime; so that vice with large opportunity comes out as infinitely worse than vice with narrow opportunity, the former receiving eternal punishment, the latter suffering correction only for a limited time. This mystery of the infinite difference between vice with large opportunity and vice with narrow opportunity—the mystery which is set forth in "lead us not into temptation"—this mystery is set forth by Plato in the *Gorgias* Myth as a mystery, without any attempt at explanation: "Men born to great power do not start with the same chance of ultimate salvation as men born to private stations." With that the *Gorgias* Myth leaves us. In the Vision of Er, however, an explanation is offered—but still the explanation, no less than the mystery to be explained, is mythically set forth—not to satisfy the understanding, but to give relief to feeling in imaginative expression. The explanation offered in the Vision of Er is that the Soul, before each incarnation, is free, within certain limits, to choose, and as a matter of fact does choose, its station in life—whether it be the station of a tyrant with large opportunity of doing evil, or that of a private person with narrow opportunity. In this way the mystery of the *Gorgias* Myth is "explained"—explained by another Myth.

So much for the "Philosophy" of the *Gorgias* Myth—so much for the great problems raised in it. Now let me add a few notes on some other points, for the better appreciation of the Myth itself as concrete product of creative imagination.

III

The judged are marked (*Gorg.* 526 B) as "corrigible" or "incorrigible". So, too, in the Myth of Er (*Rep.* 614 c) those sent to Heaven have tablets fixed in front, those sent to Tartarus tablets fixed behind, on which their deeds and sentences are recorded. The idea of tablets may have been derived from the Orphic custom of placing in the graves of the dead tablets describing the way to be taken and the things to be done on the journey through the other world.[1]

Before Dante enters Purgatory the Angel at the Gate marks him with "seven P's, to denote the seven sins (*peccata*) of which he was to be cleansed in his passage through Purgatory"—

> Seven times
> The letter that denotes the inward stain
> He on my forehead, with the blunted point
> Of his drawn sword, inscribed. And "Look," he cried,
> "When entered, that thou wash these scars away."[2]

The judgment-seat of Minos, Rhadamanthys, and Aeacus is "in the meadow, at the meeting of three ways from which the two roads lead away, the one to the Islands of the Blest, the other to Tartarus." (*Gorg.* 524 A). The

---

[1] See Comparetti, *J. H. S.* iii. 111, and Dieterich, *Nekyia*, 85, on the gold tablets of Thurii and Petelia; and cf. p. 156 ff. *infra*. The Orphic custom itself may have come from Egypt, where texts from the *Book of the Dead* were buried with the corpse. The *Book of the Dead* was a guide-book for the *Ka*, or Double, which is apt to wander from the body and lose its way. See Jevons' *Introduction to the History of Religion*, p. 323, and Flinders Petrie's *Egyptian Tales*, second series, p. 124.

[2] *Purg.* ix. 101, and see Cary's note *ad loc.*

topography of this passage corresponds with that of *Rep.*
614 c ff., where, however, it is added that the meadow of
the judgment-seat is also the spot in which the souls, returned
from their thousand years' sojourn in Tartarus and Heaven
(*i.e.* the Islands of the Blessed), meet, and rest, before going
on to the place where they choose their new lives before
drinking of the water of Lethe. In the *Gorgias* the two ways
mentioned are (1) that to Tartarus, and (2) that to the
Islands of the Blessed; and the meadow of judgment is "at
the parting of the ways"—where three roads divide—no
reference being made to a third way leading to the throne
of Necessity, and thence to the Plain of Lethe. In the
parallel passage in *Rep.* 614 c ff. the ways are not mentioned
as *three;* but they are three—(1) the way to Tartarus, (2)
the way to Heaven, and (3) the way to the Plain of Lethe—
all three diverging from the meadow.

The "Three Ways", as indicated in the Myth of Er—one
to Tartarus, one to Heaven, and the third to Lethe (a river
of the surface of the Earth)—constantly occur in the literature which reflects Orphic influence.[1] They even appear in
the folk-lore represented by the story of Thomas the
Rhymer:—

> Light down, light down now, true Thomas,
> And lean your head upon my knee:
> Abide, and rest a little space,
> And I will show you ferlies three.
>
> Oh see ye not yon narrow road,
> So thick beset wi' thorns and briars?
> That is the path of righteousness,
> Though after it but few inquires.
>
> And see not ye that braid braid road,
> That lies across the lily leven?
> That is the path of wickedness,
> Though some call it the road to Heaven.
>
> And see not ye that bonny road,
> That winds about the fernie brae?
> That is the road to fair Elf-land,
> Where thou and I this night maun gae.

[1] See Dieterich, *Nekyia*, 89, 90, and especially Rohde, *Psy.* ii. 221, note.

The three parts of the *Divina Commedia* correspond, in the main, to the "Three Ways". The theological doctrine of Purgatory, to which Dante gives such noble imaginative expression, is alien to the Hebrew spirit, and came to the Church mainly from the Platonic doctrine of purification—especially as the doctrine found expression in Eschatological Myths reflecting Orphic teaching.[1]

We come now to the Myth of Er (*Rep.* 614 A ff.), the greatest of Plato's Eschatological Myths, whether the fulness of its matter or the splendour of its form be considered.

---

[1] See Thompson's note on *Gorg.* 525 B.

THE MYTH OF ER IN THE *REPUBLIC*

CONTEXT

The subject of the Republic *is Justice—that character in the individual which manifests itself in the steady performance of Duty— Duty being what a man does for the maintenance of a certain Type of Social Life, the good of which he has been educated to identify with his own good.*

What, then, is this Type of Social Life, in living for which a man does his Duty and finds his true Happiness?

The Republic *is mainly concerned with the description of it, and of the Education which fits men for it; and as the Dialogue proceeds, the reader, who enters into the feelings of the* dramatis personae, *becomes, with them, more and more convinced that true Happiness, in this world, is to be found only in the steady performance of Duty in and for a State ordered according to the spirit, if not according to the letter, of the Constitution described by Socrates. In this world, certainly, the man who does his Duty, as Socrates defines it, has his great reward. He is 729 times happier than the man who, despising the law of Duty, has fallen under the tyranny of Pleasure.*

But a greater reward awaits the Righteous man, and greater torments are prepared for the Unrighteous man, in the world to come. For the Soul is immortal; and an ontological proof of its immortality is given.

Then, as though this proof were insufficient, the Republic *ends with the Myth of Er (told by Socrates), which proves, indeed, nothing for the Understanding, but visualises, for the Imagination, the hope of the Heart.*

Republic 613 E—621 D

"Of such sort, then, are the prizes and the wages and the gifts which the just man receiveth, while he is yet alive, from Gods and Men, over and above those good things whereof I spake which Justice herself provideth."

"Yea, in truth goodly gifts," quoth he, "and exceeding sure."

"Well," I said, "they are even as nothing, for number and greatness, in comparison with those things which await each of the two, to wit, the just man and the unjust man, when he is dead. Of these thou must hear, that each of them may have full payment of that which this Discourse oweth him to be said concerning him."

"Say on," quoth he, "there is little else I would hear more gladly."

"Nay," said I, "but it is not a Tale of Alcinous I will tell thee, but the story of a mighty man, Er, the son of Armenius, of the nation of the Pamphylians.

"It came to pass that he fell in battle; and when the corpses were taken up on the tenth day already stinking, he was taken up sound; and when they had carried him home and were about to bury him, on the twelfth day, being laid on the pyre, he came to life again; and began to tell of the things which he saw there.

"He said that when his Soul went out, it journeyed together with a great company, and they came unto a certain ghostly place wherein were two open Mouths of the Earth hard by each other, and also above, two Mouths of the Heaven, over against them: and Judges were seated between these, who, when they had given their judgments, bade the righteous take the road which leadeth to the right hand and up through Heaven; and they fastened tablets on them in front, signifying the judgments; but the unjust they sent by the road which leadeth to the left hand and down, and they also had tablets fastened on them behind, signifying all that they had done. But when he himself came before the Judges they said unto him that he must be for a messenger unto men concerning the things there, and they charged him straitly that he should give diligence to hear and see all the things in the place.

"Now, he told how that he beheld the Souls departing, some by one of the Mouths of Heaven, and some by one of the Mouths of Earth, when judgment had been given unto them; also how that he beheld Souls returning by the other two Mouths, some coming up from the Earth travel-stained, covered with dust, and some coming down from Heaven, pure. And he said that all, as they came, being come belike from a long journey, turned aside with joy into the Meadow and encamped there as in a Congregation; and they that were acquaintances greeted one another, and they questioned one another—they that were come from the Earth questioned them that were come from Heaven concerning the things there, and in like manner they that were come from Heaven questioned the others concerning the things that had happened unto them. So they discoursed with one another—some of them groaning and weeping when they called to mind all the terrible things they had suffered and seen in their journey under the Earth—he said that their journey was for a thousand years; and others of them, to wit, those which were come from Heaven, telling of blessings and marvellous fair sights.

"Time would fail me, O Glaucon, to relate all that he said, but the sum thereof was this:—That according to the number of the wrongs which each man hath ever done, and the number of them whom he hath wronged, he payeth penalty for all in their course, ten times for each:—now, it is every hundred years that he payeth, for a hundred years are counted for the lifetime of a man: so is it brought to pass that the price of evil-doing is paid tenfold: thus if certain caused the death of many by betraying cities or armies, and casting men into bondage, or taking part of other iniquity, they are recompensed tenfold with torments for each one of these things; but if any have done good unto other men, and have been just and religious, they in the same measure receive their rewards. Also concerning infants that died as soon as they were born, or lived but a short while, there were things he said that are not worth remembering. As for those who dishonoured Gods and

Parents, and those who honoured them, and as for those that were murderers, he spake of their wages as even greater; for he said that he stood beside one of whom another inquired, Where Ardiaeus the Great was. Now this Ardiaeus had made himself King in a city of Pamphylia just a thousand years before that time, having slain the old man his father, and his elder brother, and having wrought many other evil deeds, as men tell. He said, then, that the one of whom inquiry was made answered saying, He is not come; nor will he ever come hither—for this, indeed, was one of the terrible things that we beheld when we were nigh unto the Mouth, and about to go up after all our sufferings; on the sudden we came in sight of him, and others, most of them kings, but there were also private men of those that had sinned greatly amongst them: these, thinking that they were already about to go up, the Mouth received not, but bellowed; for it belloweth as often as any one of those that are wicked beyond cure like unto these, or any one that hath not paid the full price of his sins, essayeth to go up. In that place he said men were standing by—savage men, as coals of fire to look upon—who, hearing and understanding the Voice of the Mouth, took hold of some in their arms and carried them away; but Ardiaeus and others they bound hand and foot and neck, and threw down, and flayed, and dragged to a place apart by the side of the way, and there carded them on thorns, signifying to all that passed by wherefore they were taken, and that they should be cast into Tartarus. Then, he said, there came upon him and his companions a fear greater than all the fears of every sort they had before; for each one of them feared lest the Voice should be for himself when he went up: and with great joy did each one go up when the Voice kept silence.

"Of such kind, then, were the judgments and the punishments; and there were blessings that answered unto them.

"Now, when both companies had been seven days in the Meadow, Er said that they were constrained, on the eighth day, to arise and journey thence, and came on the fourth day to a place whence they could behold a Straight Light extended from above through the whole Heaven and Earth, as it were a pillar, for colour most like unto the rainbow, but brighter and purer. Unto which they came when they had gone forward a day's journey, and there, at the middle part of the Light, beheld extended from the Heaven the ends of the bonds thereof: for this Light is that which bindeth the Heavens together; as the under-girths hold together ships so doth it hold together the whole round of Heaven; and from the ends extendeth the Spindle of Necessity, which causeth all the heavenly revolutions, whereof the shaft and hook are of adamant, and the whorl is of adamant and of other substances therewith.

"Now, the whorl is after this fashion. In shape it is as one of our whorls, but from what he said we must conceive of it as a great whorl, carved hollow through and through, wherein is set, fitting it, a smaller whorl of like kind, as caskets are set fitting into one another; and then in this a third whorl is set, and then a fourth, and then four others; for the whorls are together eight, set one within another, showing their lips as circles above, and making thus the even continued outside of one whorl round about the shaft; and the shaft is driven right through the middle of the eighth whorl.

"The first and outermost whorl hath the circle of its lip the broadest; the circle of the sixth is second for breadth; the circle of the fourth is third; the circle of the eighth is fourth; the circle of the seventh is fifth; the circle of the fifth is sixth; the circle of the third is seventh; the circle of the second is eighth. And the circle of the greatest is of many colours; the circle of the seventh is brightest; the circle of the eighth hath its colour from the seventh which shineth upon it; the circles of the second and fifth are like unto each other, being ruddier than the rest; the third hath the whitest colour; the fourth is pale red; and the sixth is second for whiteness.

"The spindle turneth round wholly with one motion; but of the whole that turneth round the seven circles within turn slowly contrary to the whole: and of these the eighth goeth swiftest; next, and together, go the seventh and the sixth and the fifth; third in swiftness goeth the fourth; fourth, the third; and fifth, the second.

"And the whole spindle goeth round in the lap of Necessity.

"Aloft upon each of the circles of the spindle is mounted a Siren; which goeth round with her circle, uttering one note at one pitch; and the notes of all the eight together do make one melody.

"Round about are three others seated at equal distances apart, each upon a throne: these be the Daughters of Necessity, the Fates, Lachesis, and Clotho, and Atropos. They are clothed in white raiment and have garlands on their heads; and they chant to the melody of the Sirens; Lachesis chanteth of the things that have been, and Clotho of the things that are, and Atropos of the things that shall be: and Clotho with her right hand ever and anon taketh hold of the outer round of the spindle, and helpeth to turn it; and Atropos with her left hand doeth the same with the inner rounds; and Lachesis with either hand taketh hold of outer and inner alternately.[1]

"Now he said that when they were come, it behoved them straightway to go unto Lachesis. Wherefore a Prophet did first marshal them in order; and then having taken lots out of the lap of Lachesis and Ensamples of Lives, went up into a high pulpit and said: Thus saith Necessity's Daughter, Maid Lachesis—Souls of a day, now beginneth another course of earthly life which bringeth death. For you your Angels will not cast lots, to get you, but each one of you shall choose his Angel. Let him to whom falleth the first turn, first choose the Life unto which he shall be bound of necessity. But Virtue hath no master. As a man honoureth her and dishonoureth her, so shall he have more of her and less. He who hath chosen shall answer for it. God is not answerable.

"Er said that when the Prophet had spoken these words, he threw the lots unto all, and each took up the lot which fell beside him, save only himself; for the Prophet suffered him not.

---

[1] *I.e.*, as Mr. Adam explains (note on 617 c, D), she lays hold of outer (the circle of the Same) and inner (the circle of the Other) in turn, using her right hand for the former, and her left for the latter.

"Now when each had taken up his lot, it was plain what number he had gotten. Thereafter the Prophet laid on the ground before them the Ensamples of Lives, far more than for the persons there. Now these Ensamples were of all sorts: there were Lives of all kinds of creatures, and moreover of all conditions of men; for there were kingships among them, some that lasted for a whole lifetime, and some on the way to downfall, and ending with poverty and flight and beggary. Also there were Lives of men renowned, some of them for comeliness and beauty, or for strength and prowess, some for birth and the virtues of their forefathers; likewise also there were Lives of men of no such renown. There were also Lives of women. But conditions of the Soul were not amongst the Ensamples; the reason whereof is this, that a Soul which hath chosen a certain Life is of necessity changed accordingly; but all other things both good and evil were there mixed together—riches and poverty, and health and disease, and also states between these.

"There, methinks, dear Glaucon, is man's great peril. Wherefore let each one of us give heed to this chiefly, how that, taking no thought for the knowledge of other things, he shall seek after the knowledge of one thing, if peradventure he may learn and find out who it is that shall make him able and wise, so that he may discern the good Life from the evil, and, according to his ability, alway and everywhere choose the better Life, and reckoning how all the things that have been now said, both taken together and severally, concern the Virtuous Life, may understand what good or evil, for what state of the Soul, beauty joined with poverty or riches worketh, and what good or evil noble birth, and base birth, and private station, and rule in the city, and strength, and weakness, and quickness of wit, and slowness, and the other native qualities of the Soul like unto these, and the qualities which the Soul acquireth, do work, according as they are mixed variously with one another; to the end that, having taken count of all these, he may be able to choose, having regard to the nature of his Soul, between the worse and the better Life, calling that the worse which will lead his Soul to become more unrighteous, and calling that the better which will lead it to become more righteous. All else will he let go by; for we have seen and know that this is the best choice for a man, both whilst he liveth and when he is dead. With this doctrine, then, as hard as adamant within him, must he go unto Hades, so that there also he may not be amazed at riches and such like trumpery, and may not fall into the Life of a tyrant or of some other such evil-doer, and work iniquities many and without all remedy, and himself suffer still worse things; but rather may discern to choose alway the Life between such states, and eschew the extremes on either hand, both in this Life, as far as he is able, and in all the Life hereafter: for in this lieth man's chief happiness.

"Now the Messenger who brought this Tale from that place went on and said that the Prophet then spake thus:— Even for him whose turn cometh last, if he hath chosen with understanding, there is prepared a Life, which, if only a man bear himself manfully, is tolerable, not wretched. Neither let him who cometh first be careless of his choice; nor let him who cometh at the end be downcast.

"He said that when the Prophet had spoken these words, the one that had gotten the first place, as soon as he came forward, chose the greatest kingship there; and by reason of folly and greediness looked not well enough into all before he chose it, and marked not that therein it was appointed of Fate that he should eat his own children, and that other evils should befall him. When therefore he had looked at it at leisure, he began to beat his breast and bewail his choice, not abiding by the commandment of the Prophet; for he did not blame himself for these evils, but Ill-Luck, and Gods, and any thing rather than himself. Now, he was of them that were come from Heaven, having spent his former life in a well-ordered city, and become virtuous through Custom without True Knowledge: they that were come from Heaven were not the least part, belike, of them that were caught thus; for they had not been exercised with labours; but most part of those from under the Earth, inasmuch as they themselves had endured labours, and had seen others enduring, made not their choice hastily. For this cause, as well as through the luck of the lot, a change of good and of evil befalleth most part of the Souls; for if any man, whenever he cometh into this life, seek alway with his whole heart after wisdom, and if the lot so fall that he is not of the last to choose, there is good hope, from what the Messenger said, not only that he will have happiness here, but also that the journey hence to that place and back again hither will not be under the ground and rough, but smooth and heavenly.

"Truly it was a sight worth looking at, he said, to see how the Souls severally chose their lives—yea, a pitiful sight, and a laughable, and a wonderful; inasmuch as they chose mostly after the custom of their former life; for he told how he saw the Soul that had been Orpheus's choosing a swan's Life, for that, hating womankind because women murdered him, it would not be born of a woman. Also he said that he saw the Soul of Thamyras when it had chosen the life of a nightingale; and that he saw also a swan changing, and choosing the life of a man, and other musical creatures doing likewise. And the Soul which got the twentieth place chose the life of a lion: this was the Soul of Ajax, the son of Telamon, which eschewed becoming a man because it remembered the Judgment concerning the Arms. Next came the Soul of Agamemnon; which also, out of enmity towards mankind because that it went evil with him, took in exchange the life of an eagle. The Soul of Atalanta, which had gotten her place between the first and the last, perceiving the great honour which belongeth to the life of a man who contendeth at the Games, was not able to pass by but took it. After her he saw the Soul of Epeius, the son of Panopeus, passing into the nature of a spinster; and amongst the last he saw the Soul of Thersites the jester putting on an ape. Also it chanced that the Soul of Odysseus, which had gotten the last place of all, came forward to choose, and having abated all her ambition because she remembered her former labours, went about seeking for a long while, and after much ado, found the life of a quiet private man lying somewhere despised of the others, and when she saw it said—'Had I come first I would have done the same'; and took it with great joy.

"Beasts likewise were changed into men and into one another, the unjust into those that were savage, and the just into those that were tame: yea in everywise were they mixed together.

"Now when all the Souls had chosen their lives according to the place allotted unto each, they went forward, in order, unto Lachesis; and she sent the Agnel, which each one had chosen, with him, to be the guardian of his life and to fulfil the things that he had chosen; and the Angel, bringing him first unto Clotho, taketh him beneath her hand and the revolution of the whirling spindle, and ratifieth the Portion which the man had chosen in his turn; then, from her presence, the Angel brought him unto Atropos where she span; so did he make the threads of the man's life unalterable.

"Thence, Er said, each man, without turning back, went straight on under the throne of Necessity, and when each, even unto the last, was come out through it, they all together journeyed to the Plain of Lethe, through terrible burning heat and frost; and this Plain is without trees or any herb that the earth bringeth forth.

"He said that they encamped, when it was already evening, beside the River of Forgetfulness, the water whereof no pitcher holdeth. Now, it was necessary that all should drink a certain measure of the water; but they that were not preserved by wisdom drank more than the measure; and as each man drank, he forgot all. Then he said that when they had fallen asleep and midnight was come, there was thunder and an earthquake, and of a sudden they flew up thence unto divers parts to be born in the flesh, shooting like meteors. But he himself was not suffered to drink of the water: yet by what means and how he came unto his body he knew not; but suddenly he opened his eyes, and lo! it was morning, and he was lying on the pyre.

"Thus, O Glaucon, was the Tale preserved from perishing, and it will preserve us if we believe in it; so shall we pass over the River of Lethe safely, and keep our Souls undefiled.

"This is my counsel: let us believe that the Soul is immortal, and able to bear all ill and all good, and let us always keep to the upward way, and practise justice in all things with understanding, that we may be friends both with ourselves and with the Gods, both whilst we sojourn here, and when we receive the prizes of our justice, like unto Conquerors at the Games which go about gathering their wages; and that both here, and in the journey of a thousand years of which I told, we may fare well."

Observations on the Myth of Er

I

Let us begin with the geography and cosmography of the Myth.

The Meadow of the Judgment-seat, between the two openings of Tartarus (in and out) on the one side, and the two corresponding openings of Heaven on the other side, is also the meeting-place of the Souls which return from their thousand years' sojourn in Tartarus and Heaven. From the Meadow they journey, always above ground, till they come to a "rainbow-coloured light, straight like a pillar, extended from on high throughout the Heaven and the Earth." This Light is the axis, I take it, on which the whole heavenly system revolves, the Earth fixed in the centre of the system being a globe on the line of the axis. The destination of the Pilgrim Souls is that part of the surface of the globe at which, in the hemisphere where they are, the axis enters on its imaginary course through the centre of the Earth, in order to come out again at the antipodal point in the other hemisphere. The Souls, arrived at the very point where, in the hemisphere where they are, the axis of the Cosmos enters the Earth, are in the place of all places where the Law which controls all things is intuitively plain—they see the Pillar of Light as the Spindle of Necessity. Then, suddenly, the outlook presented to us in the Myth changes like the scene in a dream. It is no longer such a view of the Cosmos from within as we had, a moment ago, while we stood with the Pilgrims on the surface of the Earth, looking up at the Pillar of Light in the sky: we are now looking at the Cosmos from the outside, as if it were an orrery—a model of concentric cups or rings; and Necessity herself is holding the model in her lap, and the three Fates are seated round, and keep turning the eight cups, on each of which, on its edge, a Siren is mounted who sings in tune with her sisters. But the Pilgrim Souls are standing near, looking on at this spectacle. They are on their way, we

K

know, from the Meadow to the Plain of Lethe, both places on the surface of the Earth: it is on the Earth then, after all, that the throne is placed on which Necessity sits holding in her lap the model, which, like a true dream-thing, is both a little model and the great Cosmos itself.[1]   In this place, in the presence of Necessity on her throne, the Pilgrim Souls are addressed by the Prophet from his pulpit; then choose, in the turns which the lots determine, lives of men or beasts scattered, it would seem, as little images at their feet;[2] then go before the three Fates, who ratify the chosen

---

[1] Let me illustrate this characteristic of the "dream-thing" from the Dream in the Fifth Book of Wordsworth's *Prelude*:—

> On poetry and geometric truth,
> And their high privilege of lasting life,
> From all internal injury exempt,
> I mused; upon these chiefly: and at length,
> My senses yielding to the sultry air,
> Sleep seized me, and I passed into a dream.
> I saw before me stretched a boundless plain
> Of sandy wilderness, all black and void,
> And as I looked around, distress and fear
> Came creeping over me, when at my side,
> Close at my side, an uncouth shape appeared
> Upon a dromedary, mounted high.
> He seemed an Arab of the Bedouin tribes:
> A lance he bore, and underneath one arm
> A stone, and in the opposite hand a shell
> Of a surpassing brightness. . . .

>   *   *   *   *   *   *

> . . . The Arab told me that the stone
> Was "Euclid's Elements"; and "This," said he,
> "Is something of more worth"; and at the word
> Stretched forth the shell, so beautiful in shape,
> In colour so resplendent, with command
> That I should hold it to my ear. I did so,
> And heard that instant in an unknown tongue,
> Which yet I understood, articulate sounds,
> A loud prophetic blast of harmony;
> An Ode, in passion uttered. . . .

>   *   *   *   *   *   *

> While this was uttering, strange as it may seem,
> I wondered not, although I plainly saw
> The one to be a stone, the other a shell;
> Nor doubted once but that they both were books,
> Having a perfect faith in all that passed.

[2] I think that Plato may have borrowed his "patterns of lives" here from votive images of trades and callings, and of animals: "The Argive Heraeum," says Mr. Rouse (*Greek Votive Offerings*, p. 298), "yielded hundreds of animals

doom of each; then pass severally under the throne of Necessity; and thence travel together, through a hot dusty region, till they come to the Plain of Lethe, where no green thing grows, and to the River the water of which no pitcher can hold. When the Souls have drunk of this water—the foolish, too much—they fall asleep; but at midnight there is an earthquake and thunder, and suddenly, like meteors, they shoot up to be born again, in terrestrial bodies, in our part of the Earth.

The account given by Plato here is strictly in accordance with the popular belief, which makes Lethe a river entirely above ground, never counts it among the rivers of Tartarus.[1] Virgil, in *Aen*. vi. 705, 714, may be thought to place it under ground; but his description suffers in clearness from compression; and it is not likely that he willingly deserts traditional authority in a matter of such importance as the position of Lethe. His Journey to the Dead, as a whole, is derived from a source (considered by Rohde and Dieterich to be the Descent to Hades) common to himself with Pindar, Plato, Plutarch, Lucian, and (according to Dieterich, though here Rohde does not agree with him)[2] the writers of certain sepulchral inscriptions which I shall describe in the next section; and where Lethe appears in any of these authors, it never, I believe, appears as one of the infernal, or subterranean, rivers. Indeed, all reasonable doubt as to Virgil's orthodoxy seems to be barred by his statement that the plain in which Souls about to be born again are gathered together near the banks of Lethe has its own sun (*Aen*. vi. 641). It is evidently above ground somewhere—the writer

---

in bronze and clay: bulls, cows, oxen and oxherds, goats, sheep, cocks, ducks, and other birds, including perhaps a swan." These animals (to which may be added horses, pigs, doves), were, Mr. Rouse supposes, either sacrificial victims or first-fruits of hunting. Referring to human figures he says, p. 79, "It is at least probable that a successful huntsman, artist, craftsman, trader, would dedicate a figure, in character, as a thank-offering for success in his calling." If I remember rightly, a little figure, recognised as that of a "Philosopher", was discovered in the tomb of "Aristotle" found near Chalcis some years ago.

[1] See Thiemann, *Platonische Eschatologie*, p. 18.

[2] Dieterich, *Nek*. 128 f., 135, and Rohde, *Psy*. ii. 217.

of the *Axiochus* would perhaps say in the antipodal hemisphere of the Earth.

II [1]

The object of this section is to point to a detail—the twin-streams, Eunoè and Lethe, of the Earthly Paradise (*Purg.* xxviii.)—in which Dante's vision of Purgatory reproduces—I think, independently—a distinctive feature of that Orphic ritual and mythology to which Plato is largely indebted for his account of the Soul's purification as a process of forgetting and remembering—as a series of transmigrations through which the particulars of sense, the evils and sins of the flesh, are forgotten or left behind, and the universal *Ideas*, long obscured, are, at last, so clearly remembered that they can never be forgotten any more, but become the everlasting possession of the Soul, finally disembodied and returned to its own star.

It is easy to account, from the literary sources open to Dante, for the presence of rivers, and more particularly of Lethe, in his Earthly Paradise. On the one hand, the description of Eden in *Genesis* would suggest the general idea of rivers girding the Earthly Paradise;[2] while, on the other hand, the proximity of Purgatory to the Earthly Paradise makes it natural that Lethe should be one of these rivers—that first reached by one coming up from Purgatory. The drinking of Lethe, according to *Aen.* vi. and the current mythology, is the act with which a period of purgatorial discipline is closed by those Souls which are about to pass again into the flesh. In placing the Earthly Paradise on the top of a lofty mountain Dante followed a prevalent medieval belief; and, although he seems to have drawn on his own imagination in placing Purgatory on the slopes of this mountain, it was natural, and in accordance with the current mythology, that he should place it there, close to

---

[1] It ought to be mentioned that this section was written, and the substance of it read in the course of a public lecture, and also to a private society, before the appearance of Miss Harrison's *Prolegomena to the Study of Greek Religion*, and her "Query" in *The Classical Review*, Feb. 1903, p. 58.

[2] See Vernon's *Readings on the Purgatorio*, ii. 285-293. Lethe girds the Earthly Paradise on the side of Earth, Eunoè on the side of Heaven.

the Earthly Paradise or Elysium; for the Lethe of *Aen.* vi. is evidently in the same region as Elysium—

> Meanwhile Aeneas saw in the remote valley, a hidden grove, and bushes resounding with woodland noises, and the Lethaean stream, which flows before the abodes of peace.[1]

The presence, then, of Lethe, the purgatorial stream, in Dante's Earthly Paradise is easily accounted for by reference to the mythological authorities open to him. But for the association of Eunoè, the stream of Memory, with Lethe, the stream of Forgetfulness, it does not seem possible to account in this way. The common mythology gives Lethe alone. It is not likely that Dante had heard of the twin streams—Lethe and Mnemosyne—of the Orphic cult; at any rate, in the absence of evidence that he had heard of them, it seems better to suppose that the very natural picture of a stream of Memory beside the stream of Forgetfulness occurred to him spontaneously, as it had occurred to others, who, like himself, were deeply concerned to find expression for their hope of purification.

For the twin streams of the Orphic cult which resemble Dante's Lethe and Eunoè so closely, we must turn to the sepulchral inscriptions mentioned at the end of the last section. These are certain directions for the ghostly journey to be made by initiated persons, written in hexameter verse on gold tablets found in graves at Thurii and Petelia in South Italy, and now preserved in the British Museum. These tablets were described by Comparetti in the *Journal of Hellenic Studies*, iii. p. 111 ff., and are printed by Kaibel in his *Insc. Gr. Sic. et It.* p. 157. Kaibel assigns them to the third or fourth century B.C. I shall quote the one that was found at Petelia.[2] It gives directions to an initiated person who hopes to get out of the Cycle of Incarnations,[3] having been completely purified. Such a person, the verses say, must avoid the fountain on the left hand with a white

---

[1] Virg. *Aen.* vi. 703.
[2] For further description of the Petelia Tablet (in the Brit. Museum, Gold Ornament Room, Table-case H) and other Orphic golden tablets (*e.g.* the Eleuthernae Tablet from Crete, in the National Museum, Athens), the reader may consult Miss Harrison's *Prolegomena to the Study of Greek Religion*, pp. 573 ff., with Appendix by Mr. G. G. A. Murray, pp. 660 ff.
[3] See Lobeck, *Aglaoph.* p. 800.

cypress growing near it, evidently the water of Lethe, although the tablet does not name it. It is to the right that the purified Soul of the initiate must turn, to the cool water of Mnemosyne. The guardians of the well he must address in set form of words, thus—"I am the child of Earth and Heaven: I am parched with thirst; I perish; give me cool water to drink from the well of Memory." And the guardians will give him water to drink from the holy well, and he will be translated to dwell for ever with the Heroes:—

> You will find on the left of the house of Hades a Spring,
> And standing beside it a white cypress.
> To this spring do not draw nigh.
> But you will find another cool stream flowing from the Lake
>   of Memory,
> And there are Guardians before it.
> Say, 'I am the child of Earth and starry Heaven,
> But my race is from the Heavens. This you yourselves also
>   know:
> I am parched with thirst and dying. Give me quickly
> The cool water which flows from the Lake of Memory.'
> And they will give you to drink from the sacred well,
> And after that you will dwell on high among the other heroes.

The Myth of Er indeed differs from the Petelia Tablet in being concerned with those who must still drink of Lethe, and be born again in the flesh, not with those who have been thoroughly purified and drink of Mnemosyne, and so enter into the eternal peace of the disembodied state; yet there is a touch in the Platonic Myth which reminds us that the journey taken is the same as that which the Orphic initiate had to take with the golden tablet in his hand. The journey to the plain of Lethe, according to the Platonic Myth, is through a dry, torrid region, and the temptation to drink too deeply of the water of Lethe is strong, and wisdom, in the imperfectly purified Soul, is needed in order to resist it. Similarly, the purified initiate is warned by his tablet not to quench his burning thirst in Lethe, for the cool water of Mnemosyne is at hand. The drinking of Lethe is the act with which each successive period of the purgatorial discipline ends; the drinking of Mnemosyne is the act which completes the whole series of periods in the discipline.

Both streams, or fountains, are in the place—above ground, not subterranean—to which Souls journey in order that from it they may be either translated to the True Heaven, or sent back to be born again in this world.   Similarly Dante places these two streams side by side on the top of the mount of Purgatory, Lethe running west and north on the left hand of one standing on the south side of their common source and looking north; Eunoè running east and north on his right hand.   Dante, not having to set forth his doctrine of purification in the form of a myth of metempsychosis, makes the purified Soul, before it passes from the Mount of Purgatory up into Heaven, drink only once of Lethe, at the completion of all its purgatorial stages, in order that it may forget its sins; and then of Eunoè, that it may retain the memory of its meritorious deeds (*Purg.* xxviii. 130).   Sins are wiped out after penance, and so fully pardoned, that the sinner does not even remember that he has sinned; but, on the other hand, he does not begin his heavenly existence as a *tabula rasa*—the continuity of his conscious life is preserved by the memory he retains of his good actions.   Here Dante sets forth the thought on which the Platonic doctrine of recollection rests.   It is the flesh, with its sins, that the Philosopher in the *Phaedrus* forgets; but of the things of the mind—of truth and virtue— he gains always clearer and clearer memory, working out his purification as a devotee of the true "mysteries"— "Therefore only the mind of the philosopher has wings, for he ever keeps in memory, as far as he is able, those things by which God is Divine. The man, therefore, who rightly uses these memorials, being ever initiated into perfect Mysteries, he alone becomes perfect." (*Phaedrus*, 249 c). The parallel between the philosopher who "always, as far as he can, cleaves in memory to those things by cleaving to which the Deity is divine," and the purified initiate who finally drinks of the well of memory, is plainly in Plato's mind here, as Dieterich (*Nekyia*, pp. 113, 122) and others have noticed.[1]   Similarly, in the *Phaedo*, 114 c, he says

---

[1] Dieterich (*Nek.* p. 122) says: "Plato's myths entirely correspond with the tablets from Thurii and Petelia, so far as we can judge from existing remains. We find in both the celestial origin of the soul, the sorrowful cycle, the expiation of guilt due to past transgressions, the entry into the Elysian

"those who are sufficiently purified by Philosophy, live without bodies", speaking of those who are translated from the Earthly to the Celestial Paradise, *i.e.* from the True Surface of the Earth, or the Islands of the Blessed, to "even fairer abodes".

I may perhaps be allowed to notice here, in passing, a curious point of contact between Plato's representation of purification as effected through a series of metempsychoses, and Dante's representation of it as an ascent from terrace to terrace of the Mount of Purgatory. In the Myth of Er Plato says that the Souls come to Lethe in the evening, and drink of the water, and fall asleep; and at midnight there is thunder and an earthquake, and they shoot up like meteors to be born again in the flesh. Similarly, Dante tells us (*Purg.* xx. and xxi.) that when a Soul passes to a higher terrace in the course of its purification, the Mount of Purgatory is shaken, and there is a great shout of the spirits praising God. The Soul of the poet Statius, which had just passed to a higher terrace, thus explains the matter to Dante (*Purg.* xxi. 58 ff.):—The Mountain, it says,

> Trembles when any spirit feels itself
> So purified, that it may rise, or move
> For rising; and such loud acclaim ensues.

* * * * * *

Fields (though Persephone plays no part in Plato's works); in the Republic as in the Inscriptions, those to be rewarded go to the right, those to be punished to the left; Lethe is on the left in either tradition. Should we now be able to understand Plato's allusion to the Memory of enlightened philosophic souls 'for to those things they always cleave in memory'. (*Phaedrus* 249 C), and closely connected to this, the characterization of such knowledge as an initiation? When it is said of Pythagoras that he has always possessed Mnēmē (Diog. Laert. VIII. 4), the meaning is the same. What Plato says in abstract terms, becomes, in concrete, symbolic form, the Myth of the Well-spring of Memory. The memory of that which the soul once contemplated in its divine Homeland, helps to redeem it. Whoever receives it is redeemed.

Would it be too daring as yet, to look for a source of Plato's *anamnesis* in the ideas belonging to South Italian Mysteries, which are clearly of a much earlier date; ideas which have only now come to light for us in tablets which are roughly contemporary with Plato? A mere suggestion must suffice here, otherwise it could be made clear that this doctrine of the Mysteries generally influenced the entire psychology and even the doctrine of Ideas to a far greater extent than has been hitherto acceptable."

And I, who in this punishment had lain
Five hundred years and more, but now have felt
Free wish for happier clime.   Therefore thou felt'st
The mountain tremble; and the spirits devout
Heard'st, over all its limits, utter praise
To the Liege Lord, whom I entreat their joy
To hasten.[1]

The earthquake and sound of shouting which attended the
passage of the Soul of Statius to a higher terrace are compared with the shaking of Delos when Latona "couched to
bring forth the twin-born Eyes of Heaven", and with "the
song first heard in Bethlehem's field".   An earthquake and
a great sound—of thunder or shouting—are thus associated
both by Plato and by Dante with the new birth.   The
ascent of Souls from terrace to terrace of the Mount of
Purgatory is a series of spiritual new births, and answers in
Dante to the series of re-incarnations in Plato's mythological
representation of the doctrine of purification.

   That the Orphic mythology of the two fountains of
Lethe and Mnemosyne in the world of the departed—
vouched for by the gold tablet—originated in ritual practised by those who consulted oracles of the dead, is rendered
probable by a passage in Pausanias ix. 39 (which Dante
cannot be supposed to have known), in which the method of
consulting Trophonius at Lebadeia is described.   The
priests of Trophonius, before they take the applicant to the
oracle, lead him to certain fountains, Lethe and Mnemosyne,
which are very close to each other.   First, he must drink of
Lethe that he may forget all that he thought of before; then
he must drink of Mnemosyne that he may have power given
him to remember what he sees when he goes down into the
Cave of Trophonius.   There is evidently a connection
between the mythology of the Descent into Hades and the
practice of consulting oracles of the dead like that of
Trophonius.   It is to consult his father Anchises that Aeneas
goes down into Avernus; and even the inmates of Dante's
Inferno (for instance, Farinata, *Inf*. x.) have prophetic power.

   To summarise the results so far reached:—Dante was
true to mythological data at his disposal in placing Lethe

[1] *Purg.* xxi. 58 ff., Cary's Translation.

in, or near, Elysium or the Earthly Paradise, and making it a stream, not subterranean, but on the surface of the Earth; but there is no evidence to show that he had any knowledge of the Orphic mythology of the twin-streams as we have it in the Petelia inscription. Nor can we suppose that he knew of Pausanias' (ix. 39) mention of the streams of Lethe and Mnemosyne at the entrance of the Cave of Trophonius.[1] The safest course is to allow that Dante, taking the general idea of streams encircling the Earthly Paradise from *Genesis*, and the idea of Lethe as one of these streams from *Aen.* vi., may have hit, quite independently of mythological tradition, on the very natural idea of a stream of Memory to contrast with the stream of Oblivion, although his description of the attributes of Eunoè as stream of Memory certainly resembles Platonic and Neo-Platonic passages in which the process of purification is identified with that of recollection.

With regard to the *name* Eunoè (not a name obviously appropriate to the stream of *Memory*) I have a suggestion to make, which, if it goes in the right direction at all, perhaps does not go very far. I offer it, however, for what it may be worth, as a contribution to a difficult subject. My suggestion is that Dante's use of the name Eunoè may have some connection with the idea of coolness, which apparently found its way into Christian literature[2] from the early Christian epitaphs which reproduce the cold water of the pagan epitaphs. Thus, we have such pagan epitaphs as the following published by Kaibel, and referred to by Dieterich in his *Nekyia* and Rohde in his *Psyche:* May Aidoneus, Lord of those below, give you cold water (Kaibel, *I. G.*, 1842)— May you fare well and may Osiris give you cold water. (Kaibel, *I. G.*, 1488)—To the Gods of the other world— Julia Politike. May Osiris give her the cold water (inscription found in Via Nomentana, Rome; Kaibel, *I. G.*,

---

[1] It is possible that he may have seen Pliny, *H. N.* xxxi. 15. For Dante's acquaintance with Pliny, see Toynbee's *Dante Dictionary*, art. "Plinius", and his *Index of Authors quoted by Benvenuto da Imola in his Commentary on the D. C.*, published as Annual Report of the Dante Society (Cambridge, Mass.), 1900, art. "Plinius".

[2] Tertullian, *Apologeticus*, xxxix., speaking of the Lord's Supper, says, "We give help to every man who is needy, with that refreshment"; and Dante, *Par.* xiv. 27, has "The refreshment of the eternal shower".

1705; cf. Dieterich, *Nek.* p. 95); and such Christian epitaphs (quoted by Dieterich, *Nek.* p. 95, and Rohde, *Psyche*, ii. 391) as "may your soul be in coolness and peace. May God make you cool. May God make cool your spirit."

I suggest, then, that the name Eunoè—eunoia, loving-kindness—was chosen by Dante, or rather by an unknown authority from whom he borrowed it, to indicate that a boon was graciously bestowed by God through the water of this stream—the boon of coolness. "May Aidoneus, Ruler of those below, give you cold water." "May the Lord refresh you." Dante's Eunoè would thus mean the Stream of the Loving-kindness and Grace of God.

Considering the probable descent of the Christian coolness (the idea of which makes itself felt in the lines with which the *Purgatorio* ends), through epitaphs, from the Orphic cold water, I am inclined to think that it is to Christian epitaphs that we ought to go for the more immediate source of Dante's Eunoè. If the word were found there in connection with coolness, we might infer with some confidence that it had occurred in Orphic epitaphs.[1]

---

[1] In the "Query" in the *Classical Review*, Feb. 1903, p. 58, referred to on p. 160 *supra*, Miss Harrison conjectured *Of loving-kindness* in Kaibel, *I.G.S.I.* 642. In a note on "The Source of Dante's Eunoè" in the *Classical Review*, March 1903, pp. 117, 118, in reply to Miss Harrison's "Query", I wrote:— "Until Miss Harrison's *Of loving-kindness*, has been proved to belong to the original text of Kaibel, *I.G.S.I.* 642, and the reference in that inscription has been shown to belong certainly to the Orphic *Wellspring of Recollection*, it will be enough to admit that an Orphic writer in the third century B.C. might very naturally speak of the Guardians of the Well of Memory, as well-disposed towards those initiates on whom they bestowed the cold water, and that he might very naturally describe that Well itself as the Fountain of Loving-kindness."

Since writing the above I have been reminded by a reference in Dieterich's *Eine Mithrasliturgie* (1903), p. 74, n. 1, that Plutarch, in his *Is. et Osir.* ch. 47, says that the Persian god Ormuzd made six gods, the first of whom is the God of "Loving-kindness—for Oromazes out of the purest light, and Ariman out of darkness, fight each other. And the former created among the Gods, first Loving-kindness, second Truth, third Fair Law, and among the rest Wisdom and Wealth, the creator of sweets for the good. But the latter made as it were antitheses to them, equal in number." Here, I take it, the first is the first counted from Ormuzd himself; so that the God of Loving-kindness would be the last reached by the ascending Soul of the initiated person on its way up the Mithraic seven-runged ladder. It is a strange coincidence that the last stage in Dante's ladder of purification—the Mount of Purgatory—should also be Loving-kindness, having passed which his candidate is
Pure and fit to leap to the stars.
Miss Harrison (*Prolegomena*, p. 584) refers to tomb-inscriptions with "*by grace of loving-kindness and memory*". This only means, I take it, "in affectionate remembrance," and can hardly give the clue to the problem of Dante's Eunoè—Mnemosyne.

III

Dante's Mount of Purgatory has characteristics belonging
to the Islands of the Blessed, or mansions upon the earth,
to the Plain of Lethe, and to Tartarus, as these places are
described in Plato's Myths. The Earthly Paradise on the
aethereal top of the Mount of Purgatory answers to the
mansions—"on the True Surface of the Earth." Lethe, as
well as Eunoè, is on the top of the Mount of Purgatory;
and the disciplinary punishment undergone by those not
incorrigibly wicked, in Plato's Tartarus, answers in part to
the penance undergone on the various cornices or terraces
of Dante's Purgatory. Looking at the composition of the
Myth of Er as a whole, we may say that in this Myth we
have the sketch of a *Divina Commedia*, complete with its three
parts—*Inferno*, *Purgatorio*, and *Paradiso*. The *Inferno* is
painted with a few touches, where the torments of Ardiaeus
are described. The *Purgatorio* is given in more detail, not
only in the reference to what those who come out of Tartarus
have suffered during their imprisonment, but also in the
account of the march of these Souls to the throne of Necessity,
and their choosing of new Lives, and further journey on to
the water of Lethe: these experiences, leading up, as they
do, to birth in the flesh, are all parts of a purgatorial discipline. Lastly, we have the *Paradiso* of the Myth of Er in
the vision of the orrery—the little model of the great
Universe, by means of which the astronomical theory of
Plato's age—essentially the same as that of Dante's age—is
illustrated and presented in a form which appeals to poetical
fancy, and yet—so Plato thought—is scientifically correct.
This ancient astronomy, first poetised by Plato, has indeed
played a notable part in the history of poetry. Dante's
Paradiso is dominated by it—renders it into poetry, and yet
leaves it "scientific"; and Milton, although he was acquainted with the Copernican system, adheres, in *Paradise Lost*, to
the old astronomy with its concentric spheres revolving
round the Earth.[1] But when we say that Dante's *Paradiso*—
the noblest of all Eschatological Myths—is dominated by
the ancient astronomy—renders its theory of the heavens

---

[1] See Masson's *Milton's Poetical Works*, vol. i. pp. 89 ff.

into poetry and still leaves it "scientific"—we must not forget that the theory came down to Dante already touched into poetry by an influence not commonly considered poetical, to which, however, Dante's rendering owes much of its poetical effect. I refer to the influence of Aristotle. He put poetry into astronomy when he explained the revolutions of the spheres as actuated by the attraction of God—the Best Beloved, Who draws all things unto Himself with strong desire (see *Met.* Λ 7; *On the Heavens*, ii. 2; and Mr. A. J. Butler's note, *The Paradise of Dante*, p. 8). It is Aristotle who dictates the first line of the *Paradiso*—

> His glory by whose might all things are moved.
>> CARY;

and it is with Aristotle's doctrine—or poetry—that the *Paradiso* ends—

> Here vigour failed the towering fantasy;
> But yet the will rolled onward, like a wheel
> In even motion, by the Love impelled
> That moves the Sun in Heaven and all the Stars.
>> CARY.

The Aristotelian doctrine—or poetry[1]—of these lines is set forth fully in the *Banquet*, ii. 44:

> There are nine moving heavens, and the order of their position is as follows: The first that is reckoned is that of the Moon; the second, that in which Mercury is; the third, Venus; the fourth, the Sun; the fifth, Mars; the sixth, Jupiter; the seventh, Saturn; the eighth is that of the Stars; the ninth is that which can only be perceived by the move-ment above mentioned, which is called the crystalline or diaphanous, or wholly transparent. But outside of these, Catholics suppose the Empyrean Heaven, which is as much as to say the Heaven of Flame, or the luminous; and they suppose this to be immovable, since it has, in itself, in respect of every part, that which its matter requires. And this is the reason why the *primum mobile* has most rapid movement: because by reason of the fervent longing which every part of it has to be joined to every part of that most divine motionless Heaven, it revolves within that with so

---

[1] Against the view here advanced—that Aristotle's doctrine of God is "poetry"—the reader may consult an interesting article on "The Conception of energy of the unmoving", by Mr. F. C. S. Schiller, in *Mind*, Oct. 1900, republished in revised and expanded form, under the title of *Activity and Substance*, as Essay xii. in Mr. Schiller's *Humanism* (1903).

great desire that its velocity is, as it were, incomprehensible.
And this motionless and peaceful Heaven is the place of that
Supreme Deity which alone fully beholds itself. This is the
place of the blessed spirits, according as Holy Church, which
cannot lie, will have it; and this Aristotle, to whoso understands him aright, seems to mean, in the first book *On the
Heavens*.[1]

This is myth—as truly myth as the Spindle of Necessity
in the Vision of Er; which Dante sufficiently recognises in
Conv. ii. 3, where he says that although, as regards the truth
of these things, little can be known, yet that little which
human reason can know has more delectation than all the
certainties of sense.

To pass now to another point:—The back, or continuous
surface formed by the edges or lips of the concentric whorls
of the orrery (*Rep.* 616 E), has been identified by some with
the *back of the sky* of *Phaedrus*, 247 C—the outside of the
outermost sphere of the sensible Cosmos, on which the
Chariot-Souls emerge in sight of the Super-sensible Forms.
Hence, it is inferred, the place where the Souls of the Myth
of Er are assembled before the throne of Necessity, and
where they choose new Lives before they journey on to the
Plain of Lethe, is outside the sensible Cosmos.[2] I do not
think that this inference is certain, or even probable. It is
a model of the Cosmos, I think—and an old-fashioned model,
with rings instead of spheres[3]—not the outside of the actual

---

[1] A. J. Butler's Translation of Scartazzini's *Companion to Dante*, p. 420.
[2] See R. L. Nettleship's *Philosophical Lectures and Remains*, ii. 361, n. 3.
[3] *Rep.* 616 D: see Burnet, *Early Greek Philosophy*, p. 202, and §78 generally.
Sphonduloi, Prof. Burnet points out, are not spheres, but rings, what *Parmenides*
(adopting a Pythagorean idea) calls *stephanai*. According to the *sphonduloi*-
scheme, the Earth and the Heavens are not spherical, but annular. As the
astronomy accepted by Plato undoubtedly made the Earth spherical, in a
spherical Cosmos (see Zeller's *Plato*, Eng. Transl. p. 379), we must conclude
that the system of rings or *sphonduloi*, in *Rep.* 616, is that of a model only—
either an old-fashioned Pythagorean one, or an up-to-date one, in which,
however, only the half of each sphere was represented, so that the internal
"works" might be seen. That astronomical models were in use we know
from *Timaeus*, 40 D, where the speaker says that without the aid of a model
of the Heavens it would be useless to attempt to describe certain motions; and
cf. Fabricii *Bibl. Gr.* Liber iv. pp. 457 ff., on astronomical models in antiquity.
    With regard to the breadth of the rims of the *sphonduloi*, see Mr. Adam's
note on 616 E, and Appendix vi. Although the view supported by the earlier
and more ancient records mentioned by Proclus—that the breadth of the
rims of the *sphonduloi* is proportionate, but not equal, to the diameters of
the planets—is plausible, it seems better to take it that the supposed distances
of the orbits from each other are signified by the breadth of the rims.

Cosmos, that the Pilgrim Souls of the *Republic* see. In the vision of this model, or orrery, we have what is really a vision within the larger vision of the whole Myth of Er. The Pilgrim Souls are still somewhere in the sensible Cosmos —indeed, they are on the surface of the Earth somewhere. In this place, on the surface of the Earth, Necessity and the three Fates, and the rest of the pageant, appear to them, in the form of an image, as the Saints appear to Dante in the lower Spheres where they really are not.[1] Standing in this place, on the surface of the Earth—it may be on the antipodal surface of the Earth—the Pilgrim Souls see on the knees of Necessity the model of the Cosmos, with the lips of its rings making a continuous surface. It is true that in the *Phaedrus* Souls about to be born actually visit the back of the sky, and see thence the region above the Heavens, but in the *Phaedrus* these Souls have wings and can fly to the flaming ramparts of the world, whereas, in the Myth of Er the Souls plod on foot. This seems to me to make a great difference. In interpreting the details of a Platonic Myth we do well always to take account of the poet-philosopher's power of exact visualisation, in respect of which he can be compared only with Dante. I think, therefore, that *in the Myth of Er* the Souls about to be born again do not actually visit the back of the sky.

Be this as it may, the region of the back of the sky, as described in the *Phaedrus*, is either the actual abode, or in close touch with the stars (*Tim.* 42 B), which are the actual abodes, of the purified ones who have drunk of Mnemosyne, and "always remember"—"philosophers", who have been translated from the "True Surface of the Earth", as we read in the *Phaedo* (114 C): "And of those, the Souls which have sufficiently purified themselves by philosophy, live without earthly bodies to the end of time, and reach yet fairer abodes, which it is not easy to describe, nor is there now sufficient time to do so." The abode of these purified ones, in or within sight of the super-sensible region, corresponds to the Empyrean or motionless Heaven of Dante, the tenth and outermost Heaven, in which the blessed really dwell,

---

[1] *Par.* iv. 34 ff. Cf. *Odys.* xi. 600, "and after him I beheld the might of Heracles; his phantom, for he himself was with the immortal Gods."

although they appear, in the form of an image, in all the nine moving Spheres to the poet as he ascends.[1]

I wish to conclude this section of my observations on the Myth of Er with a few words about the view maintained by Mr. Adam in his note on *Rep.* 617 B, 11:—

> Knees of Necessity.—Plato means us to imagine Necessity as seated in the centre of the Universe. The notion is probably Pythagorean; for Parmenides, who attaches himself to the Pythagoreans in this part of his system (Zeller,[5] i. p. 572), speaks of a central Necessity as the cause of all movement and birth; see Diels, *Dox. Gr.* 335. 12 ff.—"Of the rings that are associated, the midmost is the parent of all motion and of the beginning of generation. Her also as divine Guide and Portress he calls Justice and Necessity"; and Zeller, *l.c.* p. 577, n. 3 (Zeller identifies this Necessity with the central fire of the Pythagoreans). The same school seem also to have held that Necessity surrounds and holds the world together (Diels, *l.c.* 321), and Zeller thinks it is this external Necessity of which Plato here avails himself (*l.c.* p. 434, n. 3). But it is quite clear that Plato's Necessity is in the middle.

I agree with Mr. Adam in rejecting Zeller's view that it is the external Necessity of which Plato here avails himself, and in thinking that Plato's Necessity is in the middle. But in what middle? Not in the Pythagorean middle of the Universe, which is not the Earth, but the Central Fire. The throne of Necessity is certainly placed by Plato either on or within the Earth, which is in the middle of his Universe. Mr. Adam, with, I venture to think, too much regard for precision, maintains that it is *within*, not on the surface of, the Earth. "If the light is 'straight like a pillar'," he writes (note on 616 B, 13), "and stretches 'through all the Heaven and the Earth', it follows that as the Earth is in the middle of the Universe, the 'middle of the light' will be at the centre of the Earth. No other interpretation of 'in the midst of the light' is either natural or easy. It would seem, therefore, that at the end of the fourth day after leaving the Meadow the Souls are at the central point both

---

[1] *Par.* iv. 28-39. The appearance of a certain Saint in a certain moving Sphere is a *sign* of his or her position in the graded hierarchy of the Empyrean, or Unmoved Heaven, in which all the Saints have their real abode. A Saint who appears to Dante in the Lunar Sphere, for example, has a lower position in the Empyrean than one who appears in the Sphere of Jupiter.

of the Universe and of the Earth, as is maintained by, among others, Schneider and Donaldson; and this view is also in harmony with some of the most important features of the remaining part of the narrative."

My view is that the throne of Necessity is on the surface of the Earth, at that spot where the pillar of light—the axis on which the Cosmos revolves—was seen, by the Pilgrim Souls as they approached, to touch the ground—seen, *with the accompanying knowledge* (so characteristic of dream-experience) that it goes through the Earth and comes out at the antipodal spot. I do not think that we ought to press the phrase "in the midst of the light", as Mr. Adam does. Apart from the fact that the Pythagorean or Parmenidean central Necessity was not in the centre of the *Earth*, the whole scenery of the Myth and its general fidelity to mythological tradition seem to me to be against putting Plato's throne of Necessity, as Mr. Adam does, in the centre of the Earth. The Myth begins by telling us that the Souls came, some of them out of the Earth, some of them down from "Heaven", to the Meadow. The Meadow is certainly on the surface of the Earth. Their journey thence to the throne of Necessity is evidently on the surface of the Earth—they have the sky above them; they see the pillar of light in the sky before them for a whole day, the fourth day of their march, as they approach it. There is no suggestion of their going down on that day into Tartarus in order to reach the "middle of the light" at the centre of the Earth. Those of them who came out of Tartarus are still out of it, and are not going back into it. And those who came out of the region described as "Heaven", are still out of that region. Hence, if I am right in identifying the Heaven of the *Rep.* with the "True Surface of the Earth" of the *Phaedo* Myth, Mr. Adam cannot be right when he says, 616 B, 11 (cf. 614 C, n.), that "Plato in all probability thinks of the Meadow as somewhere on the True Surface of the Earth described by him in the Myth in the *Phaedo*, and it is apparently along this surface that the Souls progress until they come in view of the light." The True Surface of the Earth and Tartarus, according to my view, were both equally left when the Meadow was reached. The Souls are now

L

journeying along the "Third Way", which leads, under the open sky, by the throne of Necessity, and then by the River of Lethe, to birth. The River of Lethe does not appear in the list of the subterranean or infernal rivers given in the *Phaedo*;[1] the mythological tradition (observed even by Dante, as we have seen) places it under the open sky— probably the sky of the *under-world*—the antipodal hemisphere of the Earth. And "they were borne upward into generation like shooting stars" (621 B), from which Mr. Adam (citing *Aen.* vi. 748 ff.) infers "that the Souls, just before their re-incarnation, are underground," seems to me, on the contrary, entirely in accordance with the view that, encamped near the River of Lethe, they are on the surface of the Earth, under the open sky, up into which they shoot in various directions like meteors—surely an inappropriate picture if they were down in a cavern somewhere at the centre of the Earth.

The whole movement, in short, of the Myth of Er, from the meeting of the two companies of Souls at the Meadow onwards, is above ground, under the open sky. From afar they see a pillar of light reaching down through the sky to the Earth; and, because Plato, the Dreamer of the Myth, recognises this pillar as the axis of the Cosmos—the cause of its necessary revolutions—lo! when the Souls are come to the foot of the pillar, it is no longer a pillar reaching down through the sky that they see, but Necessity herself sitting on Earth, on her throne, with a model of the Cosmos revolving in her lap.

There is another point on which I feel obliged to differ from Mr. Adam. "It is clear," he says (note on *Rep.* 616 C), "that the light not only passes through the centre of the Universe, but also, since it holds the heavens together like

---

[1] Olympiodorus, *Schol. in Phaedonem*, connects the list of infernal rivers with Orphic tradition—"The four rivers given there according to the arrangement of Orpheus they assign to the regions beneath the earth, and to the elements and points between two opposites; Pyriphlegethon to fire, and sunrise, and Cocytus to earth, and sunset, and Acheron to air and noon. These Orpheus laid down thus, but he himself dwells near the water of Ocean and the North." Here the River of Lethe does not appear.

Roscher (art. "Lethe") gives the following mentions of Lethe: Simonides, *Epig.* 184 (Bergk)—this is the first mention, but the authorship is doubtful; Aristoph. *Ranae*, 186; Plato, *Rep.* 621; Plutarch, *Cons. ad Apoll.* ch. 15, in quotation from a dramatic writer; Virg. *Aen.* vi. 705, 715; Lucian, *de luctu*, §§ 2-9; *Mort. Dial.* 13. 6, 23. 2; Ovid, *Ep. ex Pont.* 2, 4, 23.

the undergirders of men-of-war, round the outer surface of the heavenly sphere"—*i.e.* the ends of the light which passes round the outer surface are brought inside the sphere, and, being joined in the middle, form the pillar. This seems to me to make too much of the man-of-war, or trireme. It is enough to take Plato to say that the pillar (which alone is mentioned) holds the Universe together in its particular way, as the undergirdings, in their particular way, hold the trireme together. And if there is a light passed round the outer surface of the Heaven, as well as one forming its axis, why do the Pilgrim Souls see only the latter? The Heavens are diaphanous. The Pilgrims ought, if Mr. Adam's view is correct, to see not only the pillar of light rising vertically from the horizon at a certain fixed point towards which they journey, but also another band of light—that which surrounds the outside of the Universe—travelling round with the motion of the sphere of the fixed stars from East to West.

IV

I shall now conclude what I have to say about the Myth of Er with a few words on the great philosophical question raised in it. I mean the question of How to reconcile Free Will with the Reign of Law. Both are affirmed in the Myth. The Pilgrim Souls are conducted to a spot at which they see, with their own eyes, the working of the Universal Law— they stand beside the axis on which the Cosmos revolves, and see clearly that the revolutions "cannot be otherwise". They see that the axis of the Cosmos is the spindle of Necessity:—and, behold! there sits Necessity herself on her throne, and there are the three Fates, with solemn ritual, ordering the succession of events in time according to the law of Necessity. Yet, within the very precincts of the court of Necessity in which they stand, the Pilgrim Souls hear the Prophet telling them in the words of Lachesis, that "they are free to choose, and will be held responsible for their choice". Plato here presents the Idea of Freedom mythically under the form of a prenatal act of choice—the choice, it is to be carefully noted, not of particular things, but of a Whole Life—the prenatal "choice" of that whole complex of circumstances in which particular things are chosen in this earthly life. Each Soul, according to its nature, clothes itself in certain circumstances—comes into, and goes through, this earthly life in circumstances which it has itself chosen—that is, in circumstances which are to be regarded not as forcing it, or dominating it mechanically from without, but as being the environment in which it exhibits its freedom or natural character as a living creature.[1] Among the circumstances of a Life "chosen", a fixed character of the Soul itself, we are told, is not included (*Rep.* 618 B)—because the Soul is modified by the Life which it chooses. This means that the Soul, choosing the circumstances, or Life, chooses, or makes itself responsible for, its own character, as afterwards modified, and necessarily modified, by the circumstances, or Life. In other words, a man is responsible here on Earth for actions proceeding from a connate character which is modified here in accordance with the circumstances of a general scheme of life made unalterable by Necessity and the Fates before he was born— "Let him choose the life to which he shall be bound by Necessity" (*Rep.* 617 E).

In presenting Moral Freedom under the Reign of Natural Law mythically, as Prenatal Choice made irevocable by Necessity, Plato lays stress, as he does elsewhere, on the unbroken continuity of the responsible Self evolving its character in a series of life-changes. It is the choice made before the throne of Necessity which dominates the behaviour of the Soul in the bodily life on which it is about to enter; but the choice made before the throne of Necessity depended itself on a disposition formed in a previous life; the man who chooses the life of a tyrant, and rues his choice as soon as he has made it, but too late, had been virtuous in a previous life—his virtue had been merely "customary", without foundation upon consciously realised principle (*Rep.* 619 C). Plato thus makes Freedom reside

---

[1] It was chiefly in order to express this relation between living creature and environment that Leibniz formulated his theory of Pre-established Harmony. We may say of Leibniz's theory what he says himself of Plato's doctrine of recollecion—that it is "myth"—"toute fabuleuse" (*Nouveaux Essais*, Avant-propos, p. 196 b, ed. Erdmann).

in being, not in action.[1] To be free is to be a continuously
existing, self-affirming, environment-choosing personality,
manifesting itself in actions which proceed, according to
necessary law, from itself as placed once for all in the
environment which it has chosen—its own natural environment—the environment which is the counterpart of its own
character. It is vain to look for freedom of the will in some
power of the personality whereby it may interfere with the
necessary law according to which character, as modified up
to date, manifests itself in certain actions. Such a power,
such unfettered judgment without discrimination, would
be inconsistent with the continuity, and therefore with the
freedom and responsibility, of the Self. It is, in other
words, the freedom of the "noumenal", as distinguished
from the "phenomenal" Self, which Plato presents as the
"prenatal choice of a Life"—mythically; which is, indeed,
the only way in which such a transcendental idea can be
legitimately presented. "Let him choose the life to which
he shall be bound by Necessity. Virtue has no master." A
certain Life, with all its fortunes and all its influences on
character, when once chosen, is chosen irrevocably.[2] But,
none the less, it is a life of freedom, for "Virtue is her own
mistress". In being conscious of Virtue—that is, of Self as
striving after the good or self-realisation—the Soul is
conscious of its own freedom. This consciousness of "freedom", involved in the consciousness of "Virtue", is better
evidence for the reality of freedom than the inability of the
logical faculty to understand freedom is against its reality.
As Butler says, "The notion of necessity is not applicable
to practical subjects, *i.e.* with respect to them is as if it

---

[1] For the distinction, see Schopenhauer, *Parerga und Paralipomena*, ii. §
117; *Die Welt als Wille u. Vorstellung*, vol. ii. pp. 364, 365; and *Die Grundlage
der Moral*, § 10. In the last of these passages Schopenhauer (explaining the
distinction between the "intelligible" and the "empirical" character, the
latter of which is related to the former as action is to existence—action
follows being) quotes Porphyry (in Stobaeus, *Ecl.* 8. §§ 37-40): "For such
seems to be Plato's whole meaning: that souls are self-existent before they
descend into bodies and different lives, and to this end they have the choice
of one life rather than another."

[2] Hobbes' "Sovereign, once shosen, ever afterwards irremovable," is a
"foundation-myth"; the social order which constrains individuals to conformity is accounted for "mythically" by a prehistoric act of choice exercised
by individuals. They willed themselves into the social order, and may not
will themselves out of it. A "categorical imperative" is laid upon them to
act as social beings.

were not true. . . . Though it were admitted that this opinion of necessity were speculatively true, yet with regard to practice it is as if it were false."[1]

One other point and I have done with the Myth of Er: The momentary prenatal act of choice which Plato describes in this Myth is the pattern of like acts which have to be performed in a man's natural life. Great decisions have to be made in life, which, once made, are irrevocable, and dominate the man's whole career and conduct afterwards. The chief use of education is to prepare a man for these crises in his life, so that he may decide rightly. The preparation does not consist in a rehearsal, as it were, of the very thing to be done when the crisis comes—for the nature of the crisis cannot be anticipated—but in a training of the will and judgment by which they become trustworthy in any difficulty which may be presented to them. The education given to the Guardians of Plato's Beautiful City is a training of this kind. Its aim is to cultivate faculties rather than to impart special knowledge. It is a "liberal education" suitable to free men of the governing class, as distinguished from technical instruction by which workmen are fitted for the routine of which they are, so to speak, the slaves.

[1] *Analogy,* i. 6.

THE *POLITICUS* MYTH

We have now done with the three purely Eschatological Myths, and enter on a series of Myths which are mainly Aetiological. We begin with the Myth of the Alternating World-periods in the *Politicus*.

The Cosmos has alternating periods, according as God either goes round with and controls its revolution, or lets go the helm and retires to his watch-tower. When God lets go the helm, the Cosmos, being a living creature with its own innate desire, and subject, like all creatures, to destiny, begins to revolve in its own direction, which is opposite to God's direction. The change of direction—the least possible change if there is to be change at all—we must ascribe to the changeable nature of the material Cosmos, and not either to God, who is unchangeable, imparting now one motion and then its contrary, or to the agency of another God. When God, then, lets go the helm, the Cosmos begins of itself to revolve backwards; and since all events on Earth are produced by the revolution of the Cosmos, the events which happened in one cosmic period are reproduced backwards in the next. Thus the dead of one period rise from their graves in the next as grey-haired men, who gradually become black-haired and beardless, till at last, as infants, they vanish away. This is the account of the fabled Earth-born. They were men who died and were buried in the cosmic period immediately preceding that of Cronus—the Golden Age of Cronus, when the Earth brought forth food plenteously for all her children, and men and beasts, her common children, talked together, and daemons, not mortal men, were kings (cf. *Laws*, 713). But at last the stock of earthen men ran out—"the earth-born race had all perished" (*Pol.* 272 D)—and the age of Cronus came to an end: God let go the helm, and the Cosmos changed the direction of its revolution, the change being accompanied by great earthquakes which destroyed all but a few men and animals. Then the Cosmos calmed down, and for a while, though revolving in its own direction, not in God's, yet remembered God, and fared well; but afterwards forgot him, and went from bad to worse; till God, of his goodness, saved struggling men, now no longer earth-born, from destruction by means of the fire of Prometheus and the arts of Athena and Hephaestus. In due time he will close the present period—that of Zeus—by again taking the helm of the Cosmos. Then will be the Resurrection of the Dead. Such, in brief, is the Myth of the Changing World-periods in the *Politicus*.

Like the Myths already examined, this one deals with God's government of man as a creature at once free to do good and evil, and determined by cosmic influences over which he—and even God the Creator himself, whether from lack or non-use of power hardly matters—have no control. The Myth differs from those which we have examined in not being told by Socrates himself. It is told by an Eleatic Stranger, who says that the younger Socrates, who is present with the elder, will appreciate a story. Similarly, Protagoras prefaces the Myth which he tells (*Prot.* 320 c) by saying that it will suit Socrates and the others—younger men than himself.

The Eleatic Stranger in the *Politicus* tells his Myth ostensibly in order to bring it home to the company that they have defined "kingship" too absolutely—as if the king were a god, and not a human being. Gods directly appointed by the great God were kings on this Earth in a former period; but in the period in which we now live men are the only kings. Kingship must now be conceived "naturalistically" as a product of human society; and human society itself, like the whole Cosmos of which it is a part, must be conceived "naturalistically" as following its own intrinsic law without divine guidance from outside. To enforce a "naturalistic" estimate of kingship is the ostensible object of the Myth; but it soars high, as we shall see, above the argument which it is ostensibly introduced to serve.

CONTEXT

The subject of the Politicus *is the True Statesman.*

The best form of government, if we could get it, would be the rule of one eminently good and wise man, who knew and desired the Chief Good of his People, and possessed the art of securing it for them. His unlimited personal initiative would be far better than the best administration of "laws" made only because he could not be found, and because such rulers as were actually available could not be trusted with unlimited initiative.

But before we try to determine exactly the nature of the True Statesman—the man whom we should like to make King, if we could find him; and before we try to define his Art, and distinguish it from all other arts—and we must try to do this, in order that we may get a standard by which to judge the work-a-day rulers, good and bad, whose administration of the "laws" we are obliged to accept as substitute for the personal initiative of the True Statesman—before we try to formulate this standard, let us raise our eyes to an even higher standard: God is the True Ruler of men; and in the Golden Age he ruled men, not through the instrumentality of human rulers, but Gods were his lieutenants on Earth, and lived among men, and were their Kings.

It is with this Golden Age, and the great difference between it and the present age, and the cause of the difference, that the Myth told to the elder and the younger Socrates, and to Theodorus the mathematician, by the Stranger from Elea, is concerned.

Politicus, 268 E—274 E

Stranger. Here beginneth my wonderful Tale! Be as a
child, and listen! for indeed not far art thou gotten from the
years of childish things.

Socrates.[1] Let us hear it.

Stranger. Well, of those things which have been told from
old time, there be many which came to pass, and shall yet
again come to pass: whereof I count the Sign which
appeared when that Strife the Old Story telleth of was
between Atreus and Thyestes; for, methinks, thou hast heard
what they say came then to pass, and rememberest it well.

Socrates. Is it of the marvel of the Golden Lamb that
thou speakest?

Stranger. Not of that, but of the change in the setting
and rising of the sun and stars; for the story goes that in the
quarter whence they now rise in that did they then set, rising
from the opposite quarter; but that God, bearing witness
for Atreus, changed them into the way which they now keep.

Socrates. That story also I know.

Stranger. And of the kingship of Cronus, too, have we
heard many tell.

Socrates. Yea, very many.

Stranger. And, moreover, do they not tell of how men at
first grew out of the earth, and were not begotten of their
kind?

Socrates. That also is one of the old stories.

Stranger. Well, of all these things one thing is cause; yea,
of innumerable other things also which are more wonderful
than these things; but by reason of length of time most are
vanished, and of the rest mention is made separately of each,
as of that which hath no fellowship with the other things.
But of that which is the cause of all these things no man
hath spoken. Let it therefore now be told; for when it hath
been set forth, it will help to our proof concerning the King.

Socrates. Good! Go on, and leave out nothing.

Stranger. Hearken! This Universe, for a certain space of

---

[1] *Socrates the Younger* is the interlocutor throughout the whole passage
translated.

time, God himself doth help to guide and propel in the
circular motion thereof; and then, when the cycles of the
time appointed unto it have accomplished their measure,
he letteth it go. Then doth it begin to go round in the
contrary direction, of itself, being a living creature which
hath gotten understanding from him who fashioned it in the
beginning. This circuit in the contrary direction belongeth
of necessity to the nature of the Universe because of this—

Socrates. Because of what?

Stranger. Because that to be constant in the same state
alway, and to be the same, belongeth only to those things
which are the most divine of all; but the nature of Body is
not of this order. Now, that which we call Heaven and
Universe hath been made, through him who begat it,
partaker of many blessed possessions; but, mark this well,
Body also is of the portion thereof. Wherefore it is not
possible that it should be wholly set free from change,
albeit, as far as is possible, it revolveth in the same place,
with one uniform motion: for this reason, when it changed,
it took unto itself circular motion in the contrary direction,
which is the smallest possible alteration of the motion which
belongeth unto it. Now, to be constant alway in self-motion
is, methinks, impossible save only with him who ruleth all
the things which are moved; and move them now in this
direction and again in that he may not. From all this it
followeth that we must not say that the Universe either of
itself moveth itself alway, or again is alway wholly moved
by God to revolve now in one direction and then in the
contrary direction; nor must we say that there be two Gods
which, being contrariously minded, do cause it so to revolve;
but we must hold by that which was just now said and
alone remaineth, to wit, that at one time it is holpen and
guided by the power of God supervening, and hath more life
added unto it, and receiveth immortality from the Creator
afresh; and then, at another time, when it is let go, it
moveth of itself, having been so opportunely released that
thereafter it journeyeth in the contrary direction throughout ages innumerable, being so great of bulk, and so evenly
balanced, and turning on so fine a point.

Socrates. All this, methinks, hath great likelihood.

Stranger. Let us then reason with ourselves, and comprehend from this that which, coming to pass, is, as we said, the cause of all these wonders. Well, it is this.

Socrates. What?

Stranger. The circular motion of the Universe going as it now goeth, and then at another time going in the contrary direction.

Socrates. How?

Stranger. This alteration we must needs deem to be of all the changes which are accomplished in the Heaven the change which is greatest and most complete.

Socrates. So it would seem.

Stranger. And we must conclude that by reason of it the greatest changes are then accomplished for us who dwell within this Universe.

Socrates. That also is likely.

Stranger. Now, when changes many and great and of all sorts come to pass, is it not true that the nature of living creatures hardly endureth them?

Socrates. Yea, 'tis true.

Stranger. So it is then, of necessity, that beasts do perish most, and of mankind only a little remnant is left; and unto these men do many things strange and new happen, but the strangest is that which attendeth the rolling back of the Universe when the motion contrary to this which is now established cometh to be.

Socrates. What is that?

Stranger. Then cometh it to pass that the age of every creature, according as his time of life is, first standeth still, and mortals are all stayed in that course which maketh them look older and older: but presently they begin to go in the contrary direction—that is to say, they grow younger and more tender; and the hoary locks of the old man become black, and the cheeks of the bearded man become smooth, and he is restored to the bygone springtime of his life; and the lad becometh smooth again, and smaller day after day and night after night, till he cometh back, soul and body, unto the nature and likeness of a new-born child; and thereafter he ever dwindleth away, and at the last utterly

vanisheth. Likewise the corpses of them that have died by
violence at this time go through the same changes quickly,
and in a few days are dissolved and gone clean out of sight.

Socrates. But how were creatures then brought forth,
and after what manner were they begotten of their kind?

Stranger. It is manifest, O Socrates, that none was then
naturally begotten of his kind, but that the earth-born kind
they tell of was that which came up again from the earth in
those days, whereof our first forefathers had remembrance
who lived in the time next after the end of the former
Period, being born at the beginning of this present one.
From their mouth hath word concerning these things
come down unto us: which of many is not believed; but
herein they err; for consider what followeth next:—After
the old men who go back to childhood, there follow in their
turn the men who are already dead and lying in their
graves; these begin therein to be compacted anew out of
their elements, and when his time cometh unto each of them
in the cycle of generation whose motion is contrary to the
former motion, he riseth from the dead. Thus were men, of
necessity, earth-born in those days, and this name of earth-
born which we have received is the true name of them all,
save of those whom God translated to some other portion.

Socrates. Yea, indeed, this followeth from that which
went before. But tell me—the life thou sayest men led
when Cronus reigned, was it in that Period or in this?
For 'tis plain that the change whereof thou speakest in the
course of the stars and the sun falleth to happen in each.

Stranger. Well hast thou followed the argument; and thy
question is to be answered thus:—That the age when all
things came forth spontaneous for the use of man congrueth
not with this present motion, but with that which was
before; for then did God control with his providence the
whole revolution, and all the parts of the Universe everywhere were divided amongst gods appointed to rule over
them, as now gods rule over certain places; and, moreover,
living creatures, according to their kinds, were assigned unto
angels, as flocks unto divine shepherds, each angel being
wholly sufficient in all things for his own flock, so that there
was then no savagery, no devouring of one another, no war

or sedition at all: nay, time would fail to tell of all the consequences of that dispensation.

Now, therefore, hearken, and I will declare the truth that is in the old Tale of the time when all things came forth spontaneous. God himself was then the Overseer and Shepherd of men, even as now man, being as a god amongst the creatures which are beneath him, is the shepherd of their tribes. When God was our Shepherd there was no civil government, and men had not wives and children, but all came up into life again from the Earth, without remembrance of aught before. Instead of these things they had in abundance, from trees and other plants, fruits which the Earth without husbandry brought forth spontaneous. For the most part they lived without raiment and without couches, in the open air; for the seasons were tempered to do them no hurt; and soft beds had they in the grass which sprang abundantly from the Earth.

Now have I told thee, Socrates, of the life which was when Cronus reigned; as for the life which now is, which they say is under the rule of Zeus, thou art here thyself and knowest what it is. Canst thou, and wilt thou, determine which of these two lives is the happier?

Socrates. I cannot.

Stranger. Shall I then determine this for thee after some sort?

Socrates. Prithee do.

Stranger. Well then, if the nurslings of Cronus, having so great leisure and faculty of joining in discourse not only with men but with beasts, made use of their opportunity all for the getting of wisdom, conversing with beasts and one with another, and inquiring everywhere of Nature if haply any part thereof had some peculiar faculty, and perceived, better than another part, aught which might be of advantage for the ingathering of true knowledge—if this, I say, was their manner of life, 'twould be no hard matter to determine our question: they were a thousand times happier than we are. And even if, after they had eaten and drunken their fill, they passed the time telling tales one to another and to the beasts—such tales as even to this day are told of them— 'twould still, I declare, be easy to determine our question;

nevertheless, let us put it away, until some one shall appear who is able to show us credibly which way these ancients were inclined in regard of knowledge and discourse: meanwhile let us speak of that for the sake whereof this Tale was started, that the next part of our argument may go forward.

When the time of all these men was fulfilled, and the change must needs come, and of the generation of them that arose out of the Earth there was none left, and every Soul had rendered her tale of births, according to the number of times appointed for her to fall and be sown upon the Earth, then did the Governor of the Universe let go, as it were, the tiller, and depart into his own watch-tower, and Fate and inborn Impulse began to cause the Universe to revolve backwards again. Straightway all the gods which, in their several places, bore rule together with the Great God, when they knew what was done, likewise left their provinces without oversight. Then was the Universe shaken as with a great earthquake through his depths by reason of the concussion of the reversed revolution and the strife betwixt the two contrary motions whereof the one was ending and the other beginning; whereby was wrought a fresh destruction of living creatures of every kind.

Thereafter, when the due time was accomplished, the Universe at last ceased from tumults and confusion and earthquakes, and coming into a calm, and being set in order for the course wherein it useth to go, therein went, itself having superintendency and dominion over itself and all that in it is, calling to mind alway, as it was able, the teaching of the Maker and Father of all.

At first the things which it brought forth were more perfectly wrought, but at last more roughly: the cause whereof was the corporeal part which was mixed in the original nature of things, the which was full of confusion before that it came unto the present order. From Him who composed it the Universe hath all things fair and good; but from the former state thereof come all the things difficult and unrighteous which in itself it hath, and bringeth to pass in the creatures which it fashioneth. Therefore when it was with the Governor, the evil creatures it brought forth were few, and the good were in abundance; but when it was separated from him, at first for a while after the separation it performed all things exceeding well; and then, as time went on, and forgetfulness grew more and more within it, discord, inherent from of old, gained ever greater mastery and at last burst forth; and things good that were produced being few, and the admixture of the opposite sort being great, the Universe came into danger of being destroyed together with all that was in it.

Wherefore, when things were come to this pass, God, who fashioned this Order, perceiving that it was in distress, and careful lest, being tossed in the storm of so great a tumult, it should be loosed asunder and founder down into the measureless deep of Confusion, again took up His post at the helm; and having turned round that which was gone the way of disease and dissolution in the former Period when the Universe was left to itself, put all in order, and restored the Universe to the right way, and made it exempt from death and old age.

Here endeth the Tale: now let us return, and take up the beginning thereof, which will suffice for our setting forth of "The King".

When the Universe was turned back, and went the way of this present sort of generation, then again did man's age first stand still, and thereafter straightway began to bring forth things new, in the order contrary to that of the former period; for those creatures which, by reason of their smallness, were all but vanished away, began to grow bigger, and the bodies of men newly come forth from the Earth, which were born grey-headed, died again, and went down into the Earth; and all other things were likewise changed, according to the changed condition of the Universe, their Example and Controller; and among these things which were of necessity so changed were the Conception and Birth and Nourishment of living creatures; for no longer could a living creature grow in the Earth, compacted together out of his elements by others, but even as it was ordained unto the Universe to be master of his own path, so also was it ordained, by the like law, that the parts of the Whole, of themselves, as far as might be, should bring forth, and beget, and provide nourishment.

Now, therefore, are we come whither our Whole Discourse was bound.

As for the beasts of the field, to tell how and by what causes they were changed would be a long story; but our proper concern is man, and a shorter story will suffice.

When we were bereft of the care of the god which had gotten us to keep and tend, then came it to pass, because the multitude of wild beasts, being fierce by nature, were become more savage, and we ourselves were become weak and defenceless, that we were harried by them; and, moreover, at first, we were helpless, and without the aid of the arts; for the food which grew spontaneous was now lacking, and we knew not yet how to provide food, because that aforetime need had not constrained us to make provision. By reason of all these things were men in sore straits: wherefore it came to pass that those Gifts from the Gods whereof the old stories tell were bestowed upon us, together with the teaching and training which were needful; to wit, fire from Prometheus, and the arts from Hephaestos and his mate; and seeds and herbs from others: yea, all things which have furnished man's life were thus brought forth, ever since the time when the watch kept over us by the Gods, as I said just now, failed us, and it behoved us to spend our lives by ourselves, caring for ourselves; even as the whole Universe must care for itself; the which we imitating and following alway throughout all ages do live and grow up, now after this manner, and then again after that manner.

Here endeth our Tale; the use whereof will be to make us see how wrongly we set forth the nature of the King and Statesman in our former Discourse.

Before I go on to offer observations on the *Politicus* Myth, I will supplement the foregoing translation of it by giving a translation of the Myth of the Golden Age of Cronus as it appears also in *Laws* 712 E—714 A.

M

THE MYTH OF THE GOLDEN AGE

Athenian Stranger. The cities whereof we just now spake are not *polities*, or true cities, but mere dwelling-places, the inhabitants whereof are slaves in subjection unto certain ones among themselves; and each one of these dwelling-places is called "the government of such and such", after them that be masters therein: but, if it is meet that a city should be called after her masters, the True City will be called after God, who verily ruleth over men of understanding.

Cleinias. And who is this God?

Ath. I must still, for a little while, use Fable for the more convenient answering of thy inquiry—what thinkest thou?

Cleinias. Yea—Fable.

Ath. Before that those cities were, the inhabitation whereof we have set forth in the former part of this Discourse —yea, very long time before these—it is told that there was a Government and Settlement when Cronus was King; whereof the blessedness was great, and whichsoever city is now ordered best is an image of that exemplar.

$$*\qquad*\qquad*\qquad*\qquad*\qquad*$$

This, then, is the Tale which we have received concerning the blessed life of the men who lived in those days: It telleth that they had all things, without stint, spontaneous, and that the cause thereof was this: Cronus, saith the Tale, knowing that Human Nature could in no wise be left with sole authority in the administration of all things human and yet not become a vessel filled with insolency and injustice, took thought of the matter, and set over our cities, to be kings and rulers thereof, not men, but those of a more divine and excellent sort, to wit, Daemons; just as we ourselves do with our cattle and flocks—for we set not oxen over oxen, or goats over goats, but we ourselves rule over them, being of a race more excellent than theirs. In like manner God, they say, of his loving-kindness toward men, set over us the race of Daemons, which is more excellent than ours; and they, to their own great content and to ours, caring for us, and providing for us peace, and modesty, and good government, and justice without stint, made the nations of mankind peaceable and happy.

This Tale, then, hath in it truth, inasmuch as it signifieth that whichsoever city hath not God, but a mortal man, for ruler, hath no way of escape from evils and troubles: wherefore, according to the admonition of the Tale, must we by all means make our life like unto the life which was when Cronus was King; and in so far as that which is Immortal dwelleth in us, must we be obedient unto the voice thereof in all our doings private and public, and govern our households and cities according to *Law*, which, being interpreted, is *the Award of Reason*.[1]

---

[1] This Myth ought to be taken in close connection not only with the *Politicus* Myth, but with the Discourse of Diotima, in the *Symposium*, and the doctrine of Daemons set forth in that Discourse; for which see pp. 384 ff. *infra.*

Observations on the *POLITICUS* Myth

I

I cannot do better at the outset than refer the reader for the general characteristics of the *Politicus* Myth to Jowett's Introduction to the *Statesman* (*Dialogues of Plato*), where his admirable remarks, indeed, leave little to be added. The philosophical import of the Myth, it will be gathered from Jowett's remarks, consists in its presentation of the "distinctions between God causing and permitting evil, and between his more or less immediate government of the world." Interesting observations will also be found on the art with which Plato gives verisimilitude to his own Myth "by adopting received traditions (as the tradition about the sun having originally risen in the West and that about the earth-born)—traditions of which he pretends to find an explanation in his own larger conceptions." We have had instances of this art in the Platonic Myths already examined, which we have found securing credit to themselves by explaining not only old traditional Myths, but the facts and doctrines of "modern science"; and we have found the same art employed by Dante.

Having referred to Jowett's Introduction[1] for a general view of this Myth, I will now add some observations on special points.

The doctrine of periodical terrestrial "catastrophes", universal or local, leaving on each occasion a few scattered survivors to build up society afresh, mythologically explained in the *Politicus*, was part of the "science" of Plato's day,[2] and was afterwards a prominent tenet of the Peripatetics.[3]

It was also "scientific" in Plato's day to explain at least the general course of terrestrial phenomena as caused by the motion of the Heavens. It is thus that the phenomena of birth and decay in this sublunary region are accounted for by Aristotle.[4]

---

[1] I would also refer to Grote's *Plato*, ii. 480, note *s*—a long and instructive note; and to Stallbaum's Prolegomena to the *Politicus*.

[2] *Laws*, iii. 676 ff.

[3] See Newman's notes on Arist. *Pol.* ii. 5. 1269 a 5 and 6.

[4] *De Gen. et Corr.* ii. 10, 336 a 26, and cf. Zeller's *Aristotle*, Eng. Transl. i. 580 ff.

Putting together the occurrence of terrestrial catastrophes (cf. *Tim.* 22 ff.) and the influence of the motion of the Heavens, both vouched for by "science", Plato imagines the catastrophes as shocks produced by sudden changes in the direction of the motion. The western rising of the sun in the Atreus Myth may have suggested this explanation to him; or he may have known the Egyptian tradition recorded by Herodotus (ii. 142), that during eleven thousand three hundred and forty years of Egyptian history the sun on four occasions altered his course, "twice rising where he now sets and twice setting where he now rises." Although another rationale of the Egyptian tradition (or of Herodotus's version of it) has been given,[1] I venture to suggest that whereas East is left and West is right as one faces the midday sun in the northern hemisphere, while East is right and West is left to the spectator in the southern hemisphere, the "Egyptian tradition" was awkwardly built upon the tale of some traveller coming from south of the equator, who said truly that he had seen the sun rise on his right hand and set on his left.

II

Zeller (*Plato*, Eng. Transl. p. 383, n. 44) says, "Of course (cf. *Tim.* 36 E, and elsewhere) Plato is not in earnest in supposing that God from time to time withdraws from the government of the world."

Since the supposition of God's intermittent agency is made in a Myth, Plato is certainly not "in earnest" with it, in the sense of laying it down dogmatically as a scientific axiom. But is he more "in earnest" with the supposition of the continuous agency of God in the *Timaeus*? That supposition is equally part of a Myth; "The *Timaeus* itself is wholly mythical."[2] The truth is that, however Plato represents God—and he sometimes represents him in immense cosmic outlines, sometimes on a smaller scale and more anthropomorphically—the representation is always for the imagination, mythical. And it ought not to be forgotten that the supposition of God's intermittent agency is advanced

---

[1] See Rawlinson's note *ad loc.*
[2] Couturat, *de Platonis Mythis*, p. 32.

in the *Politicus* in order to explain (mythologically, of course) the fact which Plato does not shut his eyes to even in the *Timaeus*, where he supposes (still in Myth) the continuity of God's government—the fact of the existence of evil, both physical and moral, in a world supposed to be governed by God. In maintaining the existence of evil Plato is certainly "in earnest".

It is worth noting that the representation given by the *Politicus* Myth of the opposition between God and Matter—good and evil—as an opposition of motions is common to the Myth with the astronomy of Plato's day; but whereas the *Politicus* Myth makes motion in God's direction alternate with motion in the world's direction, astronomical theory makes the two motions go on for ever simultaneously, *i.e.* the eternal motion of the whole Cosmos from East to West carries round the inner spheres, whose own motions take place from West to East.

For a full discussion of the astronomy of the *Politicus* Myth I would refer the reader to Mr. Adam's *Republic*, vol. ii. 295 ff. Mr. Adam's view is that the two cycles (the motion in God's direction, and that in the opposite direction) are of equal length, and that each of them represents a Great Year—the Great Year being 36,000 years.

III

"And now the earth-born race had all perished" (*Politicus*, 272 D). The "Resurrection" of the *Politicus* Myth and "Metempsychosis" may be regarded as parallel products of imagination. Metempsychosis assumes a fixed number of souls created once for all and continuing always in existence. New souls are not created; the souls which animate the bodies of men in each successive generation are always souls which had been incarnate in former generations. In *Rep.* 611 A, Plato expressly lays it down that the number of souls in existence is always the same without augmentation or diminution.[1] This tenet involved in Metempsychosis Plato

---

[1] Cf. Rohde, *Psyche*, ii. 279.

shares with the aborigines of Australia.   Messrs. Spencer
and Gillen say:[1]

> The idea is firmly held that the child is not the direct
> result of intercourse[2]—that it may come without this, which
> merely, as it were, prepares the mother for the reception and
> birth of an already formed spirit child who inhabits one of
> the local totem centres . . . In the native mind the value of
> the Churinga (stone or wooden objects lodged in a cave or
> other storehouse, near which women do not pass) lies in the
> fact that each one of them is intimately associated with,
> and is indeed the representative of, one of the Alcheringa
> ancestors, with the attributes of which it is endowed.   When
> the spirit part has gone into a woman, and a child has, as
> a result, been born, then that living child is the re-incarnation
> of that particular spirit individual.[3]

As Metempsychosis makes the same soul, so Resurrection
makes the same body, serve more than one life.   There is a
store of old bodies, as there is of souls, upon which a new
generation draws.   The store of souls assumed by Metempsychosis is never exhausted, being recruited as fast as it is
drawn upon; but the store of adult bodies in the "Resurrection" of the *Politicus* Myth is at last exhausted, for each
adult body, when in its turn it rises from the dead, grows
smaller and smaller till it becomes the body of an infant
and vanishes away.

One might develop Plato's myth, and say that it is these
vanished infants which reappear after the manner of ordinary
birth, and grow back into adult size, when the revolution
of the Cosmos is reversed.   This would be in accordance

---

[1] *The Native Tribes of Central Australia*, p. 265.

[2] Cf. Myer and Nutts' *Voyage of Bran*, ii. 82, on the widespread idea of
conception, without male intervention, through swallowing a worm in a
drink, or through some other means.

[3] Spencer and Gillen's *Native Tribes of Central Australia*, p. 138.   Before
going to press I have not had an opportunity of seeing Messrs. Spencer and
Gillen's new book, *The Northern Tribes of Central Australia*, but I transcribe
the following sentences from a notice of it in the *Athenaeum* (July 9, 1904):—
"These tribes believe that in every child the soul of a mythical Alcheringa
ancestor of a given totem is re-incarnated.   Those totem souls haunt the
places, marked by a tree or rock, where the ancestors 'went into the ground'.
There the dying ancestors left stone amulets of a type familiar in Europe and
America, styled *churinga*.   When a child is born his ancestral churinga is
sought, and often is found near the place where the totem spirit entered his
mother."   Are the "articles belonging to the deceased", referred to p. 401
infra, parallel to these Australian amulets?

with the belief, by no means confined to such primitive
minds as those of the Australian aborigines, observed by
Messrs. Spencer and Gillen, that intercourse is after all not
the real cause of the birth of a child: that the child—
hardly distinguished as "soul" *and* "body"—is one who
returns from the world of the departed and enters into the
mother. The relationship between such a view of the
nature of procreation and the custom of counting kinship
through the mother, not through the father, is of course
obvious.

That the notion of Resurrection, then, recommends itself
to the imagination in much the same way as the notion of
Metempsychosis is what I wish to suggest to the student of
the *Politicus* Myth. The two notions are closely allied and,
indeed, tend to coalesce. The distinction between soul and
body is a hard one for the imagination to maintain; thus it
is very imperfectly maintained in the following instance:
"The Jesuits relate that among the Hurons there were
special ceremonies for little children who died at less than
two months old; their bodies were not put in coffins in the
cemeteries, but buried upon the pathway in order that they
might enter into the body of some passing woman and so be
born again;"[1] and it is practically given up in the Christian
Eschatology which insists on the ultimate union of the soul
with its risen body.

IV

My remarks in this section will serve as introduction to
the "Creation Myths", which we shall examine next.

The *Politicus* Myth may be distinguished as Aetiological
from the Eschatological Myths which we have examined in
the *Phaedo*, *Gorgias*, and *Republic*. The Eschatological Myths
are concerned immediately with the Ideas of Reason. They
set forth the Idea of Soul as subject of God's government in
the Cosmos, by depicting the future vicissitudes of the Soul,
not, of course, without reference to its past out of which its

---

[1] J. E. King on "Infant Burial", in *Classical Review*, Feb. 1903, p. 83.
The souls of infants seem always to have caused difficulty; see Rohde, *Psyche*,
ii. 411-413, on untimely births, and Adam's note on *Rep.* 615 c, "About
infants that died as soon as they were born, or only lived a short while, he
spoke other things that are not worth mentioning."

future grows. The Aetiological Myth, on the other hand, may set forth either Ideas of Reason or Categories of the Understanding. Thus the *Timaeus* (which is one great Aetiological Myth) sets forth the Ideas of Soul and Cosmos, by tracing their imaginatively constructed objects back to causes which are unfolded in an account of the Creation of the Soul and of the material world. The *Phaedrus* Myth, again, sets forth the Categories of the Understanding aetiologically, by showing that the *a priori* conditions of our knowledge of sensible phenomena are abiding mental impressions caused by a prenatal vision of the Eternal Forms in the region above the Heavens. There are other myths which cannot be called either Aetiological or Eschatological, but are merely Expository either of Ideas of Reason or of Categories of the Understanding—thus Diotima's Myth is an imaginative exposition of the Idea of Soul as Love of Truth and Immortality, while the functions of the Understanding are described imaginatively in the *Timaeus* as revolutions like those of the Cosmos.

The *Politicus* Myth, setting forth as it does the Idea of Soul as subject of God's government in the Cosmos, is Aetiological in supplying a cause for the Evil which exists in the world and man's life under God's government.

How does Plato think that we are helped out of the profound difficulty about the existence of Evil by an Aetiological Myth of Changing World-periods? The answer, if we could give it, would be a complete theory of the influence which Aetiological Myths exercise over the mind of man. Here is the greatest difficulty of morals; and it is easily solved by a fantastic story of the origin of the thing which makes the difficulty!

Let me try to explain how Plato comes to attach such value to this Aetiological Myth. First, Plato thinks that the immensity of the difficulty is best illustrated in this way—as the tragic import of a great crisis on the stage or in real life is sometimes illustrated by the trifling comment or behaviour of some one present—it may be of a child. Plato thinks that his Myth, with its childish unconsciousness of difficulty, is valuable as enhancing our sense of the immensity of the difficulty, and so helping us to remove the difficulty—the

very difficulty which it makes appear more immense. When
we know the real cause of any particular difficulty of detail
we have got a grip of it, as it were, and can generally overcome it. We can never get this sort of grip of the difficulty
about the existence of Evil; for it is not a particular difficulty
with a particular discoverable solution, but a universal
difficulty—a contradiction inherent in the very nature of
the system under which we live—it puzzles us, and paralyses
us the more we try to remove it by arguing about the cause—
by particular explanations, after our fashion. But Plato's
Myth puts the difficulty once for all in its true place—
exhibits it, in its immensity, as universal; and the moral is—
You cannot solve it as you solve a particular difficulty.
Do not try to do so. See how immense it is! "Put it by"—

> The cloud of mortal destiny,
> Others will front it fearlessly—
> But who, like him, will put it by?

This is the first part of the answer which I venture to
offer to the question, How does Plato think that we are
helped out of a profound difficulty by a childish Myth?

The second part of the answer I venture to state as
follows: It is very hard to "put it by"—impossible unless
one fancies—it is enough merely to fancy—that one has
somehow, at least partly, solved the difficulty which one is
asked to "put by". An attempt to solve a fundamental or
universal difficulty logically, by a thin process of reasoning,
can only end in a sense of failure; but a childish Myth,
touching, as it is apt to do, a vast complex of latent sensi-
bilities, may awaken a feeling of vague satisfaction. A
childish Myth may thus, after all, seem to solve a fundamental difficulty, so far as to warrant one in "putting it by"
—the one important thing being that we should "put it by",
and act, not think about it and hesitate. I suggest, then,
that Plato's love of the Aetiological Myth is due to the
instinctive sympathy of his many-sided genius with this—
shall I call it weakness?—of human nature, which finds,
amid doubts and difficulties, some satisfaction in fantastic
explanation. Let me illustrate this weakness, with which I
suggest that Plato is in artistic sympathy, by an instance of

the use of the Aetiological Myth in Finnish mythology—by
the Story of the Birth of Iron in the *Kalewala*. But first let
me say a few words about the *Kalewala* by way of introduction to this story.

The great Finnish Epic, the *Kalewala*, was pieced together
about seventy years ago by Lönnrot out of Runes or Cantos
which had been, as they still are, sung separately by the
popular Laujola, or Minstrels. The Rune, or Canto, is the
unit of Finnish poetry, and may be fairly described as an
Aetiological Myth growing out of the magician's charm-
formula.

The chief personages in the *Kalewala* are not national
kings and warriors, as in other epics, but great magicians;
and the interest of the poem, or poems, is connected mainly
with the manner in which these great magicians show their
power over Nature, and Spirits, and Men. According to the
Finnish belief, everything done in life, even the simplest
thing done by the most ordinary person, has its appropriate
charm-formula—is successfully done in virtue of the
accompaniment of the suitable word or words—*e.g.* there is
a word for successfully laying the keel of a boat, and another
for fixing the ribs, and so on. If ordinary acts depend on
the utterance of the proper words, much more do the
extraordinary acts of great magicians. Wäinämöinen, the
chief magician-hero of the *Kalewala* Runes, when he was
building his magic boat forgot three necessary words, and
wandered over the whole Earth, and at last found his way
into the World of the Dead, in his search for these lost
words. Now these mighty words, which are the arms
wielded by the magician-hero, are mighty in that they
contain the *cause* of the thing on which he exercises his
power. He is confronted with difficulties and dangers in his
adventurous career, and it is by telling a difficult or dangerous thing its origin that he conquers it. If it is a wound
to be cured it is the Birth of Iron that the magician must
know and relate (*Kal.* ix. 29 ff.). If it is a monstrous bear
that he has to overcome he must first tell the story of the
Origin of the Bear (*Kal.* xlvi. 355). If it is a disease that
he has to exorcise, he can only do that by telling the disease
its hidden name, and the place from which it came, and

the way by which it came (*Kal.* xlv. 23). If it is a snake-bite to be healed, he must know the Ancestry of Snakes (*Kal.* xxvi. 695). Thus, out of the charm-formula of the magician-hero the Aetiological Myth arises—especially when the singer of the Rune, identifying himself, as he often does, with his magician-hero, uses the first person.

The *Kalewala* is a loosely connected collection of Cantos, in which magicians are the heroes, and charms the weapons, the charms being words which reveal the nature and origin of the things or persons overcome—magic words which the Finnish Rune-singers expanded into elaborate Aetiological Myths. Among other races it is the prayer at the sacrifice or offering, as Comparetti[1] observes, which is developed into the Hymn, and then into the Myth; it is only among the Finns that the charm-formula is so developed. Sorcery, not as elsewhere ritual and custom, is here the germ of the Aetiological Myth.

THE STORY OF THE BIRTH OF IRON[2]

Wäinämöinen, with blood streaming from a wound in his knee made by his axe when he was building a boat, hurries from place to place in his sledge, asking if any one knows the mighty words which will heal the "Iron's outrage". No one knows them. At last he comes to a house in which there is a little grey-bearded old man by the fireside, who, in answer to Wäinämöinen's question, calls out to him as he sits in his sledge at the door: "Wilder streams, greater rivers than this have ere now been tamed by three words of the High Creator." Wäinämöinen rose out of his sledge and crossed the courtyard and entered the house. A silver cup and a golden tankard were brought and soon were full of blood, and overflowing. The little old man cried out from the fireside: "Speak, who art thou amongst men, of what people and nation, that already seven great basins and eight tubs are filled with thy blood? All magic words I know, save only that one word, which declareth how Iron was fashioned how the rusty metal arose."

---

[1] *Der Kalewala, oder die traditionelle Poesie der Finnen*, p. 169 (German edition, 1892).
[2] I have translated this story (with considerable compression and omission) from the German version of the *Kalewala* by Hermann Paul, published at Helsingfors in 1885 to commemorate the fiftieth anniversary of the first publication of the Finnish Epic.

Then Wäinämöinen answered and said: "I myself know the source of Iron, and the first beginning of Steel.

"Heaven is the primaeval mother, Water is the eldest child, Iron is the youngest of the brethren, Fire is the middle son.

"Ukko, the Almighty Creator, the Ruler of the wide world, separated Heaven from Water, separated dry Land from Water, before that Iron grew up, before that the rusty metal arose.

"The Creator of Heaven, Ukko, rubbed together his right hand and his left and pressed his two hands together, and laid them both upon his knee; and straightway there came into being three fair women, lovely daughters of Nature, who caused Iron to come into being and the blue flashing Steel.

"Lightly the fair women floated away by the edge of the clouds, and their swelling breasts were full of milk. The milk ran down over the earth continually, over the fields, over the fens, over the still waters and lakes. Black it flowed from the breasts of the eldest, white in bright drops it fell from the breasts of the second, red from the breasts of the youngest. She from whom the black drops fell caused the soft Iron to come forth, she from whom the white drops fell produced the glancing Steel, she from whom the red drops fell brought forth the brittle Iron.

"After a while Iron would a-wandering go, to visit his elder brother Fire. But Fire was evilly minded towards him, and blazed up, and would have consumed him; but Iron escaped out of the hands of his fierce brother, out of the mouth of the devouring Fire, and hid himself under the earth, in the bog, in the deep-hidden spring, on the wide expanse of the fen where the swans build their nests, on the ridge of the mighty cliff where the eagle watches over his brood.

"So Iron lay deep in the moist fen, kept himself there for two years hidden; yea, even in the third year lay quiet between the crooked trunks, under the rotten birch-leaves.

"Yet could he not escape out of his brother's hands; again must he return into the power of wicked Fire, and be forged into tools and weapons.

"One day the Wolf ran over the fen, one day the Bear trotted growling over the moor. The footprints of the Wolf were plain, the Bear left his track behind; and lo! there the rusty Iron appeared, there the glancing Steel, in the broad footprints of the Wolf, in the Bear's great track.

"Ilmarinen, the cunning Smith, came into the world, was born on a coal-heap, grew up on the murky hill, with a hammer in his hand, and little tongs under his arm. In the night was he born, and on the morrow went forth to seek a smithy and a place for his bellows. He saw a piece of fenland, a wet morass; he went near to look at it; and there he built him his smithy and put up his bellows.

"Soon he marked the footprints of the Wolf and the track of the Bear on the fen, and saw the rusty Iron, found the Steel, discovered in the Wolf's broad footprints, in the Bear's great track.

"Then spake the Smith: 'O unhappy Iron! What is happened unto thee! What unworthy place is this that thou hast, under the Wolf's heavy feet, in the track of the clumsy Bear?'

"Thereafter he bethought him, and whispered to himself; 'What would come of it, if I cast the Iron into the Fire, into the sparkling glow?'

"Then did the anguish of the fear of death take hold of the Iron, when it heard the terrible name of Fire.

"But the Smith lifted up his voice, and said: 'Fear not, poor Iron; Fire hurteth not his brother. If thou enterest into the smithy, and layest thyself down in the furnace, thou shalt rise up again more beautiful, thou shalt become a sharp sword for men, a useful instrument for women.'

"The Smith took the Iron, and cast it on the glowing hearth, and on the first day stirred up the flame, and yet again on the second day, and the third. Slowly the glowing Iron was melted, and boiled up in bubbles, and spread itself, like leavened dough, within the flames of the mighty Fire.

"Then cried the Iron in anguish: 'O Smith, have compassion upon me; take me out of the burning Fire, out of the hot flaming glow!'

"Then answered the Smith: 'If I take thee now out of the Fire, thou mightest grow up to be evil, and all too dangerous; thou mightest murder thy nearest-of-kin, regarding not thine own brother.'

"Then Iron lifted up his voice, and swore a great oath, and said: 'There are still trees enough to fell, and stones enough to break: never will I hurt my brother, or do harm unto my nearest-of-kin. Better and fairer and more honourable 'tis to live as companion and servant of man, to be his friend, the weapon of his hand, than to be the enemy of one's kinsman, the destroyer of one's brother.'

"Then took Ilmarinen the Smith, the famous Smith, the poor Iron out of the Fire, and laid it on the anvil, and hammered it till it was bent to use; and therefrom he made sharp tools, axes and swords, and implements of every sort.

"Yet something was still lacking to the Iron, the Steel still needed something. The Iron's tongue lacked hardness, his mouth lacked the due sharpness. The Iron could not be forged hard, unless Water wetted it.

"The renowned Smith bethought him what he should do; and then he sprinkled a little ash upon Water, and dissolved it therein, and made a pungent bath, for to give hardness to the Iron and strength to the Steel.

"Carefully did he prove the Water with his tongue, and then said: 'The Water is not yet made fit to harden the rusty metal and the blue glancing Steel.'

"Behold a Bee came flying over the grass, sporting high and low on bright wings, flitting and humming round him.

"Then spake the renowned Smith: 'Here! Busy Bee! Bring me honey on thy wing, bring hither the noble juice, suck it from the cups of the flowers, to give the right hardness to the Iron, to give strength to the Steel.'

"Hiisi's evil bird, the Wasp, overheard the talk, as she peeped down from the roof. She gave heed secretly to all, she saw the rusty metal prepared, she saw the glancing Steel brought forth.

"In haste away flew the Wasp from thence, and gathered together Hiisi's horrors; she brought the black venom of the serpent, and the deadly poison of the adder, and the bitter froth of worms, and the corroding liquor of the toad, to give hardness to the Iron and strength to the Steel.

"Ilmarinen, the cunning workman, the renowned Smith, thought that the Busy Bee had brought him honey, had given him the noble juice; and he said: 'Now is the bath right to harden the rusty metal, to give strength to the blue Steel.'

"In the bath he dipped the Iron, without heed he cast the metal therein, when he had drawn it out of the Fire, out of the glowing forge.

"Then came it to pass that Iron was made hurtful, and did rend Honour even as a dog rendeth flesh, and broke the sacred oath which he sware, and murdered his own brother, and bit wounds into him with sharp mouth, and opened paths for the blood, and poured it out in foaming stream."

The little old man at the fireside cried aloud, and rocked his head to and fro, and sang: "Oh, now I know the Beginning of Iron, now I know who drave it to evil. Woe unto thee, thou luckless Iron! woe unto thee, thou deceitful Steel! Poor metal, taken captive by witchcraft! Is it thence that thou art sprung? Is it for this reason that thou art become a terror and hast too great mastery?

"Who moved thee to wickedness, who drave thee to treason? Was it thy Father or thy Mother? Was thy eldest Brother guilty of this? Was it thy youngest Sister, or some Friend, who counselled thee and turned thee to the evil deed?

"Neither Father nor Mother nor eldest Brother nor youngest Sister nor any Friend gave thee this counsel. Thyself hast thou done this wickedness, thyself hast thou accomplished the bloody deed.

"Iron! Look at this wound! Heal the evil thou hast done ere I go in anger with complaint against thee to thy Mother. The sorrow of the old woman thy Mother is increased if her child turneth himself to evil and doeth wickedness.

"Leave off, and run no more, thou foaming blood! hold in thy course, spout forth no more in long-curved bow, bespattering my head and breast! Stand like a wall immovable, like a fence, like the sedge by the water's side, like the grass in the slimy fen! Stand like the rocks upon the firm earth, like the cliff in the raging storm!

"If thou heedest not these words, I will devise other means: hither do I call Hiisi's Kettle to seethe the foaming blood therein, to make hot the red juice, so that not a drop shall flow away, so that the purple gore shall run down thereinto, and wet not the earth nor stream foaming over the ground.

"And if power be withheld from me myself to stay the endless flood, to become master of the wild stream, know that in Heaven there liveth a Father, a God dwelling above the clouds, who is the mightiest leech for the closing-up of bleeding wounds.

"Ukko, High Creator, Everlasting God of Heaven, hear me when I call unto thee in time of need! Lay thy soothing hand, thy finger which bringeth healing, on the wound, and be as a sure lock to close it.

"Take, O Lord, a healing leaf, spread a water-lily leaf to cover the opening, stay the strong current of the blood, so that it stain not my cheeks nor stream over my garments."

Therewith the old man shut the mouth of the wound, stayed the swift course of the blood; then sent he his son into the smithy to prepare a salve of the finest threads of the grass, of a thousand herbs of the field, of the flowers whence honey, healing balm, droppeth.

The boy brought the salve to his Father, saying: "Here is strong healing salve, able to cement stones together into one rock."

The Father proved it with his tongue, and found it good; and therewith he anointed the wounded man, saying: "Not by my own power do I this, but only through the power of the Highest."

Then he bound up the wound with silken bands, saying: "May the silk of the Eternal Father, the bands of the Almighty Creator, bind up this wound. Be gracious, O Heavenly Father, look down and help, put an end unto the bitter anguish, heal this wound without the sharpness of pain."

Then did Wäinämöinen, on a sudden, feel that he was healed; and soon thereafter the wound grew together, and was closed.[1]

A Myth like this of the Birth of Iron, amplified, indeed, and embellished by poetical art, but originally inspired by the childish belief in the value of words which set forth the cause, helps us, I think, to understand Plato's employment of the Aetiological Myth. Confronted by some profound difficulty, he lays it, or "puts it by", by means of a fanciful account of the origin of the state of things which presents the difficulty. He seems to feel that an Aetiological Myth is "a comfortable thing",[2] and a charm to conjure with when one is hard pressed.

The transition is easy from the point which we have now reached to Plato's Creation Myths—his Aetiological Myths *par excellence*. These are the *Timaeus* (which is one great Myth) and the Myth of Prometheus and Epimetheus in the *Protagoras* (320 c ff.).

In distinguishing these Myths as Aetiological from the strictly Eschatological Myths of the *Phaedo, Gorgias*, and the *Republic*, I do not ignore the eschatological prospect which is presented in them, especially in the *Timaeus;* but aetiological retrospect is what is really characteristic of them. It is the origin of the Universe, and of Man, Soul and Body, not the future life of Man's Soul, that these Myths are properly concerned with. They set forth the Ideas of Reason, Soul, Cosmos, and God, aetiologically in a Vision of Creation; and supply, moreover, a mythological deduction of Categories of the Understanding and Moral Virtues, which lies outside the scope of the strictly Eschatologi. al Myths; *i.e.* they deduce Categories and Virtues from their causes in the nature of God and the make of the Cosmos—they picture

---

[1] *Kalewala*, Runes 8 and 9, vol. i. pp. 95-124, German version by Hermann Paul (Helsingfors, 1885).

[2] "Prisms are also comfortable things" (Bacon, *Nat. Hist.* cent. x. 960).

N

for the imagination the orderly constitution of nature as
expressing the wisdom and goodness of God, and explain—
always for the imagination—the harmony subsisting between
that constitution and the faculties of the Soul.   Thus in
Timaeus 40 E - 42 E the *a priori* conditions of thought, the
modes in which the Understanding brings order into the
manifold of sense-experience, are set forth as due to impressions received by the Soul in its speculative journey
round the Heavens, when it rode on its star-chariot, and
saw the eternal laws of the Universe, and learned to move in
orbits of rational thought, similar to those which rule the
stars.

It will be convenient to begin our study of the Creation
Myths with the *Protagoras* Myth. It is on a small scale, and
by looking at it first the eye of imagination may perhaps be
prepared for the contemplation of the vast *Timaeus*. Although
it is only a small part of the *Timaeus* that the limits of this
work allow me to translate and comment on, I would ask the
reader to regard the whole book as one great Myth in which
the Ideas of Soul, Cosmos, and God are set forth in great
shapes for our wonder—in which the relation of the Created
Soul—World Soul and Human Soul—to the Creator, the
relation of the Human Soul to the Human Body, the Origin
of Evil, the Hope of Salvation, and other things which concern our peace, are made visible. The *Timaeus* is a Myth,
not a scientific treatise, although it was its fortune from the
very first to be treated as if it were the latter. No other
work of Plato's was so much read and commented on in
antiquity, and throughout the Middle Age, as the *Timaeus;*
and that chiefly because it was regarded as a compendium
of natural science, all the more valuable because its "natural
science" was not presented as something apart by itself, but
"framed in a theological setting". Aristotle, of course, treats
it *au pied de la lettre*.[1] With the Christian Platonists it took
rank as a scientific and theological authority along with the

---

[1] The reader may test the justice of this statement by referring to the
passages quoted in the *Index Arist.* s.v. "Timaeus Platonis dialogus"; and see
Zeller, *Plato*, p. 344, Eng. Transl.

Book of Genesis.[1] Dante's references to Plato's actual text are, I believe, all to passages contained in the *Timaeus*.[2]

Like the *Politicus* Myth, the *Protagoras* Myth is not spoken by Socrates; and Protagoras, the speaker, like the Eleatic Stranger in the *Politicus*, says that a Fable will come well from himself, an older man addressing younger men—Socrates and the others present.

---

[1] "Numenius the Platonist speaks out plainly concerning his master: What is Plato but the Attic Moses?" (Henry More's *Conjectura Cabbalistica*, Preface, p. 3; ed. 1662.) It was practically as author of the *Timaeus* that Plato was "*Moses Atticus*". Jowett (*Dialogues of Plato*, Introd. to *Timaeus*) has some interesting remarks on the text—"The influence which the *Timaeus* has exercised upon posterity is partly due to a misunderstanding."

[2] See Moore's *Studies in Dante*, first series, pp. 156 ff., and Toynbee's *Dante Dictionary*, arts. "Platone" and "Timeo [2]".

THE *PROTAGORAS* MYTH

CONTEXT

The scene of the Protagoras *is the house of Callias, a wealthy Athenian gentleman, to which Socrates takes his friend Hippocrates, that he may introduce him to the celebrated teacher of Rhetoric—or the Art of getting on in Life—Protagoras, who happens to be staying with Callias. Besides Protagoras they find two other Sophists of repute there, Hippias and Prodicus, also Critias and Alcibiades. Hippocrates wishes to become a pupil of Protagoras; and Socrates, after communicating his friend's wish to the great man, asks him, "What he will make of Hippocrates?" and Protagoras answers, "A better and wiser man"—that is, he will teach him how to do the right thing always in private and public life. Socrates expresses doubt as to whether the science of right conduct, or virtue private and political—for that is what Protagoras professes to be able to teach—can really be taught. The Athenians, as a body, apparently do not think that it can be taught, for they do not demand it of their politicians; nor do the wisest and best citizens think that it can be taught, for they never attempt to impart it to their sons.*

The Myth (together with the Lecture of which it is a part) is the answer which Protagoras now gives to the difficulties raised by Socrates. The object of the Myth and Lecture is to show, that virtue—or rather, the virtues, for Protagoras enumerates five: wisdom, temperance, justice, holiness, courage—can be taught.

When Protagoras has finished his Myth and Lecture, conversation is resumed between him and Socrates, and results in making it plain that the five virtues must be reduced to one—viz., to knowledge, which is represented as the art of measuring values—the values of the various objects which conduct sets before itself.

Thus it has been brought about that Protagoras must admit the conclusion that virtue is knowledge, unless he would contradict his own thesis that it can be taught; while Socrates, in showing that it is knowledge, confirms that thesis, which he began by disputing.

Protagoras 320 c—323 a

Time was when there were Gods, but mortal creatures after their kind were not. Now when the appointed time came unto these also that they should be born, the gods fashioned them under the Earth, compounding them of earth, and of fire, and of whatsoever is made by the mingling of fire and earth. Now when they were ready to bring them to light, they gave commandment unto Prometheus and Epimetheus to adorn them, and distribute unto each the powers that were meet. But Epimetheus entreated of Prometheus to let him distribute. "When I have distributed," quoth he, "do thou see whether it is done well."

So he prevailed with him, and distributed: and unto some he gave strength without swiftness, but the weaker he adorned with swiftness; unto others he gave weapons; and for those unto whom he gave not weapons he contrived other means of safety; to wit, unto those of them which he clothed with smallness he appointed winged escape, or habitation under ground; and unto those which he increased with bigness, the safety which cometh therefrom. After this fashion, then, did he distribute, ever making one gift equal unto another. These things he contrived, lest perchance any race should be cut off. But when he had furnished them with means for escaping destruction from one another, he contrived for them convenient defence against the seasons of the year, clothing them with thick hairs and stout hides sufficient to keep off the cold of winter and the burning heat; the which might also be for couches proper and native unto each one of them, when they went to their lairs. Moreover, he shod some of them with hoofs, and others with hairs and thick skin without blood. After that he appointed unto them different kinds of food: unto some the herbs of the earth, unto others the fruits of the trees, unto others roots; and some there were unto which he appointed for food the flesh of other beasts. And he ordained that they should bring forth young, some few, and others, which were devoured of these, many, that their race might be preserved.

Now, inasmuch as Epimetheus was not very wise, he unwittingly spent all the qualities he had upon the brutes; and lo! mankind was still left unto him unadorned, and he knew not what he should do concerning them.

While he yet doubteth, Prometheus cometh unto him to look into his distribution; and perceiveth that all other creatures are duly furnished in all things, but that man is naked and without shoes or bed or weapons: and now was come the appointed day on the which man also should go forth from the earth into the light.

Wherefore Prometheus, being brought to his wits' end to devise any means of safety for man, stealeth the cunning workman's wisdom of Hephaestus and Athena, together with fire—for without fire none can get this wisdom or use it; and this he giveth as a gift unto man.

Thus did man get the mechanic wisdom needful for his bare life; but the wisdom which is needful for the life political he had not, for it was with Zeus; and unto Prometheus it was no longer permitted to enter into the citadel, the dwelling-place of Zeus; moreover, the guards of Zeus were terrible; but into the common dwelling of Athena and Hephaestus, wherein they plied their craft, he secretly entered, and stole the fiery art of Hephaestus, and also Athena's art, and gave them unto man. Whence came convenient living unto man; but as for Prometheus, he was afterwards arraigned for theft because of Epimetheus, as the story telleth.

Now man, having been made a partaker of the divine lot, by reason of his kinship with the Godhead, alone among living creatures believed in Gods, and began to take it in hand to set up altars unto them and make graven images of them. Then soon with cunning device did he frame articulate speech and names, and invented houses to dwell in, and raiment and shoes to put on, and beds for rest, and food from the fruits of the earth.

Thus furnished, men at first dwelt scattered abroad, and there were no cities. Wherefore men were continually devoured by wild beasts, for they were altogether weaker than the beasts, and their craftsman's art could help them to get food enough, but was not sufficient for their war with the wild beasts; for they had not yet the art political, whereof the art of warfare is a part.

Wherefore they sought to assemble themselves together, and save themselves by building cities.

Now when they were assembled together, they wronged one another, because they had not the art political; so they were again scattered abroad, and were like to be destroyed.

But Zeus, fearing lest our race should perish utterly, commandeth Hermes to go unto men bearing modesty and justice, for the ordering of cities, and to be bonds joining men together in friendship. Hermes inquireth of Zeus how he shall give justice and modesty unto men. "Are these," quoth he, "to be distributed as the arts are distributed, the which are distributed after this wise—one man hath the art of physic, or some other art, and is sufficient unto many who have it not? Shall I distribute justice and modesty among men thus, or give them unto all?" "Unto all," said Zeus, "and let all be partakers of them. For if few were partakers as of the arts, cities would not arise. Also make it a law from me, that he who cannot partake of modesty and justice shall be put to death, for he bringeth plague into the city.

For this reason, O Socrates, the Athenians and others, when they consult about things which need the skill of the carpenter or other handicraftsman, think that few advisers are enough, and if any one who is not of those thrust himself forward to advise, they will have none of him. Thus do they, thou sayest. And I say 'tis but reasonable they should do this. But when they enter into counsel concerning those things that pertain unto virtue political, which must needs walk alway in the path of righteousness and temperance, then with reason do they bear with any man as a counsellor, considering that all men must partake of this virtue, else there could be no city.

Observations on the *PROTAGORAS* Myth

I

Before calling attention to some important points in this Myth, I must allude to a view maintained by some critics— that it is not a Platonic Myth at all, but only a Sophistic Apologue, or Illustrative Story, like Prodicus's *Choice of Hercules*. This view is stated, and objected to, by Grote in the following passage:[1]—

> The speech is censured by some critics as prolix. But to me it seems full of matter and argument, exceedingly free from superfluous rhetoric. The fable with which it opens presents, of course, the poetical ornament which belongs to that manner of handling. It is, however, fully equal, in point of perspicuity as well as charm—in my judgment, it is even superior—to any fable in Plato.
>
> When the harangue, lecture, or sermon of Protagoras is concluded, Sokrates both expresses his profound admiration of it, and admits the conclusion—that virtue is teachable— to be made out, as well as it can be made out by any continuous exposition.
>
> Very different, indeed, is the sentiment of the principal Platonic commentators. Schleiermacher will not allow the mythus of Protagoras to be counted among the Platonic myths. He says that it is composed in the style of Protagoras, and perhaps copied from some real composition of that Sophist. He finds in it nothing but a "coarsely materialistic way of thinking, which does not use philosophy beyond the physical experience" (*Introduction to the Pythagoras, vol. i*, pp. 233, 234).
>
> To the like purpose Ast (*Plat. Leb.* p. 71), who tells us that what is expressed in the mythus is, "The vulgar and mean sentiment and manner of thought of the Sophist; for it deduces everything, both arts and the social union itself, from human wants and necessity." Apparently these critics, when they treat this as a proof of meanness and vulgarity, have forgotten that the Platonic Sokrates himself does exactly the same thing in the *Republic*—deriving the entire social union from human necessities (*Republ.* ii. 369 c).
>
> K. F. Hermann is hardly less severe upon the Protagorean discourse (*Gesh. und Syst. der Plat. Phil.* p. 460).
>
> For my part, I take a view altogether opposed to these learned persons. I think the discourse one of the most

[1] *Plat.* ii. pp. 46, 47.

striking and instructive portions of the Platonic writings; and
if I could believe that it was the composition of Protagoras
himself, my estimation of him would be considerably raised.

Steinhart pronounces a much more rational and equit-
able judgment than Ast and Schleiermacher upon the
discourse of Protagoras (*Introduction to the Protagoras*, pp.
422, 423).[1]

I entirely agree with Grote; and hope that I shall be
able in the following observations to show reason for the
opinion that this is not a mere illustrative story, designed to
put popularly in a picture what might be put abstrusely,
but a genuine Myth containing suggestions of the kind which
must be put in the form of a myth or not at all. The mark
of a true Myth, it must be remembered, is that it sets forth
the *a priori* elements in man's experience. An Illustrative
Story or Allegory, as such, merely makes easier and more
pleasant the task of receiving and recalling *a posteriori* data.
This is the broad distinction between Myth and Allegory—
a distinction which we must not lose sight of, although we
observe that Allegory in the hands of a man of genius, like
Plato, or Dante, or Bunyan, always tends to become Myth;
and that there are few Myths, as distinguished from Allegories, which are not built up of parts, some of which are
Allegories.

While contending strongly for the view that the discourse
delivered by Protagoras is a true Myth, not an Allegory, I do
not forget that it is delivered by Protagoras. But even this,
I submit, is quite consistent with its being a Myth, and that,
even if Stallbaum (Note on *Protag.* 320 c) is right in thinking
that Plato is parodying Protagoras's style and borrowing
from his book *Concerning what was established at the beginning.*
The *Timaeus*, at any rate, is a Myth, although it is not
spoken by Socrates and imitates a style very different from
that of the Myths spoken by Socrates. If we are to take
the concrete view necessary to the proper understanding of
Plato's Myths as they come up individually for critical

[1] Professor Campbell (*Politicus*, Introd. p. xxxii.) is apparently with the
critics from whom Grote differs:—"The myth in the *Protagoras* . . . is meant
to convey an idea which Socrates combats, and which Plato evidently does
not fully accept. So also the elaborate myth of Aristophanes in the *Symposium*
contains a phase of thought about the Origin of Love which is afterwards
glanced at as an hypothesis of little value (*Sympos.* 205 E)."

judgment, we must allow for the dramatic circumstances of each case. The Myth told in the *Symposium* by Aristophanes, being told by Aristophanes, has a comic vein; similarly, the Myth put into the mouth of Protagoras is somewhat pompous and confused. None the less, these, I would contend, and the other non-Socratic Myths are. true Platonic Myths. It is always Plato the Dramatist who, through the mouth of Aristophanes, or Protagoras, or the Eleatic Stranger, sets forth for the Imagination the Universal of which the Scientific Understanding can give no account.

II

The second observation I have to make on the *Protagoras* Myth is that it sets forth the distinction between the Mechanical and the Teleological explanations of the world and its parts—the distinction with which Kant is occupied in his *Critique of Judgment*. According to Kant, the antinomy between these two explanations exists for the Determinant Judgment (the Judgment which, given the Universal, brings the Particular under it) but not for the Reflective Judgment (the Judgment which, given the Particular, finds a Universal by which to explain it). The Universal of Teleology—a Purpose, to serve which all things in the world are designed by a Personal God—is a Principle, or Universal, which may be posited by the Reflective Judgment, without contradiction, by the side of the mechanical principle of explanation—indeed, must be posited, for without the *guidance* it affords we could not understand the world at all; but, for all that, we are not warranted in assuming that it is a principle objectively existing and operative in the world. Natural objects which we can understand only as results of purpose may very well be due to mere mechanism. "Purposiveness is a concept which has its origin solely in the Reflective Judgment";[1] *i.e.* it is a Universal which we think of, which we find useful; but it does not, therefore, exist independently of our thought, as a real cause.

What[2] in the end does the most complete teleology prove? Does it prove that there is such an Intelligent Being? No.

---

[1] Bernard's Transl. of the *Critique of Judgment*, p. 18.
[2] Bernard's Transl. of the *Critique of Judgment*, pp. 311, 312, and 260, 261.

It only proves that according to the constitution of our cognitive faculties . . . we can form absolutely no concept of the possibility of such a world as this save by thinking a *designedly working* Supreme Cause thereof. . . . If we expressed ourselves dogmatically, we should say, "There is a God". But all we are justified in saying is, "Things are so internally constituted as if there were a God"; *i.e.* we cannot otherwise think that purposiveness which must lie at the bottom of our cognition of the internal possibility of many natural things, than by representing it, and the world in general, as a product of an Intelligent Cause—a God. Now, if this proposition, based on an inevitably necessary maxim of our Judgment, is completely satisfactory, from every *human* point of view, for both the speculative and practical use of our Reason, I should like to know what we lose by not being able to prove it as also valid for higher beings, from objective grounds (which are unfortunately beyond our faculties). It is, indeed, quite certain that we cannot adequately cognise, much less explain, organised beings and their internal possibility, according to mere mechanical principles of nature; and, we can say boldly, it is alike certain that it is absurd for men to make any such attempt, or to hope that another Newton will arise in the future, who shall make comprehensible by us the production of a blade of grass according to natural laws which no design has ordered. We must absolutely deny this insight to men.[1] But then, how do we know that in nature, if we could penetrate to the principle by which it specifies the universal laws known to us, there *cannot* lie hidden (in its mere mechanism) a sufficient ground of the possibility of organised beings, without supposing any design in their production? Would it not be judged by us presumptuous to say this?

Probabilities here are of no account, when we have to do with judgments of the Pure Reason; we cannot, therefore, judge objectively, either affirmatively or negatively, concerning the proposition: Does a Being, acting according to design, lie at the basis of what we rightly call natural purposes, as the cause of the world, and consequently as its author? . . . The teleological act of judgment is rightly brought to bear, at least problematically, upon the investigation of nature, but only in order to bring it under principles of observation and inquiry according to the *analogy* with the causality of purpose, without any pretence to *explain* it thereby. It belongs, therefore, to the Reflective and not to the Determinant Judgment. The concept of combinations and forms of nature in accordance with purposes is then at least *one principle more* for bringing its phenomena under

---

[1] Is Kant right here? This is the great Question of Philosophy.

rules where the laws of simply mechanical causality do not
suffice. For we bring in a teleological ground, when we
attribute causality in respect of an Object to the concept
of an Object, as if it were to be found in nature (not in
ourselves),[1] or rather when we represent to ourselves the
possibility of the Object after the analogy of that causality
which we experience in ourselves, and consequently think
nature technically as through a special faculty. If, on the
other hand, we did not ascribe to it such a method of
action, its causality would have to be represented as blind
mechanism. If, on the contrary, we supply to nature causes
acting *designedly,* and consequently place at its basis teleology, not merely as a *regulative* principle for the mere
judging of phenomena, to which nature can be thought as
subject in its particular laws, but as a *constitutive* principle of
the *derivation* of its products from their causes, then would
the concept of a natural purpose no longer belong to the
Reflective but to the Determinant Judgment. Then, in fact,
it would not belong specially to the Judgment (like the
concept of beauty regarded as formal subjective purposiveness), but as a rational concept it would introduce into a
natural science a new causality, which we only borrow
from ourselves and ascribe to other beings, without meaning
to assume them to be of the same kind with ourselves.

Now let us return to the *Protagoras* Myth, which I have
said sets forth the distinction between the teleological and
the mechanical methods of explaining the world and its parts.

In the animals as equipped by Epimetheus, Afterthought,
"who was not very wise," the world and its parts are presented as products of mere mechanism which are regarded by
foolish Afterthought as due to his own design. The qualities
with which Epimetheus equips the animals are only those by
which they barely survive in their struggle for existence. An
animal that is small and weak burrows in the earth, and
survives. But to suppose that its power of burrowing was
designed with a view to its survival is to forget that it was
only Afterthought who conferred the power, not Forethought.
To suppose design here is as unnecessary surely as it would
be to suppose that gold ore was hidden in the quartz in order
that men might have difficulty in finding it. As a matter of
fact, small weak animals that burrow are not generally found
by their enemies; as a matter of fact, animals with thick fur

---

[1] The proper understanding of the Doctrine of Ideas seems to me to
depend on the proper appreciation of the point here put by Kant.

do not generally perish in a cold climate; as a matter of fact, swift animals are not generally caught; as a matter of fact, prolific animals generally do not die off fast enough to become extinct. And yet Afterthought takes credit to himself for all this!

In such cases there is really no design—no Forethought, —merely the inevitable consequence of blind natural law; and it is only foolish Afterthought who pretends that there is design—Afterthought who always begins to reflect after the *fait accompli*, Afterthought the Father, as Pindar says, of Pretence.[1] But the pretence of Epimetheus is found out. He has nothing left wherewith to equip Man. He can seem to "design" only where mechanism really does the work— really produces the results which he pretends to produce by his "design". The various modes of structure and habit by which the lower animals correspond with their various environments (and the summary list of these modes given in the Myth shows that Plato has the eye of the true naturalist)—the various modes of animal correspondence— are indeed best accounted for mechanically, without any Epimethean pretence of teleology. But when we pass from the compulsion of mere animal survival to the beauty of human civilisation, we pass, Plato in this Myth seems to tell us, into another order of things. The mere survival of animals is not such a great thing that we must think of it as caused by Prometheus—as designed in the true sense; but the civilised life of Man is too beautiful and good a thing not to be designed in the true sense—not to be an end consciously aimed at by the Creator, who uses as his means the Art which Prometheus gave to a few, and the Virtue which Hermes placed within the reach of all. In short, Plato seems to say in this Myth that a teleological explanation of Man's Place in the Cosmos is indispensable. But let us note that the teleological explanation which he offers is conveyed in Myth. Plato's attitude here towards teleology is not different from Kant's, if allowance be made for the difference between the mythical and the

[1] Pindar, *Pyth.* v. 34.

critical ways of expression. "Though not for the Determinant, yet for the Reflective Judgment," says Kant,[1] we have sufficient ground for judging man to be, not merely, like all organised beings, a *natural purpose*,[2] but also the ultimate purpose of nature here on earth." It need hardly be said that the assumption or working hypothesis which Kant here makes on behalf of Man does not stand alone. If oaks could speak, they would say that the Oak is "the ultimate purpose of nature here on earth".

III

My next observation is on the account given of the origin of Virtue in the *Protagoras* Myth.

The gift of Epimetheus is nature—bodily structure and function, with the instincts and habits thereon dependent, whereby the lower animals correspond accurately, but blindly, with a narrow immediate environment; the gift of Prometheus to Man, whose mere nature is not adequate to the wider environment into which his destiny advances him, is Art, which, though imparted to few, benefits the whole race by completing nature, to borrow the phrase in which Aristotle[3] expresses the close relation existing between Nature and Art. Plato, too, wishes us to look at the relation as a close one; for in the Myth Prometheus takes up his brother's unfinished work. But morality (as distinguished, on the one hand, from natural constitution—the gift of Epimetheus to animals, and, on the other hand, from acquired skill in some department—the gift of Prometheus to a few men)—virtue, as distinguished from nature and art, is distributed by Hermes to all men. All men have implanted in them what may be called "an original moral sense", which education appeals to and awakens. All men are capable of morality as they are capable of speech. Virtue is "learnt" as one's mother tongue is learnt, without

---

[1] Bernard's Transl. of the *Crit. of Judgment*, p. 35.

[2] "An organised product of nature (a natural purpose) is one in which every part is reciprocally purpose (end) and means." Bernard's Transl. of *Crit. of Judgment*, p. 280; cf. Watson's *Selections from Kant*, p. 345.

[3] *Phys.* ii. 8, 199 a 15.

any special instruction like that through which some particular art or craft is acquired by a person specially capable
of acquiring it.   Here the resemblance and difference
between Virtue and Art—a subject approached by Plato
from many sides—is viewed from yet another side, in Myth,
and, therefore, we may take it, with deep insight into its
metaphysical import.   Art, though it is the gift of Prometheus,
and distinguishes Man, as working for consciously realised
future ends, from the brutes, which, at most, live in a
dream of the present, is still only "a completion of nature",
and Man does not yet live the true life of Man under the
régime of Prometheus.   The gift of Prometheus, indeed,
came from Heaven, but it was stolen.   The Godlike intelligence of Man employs itself in the pursuit of objects which,
though really means under the providence of the Creator
to the ultimate realisation of the true human life, are not
yet regarded by Man himself as more than means to the
convenient life of the dominant animal on earth.   Man,
having received the stolen gift, conquers the lower animals;
yet still man is a wolf to man.   But the gift which makes him
see, with the eye of justice and respect, his fellow-man as
an End along with himself in a Kingdom of Ends—this
gift was not stolen, but is of the Grace of God.   It is given
to all men, or at least is a godsend which all may hope in
the course of life to find; and it is given in greater measure
to some men than to others.   Great teachers of the moral
ideal arise, like great poets, specially inspired; and their
power, whether manifested in the silent example of their
lives, or in the prophetic utterance of Myth, is felt in its
effects by all; but the secret of it is incommunicable.[1]

The gift of virtue in greater measure is not, indeed,
alluded to in the *Protagoras* Myth, but it is, after all, merely
an eminent instance of the gift as described in that Myth.
The gift of virtue, whether in less or greater measure, is of
the Grace of God.   Such a doctrine is properly conveyed
in Myth; and the discourse of Protagoras in which it is
conveyed is, I submit, a true Myth, because it sets forth the

[1] See *Meno,* 99, 100.

a priori, not, as Schleiermacher and some other critics maintain, a mere Sophistic Apologue or Allegory illustrating and popularising *a posteriori* data.

"As to the myth brought forward by Protagoras," says Schleiermacher,[1] "there is no need to number it as some have done, good-naturedly raising it to an exalted rank, among those of Plato's own; on the contrary, if not the property of Protagoras himself, as seems likely, though there is no evidence to confirm the supposition, yet the manner in which Plato applies it makes it much more probable that it is, at all events, composed in his spirit. For precisely as is natural to one of a coarsely materialistic mode of thinking, whose philosophy does not extend beyond immediate sensuous experience, the reasoning principle in men is only viewed as a recompense for their deficient corporeal conformation, and the idea of right with the feeling of shame, as requisite for a sensuous existence, and as something not introduced into the minds of men until a later period."

"Not introduced into the minds of men until a later period!" This objection appears to me to be founded on a misunderstanding of what a Myth is and does. It is of the very essence of a Myth to represent as having a history in time what in itself is out of time. The Soul, which is the Subject of all experience in time, is mythologically set forth as an Object or Thing whose creation, incarnation and earthly life, disembodied state and penance, re-incarnation and final purification or damnation, can be traced as events in time. How absurd to draw inferences from the chronology of such a history! It is not the historical question, When the mind received the idea of Virtue, whether later or sooner, that Plato is really concerned with; but the philosophical question, What is the true nature of Virtue—of the Virtuous Soul—of the Soul itself at its best? "The Soul to Plato," as Hegel[2] says, "is not a *Thing* the permanence or non-permanence of which we may discuss, but a *Universal*." Yet in Myth this Universal is necessarily set forth as a *Thing* permanent throughout a succession of changes in

---

[1] *Introduction to the Protagoras*, p. 96, Dobson's Transl.
[2] *Gesch. der Phil.* vol. xiv. p. 187 (1842).

time. It is indeed no easy matter always to remember that a Myth is a Myth.

IV

A Myth may be told in painting, or embroidery, or sculpture, as well as in words; and I am going to conclude these remarks on the *Protagoras* Myth by asking the reader to look at a sarcophagus in the Capitoline Museum on which the mystery of Man's birth and life and death is rendered for the eye in a relief representing, naively enough, the history of the Butterfly-Soul and its Clay Body, the handiwork of Prometheus.[1]

There sits Prometheus with a basket of clay beside him; on his knees a little human figure standing, which he supports with his left hand; while his right hand, holding the modelling stick, is drawn back, its work finished. On the head of the little human figure Athena lightly sets a butterfly. Behind and above, Clotho spins the thread of life, and Lachesis draws the horoscope on a globe of the Heavens. It is morning, for Helios with his chariot and horses is rising on the left hand. Beneath him is seated Gaia with her horn of plenty; near him lies Oceanus with his rudder in his hand; while the Wind-God blows through his shell; and, half hidden among these elemental powers, Eros kisses Psyche.

Now let us turn from the Morning and Day of the sculptured Myth, and look at its Evening and Night. On the right of the two central figures, Prometheus and Athena, close by Athena with her butterfly, stands Night, a tall draped woman, above whom is Selene in her car, with her veil making a crescent behind her in the wind as she rides. At the feet of Night lies a Youth, dead, with his butterfly-soul fluttering near. Death, with down-turned torch, is bending over the corpse, and Fate sits at its head unrolling a scroll on her knee; while the Soul of the Youth—now a

---

[1] The version of the Myth presupposed by the Capitoline artist is plainly Neo-Platonic. In the Myth as Plato has it in the *Protagoras*, Prometheus does not make Man. On the Capitoline sarcophagus (No. 446 [13], described by Helbig, *Führer durch die öffentl. Sammlungen klass. Alterth. in Rom.*, vol. i. p. 341; and cf. Mitchell, *History of Anc. Sculpture*, p. 693), he does; just as, in Plotinus, *Enn.* iv. 3. 13 (quoted p. 230 *infra*), he—not, as in Hesiod, *O. et D.* 49 ff., Hephaestus—makes Pandora.

O

little-winged human form—led by Hermes, is already on its westward way to Hades.

This is the front of the sarcophagus; and the two ends include the mystery of the front in a larger mystery. On the one end is Hephaestus at his forge, and the fire is burning which Prometheus stole. On the other end the sin is punished—Prometheus lies bound upon Caucasus, and the vulture sits over him; but Heracles, with his bow bent, is coming to deliver him.

V

(*Excursus on Allegory*)

The story of Prometheus, whether as told in the *Protagoras*, or as represented on the Capitoline sarcophagus, is, I am prepared to maintain, a genuine Myth—sets forth a mystery which the scientific understanding cannot fathom. At the same time, it is a Myth which evidently lends itself more easily than those which we have hitherto examined to allegorical interpretation, and, indeed, in Neo-Platonic hands became the subject of very beautiful allegorical interpretation. It would seem, then, that at the *Protagoras* Myth we have reached the stage in our review of the Platonic Myths at which some connected remarks may be offered on a point which has been already alluded to—the Difference between Myth and Allegory; and along with Allegory we may consider Parable.

I remarked a little while ago that a composition which, as a whole, is a Myth, and not an Allegory, is often found to be built up of parts, some of which are Allegories. The *Phaedrus* Myth and the *Divina Commedia* are compositions of this build. This partly explains the circumstance that even the noblest Myths have so often fallen an easy prey to allegorical interpretation. Because the parts are plainly Allegories, it is supposed that the whole is an Allegory. And there are no limits to allegorical interpretation. Any Myth—nay, any true account of historical events or of natural phenomena—can be interpreted as an Allegory, setting forth any dogma, religious, philosophical, or scientific.

The importance of the part played by the allegorical interpretation of Homer in the Greek philosophical schools, of the Old Testament History among the Alexandrine Jews and Christian Fathers, and of the Platonic Myths among the Neo-Platonists,[1] cannot easily be over-estimated by the historian of philosophical and religious thought. As early as the time of Xenophanes[2] it was felt that the tendency of the popular mythology was immoral. "Homer and Hesiod," he says, "have ascribed to the Gods all things that are a shame and a disgrace among men—thefts and adulteries, and deception of one another." With this verdict Plato is in entire agreement (*Rep.* 378 D); but not with the method of allegorical interpretation (see *Phaedrus*, 229), which attempted to save both Homer and morality.[3] Plato, objecting to the allegorical interpretation of Myth on literary and philosophical grounds, as well as on the practical ground alleged in *Rep.* 378 D—that children cannot distinguish between allegorical and literal meaning—banishes Homer from the educational curriculum, and in lieu of his stories, since children must begin with stories, substitutes newly invented stories—moral tales, we may suppose, for he gives no specimens—in which Gods and human beings behave in a manner which can, and ought to, be imitated, just as the good people behave in some modern story-books for the young.

But in his objection to the allegorisation of Homer Plato stands almost alone. The line generally taken by the Greeks after, as well as before, Plato's time was that Homer is an inspired teacher, and must not be banished from the curriculum. If we get beneath the literal meaning, we find him teaching the highest truth. The allegorical interpretation of Homer began doubtless in the spirit of apology for revered scriptures found to conflict with modern notions; but it soon became an instrument of historical research and meta-

---

[1] "The Myths were accepted by common consent as the text for the deepest speculations of the later Platonic schools, and so have contributed, through them, more largely that any other part of Plato's writings to the sum of common thoughts."—Westcott's *Essays in the History of Religious Thought in the West* ("The Myths of Plato"), p. 46.

[2] He was alive in 479 B.C.; see Burnet, *Early Greek Philosophy*, 1st Ed., p. 111.

[3] On the allegorisation of Homer, beginning with Theagenes, see Lobeck, *Aglaoph.* pp. 155 ff.; the feeling which prompted it is expressed in the aphorism, "Homer blasphemed, unless he was using allegory".

physical speculation.[1] Few were content to confine themselves with Plutarch to the plain ethical lessons to be drawn
from Homer and the poets as picturing human life and
nature—to read, for example, the story of *The Intrigue of
Aphrodite and Ares*, if not simply for the story, at any rate
for nothing more abstruse than the lesson that luxury leads
to such intrigue.[2] Such simple teaching did not satisfy
either the historians or the philosophers.

The Centaurs (Palaephatus tells us) were a body of
young men from the village of Nephelê in Thessaly, who
first trained and mounted horses for the purpose of re-
pelling a herd of bulls belonging to Ixiôn, King of the
Lapithae, which had run wild and done great damage;
they pursued these wild bulls on horseback, and pierced
them with their spears, thus acquiring both the name of
Prickers[3] and the imputed attribute of joint body with the
horse. Aktaeôn was an Arcadian, who neglected the cultivation of his land for the pleasures of hunting, and was
thus eaten up by the expense of his hounds. The dragon
whom Kadmus killed at Thêbes was in reality Drako, King
of Thêbes; and the dragon's teeth which he was said to

[1] —and perhaps also of literary embellishment. "Ion's allusion to his
embellishments of Homer, in which he declares himself to have surpassed
Metrodorus of Lampsacus and Stesimbrotus of Thasos, seems to show that,
like them, he belonged to the allegorical school of interpreters" (Jowett's
Introduction to the *Ion*).

[2] Plutarch, *de Audiendis Poetis*, c. 4. The *de Aud. Poet.* is worth careful
study in connection with the allegorisation of Homer, against which it is a
protest. On the one hand, Poetry is to be read for the entertainment which
may be derived from a "good story" simply as a "good story"; thus Homer
bids Odysseus look carefully at the things in Hades, *in order that he may go
and tell his wife about them*—

> But strive quickly to return to the light, and ponder all
> these things, in order that you may tell them to your
> wife hereafter.

On the other hand, Poetry is to be read for the lessons in morality and
worldly wisdom which may be learnt from the characters and conduct of
the personages portrayed; but let not the young think that these personages
are abstract types—all-good or all-bad; the poets draw for us real men,
mixed of good and bad qualities. Poetry is "the imitation of characters and
lives of men who are not perfected and pure . . . of those who are mixed in
feelings and false opinions; through their finer nature, however, often turning
towards what is better" (c. 8). These are the advantages to be derived
from Poetry. We must partake of it with caution, however, for it is like the
polypus—pleasant to eat, but often gives bad dreams (c. 1).

It ought to be noted that, where Egyptian Myths are concerned, Plutarch
does not eschew the method of allegorical interpretation; but see remarks on
de Is. et Osir. § 78, in Prof. Dill's *Roman Society in the Last Century of the Western
Empire*, pp. 76, 77.

[3] *Kentores.*

have sown, and from whence sprung a crop of armed men, were in point of fact elephants' teeth, which Kadmus as a rich Phoenician had brought over with him: the sons of Drako sold these elephants' teeth and employed the proceeds to levy troops against Kadmus. Daedalus, instead of flying across the sea on wings, had escaped from Krête in a swift sailing-boat under a violent storm; Kottus, Briareus, and Gygês were not persons with one hundred hands, but inhabitants of the village of Hekatoncheiria in Upper Macedonia, who warred with the inhabitants of Mount Olympus against the Titans; Scylla, whom Odysseus so narrowly escaped, was a fast-sailing piratical vessel, as was also Pegasus, the alleged winged horse of Bellerophôn.[1]

While those interested in history adopted this method of "natural explanation"[2] in dealing with Myths, the philosophers adopted the method to which it is best to confine the description "allegorical interpretation". Homer's whole story, and the proper names which occur in it, have a hidden religious, philosophical, scientific meaning which it is the work of the method to unfold, by discovering analogies and etymologies. So far as etymologies were concerned, this method probably owed something to the lead given by Plato himself in the *Cratylus;* but while Plato's etymologies are put forward playfully, and as it were in the guise of myths, the etymologies of the Stoics and other allegorisers of Myth seem to be seriously offered as the meanings which Homer really had in his mind when he used the names. "Zeno first," says Cicero,[3] "after him Cleanthes and then Chrysippus, took quite unnecessary pains to interpret the meaning of imaginary tales, and to explain the reasons why each of their names should be called what it is." Two examples of the Stoic method will be sufficient, with a general reference to Zeller's *Stoics, Epicureans, and Sceptics*, pp. 334 ff. (Eng. Transl.).

The one God of many names is called Zeus from living ($z\bar{e}n$): as manifest in air he is called Hera, from *aer:* as manifested in water he is called Poseidon, from *posis:* as manifested in aether he is called Athena, from *aither:* and so on.[4]

[1] Grote's *Hist. of Greece*, part i. ch. 16, vol. i. pp. 342, 343, edit. 1862.
[2] See Zeller's *Stoics, Epicureans, and Sceptics*, p. 335, n. 1, Engl. Transl.
[3] Cic. *de Nat. Deor.* iii. 24, 63.
[4] Diog. Laert. vii. 147.

"If Hephaestus," says Heraclitus the Stoic, "intended
the shield of Achilles to be a representation of this world,
what else is thereby meant but that, by the influence of
primary fire, matter has been shaped into a world?"[1]

The Jews, Palestinian and Alexandrine, before and
after Philo's time,[2] following the lead given by the Greek
interpreters of Homer, applied the allegorical method to
the Old Testament scriptures. One may estimate the
length to which allegorical interpretation of the Old Testament was carried by Guilds[3] and others before Philo's time

[1] See Zeller's *Stoics, etc.*, p. 340, Eng. Transl. "The Stoics", says Dr.
Bigg (*The Christian Platonists of Alexandria*, p. 146), "assure us that the heathen
deities are but symbols of the forces of nature, and turn the hideous myths
of Zeus or Dionysus into a manual of physical science."
  On the general subject of the allegorisation of Homer, both before and
after Plato's time, the reader may consult, in addition to Lobeck, referred to
above, Mr. Adam's note on *Rep.* 378 D, 24, with authorities cited there;
Zeller's *Stoics, Epicureans, and Sceptics*, pp. 334 ff., Eng. Transl.; Jowett's
Dialogues of Plato, Intod. to *Rep.* p. xxxviii.; and Grote's *History of Greece*,
part i. ch. 16, from which I extract the following passage (vol. i. p. 344, edit.
1862):—"It remains that we should notice the manner in which the ancient
myths were received and dealt with by the philosophers. The earliest expression which we hear, on the part of philosophy, is the severe censure
bestowed upon them on ethical grounds by Xenophanes of Kolophôn, and
seemingly by some others of his contemporaries. It was apparently in reply
to such charges, which did not admit of being directly rebutted, that
Theagenês of Rhegium (about 520 B.C.) first started the idea of a double
meaning in the Homeric and Hesiodic narratives—an interior sense, different
from that which the words in their obvious meaning bore, yet to a certain
extent analogous, and discoverable by sagacious divination. Upon this
principle he allegorised especially the battle of the Gods in the *Iliad*. In
the succeeding century, Anaxagoras and Metrodôrus carried out the
allegorical explanation more comprehensively and systematically; the former
representing the mythical personages as mere mental conceptions invested
with name and gender, and illustrative of ethical precepts—the latter
connecting them with physical principles and phaenomena. Metrodôrus
resolved not only the persons of Zeus, Hêrê, and Athênê, but also those of
Agamemnôn, Achilles, and Hectôr, into various elemental combinations and
physical agencies, and treated the adventures ascribed to them as natural
facts concealed under the veil of allegory. Empedocles, Prodicus, Antisthenes,
Parmenides, Heracleides of Pontus, and, in a later age, Chrysippus and the
Stoic philosophers generally, followed more or less the same principle of
treating the popular Gods as allegorical personages; while the expositors of
Homer (such as Stesimbrotus, Glaucôn, and others, even down to the Alexandrine age), though none of them proceeded to the same extreme length
as Metrodôrus, employed allegory amongst other media of explanation for
the purpose of solving difficulties, or eluding reproaches against the poet."
  Grote, in a footnote (p. 345, n. 1) to the foregoing passage, calls attention
to the ethical turn given to the stories of Circe, the Sirens, and Scylla, by
Xenophon, *Mem.* i. 3, 7, and ii. 6, 11-31.
[2] The allegorising Jewish school began two hundred years before Philo
(fl. A.D. 39); see Gfrörer, *Urchristenthem*, i. 83.
[3] See Conybeare's *Philo, de Vita Contemplativa*, p. 293: the Servants (also
called suppliants—ascetic Jewish congregations or guilds) allegorised the
Pentateuch. This was necessary in order to make Gentile converts, who
looked for Plato in Moses.

from the circumstance that even Philo himself was alarmed. The allegorising of the Law, he thought, makes for laxity in the observance of it.[1] The wise man will *both* seek out the hidden meaning, *and* observe the letter of the Law. He will allegorise without breaking with old custom.[2] But where the allegorisation, not of the Law, but of the History of the Old Testament scriptures, is concerned, Philo proceeds without fear. At once an ardent Platonist and a Hebrew of the Hebrews, he assumed the substantial accuracy of the narrative of events given in the Old Testament from the creation of the world downwards throughout the whole history of his Race; and, at the same time, he believed that the history of his Race was not mere history—it was philosophy, or rather theology, as well as history. The events recorded were not only true in fact; they constituted also a continuous revelation of hidden meaning. He looked at the history of his Race both as a chronicle of actual events, and as a great miracle-play in which dogma was put on the stage of this visible world. This double point of view is very difficult to enter into; but we must enter into it, so far, at least, as to treat it very seriously, if we are to understand the "tendency" of certain currents of religious and philosophical thought which have prevailed since his day, even down to the present time. Here is a passage from his book *Concerning the Sacrifices of Abel and Cain*,[3] in which the allegorical interpretation of "sacred history" reminds us of the method by which not only "sacred history" but traditional dogma is, in our own day, being rewritten as "philosophy":—

For Abraham, coming with great haste and alacrity, commands Virtue, Sarah, to hasten and ferment three measures of meal, and to make cakes under the ashes, when God, attended by two Supreme Powers, Dominion and Goodness, Himself one in the middle, produced three images in the visual soul, each of which it is impossible to measure (for His Powers also are not to be circumscribed), but they measure all things. His Goodness is the measure of the good, His Dominion the measure of things subject; and the Ruler Himself the measure of every thing corporeal

[1] See Conybeare's *Philo, de Vita Cont.* pp. 300, 301.
[2] See Gfrörer, *Urchristenthum*, i. 104.
[3] *De Sacrif. Ab. et Caini*, (15), 59, ed. Cohn, p. 173, Mangey.

and incorporeal. . . . It is good for these three measures
to be fermented, as it were, and commingled in the soul,
that being persuaded of the existence of a supreme God,
who surpasses His Powers, and is either seen without them,
or appears with them, it may receive impressions of His
might and beneficence, and be initiated in the most perfect
mysteries.

In the Old Testament history, then, Philo recognises at
once a higher, or mystic, and a historical, or literal, sense—
definition according to the hidden meaning—allegory, and
the literal determination.[1] The personages in the book of
Genesis are at once historical, and "modes of the soul".
Adam is "the earthborn Man"; the fact of his existence is
historical, but the details of his history are mythical, and
must be interpreted allegorically: thus his rib is legendary—
nobody can take it literally.[2] Noah is justice, Enoch hope,
Moses the prophetic reason. Similarly, Egypt is the body,
Canaan piety.[3] Again—and here Philo's Platonism prevails
—it was not God, but the Logos, who appeared in the
burning bush.[4] Spiritual men are satisfied, he says, with
the truth that God exists; but the many need an anthro-
pomorphic God. Moses gives God feet and hands, on
account of the weak understanding of his readers. This is
as it ought to be. Moses is like the physician who must
keep his patient in ignorance of the truth. But for the educated
reader such representations of God are dangerous. They
lead to Atheism, and the only true method of dealing with
them is that of Allegory.[5] The allegorical wisdom, the
possession of the few wise, is compared by Philo to the
Hellenic Mysteries: "Receive these Mysteries, Candidates,
with purified ears, for they are holy."[6] Here, of course, Philo
borrows directly from Plato,[7] who often compares Philosophy,
especially when Myth is its vehicle, to initiation, as in
Sympos. 209 E, 210 A, and in *Phaedrus*, 249 C, 250 B.[8] But
it is only a phrase that Philo borrows from Plato. What a

---

[1] Gfrörer, *o.c.* i. 84. [2] Gfrörer, *o.c.* i. 98, 99.
[3] Gfrörer, *o.c.* i. 88. [4] Gfrörer, *o.c.* i. 87.
[5] Gfrörer, *o.c.* i. 97.
[6] Philo, *de cherubim*, Mang. i. 147; Gfrörer, *Urchristenthum*, i. 100.
[7] As he does also at the end of the passage quoted above from the *de
Sacrif. Ab. et Cain.*
[8] See Couturat, *de Platonis Mythis*, p. 55.

Myth is Philo does not understand. A Myth is indeed a mystery and remains a mystery. Philo and his following are only concerned to make it something understood.

For the employment of the method of allegorical interpretation by the Christian Fathers I cannot do better than refer the reader generally to Dr. Bigg's *Christian Platonists of Alexandria*, especially to Lecture iv., and to Hatch's *Hibbert Lectures*, 1888, Lecture iii., on *Greek and Christian Exegesis*. To these references I would add a quotation from Professor G. Adam Smith's *Modern Criticism and the Preaching of the Old Testament*, pp. 226-228:—

> The early fathers were interested in the Old Testament mainly for its types and predictions of Christ. The allegorical became the orthodox exegesis, and was at last reduced to a theory by Origen, and elaborated into a system by the school which he founded. . . . When the heretics began to outdo the orthodox in allegorical exposition, the latter awoke to the dangers of the habit they had fostered, and loudly proclaimed the need of sobriety and reason in the pursuit of it. But the historical sense of the age was small, and till the close of the 4th century no exegete succeeded in finding his feet on a sound historical basis. [Theodore of Mopsuestia (350-429) was the father of historical exegesis.] To Theodore the types and prophecies of the Old Testament had, besides their references to the future, a prior value in themselves and for the age in which they were delivered.[1]

It is perhaps worth reminding the reader that the Christian Fathers had high authority for their allegorical interpretation of the Holy Scriptures. St. Paul (*Gal.* iv. 22-26) had authorised such interpretation:—

> It is written that Abraham had two sons, the one by a bondmaid, the other by a freewoman. But he who was of the bondwoman was born after the flesh; but he of the freewoman was by promise. Which things are an allegory:

[1] Chrysostom, in his commentary of Isaiah (vol. vi. p. 17, ed. Montfaucon), took the same line:—"But I," he says, "do not despise this interpretation" (allegorical), "and the other" (historical) "I declare to be more exact." Commenting on the new line of exegesis taken by Theodore and Chrysostom, Professor G. Adam Smith brings out its significance in one admirable sentence (p. 321): "Recognise that the fundamental meaning of the prophecies must be that which they bore to the living generation to whom they were first addressed, and you are at once inspired by their message to the men of your own time."

for these are the two covenants; the one from the Mount
Sinai, which gendereth to bondage, which is Agar. For
this Agar is Mount Sinai in Arabia, and answereth to
Jerusalem which now is, and is in bondage with her
children. But Jerusalem which is above is free, which is
the mother of us all.[1]

In the Philosophy of Plotinus and the Neo-Platonic
School the allegorical interpretation of Myths—especially of
those which describe and account for the Fall and Ascension
of Souls after the manner of the *Phaedrus* Myth and the
Discourse of Diotima—holds a position the importance of
which it would be difficult for the student of the development
of religious thought to exaggerate. No more can be attempted here than to give a general idea of the Neo-
Platonic method of dealing with these Myths; and perhaps
the following specimens may be sufficient for this purpose.

Plotinus (*Enn.* iv. 3. 13), adhering to the Orphic doctrine
which Plato sets forth in the *Phaedrus* Myth, speaks of the
Descent of Souls into the bodies prepared for them as taking
place, for each Soul, at an appointed time:—"To each soul
its own point of time. When that comes it descends as at
the cry of a herald, and enters the appropriate body."
Their descent, he says, is fated or determined by universal
law; and yet it is free, for, in embodying themselves, Souls
obey a universal law which is realised *in themselves*. They
are free, as Intelligence is free, for they obey the necessity
which is that of their own nature:—"And the Mind, which is
before the world, is destined to remain wholly there above,
and to send downwards. What is sent is the Particular
which exists in the System of the Universal. For the
Universal lies in close relation with the Particular, and the
Law does not hold from outside the power by which it is
fulfilled, but is given among those existences in whom it
lives, and they bear it with them."

"This Cosmos, then," he continues, "having many Lights,
and being illumined by Souls, receiveth beauty added unto
beauty from the great Gods and from the Intelligences which

---

[1] Similarly in 1 *Peter* iii. Noah's ark, wherein "eight souls were saved by
water", is allegorically interpreted as Baptism. In the Old Testament,
Hosea (xii. 1-5) allegorises, according to the writer of art. "Allegorical
Interpretation" in the *Jewish Encycl.*

bestow Souls. And this, methinks, is the meaning of that Myth which telleth how that, when Prometheus—that is Forethought—had fashioned a woman,[1] the other gods did thereafter adorn her: one gave unto this creature of earth and water human speech, and beauty as of a goddess; and Aphrodite gave unto her one gift, and the Graces another, and all the other gods added their several gifts; and she was called Pandora, because that all gave unto her who was fashioned by the Forethought of Prometheus. But whereas Epimetheus, who is Afterthought, rejected this gift of Prometheus, the Myth thereby signifieth that the choice of that which partaketh more of the nature of the Intelligible is the better choice. Yea, the Maker is himself bound, for he hath contact of some sort with that which hath proceeded from him, and is therefore constrained by bonds which are without. But whereas Heracles releaseth him from his bonds, the Myth signifieth that he hath in him a Power whereby he is yet able to attain unto deliverance from these bonds."[2]

Another Myth from which the Neo-Platonists drew largely was that of Narcissus.[3] Their interpretation of this Myth hinges on the identification of the "Mirror of Dionysus" with the "Bowl of Dionysus."[4] The Soul remains at peace in its heavenly home, till it sees its own image in the water of this mirror. It plunges into the water to embrace the image, and drinks forgetfulness of its heavenly estate:— "For seeing," says Plotinus (*Enn.* I. vi, 8), "those beauties which appear in bodies, he must not run after them, but knowing them to be images and vestiges and shadows, he must flee to that of which they are the images. And if any one should pursue them, wishing to take them as real, they would be like a fair image borne on water, and when

---

[1] In Hesiod, *O. et D.* 49 ff. Hephaestus, not Prometheus, makes Pandora; and Prometheus warns his brother not to accept her, but he pays no heed to the warning.

[2] Plot. *Enn.* iv. 3. 14; and see A. Ritter, *die Psychologie des Plotin* (1867), p. 42. Pandora is the World endowed by the Soul with ideal gifts.

[3] See Ovid, *Met.* iii., and Pausanias, ix. 31, for this Myth.

[4] See Macrobius, *in Somn.* i. 12. 66: "This is what Plato noted in the *Phaedo*, (*sic*) that the mind is drawn into the body shivering with fresh intoxication, wishing it to be understood as a new material inundation, in which it is with difficulty controlled. The sign of this mystery is the starry bowl itself of Father Liber and this is what the ancients called the River of Lethe, and Father Liber himself the Orphics believe is to be understood as *material intelligence*." Lobeck, who quotes this passage from Macrobius (*Aglaoph.* p. 736), criticises it as departing from the original conception of the *bowl*, which is that of the bowl in which Plato's Demiurgus mixes the ingredients, first of the World-Soul, and then of human souls.

he desires to seize it (as some allegory describes in riddles, it seems to me), plunging to the bottom of the stream, he disappears. In the same way, he who grasps beautiful bodies and will not let them go, is submerged not only in body but in soul, within the dark depth hateful to his own mind, where, remaining blind in Hades, he dwells among shadows, there as here.

"Let us flee then, to the beloved Fatherland, as one should more soundly advise. What then is this flight?" etc.: and again in *Enn.* IV. iii. 12 he says—"The souls of men, seeing their own images as if in the mirror of Dionysus, leaped down from above, but were not cut off from their source in the divine mind. For not with Mind did they come, but though they have descended as far as the earth, their heads have remained above the heavens. It befell them to go deeper, since that midmost part of them was forced by the bondage of the mind to have regard for that to which it was fixed. But Father Zeus, pitying their toils, makes the bonds in which they labour, perishable, and gives cessation in time, freeing them from their bodies, in order that they may dwell there, and be themselves, where the Soul of all ever is, not concerned with this world."[1] Souls, then, descending, at their appointed times, come to the water which is the Mirror of Dionysus, and enamoured of their own images reflected therein—that is, of their mortal bodies—plunge into the water. This water is the water of oblivion, and they that drink of it go down into the cave of this world.[2] The wise soul drinks moderately; for to drink deeply is to lose all recollection of the intelligible world. The wise soul is thus the "dry" soul, as the phrase of Heraclitus[3] seems to be understood by the Neo-Platonists who quote it.[4] The dry soul hearkens, in this life, to the genius who accompanies her in her descent: but, over all the genii of

---

[1] See Lobeck (*Aglaoph*, p. 555, for the place of the mirror in the Zagreus Myth; and Rohde (*Psyche*, ii. 117) for Zagreus as a type, along with Narcissus, of the passage of the Unity of the World-Principle into the multiplicity of sensible phenomena.

[2] "To the soul the body is a chain and tomb, and the world a cavern and grotto," Plot. *Enn.* iv. 8. 3; and cf. iv. 8. 1, where the doctrine of the Fall or Incarnation of Souls, as set forth by Plato in the *Phaedrus* and *Timaeus* and by Empedocles, is reviewed.

[3] See Bywater's *Heracliti Eph. Reliquiae*, lxxiv. lxxv.

[4] See Creuzer, *Plotinus de Pulch.* p. xxxvi.

particular souls, Eros rules as chief genius. Creuzer[1] mentions a picture in which Narcissus is represented as gazing at his own image in the water, and the Heavenly Eros as standing with a sad countenance behind him. "The youthful Narcissus," says Ficino,[2] "that is, the mind of a thoughtless and untried man, does not see his own face. He turns his regard by no means to his proper substance and worth, but pursues his reflection in water and tries to embrace it. That is to say, he admires beauty in a perishable body, like moving water, which is the shadow of his own rational soul."

The moral of the Narcissus Myth is: Free thyself by "ecstasy" from the life of flux and sensible appearances— escape from the Stream of Pleasure and the Flesh[3]—the Stream of Generation, which is the "Mirror of Dionysus".[4]

With the Myth of Narcissus thus allegorised, the Neo-Platonists brought the story of Odysseus into very close relation. Thus the passage quoted above from *Enn.* i. 6. 8, in which the immersion of the Soul in the Stream of Sense is described, is immediately followed by a passage in which the deliverance from that stream is compared to the flight of Odysseus from the enchantments of Circe and Calypso:— "But what is this flight? How shall we conduct it? As they say allegorically that Odysseus did, fleeing from the enchantress Circe, or Calypso.

"He took no joy in his sojourn with them, although participating in pleasures of sight and loveliness of sense. That is our Fatherland, whence we came, and there our Father resides. What then is this journey and this flight? It is unnecessary to travel with feet, for feet carry one only from one country to another. Nor is it necessary to prepare a chariot with horses, or a seafaring craft, but you must lay aside all these and not regard them, but close your eyes to arouse and awaken another sight, which everyone possesses, but few put to use."

Similarly, Numenius (quoted by Porphyry, *de Ant.*

[1] *Plot. de Pulch.* p. lxiii.

[2] Ficinus, *in Plat. Sympos.* cap. 17, quoted by Creuzer, *Plot. de Pulch.* p. lxviii.

[3] See Creuzer, *Plot. de Pulch.* pp. lvi. lvii.

[4] I take it that the Mirror of Dionysus of the Neo-Platonists is due to a "conflation" of the Narcissus Myth and the Zagreus-Dionysus Myth.

Nymph. cap. 34)[1] makes Odysseus the image of intellect gradually, through various incarnations, freeing itself from the flesh—"the image of what goes through the succession of generation, and is thus restored to the infinite, outside all waves and the sea."

Again, a Pythagorean quoted by Stobaeus, *Ec. Phys.* i. 52, p. 1044, says, "Homer calls the revolution in the cycle and circuit of rebirth, Circe, daughter of the Sun: and Eustathius, in *Od.* i. 51 says: About Calypso, if she was a queen, as the geographers have handed down, the ancients have hardly exaggerated. For they reshape her in allegory as our body, as concealing within, justice and the pearl of the soul who herself took possession of Odysseus the philosopher, as a man imprisoned in the flesh. And to speak allegorically, in the seagirt island which was embowered in woods, which was the navel of the sea, this is to be in the moist element, and as Plato would say, ebbing and flowing (*Timaeus* 43 A) . . . of Hermes, indeed, the poet spoke in riddles that he acted as a mediator, that is, the Logos, and became according to philosophy the longing for his native land, and guided him to the intelligible world, which is, according to the followers of Plato, the true fatherland of souls. Similarly, released and delivered from this Calypso, he found Penelope, or philosophy." With words to the same effect Apuleius closes his treatise *de Deo Socratis:*—"Nor does Homer teach you otherwise regarding that same Ulysses, who always desired Prudence for his companion, whom he called Minerva by poetic custom. Therefore in her company, he encountered all dangers and overcame all adversity. So by her counsels he entered the cave of the Cyclops but emerged again, he saw the oxen of the sun, but abstained from taking them, he descended to the lower world but came up again. Accompanied by that same Wisdom he sailed past Scylla, and was not seized: he was enclosed by Charybdis, but not held: he drank the potion of Circe, but was not transformed: he reached the Lotus-eaters, but did not remain with them: he listened to the Sirens, but did not visit them."[2]

---

[1] See Creuzer, *Plot. de Pulch.* p. lxxii.

[2] Bacon's allegorical interpretation of three myths—that of Pan, that of Perseus, and that of Dionysus—in his *de Augmentis Scientiarum*, ii. cap. 13, is worth comparing with the Neo-Platonic examples given above.

Beautiful as the Neo-Platonic allegorisation often is, I venture to think that the less we associate it with our reading of Plato's Myths the better. The Neo-Platonists did not understand the difference between Myth and Allegory. Allegory is Dogma in picture-writing; but Myth is not Dogma, and does not convey Dogma. Dogma is gained and maintained by Dialectic, which, as Stallbaum says (note on *Rep.* 614 B), "cannot be applied to the elucidation of the subjects with which Myth deals, any more than it can, at the other end of the series, be applied to the elucidation of the particulars of sense, as such."

For light in understanding Plato's Myths, it is to the independent creations of other great mythmakers, such as Dante, that we must go, not to the allegorical interpretations of the Neo-Platonists and their like.[1]

What Plato himself thinks of allegorical interpretation we know from a passage near the beginning of the *Phaedrus* (229):—In reply to the question of Phaedrus, whether he thinks that the story about Orithyia being snatched away by Boreas from the height overlooking the Ilissus is a true story, Socrates says, that if he took the learned line, he might answer, "Yes, it may be true that once upon a time a girl called Orithyia was blown by the wind over the cliff and killed". But such rationalism, imposing and ponderous, is surely not very happy as a method, for if you begin to employ it, where are you to stop? You will have to rationalise all the stories in Greek mythology, expending a great deal of matter-of-fact cleverness on an interminable task, and leaving no time for anything worth doing. As for himself, he declares that, not yet having satisfied the Delphic injunction, "Know thyself," he should be acting ridiculously if he spent his precious time over the interpretation of these stories: he is willing to receive them as they are told, and believe them just as other people believe them.[2]

---

[1] For Zeller's opinion of the Neo-Platonic interpretation of Diotima's Myth in the *Sympos.* see his *Plato*, p. 194, n. 66 (Engl. Transl.).

[2] Grote, *Hist. of Greece*, part i. ch. xvi. vol. i. pp. 362 ff. (ed. 1862), has remarks of exceptional value on this passage, and generally on Plato's attitude to the old mythology. "Plato," he says, "discountenances all attempts to transform the myths by interpretation into history or philosophy, indirectly recognising the generic difference between them. . . . He shares the current faith, without any suspicion or criticism, as to Orpheus, Palamedes, Daedalus, Amphion, Theseus, Achilles, Chiron, and other mythical personages; but

Dr. Westcott, in his charming and suggestive essay on "The Myths of Plato" (the first of his *Essays in the History of Religious Thought in the West*), to which every student of the subject must feel himself under great obligation, contrasts Myth and Allegory in the following words:—

> In the allegory the thought is grasped first and by itself, and is then arranged in a particular dress. In the myth, thought and form come into being together: the thought is the vital principle which shapes the form; the form is the sensible image which displays the thought. The allegory is the conscious work of an individual fashioning the image of a truth which he has seized. The myth is the unconscious growth of a common mind, which witnesses to the fundamental laws by which its development is ruled. The meaning of an allegory is prior to the construction of the story: the meaning of a myth is first capable of being separated from the expression in an age long after that in which it had its origin.

It will be understood that I do not agree with the suggestion contained in the last sentence. I do not recognise the competence of interpretation to separate the "meaning" from the "expression" of a Myth. I hold that Myth has no *dogmatic* meaning behind its literal sense. Its "meaning" is, first, its literal sense—the story which is told; and then, beyond this, the *feeling* which it calls up and regulates. The further one is removed from the age in which a Myth had its origin, the more difficult it must be to recover its "meaning" of this second sort—that is, the feeling which it called up and regulated in its maker and his immediate audience. Our task is not the facile one of reading our own

---

what chiefly fills his mind is the inherited sentiment of deep reverence for these superhuman characters and for the age to which they belonged. . . . The more we examine this sentiment, both in the mind of Plato, as well as in that of the Greeks generally, the more shall we be convinced that it formed essentially and inseparably a portion of Hellenic religious faith. The myth both presupposes, and springs out of, a settled basis and a strong expansive force of religious, social, and patriotic feeling, operating upon a past which is little better than a blank as to positive knowledge. It resembles history, in so far as its form is narrative; it resembles philosophy, in so far as it is occasionally illustrative; but in its essence and substance, in the mental tendencies by which it is created, as well as in those by which it is judged and upheld, it is the popularised expression of the divine and heroic faith of the people." See further, vol. i. pp. 370 ff., for a summary of Grote's whole discussion of Greek Myths in part i. of his *Hist. of Greece.* I am acquainted with no discussion of them which appears to me so informing and suggestive as Grote's.

doctrines into a Myth which has come down to us, but the vastly difficult one of entering sympathetically into the life of a prophet in a bygone world.

While the conversion of old narratives, mythical or historical, into Allegories has most often been the congenial work of prosaic persons, "using an unpolished skill," it has sometimes been taken up by the great poets themselves with happy effect. Let me conclude this part of the subject with one instance of this—Dante's beautiful allegorisation of the story of the three Marys at the Sepulchre:—

> Mark saith that Mary Magdalene, and Mary the mother of James, and Mary Salome went to find the Saviour at the Sepulchre and found Him not, but found a young man clothed in a white garment, who said unto them: "Ye seek the Saviour; I say unto you that He is not here; but be not affrighted; go and tell His disciples and Peter, that He will go before them unto Galilee; and there shall ye see Him, as He said unto you."
>
> By these three women are signified the three sects of the active life, the Epicureans, the Stoics, and the Peripatetics, which go unto the Sepulchre, to wit, this present World, which is the receptacle of corruptible things, and seek for the Saviour, to wit, beatitude, and find it not; but they find a young man clothed in a white garment, who, according to the testimony of Matthew and also of the others, was the Angel of God; thus, Matthew saith, "The Angel of God descended from heaven, and came and rolled back the stone and sat upon it, and his countenance was like lightning, and his raiment like snow."
>
> This Angel is the Nobility of our Human Nature which cometh, as it is said, from God, and speaketh in our Reason, and saith unto each of these sects—that is, unto every man who seeketh beatitude in the active life—"It is not here; but go and tell the disciples and Peter"—that is, those who go about seeking it, and those who have erred from the right way, like Peter who had denied Him—"that He will go before them into Galilee"—that is, that beatitude will go before them into Galilee—that is, into the life of Contemplation. Galilee signifieth *whiteness;* and as whiteness is more full of corporeal light than any other colour, so is Contemplation more full of spiritual light than any other thing here below. And he saith, "will go before": he saith not, "shall be with you"; thus giving us to understand that God alway goeth before our Contemplation; here can we never overtake Him who is our highest beatitude. And he saith, "There shall ye see Him, as He said"—that is, there

P

ye shall have of His joy, to wit, felicity, as it is promised
unto you here—that is, as it is surely ordained that ye may
possess it.

Thus it appeareth that we can find our beatitude (which
is this felicity of which we speak), first imperfect in the
active life, that is, in the conduct of the moral virtues, and
then perfect—after a certain fashion—in the conduct of the
intellectual virtues.[1]

Hitherto we have considered the allegorical interpretation of narratives, mythical or historical, which the interpreters found ready to hand. Let us now pass to narratives
deliberately constructed for the illustration of doctrine or
the inculcation of moral conduct. When doctrine is illustrated with more or less detail, such narratives are best
called Allegories; when moral conduct is inculcated, Parables
—that term being retained for little vignette-like stories
which present some bit of conduct to be carefully noticed,
imitated, or avoided.

In Plato himself we have examples of deliberate allegorical composition in the Allegory of the "Cave" (*Rep.* 514 ff.),
in that of the "Disorderly Crew" (*Rep.* 488 A ff.), and in
that of the "Birdcage" (*Theaet.* 197 c). The "Choice of
Hercules", composed by Prodicus (Xen. *Mem.* ii. 1. 21 ff.),
is another example; the piece known as "The Tablet of
Cebes" is another; and the beautiful story of "Cupid and
Psyche", told by Apuleius (*Met.* iv. v. vi.),[2] is another.
The story of Pandora also, as given by Hesiod (*O.D.* 49 ff.),
has much in it which must be ascribed to deliberate intention. The class of Parables, strictly so called, is represented by many of the Parables of the Old Testament and
of the Gospels—by stories like "The Prodigal Son", as
distinguished from stories like "The Sower", which are
really Allegories.

---

[1] *Conv.* iv. 22.

[2] Mr. A. Lang, in his Introduction to William Adlington's *Translation of
the Cupid and Psyche of Apuleius* (1566), shows how dependent the maker of an
allegorical story often is on Myth. The Allegory of "Cupid and Psyche" is
composed on the framework of a Myth which explains a custom—the widely
distributed custom according to which the bridegroom must, for some time
after marriage, seek the bride secretly in the dark. See also *Custom and Myth*,
pp. 64 ff. Dr. Bigg (*Neoplatonism*, pp. 128-133) gives a charming epitome of
the story, with its interpretation. Referring to Mr. Lang's folk-lore, he says
(p. 129), "This artistic composition has very little indeed to do with Hottentots
or Zulus. It is really a very elaborate piece of allegory, metaphysics without
tears." I agree with both Mr. Lang and Dr. Bigg.

There are also narratives with a purpose, which, like *The Pilgrim's Progress*, are at once Allegories and Parables as distinguished from Allegories. What strikes one most in these narratives originally written to be Allegories or Parables is: How much more effective they are than old Myths tampered with by rationalism and converted into Allegories. These Allegories originally written to be Allegories, indeed, present doctrine often thinly disguised, but their makers have to exercise creative imagination, not merely scholastic ingenuity. The best of them are true Myths as well as Allegories, and appeal to us, at any rate, by their tales of mankind, if not always by power of calling up Transcendental Feeling—a power which properly belongs to less consciously planned products of genius. Why is *The Pilgrim's Progress* a Possession for Ever? Not because it is an ingenious Allegory setting forth doctrine rigorously held by its author; not because it has a good moral tendency, like Plato's tales for children; but because it is a Myth—an interesting, touching, humorous, mysterious story about people—because its persons, albeit "allegorical", are living men and women, sometimes, like Molière's or Shakespeare's, active in the dramatic movement of the story, sometimes sketched as they stand, like the people in the *Characters* of Theophrastus.

And I slept, and dreamed again, and saw the same two Pilgrims going down the Mountains along the High-way towards the City. Now a little below these Mountains, on the left hand, lieth the Country of *Conceit;* from which Country there comes into the way in which the Pilgrims walked, a little crooked Lane. Here, therefore, they met with a very brisk Lad, that came out of that Country. So *Christian* asked him *From what parts he came, and whither he was going?*

Ignor. Sir, I was born in the Country that lieth off there a little on the left hand, and I am going to the Celestial City.

Chr. But how do you think to get in at the Gate, for you may find some difficulty there?

Ignor. As other good people do, said he.

Chr. But what have you to shew at that Gate, that may cause that the Gate should be opened to you?

Ignor. I know my Lord's will, and I have been a good liver; I pay every man his own; I pray, fast, pay tithes, and give alms, and have left my Country for whither I am going.

Chr. But thou camest not in at the Wicket-Gate that is

at the head of this way; thou camest in hither through that same crooked Lane, and therefore I fear, however thou mayest think of thyself, when the reckoning day shall come, thou wilt hear laid to thy charge that thou art a Thief and a Robber, instead of getting admittance into the City.

Ignor. Gentlemen, ye be utter strangers to me, I know you not; be content to follow the Religion of your Country, and I will follow the Religion of mine. I hope all will be well. And as for the Gate that you talk of, all the world knows that that is a great way off of our Country. I cannot think that any man in all our parts doth so much as know the way to it, nor need they matter whether they do or no, since we have, as you see, a fine pleasant Green Lane, that comes down from our Country the next way into the way.

When *Christian* saw that the man was wise in his own Conceit, he said to *Hopeful* whisperingly, *There is more hopes of a fool than of him.* And said, moreover, *When he that is a fool walketh by the way, his wisdom faileth him, and he saith to everyone that he is a fool.* What, shall we talk further with him, or outgo him at present and so leave him to think of what he hath heard already, and then stop again for him afterwards, and see if by degrees we can do any good of him?

*   *   *   *   *   *

So they both went on, and *Ignorance* he came after.

*   *   *   *   *   *

I saw then in my Dream that *Hopeful* looked back and saw *Ignorance*, whom they had left behind, coming after. Look, said he to *Christian*, how far yonder youngster loitereth behind.

Chr. Ay, ay, I see him; he careth not for our company.

Hope. But I tro it would not have hurt him, had he kept pace with us hitherto.

Chr. That's true, but I warrant you he thinketh otherwise.

Hope. That I think he doth, but, however, let us tarry for him. So they did.

Then *Christian* said to him, Come away man, why do you stay so behind?

Ignor. I take my pleasure in walking alone, even more a great deal than in Company, unless I like it the better.

Then said *Christian* to *Hopeful* (but softly), Did I not tell you he cared not for our company? But, however, said he, come up, and let us talk away the time in this solitary place. Then directing his speech to *Ignorance*, he said, Come, how do you? How stands it between God and your Soul now?

Ignor. I hope well; for I am always full of good motions, that come into my mind to comfort me as I walk.

Chr. What good motions? pray tell us.

Ignor. Why, I think of God and Heaven.

Chr. So do the Devils and damned Souls.

Ignor. But I think of them and desire them.

Chr. So do many that are never like to come there. *The Soul of the Sluggard desires, and hath nothing.*

Ignor. But I think of them, and leave all for them.

Chr. That I doubt, for leaving all is an hard matter— yea, a harder matter than many are aware of. But why, or by what, art thou persuaded that thou hast left all for God and Heaven.

Ignor. My heart tells me so.

Chr. The wise man says, *He that trusts his own heart is a fool.*

Ignor. This is spoken of an evil heart, but mine is a good one.

Chr. But how dost thou prove that?

Ignor. It comforts me in hopes of Heaven.

Chr. That may be through its deceitfulness, for a man's heart may minister comfort to him in the hopes of that thing for which he yet has no ground to hope.

Ignor. But my heart and life agree together, and there-fore my hope is well grounded.

Chr. Who told thee that thy heart and life agree together?

Ignor. My heart tells me so.

*   *   *   *   *   *

Now while I was gazing upon all these things, I turned my head to look back, and saw *Ignorance* come up to the River-side; but he soon got over, and that without half that difficulty which the other two men met with. For it happened that there was then in that place one *Vainhope*, a Ferry-man, that with his Boat helped him over; so he, as the other I saw, did ascend the Hill to come up to the Gate, only he came alone; neither did any man meet him with the least en-couragement. When he was come up to the Gate, he looked up to the writing that was above, and then began to knock, supposing that entrance should have been quickly administered to him; but he was asked by the men that looked over the top of the Gate, Whence came you? and what would you have? He answered, I have eat and drank in the presence of the King, and he has taught in our Streets. Then they asked him for his Certificate, that they might go and shew it to the King. So he fumbled in his bosom for one, and found none. Then said they, Have you none? But the man answered never a word. So they told the King, but he would not come down to see him, but commanded the two Shining Ones that conducted *Christian* and *Hopeful* to the City, to go out and take *Ignorance*, and bind him hand and foot, and have him away. Then they took him up, and carried him through the air to the door that I saw in the side of the Hill, and put him in there. Then I saw that there was a way to Hell even from the Gates of Heaven, as well as from the City of *Destruction*. So I awoke, and behold it was a Dream.

Now the day drew on that *Christiana* must be gone. So the Road was full of People to see her take her Journey. But behold all the Banks beyond the River were full of Horses and Chariots, which were come down from above to accompany her to the City Gate. So she came forth and entered the River, with a beckon of Farewell to those that followed her to the River-side. The last word she was heard to say here was, *I come, Lord, to be with thee and bless thee.*

So her Children and Friends returned to their place, for that those that waited for *Christiana* had carried her out of their sight. So she went and called, and entered in at the Gate with all the Ceremonies of Joy that her Husband *Christian* had done before her.

*   *   *   *   *   *

In process of time there came a Post to the Town again, and his business was with Mr. *Ready-to-halt*. So he enquired him out, and said to him, I am come to thee in the name of him whom thou hast loved and followed, tho' upon Crutches; and my message is to tell thee that he expects thee at his Table to sup with him in his Kingdom the next day after *Easter*, wherefore prepare thyself for this Journey.

Then he also gave him a Token that he was a true Messenger, saying, *I have broken thy golden bowl, and loosed thy silver cord.*

After this Mr. *Ready-to-halt* called for his fellow Pilgrims, and told them, saying, I am sent for, and God shall surely visit you also. So he desired Mr. *Valiant* to make his Will. And because he had nothing to bequeath to them that should survive him but his Crutches and his good Wishes, therefore thus he said, *These Crutches I bequeath to my Son that shall tread in my steps, with a hundred warm wishes that he may prove better than I have done.*

Then he thanked Mr. *Great-heart* for his Conduct and Kindness, and so addressed himself to his Journey. When he came at the Brink of the River he said, *Now I shall have no more need of these Crutches, since yonder are Chariots and Horses for me to ride on.* The last words he was heard to say was, *Welcome Life.* So he went his way.

The test, indeed, of a good Allegory is that it is also a good Myth, or story, for those who do not understand, or care for it, as a vehicle of doctrine. To this test the Parables spoken by Jesus appear to have been consciously accommodated. He often spoke to the common people in Parables without interpreting them. These Parables were received by the common people as Myths; afterwards He interpreted them as Allegories to His disciples. Many of His Parables, indeed, as was suggested above, have no interpretation. Stories like the Parables of the Prodigal Son, of the Rich Man who proposed to build barns, of Dives and Lazarus, of the Good Samaritan, are not Allegories to be interpreted— for they have no "other meaning"—but rather little dramas "which reduce to a single incident what is continually occurring in man's experience".[1]

And even those Parables which are Allegories and admit of detailed doctrinal interpretation, such as the Parable of the Sower, have an intrinsic value apart from the doctrine which they convey—the value of pictures in which common things stand *reflected*—stand as images, or doubles, for our wonder, in another world, under another sky.[2] When one looks at Millet's "Sower",[3] it is easy to put oneself in the place of those who heard Parables gladly without asking for the interpretation of them.

Let us now look at Plato's two most elaborate "Allegories" —the "Cave", and the "Disorderly Crew"; and let us remind ourselves of the features of the former[4] by first referring to *Republic*, 532 B, C, where a summary of the whole is given in one sentence:—" 'On the other hand,' I said 'the release from their bonds and their transition from the shadows of the images to the images themselves and to the light, and their ascent from the cave into the sunlight, and the fact that even when they are still unable to see the animals and plants and the light of the sun, except as reflections in water, which are indeed divine, and shadows of reality, and not shadows of images thrown by another such light as may itself be called an image when compared

[1] Réville, *Prolégomènes de l'Hist. des Religions* (Engl. Transl. by Squire), p. 110.

[2] See Shelley's poem, *The Recollection*, quoted *infra*, p. 357, where I attempt to show that a charm like that belonging to reflected images, or doubles, of natural objects—as of trees (or of Narcissus himself) in a pool— enters into the effect produced by the word-pictures of Poetry.

[3] In the gallery of the Metropolitan Museum of Art, New York.

[4] *Republic*, 514 A ff.

with the sun—all this work of the arts which we have
described, has this power of exalting the noblest part of the
soul towards the contemplation of the highest reality, as in
that other instance the clearest organ in the body was led
to the contemplation of what was brightest in the visible
world'."—There is a Cave in form of a long tunnel which,
retaining throughout the dimensions of its entrance, runs
down, with a steep decline, into the earth. Some way
down, where the daylight at last fails, a great Fire is
burning, and beyond the Fire there is a low wall built
across the Cave at right angles to its direction. Over the
top of this wall showmen hold up and move about little
images of men and animals. The shadows of these images
are thrown on the rock with which the Cave ends some
way beyond.[1] Facing this end-rock of the Cave and the
shadows thus thrown on it are Prisoners bound so that they
cannot turn round. These Prisoners, whose knowledge is
confined to shadows of images, represent people who have
nothing better than second-hand, hearsay knowledge of
"particular facts". But the "Philosopher" comes down from
the daylight into the Cave, and unbinds some of them, and
"converts" them—turns them round, so that they see the
showmen's little images, the "realities" of these shadows.
These converted ones represent people who have direct,
first-hand knowledge of "facts". Some of these the Philosopher is able to lead up the steep floor of the Cave, past
the Fire, which is the Visible Sun, and out into the daylight,
which is the light of the Intelligible Sun, the Good, the
source of existence and true knowledge. At first the released
prisoners are so dazzled by the daylight that they cannot
bear to look at the things illuminated by it—men, animals,
trees—much less at the Sun itself, but can look only at
shadows of men and animals and trees on the ground, or
reflections of them in water. These shadows and reflections,
however, differ from the shadows seen on the end-rock of
the Cave, in being shadows, not of images of real things,

---

[1] In the Pitt-Rivers Museum at Oxford there is a Javanese *Wayang
Kulit*, used, in the Historical and Mythological Drama, for the production of
shadow-representations.   The shadows of puppets (made of leather) are
thrown on a screen, the performer manipulating the puppets from behind,
and working their arms by means of sticks.

but of real things themselves—they represent the diagrams of geometry, and, generally, the symbols and concepts employed in the deductive sciences to express the principles or laws with which the inquiry is really concerned. In time, the eyes of the released prisoners become accustomed to the daylight, and men, animals, trees, the moon and stars, and, last of all, the Sun, can be looked at. We have now reached the end of all education—the direct apprehension of the ideas, or Principles, which severally, and as connected system, explain particulars, just as the living man once seen "explains" the showman's image of him.

I have called the "Cave" an Allegory. It certainly is an Allegory, and is offered as such together with its interpretation.[1] But when a great poetic genius like Plato builds an Allegory, the edifice, while serving its immediate purpose as an Allegory, transcends that purpose. Plato *sees* the Cave and *makes us see* it, and there is much more to be seen there than the mere purpose of the Allegory requires. Perhaps Plato, when he was at Syracuse, saw such a gallery in the stone quarries (there are such galleries still to be seen in the *Latomie* at Syracuse) lighted up with a fire, and the miners— it may be slaves or convicts in chains—working at the far end with their backs to the fire, while their shadows and the shadows of people and things behind them flitted on the walls. Be this as it may, Plato's Cave is a mysterious place. We enter it wondering, and soon forget, in our wonder, that there is "another meaning". We acquiesce in what we see— the prisoners among the shadows, and the Redeemer coming down through the dimly-lighted gloom, like Orpheus,[2] to lead them up into the daylight. The vision which Plato's "Allegory" calls up is such as his great Myths call up; it is a vision which fills us with amazement, not a pictorial

---

[1] See Couturat, *de Plat. Myth.* p. 51, who regards the "Cave" as an Allegory. Schwanitz, *die Mythen des Plato*, p. 9, on the other hand, calls the "Cave" a *myth*, and brings it into close comparison with the Prometheus-and-Epimetheus Myth in the *Protagoras*:—"If the images of the cave alluded to the differences in human knowledge, which depended on the degree to which the bonds which hold it back had been discarded, then the myth of Prometheus and Pandora, on the other hand, is a prelude to the truth that God has impressed on all souls the image of the One, that all participate in the One, in respect for virtue, in a sense of justice, and the communal bonds which link states together."

[2] The book *Descent to Hades* (see Lobeck, *Aglaoph*, p. 373) may have been in Plato's mind.

illustration which helps us to understand something.[1] Its nearest parallel in literature is that vision which Dante on a sudden calls up before our eyes in *Inferno*, iv. 46-63:—

'Tell me, Master, tell me Lord', I began, desiring to be assured of that Faith which overcomes every error,

'Did any, by his own merit of that of another, issue from here, who was afterwards blessed?' And he, who understood my veiled words, replied: 'I was new to this condition, when I saw a Mighty one arrive, crowned with the insignia of victory.

He removed from among us the shade of our first parent, of Abel his son, and that of Noah, of Moses the Lawgiver who was obedient.

Abraham the Patriarch; David the King; Israel with his father and his children, and Rachel for whom he laboured so long; And many others, and made them blessed. I desire you to know that before these, no human spirits were saved.'

The "Disorderly Crew" is also an Allegory and offered as such; but, like the "Cave", it has an interest independent of its "other meaning". Without being, like the "Cave", an impressive Myth as well as an Allegory, it is still, apart from its interpretation, a bit of highly interesting story of mankind. Plato makes the crew of a Greek trading vessel live and move before our eyes. And how like the ancient crew is to the modern one! Let me place Plato's sketch of the Disorderly Crew and the brilliant description in *Eothen* of the "politics" of the Greek brigantine caught by a sudden squall side by side:—

"Imagine," says Socrates, "a shipowner bigger and stronger than all the other men in the ship, but rather deaf, and rather short-sighted, and with a corresponding knowledge of seamanship; and imagine a crew of sailors all at variance with one another about the steering of the ship, each thinking that he himself ought to steer, although not a man among them has ever learnt the art of steering a ship, or can point to anybody who ever taught him, or can mention a time during which he used to receive instruction: imagine them even asserting that the art cannot be taught at all, and ready to cut down anybody who says that it can, and themselves always mobbing the shipowner, their

---

[1] This notwithstanding its close connection with the "Divided Line", *Rep.* 509 D ff.

master, and entreating him, with every argument they can lay hold of, to let them have the tiller; sometimes, if one faction fails to move him, and another is more successful, the unsuccessful killing the successful or casting them out of the ship, and taking the fine old owner, and drugging him, or making him drunk, or perhaps putting him in irons, and then taking themselves the command of the ship, and using the stores, and drinking and feasting, and sailing the ship as such revellers are likely to sail her; and, to put the finishing touch to our picture, imagine them praising— describing as a 'true seaman', a 'true pilot', a 'man thoroughly qualified in navigation'—any one who is great in the art of capturing the owner by argument or force, and securing the command of the ship to themselves; and imagine these men finding fault with one who cannot do this, and saying that he is 'of no use'—men who have no conception at all of what the true pilot must be—that one must make a study of the seasons, and the sky and the stars, and the winds and all things that belong to navigation, if one is to be really fit to take command of a ship—men, I say, who have no conception whatever of this—men who think that there is no art of *how* a pilot shall steer whether some people wish him to steer or not—no art of steering *as such*—to be studied and learnt. With such a state of things as this on board, don't you think that the truly qualified pilot is sure to be called a 'star-gazer', a 'mere theorist', and 'of no use to us', by sailors in a ship so appointed?"

"Yes, indeed," said Adeimantus.

"Then," said I, "I don't think you want to have the simile analysed, in order to understand that it figures a city in its attitude to true Philosophers. You understand that?"

"Yes," said he.[1]

I sailed (writes Kinglake)[2] from Smyrna in the *Amphitrite*, a Greek brigantine which was confidently said to be bound for the coast of Syria; but I knew that this announcement was not to be relied upon with positive certainty, for the Greek mariners are practically free from the stringency of ship's papers, and where they will, there they go.

*   *   *   *   *   *
*   *   *   *   *   *

The crew receive no wages, but have all a share in the venture, and in general, I believe, they are the owners of the whole freight; they choose a captain to whom they entrust just power enough to keep the vessel on her course in fine weather, but not quite enough for a gale of wind; they also elect a cook and a mate.

---

[1] *Rep.* 488 A ff.   [2] *Eothen*, ch. vi.

*   *   *   *   *   *
*   *   *   *   *   *

We were nearing the isle of Cyprus, when there arose half a gale of wind, with a heavy, chopping sea. My Greek seamen considered that the weather amounted, not to a half, but to an integral gale of wind at the very least; so they put up the helm, and scudded for twenty hours. When we neared the mainland of Anadoli, the gale ceased, and a favourable breeze springing up, soon brought us off Cyprus once more. Afterwards the wind changed again, but we were still able to lay our course by sailing close-hauled.

We were at length in such a position, that by holding on our course for about half an hour, we should get under the lee of the island, and find ourselves in smooth water, but the wind had been gradually freshening; it now blew hard, and there was a heavy sea running.

As the grounds for alarm arose, the crew gathered together in one close group; they stood pale and grim under their hooded capotes like monks awaiting a massacre, anxiously looking by turns along the pathway of the storm, and then upon each other, and then upon the eye of the Captain, who stood by the helmsman. Presently the Hydriot came aft, more moody than ever, the bearer of fierce remonstrance against the continuing of the struggle; he received a resolute answer, and still we held our course. Soon there came a heavy sea that caught the bow of the brigantine as she lay jammed in betwixt the waves; she bowed her head low under the waters, and shuddered through all her timbers, then gallantly stood up again over the striving sea with bowsprit entire. But where were the crew? It was a crew no longer, but rather a gathering of Greek citizens—the shout of the seamen was changed for the murmuring of the people—the spirit of the old Demos was alive. The men came aft in a body, and loudly asked that the vessel should be put about, and that the storm be no longer tempted. Now, then, for speeches:—the Captain, his eyes flashing fire, his frame all quivering with emotion—wielding his every limb, like another and a louder voice—pours forth the eloquent torrent of his threats, and his reasons, his commands, and his prayers; he promises—he vows—he swears that there is safety in holding on—safety, *if Greeks will be brave!* The men hear and are moved, but the gale rouses itself once more, and again the raging sea comes trampling over the timbers that are the life of all. The fierce Hydriot advances one step nearer to the Captain, and the angry growl of the people goes floating down the wind; but they listen, they waver once more, and once more resolve, then waver again, thus doubtfully hanging between the terrors

of the storm and the persuasion of glorious speech, as though
it were the Athenian that talked, and Philip of Macedon that
thundered on the weather bow.

Brave thoughts winged on Grecian words gained their
natural mastery over terror; the brigantine held on her
course, and smooth water was reached at last.

Let me close these remarks on the relationship between
"Myth" and "Allegory" with a reference to "Ritual", in
which the characteristics of both seem to be united. A
"ritual performance" or "rite" is made up of "symbols".[1]
A symbol is a thing, or an act, taken to represent something
else. That something else—generally something of great
importance—may be a transaction (such as a sale of land,
symbolised in the Roman law by the act of transferring a
clod of earth), or a belief (such as the doctrine of baptismal
regeneration, symbolised by sprinkling with water), or a
concept (such as that of justice, symbolised by a figure
holding an even balance), or a nation (symbolised by its
flag). In most cases the symbol has some analogical resemblance, close or remote, to that which it represents; in
some cases it is a badge which has for some other reason
become attached. The habit of symbolic representation is
one of the most primitive and persistent tendencies of human
nature. It was present in the first efforts of language, and
the highest flights of science are still entirely dependent on
the development of it; while without the development of it
in another direction there could have been no poetry—the
primrose would always have been but the yellow primrose;
and even no courtesy of manners—everybody would always
have called a spade a spade.

Now, a ritual performance, or rite, is a composition
made up of symbols so put together as to produce solemn
feeling in those who celebrate and assist. This effect produced is a massive experience of the whole, and may be,
indeed ordinarily is, received without conscious attention to
the significance of the separate parts—the symbols which
together make the whole rite. The rite, if effectually received, is received devoutly as a Myth, not critically apprehended as an Allegory. In its origin and composition it is

[1] See Réville, *Prolégomènes de l'Hist. des Religions*, p. 125 (Eng. Translation
by Squire).

an Allegory—a mosaic of symbols; but as time goes on this is largely lost sight of; the corporate genius of the religious society to which it belongs transforms it for the devout into a Myth. Plato compares that enthusiastic Philosophy, of which Myth is the vehicle, to the Mysteries.[1] The devout went to Eleusis, not to get doctrine out of allegorical representations, but to have their souls purified by the awe of the "Blessed Sights" presented in the acted Myth.

The procession in *Purgatorio*, xxix., like Ezekiel's visions, to which it is indebted, is an elaborately ordered series of symbolical creatures and objects; in the fresco on the left wall of the Spanish Chapel of S. Maria Novella in Florence, every figure, either in itself, or in the position which it occupies in the group, is a symbol. It is true, of course, that to appreciate the beauty of either composition fully one must have at least a general acquaintance with the meaning of the symbols employed; yet finally it is as a great spectacle that the procession of the twenty-ninth Canto of the *Purgatorio* or the fresco in the Spanish Chapel appeals to one. Indeed, it is because it so appeals that one is anxious to spell out the symbolical meaning of its separate parts, so that, having spelt this patiently out, one may find one's self all the more under the enchantment of the whole which transcends the sum of its parts so wondrously.[2]

Similarly, to take a third instance, it is because the Story, in the Second Book of the *Fairy Queen*, of the Adventures at the Castle of Medina, is very readable as a story, and contains beautiful passages of poetry, that we are pleasurably interested in following its elaborate translation of the dry Aristotelian doctrine of "Mean and Extremes" into pictures.

I would add that the effect produced by a great professedly allegorical composition like the procession in *Purgatorio*, xxix., or the Spanish Chapel fresco, is sometimes produced by a poem—sometimes even by a single line or stanza of poetry—in which the poet's art, instead of definitely presenting, distantly suggests a system of symbols. A symbol or system of symbols definitely presented is often enough a mysterious thing; but a symbol or system of symbols distantly

[1] See *supra*, p. 228.

[2] The symbolism of the fresco alluded to above is dealt with by Ruskin in his *Mornings in Florence*, iv. and v.

suggested "teases us out of thought", and arouses in no ordinary degree that wonder, at we know not what, which enters into the effect produced by Poetry as such.

I do not think that a better example of what may be called suppressed symbolism, and of its wonderful poetical effect, could be found than that afforded by Dante's canzone beginning—

Three ladies have gathered round my heart.[1]

a poem on which Coleridge's record of its effect upon himself is the best commentary. He begins[2] by describing it as "a poem of wild and interesting images, intended as an enigma, and to me an enigma it remains, spite of all my efforts." Then, in an entry dated Ramsgate, Sept. 2, 1819, he writes: "I *begin* to understand the above poem (Three ladies have gathered round my heart, etc.), after an interval from 1805, during which no year passed in which I did not re-peruse, I might say, construe, parse, and spell it, twelve times at least—such a fascination had it, spite of its obscurity! It affords a good instance, by the bye, of that soul of *universal* significance in a true poet's composition, in addition to the specific meaning."

[1] Canzone xx. p. 170, Oxford Dante.
[2] *Anima Poetae*, from the unpublished notebooks of S. T. Coleridge, edited by E. H. Coleridge, 1895, p. 293.

THE *TIMAEUS*

CONTEXT

The subject of the Timaeus *is the Creation of the Universe (soul and body) and of Man (soul and body). The speaker in whose mouth the whole Discourse, or Myth, treating of this subject is put is Timaeus, the great Pythagorean Philosopher of Locri in Italy.*

The Discourse, or Myth, is part of the general scheme which is worked out in the Trilogy consisting of the Republic, Timaeus, *and* Critias.

The assumed chronological order of the pieces is Republic, Timaeus, Critias: *i.e. the Conversation at the house of Cephalus is repeated next day by Socrates to Timaeus, Critias, Hermocrates, and another—this is the* Republic; *the day after that again, Socrates, Timaeus, Critias, and Hermocrates meet, and the Conversation and Discourse which constitute the* Timaeus *are held, followed by the Myth related by Critias in the unfinished piece which bears his name. Thus we have first an account of Man's education; then an account of his creation; and lastly the story of the Great War for which his education fits him.*

But, of course, the logical order is Timaeus, Republic, Critias:—*God, because he is good, makes, in his own image, the Universe of which Man is part—not, however, a mere part, but a part which, after a fashion, is equivalent to the whole, in so far as it adequately represents the whole—a microcosm in the macrocosm. Man, as microcosm, is an image of God as adequate as the great Cosmos itself is; and, like God whose image he is, is a creator— makes in turn a Cosmos, the State. We have thus the analogy:— God: Cosmos : : Man : State. Upon God's creation of the Cosmos, in the* Timaeus, *there follows, in order, Man's creation of the State, in the* Republic; *while the* Critias *comes last with the representation of the State performing the work for which it was created.*

Timaeus 29 D—92 C

Let the cause of the creation of this Universe be declared, to wit, that the Maker thereof was Good; with the Good there is no grudging of aught at any time: wherefore, being altogether without grudging, God wished all things to be made as like unto Himself as might be.

*   *   *   *   *   *

Now God, wishing that all things should be good so far as might be, and nothing evil, having received all that was Visible into His hands, and perceiving that it was not at rest but moved without measure and without order, took and brought it out of that disorder into order, thinking that this state was altogether better than that. For He Who is Best might not then—nor may He now—do aught save that which is most excellent. Wherefore He took thought and found out that, amongst those things which are by nature Visible, no work which is without Reason would ever, in the comparison, be fairer than that which hath Reason; and again, that Reason could not, without Soul, come and abide with anything. For this cause He put Reason in the Soul, and Soul in Body, when he fashioned the Universe; to the end that the creature of his workmanship might be the fairest by nature and the most excellent.

Our discourse, then, following alway the way of likelihood, hath brought us thus far—that this Universe is a Living Creature, which hath in truth gotten Soul and Reason through the Providence of God.

Next must we tell in the likeness of what Living Creature the Maker made it. Unto none of those creatures which are by nature Parts of the Whole let us compare it; for naught fair could ever come forth in the likeness of that which is imperfect; but unto That whereof the living creatures, severally and according to their kinds, are parts must we deem it most like. Now That containeth in itself all Intelligible Creatures, even as this Universe containeth us and all his other nurslings which were created to be Visible: for unto That which is the fairest of Things In-

Q

telligible and altogether perfect did God wish to liken it; wherefore made He it a Living Creature, One, Visible, having in itself all Living Creatures which are by nature kin unto it.

Have we rightly called the Heaven One? Or were it more right to say that there are Heavens many—nay, infinite in number?

One Visible Heaven there must be, if it is to be fashioned according to the pattern of That which, inasmuch as it containeth all Intelligible Creatures which are, could never be a second with another; for if it were a second with another, then must there be another Creature including these two, whereof they would be parts; and it would no longer be right to say that this Visible Universe was made after their likeness, but rather after the likeness of That which included them. Wherefore that this Universe might be One only, like unto the One only, All-perfect, Living Creature, the Maker made neither two Universes nor Universes infinite in number, but this One Only Begotten Heaven which was made, and is, and ever shall be.

*   *   *   *   *   *

For this cause, and out of these elements, being of such sort and four in number, was the Body of the Universe brought forth at one with itself through the proportional disposition of elements. Whence also it got Love, so that it was knit together with bonds which cannot be loosed, save by Him Who did bind.

Now, the making of the Universe took up the whole of each of the four elements: for the Maker of the Universe made it of all the fire that was, and all the water, and all the air, and all the earth, and left not any part or virtue of any of these without; to the end, first, that it might be a Living Creature, Whole, so far as might be, and Perfect, with the parts thereof perfect; and secondly, that it might be One Only, since naught was left over of which another like unto this could be made; and thirdly, that it might be without old age or disease; for He knew that if things hot and cold, and all such as have strong powers, encompass the composite body from without, and strike against it un-

seasonably, they dissolve it and bring disease and old age
upon it, and so cause it to decay.

*   *   *   *   *   *

That shape likewise gave He unto it which is fit and
proper. Inasmuch, then, as that shape which comprehendeth
in itself all the shapes is fit for the Living Creature which
should contain in itself all Living Creatures, for this cause
did He turn it to be like a ball, round, with boundary at
every point equally distant from centre. Thus gave He unto
it that which of all shapes is the most perfect, and most like
unto itself, deeming that which is like unto itself fairer by
far than that which is unlike. Moreover, without He made
it perfectly smooth all round, for reasons many:—eyes it
needed not, because nothing visible was left remaining
without; nor ears, because there was nothing without
audible; nor was there air round about it that it should
breathe; nor did it need to have any organ for the taking
in of food, or for the putting out of that wherefrom the
juices were already expressed; for nothing went forth, and
nothing came unto it from anywhere; for without there was
nothing. Yea, it was fashioned cunningly that it should
afford nourishment unto itself, through the wasting of itself,
and should receive and do all within itself and through itself;
for He Who made it thought that if it were sufficient unto
itself, it would be better than if it had need of other things
added unto it. Wherefore, inasmuch as it needeth not
hands for taking hold of aught or withstanding any
adversary, He deemed it not meet to give unto it hands to
no purpose, nor feet, nor any instrument of walking; for the
motion that He allotted unto it was the motion proper unto
such a body, to wit, that one of the Seven Motions which
appertaineth most unto Reason and Understanding. Wherefore He turned it round and round, with the same quickness,
in the same place, about itself; but the other motions, all
save circular motion, He took away from it, and stablished
it without their wanderings. Inasmuch, then, as for this
revolution there was no need of feet, He created it without
legs and feet.

Thus did God, Who is alway, reason with Himself
concerning the god who should be, and made him to be

smooth, and even, with boundary at every point at equal distance from the centre—a Body whole and perfect, composite of bodies perfect.

And in the midst thereof He put Soul, and spread it throughout the whole, and also wrapped the Body round about on the outside therewith; and made the Universe a revolving sphere, one only, and solitary, but, by reason of the virtue which belonged unto it, able to consort with itself, having need of no other, being itself acquaintance and friend unto itself in full measure. A god, then, in regard of all these things blessed, begat He it.

But, albeit Soul cometh second in our discourse, yet was she not created by God younger than Body; for of these twain which He joined together He would not have suffered the elder to be governed by the younger.

*   *   *   *   *   *

The mistress and ruler of the Body did God fashion Soul, out of these elements, after this manner: betwixt that Substance which is undivided and alway the same, and that which cometh into being and is divided in bodies, He made, by the mixing of them both, a third sort of Substance in the middle betwixt the Same and the Other.

*   *   *   *   *   *

These Substances, being three, He took and mixed all together, so that they became one Form; and the Nature of the Other, which was hard to mix, He joined by force unto the Same, and these He mingled with the Third Substance; and of the three made one: then again divided this whole mass into as many parts as was meet, whereof each one was compounded of the Same and the Other and the Third Substance.[1]

[35 B - 36 D.—These parts, all standing in specified numerical ratios to one another, are cut off in specified order, until the whole soul-mass is used up. They are pieced together in the order in which they are cut off, and make a soul-strip, as it were, which is then divided lengthwise into two equal bands, which are laid across each other

---

[1] "The Third Substance" is "the Unity of Apperception"—"Self-consciousness".

like the two strokes of the letter X, the point at which they cross being the middle of each. Each of these crossed bands is then bent (say, up) into a hoop, so that its ends and the ends of the other band meet at the point, in the two circumferences thus formed, which is opposite that at which the bands cross each other. "Thus," as Mr. Archer-Hind says,[1] "we have two circles bisecting each other, and, as the shape of X implies, inclined at an acute angle." One of these hoops, called the outer, is the Circle of the Same, the inner is the Circle of the Other. The former revolves from left to right (from east to west), the latter from right to left. The Circle of the Same remains one and undivided, but the Circle of the Other is subdivided into seven concentric circles—those of the seven planets—each with its own proper motion.[2]]

Now, when the making of the Soul had been fully accomplished according to the good pleasure of her Maker, then did He fashion within her all that is corporeal, and draw these two, Soul and Corporeal Body, together, and join them middle to middle, and the Soul was inwoven everywhere from the middle of the Heaven even unto the borders thereof, and spread round the Heaven without, for a covering, and, turning round within herself, made beginning of her divine life of Reason, which continueth without end for evermore.

The Body of the Heaven was created visible; but she, to wit, the Soul, invisible, and a partaker of Reason and Harmony; being the most excellent of the things created, for that she was created by Him Who of Beings Intelligible and Eternal is the most excellent.

Inasmuch, then, as she was compounded of the Same and of the Other and of Substance, these three, and was divided and bound together according to due proportions, and alway returneth unto herself, when she toucheth anything whose substance is scattered, or aught whose substance is undivided, she is moved throughout all her nature, and

---

[1] *Timaeus*, note on 36 c, p. 111.
[2] See *de An.* i. 406 b 25-407 b 13, where Aristotle summarises this account of the formation of the Soul, and criticises it in a manner which shows that he entirely misapprehends the *Timaeus*—fails to see that its "doctrines" are conveyed by myth, not by teaching. *In a Myth* it is allowable to speak of the soul as having size.

declareth wherewith that thing is the same, and wherefrom it is different.

*   *   *   *   *   *

Now, when the Father Who begat this created image of the eternal gods saw that it moved and lived, He was glad; and, being well pleased, took thought to make it even more like unto the pattern thereof. Inasmuch, then, as that pattern is an Eternal Being, even such, so far as might be, did He seek to make this Universe likewise. Now, the nature of the Being which is the pattern thereof is eternal. And this nature could not be joined in any wise unto the created thing: wherefore He took thought to make a Moving Image of Eternity; and whilst He was ordering the Heaven, He made of Eternity which abideth in Unity an Image Eternal progressing according to Number, to wit, that which we have called by the name of *Time*. For days and nights and months and years, which were not before the Heaven was created, He fashioned and brought forth together with the Heaven when He framed it.

*   *   *   *   *   *

Time was created together with the Heaven, so that, having been created together, together they might be dissolved, if dissolution should ever befall them: and after the pattern of the Eternal Nature was it created, that it might be as like thereto as possible; for the pattern is existent throughout all Eternity, and the Image thereof was made, and is, and shall be continually, throughout all Time. Wherefore, according to this counsel of God for the creation of Time, the sun and the moon and the other five stars, which are surnamed planets, were created for the dividing and safeguarding of the numbers of Time. And God, when He had made the bodies of each of these, set them in the orbs wherein the circuit of the Other was moving, seven stars in seven orbs.

*   *   *   *   *   *

Now, until Time was brought forth, all else had been fashioned in the likeness of That whereunto it was made like; but inasmuch as all the kinds of living creatures, which the Universe should comprehend within itself, were not yet created, therein was it still unlike.

This part, therefore, of the Universe which remained unfinished He now finished, moulding it to the nature of the
pattern. All the Forms which Reason perceiveth to be present
in the Intelligible Living Creature, these, after their kinds,
did He think it meet that this Universe also should contain.
Now, these Forms are four: first, there is the heavenly race
of the gods; then the race of winged fowls of the air; third,
the kind that liveth in the water; and fourth, the kind that
walketh on the dry land.

The Form of the Godhead He consecrated and made for
the most part of fire, that it might be brightest of all and
fairest to look upon; and likening it unto the Universe He
made it spherical, and set it in the Path of the Wisdom of
the Highest to go therewith, and distributed it over all the
spangled round of Heaven, to be a true adornment thereof.
And unto every one of the divine stars He gave two motions—
the one motion in the same place, and itself the same without
changing, which is the motion of him who is true unto
himself and thinketh alway the same thoughts concerning
the same things; and the other motion forward, controlled
by the revolution of the Same and the Like: but in respect
of the other five motions He made it stand still. For this
cause were those stars created which wander not, but,
turning round with uniform motion, each one in his own
place, therein alway abide, being living creatures divine and
eternal.

As for the stars which wander, they were created in the
manner which hath been told.

And Earth, our nursing mother, which is wrapped round
about the line which extendeth from pole to pole, she was
fashioned to be the guardian and maker of night and day,
the first and eldest of the gods which were created within
the Heaven.

    *   *   *   *   *   *

Of Earth and Heaven were born Ocean and Tethys; of
these were born Phorkys and Cronus and Rhea and their
brethren; and of Cronus and Rhea were born Zeus and Hera
and their brethren, whose names are made mention of; and
these, again, had children.

Now, when all the gods were born—both gods visible in their heavenly courses, and gods which make themselves visible as it pleaseth them—then spake unto them the Begetter of this Universe, saying: Gods of gods whose Maker and Father I am, ye are the creatures of my handi-work, and without me are ye not loosed asunder; for verily that which is bound together can alway be loosed asunder; but none save an evil one would desire to loose asunder that whereof the parts are well joined together and the whole state is goodly.   Wherefore, being creatures, ye are not altogether set apart from death so that ye cannot be loosed asunder: nevertheless, loosed asunder ye shall not be, nor shall ye partake of death, because that my will, which is your portion, is a greater bond and prevaileth more than all those bonds wherewith your parts were bound together when ye were created.

Now give ear unto that which I declare unto you. Three mortal kinds are yet uncreated. If these be not brought forth, the Heaven will be imperfect; for it will not have in itself all the kinds of living creatures; yet must it have all, if it is to be fully perfect. But if these were brought into being by me, and by me made partakers of life, they would be equals to gods. Wherefore, to the end that they be mortal and that this Universe—this All, be truly All, turn ye, according to nature, to the making of living creatures, having the faculty, for an ensample, wherewith I created you.

That part of them whereunto it belongeth to partake in the name of *immortal*—that part, to wit, which is called divine and is leader in them of those parts which alway do desire to follow after righteousness and after you—that part I, having sown to be a beginning, will deliver unto you. Thereafter do ye, weaving the mortal upon the immortal, fashion living creatures and beget them, and giving them nourishment increase them, and when they die receive them again. Thus He spake, and again He took the bowl wherein afore He compounded and mixed the elements of the Soul of the All, and into this bowl He poured that which was left over of the elements, mixing them as afore; yet now were they not so pure as at first, but second and third in quality.

Then, when He had made of them one mixture, He took and divided Souls therefrom, as many as there are stars, and to each star he assigned a Soul, and caused each Soul to go up into her star as into a chariot, and showed unto her the nature of the All, and declared the laws thereof which are fixed and shall not be moved, to wit, that it was appointed that the first birth should be for all the same, so that no Soul should fare worse at His hands than another, and that all, having been cast as seed upon the Instruments of Time, each upon the Instrument suitable for her, must first be born in the flesh of that living creature which feareth God most; and, since human nature hath two kinds, in the flesh of that kind which is the better, which thereafter should be called *Man*. Therefore, whereas Souls of necessity should be implanted in Bodies, and of the Body there should be that which cometh and that which goeth, first must all Souls have implanted in them at their birth one sense collected from the passions which assault them; moreover, all must have born in them love made up of pleasure and pain, and in addition thereto fear and anger and all the other passions which do go together with these, and also as many as are by nature contrary to these—and if any man should hold these passions in subjection, his life would be righteous; but unrighteous, if he should be overcome of them; and whosoever lived virtuously all the time appointed unto him should journey back to his kindred star and dwell there, and there should have a life blessed and conform unto his nature: but whosoever fell short of this, he in the second birth should pass into the nature of Woman; and if therein he refrained not from wickedness, then, according to the likeness of that wickedness whereunto he turned him, should he pass alway into the nature of some Beast, and should not be rid of the labour of these changes until, having closely followed the Circuit of the Same and the Like which is in himself, he should, by the might of reason, overcome all that unreasonable, tumultuous crowd which was afterward gathered about him from the elements of fire and water and air and earth, and should come again unto his first and best estate.

He having made all these ordinances for them, that He

might be blameless as touching the wickedness which should
be thereafter in each one of them, sowed some on the Earth
and some on the Moon and some on the other Instruments of
Time; and all that should come after the sowing He delivered
unto the Young Gods, to wit, the moulding of mortal bodies
and the fashioning of all parts (together with all their
appurtenances) that yet remained of man's Soul which must
be added thereto: all this did He deliver unto the Young
Gods, that thereby they might have rule over the living
creature which is mortal, and might guide it, after their
ability, to walk in the most honourable and perfect way,
without evil, save that which it should itself bring upon itself.

All these things did He ordain, and thereafter abode in
His own proper nature. Therein He abode; and His sons,
having comprehended their Father's ordinance, were
obedient unto it, and having received the immortal beginning
of the living creature which is mortal, they took their own
Maker for an ensample, and borrowed from the Universe
portions of fire and earth and water and air which should
be restored again: these they took and cemented together,
not with the bonds which cannot be loosed wherewith they
themselves were held together; but with bolts innumerable,
invisible by reason of smallness, they welded them, and out
of them all fashioned one body for each living creature,
binding the Circuits of Immortal Soul within Body that
consisteth in perpetual influx and efflux.

Now the Circuits of the Soul, having been bound within
the River of the Body which floweth mightily, neither had
the mastery over it, nor were they mastered, but were pushed
about, and did push with violence, so that the whole creature
was moved, and went hither and thither disorderly, by
chance, without forethought, having all the six motions;
for forward and backward, and to the right and to the left,
and down and up, did the creatures go, wandering towards
all the six points; because that the flood was great which
did swell up over them supplying their nourishment, and
then again did flow away from them; and yet greater was
the commotion that was made in them by the blows of
those things which did strike against them—to wit, when
the body of any living creature happened on something

without, foreign from itself, and therewith had contact—
with fire, or with solid earth, or smoothly sliding water, or
if at any time it was overtaken by the blast of winds borne
along in the air; and then the motions caused by all these
were carried through the Body into the Soul and beat upon
her. Wherefore were all these motions together called
aesthêses,[1] and still are so called.

*   *   *   *   *   *

By reason of these assaults of the passions which are
made upon her, the Soul now, as in the beginning, loseth
understanding when she is first bound unto the mortal body;
but when the stream of growth and nourishment abateth of
his influx, and the Circuits of the Soul are gotten into smooth
waters, and go their own way, and are become more constant as time passeth on, then at last are they brought into
the perfect form of the natural motion which is proper unto
each of the Circles, and marking and naming the Other and
the Same aright, they cause him who possesseth them to
have understanding; and if right teaching also take part in
the work, he becometh whole and altogether sound, having
escaped that disease which is the greatest of all; but if he
give not heed unto this teaching, he journeyeth halt through
this present life, and, without initiation, and without understanding, cometh again unto Hades.

But these be things which come to pass afterward; it
behoves us rather to tell more exactly concerning the matter
which now we have in hand, and concerning the matter
which is precedent thereto, to wit, concerning the generation
of the Body with the parts thereof, and concerning the Soul
and the causes and purposes of the Gods by reason whereof
she was generated. All these things, therefore, let us ex-
pound, alway holding fast in our discourse unto that which
seemeth most likely.

The Young Gods, taking for a pattern the shape of the
Universe which is a globe, bound the Divine Circles, which
are twain, within this corporeal ball which we now call
Head, which is the divinest of our parts, and hath lordship

---

[1] Plato seems to derive *aisthêsis*, "sensation," from *aïssein*, "to rush
violently".

over them all. Unto the Head, to minister unto it, the Gods
gave the whole Body which they had compacted together;
for they perceived that unto the Head belonged all the
motions which should be. Wherefore, that it might not go
rolling upon the earth, which hath heights and depths of
every sort, finding no way of getting over those or out of
these, to this end gave they unto it the Body for a carriage,
to make the way easy for it. Wherefore the Body got length,
and put forth limbs which were able to be stretched out and
to be bent, four in number; for thus did the Gods devise
means of going about, so that the Body, therewith taking
hold and pushing off, could go through all places, bearing
aloft the temple of that which in us is the most divine and
the most holy. In this wise, then, and for this end, were legs
and hands put forth and added unto all men: and the
Gods, thinking that that which is before is more honourable
than that which is behind, and more able to lead, made
man to go for the most part forward; wherefore must he
needs have the forepart of his body distinct from the hind
part and dissimilar. For this reason they first put the face
on the forepart of the vessel of the Head, and fixed therein
the instruments which should minister in every way unto
the forethought of the Soul, having ordained that that which
hath ability to lead should be that which is by nature
before.   First of these instruments they fashioned light-
bringing eyes, and fixed them in, after this wise.   Out of
that fire which hath not the power of burning, but is able
to give gentle light—that light, to wit, which belongeth to
day—they contrived and made a body; for the pure fire,
twin-born therewith, which is within us they did cause to
flow through the eyes, having compressed their substance
throughout, but most of all in the mid part thereof, so that
it was made smooth and dense, and held in whatsoever in
the light was thick, and let only the light itself strain through
in a pure stream.   When, therefore, the light of day is
round about the visual stream, then doth the stream, going
forth, like unto like, compactly join itself unto that stream
without against the which the stream that cometh from
within doth thrust itself, and these two being blended together make one body which is extended in a straight line

from the eyes. The visual stream, then, since it is compact
of parts altogether like, receiveth altogether like affections;
and when it toucheth anything, and something else toucheth
that, it passeth their motions on throughout the whole Body,
until they come unto the Soul, and so it causeth that sense
wherewith we say that we *see*. But when the kindred fire is
gone away into night, then is the visual stream cut off; for,
going forth into that which is unlike itself, it is changed and
quenched, no longer becoming consubstantial with the air
round about, because that the air hath in it no fire.

*   *   *   *   *   *

Now these be all auxiliary causes which God maketh
subservient unto His design of bringing the Idea of the Best
into act, as far as is possible; but most men are of opinion
that they are not auxiliary causes, but true causes which, by
cooling and heating, and thickening and thinning, and the
like, do produce all things. And yet these operations can in
no wise have in them understanding or design of aught; for
of things which be, unto one alone it belongeth to have
understanding, and that one, let it be declared, is Soul; which
is invisible; but Fire and Water and Earth and Air all are
visible creatures. Wherefore the lover of understanding and
knowledge must first follow after those causes which apper-
tain unto the Intelligible World, and then, secondly, after
those which are made manifest when one thing, being moved,
moveth another thing of necessity.

This, then, must we also do, speaking concerning both
kinds, but making separation between those causes which
with understanding are artificers of things fair and good, and
those which without knowledge produce disorderly what
chanceth at any time. Concerning the auxiliary causes
which helped to give unto eyes that faculty which they now
have, enough hath been said; now, therefore, let us declare
that benefit wrought by eyes—great above all benefits—for
whose sake God bestowed them upon us.

Eyesight, methinks, hath been the cause unto us of the
greatest benefit, inasmuch as no word of our present discourse concerning the Universe would have been spoken, if
we had seen neither stars nor sun nor heavens: whereas

now day and night and the months and the circuits of the
years, passing before our eyes, have discovered unto us
Number, and given unto us a notion of Time, and set us
a-seeking to know the nature of the All: whence we have
gotten us Philosophy, than which no greater good hath come,
nor ever shall come, as gift from gods unto mortal kind.

I say, then, that this is the greatest good from eyes; and
the other benefits therefrom which are all less than this,
wherefore should I recount them? Let the man who is
without Philosophy break out into vain lamentations,
because, forsooth, he is blind and hath not these small
things: as for ourselves, we will declare the cause of vision
in this wise and the chief end thereof:—God invented
vision and gave it unto us for a gift, to the end that, having
observed the Circuits of Intelligence in the Heaven, we
might use them for the revolutions of Thought in ourselves,
which are kin, albeit perturbed, unto those unperturbed
celestial courses; and having throughly learnt and become
partakers in the truth of the reasonings which are according
to nature, might, by means of our imitation of the Circuits
of God which are without error altogether, compose into
order the circuits in ourselves which have erred.

Concerning Sound and Hearing let the same thing be
said—that they also have been bestowed by the Gods to the
same end as Sight. For to this end also hath Speech been
ordained, and maketh thereto the largest contribution; and,
moreover, all that part of Music which is for the service of
the Voice and Hearing hath been given unto us for the sake
of Harmony; and Harmony, having her courses kin unto
the revolutions in our Soul, hath been given by the Muses
to be a helper unto the man who, with understanding, shall
use their art, not for the getting of unreasonable pleasure—
which is commonly esteemed the use of Music—but for the
ordering of the circuit of our Soul which hath fallen out of
harmony, and the bringing thereof into concord with itself;
and Rhythm also, because that the state of most men is
without measure and lacketh grace, hath been given unto
us for the same end, to aid us, by the same Benefactors.

Hitherto hath this discourse been for the most part concerning those things which are of the workmanship of

Reason; but now must it set by the side of these that which
cometh to pass of Necessity; for, in truth, the generation of
this Universe was a mixed generation, sprung from the
concurrence of Necessity and Reason.

Reason exercised authority over Necessity by persuading
her to bring the most part of the things which were made
unto the Best Issue. According to this scheme, in the
beginning, was the Universe established through the instrumentality of Necessity working in obedience unto the
admonition of Wisdom. If any man, therefore, would tell
truly how this Universe is come into being, he must include
the natural operation of the Cause Errant.[1] Let us then
turn back, and, having taken up this other proper principle
of things created, begin again from the beginning, even as
we began the former inquiry.

Wherefore let us search out the natures of Fire and
Water and Air and Earth, which were before the Heaven
was brought forth; and also the state which was before these
natures themselves were.

*　　　*　　　*　　　*　　　*　　　*
*　　　*　　　*　　　*　　　*　　　*

As was said at the beginning, these things, being without
order, God took, and put into them all those measures of
Proportion and Symmetry whereof they were capable, each
one in respect of itself, and all in respect of one another.
For before that there was nothing which partook of these
measures save by chance; nor was there any of the things
which now have names which was then worthy at all of
being named, neither Fire nor Water nor any of the other
Elements; but all these did He first set in order, and then
out of them instituted this Universe, One Living Creature,
which hath in itself all living creatures mortal and immortal.
Of those which are divine He himself is the Maker; but the
creation of those which are mortal He appointed unto His
own offspring, to be their work; and they following His
example, when they had received of Him the immortal
principle of the Soul, thereafter fashioned round about her
this mortal Body, and gave it all unto her to be her vehicle;

---

[1] I have adopted this translation of *he planomene aitia* from Mr. Archer-
Hind.

and, moreover, they constructed another kind of Soul, and put it also into the Body, to wit the Mortal Soul which hath in itself passions terrible, of necessity inherent—first, Pleasure, evil's best bait, then Pains that banish good things, also Confidence and Fear, two heedless counsellors, and Wrath hard to entreat, and Hope easily led astray. These did they mix with Sense that lacketh Reason, and Love that dareth all, and so builded the mortal kind of Soul.

Wherefore, fearing to defile the divine more than was inevitable, they appoint a dwelling-place for the mortal apart therefrom, in another region of the body, having built an isthmus and boundary between the Head and the Breast, to wit, the Neck, set between them that they might be separate. In the Breast, then, or what is called the Chest, they enclosed the mortal kind of Soul; and inasmuch as one part thereof was by nature better, and the other part worse, they also built a wall of partition to divide the vessel of the Chest, as a house is divided into the women's quarters and the men's quarters; so did they put the Midriff as a barrier betwixt these two parts.

That part of the Soul, therefore, which partaketh of courage and spirit, loving strife, they established nearer unto the Head, betwixt the Midriff and the Neck, to the end that, being within hearing of the Reasoning Part, it might, together with it, keep down the brood of appetites by force when they would not obey the word of command from the castle; and the Heart, which is the knot of the veins and the fountain of the blood which floweth everywhere mightily through all the members, they set to be the guardhouse, so that when the fierceness of wrath boileth, what time Reason doth pass the word that some wickedness is being done around them without, or haply by the Appetites within, then the whole sensitive system of the Body, keenly apprehending through all the narrow passages thereof the exhortations and threats uttered, should become obedient and tractable altogether, and so should let the Best Part be the leader of them all.

* * * * * *

As for that part of the Soul which desireth meat and drink and the other things which it needeth by reason of the nature of the Body, this they established in the region which lieth between the Midriff and the borders of the Navel, having framed, as it were, a manger to extend throughout all this place for the nourishment of the Body. Here they bound this part of the Soul like a wild beast which nevertheless must be kept joined unto the rest and reared, if there was to be a mortal race at all. Accordingly, that, always feeding at the manger and dwelling as far as possible from the part which taketh counsel, it might raise as little tumult and uproar as possible, and let the Chief Part take counsel in peace concerning the common good, for this cause did they post it here. And knowing this concerning it that it would not be able to understand Reason, and that even if it attained somehow unto some empiric knowledge of reasonable truths, it was not of such a nature as to give heed thereto, but for the most part would follow the ghostly conduct of Images and Phantasms by night and by day, God sought out a device against this, and put the Liver close by the dwelling-place of the Appetitive Soul, having fashioned it close and smooth and shining and sweet and bitter too, so that the thoughts which come from the Intelligence, striking upon it as upon a mirror which receiveth impressions and causeth images to be seen, might fill the Appetitive Soul, at one time, with fear, . . . at another time might make it mild and gentle, and give unto it a space of calm at night, wherein it should receive the Oracles of Dreams, meet for that which is without Reason and Understanding; for they who made us were mindful of that which their Father spake, commanding them to make the mortal race as perfect as possible; therefore did they regulate even the base part of us after this wise, that it might lay hold of truth somehow, and therefore did they establish a Place of Oracles therein.

*   *   *   *   *   *

Now, as touching the three sorts of Soul implanted in us, whereof we have oft-times spoken, and the proper motions of each, let this be now said shortly, that any one of them which continueth in abeyance, having her motions stopped, must needs become weaker; but any one which exerciseth herself becometh stronger. Wherefore we must take heed

R

that they all, in regard to one another, have their motions accomplished in due measure.

But as touching that kind of Soul in us which hath most authority, let this be understood, that God hath given it unto each man to be his Genius, to wit, that Soul which, we say, dwelleth in the topmost part of the Body, and lifteth us up from Earth towards our birthplace in the Heaven, forasmuch as we are not earthly creatures but heavenly: this we say, and most truly say; for from that Place whence the Soul first sprang the Divine Principle suspendeth our head and root, and so causeth the whole Body to stand upright. Wherefore if any man have followed after the lusts of the flesh, or after contention, and busied himself wholly therewith, all his thoughts within him must needs be mortal, and so far as it lieth in him to become mortal, he cannot fail at all of this; for this hath he fostered: but if any man have earnestly pursued learning and the knowledge of Truth, and have exercised most his faculty of thinking, he must needs have thoughts immortal and divine if he lay hold of Truth; and so far as Human Nature may have part in Immortality, he cannot fall short thereof at all: and inasmuch as he serveth the Divine Part, and hath the Genius which dwelleth in him ordered aright, he must needs be blessed exceedingly:[1] and the service required of every man is the same alway—to wit, he must apportion unto each part the kind of nourishment and motion proper thereto. Now unto the Divine Part in us the motions which are kin are the Thoughts and Circuits of the All. These must every man follow, that he may regulate the Revolutions in his Head which were disturbed when the Soul was born in the flesh; and, by throughly learning the Harmonies and Circuits of the All, may make that which understandeth like unto that which is understood, even as it was in the beginning; and having made it like, may attain unto the perfection of that Best Life which is offered unto men by the Gods, for this present time and for the time hereafter.

Now is the commandment which came unto us in the beginning, that we should declare the nature of the All,

---

[1] Cf. Arist. *E.N.* x. 7. 8. 177 b 26 ff., and *E.N.* viii 3. (vii 15) 1249 b 20, where "to serve and contemplate God" seems to be an echo of "as he serveth the divine part" *Tim.* 90 c.

even unto the generation of Man, well-nigh brought to fulfilment; for the way of the generation of the other living creatures we may tell shortly, if it so be that it needeth no long history. Thus methinks shall a man set proper bounds unto his discourse concerning them.

Let this, then, be said, that of those which were born Men, it is most likely that as many as were cowardly, and passed their life in unrighteousness, were changed into Women when they were born the second time.

*   *   *   *   *   *

Thus were Women and the whole female sex brought forth.

The tribe of Birds, putting forth feathers instead of hair, was the transformation of men that were guileless, but lightwitted; who were observers of the stars, but thought foolishly that the surest knowledge concerning them cometh through Sight.

The tribe of Beasts which walk on the Earth sprang from those men who sought not Wisdom at all for an help, nor considered the nature of the Heaven at all, because that they no longer used the Revolutions in the Head, but followed the Parts of the Soul which are about the Breast, making them their guides. By reason of this manner of living their four limbs and their heads were drawn down unto kindred earth, and thereon did they rest them; and they got head-pieces of all sorts, oblong, according as the circuits of each, not being kept in use, were crushed in. For this cause their kind grew four-footed and many-footed, for God put more props under those which were more senseless, that they might be drawn the more toward the earth. But the most senseless of them all, which do stretch their whole body altogether upon the earth, since they had no longer any need of feet, the Gods made without feet, to crawl on the earth.

The fourth kind was born, to live in the water, from those men who were the most lacking in Understanding and Knowledge; whom they who fashioned them afresh deemed not worthy any more even of pure air to breathe, because that they had made their Souls impure by all manner of wickedness: wherefore the Gods gave them not thin pure air to breathe, but thrust them down into the waters, to draw thick breath in the depths thereof. From these men is sprung the nation of Fishes, and of Oysters, and of all that live in the water, which have gotten for recompense of uttermost ignorance the uttermost habitations.

*   *   *   *   *   *

Now may we say that our discourse concerning the All is come to its ending. For this Universe, having taken unto itself Living Creatures mortal and immortal, and having been filled therewith, hath been brought forth a Creature Visible, containing the things which are visible; the Image of his Maker, a God Sensible, Greatest, Best, Fairest, and Most Perfect—this One Heaven Only Begotten.

OBSERVATIONS ON THE *TIMAEUS* MYTH

I

It lies outside the scope of this work to select for separate comment even a few of the most important questions and topics contained in the vast *Timaeus*, related as these are, not only to Plato's Philosophy itself as a whole, but to subsequent Philosophy and Theology and Natural Science as influenced by this Dialogue, perhaps the most influential of all Plato's Dialogues.

I keep clear of the *Timaeus* as an Essay on Physics and Physiology profoundly interesting to the student of the history of these branches.

I do not wish to ransack it for its anticipations of later metaphysical doctrine, such as that of the subjectivity of space, which may, or may not, be taught in the passages treating of Space and the Receptacle.

I do not trouble myself or my readers with the lucubrations of Proclus and his like on it.

I do not say a word about the theological doctrine which Christian exegesis has found in it in such abundant store.

For these things the reader must turn to editions of the *Timaeus*, and Histories of Philosophy where the *Timaeus* is discussed.

Here we are concerned with it merely as one in the series of Plato's Myths; and as most of the observations which have been made in connection with the other Myths already examined apply equally to this Myth, special observations on it need not be numerous or long. Indeed, the translation which I have made, if read in the light of these former observations, almost explains itself.

More might have been translated, for the whole Discourse delivered by Timaeus is a Myth; or other parts might have been substituted for some here translated. I had to use my judgment in choosing what to translate, as I could not translate the whole, and my judgment may have sometimes erred; yet, after all, I venture to think that what I have translated presents the *Timaeus* in the aspect in which it is the object of this work to present it—as a great Myth in the series which we are reviewing.

This Myth sets forth, in one vast composition, the three Ideas of Soul, Cosmos, and God: in one vast composition; perhaps nowhere else in literature are they set forth so as to produce such a convincing sense of their organic inter-connection. And the impressiveness of this vast composition is wonderfully enhanced by the context in which it is framed. Indeed, what is new in the presentation of the Ideas of Soul, Cosmos, and God in the *Timaeus*, as compared with other Platonic Myths in which they are presented, is derived from the context in which this Myth frames them. The *Timaeus*, as we have seen, and shall see better when we reach the *Critias*, follows on after the *Republic*. It begins with a re-capitulation of the five books of the *Republic*, which Socrates offers in order that he may say: "Here you have the *structure* of the Perfect State set forth; now let us see that State exerting *function* in accordance with its structure. Its structure is that of a highly organised military system. Let us see it engaged in a great war." In answer to this demand Critias introduces and outlines the Atlantis Myth (afterwards resumed in the unfinished Dialogue which bears his name), the History of the Great Antediluvian War in which Athens—representing the Beautiful City of the *Republic*—maintains the civilisation of Hellas against the outer barbarian. That is the immediate context of the Discourse, or Myth, delivered by Timaeus. But the Myth breaks away from the sequence of that context in the most startling manner, and soars, on a sudden, above the mundane outlook of the first five books of the *Republic* and the *History of the Great War*, with which the company were up to the moment engaged, and constrains them to give all their thoughts to the world eternal.

Two things Timaeus seems to tell them in this Myth.

First, the State must be framed in the Cosmos. You cannot have any scientific knowledge of the Social Good till you understand it as part of the Absolute Good realised in the Cosmos which is the Image of God. The knowledge of the Idea of the Good which the *Republic* (in a passage subsequent to the books epitomised by Socrates in the *Timaeus*) requires of the True Statesman is, indeed, nothing but the apprehension of the Social Good as determined by the Cosmic Good. The method of the *Republic* was to write the goodness of the Individual large in the goodness of the State. But we must not stop here. The goodness of the State must be written large in that of the Universe: written, not, indeed, in characters which the scientific faculty can at last be sure that it has deciphered, but in the hieroglyphics, as it were, of a mysterious picture-writing which, although it does not further definite knowledge, inspires that Wonder which is the source of Philosophy, that Fear which is the beginning of Wisdom.

But, secondly, Timaeus goes far beyond the mere recommendation of a study of Cosmology for the sake of the better realisation of the political end. He tells the company, in this Myth, that the political end is not the only end which man may propose to himself. The life of the State and of Man as member of the State, however it may be ennobled and made to seem more choice-worthy by being viewed as part of the blessed life of the One, Only Begotten, Living Creature which is the express image of God, is nevertheless an end in which it is impossible to acquiesce. The best-ordered State cannot escape the Decline and Fall which await all human institutions; and the life of the citizen is incomparably shorter than that of his earthly city. If Man is to have any abiding end it must be in a life of the Soul which lies beyond death, outside the cycle of birth.[1]

To be remembered, and even to be worshipped, by future generations on earth is an "immortality" which can satisfy no man; and still less satisfying is the "immortality" of absorption in the Spirit of the Universe. The only immortality which can satisfy a man, if he can only believe in it, is a personal life after bodily death, or, it may be, after many bodily deaths, when he shall return to his "native star", and be there for ever what the grace of God and his own efforts after purification have made him.

---

[1] "In Plato the State, like everything else upon Earth, is essentially related to the other world, whence all truth and reality spring. This is the ultimate source of his political idealism. . . . The State, therefore, serves not only for moral education, but also as a preparation for the higher life of the disembodied spirit into which a beautiful glimpse is opened to us at the end of the *Republic*" (Zeller, *Aristotle*, ii. 212, Engl. Transl.; cf. Rohde, *Psyche*, ii. 293). The latter half of the *Republic*, as has been pointed out, is not before us in the *Timaeus*.

This third sort of immortality obviously holds the field against the two other sorts mentioned; for, first, it is worth believing, which the second sort, however easy to believe, is not; and, secondly, it is more worth believing than the first sort, because it is a true "immortality"—a personal life for ever and ever—whereas the first sort, consisting in the lapsing memory of the short-lived individuals of a Race itself destined in time to disappear from the earth, is not a true immortality, however comforting it may be to look forward to it as a brief period in the true immortality. Lastly, the third sort of immortality, being worth believing, is, in addition to that, easy to believe, because no evidence drawn from the Natural World can ever be conclusive against it. It is not like a miracle alleged to have occurred in the Natural World in opposition to the recognised Laws of that World. No objective Law of Nature is violated by the personal immortality of the disembodied Soul. The evidence against it, as for it, is subjective only. Does belief in personal immortality comfort men? If it does, they will be found believing—a few, fervently, the majority, perhaps, in passive fashion.

So far I have tried to express the thought and feeling which seem to be in unison with the note of the *Timaeus* Myth. But there is another type of thought and feeling, on this great subject, which we cannot ignore, although the *Timaeus* Myth ignores it entirely. We must remember that for the Buddhist East personal immortality has little or no attraction. Final sleep seems to be the ideal for a large portion of the human race.

It would be foolish, then, to say that belief in personal immortality is at all a subjective necessity. All that we are entitled to say is that, as a matter of fact, this belief has prevailed among the races which hitherto have taken the lead in the world. Whether or no it is bound to remain prevalent it is impossible to say. The overworked and the indolent, in modern Europe, easily acquiesce in—nay, gladly embrace, the ideal of eternal sleep; and even for some energetic constructive minds the time comes when they simply wish to rest from their labours, contented to think, or hope, that the mundane system, political, industrial, or scientific, for which they have worked hard, will continue to prosper when they are gone. The ideal of work or duty done is the ideal which, in the West, now competes most seriously with the ideal of personal immortality:—

Stranger, report to the Lacedaemonians that here we lie, obedient to their laws.

II

(*Timaeus*, 42, and 91 D ff.)

The lower animals were created after (1) man, and (2) woman, to embody the Souls of human beings who had lived unrighteously.

Here, as elsewhere in Plato—in the *Phaedrus* Myth; in the Myth of Er; in *Phaedo*, 81, 82; in *Laws*, ix. 872 E— the *raison d'être* of metempsychosis is Correction and Purification—its *raison d'être* also in the Orphic teaching and in Buddhism. But we must not suppose that belief in metempsychosis is necessarily associated with the notions of Correction and Purification. Metempsychosis recommended itself to the imagination of man as Natural History long before it was used for an ethical purpose.[1] The notion that there is a fixed number of souls always in existence— perhaps a fixed number of bodies—and that all the people successively born on earth are dead people who return from the place of spirits or from their graves, by some law of nature in the presence of which sexual intercourse has quite a subordinate place, is a notion which prevails widely among primitive races, and is entertained merely as an item of Natural History—as a theory of generation, and has no ethical import.

Now it seems to me that the difference between men and beasts which belief in metempsychosis as process of Correction and Purification makes little of, is one which belief in metempsychosis as mode of generation is bound to regard as very real. It may conduce to the purification of a man's Soul that it should be incarnate afterwards in the body of a lion or a swan; but if mere generation is all that is effected

---

[1] The ideas of retribution and purification seem to be entirely absent from Irish transmigration stories: see *The Voyage of Bran*, by Myer and Nutt, ii. 96.

by metempsychosis it is natural to suppose that the Souls re-incarnated in one generation of men are those which appeared on earth in a former generation of men, and will reappear in some future generation of men. Where a beast becomes a man or a man a beast, and the change is not conceived as promoting purification, we have something exceptional—not a case of the normal metempsychosis by which the human race is propagated, but rather a case of metamorphosis due to some particular act of magic, like Circe's, or some other extraordinary cause like that which changed the daughters of Pandion, one into a nightingale, and the other into a swallow. The notion of a man's being able to transform himself or another man into a beast by magic is as primitive and as deeply rooted as that of metempsychosis, but in itself has nothing in common with the notion of metempsychosis.

I would therefore distinguish sharply between belief in the reappearance, in human bodies, of departed human souls—or perhaps I ought to say the reappearance of departed human beings, Soul and Body not being regarded as separate entities—the normal generative process by which the human race is maintained on earth, and belief in the sudden bodily transformation, by magic or other cause, of men into beasts and beasts into men—an exceptional occurrence.

Having distinguished two beliefs which I think ought to be distinguished, I am ready to admit considerable "contamination" of each by the other, even before the advent of the notion of purification as an end served by re-incarnation of human Souls, not only in human bodies, but also in the bodies of beasts.

We see how natural it is that such "contamination" should take place, if we consider the mental condition which expresses itself in the Beast-Fable. It is a state of chronic dream-consciousness. The Beast-Fable is a dream in which men and beasts talk and act together; in which the transformation of a man into a beast, or a beast into a man, is taken as a matter of course; in which beasts, in short, are at once men and beasts.

The mental condition which expresses itself in the dream

of the Beast-Fable easily lends itself to belief in bodily transformations of men into beasts, and beasts into men, effected supernaturally by magicians; or sometimes taking place naturally, so that one who was a man in a former generation is born again in this generation as a beast, and may reappear in a future generation as a man. Here the originally independent notions of metempsychosis and metamorphosis begin to "contaminate" each other. Metamorphosis, which is properly the supernatural bodily transformation of a man into a beast, or a beast into a man, appears as the re-birth, in due natural course, of a beast as a man, or a man as a beast: metamorphosis has insinuated itself into the place occupied by metempsychosis, and has become a sort of metempsychosis; while metempsychosis, originally a kind of re-birth of departed human beings as human beings, now includes the notion of departed human beings reappearing in new births as beasts, and of beasts as human beings.[1]

As soon as the notions of retribution and purification came to be connected with the notion of metempsychosis, the modification produced in that notion by the notion of magical metamorphosis would be greatly accentuated: to be born again as a beast would in many cases seem to be more appropriate, from the point of view of retribution and purification, than to be born again in the natural course as a human being.

III

Timaeus, 41 D, "And making them of one mixture, he divided the souls according to the number of the stars."

Susemihl (*Genet. Entw.* ii. 369) and Archer-Hind (*Tim.* ad loc.) think that the Creator assigned to the fixed stars, not already differentiated individual Souls, but masses of the, as yet, undifferentiated Soul-stuff which he had compounded in the bowl. Only when the time came that Souls

---

[1] The case of Tuan Mac Cairill, in Irish legend, may be quoted as illustrating the manner in which the ideas of metamorphosis, metempsychosis, and pregnancy without male intervention, run into one another. Tuan became, in succession, a Stag, a Bear, an Eagle, and a Salmon. The Salmon was boiled and eaten by a woman, who thereupon conceived, and brought forth Tuan again in human form. See *The Voyage of Bran*, by Myer and Nutt, ii. 76.

should be "sown" on the instruments of Time, the planets and earth, were these masses of Soul-stuff in the fixed stars taken and differentiated into individual Souls. I agree with Zeller (*Plato*, pp. 390, 391, Engl. Transl.) in holding that the Souls are differentiated as individuals when they are assigned each one to its fixed star; and that it is these individual Souls which, on the completion of their speculative journey round the outer sphere of the Heaven, are transferred to the earth and planets in order to partake of their first birth in the flesh.

Mr. Archer-Hind asks (note, *ad loc.*) what is the purpose of this distribution of (as he supposes) masses of undifferentiated Soul-stuff among the fixed stars; and finds the explanation in *Phaedrus*, 252 C, D, where different gods are assigned as patrons for persons of various temperament. If the reader will turn to the passage in the *Phaedrus* referred to by Mr. Archer-Hind, he will find that the patron gods, *i.e.* stars, are not the fixed stars, but the planets, Jupiter, Mars, the Sun; and this is only in accordance with the prevailing belief—that it is from the planets that the varieties of temperament are, at least, chiefly derived. The purpose of the distribution of Souls (in my view, individual Souls, not masses of Soul-stuff) among the fixed stars is what Plato distinctly says it is—that these Souls may learn the Laws of the Universe—the Nature of the Whole.

THE *PHAEDRUS* MYTH

CONTEXT

The subject of the Phaedrus *is "Rhetoric and Love".*

Socrates and the young Phaedrus take a walk together outside the Walls, and rest under a plane-tree by the bank of the Ilissus.

There Phaedrus reads to Socrates a rhetorical piece, which he has just heard delivered by Lysias, in praise of the non-lover as distinguished from the lover.

Socrates does not think much of the performance, and delivers a better speech on the same subject—in dispraise of the lover and praise of the non-lover.

When he has finished his speech, he rises to go away, but is stopped by his Divine Sign, or Familiar Spirit, and stays to deliver a Recantation of his blasphemous dispraise of Love.

The sanity of the non-lover, on which he had enlarged, is indeed a paltry thing, he now says, as compared with the madness of the lover. Madness is the gift of God. There are four kinds of divine madness: the first is prophetic inspiration—as the name mantike, *derived from* manike, *shows; the second is religious exaltation— the feeling of the mystic, or initiated person; the third is poetic genius; and the fourth is the Love by which the immortal Soul is winged for her flight to Heaven.*

The Myth *describes the birth and growth of this Love, which it presents as the nisus of the Soul after the True, the Beautiful, and the Good—in one word, as Philosophy.*

When the Myth is finished, conversation is resumed, and returns to the subject of Rhetoric, or the Art of Public Speaking, which is now discussed by Socrates with a deep sense of the importance of Truth. To be a really good speaker, a man must know the Truth, and be able to recommend it to his audience. Genuine Rhetoric is based on Philosophy; and the highest kind of such Rhetoric, on that enthusiastic Philosophy which is the gift of Eros. Let Lysias keep this in mind.

Phaedrus 246 A—257 A

Concerning the Immortality of the Soul enough hath been spoken: now let it be told of what fashion she is, with this preface, to wit, that *her fashion, as it truly is, only the tongue of a God, using long discourse, could declare; but what she is like unto, a Man may tell, speaking more shortly.*

Let it then be said of the Soul, that she is like unto a Power composite of two Winged Horses harnessed, and a Charioteer.

All the Horses and Charioteers of the Gods are themselves good, and of good stock; but of the other Souls the goodness is mixed: for 'tis a Yoke of Horses that the Charioteer of Man's Soul driveth, and, moreover, of his Horses the one is well-favoured and good, and of good stock, the other of evil stock and himself evil. Wherefore a hard thing, and a contrarious, the driving of our Chariots must needs be.

Now let it be told how it hath come to pass that of living creatures some are called mortal and some immortal. All that is called by the name of *Soul* watcheth over all that is without Soul, and maketh circuit of the whole Heaven, and appeareth now in this shape now in that. If a Soul be perfect, and keep her wings full of feathers, she flieth high and encompasseth the whole world with her government. But there be Souls that have shed their wings, and fall down headlong till they lay hold on that which is corporeal, and there they make their abode, having taken unto themselves earthly bodies. The earthly body, albeit without the power of the Soul it is not moved, seemeth to move itself; and the whole, compacted together of Soul and Body, is that which we call by the name of *"living creature"*, thereunto adding *"mortal"*.

Of that which is *"immortal"* we have no understanding; but make for ourselves an image thereof; and God, whom we have not seen neither have rightly comprehended, we conceit as One who liveth and is immortal and hath Soul and Body; and in him we say are these two joined together for evermore.

Let these things and the telling of them be as it pleaseth God; but of the falling off of the wings, and wherefore the

Soul sheddeth them, let the cause be now discovered. It is after this wise.

The nature of wings consisteth in the power of lifting that which is heavy up into the height where the generation of the Gods dwelleth; and unto wings, amongst the bodily parts, belongeth the largest portion of that which is of God. Now that which is of God hath beauty, and wisdom, and goodness, and all perfection; by these, therefore, the growth of the wings of the Soul is chiefly nourished and increased; whereas by the things which are contrary to these, to wit, by all things hateful and evil, are her wings caused to pine away, and utterly destroyed.

Zeus, the great Captain of the Host of Heaven, mounted upon his winged chariot, rideth first and disposeth and over-seeth all things. Him followeth the army of Gods and Daemons in eleven orders—for Hestia alone abideth in the House of the Gods; but all the other Gods which are of the number of the Twelve go forth and lead each one the order whereof he is appointed to be captain.

Many holy sights there be for eye to behold of blessed Gods in their courses passing to and fro within the firmament of Heaven, each one doing his own business: and whosoever willeth, and is able, followeth; for Envy standeth afar from the Heavenly Choir.

Now, as often as they go to eat at the banquet, their path is ever up by the steep way close under the roof of the Heaven. The Chariots of the Gods, going evenly and being alway obedient to the hand of the Charioteer, accomplish their journey easily; but the other Chariots hardly, with great labour, for the Horse which is by nature froward is as a weight, and ever inclineth towards the Earth, and, except the Charioteer hath brought him into subjection, draweth the Chariot down. Herein standeth the cause to the Soul of trouble and trial exceeding great and sore which are prepared for her.

The Souls which are called *immortal*, when they are come to the top of the Heaven, journey out therefrom and stand upon the Roof thereof without, and standing are carried round by the circuit, and behold those things which are without the Heaven.

Now, the Place which is above the Heaven no poet here hath ever praised, nor shall praise, worthily. The Place is after this wise: for he especially whose discourse is concerning Truth must make bold to say what is true concerning it.

The Substance which Verily Is, which hath no colour and no shape, and hand cannot touch, is comprehended only by the Governor of the Soul, to wit, by Reason. Round about this Substance, in this Place, dwelleth True Knowledge. The Mind of God—yea, that Part wherewith every Soul seeketh after the food convenient for herself—is fed with Reason and True Knowledge undefiled. Wherefore beholding again at last That Which Is, it is satisfied, and the sight of That which is True feedeth it, and maketh it glad, until the circuit shall have brought the Soul round again unto the same Place. In the journey round the Soul beholdeth Justice Itself, she beholdeth Temperance Itself, she beholdeth True Knowledge: not that knowledge which is with generation, and differeth in respect unto different of those things concerning which we now say that *"they are";* but the knowledge which standeth in That which Verily Is. The Soul, then, having beheld these and also all other things Which Verily Are, and having eaten of this feast, sinketh down again into the inward part of the Heaven and cometh home unto her House. And when she is come, the Charioteer maketh the Horses to stand at the manger, and casteth ambrosia before them, and thereafter giveth them nectar to drink.

This is the life of the Gods. Of the other Souls, whichsoever followeth God best, and is made most like unto Him, keepeth the head of her Charioteer lifted up into the Place without the firmament, and is carried round with the circuit thereof, being troubled by the Horses, and hardly beholding the Things Which Are; after her cometh the Soul which for a space keepeth the head of her Charioteer lifted up, and then again sinketh down, and because of the violence of the Horses, seeth some of the Things Which Are, but some she seeth not.

Beside these there follow other Souls which all do strive after that which is above, but are not able to reach unto it, and are carried round sunken beneath the face of the Heaven, trampling upon one another, and running against one another, and pressing on for to outstrip one another, with mighty great sound of tumult and sweat of the race; and here, by reason of the unskilfulness of the Charioteers, many Souls are maimed, and many have their wings broken; and all, greatly travailing, depart uninitiated, not having seen That Which Is, and turn them to the food of Opinion.

Now these are the causes wherefore they so vehemently desire to see the Place where the Plain of Truth is: because the pasture convenient for the Best Part of the Soul groweth in the Meadow there, and the power of wings, whereby the Soul is lightly carried up, is nourished by that pasture; and because Adrasteia hath made a decree that the Soul which hath been the companion of God, and seen some of the Things Which Are, shall be without affliction all the time until another journey round the Heaven beginneth for her; and if she can alway behold Those Things she shall be without hurt alway: but when a Soul, having seen Those Things aforetime, is now not able to follow, and seeth them not, being overtaken by some evil chance, and filled with forgetfulness and wickedness, and made heavy so that she sheddeth the feathers of her wings and falleth unto the Earth, then the law is that she shall not be planted in the body of any Beast in the first generation: but the Soul which hath seen most shall pass into the seed of a man who shall become a Seeker after the True Wisdom, a Seeker after the True Beauty, a Friend of the Muses, a True Lover; the Soul which cometh second shall enter into the seed of a King who shall rule justly, or of a Warrior and Commander of the Host; the Soul which cometh third shall enter into the seed of a man who shall busy himself with the affairs of a City, or with the stewardship of a household, or with merchandise; the Soul which is fourth shall enter into the seed of a man who shall endure hardness for the sake of the crown of victory, or shall be a healer of the diseases of the body; the Soul which is fifth shall have the life of a Prophet or Priest; unto the sixth shall belong the life of a Poet or some other of the tribe of Copiers; unto the seventh the life of a Workman or Husbandman; unto the eighth the life of

S

a Sophist or Demagogue; unto the ninth the life of a Tyrant. In all these lives, whosoever walketh righteously hath a better portion; whosoever walketh unrighteously, a worse.

Now into the same Place from whence each Soul cometh she returneth not again until ten thousand years have been accomplished; for sooner is no Soul fledged with wings, save the Soul of him who hath sought after True Wisdom without deceit, or hath loved his Comrade in the bonds of Wisdom. The Souls of such men, when the third course of a thousand years is finished, if they have chosen this life three times in order, being fledged with wings, do then depart.

But the other Souls, when they have ended their first life, are brought before the judgment-seat; and when they have received sentence, some go to the prisons under the Earth, and there pay the penalty: and some by the sentence are exalted and go into a certain place of the Heavens, where they fare as beseemeth the life which they spent when they had Man's form.. But in the thousandth year both sorts, being come to the casting of lots and to the choosing of the second life, choose, every Soul, the life which pleaseth her. And now it cometh to pass that a Soul which was a Man's goeth into the life of a Beast, and the Soul of a Beast which aforetime was a Man goeth again into a Man; for unto Man's shape no Soul attaineth which never beheld the Truth; the cause whereof is this—Man must needs understand the Specific Form which proceedeth from the perceiving of many things, and is made one by Thought. This is the Recollection of Those Things which each Soul erewhile saw when she journeyed together with God, despising the things which we now say are, and holding herself up to look at That which Verily Is. Wherefore of right only the Mind of the Lover of Wisdom is winged; for he alway cleaveth in Memory, so far as he is able, unto Those Things by cleaving unto which God is verily God. The man, therefore, who useth these memorials aright, and is alway a partaker in the perfect mysteries, he alone becometh verily perfect; but inasmuch as he escheweth the things which men do strive after, and giveth himself unto God, they that are of the world rebuke him, saying that he is beside himself; for they perceive not that he hath inspiration of God.

It is come to pass, then, that this Discourse is now returned unto whence it came, to wit, unto the Fourth Sort of Madness: for when a man beholdeth the beauty which is here, and then calleth to mind the True Beauty, and getteth wings and desireth with them to fly up, but is not able—looking up into the sky like a bird, and heeding not the things beneath—he is accounted as mad after the manner of the Fourth Sort of Madness; because that the spirit of his Madness wherewith he is possessed is the best, proceeding from the best for him who hath it, and for him who partaketh of it; and because that he who loveth things beautiful with the spirit of this Madness upon him hath the name of *Lover;* for, as hath been said, every Soul which is a Man's hath of necessity seen the Things which Verily Are—else would it not have entered into this creature; but to call Those Things to mind, by means of these, is not easy for every Soul; neither for those Souls which saw the Things There for a little space, nor for those unto which, when they were fallen down to the Earth, evil happened, so that they are turned to iniquity by evil communications, and forget holy things which they saw aforetime. Verily few are they which are left having Memory present with them in sufficient measure.

These, when they see any likeness of the Things There, are amazed and cannot contain themselves any more; but what it is that moveth them they know not, because that they perceive nothing clearly.

Now of Justice and Temperance and all the other Precious Things of the Soul no glory at all shineth in the likenesses which are here; but using dull instincts and going unto images, hardly do a few men attain unto the sight of that One Thing whereof they are the images. Beauty Itself, shining brightly, it was given unto them then to behold when they were of the blessed choir and went—we in the train of Zeus, and other Souls led by other Gods—and saw that great and holy sight, and were made partakers of those Mysteries which it is meet to call the most holy: the which they did then celebrate, being themselves altogether fair and clean, and without taste of the miseries prepared for them in the time thereafter, and being chosen to be eyewitnesses of visions which are altogether fair, which are true with all singleness, which are without variableness, which contain the fulness of joy. These are the Things which our Souls did then see in pure light, being themselves pure and without the mark of this which we call body, and now carry about with us, as the fish carrieth the prison-house of his shell.

Let these words, then, be offered for a thanksgiving to Memory, for whose sake we, as remembering our joys that are past, have lengthened this Discourse.

Now, as touching Beauty:—We beheld it shining, as hath been said, amongst those other Visions; and when we came hither, we apprehended it glittering most clearly, by means of that sense which in us is the most clear, to wit, eyesight, which is the keenest sense that the body conveyeth. But the eye seeth not Wisdom. O what marvellous love would Wisdom cause to spring up in the hearts of men, if she sent forth a clear likeness of herself also, even as Beauty doth, and it entered into our eyes together with the likenesses of all the other Things which be worthy of Love! But only unto Beauty hath this portion been given. Wherefore Beauty is the most evident of all, and the best beloved.

Now, he who hath not lately partaken of the heavenly Mysteries, or hath been corrupted, is not quickly carried hence to that Other Place and to Beauty Itself, when he seeth the things which here are called after the name thereof. Wherefore, looking upon these, he giveth them not reverence, but, delivering himself up to pleasure, after the manner of a beast he leapeth upon them, desiring to beget offspring according to the flesh, and feareth not to have his conversation in lasciviousness, nor is ashamed of following after pleasure contrary to nature. But he who hath lately partaken, who hath beheld many of the Things There, when he seeth a face, or the figure of a person, made in the very likeness of Beauty, first his flesh trembleth, and awe of those things which he saw aforetime entereth into his heart; then he looketh, and worshippeth the Beautiful One as a God, and, were he not afraid that men should account him a maniac, would offer sacrifice to his Beloved, as to a graven image and a God. Then while he looketh, after the trembling, as it useth to happen, sweating and unwonted heat

take hold of him, for he hath received the effluxion of
beauty through his eyes, and is made hot, so that the wings
in him are watered; for when he is made hot, the parts
where the wings sprout are melted, which before were
closed by reason of their hardness and hindered the feathers
from growing. When, therefore, the nourishment floweth
unto them, the stalks of the feathers swell, and are moved
for to grow from their roots under the whole surface of the
Soul; for aforetime the whole Soul was feathered. It cometh
to pass then that the whole Soul doth boil and bubble; and
as it happeneth unto those who are teething, when their
teeth are lately begun to grow, that there is an itching in
their gums and distress, even so doth it happen unto the
Soul of him who beginneth to put forth wings; for his Soul
boileth and is in distress and itcheth when she putteth forth
her feathers. When, therefore, she looketh upon the beauty
of her Beloved, parts (*merē*) come thence unto her in a
stream (which for this cause are called *himeros*); and she,
receiving them, is watered and made hot, and ceaseth from
her pain and rejoiceth. But when she is parted from her
Beloved and waxeth dry, the mouths of the passages whereby
the feathers shoot forth, being parched and closed up,
hinder the sprouting of the feathers, which is shut in together with Desire, and leapeth as a man's pulse, beating
against each passage that withstandeth it, so that the whole
Soul, being pricked on every side, is filled with frenzy and
travaileth: but contrariwise, having memory of the Beautiful
One, she rejoiceth; so that this strange thing happeneth
unto her—her pain is mingled with joy, and she is be-
wildered, and striveth to find a way, but findeth none; and,
being filled with madness, she cannot sleep by night nor
stay in one place by day, but runneth to and fro wistful, if
perchance she may behold the One who possesseth that
Beauty. And, beholding, she draweth Desire from the
channel thereof unto her, and the entrances which were
shut are opened, and she taketh breath and ceaseth from
her prickings and travail, and instead thereof reapeth the
sweetest pleasure for the present time. Wherefore willingly
she departeth not, esteeming no one more highly than the
Beloved; but mother, and brethren, and all her friends, she

forgetteth, and thinketh it of no account that her substance
is wasted through neglectfulness; and the things which are
approved of men and of good report, wherein she did aforetime take pride, all these she now doth despise, and is willing
to be a slave, and make her lodging wheresoever she may
come nearest unto her Love; for she cometh not to worship
only, but because she hath found that the One who possesseth that Beauty is the sole physician of her greatest troubles.

Now this affection, fair boy, unto whom my whole Discourse is dedicate, men call Eros; but as touching the name
which the Gods call it, when thou hearest it haply thou
wilt laugh because it is new—for some of the disciples of
Homer, out of the Secret Verses, recite two verses unto
Eros, whereof one is very impudent, and not good in metre.
Now these are the verses of their hymn:—

> Men call him Eros by name, surnaming him Eros the
> Flyer;
> Gods call him Pteros, because that he haunteth on
> Wings and compelleth.

These things, then, it is permitted to a man to believe, or
believe not, as he is minded. Nevertheless, the case of those
that be in love, and their state, is that which hath been said.

Now, if it be one of the train of Zeus that is taken, he is
able more stoutly to bear the burden of him whose name is
Winged; but they who be servants of Ares, and made the
circuit along with him, when they are taken by Eros, and
think that they are injured in aught by the Beloved One, are
ready to shed blood and make a sacrifice of themselves and
the Beloved One. As each, then, was of the choir of a
certain God, him he honoureth alway, and maketh his
example according to his ability, so long as he is uncorrupt
and liveth the life of the first birth here; and in this manner
likewise he behaveth himself in his conversation toward the
Beloved Ones and other men.

It cometh to pass, then, that each man, according to his
natural temper, chooseth his Beloved and maketh him his
God, and fashioneth and adorneth him as a graven image,
to honour him and celebrate mysteries before him. They,
therefore, who are of the company of Zeus, seeking for a
Beloved One like unto Zeus in soul, inquire whether some

one be by nature a lover of True Wisdom and able to rule; and when they have found what they seek, and are fallen in love, they do all so that the Beloved One shall be altogether such as they seek, to wit, like unto Zeus. Then, indeed, if they have not already made a beginning of this endeavour, do they take the matter in hand, and both learn from whomsoever they are able to learn, and themselves pursue the knowledge thereof: and questioning in their own souls to find therefrom the nature of their own God, they seek not in vain, because that they are constrained to look steadfastly upon their God, and by memory lay hold on him, and, being filled with his spirit, receive of him their habitudes and way of life, so far as man can partake of God. Whereof they account the Beloved One the cause, and therefore have they the more pleasure in him; and if the river, wherefrom even as Bacchae they draw their nourishment, flow from Zeus, then do they turn the waters thereof upon the Soul of the Beloved One, and make it as like unto their own God as is possible.

He who was of the train of Hera seeketh after one who is Royal, and having found, doth in all things as the follower of Zeus doth. He who was of the train of Apollo or of any other God, observing the nature of his own God, seeketh to have a comrade of the like nature; and when he hath gotten such an one, he taketh the God for an example unto himself, and teaching and guiding, bringeth the Beloved One also unto the way and likeness of the God as far as can be, striving without envy or grudging or malice by all means to bring the Beloved One unto the full likeness of himself and of whichsoever God he himself honoureth.

The Desire, then, of them that truly love, and their Initiation, if they accomplish that which they desire, is verily a fair and blessed boon bestowed, by the friend whom Love hath made mad, upon him whom he hath chosen for his friend, and caught. Now, it is after this wise that he is caught. Whereas at the beginning of this Tale we said that each Soul hath three parts—two thereof in the form of Horses, and the third part in the form of a Charioteer; so now we would have this remain as it was then told, and that one of the Horses is good and the other is not. But what is the virtue of the good Horse and the illness of the evil Horse we did not declare; now, therefore, must we tell it.

That one of the two which hath the more honourable station, in form is straight and well-knit, with a high neck and an arched nose, in colour white, with black eyes, a lover of honour in all temperance and modesty, a friend of true glory, needing not the whip, being guided by the mere word of the Charioteer. But the other Horse is crooked, lumpish, ill-jointed, with a stiff neck, a short throat, a snub nose, in colour black, with grey eyes, sanguineous, a friend of lust and boastfulness, hairy about the ears, deaf, hardly submitting himself to the lash and the pricks.

Now when the Charioteer beholdeth the Vision of Love, and his whole Soul is warmed throughly by the sight, and he is altogether full of itchings and the prickings of desire, then that Horse which is obedient to the Charioteer, being constrained then and alway by modesty, holdeth himself back from rushing upon the Beloved One; but the other Horse careth no longer for the Charioteer's pricks nor for his whip, but pranceth, and with violence chargeth, and, striving with his fellow and with the Charioteer, compelleth them to go unto the Beloved One and make mention of the sweetness of carnal love. At first the twain resist, taking it ill that they are constrained unto wickedness; but at the last, since their evil state hath no ending, they go as the evil Horse leadeth, yielding themselves up, and consenting to do what he biddeth. Moreover, now are they come near, and see the countenance of the Beloved One gloriously shining. Which when the Charioteer seeth, his memory is straightway carried back unto the Form of the Eternal Beauty. Her he again beholdeth standing girt with temperance upon her holy pedestal; and, beholding her, he is filled with fear and reverence, and falleth backward, and thereat must needs pull the reins back with force, so that he bringeth both the Horses down upon their haunches—the one willingly, because that he resisteth not, but the lascivious one against his will altogether.

Now when the two Horses are come away a little further from the Beloved, the one, by reason of his shame and panic, wetteth all the Soul with sweat; and the other, having ceased from the pain which he had from the bit and from his falling down, hardly recovering breath, in anger up-braideth, and heapeth curses upon, the Charioteer and his fellow Horse, saying that, because of cowardice and weak-heartedness, they have left their place appointed unto them and the promise which they made.

Then again, when they are not willing to go near, he constraineth them, and hardly consenteth when they beseech that the matter may be deferred to some other time: and when the time agreed upon cometh, and the two make pretence of not remembering, he putteth them in mind, and pulleth them with force, neighing, and compelling them again to come near for to speak the same words unto the Beloved; and when they are come near, he bendeth down his head, and stretcheth out his tail, and biteth the bit, and pulleth it shamelessly. But the Charioteer, being moved in his heart this second time as the first time, yea more ex-ceedingly, falleth backward as it were from before the barrier at the starting place of the racecourse, and more violently doth draw the bit unto him from the teeth of the lascivious Horse, and maketh his cursing tongue and his jaws bloody, and presseth his legs and haunches to the earth, and delivereth him up to torment.

Now when the evil Horse, having oft-times suffered the same correction, ceaseth from his wantonness, being humbled he followeth the guidance of the Charioteer, and, whenever he seeth the Beautiful One, is brought to naught with terror. So it cometh to pass in the end that the Soul of the Lover followeth the Beloved One in reverence and fear.

The Beloved then being served as a God with all service, by one who maketh not a pretence of love but loveth truly, and being by nature a friend unto him who serveth, even though in time past fellow disciples and others have made mischief with their tongues, saying that it is not seemly to come near unto a Lover, and though by reason of this the Beloved hath rejected the Lover, yet in process of time do ripeness of age and need of him cause the Beloved to receive the Lover into companionship; for surely it hath never been ordained that evil shall be friend to evil, or good shall not be friend to good.

When, therefore, the Beloved receiveth the Lover, and hath accepted his speech and companionship, then doth the good-will of the Lover drawing very nigh fill the Beloved with amazement; and lo! in comparison with this friend who hath in him the spirit of God, not even the whole company of other friends and kinsfolk provideth any portion at all of friendship!

Now when the Beloved continueth for awhile in this, and cometh near unto the Lover, touching him in the gymnasia and other places where they meet, then at last the fountain of that stream which Zeus, loving Ganymede, called by the name of *Himeros*, floweth mightily toward the Lover, and part thereof goeth down into him, and, when he is filled to overflowing, the other part runneth out: and even as the wind, or a voice, leapeth back from the smooth rock and rusheth to the place whence it came, so doth the Stream of Beauty return unto the Beautiful One through the Eyes, which is the natural way unto the Soul; and when it is come thither, it giveth the Soul wings—it watereth the passages of the feathers, and causeth them to sprout; and the Soul of the Beloved also is filled with love. The Beloved loveth, but knoweth not whom, nor hath understanding of what hath come to pass, for to tell it; but is like unto a man who hath been smitten with disease of the eyes by another man, but cannot tell the cause thereof; or like unto one who seeth himself in a glass, and knoweth not that it is himself, so doth the Lover stand as a glass before the Beloved: and when the Lover is present, the Beloved ceaseth from the pain of Love, even as the Lover also ceaseth; and when the Lover is absent, the Beloved longeth after him and is longed after, having Love-for-Love which is the Image of Love, yet calling and deeming it not Love but Friendship; and the Beloved desireth, even as the Lover desireth, but less vehemently, to see, to touch, to kiss, to embrace—and doeth this quickly thereafter, as is like; concerning which the lascivious Horse of the Lover's Soul hath somewhat to say unto the Charioteer, and demandeth of him a little enjoyment as the reward of many labours. But the Horse of the Beloved hath nothing to say, but being swollen with desire, and knowing not what he doeth, throweth his arms round the Lover and kisseth him, greeting him as a dear friend, and when, they are come close unto each other, is ready to grant unto him all that he asketh; while the fellow Horse, obedient unto the Charioteer in all modesty and reasonableness, withstandeth. Wherefore, if then the better parts of the mind prevail, and lead the Soul into a constant way of life and true wisdom, then are men, all the days of their life here, blessed and at peace with themselves, having the mastery over themselves, doing all things in order, having brought into bondage that part of the Soul wherein wickedness was found, and having made that part free wherein virtue dwelleth; and after this life is ended, they rise up lightly on their wings, having gained the victory in the first of the three falls at the True Olympic Games, than which victory no greater good can the Temperance of Man or the Madness from God bestow on Man.

But if any take unto themselves a baser way of life, seeking not after true wisdom but after honour, perchance when two such are well drunken, or at any time take no heed unto themselves, their two licentious Horses, finding their Souls without watch set, and bringing them together, make choice of that which most men deem the greatest bliss, and straightway do enjoy it; and having once enjoyed it, they have commerce with it afterward alway, but sparingly, for they do that which is not approved of their entire mind.

Now these two also are friends unto one another, but in less measure than those I before spake of, because they live for a while in the bonds of love, and then for a while out of them, and think that they have given and received the greatest pledges betwixt each other, the which it is never allowed to break and come to enmity one with another. When such do end their life here and go forth from the body, they are without wings, but have a vehement desire to get wings; which is no small recompense they receive for Madness of Love. Wherefore they are not compelled to go down unto the darkness and the journey under the Earth, seeing that they have already made a beginning of the heavenly journey; but they pass their time in the light of day, and journey happily together Lover and Beloved, and when they get wings, of the same feather do they get them, for their Love's sake.

These are the gifts, dear boy—behold how many they are and how divine!—which the friendship that cometh from the Lover shall bestow on thee: but the conversation of him who is no Lover, being mingled with the temperance of this mortal life, and niggardly dispensing things mortal, begetteth in the Soul of his friend that Covetousness which the multitude praise as Virtue, and causeth her hereafter to wander, devoid of understanding, round about the Earth and under the Earth, for a thousand years nine times told.

OBSERVATIONS ON THE *PHAEDRUS* MYTH

I

I think it necessary, at the outset of my observations on the *Phaedrus* Myth, to take notice—let it be brief—of the tolerant, nay sympathetic, way in which Plato speaks (256 C-E) of the madness of love of those who are not "true lovers". He speaks eloquently of it as a bond which unites aspiring souls in the after life. He speaks of those united by this bond as getting wings of the same feather in Heaven for their love's sake. His language is as sympathetic as the language in which Dante expresses his own sympathy, and awakens ours, with a very different pair of winged lovers— Francesca and Paolo flying together like storm-driven birds in Hell.[1] It is astounding that Plato should allow himself to speak in this way. The explanation offered by Thompson[2] does not enable me to abate my astonishment:—The concluding portion of the Myth, he tells us, "which stands more in need of apology," ought to be considered in connection with the fact that the entire Discourse is intended as a pattern of philosophical Rhetoric, and is adapted, as all true Rhetoric must be, to the capacity of the hearer—in this case, of Phaedrus, who is somewhat of a sensualist. It is still to me astounding that Plato—even as dramatist in sympathy with the sensualism of one of his *dramatis personae*, the youth to whom his "Socrates" addresses this Rhetorical Paradigm, if that is what the *Phaedrus* Myth is[3]—should have ventured to speak, as he does here, of what he indeed elsewhere[4] condemns as unequivocally as Aristotle condemns it.[5]

The reflection, in most cases a trite one, that even the best men are apt to become tolerant of the evil which prevails in the manners of their age, is hardly, in this case, a trite reflection, for it is such an oppressively sad one.

---

[1] *Inferno*, v.

[2] *Phaedrus*, p. 163.

[3] I entirely dissent from the view that this Myth is merely a pattern of philosophical Rhetoric; and also from the consequential view (Thompson's Introduction to *Phaedrus*, p. xix.), that it is mostly "a deliberate allegory", unlike, it is added, other Platonic Myths in which the sign and the thing signified are blended, and sometimes confused. See *infra*, p. 300.

[4] *Laws*, viii. 841 D.

[5] *E. N.* vii. 5. 3. 1148 b 29.

II

In passing to the *Phaedrus* Myth (with which the *Meno* Myth must be associated), we pass to a Myth in which the "Deduction of the Categories of the Understanding" occupies perhaps a more prominent place, by the side of the "Representation of Ideas of Reason", than has been assigned to it even in the *Timaeus*.

The mythological treatment of Categories of the Understanding stands on a different footing from that of "Ideas of Reason" in this important respect, that it is not the only treatment of which these Categories are capable. The Ideas of Reason, Soul, Cosmos, and God, if represented at all, must be represented in Myth; and it is futile to attempt to extract the truth of fact, by a rationalising process, out of any representation of them, however convincing, as a representation, it may appear to our deepest instinct. On the other hand, Categories of the Understanding (*e.g.* the notions of Substance and of Cause), though, as *a priori* conditions of sensible experience, they cannot be treated as if they were data of that experience, are yet fully realised, for what they are, in that experience, and only in it. Hence, while their *a priori* character may be set forth in Myth, the fact that, unlike the Ideas of Reason, they are fully realised in sensible experience, makes them also capable of logical treatment. That they are capable of such treatment is obvious, when one considers the advance, sound and great as measured by influence in the physical sciences, which Logic has brought about in our interpretation of the Notion, or Category, of Cause, and that by discussions carried on quite apart from the question of whether the Notion is present *a priori*, or is of *a posteriori* origin. We may say, however, that treatment of Categories of the Understanding tends to become less mythological and more logical as time goes on; but yet the mythological treatment of them can never become obsolete—it still remains the legitimate expression of a natural impulse, the power of which—for evil— Kant recognises in his Transcendental Dialectic. I call the mythological expression of this impulse legitimate, because it is mythological, and not pseudo-scientific.

I take the *Phaedrus* Myth, along with the *Meno* Myth, as an example of the Mythological Deduction of Categories of the Understanding. The Eternal Forms seen by the Soul in its prenatal life, as "remembered" in this life when objects of sense present themselves, are Categories, although the list of them is redundant and defective if we look at it with Kant's eyes, which I do not think we need do.

But although the *Phaedrus* Myth deduces Categories, it represents Ideas as well. Plato, as I have been careful to point out, does not anywhere distinguish Categories and Ideas formally; and the *Phaedrus* Myth, in particular, is one of the most complex, as well as comprehensive, in the whole list of the Platonic Myths. It deduces Categories, sets forth the Ideas of Soul, Cosmos, and God, is Aetiological and Eschatological, and, though a true Myth, is very largely composed of elements which are Allegories. Its complexity and comprehensiveness are indeed so great that they have suggested the theory—that of Düring,[1] with which, however, I cannot agree—that the Myth is a Programme—a general view of a whole consistent Eschatological Doctrine, which is worked out in detail in the *Gorgias*, *Phaedo*, and *Republic* Myths.[2] In the *Phaedrus* Myth alone, Düring maintains, we have a complete account of the whole History of the Soul— its condition before incarnation, the cause of its incarnation, and the stages of its life, incarnate, and disembodied, till it returns to its original disembodied state. All this, he argues, is so summarily sketched in the *Phaedrus* that we have to go to the other Dialogues mentioned, in order to understand some things in the *Phaedrus* rightly. In the *Phaedrus* Myth, in short, we have "the summarized rendering of an imaginative concept, visualized in greater detail." The *Phaedrus* Myth thus dealing, for whatever reason, with everything that can be dealt with by a Myth, we shall do well not to separate its Deduction of Categories, or Doctrine of recollection, too sharply from the other elements of the composition.

[1] *Die eschat. Myth. Platos*, p. 476 (*Archiv für Gesch. d. Philos.* vi. (1893), pp. 475 ff.).
[2] Cf. Jowett and Campbell's *Republic*, vol. iii. p. 468. "The attempts of Numenius, Proclus, and others to connect the Myth of Er with those in *Gorg.*, *Phaed.*, *Phaedr.*, *Tim.*, so as to get a complete and consistent view of Plato's supra-mundane theories, only show the futility of such a method."

This Myth is part of the Discourse which Socrates delivers, by way of recantation, in praise of Love. The non-lover, indeed, is sane, but the madness of the lover is far better than the other's sanity. Madness is the source of all that is good and great in human effort. There are four kinds of it[1]—(1) the Prophet's madness; (2) the madness of the Initiated; (3) the madness of the Poet; and (4) the madness of the True Lover who is the True Philosopher. It is the Transcendental History of the Soul as aspiring after this True Love that is the main burden of the Myth. And here let me say a few words, in passing, on the view maintained by Thompson in his Introduction to the *Phaedrus* (p. xix.),[2] that this Myth is, for the most part, "a deliberate Allegory". With this view I cannot agree. It ignores the fact that a Myth is normally composed of elements which are Allegories. The Chariot, with the Charioteer and two Horses, is allegorical—it puts in pictorial form a result already obtained by Plato's psychological analysis, which has distinguished Reason, Spirit, and Appetite as "Parts of the Soul". But if the Chariot itself is allegorical, its Path through the Heavens is mythic. Allegory employed as rough material for Myth is frequent in the work of the Great Masters, as notably in the greatest of all Myths—in the *Divina Commedia*. A striking instance there is the Procession, symbolic of the connection between the Old Dispensation and the New, which passes before the Poet in the Earthly Paradise (*Purg.* xxix. ff.). The Visions of Ezekiel, to which Dante is here indebted for some of his imagery, may also be mentioned as instances of mythological compositions built largely out of elements which are allegories. It is enthusiasm and a living faith which, indeed, inspire the mythopœic or prophetic architect to build at all; but his creative enthusiasm is often served by a curious diligence in the elaboration of the parts.

III

I have identified the prenatal impression produced in the Soul by the Eternal Forms seen in the Super-Celestial place

---

[1] *Phaedrus*, 244. [2] Alluded to *supra*, p. 297.

with Categories, or *a priori* conditions of sensible experience, and regarded the "recollection" in this life of these Forms seen in the prenatal life as equivalent to the effective operation of *a priori* Categories, or functions of the Understanding, on the occasion of the presentation of objects of sense. I wish now to meet an objection which may be brought against this identification. Let us first look at the list of Eternal Forms given in the Myth (247 C, and 250 B). They are Justice Itself; Temperance Itself; True Knowledge; Beauty Itself; and are described as really existent, and without colour, without shape, intangible. Now Justice Itself and Temperance Itself in this list cannot be called Categories of the Understanding. They would seem to correspond rather to "Categorical Imperative". True knowledge, on the other hand, does cover the ground occupied by Categories of the Understanding, if it does not cover more. Knowledge is distinguished in the *Meno* (97, 98), as knowledge of the effect through its cause, from right opinion, empirical knowledge of the detached effect; and the recognition of necessary causal connection, thus identified with knowledge, is expressly said (98 A) to be recollection. If we consider how close the Myth of recollection in the *Meno* (81 B) stands to the *Phaedrus* Myth, we are bound to conclude that the true knowledge, mentioned as one of the existences seen by the Soul in the region above the heavens, covers the *a priori* Category of Cause, and, it is fair to add, the other Categories of the Understanding by the use of which, within the limits of possible experience, scientific truth is attained. Further, while the presence or true knowledge among the Eternal Essences or Forms entitles us to speak of *a priori* Categories as domiciled in the region above the heavens[1] of the *Phaedrus* Myth, we need not quarrel with the presence of Justice itself, Temperance itself, Beauty itself in a list of Categories; the distinction between Categories of the Understanding and Ideas of Reason, as I have pointed out, is not provided for in Plato's philosophical language, and it is to be noticed that, in describing these Eternal Essences or Forms of Justice,

---

[1] These are "Categories which are already in things", to use Professor Pringle-Pattison's expression (*Scottish Philosophy*, p. 140).

T

Temperance, and Beauty, he describes them as if they were Categories "empty without sense"—that is, empty except as "recollected" in this life on the occasion of the presence of objects of sense; just as in the parallel passage in the *Meno* (81 c), he speaks of the prenatal knowledge of goodness as "recollected" in this life. It will be fair, then, I think, to call the list of Essences or Forms in the *Phaedrus* Myth a list of Categories of the Understanding (included under true knowledge), and of certain other *a priori* Forms described as if they were Categories. As in the *Timaeus*, so in the *Phaedrus* Myth, the fact (ascertained, we may suppose, by Plato as by Kant through introspection) that man brings *a priori* principles to bear on his individual experience is explained by an Aetiological Myth telling how the Soul in its prenatal state goes round, so far as it is not hindered by earthward inclination, with the revolution of the outermost heavenly sphere, from the back, or convex surface, of which is seen the region above the heavens—the plain of truth, where the true food of the mind grows. The Eternal Truths which grow on this Plain are apprehended by the gods perfectly; by other Souls, which are still within the cycle of generation, only in an interrupted and partial view; but, we may suppose, in godlike manner by human Souls which have been finally purified and released from the flesh for ever. In proportion as a human Soul has "recollection" of these truths while it is in the flesh, in that proportion is it purified. Among the Eternal Essences of the region above the heavens the Beauty Itself is that which is most easily "remembered", because it is more apparent in its visible copies than the other Essences are in theirs (*Phaedrus*, 250 D). The Eternal Beauty manifests itself to the eye in beautiful things more clearly than the Eternal Justice, for instance, manifests itself to the "moral sense" in actions, laws, and institutions. Love, awakened by the sight of "beautiful things", is the form taken by this "recollection" of the Eternal Beauty—an impulse, at once emotional and intellectual, of the whole man, by which he is carried on, through the apprehension of that Essential Principle which is most easily apprehended, to the apprehension also of the Essential Principles of Conduct and Science. Hence love, recollection, and philosophy are practically convertible terms,[1] and mean the intellectual love of God. This enthusiastic love of the beautiful "intelligible world", sharpening recollection till all forgetfulness is overcome, and the Soul is made perfectly pure, and is redeemed from the flesh for ever—this philosophy (to sum up all in a single word), being a nisus which engages the whole man in one concentrated endeavour, can only be felt and affirmed, cannot be explained. It is the very Life of the Subject of all experience, and cannot be treated as if it were an Object to be explained scientifically in its place among other Objects like itself.

The Philosopher as conceived by Plato is an ardent Lover. He lives all his earthly life in a trembling hope, and, out of his hope, sees visions, and prophesies.

Plato, keenly appreciating the power with which expression of thought or feeling reacts on thought or feeling, spares no pains in showing how to give artistic form to Myth, the natural expression (if only as by-product) of the enthusiastic philosophic nisus after self-realisation or purification. This is the justification of the artistic Myth, for the construction of which Plato supplies models—that it helps to moderate and refine and direct the aspirations, the hopes, the fears, the curiosity, of which Myth is the natural expression. It will be remembered what importance is attached, in the scheme of education sketched in the *Republic*, to "good form" in the mode of expressing not only literary meaning and musical feeling, but also athletic effort. The form of expression is, as it were, the vessel which contains and gives contour to the character which expresses itself. We must be careful to see that we have in our system of education good models of expression into which, as into moulds, young character may be poured. Apart from its bearing on education, the whole question of the reaction of expression on that which expresses itself is an interesting one, and may be studied in its biological rudiments in

---

[1] So Dante (*Conv.* iii. 12), says, "Philosophy is a loving exercise of Wisdom": Amor is the Form, and Sapienza the Subject Matter of Filosofia (*Conv.* iii. 13, 14). So also Wordsworth, substituting "Poetry" for "Philosophy" (Pref. to *Lyrical Ballads*), "Poetry is the breath and finer spirit of all knowledge: it is the impassioned expression which is in the countenance of all Science".

Darwin's work on the *Expression of the Emotions in Man and Animals.*

I said that we should do well, considering the complexity of the *Phaedrus* Myth, not to detach its Deduction of Categories or doctrine of recollection too much from the general context. The doctrine of recollection is treated by Plato, in the *Phaedrus* and *Meno*, as inseparable from the doctrine of the prenatal existence and immortality of the Soul, and is closely bound up with the Orphic doctrine of purification and his own version of it—the doctrine of philosophic love. It is impossible, then, to pledge Plato to belief in the literal truth of the doctrine of recollection, unless we are prepared to go with Zeller the length of thinking that he is in earnest in believing that the Soul actually existed as a separate person before it was born into this body, and will pass through a series of incarnations after the death of this body. "If it be impossible," writes Zeller (*Plato*, pp. 404 ff., Eng. Tr.), "to imagine the soul as not living, this must equally hold good of the future and of the past; its existence can as little begin with this life as end with it. Strictly speaking, it can never have begun at all; for the soul being itself the source of all motion, from what could its motion have proceeded? Accordingly Plato hardly ever mentions immortality without alluding to pre-existence, and his expressions are as explicit and decided about the one as the other. In his opinion they stand or fall together, and he uses them alike to explain the facts of our spiritual life. We therefore cannot doubt that he was thoroughly in earnest in his assumption of a pre-existence. And that this pre-existence had no beginning is so often asserted by him[1] that a mythical representation like that of the *Timaeus* can hardly be allowed any weight to the contrary. We must, nevertheless, admit the possibility that in his later years he did not strictly abide by the consequences of his system, nor definitely propound to himself whether the soul had any historical beginning, or only sprang to its essential nature from some higher principle.

"If the two poles of this ideal circle, Pre-existence and Immortality, be once established, there is no evading the

[1] *Phaedrus*, 245 C, D; *Meno*, 86 A.

doctrine of Recollection which lies between them; and the notions of Transmigration and of future rewards and punishments appear, the more we consider them, to be seriously meant. With regard to Recollection, Plato speaks in the above-cited passages so dogmatically and definitely, and the theory is so bound up with his whole system, that we must unconditionally reckon it among the doctrinal constituents of that system. The doctrine is an inference which could not well be escaped if once the pre-existence of the soul were admitted; for an existence of infinite duration must have left in the soul some traces which, though temporarily obscured in our consciousness, could not be for ever obliterated. But it is also in Plato's opinion the only solution of a most important scientific question: the question as to the possibility of independent inquiry—of thought transcending sensuous perception. Our thought could not get beyond the Immediate and the Actual; we could not seek for what is as yet unknown to us, nor recognise in what we find the thing that we sought for, if we had not unconsciously possessed it before we recognised and were conscious of it.[1] We could form no conception of Ideas, of the eternal essence of things which is hidden from our perception, if we had not attained to the intuition of these in a former existence.[2] The attempt of a modern work to exclude the theory of Recollection from the essential doctrines of the Platonic system[3] is therefore entirely opposed to the teaching of Plato. The arguments for the truth and necessity of this doctrine are not indeed, from our point of view, difficult to refute; but it is obvious that from Plato's they are seriously meant."

I venture to think that the doctrine of recollection, in itself, and in its setting, is not intended by Plato to be taken literally—that it is not Dogma but Myth. This view, for which I may appeal to the authority of Leibniz and Coleridge,[4] seems to me to be borne out by the passage in the

---

[1] *Meno*, 80 D ff.
[2] *Phaedo*, 73 C ff. and 76 D.
[3] Teichmüller, *Studien zur Gesch. d. Begriffe*, pp. 208 ff.
[4] Leibniz (*Nouv. Ess.* Avant-propos) describes the Platonic doctrine of Reminiscence as entirely imaginary; and Coleridge (*Biog. Lit.* ch. 22), speaking of Wordsworth's *Ode on the Intimations of Immortality from Recollections of Early Childhood*, says: "The ode was intended for such readers as had been accustomed to watch the flux and reflux of their inmost nature, to venture at times into the twilight realms of consciousness, and to feel a deep interest

Meno[1] dealing with recollection: recollection is presented there, in accordance with Orphic belief, as becoming clearer and clearer at each incarnation, till the soul at last attains to the blessed life of a daemon. Can it be maintained that Plato is in earnest with all the Orphic details of this passage?—and, if not with all, with any? It is to be noted, too, that Socrates ends by recommending his tale about recollection entirely on practical grounds, as likely to make us more ready to take the trouble of seeking after knowledge. Here we are in this world, he says in effect, with mental faculties which perhaps deceive us. How are we to save ourselves from scepticism and accidie? Only by believing firmly that our mental faculties do not deceive us. Science cannot establish in us the belief that our mental faculties do not deceive us; for our mental faculties are the conditions of science. The surest way of getting to believe that our mental faculties do not deceive us is, of course, to use them: but if the absence of scientific proof of their trustworthiness should ever give us anxiety, the persuasiveness of a Myth may comfort us; that is, a Myth may put us in the mood of not *arguing* about our mental faculties, but believing in them. Meno, in argumentative mood, asks how it is possible to investigate a thing about which one knows absolutely nothing—in this case, Virtue, about which Socrates professes to know nothing himself, and has shown that Meno knows nothing. One's investigation, Meno argues, having no object whatever before it, might hit by accident on some truth—but how is one to know that it is the truth one wants? To this Socrates replies: I understand your meaning, Meno. But don't you see what a verbal sort of argument it is that you are introducing? You mean "that one can't investigate either what one knows or what one does not know; for what one knows one knows, and investigation is unnecessary; and what one does not know one does not know, and how can one investigate one knows not what?"

in modes of inmost being, to which they know that the attributes of time and space are inapplicable and alien, but which yet cannot be conveyed, save in symbols of time and space. For such readers the sense is sufficiently plain, and they will be as little disposed to charge Mr. Wordsworth with believing the Platonic pre-existence in the ordinary interpretation of words, as I am to believe that Plato himself ever meant or taught it."

[1] *Meno*, 81.

Meno. Exactly; and you think it is a good argument?

Socrates. No, I don't.

M. Why, pray?

S. I will tell you. I have heard from men and women who are wise concerning divine things—

M. What have you heard?

S. A Tale, true I believe, and great and glorious.

M. What was it? Who told you?

S. Those priests and priestesses whose continual study it is to be able to give an account of the things which are their business; and also Pindar, and many other divine poets. And their Tale is this—it is for you to consider whether you think it a true Tale: they say, "That the Soul of Man is immortal, and to-day she cometh to her End, which they call Death; and then afterwards is she born again, but perisheth never. Wherefore it behoveth us to go through our lives observing religion alway: for *the Souls of them from whom Persephone hath received the price of ancient Sin, she sendeth back to the light of the Sun above in the ninth year. These be they who become noble kings and men swift and strong and mighty in wisdom, and are called Blessed of them that come after unto all generations."*

Since the Soul, then, Socrates continues, is immortal, and has often been incarnate, and has seen both the things here and the things in Hades, and all things, there is nothing which she has not learnt. No wonder, then, that she is able, of herself, to recall to memory what she formerly knew about Virtue or anything else; for, as Nature is all of one common stock and kind, and the Soul has learnt all things, there is no reason why, starting from her recollection of but one thing (this is what is called "learning"), a man should not, of himself, discover all other things, if only he have good courage, and shirk not inquiry—for, according to this account, all inquiry and learning is "remembering". So, we must not be led away by your verbal argument. It would make us idle; for it is an argument that slack people like. But my account of the matter stirs people up to work and inquire. Believing it to be the true account, I am willing, along with you, to inquire what Virtue is.[1]

---

[1] *Meno,* 80 D-81 E.

The practical lesson to be drawn from the Myth contained in this passage is indicated by Socrates a little further on:[1]—There are things, he says, in the Doctrine, or Myth, of Reminiscence on which it is hardly worth while to insist, if they are challenged; but there is one thing in its teaching which is worth maintaining against all comers—that, if we think that we ought to investigate what we do not know, we are better men, more courageous and less slothful, than if we think that what we do not know is something which it is neither possible to ascertain nor right to investigate.

Zeller's reason for maintaining that the doctrine of recollection, set forth in this passage and in the *Phaedrus* Myth, is to be taken literally seems to be that the doctrine is propounded by Plato as the sole explanation of what he certainly accepted as a fact—the presence of an *a priori* element in experience, and, moreover, is an explanation involving the doctrine of Ideas which, it is urged, Plato wishes to be taken literally.

I do not think that because introspection makes Plato accept as a fact the presence of an *a priori* element in experience, it follows that even the only "explanation" which occurs to him of the fact is regarded by him as "scientific". The "explanation" consists in the assumption of Eternal Ideas which are "recollected" from a prenatal experience on the occasion of the presentation, in this life, of sensible objects "resembling" them. I go the length of thinking that the Eternal Ideas, as assumed in this "explanation", are, like their domicile, the Plain of Truth, creations of mythology.[2] It is because Aristotle either could not or would not see this, that his criticism of the doctrine of Ideas[3] is off the

---

[1] *Meno*, 86 A, B, C.

[2] This view of the Ideas as we have them in the *Phaedrus* Myth is, of course, quite consistent with an orthodox view of their place in Logic. In Logic the ideas are scientific points of view by means of which phenomena are brought into natural groups and explained in their causal context. Answering to these scientific points of view are objectively valid Laws of Nature. Couturat (*de Plat. Mythis*, p. 81), after pointing to certain differences in the accounts given in the *Tim.*, *Phaedo*, *Republ.*, and *Sophistes*, respectively, of the ideas, ends with the remark that we might complain of "inconsistency" were it not that the *whole doctrine* of ideas is "mythical". This, I think, is going too far. It is interesting to note that Dante (*Conv.* ii. 5) draws a close parallel between the Platonic ideas and "Gods": so far as the parallel goes, the former will belong to "mythology" equally with the latter.

[3] *Met.* xii.

mark.   Milton's poem "*On the Platonic Idea, as Aristotle under-stood it*" seems to me to express so happily the state of the case—that the doctrine of Eternal Ideas set forth by Plato in Myth is erroneously taken up by Aristotle as Dogma—that I venture to quote it here in full:[1]—

Tell me, Goddesses who protect the sacred groves, and thou, Mother Memory, greatly blessed in the ninefold divinity, who as tranquil Eternity reclinest far away in the tremendous Cave, preserving the memorials and the fixed laws of Jove, and the daily records of Heaven and the Gods, Who is He that first formed expertly in his image the human race?   He the eternal, incorruptible, coeval with the heavens; the single and universal likeness of God?

Not he, twin brother of virgin Pallas, dwells as progeny within the mind of Jove, but although his nature may be shared with all, he yet exists above and apart, according to the will of the One.   And wonder! is confined in a fixed region of space: whether he, the eternal comrade of the stars, roams through the tenfold orders of Heaven, or inhabits the orb of the Moon, which is nearest to the Earth; or seated among souls about to enter the body, numbs the forgetful by the waters of Lethe; or else perchance in remote regions of the earth he strides, a great giant, arche-type of man, and terrifies the Gods as he lifts his lofty head, huger than Atlas, supporter of the stars.

Not he to whom blindness gave profound light, the Dircaean seer, perceived him in his deep heart, nor in the silent night did Plëione's swift-thoughted grandson show him to the wise choir of prophets.   The Assyrian priest did not know him, though he commemorated the far-distant ancestors of ancient Ninus, and primeval Belos, and re-nowned Osiris.   Not he, glorious in the triple name, Thrice Greatest Hermes (as thus conversant with the Mysteries), left such a tale to the worshippers of Isis.

But you,[2] perennial glory of the Garden of Academus (if you first brought this monstrosity into the schools) now, now you shall recall the Poets, exiles from your city; yourself the greatest teller of tales, or else depart yourself, its founder, from the gates.

---

[1] Masson's *Poetical Works of John Milton*, vol. iii. p. 76.

[2] Prof. Masson (*o.c.* iii. 527) says: "'You' is, of course, Plato; and here, it seems to me, Milton intimates at the close that he does not believe that the Aristotelian representation of Plato's Idea, which he has been burlesquing in the poem, is a true rendering of Plato's real meaning.   If it were so—if Plato had really taught any such monstrosity, then, etc.   I rather think commentators on the poem have missed its humorous character, and sup-posed Milton himself to be finding fault with Plato."

To put the matter briefly: I regard the whole doctrine of recollection, and of ideas *qua* involved in that doctrine, as an Aetiological Myth—plausible, comforting, and encouraging—to explain the fact that Man finds himself in a World in which he can get on. The Myth is a protest against the Unknown Reason of Meno and his like—the sophistry which excuses inactivity by proving, to the satisfaction of the inactive, that successful advance in knowledge and morality is impossible.

IV

Phaedrus, 248 D, E

The fact that the Philosopher and the Tyrant are respectively first and last in a list of *nine* can be explained only by reference to the importance attached by Plato to $9 \times 9 \times 9 = 729$, which, in *Republ.* 587 D, E (see Adam's notes), marks the superiority of the Philosopher over the Tyrant in respect of Happiness. The number 729 had a great vogue in later times. Plutarch, in his *On the creation of the soul, from the Timaeus*, ch. 31, makes it the number of the Sun, which we know from the *On the face in the disc of the Moon*, ch. 28, stands for the intellect, and that the Sun itself is number 729, which is at once the square and the cube. It is also involved in the "mysterie of the Septenary, or number seven", which is of two kinds—the 7 which comes in the series 1, 2, 3, 4, 5, 6, 7, 8, 9, 10; and the seventh term from unity in the series 1, 3, 9, 27, 81, 243, 729. This is both a square (=incorporeal substance) and a cube (=corporeal substance), *i.e.* 27×27 and $9 \times 9 \times 9$ both $= 729$. This is worked out by Philo in a passage of his *Cosmopoeia Mosaica*, quoted by Dr. Henry More in his *Defence of the Moral Cabbala*, ch. ii. p. 164 (ed. 1662); and More's application is worth quoting: "Seven hundred and twenty-nine is made either by *squaring* of twenty-seven, or *cubically* multiplying of nine, and so is both *cube* and *square*, *Corporeal*, and *Incorporeal*. Whereby is intimated that the World shall not be reduced in the *Seventh day* to a mere spiritual consistency, to an *incorporeal* condition, but that there shall be a cohabitation of the Spirit with Flesh in a mystical or moral sense, and that God will pitch his Tent amongst us. Then shall be settled everlasting Righteousness, and rooted in the Earth, so long as mankind shall inhabit upon the face thereof."

Again, Dante makes 9 the number of Beatrice. She was in her ninth year when he first saw her (*Vita Nuova*, 2); his first greeting he received from her nine years afterwards at the ninth hour of the day (*V. N.*, 3); and she departed this life on the ninth day of the ninth month of the year, according to the Syrian style (*V. N.* 30):—"This number was her very self; by likeness I mean, and I understand it in this way: Number three is the root of nine, because without any other number, multiplied by itself it makes nine, as we see manifestly that three times three makes nine. Therefore, if three is the only factor of nine, and the only factor of miracles is three, that is, Father, Son and Holy Ghost, who are three and one, this lady was accompanied by the number nine to make us understand that she was a nine, that is, a miracle whose root is in the marvellous Trinity alone." With this may be compared a passage in *Convivio*, iv. 24, in which Dante, referring to Cicero, *de Senectute* (§ 5), as authority, says that Plato died aged eighty-one (cf. Toynbee, *Dante Dict.*, art. "Platone," at the end, for a quotion from Seneca, *Ep.* 58, to the same effect); and adds: "And I believe that, if Christ had not been crucified, and if he had lived for that period of time which his life might have covered in accordance with nature, he would have been transformed in his eighty-first year from a mortal body to an eternal one."

V

The contrast between the celestial *mise en scène* of the History of the Soul represented in the *Phaedrus* Myth, and the terrestrial scenery of the great Eschatological Myths in the *Phaedo, Gorgias,* and *Republic,* is a point on which some remarks may be offered.

In the *Phaedrus* Myth we are mainly concerned with the Fall and Ascension of human Souls through the Heavenly Spheres intermediate between the Earth and the Meadow of Truth. Reference to the Sublunary Region which includes

Tartarus, the Plain of Lethe, and the Earthly Paradise (Islands of the Blessed, True Surface of the Earth, what is round the Earth=Heaven), is slight and distant. In the *Phaedrus* Myth we have light wings and a *Paradiso;* in the three other Myths mentioned, plodding feet and an *Inferno* and a *Purgatorio.*

This distinction answers to a real difference in the sources on which Plato drew for his History of the Soul. On the one hand, he was indebted to the Pythagorean Orphics, who put purification in the forefront of their eschatology. On the other hand, he had at his disposal, for the selection of details, the less refined mythology of the *Descent to Hades,* as taught by the Priests denounced in the *Republic.*[1]

The eschatology of the Pythagorean Orphics may be broadly characterised as celestial and astronomical. The Soul falls from her native place in the Highest Heaven, through the Heavenly Spheres, to her first incarnation on Earth. By means of a series of sojourns in Hades, and re-incarnations on Earth (the details of which are mostly taken from the mythology of the *Descent to Hades*), she is purified from the taint of the flesh. Then, at last, she returns to her native place in the Highest Heaven, passing, in the upward flight of her chariot, through the Heavenly Spheres, as through Stations or Doors.

The earliest example which has come down to us of this celestial eschatology is that which meets us in the passage with which Parmenides begins his Poem. Parmenides goes up in a chariot accompanied by the Daughters of the Sun; he rides through the Gate of Justice where the paths of Day and Night have their parting; and comes to the Region of Light, where Wisdom receives him.[2]

In contrast to this celestial eschatology, the eschatology of the Priests denounced in the *Republic* may be described as terrestrial. All Souls go to a place on Earth, or under the Earth, to be judged, and the good are sent to the right to eternal feasting (everlasting drunkenness, *Rep.*

---

[1] 363 c, d; 364 b ff.
[2] See Burnet's *Early Greek Philosophy,* First Edition pp. 183 ff.; and Dieterich, *A Mithraic Liturgy,* p. 197. The passage does not express the views of Parmenides himself; but is borrowed from the Pythagorean Orphics, probably for the mere purpose of decoration. The Soul-chariots of the *Phaedrus* Myth are derived from the same source.

363 D), and the wicked to the left, to lie for ever in the Pit of Slime. Of the true purification effected by a secular process of penance and philosophic aspiration these Priests have no conception. The only purification which comes within the range of their thought is that effected, once for all in this life, by ritual observance. The purification thus effected in this life is all that is needed to bring the Soul to the very "earthly" Paradise of their eschatology.

Although Plato leaves us in the *Gorgias* with only the Islands of the Blessed and the Pit of Tartarus of this terrestrial eschatology, he makes it plain in the *Phaedo* Myth, not to mention the *Timaeus* and the *Phaedrus* Myth, that the ultimate destination of the virtuous Soul is not any Terrestrial Paradise of sensual delights (which might well be that secured by mere ritual purification), but a Celestial Paradise, to which the Pure Intelligence rises by its own strenuous effort, recalling to memory more and more clearly the Eternal Truth which it ardently loves.

It was through what may be called its astronomical side, and not through that side which reflects the mythology of the *Descent to Hades*, that the Platonic eschatology influenced subsequent religious thought and practice. The doctrine of purification effected by personal effort in a Cosmos governed by God, which, after all, is the great contribution made by Plato to the religious thought and practice of Europe, found its appropriate vehicle in the large astronomy which meets us in the *Timaeus* and *Phaedrus*—an astronomy which was afterwards elaborated, with special reference to the aerial and aethereal habitats of Daemons and disembodied human Souls, by the Stoics no less than by the Platonists. Dieterich, in his *A Mithraic Liturgy* (1903), mentions the Stoic Posidonius, Cicero's teacher, as the writer who did most to unite the Pythagorean and Platonic tradition with the doctrines of the Stoa. As result of his accommodation of Platonic eschatology to Stoic doctrine, reference[1] to a subterranean Hades disappears, and the History of the Soul after Death is that of its ascent from Earth to Air, from Air to Aether, and through the Spheres of the Planets to the Sphere of the Fixed Stars. The substitution of ascent for descent, even in

[1] *Eine Mithrasliturgie*, pp. 79 and 202.

the case of the Souls of the wicked, connects itself closely with the "physical science" of the Stoics. In the *Phaedrus* Myth the Soul has wings and flies up; but the Stoics give a "scientific" reason for its ascent—the "matter" of which it is made is so rare and light that it rises of necessity when it is separated from the terrestrial body. To Posidonius, and through him to Plato and the Pythagorean Orphics, Dieterich[1] carries back the eschatology of Cicero's *Dream of Scipio* and *Tusculan Disputations*,[2] and of Seneca's Letter to *Marcia*[3]—an eschatology in which the Soul is represented as ascending through Heavenly Stations; while the astronomy of the pseudo-Aristotelian *Concerning the Universe*—a work of the first century after Christ, translated in the second century by Apuleius—he contends, is essentially that of Posidonius. The latest embodiment of the Type first made known to us in the Poem of Parmenides and the *Phaedrus* Myth is Dante's *Paradiso*, the scheme of which is "The Ascension of a Purified Soul through the Moving Heavens into the Presence of God in the Unmoved Heaven". Let us try to follow the line, or lines, along which the influence of the *Phaedrus* Myth (for the Poem of Parmenides scarcely counts beside the *Phaedrus* Myth) was transmitted to the *Paradiso*.

It was transmitted to the *Paradiso* along two main lines. The first passed through the Aristotelian *Metaphysics* and *On the Heavens*—the influence thus transmitted showing itself in the definite astronomical framework of the *Paradiso*, and the notion of "The Love which moves the Sun and the other stars". The second line (which I believe to be necessary, with the first, for the full explanation of the scheme, and more especially of the character of the *Paradiso*) has two strands, one of which consists of the *Dream of Scipio*, and its antecedents, chiefly Stoical; the other, of certain astronomical apocalypses, chiefly Christian—these apocalypses being closely related to certain sacramental rites, or mysteries, which embody the eschatology of the *Phaedrus* Myth.

Let me enlarge a little on these two lines of influence; and, first, try to indicate how the Myth of the Region above the Heavens—the goal of all volition and intellection—

---

[1] *o.c.* p. 201.   [2] i. 18, 19.   [3] Ch. 25.

passes through Aristotle into the Christian mythology of Dante.

The "back of the sky" of the *Phaedrus* Myth (247) is the convex surface of the eighth Sphere—the Sphere of the Fixed Stars, which includes, according to Plato's astronomy, all the other Spheres, and carries them round with it in its revolution from east to west, while they have their own slower motions within from west to east.[1]

The gods, sitting in their chariots, are carried round on this outer Sphere, throughout its whole revolution, in full sight of the Eternal Region beyond, while human Souls, at least till they are perfectly purified, obtain only broken glimpses of it. We must suppose that it is in order to get a connected view of this Super-celestial Region that the newly

---

[1] See *Timaeus*, 36 B; *Republic*, 616 B ff.; and Boeckh, *Another commentary on the Platonic System of Celestial Globes and on the inward truth of Philosophic Astronomy* (Heidelberg, 1810), p. 5. According to the system accepted by Plato as scientifically true, the Earth occupies the centre, round which the Heavens revolve; but the Earth does not revolve on its own axis; the *eillomenen* of *Tim.* 40 B means "wrapped, or globed round", not "revolving" as Arist. *de Coelo*, ii. 293 b 30, falsely interprets. If Plato made the Earth revolve on its axis, that would neutralise the effect of the revolution of the Sphere of the Fixed Stars (Boeckh, *o.c.* p. 9). In the *Phaedrus* Myth, however, Boeckh (p. 28) is of opinion that Plato deserts the system which he accepts as scientifically true, and follows the Pythagoreans, who put Hestia, the Watchtower of Zeus, in the centre of the Universe (see Burnet *op. cit.*, § 125, pp. 319 ff.). The "For Hestia alone among the Gods remains at home", of *Phaedrus*, 247 A, is in favour of Boeckh's opinion; but, apart from this one clause, there is nothing in the Myth to suggest that Plato does not think of the Earth as fixed in the midst of the Heavens. If he thought of the Earth as one of the planets revolving round a Pythagorean central fire, why does the Earth not appear with the other planets, in this Myth, as one of the planet-gods in the train of Zeus? "The planet-gods," Plato in effect says, "after their journey come 'home'. Hestia, the 'hearth' is the 'home' to which they come." This is a quite natural sequence of ideas; and I think it better to suppose that it passed through Plato's mind, than to have recourse to the view that he abandoned the doctrine of the centrality of the Earth, without which, indeed, it would be very difficult to visualize the Fall and Ascension of human Souls—the main "incident" of the Myth. The statement of Theophrastus recorded by Plutarch, that Plato in his later years regretted that he had made the Earth the centre in the *Timaeus*, is doubtless justly suspected by Zeller and other scholars: see Zeller's *Plato*, p. 379, n. 37, Eng. Transl.

I have spoken of the choir of Zeus as "planet-gods"; but, as there are seven planets and twelve gods—or eleven in the absence of Hestia—the expression is only approximately exact. Cf. Thompson's *Phaedrus*, p. 159.

For later developments of the geocentric system accepted by Plato, see Arist. *Met.* xi, 1073 b 17 ff. (xi is judged to be post-Aristotelian by Rose, *de Arist. lib. ord. et auct.* p. 242), where the system of Eudoxus with 27 spheres, that of Callippus with 34 spheres, and that of the writer himself with 56 spheres, are described. Cf. Zeller's *Arist.* i. 499-503, Engl. Transl. These spheres were added to explain the phenomena.

created Souls in the *Timaeus* (40 E - 42 E) are sent, each in
its star-chariot, on a journey round the Heavens. It is the
invincible desire of seeing the Super-celestial Region which
draws all Souls, divine and human, up to the "back of the
sky", and obliges them to go round with the revolution of
the heaven—moving in order to apprehend the whole extent
of that which is unmoved. Human thought here on Earth is
rational in so far as it reproduces, or "imitates", within the
microcosm of the circular brain, the orbit in which the
Heavenly Sphere moves in the presence of this Unmoved
(*Timaeus*, 47 B).

Aristotle, although he omits the mythology of Souls in
their chariots, retains the motive of the *Phaedrus* Myth, and,
indeed, much of its language,[1] in his doctrine that the Outer
Sphere—the *Primum Mobile*—is itself moved by the attraction
of something beyond which is unmoved; and this ultimate
unmoved source of the heavenly motion he identifies with
God, described as an immaterial, eternally active, Principle,
final object at once of knowledge and desire, Who moves
the Heavens as One Beloved moves a Lover—"it moves as
the object of love."[2] Now this is Myth. God the Best
Beloved, the Final Truth, takes, in Aristotle's theory, the
place of the Meadow of Truth which the Souls, in Plato's
Myth, eagerly seek to see. The language of the Aristotelian
passage, too, is worthy of the dignity of the Myth. With all
its technicalities the passage is a lofty hymn which has
deeply influenced the religious imagination of all after ages.

The Region above the Heavens, or Meadow of Truth,
of the *Phaedrus* Myth—the God of *Met.* xi, Who, unmoved
object of volition and intellection, moves the Heavens—
appears in the Christian doctrine, which Dante poetises, as
the Quiet Heaven, the Empyrean, the unmoved dwelling-
place of God and all the blessed spirits. This, in the
mediaeval astronomy, is counted as the Tenth Heaven, for
between it and the Eighth Sphere of the Platonico-Aristote-
lian system the Ninth Starless Sphere, the Crystalline Sphere,
had been interpolated as *primum mobile*. Let us turn again
to the passage in the Banquet (ii. 4) in which Dante speaks

---

[1] *Phaedrus*, 245 C, is the source of the thought and phraseology of Arist.
Met. xi, 1072 a 23 ff.

[2] See Arist. *Met.* xi, 1072 a 21-1072 b 30.

of the Tenth Heaven, and read it afresh[1] in the light of what has been said about the plain of Truth and the Aristotelian God:—

"There are nine Moving Heavens; and the order of their position is as follows: The first that is reckoned is that of the Moon; the second that in which Mercury is; the third Venus; the fourth the Sun; the fifth Mars; the sixth Jupiter; the seventh Saturn; the eighth is that of the Stars; the ninth is that which can only be perceived by the movement above mentioned, which is called Crystalline, or diaphanous, or wholly transparent. But outside of these Catholics suppose the Empyrean Heaven, which is as much as to say the Heaven of Flame, or the Luminous; and they suppose this to be immovable, since it has in itself, in respect of every part, that which its matter requires. And this is the reason why the *primum mobile* has most rapid movement: because by reason of the fervent longing which every part of it has to be joined to every part of that most divine Motionless Heaven, it revolves within that with so great desire that its velocity is, as it were, incomprehensible. And this Motionless and Peaceful Heaven is the place of that Supreme Deity which alone fully beholds itself. This is the place of the blessed spirits, according as Holy Church, which cannot lie, will have it; and this Aristotle, to whoso understands him aright, seems to mean in the first book *On the Heavens*."

In this doctrine of the Quiet Heaven, justly said to have the authority of Aristotle in its favour, we have the motive of the whole Myth of the *Paradiso*. The ascent of Dante, through the Nine Moving Spheres, to the Unmoved Heaven, his will and intellect moved at every stage by "the Love which moves the sun and other stars", is a Myth—how valuable in its regulative influence the world knows, and may yet know better—a Myth setting forth like the Myth of the Soul-Chariots, man's personal effort to take his place in the Cosmos by "imitating" its eternal laws in his own thought and will, not content to look always down, like the brutes, at the things beneath him on the ground, but, first, lifting up his eyes to the Visible Gods—the stars in their orderly courses—and then thinking out the law of their

[1] See p. 169 *supra*.

U

order; thus, as we read in the *Timaeus* (47 A), realising the final cause of eyes, which is to awaken thought.   The ultimate identity of Thought and Will as both drawn forth by the attraction of one Object—the Object, Plato would say, of "Philosophy", of "Theology" Aristotle and Dante would say—is thus contained in the Myth of the *Paradiso*, as in the *Phaedrus* Myth.   The associations of Dante's Myth lie nearer to our modern life than those of Plato's Myth, and we may be helped to appreciate the latter through the former. In both we have models of what a refined Myth ought to be.   It ought to be based on old tradition, and yet must not fetter, but rather give new freedom to, present-day thinking. It is impossible to define, or even describe, the aid which a refined mythology, such as that of Dante, brings to a man's life, for the aid which it brings is inseparable from the charm under which his personal study of it has at last brought him: "It is necessary to sing such things over to one's self."[1]

The Meadow of Truth of the *Phaedrus* Myth, which thus answers to Aristotle's unmoved mover, or God, and to Dante's Unmoved Heaven, or Empyrean, the dwelling-place of God, holds an important position in the Neo-Platonic philosophy.   The passage in which Plotinus describes it is one of the most highly-strung pieces of philosophical writing in the whole of his *Enneads*, and need not be entered upon here;[2] but Plutarch's description of it may be given.   It occurs in his *On the failure of the oracles*,[3] where he records the doctrine of a "Barbarian Stranger", who, rejecting alike the view of Plato, that there is only one Cosmus, and the view of others, that the number of Cosmi is infinite, and that of others still, that there are five of them, maintains that there are exactly 183[4] of them, arranged in the figure of a triangle, the sides of which they form, touching one another—60 to each side, and one in each angle.   These

---

[1] *Phaedo*, 114 D.

[2] *Enn.* vi. 7. 13. Two sentences from it will show its character sufficiently:— "In itself the true mind was born to wander, moving together with those beings who were wandering with itself; for it itself is everywhere, and therefore it holds wandering within itself. Its wandering is in the Plain of Truth, from which it dare not depart."

[3] Ch. 22.

[4] Half of the number of the days in the year, as a friend suggests to me. Cf. the number of the king (729), *Rep.* 587 E.

Cosmi move round along the sides of the triangle in procession, moving round unswervingly, as in a dance; and
the area of the triangle which these moving Cosmi make is
called the Plain of Truth. In this Plain abide unmoved the
reasons, forms, patterns, of all things which ever have, and
ever shall, come into being; and round about these Eternal
Verities is spread Eternity, which flows out as Time upon
the moving Cosmi. Human Souls, if they live virtuously,
have sight of these Eternal Verities once in ten thousand
years. The holiest mysteries of this world are but a dream
of that Perfect Revelation.

"This Myth of the Barbarian Stranger," says the narrator
of it in Plutarch's Dialogue, "I listened to as though I were
being initiated. The Stranger offered no demonstration or
other evidence of the truth of it."

The Myth[1] is a good instance of the way in which the
later Platonists used Plato's suggestions—and, it must be
added, Aristotle's; for in *De Caelo*,[2] the *aeon* outside the
Heavens, where there is neither place nor emptiness,
nor time, nor change, is identified with God, whose life is
described as without suffering, most excellent, sole-governing.
Platonists had, indeed, almost as rich a mine to work in
Aristotle as they had in Plato himself.[3]

Before I leave the subject of the influence of the *Phaedrus*
Myth as transmitted to Dante through the *de Coelo* and
Metaphysics—it shows itself mainly in the definite astro-
nomical framework of the *Paradiso*, and the notion of

The Love that moves the Sun and the other stars.

I may notice another notion very prominent in the *Paradiso*
which seems to have taken form in the course of an evolution
starting from the *Phaedrus* Myth, or the eschatology of which
that Myth is the most eminent product. I refer to the
notion that the various temperaments, or characters, are
produced by the action of the stars, especially of the planets.

---

[1] Referred to by Dr. Bigg, *Neoplatonism*, p. 121.
[2] i. 9. 279 a 16.
[3] The *Axiochus* (371 B) is quite un-Platonic, and indeed singular, in its
view of the plain of Truth. The place where Minos and the other Judges of
the Dead sit is called the plain of Truth, and is on the *other side* of Acheron
and Cocytus, *i.e. down in* Tartarus; whereas the Meadow of the Judgment-
Seat in the *Phaedo* is on *this side* of these rivers, and in the *Republic* is certainly
outside of Tartarus.

This notion is deeply embedded in the structure of the *Paradiso*. The spirits whom Dante sees in the three lower spheres are seen by him there in human form because in their earthly lives they yielded to influences exerted by the Moon, by Mercury, and by Venus respectively—because they broke vows, were ambitious, were guilty of unchastity. In the four upper planetary spheres likewise Dante sees spirits whose characters on Earth were such as their various planets determined; these, however, being beyond the shadow of the Earth and its influence, are no longer in human form, but enclosed in an envelope of light—they are burning suns[1]—spherical, like the stars; for the sphere is the perfect form which the pure aethereal vehicle naturally takes. Now, if we turn from the *Paradiso* to the *Phaedrus* Myth we find that there Souls belong to the choir of, follow in the train of, various Planet-Gods, Zeus, Ares, and others, in their ascent to the Empyrean, or plain of Truth, and show corresponding temperaments of character when they are afterwards born in the flesh.

This mythological explanation of the varieties of temperament may be compared with that offered by Macrobius in his Commentary on Cicero's *Dream of Scipio*, which I cannot do better than give in Professor Dill's words:[2]—

> The Commentary on the *Dream of Scipio* enables one to understand how devout minds could even to the last remain attached to paganism. It presupposes rather than expounds the theology of Neoplatonism. Its chief motive is rather moral or devotional than speculative. The One, supreme, unapproachable, ineffable, residing in the highest heaven, is assumed as the source of mind and life, penetrating all things, from the star in the highest ether to the lowest form of animal existence. The Universe is God's temple, filled with His presence. The unseen, inconceivable Author created from His essence pure mind, in the likeness of Himself. In contact with matter mind degenerates and becomes Soul. In the scale of being the moon marks the limit between the eternal and the perishable, and all below the moon is mortal and evanescent except the higher principle in man. Passing from the divine world through the gate of Cancer (cf. Plotin. *Ennead*, iv. 3. 15), mind descends gradually, in a fall from its original blessedness,

---

[1] *Par.* x. 76.

[2] *Roman Society in the Last Century of the Western Empire*, pp. 90, 91.

through the seven spheres, and, in its passage, the divine and universal element assumes the various faculties which make up the composite nature of man. In Saturn it acquires the reasoning power, in Jupiter the practical and moral, in Mars the spirited, in Venus the sensual element. But in the process of descending into the body, the divine part suffers a sort of intoxication and oblivion of the world from which it comes in some cases deeper than in others. Thus the diffusion of Soul among bodily forms is a kind of death; and the body is only a prison, or rather a tomb, which cannot be quitted save by a second death, the death to sin and earthly passion.

Here, in the *Commentary* of Macrobius, two things kept separate in the *Phaedrus* Myth—the Fall of Souls to the Earth through shedding their wings, and their membership of the retinue of particular gods—are combined. It is in its Fall that a Soul comes into touch with the gods; and derives, it would seem, a complex temperament from touch with them all in succession.[1]

With regard to the cause of the Fall of Souls—the Neo-Platonic mythology, while retaining the wing-losing explanation given in the *Phaedrus*, dwells more particularly on the ideas of illusion and intoxication. Souls remain at peace above till, like Narcissus, they see themselves reflected in the mirror of Dionysus:[2] this is the flowing stream of sense and generation, into which they plunge, mistaking the image for reality. With the idea of illusion thus illustrated, the idea of intoxication connects itself naturally. The stream of sense, the mirror of Dionysus, is the bowl of Dionysus. Plunging into it the Soul drinks forgetfulness of Eternal

---

[1] Macrobius, *Somn.* i. 12, 68. See Lobeck, *Aglaoph.* pp. 932 ff., where other writers are quoted for this view of the formation of human temperament. The seven planets likewise connect themselves with the seven days of the week, and the seven metals (To each of the stars there is some substance assigned, to the sun gold, to the moon silver, to Mars iron, to Saturn lead, to Jupiter electron, Mercury tin, Venus copper, Schol. on Pindar, *Isthm.* v. 2); consequently the Mithraic stair, the seven-staged ladder, represented the seven planetary spheres, through which the Soul passes, by seven metals: the first step, that of Saturn, was of lead; the second, that of Venus, of tin; the third, that of Jupiter, of brass; the fourth, that of Mercury, of iron, and so on, the days of the week being taken in backward order: see Lobeck, *Aglaoph.* p. 934. Further, there are seven colours, seven strings, seven vowels, seven ages of a man's life, as well as seven planets, seven days, and seven metals (cf. Dieterich, *Mithrasliturgie*, pp. 186 ff.); also seven seals, some of them associated with differently coloured horses, and seven angels, in *Rev.* v.-viii.

[2] Plotin. *Ennead*, iv. 3. 12, vol. i. p. 247, ed. Kirchhoff.

Truth, and the world into which it is born thereafter is the cave of Forgetfulness. There are Souls which have not drunk so deeply as others of this cup. There are the "dry souls" of Heraclitus.[1] They still retain some recollection of the disembodied state, and in this earthly life hearken to the good daemon who comes with them in their descent. The comparison of the body to a Heraclitean river, which occurs in *Timaeus* (43 A), doubtless contributed to this Neo-Platonic mythology of the Fall.

The second line of influence connecting the *Paradiso* with the *Phaedrus* Myth has, as I said, two strands, the first of which consists of the *Dream of Scipio* and its antecedents, chiefly Stoical. The links between the *Phaedrus* Myth and *Dream of Scipio* (which Dante undoubtedly knew)[2] are indicated by Dieterich in passages referred to above,[3] and need not be specified here; but the second strand, consisting of the astronomical apocalypses, has scarcely received the attention which it deserves, and I venture to say something about it.

It is remarkable how little Dante is indebted in the *Paradiso* to the *Revelation of St. John*. The seven references in the *Paradiso* to that Apocalypse noted by Dr. Moore (*Studies in Dante*, First Series, Index to Quotations, 1) concern details only. The *Revelation of St. John* has indeed nothing serviceable for Dante's purpose except details, for its scheme is quite different from that of the *Paradiso*. It is very doubtful if the writer knows anything of the astronomy of the eight Moving Heavens and the Unmoved Heaven; at any rate, if he does, he makes no use of it; his scheme is not that of the Ascension of a Soul through Heaven after Heaven. The scene is always changing from Heaven to Earth, and to Hell; and the New Jerusalem, in the description of which the Vision culminates, descends out of the New Heaven, and is established upon the New Earth. It is to apocalypses of an entirely different type that the *Paradiso* is related—to

---

[1] Bywater, *Heracliti Rel.* p. 30.
[2] See Tozer (*An English Commentary on Dante's "Divina Commedia"*) on *Par.* xxii. 133 ff.; and cf. *Annual Report of the Dante Society (Cambridge Mass.)*, 1901; *Index of Authors quoted by Benvenuto da Imola*, by Paget Toynbee, art. "Macrobius".
[3] *Supra*, pp. 312-314.

apocalypses in which the whole *mise en scène* of the eschato-logical drama is astronomical, and the preoccupation of the writers is not, as that of the writer of the *Revelation of St. John* largely is, with the Reign of the Messiah on Earth over a chosen people, but with the purification of the disembodied Soul of the individual. These "astronomical apocalypses", as we may call them—some of them of Jewish authorship (like the *Book of the Secrets of Enoch*, the "Slavonic Enoch",[1] which was written, before the end of the second century B.C., at Alexandria, in the main in Greek, although portions of it reproduce a Hebrew original), the majority of them of Christian authorship—owe their astronomy mainly to Greek sources. It is true, of course, that the conception of Seven Heavens answering to the Seven Planets was familiar in the East before the Hellenistic period;[2] but the remarkable prominence which the conception suddenly assumed in that period can only, I submit, be ascribed to direct Greek influence.[3] The scheme of these apocalypses is always that of a Soul separated by ecstasy from its body, and, with some angel or daemon as guide or initiator, rising from the Earth, through air to aether, and then from planetary sphere to planetary sphere, up to the Presence of God in, or beyond, the Seventh Heaven. Thus in the *Ascension of Isaiah*,[4] Isaiah is conducted, through the seven planetary spheres, to the Presence of God the Father, and hears Him commissioning His Son to descend to the Earth. The descent of Christ through the spheres is then described; and after an account of His life on Earth, and death, and resurrection, the Apocalypse closes with His Ascension through the Heavenly Spheres to the right hand of God.

The persistence of this type—the "astronomical apocalypse"—is as remarkable as its wide distribution. Appearing

---

[1] Translated from the Slavonic by W. R. Morfill, and edited with Introduction, notes, and indices, by R. H. Charles, 1896.

[2] See Prof. Charles's Introduction to *The Book of the Secrets of Enoch*, pp. xxi. ff.

[3] Dieterich (*A Mithraic Liturgy*, p. 192) remarks that the conception of the ascension of the Soul through Heavenly Stations does not appear in Jewish literature till the Hellenistic period—in the Apocalypse of Enoch.

[4] Written in Greek, according to Prof. Charles (see his *Ascension of Isaiah*, 1900, and his articles on Apocalyptic literature in the *Encl. Brit.* and *Encl. Bib.*), between A.D. 50 and 80, translated into Latin, Ethiopic, and Slavonic, and extant now in its entirety only in the Ethiopic version.

first among the Jews in the second century B.C., it is adopted
by the Christians—Greek, Latin, Slavonic, and Ethiopian,
and at last by Islam; for the *Vision of Mahomet* is one of the
best examples of it.

The *Vision of Mahomet* is the story of the Prophet's
miraculous journey from Mecca to "the further temple" at
Jerusalem, and his ascent thence,[1] through the Circles of
Heaven, into the immediate Presence of God, far beyond
where even Gabriel could ascend. I give the story (only
briefly referred to in the *Quran* itself, ch. xvii. 1, but told
in all the earliest Lives of the Prophet) in the words of Mr.
P. de Lacy Johnstone (*Muhammad and his Power*, 1901, pp.
84 ff.):—

At the portal of the first heaven the angel knocked, and
a voice from within inquired who sought admittance.
Gabriel answered, "It is I, Gabriel." But again the voice
asked, "Is there any with thee?" and he said, "Muhammad."
Again came the question, "Hath he been called (to the office
of prophet)?" and he answered, "Yes." Then was the gate
opened, and they entered; and Adam greeted Muhammad
with the words, "Welcome, pious son and pious Prophet!"
Then Muhammad beheld, and saw two doors, the one on
Adam's right hand, and the other on his left. As oft as he
looked towards the first he laughed with delight, and there
issued therefrom a sweet savour; but as often as he turned
to the other he wept, and from it came evil odours; and the
Prophet marvelled, and asked of Gabriel what this should
mean; and it was told him that the one door led to Paradise,
and the other to Hell, and that the Father of Mankind
rejoiced over those who were saved, and wept over those
of his children who were lost. Then they soared upward
to the second Heaven, to which they entered after the same
questions and answers as at the first; and there were two
young men, John the Baptist and Jesus, and they greeted
Muhammad, "Welcome, pious brother and pious Prophet!"
Thence they passed to the third Heaven, to receive the same
welcome from Joseph, "whose beauty excelled that of all
other creatures as far as the light of the full moon surpasses
that of the stars"; then to the fourth, where Enoch greeted
them; and the fifth, where Aaron welcomed them with the
same words. In the sixth Heaven Moses welcomed him as
his brother and a Prophet; but he wept as he soared above
him—not for envy of Muhammad's glory surpassing his

---

[1] It is from the spot antipodal to Jerusalem that Dante ascends.

own, but to think that so few of his own nation were appointed to Paradise. From the Heaven of Moses the Archangel led Muhammad up to the seventh, where he showed him Abraham "his Father", who bade him "Welcome, pious son and pious Prophet!" In this seventh Heaven the Prophet beheld the wondrous Tree, the abode of Gabriel, round which fly countless myriads of angels; from its foot spring the two rivers of Paradise, and the two great rivers of Earth—Euphrates and the Nile; and "the light of God overspreads the whole Tree". There, too, was the heavenly Kaaba, the original of the Meccan, and round it went, in adoring circuit, radiant armies of angels; so vast indeed is their number that the same worshipping host never returns after once making the mystic round. Beyond the seventh Heaven Gabriel could only go with the Prophet, and that by special permission, as far as the first of the seventy veils of dazzling light (each 500 years' journey from the next) that shut in the Throne of God. As the Prophet passed each successive stage, the gracious Voice bade him "come nearer!" till at last he entered the immediate presence of God. There he was endowed with perfect wisdom and knowledge, cheered with the promise that all who received his message should be taken into Paradise, and commanded to lay on his faithful followers the duty of praying fifty times in the day. The Prophet returned from God's Presence Chamber to the lower heavens, and told Moses of the duty laid upon him. But by the old Lawgiver's advice he time after time ventured back to plead with his Lord till the burden of the daily prayers was reduced to five—the perpetual ordinance of Islam. Then with lightning speed the Prophet was returned to his chamber at Mecca, and, for all the wondrous things he had seen, yet was the bed warm when he lay down again.

There can be no doubt, of course, that the *Vision of Mahomet* was deliberately modelled on the Astronomical Apocalypse of which the *Ascension of Isaiah* may be taken as an example. Can there be any doubt that the same Type was before Dante's mind when he wrote the *Paradiso?* It would be unreasonable to suppose that a Poem, which in character as well as in astronomical scheme so closely conforms to a Type of which the examples were so widely distributed, was written in ignorance of that Type. The *Paradiso*, as it stands, cannot be accounted for by the supposition that the *Somnium Scipionis* first suggested to the Christian Poet an astronomical scheme which he elaborated on lines laid down for him by Aristotle and Alfraganus, in whose works he happened to be learned and greatly interested. It was not, I take it, because he knew the *Dream of Scipio* and was interested in the traditional astronomy that he adopted the astronomical scheme, but because he found that scheme in the Christian Apocalypse already consecrated to the subject with which his Poem is concerned (and the *Dream of Scipio* is not)—the purification of a Soul.[1]

Taking, then, the Astronomical Apocalypse of which the *Secrets of Enoch*, the *Ascension of Isaiah*, and the *Vision of Mahomet* are examples, as the Type on which Dante deliberaately modelled the *Paradiso*, with the aid of the *de Coelo*, and *Metaphysics*, and *Elementa* of Alfraganus, and *Somnium Scipionis* (itself a divergent example of the same Type), let me try to indicate the connection of this Type with the eschatology of the *Phaedrus* Myth.

The connection is to be found, I think, in the use made by scaramental ritual of the celestial *mise en scène* adopted in the *Phaedrus* Myth for the representation of the Soul's History —the sacramental ritual itself being the germ out of which the literary product—the Apocalypse—grew. Fortunately Dieterich's recent work, *A Mithraic Liturgy* (1903), enables us to form a clearer idea of the sacramental ritual referred to than was possible before.

The "Liturgy"[2] which Dieterich edits and comments on (whether a *Mithras* liturgy, as he holds, or belonging to

---

[1] The *Ascension of Isaiah*, one of the most elaborately astronomical of the apocalypses, existed in a Latin version which Dante may well have known. It was printed at Venice in 1522, and contains—6-11—the "ascension" proper. See also Mr. M. R. James (*The Revelation of Peter*, p. 40, and *Texts and Studies*, ii. 2, pp. 23 ff.) for the influence of the *Apocalypse of Paul* (a fourth or early fifth century work, which exhibits, with some confusion, the astronomical scheme which is so exactly followed in the *Ascension of Isaiah*) upon mediaeval visions and the *Divina Commedia*.

[2] The Paris Papyrus 574, *Supplément grec de la Bibliothèque Nationale*, from the text of which Dieterich restores this Liturgy, was, according to him, written at the beginning of the fourth century after Christ (see *o.c.* p. 43), not, however, in the interest of worship, but as a book of magic. A Greek Mithras liturgy composed in Egypt in the second century (see *o.c.* pp. 45, 46) was transcribed in the fourth century, and "nonsense words", interspersed through its text; and the farrago thus produced was to be recited as a spell, or series of spells.

On the origin, nature, and remarkable spread of Mithras-worship the reader may consult Cumont's *Mystères de Mithra* (1902), with map.

some other ritual, as Cumont holds[1]) is the Order to be observed in a Sacramental. Drama which conducts the candidate through stages or stations of ritual performance representing the grades of the ascent of the disembodied Soul, through the Heavenly Spheres, up to the Presence of the Highest God beyond the Pole. What happens ritually here to the initiate will be accomplished actually for his Soul after death. The ecstasy which the solemn sacrament procures and regulates through ascending grades of feeling is a preparation for, and a guarantee of, the actual ascension of the disembodied Soul.

The Liturgy begins with a Prayer which the candidate, still regarded as in the Sublunary Region, must recite. The Prayer recited, he rises, using set forms of words (some of them perhaps unintelligible names) at each stage, from the element of Earth to that of Water; then to Fire (sublunary, not celestial), and then to Air. Then, next, he stands before Doors[2] of Fire which admit to the aethereal world of the Gods—the Spheres of the Planets. Standing before these Doors, the candidate says, "I too am a star which goeth along with you, rising with his beams out of the depth: oxyoxerthouth".[3] At these words the Doorkeeper, the Fire-God, opens the Doors, and the candidate enters the Region of the Planets, where the Sun appears and goes before him to the Pole. Arrived there, he is in the Sphere of the Fixed Stars—represented by the seven Fates and the seven Rulers of the Pole, probably the Seven Stars of the Little Bear and the Great Bear round the Pole. Beyond the Pole and Sphere of the Fixed Stars is the throne of the Highest God, who guides the Great Bear, which, in turn, moves the Sphere of the Fixed Stars in a direction opposite to that in which the Planets move. Into the presence of this Highest God the initiate at last comes; and the Liturgy

---

[1] See especially M. Cumont's elaborate criticism of Dieterich's *Mithraic Liturgy* in the *Revue de l'Instruction Publique en Belgique*. The "Liturgy", according to M. Cumont, is a "magic-book" after all, reproducing the thoughts and even the style of the Hermetic treatises; but the writer, to enhance the value of his work, instead of following the ordinary method and publishing it as a revelation of Isis to Horus or of Hermes to Tât, presents it as a communication received by himself from the great foreign god Mithras through the intermediation of an archangel.

[2] There are Doors also through which Parmenides passes in his ascension.

[3] Dieterich, *o.c.* p. 8.

ends with his words of adoration—"Lord, hail, Master of water, hail, Governor of the earth, hail, Ruler of breath. Lord, I die, I am born again, having grown and been made to grow, I make an end; from coming into living generation I go to freedom from generation, as you have ransomed me, as you have ordered and wrought the mystery."[1]

Here, then, in the "Mithras liturgy" we have the order of a sacrament carried out on lines laid down in the Vision of Parmenides and the *Phaedrus* Myth—the astronomical eschatology of these pieces is embodied in a ritual—the actual ascension of the disembodied Soul is prepared for, and indeed guaranteed, in this life, by means of a dramatic representation of it, in which the candidate is the actor. Associated thus with a practical end of the highest importance—the salvation of the candidate—the astronomical scheme would be likely to hold the field against all rivals; and this is what it actually did. The notion of Ascent so completely extruded that of Descent, that we find even the Place of Torment localised somewhere in the air—as by Plutarch, in his *On the face in the disc of the Moon*[2] and his Aridaeus-Thespesius Myth;[3] in the latter the region just under the moon is designated as the furthest point reached by Orpheus when he went to seek Eurydice—the traditional *Descent of Orpheus* is actually transformed into an *Ascent of Orpheus*.

I cannot but think that the extraordinary popularity obtained by the Astronomical Apocalypse was due to the fact that behind it sacramental ritual originally stood. It is certainly remarkable that the Hellenistic and early Christian period, which produced the Astronomical Apocalypse, was also the age of innumerable Sacramental Cults. We can hardly have here a mere coincidence. The Apocalypse, I take it, was valued, at first, as setting forth, in interesting narrative, the ascension which the ritual symbolised and

---

[1] Dieterich, *o.c.* p. 14.
[2] Chapter 28.
[3] *On the postponements of the Divine Vengeance*, chapter 22. In his Introduction to *The Book of the Secrets of Enoch* (pp. xxxiv. ff.), Prof. Charles remarks that "the presence of evil in heaven caused no offence in early Semitic thought". In the northern region of the Third Heaven Enoch sees the place of the damned, and Mahomet sees it in the First Heaven.

guaranteed: indeed, it was probably valued for something more than its interesting narrative—for some sacramental value which it derived from the parent ritual. We seem to have this mysterious "something more" even in Dante's conception of his own Apocalypse. His Vision of Paradise is to him a saving sacrament of which he has partaken:—

> O Lady, in whom my hope grows strong, and who endured for my salvation to leave your footprints in the lower world;
> By your power and beneficence I recognize the grace and worth of all that I have seen.
> You have drawn me from servitude to liberty by all those paths, by all those modes, which you had the power to use.
> Preserve in me your magnanimity, so that my soul, which you have made intact, may unloose itself from the body in a manner which shall please you.[1]

In his note on this passage Mr. Tozer[2] says: "Dante's conversion and ultimate salvation were the primary object of his journey through the three realms of the spiritual world."

The close connection between sacramental ritual or initiation and apocalypse is very clearly brought out in the Myth with which Plutarch ends his *On the postponements of the Divine Vengeance*—the Vision of Aridaeus-Thespesius just now alluded to. The hero of the Myth is a wicked man called Aridaeus, who, as the result of an accident to his head, lies unconscious for three days, during which time his Soul (the rational part of it, but not the irrational) visits the world of spirits in the air, where he receives a new name, Thespesius. With this new name he returns to this world, a new man, regenerate, and lives ever after in the practice of virtue and religion. This Myth is one of a well-marked class of eschatological visions, or apocalypses, which render, in literary form, the ritual observed at initiation—initiation being viewed as a Death, and a New Birth, warranting the imposition of a New Name. Like the initiatory ritual which it renders, this type of apocalyptic vision involves what may be figured as the Death of the

---

[1] *Par.* xxxi. 79 ff.
[2] *English Commentary on Dante's "Divina Commedia"*, pp. 615, 616.

candidate—by ecstasy he passes into a state from which he returns to his ordinary life a new man.

It is as a new man—as one filled with a joy which is not of this world—that Dante returns from the apocalyptic vision, or initiation, of the *Paradiso*—

> I think that I beheld it, because more largely, in saying this I feel that I rejoice.[1]

The *Paradiso* is the last of the descendants of the *Phaedrus* Myth; and reveals its parentage in nothing so clearly as in its character of being, for its author, and even for ourselves, a mystery—a solemn ritual at which one may assist, not merely an admirable piece of literary workmanship.

Plutarch's Aridaeus-Thespesius Myth[2] seems to me to be so important for the understanding of what I have called the celestial and astronomical *mise en scène* given to eschatology by Plato in the *Phaedrus* Myth, and, after him, by Philosophers of different schools, by religious societies, more especially in the order of their sacramental ritual, by the apocalyptic writers, Jewish, Christian, and Mohammedan, and, lastly, by Dante in his *Paradiso*, that I shall give the reader the opportunity of perusing the passage in Philemon Holland's version:[3]—

> There was one Thespesius of the city of Soli in Cilicia, who having led his youthful days very loosely, within a small time had wasted and consumed all his goods, whereby he was fallen for a certain space to extreme want and necessity, which brought him also to a lewd life, insomuch as he proved a very bad man; and repenting his former follies and dispense, began to make shifts, and seek all means to recover his state again . . . he forbare no lewd, indirect, and shameful practices, so they turned to his gain and profit, and within a little while he gat together not great store of goods, but procured to himself a bad name of wicked dealing, much shame, and infamy. But the thing that made him famous, and so much spoken of, was the answer delivered unto him from the Oracle of Amphilochus, for thither had he sent, as it should seem, to know whether

---

[1] *Par.* xxxiii. 92, 93. [2] *De sera numinis vindicta*, ch. 22.

[3] *The Philosophie, commonlie called The Morals, written by the learned Philosopher Plutarch of Chaeronea, translated out of Greeke into English, and conferred with the Latine translations and the French, by Philemon Holland of Coventrie, Doctor in Physicke.* London, 1603.

he should live the rest of his life better than he had done before. Now the oracle returned this answer: That it would be better with him after he was dead; which in some sort happened unto him not long after: For being fallen from an high place with his head forward, without any limb broken, or wound made; only with the fall the breath went out of his body, and there he lay for dead; and three days after, preparation being made for his funerals, carried forth he was to be buried; but behold all on a sudden he revived, and quickly came to himself again; whereupon there ensued such a change and alteration in his life, that it was wonderful; for by the report and testimony of all the people of Cilicia, they never knew man of a better conscience in all his affairs and dealings, whiles he did negotiate and dwell among them; none more devout and religious to God-ward, none more fast and sure to his friends, none bitterer to his enemies; insomuch as they who were most inward with him, and had kept his company familiarly a long time, were very desirous and earnest with him, to know the cause of so strange and sudden alteration. . . . Thus he reported unto them and said: That when the spirit was out of his body, he fared at the first (as he thought himself) like unto a pilot, flung out of his ship, and plunged into the bottom of the sea; so wonderfully was he astonished at this change; but afterwards, when as by little and little he was raised up again and recovered, so that he was ware that he drew his breath fully, and at liberty, he looked round about him, for his soul seemed as if it had been one eye fully open; but he beheld nothing that he was wont to view, only he thought that he saw planets and other stars of an huge bigness, distant an infinite way asunder, and yet for number innumerable, casting from them a wonderful light, with a colour admirable, the same glittering and shining most resplendent, with a power and force incredible, in such sort, as the said soul being gently and easily carried, as in a chariot, with this splendour and radiant light, as it were upon the sea in a calm, went quickly whithersoever she would; but letting pass a great number of things worthy there to be seen, he said that he beheld how the souls of those that were departed this life, as they rose up and ascended, resembled certain small fiery bubbles, and the air gave way and place unto them as they mounted on high; but anon when these bubbles by little and little brast insunder, the souls came forth of them, and appeared in the form and shape of men and women, very light and nimble, as discharged from all poise to bear them down: howbeit, they did not move and bestir themselves all alike and after one sort; for some leaped with a wonderful agility, and mounted directly and plumb upright; others turned round about together like unto bobbins or spindles, one while up and another while down, so as their motion was mixed and confused, and so linked together, that unneth for a good while and with much ado they could be stayed and severed asunder. As for these souls and spirits, many of them he knew not (as he said) who they were; but taking knowledge of two or three among them who had been of his old acquaintance, he pressed forward to approach near and to speak unto them: but they neither heard him speak, nor indeed were in their right senses; but being after a sort astonied and beside themselves, refused once to be either seen or felt, wandering and flying to and fro apart at the first; but afterwards, encountering and meeting with a number of others disposed like unto themselves, they closed and clung unto them, and thus linked and coupled together, they moved here and there disorderly without discretion, and were carried every way to no purpose, uttering I wot not what voices, after a manner of yelling or a black-sanctus, not significant nor distinct, but as if they were cries mingled with lamentable plaints and dreadful fear. Yet there were others to be seen aloft in the uppermost region of the air, jocund, gay and pleasant, so kind also and courteous, that oftentimes they would seem to approach near one unto another, turning away from those other that were tumultuous and disorderly. . . . And these (by his own saying) he had a sight of a soul belonging to a kinsman and familiar friend of his, and yet he knew him not certainly, for that he died whiles himself was a very child; howbeit, the said soul, coming toward him, saluted him in these terms: God save you, Thespesius: whereat he marvelled much, and said unto him: I am not Thespesius, but my name is Aridaeus: True, indeed (quoth the other), before-time you were so called, but from henceforth Thespesius shall be your name; for dead you are not yet, but, by the providence of God and permission of Destiny, you are hither come, with the intellectual part of the soul; and as for all the rest, you have left it behind, sticking fast as an anchor to your body: and that you may now know this and evermore hereafter, take this for a certain rule and token: That the spirits of those who are departed and dead indeed, yield no shadow from them; they neither wink nor yet open their eyes. Thespesius, hearing these words, began to pluck up his spirits so much the more, for to consider and discourse with himself: looking therefore every way about him, he might perceive that there accompanied him a certain shadowy and dark lineature, whereas the other souls shone round about, and were clear and transparent within forth, howbeit not all alike; for some yielded from them pure colour, uniform and equal, as doth the full moon when she is at the clearest; others had (as it were) scales or cicatrices, dispersed here and there by certain distant spaces between; some again were wonderful hideous and strange to see unto, all to be specked with black spots, like to serpents' skins; and others had light scarifications and obscure risings upon their visage. Now this kinsman of Thespesius discoursed severally of each thing, saying: That Adrasteia the Daughter of Jupiter and Necessity was placed highest and above the rest, to punish and to be revenged of all sorts of crimes and heinous sins, and that of wicked and sinful wretches there was not one (great or small) who either by force or cunning could ever save himself and escape punishment: but of one kind of pain and punishment (for three sorts there be in all) belonged to this gaoler or executioner, and another to that; for there is one which is quick and speedy called Penalty, and this taketh in hand the execution and chastisement of those who immediately in this life (whiles they are in their bodies) be punished by the body, after a mild and gentle manner, leaving unpunished many light faults, which require some petty purgation; but such as require more ado to have their vices and sins cured, God committeth them to be punished after death to a second tormentress, named Revenge; mary those who are so laden with sins that they be altogether incurable, when Revenge hath given over and thrust them from her, the third ministress of Adrasteia, which of all other is most cruel, and named Erinnys, runneth after, chasing and pursuing them as they wander and run up and down; these (I say), she courseth and hunteth with great misery and much dolor, until such time as she have overtaken them all and plunged them into a bottomless pit of darkness inenarrable and invisible. . . . Observe well (quoth he) and consider the diverse colours of these souls of all sorts; for this blackish and foul duskish hue is properly the tincture of avarice and niggardise; that which is deep red and fiery betokeneth cruelty and malice; whereas if it stand much upon blue it is a sign that there intemperance and looseness in the use of pleasures hath remained a long time, and will be hardly scoured off, for that it is a vile vice: but the violet colour and sweetish withal proceedeth from envy, a venomous and poisoned colour. . . . But here it is a sign that the purification of the soul is fully finished, whenas all these tinctures are done away quite, whereby the soul may appear in her native hue, all fresh, neat, clear, and lightsome. . . . Now, of these souls some there be which after they have been well and thoroughly chastised, and that sundry times, recover in the end a decent habitude and disposition; but others again are such as the vehemence of their ignorance, and the flattering shew of pleasures and lustful desire, transporteth them into the bodies of brute beasts. . . they desire by the means of the body to enjoy the fruition of their appetite; forasmuch as here there is nothing at all but a bare shadow, and as one would say, a vain dream of pleasure which never cometh to perfection and fulness.   When he had thus said, he brought and led me away most swiftly an infinite way; howbeit, with ease and gently, upon the rays of the light, as if they had been wings, unto a certain place where there was a huge wide chink tending downward still, and thither being come, he perceived that he was forlorn and forsaken of that powerful spirit that conducted and brought him thither; where he saw that other souls also were in the same case; for being gathered and flocked together like a sort of birds, they fly downward round about this gaping chawne, but enter into it directly they durst not; now the said chink resembled for all the world within the caves of Bacchus, so tapissed and adorned they were with the verdure of great leaves and branches, together with all variety of gay flowers, from whence arose and breathed forth a sweet and mild exhalation, which yielded a delectable and pleasant savour, wonderful odoriferous, with a most temperate air, which no less affected them that smelled thereof than the scent of wine contenteth those who love to drink: in such sort as the souls, feeding and feasting themselves with these fragrant odours, were very cheerful, jocund and merry; so as round about the said place there was nothing but pastime, joy, solace, mirth, laughing and singing, much after the manner of men that rejoice one with another, and take all the pleasure and delight that possibly they can.   And he said, moreover, that Bacchus by that way mounted up into the society of the Gods, and afterwards conducted Semele; and withal, that it was called the place of Lethe, that is to say, Oblivion: whereupon he would not let Thespesius, though he were exceeding desirous, to stay there, but drew him away perforce; instructing him thus much and giving him to understand, that reason and the intelligible part of the mind is dissolved and, as it were, melted and moistened by this pleasure; but the unreasonable part which savoureth of the body, being watered and incarnate therewith, reviveth the memory of the body; and upon this remembrance, there groweth and ariseth a lust and concupiscence, which haleth and draweth unto generation (for so he called it), to wit, a consent of the soul thereto, weighed down and aggravated with over much moisture.   Having therefore traversed another way as long as the other, he was ware that he saw a mighty standing bowl into which diverse rivers seemed to fall and discharge themselves, whereof one was whiter than the foam of the sea or driven snow, another of purple hue or scarlet colour, like to that which appeareth

in the rainbow; as for others, they seemed afar off to have
every one of them their distinct lustre and several tincture.
But when they approached near unto them, the aforesaid
bowl, after that the air about was discussed and vanished
away, and the different colours of those rivers no more
seen, left the more flourishing colour, except only the white.
Then he saw there three Daemons or Angels sitting together
in triangular form, medling and mixing the rivers together
with certain measures.   And this guide of Thespesius's
soul said, moreoever, that Orpheus came so far when he
went after his wife; but for that he kept not well in mind
that which he there saw, he had sowen one false tale among
men; to wit, that the oracle at Delphi was common to
Apollo and the Night (for there was no commerce or fellowship at all between the Night and Apollo).   But this oracle
(quoth he) is common to the Moon and the Night, which
hath no determinate and certain place upon the Earth,
but is always errant and wandering among men by dreams
and apparitions; which is the reason that dreams compounded and mingled, as you see, of falsehood and truth,
of variety and simplicity, are spread and scattered over the
world.   But as touching the oracle of Apollo, neither have
you seen it (quoth he), nor ever shall be able to see; for the
terrene substance or earthly part of the soul is not permitted to arise and mount up on high, but bendeth downward, being fastened unto the body.   And with that he
approached at once nearer, endeavouring to shew him the
shining light of the three-feet or three-footed stool, which
(he said) from the bosom of the goddess Themis reached
as far as to the Mount Parnassus.   And having a great
desire to see the same, yet he could not, his eyes were so
dazzled with the brightness thereof; howbeit, as he passed
by, a loud and shrill voice he heard of a woman, who,
among other things delivered in metre, uttered also, as it
should seem by way of prophecy, the very time of his death:
and the Daemon said it was the voice of Sibylla; for she,
being carried round in the globe and face of the moon, did
foretell and sing what was to come: but being desirous to
hear more, he was repelled and driven by the violence of
the moon, as it were with certain whirl-puffs, clean a
contrary way; so he could hear and understand but few
things, and those very short; namely, the accident about
the hill Vesuvius, and how Dicaearchia should be consumed
and burnt by casual fire, as also a clause or piece of a verse,
as touching the emperor who then reigned, to this effect:—

> A gracious prince he is, but yet must die,
> And empire leave, by force of malady.

After this they passed on forward to see the pains and

torments of those who were punished; and there at first
they beheld all things most piteous and horrible to see to;
for Thespesius, who doubted nothing less, met in that place
with many of his friends, kinsfolk, and familiar companions,
who were in torment, and suffering dolorous pains and
infamous punishment they moaned themselves, lamenting
and calling and crying unto him. At the last he had a
sight of his own father rising out of a deep pit; full he was
of pricks, gashes, and wounds, and stretching forth his
hands unto him, was (mauger his heart) forced to break
silence, yea, and compelled by those who had the charge
and superintendence of the said punishments, to confess
with a loud and audible voice, that he had been a wicked
murderer of certain strangers and guests whom he had
lodged in his house; for perceiving that they had silver and
gold about them, he had wrought their death by the means
of poison; and albeit he had not been detected thereof in
his lifetime, whiles he was upon the earth, yet here was he
convicted and had sustained already part of his punishment,
and expected to endure the rest afterwards. Now Thespesius
durst not make suit nor intercede for his father, so affrighted
he was and astonied; but desirous to withdraw himself and
be gone, he lost sight of that courteous and kind guide of
his which all this while had conducted him, and he saw
him no more: but he might perceive other horrible and
hideous spirits who enforced and constrained him to pass
further, as if it were necessary that he should traverse still
more ground: so he saw those who were notorious male-
factors, in the view of every man (or who in this world had
been chastised), how their shadow was here tormented with
less pain, and nothing like to others, as having been feeble
and imperfect in the reasonless part of the soul, and therefore subject to passions and affections; but such as were
disguised and cloaked with an outward appearance and
reputation of virtue abroad, and yet had lived covertly and
secretly at home in wickedness, certain that were about
them forced some of them to turn the inside outward, and
with much pain and grief to lay themselves open, to bend
and bow, and discover their hypocritical hearts within, even
against their own nature, like unto the scolopenders of the
sea, when they have swallowed down an hook, are wont to
turn themselves outward: but others they flayed and
displayed, discovering plainly and openly how faulty, per-
verse, and vicious they had been within, as whose principal
part of the reasonable soul vice had possessed. He said,
moreover, that he saw other souls wound and interlaced
one within another, two, three, and more together, like to
vipers and other serpents, and these not forgetting their
old grudge and malicious ranker one against another, or

upon remembrance of losses and wrongs sustained by
others, fell to gnawing and devouring each other. Also,
that there were three parallel lakes ranged in equal distance
one from the other; the one seething and boiling with gold,
another of lead exceeding cold, and a third, most rough,
consisting of iron: and that there were certain spirits
called Daemons which had the overlooking and charge of
them; and these, like unto metal-founders, or smiths, with
certain instruments either plunged in, or drew out, souls.
As for those who were given to filthy lucre, and by reason
of insatiable avarice committed wicked parts, those they
let down into the lake of melted gold, and when they were
once set on a light fire, and made transparent by the strength
of those flames within the said lake, then plunged they were
into the other of lead; where after they were congealed and
hardened in manner of hail, they transported them anew
into the third lake of iron, where they became exceeding
black and horrible, and being cracked and broken by
reason of their dryness and hardness, they changed their
form, and then at last (by his saying) they were thrown again
into the foresaid lake of gold, suffering by the means of
these changes and mutations intolerable pains. But those
souls (quoth he) who made the greatest moan unto him,
and seemed most miserably (of all others) to be tormented,
were they who, thinking they were escaped and past their
punishment, as who had suffered sufficiently for their
deserts at the hands of vengeance, were taken again and
put to fresh torments; and those they were for whose sins
their children and others of their posterity suffered punishment: for whensoever one of the souls of their children or
nephews in lineal descent either met with them, or were
brought unto them, the same fell into a fit of anger, crying
out upon them, shewing the marks of the torments and
pains that it sustained, reproaching and hitting them in the
teeth therefor; but the other, making haste to fly and hide
themselves, yet were not able so to do; for incontinently the
tormentors followed after and pursued them, who brought
them back again to their punishment, crying out and
lamenting for nothing so much as that they did foresee the
torment which they were to suffer, as having experience
thereof already. Furthermore, he said that he saw some,
and those in number many, either children or nephews,
hanging together fast like bees or bats, murmuring and
grumbling for anger, when they remembered and called to
mind what sorrows and calamities they sustained for their
sake. But the last thing that he saw were the souls of such
as entered into a second life and new nativity, as being
turned and transformed forcibly into other creatures of all
sorts, by certain workmen appointed therefor, who, with

tools for the purpose, and many a stroke, forged and framed
some of their parts new, bent and wrested others, took
away and abolished a third sort; and all, that they might
sort and be suitable to other conditions and lives: among
which he espied the soul of Nero afflicted already grievously
enough otherwise, with many calamities, pierced thorough
every part with spikes and nails red-hot with fire: and when
the artisans aforesaid took it in hand to transform it into
the shape of a viper, of which kind (as Pindarus saith) the
young ones gnaweth through the bowels of the dam to
come into the world, and to devour it, he said that all on a
sudden there shone forth a great light out of which there
was heard a voice giving commandment that they should
metamorphose and transfigure it into the form of another
kind of beast more gentle and tame, forging a water-
creature of it, chanting about standing lakes and marishes;
for that he had been in some sort punished already for the
sins which he had committed, and besides, some good turn
is due unto him from the gods, in that, of all his subjects,
he had exempted from tax, tallage, and tribute the best
nation and most beloved of the gods, to wit, the Greeks.
Thus far forth, he said, he was only a spectator of these
matters; but when he was upon his return, he abid all the
pains in the world for very fear that he had; for there was
a certain woman, for visage and stately bigness admirable,
who took hold on him, and said: Come hither, that thou
mayest keep in memory all that thou hast seen the better:
wherewith she put forth unto him a little rod or wand all
fiery, such as painters or enamellers use; but there was
another that stayed her: and then he might perceive himself to be blown by a strong and violent wind with a trunk
or pipe, so that in the turning of an hand he was within
his own body again, and so began to look up with his eyes
in manner out of his grave and sepulchre.

Let me now call the reader's attention to some points
which ought to be noticed in the foregoing Myth.

The Myth, as I said, is one of a well-marked class of
Eschatological Myths (to which the Timarchus Myth in
Plutarch's *On the daemon of Socrates* also belongs) based on the
ritual observed at Initiation, which, indeed, they merely
transfer from the sanctuary in this world to the world of
spirits. The apparent death of Aridaeus-Thespesius stands in
the Myth for the ceremonial death which an initiated person
suffers, who, in simulating actual death by falling into a
trance, or even by allowing himself to be treated as a corpse,

dies to sin in order to live henceforth a regenerate life in this world. The accident which brings on the state of apparent death is a literary device adopted in order to give verisimilitude to the idea that the Soul of Aridaeus-Thespesius actually visits the other world, and returns to this world to tell the tale. By this device the experiences of a newly initiated person returning to ordinary life a regenerate man are transformed into those which an actual revenant from beyond the grave would have to tell. The accident which befalls Aridaeus-Thespesius is, in fact, the mythological equivalent of the terror which confounds the candidate at the beginning of his Initiation—a terror comparable with the sharpness of death, and resulting in a trance, during which he is ceremonially a dead man.

To acquire a new soul' (says M. le Comte Goblet d'Alviella)[1] 'it is necessary to renounce the old one; you must first of all die. Most initiations, also, imply an apparent death. Either the neophyte submits to a feigned sacrifice, or there is imposed on him a journey to the land of the dead. To die, said Plutarch, playing on the words, is to be initiated: *teleutan—teleisthai*. Reciprocally, let me add, to be initiated is to die. At the least it is to undergo a temporary death in order to live again in different and better conditions. In this sense initiation is regeneration. It was so among the ancients, as well as among the non-civilized peoples whose customs I have just described.[2] We see from the narrative of Apuleius that initiation into the mysteries of Isis was regarded as a voluntary death leading to another life.[3] The mysteries of Cybele included the slaughter of a bull and a ram, during which the initiate, lying in a trench, received upon his body the blood of bull or ram; from that moment he became reborn for ever in the sacrifice of bull and ram.[4] In India, even today, the young Brahmin who desires to be initiated by a Guru in the knowledge of the Vedas, must submit to a ceremony in which he pretends to return to the condition of

[1] *Eleusinia* (Paris, 1903), p. 63.
[2] *o.c.* p. 62: "In certain parts of the Congo, youths of the age to become men pretend to fall dead. Carried away by witch doctors into the forest, they spend several months, sometimes several years, there; then they return to their families, but they now have to comport themselves as if they had quite forgotten their former lives, including speech and the habit of eating. They must be educated over again, as if new born." Cf. W. H. Bentley, *Life on the Congo* (London, 1887), pp. 78 ff.
[3] *Met.* xi.
[4] *Corp. Insc. Lat.* vi. p. 97, No. 510.

an embryo.[1] Lastly, in the bosom of Christianity, baptism which constitutes the essential formality of entry into the community of believers, has always been represented as a symbolic burial preparatory to a spiritual resurrection.[2]

There is to be read on the architrave of the baptistery in the Lateran, the oldest in existing Christendom, the following couplet engraved in the fifth century by Pope Xystus III:—

> Hope for the kingdom of Heaven, ye who are
>   reborn at this font;
> The blessed life does not receive those who
>   were born once only.

In certain religious orders, the taking of the vows, which is a true initiation, comprises a celebration of the Office for the Dead over the novice lying on a bier, or stretched under a pall between four candles. After the singing of *Miserere* he gets up receiving the kiss of peace, and takes communion at the hands of the abbot.[3] From this day he takes a new name, which he keeps till death.[4]

The Place of Lethe, in the Aridaeus-Thespesius Myth, is difficult to localise; but it is evidently a place Souls come to

---

[1] *Sacred Books of the East*, vol. xliv. pp. 86-90. Perhaps we may be allowed to bring into comparison with this custom another custom mentioned by Dr. Budge: speaking of a certain prehistoric form of burial in Egypt, he says (*Egyptian Ideas of the Future Life*, p. 162 ff.): "They are buried in the ante-natal position of a child, and we may perhaps be justified in seeing in this custom the symbol of a hope that as the child is born from this position into the world, so might the deceased be born into the life in the world beyond the grave . . . The Egyptians continued to mummify their dead, not believing that their physical bodies would rise again, but because they wished the spiritual body to 'sprout' or 'germinate' from them, and if possible—at least it seems so—to be in the form of the physical body."

[2] *Rom.* vi. 4, *Coloss.* ii. 12, "Buried with him in baptism, wherein also ye are risen with him through the faith of the operation of God, who hath raised him from the dead."

[3] *Ceremoniale benedictinum*, in *Dictionnaire de Théologie Catholique* (Paris, Gaume, 1863), t. xix. pp. 184, 185.

[4] See also Dieterich (*Eine Mithrasliturgie*, pp. 158-161, 166, 175), and authorities cited by him (*e.g.* Frazer, *The Golden Bough*, iii. 442 ff.; Codrington, *The Melanesians*, 39), for the wide prevalence among primitive, as well as among civilised races, of this view of Initiation (whether Initiation at the age of puberty, or at other times) as a Death (simulated by the novice) and a New Birth, followed often by the imposition of a New Name. When ceremonial Death takes the form of actual unconsciousness, a stupefying drink is generally the agent employed. I would suggest that the drinking of the water of Lethe, in Greek mythology, by Souls about to be born again in the flesh, has its origin in this custom of administering a stupefying drink to the patients of initiatory rites, who "die to live".

"For all Greek mysteries," says Mr. A. Lang (*Homeric Hymns*, p. 93), "a satisfactory savage analogy can be found. These spring straight from human nature; from the desire to place customs, and duties, and taboos under divine protection; from the need of strengthening them, and the influence of the

in their descent from the aethereal and aerial regions, lying somewhere between these regions and the Earth. The foliage and flowers of the place remind us of the Terrestrial Paradise, midway between Heaven and Earth, in which Dante places the Stream of Lethe. Plutarch's whole description, however, reflects the doctrine, which we afterwards find in Plotinus and others of the Neo-Platonic school, of the Mirror and Bowl of Dionysus, and cannot properly be brought into line with such a description of the River of Lethe as we have in the Myth of Er. In one point, however, the two descriptions seem to be at one—the Place of Lethe is not subterranean.

The Bowl, the Oracle of Night and the Moon, at which the three Daemons sit, mixing dreams, is, I think, the Moon, above which the Soul of Aridaeus-Thespesius cannot rise, because the irrational part of it is still in the body on Earth. As we learn from the *Concerning the face on the disc of the Moon*,[1] that part, as well as the rational part, rises, at the death of the body on Earth, up to the Moon; and it is only when the death of the irrational part has taken place on the Moon that the rational part can rise to its original home, the Sun. The rational part of the Soul of Aridaeus-Thespesius, then, comes near to, but may not pass, the Moon; and can only see from afar the glory of the true Delphi which is eternal in the Heavens—the Sun, the seat of Apollo, the home of Reason. Orpheus, when he went to seek Eurydice, came, Aridaeus-Thespesius is told, only as far as the Oracle of Dreams, *i.e.* the Moon. The celestial or astronomical eschatology, which, in Plutarch, has taken the place of the terrestrial, converts, we thus see, the descent of Orpheus into an ascent.[2]

The torments of Hell or Purgatory are described in the Aridaeus-Thespesius Myth with almost Dantesque power; indeed, the three lakes and the treatment of Souls in them

elders, by mystic sanctions; from the need of fortifying and trying the young by probations of strength, secrecy, and fortitude; from the magical expulsion of hostile influences; from the sympathetic magic of early agriculture; from study of the processes of nature regarded as personal; and from guesses, surmises, visions, and dreams as to the fortunes of the wandering soul on its way to its final home."

[1] Chapters 28-30.

[2] Mr. Arthur Fairbanks (*Class. Rev.* Nov. 1901), commenting on Soph. *Ajax*, 1192, and quoting Eur. *Hel.* 1016, 1219, *Frag.* 971, *Suppl.* 1140, connects the ascension of Souls into the aether with the practice of cremation.

present a picture of terror which it would be hard to out-
match in literature. But where is the place of these torments?
Under the Earth? I think not. The following passage in
the *On the face on the disc of the Moon* seems to me to be
conclusive in favour of locating these torments in the lower
region of the air: "That all soul, mindless or intelligent,
having fallen away from the body, is set in the space between
the earth and the moon, to wander for an indefinite time.
But those that were unrighteous and spurn justice, pay the
penalty for their crimes. And that in like manner it is
necessary for souls who are so far purified, and have breathed
out from the body its plagues which were the cause of evil,
to abide for the appointed time in the mildest region of the
air, which they call the Fields of Hades."[1] The conclusion
to be drawn from the foregoing passage seems to be borne
out by the passage at the beginning of the Aridaeus-
Thespesius Myth, where Souls are seen ascending like
bubbles—Souls of all sorts, good, bad, and indifferent, each
sort distinguished by its own colour; and the gulf, which
Timarchus sees in the *On the daemon of Socrates* Myth, he
sees when he is no longer within sight of the Earth: it is
the place of torment—a seething abyss of air (I think), on
the surface of which half-submerged Souls are seen floating,
like stars or will-o'-the-wisps.[2] At the same time it must be
admitted that Plutarch's power of place-visualisation is not
so clear and distinct as to leave one without doubt as to the
locality of his Place of Torment—it may, after all, be subterranean, not aerial; I am inclined, however, to think that,
following undoubted precedent,[3] he makes it aerial—that
he localises the whole eschatological drama—Inferno, Purgatorio, and Paradiso—in the air and aether.

There is another point of interest which ought to be
noticed in connection with the Aridaeus-Thespesius Myth—
the remarkably developed power of colour-visualisation of
which it affords evidence. Effects of light, lustre, and colour

---

[1] Plutarch, *dē fac. in orbe lun.* 28.   [2] *De gen. Soc.* 22.

[3] See Rohde, *Psyche*, ii. 319, n. 4, where the Stoical doctrine of the levity
the Soul is alluded to as incompatible with its descent, and Sext. *adv. phys.* 1,
71, is quoted for this—"For it is not possible to conjecture that souls are
borne below. For being composed of minute particles they are rather carried
to the regions above by their own lightness." See *supra*, p. 328, n. 2, for the
localisation of Hell in the Third Heaven by the writer of the *Secrets of Enoch*.

constantly appeal to us. But, on the other hand, the power
of place-and-form-visualisation seems to be deficient, or, at
any rate, not to be developed equally with that of colour-
visualisation. Plutarch's other great Eschatological Myth—
that in the *On the daemon of Socrates*—likewise affords evidence
of highly developed power of colour-visualisation with, at
any rate, comparatively little power of place-and-form-
visualisation.[1] Highly developed power of visualising in
both kinds—in both colour and form—is indeed a rare gift.
Dante had it. Place and Form are as distinct in the *Inferno*
and *Purgatorio* as Light and Colour are glorious in the
Paradiso. Plato visualises Place and Form with great dis-
tinctness, but not, I think, with Dante's convincing distinct-
ness; the Abstract Thinker competed, in Plato, with the
Poet to a much greater extent than in Dante. In power of
colour-visualisation, however, Dante is greatly Plato's
superior; and comparing Plato and Plutarch in this respect,
I would say that the latter gives, at any rate, more evidence
of the possession of the power than the former does. Against
the remarkable colour effects of the Myths in the *On the
daemon of Socrates* and the *On the postponements of the Divine
Vengeance*, we can only set, from Plato's Myths, some much
more ordinary effects—that of the description, in the *Phaedo*
Myth, of the party-coloured Earth seen from above, that of
the colour of the Stygian Region in the same Myth, that of
the rainbow-coloured pillar in the Myth of Er, and certain
general effects of light conveyed by words here and there
in the *Phaedrus* Myth. This is not the place to pursue the
subject of the relation of highly developed power of colour-
visualisation and highly developed power of form-visualisa-
tion to each other and to other faculties in the Man of
Science and the Poet respectively. It is a subject which
has special importance for the psychology of the poetical
temperament, and deserves more attention, in that connection, than it has hitherto received; although invaluable
service has already been done, in the way of laying the
foundation from which any such special inquiry must start,
by Mr. F. Galton in his *Inquiries into Human Faculty and its
Development* (1883), to which the reader is now referred.

[1] This Myth is given on pp. 391 ff.

VI

"Possession and madness from the Muses."[1]

It was maintained in the Introductory Part of this work
that the Poet performs his essential function as Poet only in
so far as he rouses Transcendental Feeling in his patient,
and that he does so by inducing in him the state of dream-
consciousness. It is characteristic of this state, as induced
by the Poet, that it does not continue for any appreciable
length of time, but takes the form of fitfully recurrent lapses
in the midst of a waking consciousness, which it is also the
Poet's function—but only as skilled workman, not as
inspired Poet—to furnish with suitable objects. As workman
the Poet must have skill to tell a story, whether in narrative,
or in dramatic or in lyrical form, whether true or fictitious,
which shall be interesting to the waking consciousness as
a story—which shall appeal powerfully to our natural love
of "anthropology", and to other common sentiments of the
human breast. The interesting story, with its appeal to our
common sentiments, constitutes, as it were, the Body of the
poem, and bulks largely—

> She would na ha'e a Lowland Laird,
>   Nor be an English Lady;
> But she's awa wi' Duncan Graham,
>   An' he's row'd her in his plaidie.

This is "what the poem is about"—its subject matter, its
Body—and is always with us. But the Soul—the essential
Poetry of a poem, is apprehended only at those moments
when the common sentiments—wonder, love, pity, dread,
curiosity, amusement—roused by the workman's artistic
handling of the subject-matter, are satisfied fantastically, as
in a dream, by some image presented or suggested, or by

[1] *Phaedrus*, 245 A: "And the third possession and madness is from the
Muses, taking hold of a gentle and pure soul, rousing and exciting it to odes
and other forms of poetry such as adorn many works of the ancients and
educate their descendants. And whoever without madness from the Muses
attempts to penetrate the gates of Poetry, being persuaded that he will be
sufficiently a poet, will be unskilful himself, and poetry either of the mad
or the controlled kind will vanish."

Plato's *Ion* should be read in connection with this. It is a study of "Poetic
Inspiration".

some mysterious omen of word or phrase or cadence. It is in giving such satisfaction to natural sentiments which his art has aroused in his patient that the Poet shows his genius as distinguished from his art. His gift is a sort of "Enchantment in sleep". In sleep some ordinary sensation of cold, or heat, or of some other kind, starts an explanatory pageant of dream-images. So in the Poet's mind some common sentiment, which he experiences more vividly than other men as he tells his story, expresses itself suddenly in some image or other representation; and his reader, in whose mind he has already roused the same sentiment by his story, welcomes the image or other representation, as expressing the sentiment—as relieving the weight of it, as solving the mystery of it, as justifying it. It is in a dream, fantastically, that the relief, the solution, the justification, are found; for the Poet's image, the product in him of the dream-consciousness, becomes in the Poet's patient the producer of a state of consciousness like that which produced it in the Poet. The case is analogous to that of one mimicking or dwelling on the outward expression of a mental state in another, and having the state thereby produced by reaction in himself.

The dream-state produced in the patient by the reaction on his consciousness of the imagery, and other dream-products, supplied by the genius of the Poet, though it lasts as dream-state but for a moment, yet leaves an effect behind which persists more or less sensibly throughout the waking consciousness which follows; and if the lapses into the dream-state induced by a poem are frequent, the effect, persisting in the waking consciousness which apprehends the subject-matter, becomes always more and more impressive. This effect may be described as a feeling of having lately been in some divine region, where the true reasons of the things which happen in this world of ordinary experience are laid up; a Place in which one understood the significance of these things, although one cannot now explain what one then understood. In the *Phaedrus* Myth, where the Souls peep over the edge of the Cosmos for a moment into the Plain of Truth beyond, and then sink down into the region of the sensible, this feeling of "having just now understood the true significance of things" is pictorially rendered.

I venture to urge on those who discuss that vexed question—"What is Poetic Truth?" the importance of not neglecting this "feeling of having just now understood the true significance of things"—a feeling which, of course, is experienced pretty generally, and quite apart from the influence of Poetry, although in the case of those who come under that influence it is so elaborately procured and regulated as to become an important factor in their lives. When we are told by the exponents of "Poetic Truth", from Aristotle downwards, that it is the "Universal"—that "Poetry sets forth the Universal"—we are not asked to believe that there are Universals (in the plural) of Poetry like those of Science—principles supplied by Poetry which explain particulars, or furnish some definite guidance in respect of them, as, *e.g.*, the Law of Gravitation "explains" the orbits of the planets, or even as the "Principles of Economics" furnish guidance in particular cases arising in the course of business. If, then, the exponents of "Poetic Truth" do not claim for the "Universal" of Poetry that it provides any such explanation or guidance in detail, what do they understand it to be and do?

It seems to me that their exposition amounts to this:— The Universal of Poetry is that which does for the details of the Poet's interesting Story or Picture what "Knowledge of the Good" does for the objects of Conduct: it is as it were a Light, in which they are bathed and altered—an atmosphere of solemn elemental feeling through which we see the representations of Poetry, as we see the presentations of Social Life—its claims and temptations—through the medium of the Sense of Duty. If this is what the doctrine of the "Universal of Poetry", as expounded by those who have written on the subject, amounts to, I am entirely in agreement with them. I am merely putting their doctrine in other words when I state my own view as follows:—The "Universal of Poetry" is apprehended by us when, having entered at the beck of the Poet, our initiator, into the vast wonderland of the dream-consciousness, we presently return therefrom to the waking world of his interesting story, and see its particulars again with the eyes of *revenants* who now know their secret meaning—or rather, know that they have a secret meaning—that they represent, here in the world of our ordinary observations and sentiments, the truth of a deeper order of reality. So, Plato[1] will have his Guardians believe that the particular events of their lives here are but representative doubles of things which are accomplished in a real life behind: the Guardians are to be told that "their youth was a dream"—that they merely imagined that they were being educated here: in reality, all the while, it was elsewhere, in the womb of their Mother Earth, that they were being fashioned and nurtured.

Let me not be misunderstood. I do not underrate the importance in Poetry of all that appeals to our love of "anthropology". The *Odyssey* must be interesting as, say, the *Voyages of Columbus* are interesting; the *Songs* of Burns and Goethe must be interesting as the common sentiments and experiences which they set forth are interesting to us all in our own lives and the lives of our neighbours. Minute character-drawing, the picturesque portrayal of people as they strike the eye in their surroundings, dramatic representation of their doings and fortunes, and description of the natural world, especially as scene of man's adventures and musings—all these, in their proper places, must be supplied by the Poet; but they are what I have called the Body of Poetry—they constitute the material which the Soul of Poetry inspires. The material must, indeed, be interesting to the waking consciousness, if it is to be inspired; but it may well be interesting without being inspired. The inspiration, I have argued, if it comes, comes from the dream-consciousness. The Soul of Poetry is apprehended in its Body at the moment when we awake from the "Poet's Dream", and on a sudden see the passing figures and events of his interesting story arrested in their temporal flight, like the "brede of marble men and maidens" on the Grecian Urn, and standing still, from the viewpoint of eternity, as emblems—of what?—of Eternal Verities, the purport of which we cannot now recall; but we know that they are valid, and are laid up in that other world from which we are newly returned.[2]

[1] *Republic*, 414.
[2] See Plotinus, *Enn.* vi. 9. 9 and 10: speaking of the return from the ecstatic to ordinary consciousness, he says—"The vision is difficult to describe.

It may be objected that "Poetic Truth" is not rated highly enough when its "Universal" is identified with a "vague feeling" of some inexplicable significance attaching to objects and sentiments, within the sphere of ordinary experience, which are brought before us in the Poet's story. The patent fact that Poetry "elevates" men's lives may be urged against a view which reduces its "Truth" to the low level, it may be thought, of a feeling of the "Irrational Part of the Soul". I would meet this objection by referring to what I have said about the relation of the conscious Self of waking experience—the sensitive and rational Self—to the Self of the dream-consciousness, and of both to the unconscious Self of the "Vegetative Part of the Soul", in which they have their roots. The Vegetative Part, I argued, is the principle within us which inspires the conscious life with that which is the foundation of conduct, and (when we turn to speculation) the beginning and end of Metaphysics—that faith in reality and goodness in the strength of which we struggle on, seeking ever new experiences and adventures. I put no slight, therefore, upon the "Universal of Poetry" if I ascribe it to the inspiration of this fundamental principle making itself felt in consciousness, not in the normal form of implicit belief in the Worth of Life, but less normally as the dream-intuition of a ground of that belief. The Metaphysician is too often found trying to set forth a ground which shall be plain to the Understanding, forgetting that

> Thou canst not prove the Nameless,
> Nor canst thou prove the world thou movest in,
> For nothing worthy proving can be proven,
> Nor yet disproven.

The Poet does better: he induces the dream-intuition of a ground, and leaves us with the wonder of the vision haunting our minds when we wake to pursue the details of his interesting story.

But in what form, it will be asked, does this ground of our faith present itself to the dream-consciousness? It presents itself, I would answer, as "another world" one,

For how could anyone relate it as 'other', not seeing it as other when he beheld it, but as one with himself?"; and see *infra*, p. 349, where it is contended that the feeling of being "one with the world" is that experienced when great poetry exerts its influence most powerfully.

unchanging, good, certified, by the testimony of one swift act of perfect intuition, to exist beyond, or rather within, the world of multiplicity and change and trouble which the senses and understanding present to us; and, recapitulating all that I have said in this section, and other parts of this work, I would describe the way in which the Poet brings us to this intuition as follows:—

The Poet, by means of words, makes us, his patients, see those wondrous images of the familiar things of human life and experience which he himself sees.[1] We dream his dream. But, in a moment, our dream is past, and we see, with the waking mind's eye, the familiar things which, a moment before—or was it not ages ago?—were so wondrously transformed for the dreaming mind's-eye. Henceforth all is changed. Whatever bit of interesting human life and experience the Poet has taken for his "subject"—be it the situation which appeals to tender sentiment in a love-song, the action which appeals to pity, fear, grief, risibility, expectant curiosity, in a play, the world of nature which appeals to us as scene of man's adventures and musings, in a poem of observation and reflection—whatever be the interesting bit of human life and experience which the Poet has presented to us, it is now, for us also, no longer a mere particular experience. We now see this bit of common experience in a setting of mysterious feeling. When we try to explain to ourselves what this mysterious feeling is which can so wondrously transfigure a bit of common experience, we are fain to borrow the language of logic, and speak of it as a "Universal"—"the particular," we say, "is no longer a particular: it bears the image of the Universal, reflects the light of the Universal." But this so-called "Universal" is no conceptual product of the logical understanding: the logical understanding, like the senses, regards the World as a number of more or less connected items external to itself; but this feeling which is come over us is the feeling of being one with the World. This feeling of being one with the

[1] As the simplest and best definition of poetry, I would suggest that it is the art of stimulating the imagination with words. (Schopenhauer, *The World as Will and Idea*, ii. 484). Poetry is a kind of teaching, filled and bounded by words, but in its material loose and licentious. It is thus related to fantasy. (Bacon, *de Augm. Sc.* ii. cap. 13).

World is the reflection, in consciousness, of the condition of that unconscious "Vegetative Soul" in us which is the foundation of our conscious life—which, by its continuous activity, sustains the broken activities of our conscious life, and correlates them, and inspires us with invincible faith in a real World, as part of which, or as one with which, it is good to live. This faith is the stuff out of which the Thinking Faculty, in course of time, constructs its preposterous "ontology", or *theory* of a real World in which, and of which, it is good to be—a theory which consists in the production of *ex post facto* reasons for what Transcendental Feeling, representing, in consciousness, the condition of the unconscious "Vegetative Soul" in us, lays down as a sure first principle—that behind, or rather within, the temporal world of particular items presented to us in the life of the senses and understanding—behind the world of "phenomena which we can never explain" and "passions of which we have not yet formed clear and distinct ideas", there is an eternal World—one, unchangeable good. This is the World which the "Vegetative Part of the Soul" puts its trust in; and the other "Parts", sensitive and rational, follow its lead—with increasing hesitation and scepticism as "higher" operations of consciousness come into play: but yet they follow—

> Lead me, O Zeus, and thou, Destiny, whither I have been ordained by you. Thus I shall follow resolutely. And if unwillingly I shall be wrong, but nevertheless I will follow.

To feel of a sudden that there is surely an eternal World behind, or within, the temporal world of particular items, is to experience the purification which Poetry—one among other agencies—effects in us.

I would conclude this Section with some remarks on the place of Metrical Form—melodious and rhythmic diction—and of Imagination, or Representation, respectively in Poetry.

If the essential function of Poetry, as Poetry, is to rouse Transcendental Feeling by inducing lapses into the state of dream-consciousness, it is easy to see that metrical form is helpful towards the exercise of this function. Metrical form represents song and dance, both natural expressions of, and both powerfully reacting on, those modes of what may be called Empirical[1] Feeling which have been most influential in the development of man as social being—sympathy with kinsmen and associates, joy and sorrow, love and hatred, confidence and fear, experienced by each man in common with the other members of his tribe.[2] When we civilised men are subjected to the influence of metrical diction, we are visited, in our solitude, by faint shadows, as it were, of those actual feelings which social song and dance expressed and strengthened in primitive man. As experiencing these feelings in this shadowy form, we are, *ipso facto*, withdrawn from the current world of actual feelings, sense-impressions, and concepts of the understanding, and carried away to the confines of the dream-world into which it is the peculiar office of the Poet to transport us, in order that we may see, just for a moment, the creations with which he has filled it, and then may return, surrounded by an atmosphere of Transcendental Feeling, to see, in the waking world of his interesting story, the doubles of these creations reflecting, each with its own specific tint, the solemn light of that feeling. But is metrical form absolutely necessary to the exercise of this peculiar office of Poetry? For an answer to this question I go to a great poet, than whom there is none

---

[1] I venture to speak of "Empirical Feeling" as distinguished from "Transcendental Feeling". Empirical Feeling has such modes as love, hate, fear, anger, surprise; they are specifically marked off from one another, and are always experienced each in a set of circumstances, or in relation to some object, which is specifically marked off from other sets of circumstances or other objects. These modes of feeling accordingly, like the objects which arouse them, come into consciousness, or supervene; they are *a posteriori* data of consciousness—empirically received. But Transcendental Feeling—Faith in the Worth of Life—is not a datum of conscious experience, like this or that mode of Empirical Feeling; it does not merely supervene or come into consciousness; it is already involved in consciousness; it is the *a priori* condition of conscious activity; if we had it not, we should not endure to live and seek after the *a posteriori* data which make the content of life.

[2] "Circling in the common dance, moving and singing in the consent of common labour, the makers of earliest poetry put into it those elements without which it cannot thrive now. . . . It is clear from the study of poetic beginnings that poetry in its larger sense is not a natural impulse of man, simply as man. His rhythmic and kindred instincts, latent in the solitary state, found free play only under communal conditions, and as powerful factors in the making of society."—Gummere, *The Beginnings of Poetry* (1901), p. 473. I find much that I can agree with in Prof. Gummere's book; but I think that he (together with many others) is wrong in making metrical form *essential* to Poetry.

greater, I think, whether he be judged by power of rousing Transcendental Feeling or by mastery of the art of versification—to Coleridge. "The writings of Plato," he says,[1] "and Bishop Taylor, and the *Theoria Sacra* of Burnet, furnish undeniable proofs that poetry of the highest kind may exist without metre, and even without the contradistinguishing objects of a poem;" and again,[2] "Metre in itself is simply a stimulant of the attention . . . I write in metre, because I am about to use a language different from that of prose." The evidence of Wordsworth is to the same effect; but as he is not a great master of versification, as Coleridge is, his evidence may be thought, perhaps, to be less valuable:— "It has been shown that the language of Prose," Wordsworth says in the Preface to the Second Edition of his Poems (including *Lyrical Ballads*), "may yet be well adapted to Poetry; and it was previously asserted that a large portion of the language of every good poem can in no respect differ from that of good Prose. We will go farther. It may be safely affirmed that there neither is, nor can be, any *essential* difference between the language of Prose and metrical composition. . . . I here use the word 'Poetry' (though against my own judgment) as opposed to the word Prose, and synonymous with metrical composition. But much confusion has been introduced into criticism by this contradistinction of Poetry and Prose, instead of the more philosophical one of Poetry and Matter of Fact, or Science. The only strict antithesis to Prose is Metre; nor is this, in truth, a *strict* antithesis, because lines and passages of metre so naturally occur in writing prose, that it would be scarcely possible to avoid them, even were it desirable." If this evidence, as coming from one who is no great master of versification, be thought lightly of, it ought, on the other hand, to be remembered that Wordsworth is Coleridge's peer in power of rousing Transcendental Feeling, and exercises this power often through the medium of studiously prosaic diction. His Poetry, therefore, is evidence, apart altogether from his critical opinion just quoted, in favour at least of the view that full poetic effect can be produced where the diction is hardly distinguishable from that of prose.

[1] Coleridge, *Biogr. Lit.* ch. xiv.   [2] Coleridge, *o.c.* ch. xviii.

The view maintained by Coleridge and Wordsworth[1] is not, it would seem, orthodox. Recent critics of Poetry are generally in favour of the view that metrical form is an *essential condition* of the existence of "Poetry".[2]

Now, the difference between a great poet himself and critics of the poetic art who are not, and do not pretend to be, great poets, or even poets at all, appears to me to be worth defining; and I venture to define it as follows:—

A great poet, like Wordsworth or Coleridge, is so intent upon the End of Poetry that he uses the means with little thought of what they happen to be in themselves. Critics of Poetry, on the other hand, even when they are endowed with personal feeling for the End of Poetry, are apt, as critics, to take that End for granted, and devote their attention exclusively to the very interesting subject of the means whereby it is achieved. They assume that, of course, a great poet produces "poetic effect"; but not cherishing that effect as a personal experience to be received with undiminished wonder and joy whenever they read his poetry, they are apt, in their capacity of critics, to lose clear sight of it, and then to mistake for part of it something entirely distinct from it—the mere aesthetic effect produced by the melody and rhythm undoubtedly present in most cases where there is Poetry. This mistake, I venture to think, lurks in the following definition of "Poetry", which may be taken as expressing the view of a large, and in some respects, meritorious class of critics—those who are impressed by the "necessity of considering literature as material of science":—"Poetry is literature, usually of a high degree of Human Interest, which, in addition to its Human Interest, has in it an added Aesthetic Interest," *i.e.* appeals to "an aesthetic sense of rhythm".[3] Here it may be that "*high*

---

[1] And Shelley, *A Defence of Poetry:* "The distinction between poets and prose writers is a vulgar error."

[2] A collection of opinions on this subject, I should think pretty nearly complete, and certainly somewhat embarrassing by reason of the often very minute differences recorded, will be found in Professor Gummere's work, *The Beginnings of Poetry* (1901); see also Professor Butcher's *Aristotle's Theory of Poetry and Fine Art*, pp. 143-147, and Mr. Adam's note on *Republic*, 601 B, 9. Plato and Aristotle both make narrative the essential thing in Poetry: metre is ancillary: see *Phaedo*, 61 B, and *Poet.* 1451 b 29, quoted by Mr. Adam.

[3] *An Introduction to the Scientific Study of English Poetry*, by Mark H. Liddell (1902), pp. 72 and 65. See also Gummere, *o.c.* ch. ii., "Rhythm as the Essential Fact of Poetry"

Human Interest"—though said to be only "usually"
present—stands for the End of Poetry as Wordsworth and
Coleridge understand it; but the attainment of this end is
made entirely dependent on successful appeal to the
aesthetic sense of rhythm—metrical form is made absolutely
necessary to the exercise of the essential function of Poetry.
Indeed, so vital is the connection between "metre" and
"poetry" conceived to be, that we are asked to regard the
rhythmic structure of the diction as only the outer form of a
"rhythmic structure of ideation": there can be no Poetry
where there is not only a rhythmic structure of diction, but a
rhythmic structure of ideation.[1]

While maintaining that not only is "Verse Form
Interest"[2]—successful appeal to the aesthetic sense of
rhythm—no part of the true poetic effect, but that metrical
form is not essential, even as means, to the production of
true poetic effect, I, of course, am ready to admit that,
when metrical form is absent, poetic effect is produced with
greater difficulty than when that form is present; for the
appeal made to the Self of the dream-consciousness is so
much the weaker as being made solely through dream-
scenery, without the aid of the nascent emotion accompanying the suggested Song and Dance.   But dream-
scenery suggested by the plainest prose is often, I submit,
enough, by itself, to make the *milieu* in which it is possible
to experience the true poetic effect. This could be illustrated
abundantly from the Icelandic Sagas. On the other hand,
it is often the case that the destruction of the metrical form,
dream-scenery being left untouched, destroys that *milieu:*
of this Plato gives us an amusing example in *Republic,* 393
E ff., where *Iliad,* i. 17 ff., is turned into prose; and, as
Professor Gummere asks,[3] "What would be left in prose,
any prose, of Goethe's *Ueber allen Gipfeln ist Ruh' ?*" Nothing
of *that particular poem* certainly, the original diction of which
is metrical. But, I submit, there are poems the original
diction of which is not metrical. Because a poem, originally
composed in metrical form, is spoilt as a poem by translation
into prose, it does not follow that "prose" is impossible as the

---

[1] Liddell, *o.c.* p. 145.   [2] *o.c.* p. 74.
[3] *o.c.* p. 49.

original form in which a poem may be composed. "There
is no valid test for the historian save this test of rhythm,"
says Professor Gummere.[1] It is a rough test—convenient, I
dare say, for the purpose of the historian; but the philosophical student cannot accept it as having any value for
his own purpose.

I would class metrical form, then, along with interesting
story and skilful word-painting, as a part—an important,
but not absolutely necessary part—of the *milieu* in which the
genius of the Poet finds it possible to produce poetic effect
in his patient; that effect itself, of course, being something
essentially distinct from the interest felt in the story, from
the specific emotions roused by its incidents and scenery, or
from the emotion caused (it may be, first of all in the vocal
chords[2]) by the rhythm and melody of the words, whether
spoken or unspoken. In the *milieu* of imagery and emotion
produced by the Poet's story or description, especially when
it is couched in melodious language,[3] the Poet's patient is
ready to experience, when the "psychological moment"
arrives, that sudden flash of Transcendental Feeling in which,
I contend, the essence of poetical effect consists.

I venture to think that the exaggerated importance
attached to metrical form, regarded as an *essential condition*
of poetic effect, has been responsible for the comparatively
scanty attention paid by recent writers on the nature of
Poetry to the immensely important part played by Representation, simply as Representation, in the creation of what
I have called the poetic *milieu*, to distinguish it from poetic
effect. The Greek identification of the art of poetry with
imitation seems to me to have the root of the matter in it,
if we understand by imitation the production of the poetic
milieu, and take purification (as it appears in Aristotle's
Poetics) to stand for the poetic effect—the flash of Transcendental Feeling in that *milieu*.

---

[1] *o.c.* pp. 49, 50.

[2] "I believe that with careful self-observation many men 'with an ear for
verse' will recognise that the essential part of poetic excitation has lain in
scarcely perceptible changes of tension in the muscles of the throat" (Myers,
Human Personality, i. 102). I confess that it is with much astonishment that I
find Myers among those who make the sense of nascent melodious speech in
the vocal chords *the essential condition* of experiencing poetic effect.

[3] Mr. W. B. Yeats in his book, *The Idea of Good and Evil*, p. 16, propounds
the charming idea of "poems spoken to a harp".

The Poetic *milieu*, as I have argued throughout this work, is a state of dream-consciousness—not, indeed, shut off, as in sleep, from the waking state, but concurrent with, or inserted into, it. As we read or listen to Poetry we are in a daydream. We are, indeed, aware of the "real things" of this world round about us; and yet we are in another world, not of "real things", but of representations, imitations, pictures, reflections. These reflections resemble the "real things"—and yet, they are quite different from them—as different as the upside-down trees in the pool of water are different from the real trees of which they are reflections. The reflections of Poetry, like those of the pool, are in another world. What do they mean? They are more beautiful than the "real things" of this world. The "real things" therefore cannot account for them. They are copies surely of "eternal things" existing somewhere. Where? Such is the reasoning, and such is the final difficulty, or *impasse*, of the dream-consciousness which the Poet can induce in his patient simply by means of Representation. Sometimes the patient does not get beyond the difficulty or *impasse;* sometimes—and this is to experience the true poetic effect—the *impasse* is opened for a moment, the difficulty is solved in a swift act of intuition—too swift, alas! for the truth revealed to be retained in the memory:

> It sees her such that when it tells it to me again, I do not understand it, so subtly does it talk to the mourning heart, which makes it speak.[1]

I have spoken of objects reflected in a pool of water. The feeling which such reflections cause is, I think, very nearly akin to that which poetic imitation causes. The phantasms of real things in water, in painting, in word-painting, lend themselves to the feeling that there is "another world". They are seen in a strange light and atmosphere, and, as we look at them, the world of waking experience recedes, and we pass into dreamland—as we do sometimes on a still autumn evening when we see familiar houses and trees silhouetted against the pure sky, like things in a

---

[1] *Vita Nuova*, Sonetto xxv.

picture which we now look at for the first time with wonder
and eerie surmise.

Shelley's rendering of the feeling produced by reflections
in water is worth careful consideration as a great poet's
record of an experience which is closely related to, if not
identical with, that produced by poetical "Imitation", or
"Representation". I close this section by quoting his lines[1]
as an answer—not the less valuable because not intended by
the poet himself to be an answer—to the question, What is
the end of Poetry, and how does Imitation subserve that end?

> We paused beside the pools that lie
>   Under the forest bough,
> Each seemed as 'twere a little sky
>   Gulfed in a world below;
> A firmament of purple light,
>   Which in the dark earth lay,
> More boundless than the depth of night,
>   And purer than the day—
> In which the lovely forests grew,
>   As in the upper air,
> More perfect both in shape and hue
>   Than any spreading there.
> There lay the glade and neighbouring lawn,
>   And through the dark-green wood
> The white sun twinkling like the dawn
>   Out of a speckled cloud.
> Sweet views which in our world above
>   Can never well be seen,
> Were imaged by the water's love
>   Of that fair forest green.
> And all was interfused beneath
>   With an Elysian glow,
> An atmosphere without a breath,
>   A softer day below.

[1] *The Recollection.*

THE TWO *SYMPOSIUM* MYTHS

CONTEXT

The subject of the Symposium, *like that of its companion Dialogue, the* Phaedrus, *is Love.*

The subject is treated, from various points of view, in speeches made, in succession, by those present at a Banquet in the house of Agathon the tragedian—by Phaedrus, by Pausanias, by Eryximachus, by Aristophanes, by Agathon himself, by Socrates reporting the Discourse of Diotima the Woman of Mantinea, and lastly by Alcibiades.

Two of these speeches—that of Aristophanes, and that of Diotima, reported by Socrates—are Myths.

Symposium 189C—193D. THE MYTH TOLD BY ARISTOPHANES

Men, methinks, have altogether failed of apprehending the power of Love; for had they apprehended it, for him would they have builded the greatest temples and the greatest altars, and unto him would bring the greatest burnt offerings; whereas now no such honours are paid unto him—honours meet for him above all other gods; for he is that one of them all who loveth men most; he is the helper of mankind, and our physician where healing bringeth the greatest happiness. I will therefore endeavour to instruct you in his power; and you shall teach others.

First must be told what Human Nature is, and what are the affections thereof.

Human Nature was not originally what it now is, but different; for, in the first place, there were three genders of mankind—not as now, two—male and female, but a third in addition thereto—a common gender composite of the two. This gender itself is clean gone, and only the name thereof remaineth, *Man-Woman*, as a name of reproach. Secondly, the whole form of every human creature was round, whereof the back and sides made one circumference; and it had four hands, and likewise four legs; and two faces, altogether similar to each other, upon a round neck; and on the top of these faces, which were set opposite to each other, one head; and four ears; and there were two privy members; and all the other parts after the same manner; and these people walked upright, as men do now, whithersoever they would; and also, when they desired to go quickly, they rolled quickly round, pushing off with their eight limbs, like tumblers who tumble over and over with their legs going round in the air.

Now the genders were three, and of this sort, because the male gender was in the beginning sprung from the Sun, and the female gender from the Earth, and that which partook of both from the Moon—for the Moon partaketh of both Sun and Earth: so it came to pass that they themselves and their manner of progression were circular after the likeness of their parents: and they were terrible by reason of their strength and valour; and their hearts were proud, and they made assault upon the Gods; for that which Homer telleth concerning Ephialtes and Otus is told concerning them—that they essayed to go up into Heaven for to lay hands on the Gods.

Wherefore Zeus and the other Gods took counsel what they should do, and were in doubt; for they were not minded to slay them, as they slew the giants, with thunder-bolts, and to make men to cease utterly from the Earth, for then would the worship and the sacrifices which men render unto the Gods also cease; nor were they minded to let them go on in their iniquities. At last after a long while Zeus bethought him of this that followeth, and said: "I have found out a way, methinks, of keeping men alive, and yet making them weaker, so that they shall cease from their wickedness: I will cut each one of them in twain; and so shall they be made weaker, and also more serviceable for us, having been increased in number; and they shall walk upright on two legs; and if I see them again behaving themselves frowardly and not willing to live peaceably, I will cut them yet again in twain," he said, "so that they shall go hopping on one leg."

Having spoken thus, he straightway began to cut men in twain, as one cutteth apples for pickling, or eggs with hairs; and each one whom he cut in twain he delivered unto Apollo, and commanded him to turn round the face and half of the neck towards the cut, so that the fellow, beholding it, might behave himself more seemly; likewise the other parts did he command Apollo to dress: and Apollo turned the face round, and pulled the skin together from all parts over that which is now called the belly, even as one draweth together a purse, and the one opening which was left he closed and made fast in the middle of the belly—this is that which they now call the navel; and smoothing out all the other wrinkles everywhere, he fashioned the breasts with an instrument like unto that wherewith cobblers smooth out the wrinkles of the leather round the last; but he left a few wrinkles about the belly itself and the navel, to be for a memorial of that which had been done of old.

Now when the original creature was cut in twain, the one half, longing for the other half, went to meet it, and they cast their arms around one another, and clung unto one another, eagerly desiring to be made one creature; and they began to die for lack of food and of all other things that a man must provide for himself; for neither would eat aught save together with the other: and when one of the halves died, and the other was left, that which was left went about seeking for another half, and when it happened upon the half of that which aforetime was a woman—this half we now call woman—or upon the half of that which was a man, joined itself unto it: and thus did they perish. Then Zeus had compassion upon them, and brought forth a new device:—He brought their privy parts round to the front— for before that time their privy parts were set in the outerpart of their bodies, and they had not intercourse one with another, but with the earth, as grasshoppers. So he changed them and caused them to have intercourse one with another, to the end that, if a man happened upon a woman, there might be propagation, and if male happened upon male, there might be satisfaction, and then an end made of it, both turning to other things and minding them. Of such oldness is the love of one another implanted in us, which bringeth us again into the primitive state, and endeavoureth of two to make one and to heal the division of Human Nature. Every human creature, then, is a counterpart, being a half cut flat like unto a flounder, and alway seeketh his own counterpart.

They who are the halves of that composite nature which was then called *Man-Woman* are the kind whereof the most part of adulterers are; and of this sort likewise are women which lust for men and are adulteresses. But those women who are halves of the whole which was Woman take little heed of men, but rather turn them to companionship with women; and those males which are halves of the whole which was male, go after the male: while they are boys, inasmuch as they are slices of the male, they love men and take pleasure in companionship with men; these be of all boys and youths the best, inasmuch as they are by nature the most manly: some, indeed, say that they are without shame; but herein they speak falsely; for it is not by reason of shamelessness that they do this, but by reason of the

courage and manliness in them, which their countenance
declareth. Wherefore do they greet joyfully that which is
like unto themselves: and that this I say concerning them
is true, what followeth after showeth; for afterward when
these are grown up, they alone of all men advance to the
conduct of politiques. Now when these are grown up to be
men, they make youths their companions, and their nature
inclineth them not to wedlock and the begetting of children;
only the law constraineth them thereto: for they are content
to pass their lives with one another unwedded, being lovers
one of another, and always greeting that nature which hath
kinship with their own. When, therefore, one of these
happeneth upon the very one who is his own other half,
then are the two confounded with a mighty great amazement
of friendship and kinship and love, and will not—nay, not
for a moment—be parted from each other. These be they
who all their life through are alway together, nor yet could
tell what it is they wish to obtain of each other—for surely
it is not satisfaction of sensual appetite that all this great
endeavour is after: nay, plainly, it is something other that
the Soul of each wisheth—something which she cannot tell,
but, darkly divining, maketh her end. And if Hephaestus
came and stood by the two with his tools in his hand, and
asked of them saying, "What is it, O men, that ye wish to
obtain of each other?" and when they could not answer,
asked of them again saying, "Is it this that ye desire—to be
so united unto each other that neither by night nor by day
shall ye be parted from each other? If it is this that ye
desire, I will melt and fuse you together so that, although ye
are two, ye shall become one, and, as long as ye live, shall
both live one common life, and when ye die, shall be one
dead man yonder in Hades, instead of two dead men: see
now, if it be for this ye are lovers, and if the getting of this
is all your desire." We know well that there is none who
would say nay unto this, or show a wish for aught else; yea,
rather, each one would think that this which was now
promised was the very thing which he had alway, albeit
unwittingly, desired—to be joined unto the beloved, and to
be melted together with him, so that the twain should become

one: the cause whereof is this, that our original nature was such that we were One Whole.

Love, then, is the name of our desire and pursuit of the Whole; and once, I say, we were one, but now for our wickedness God hath made us to dwell separate, even as the Arcadians who were made to dwell separate by the Lacedaemonians; and even yet are we in danger, if we are not obedient unto the Gods, to be again cut in twain, and made to go about as mere tallies, in the figure of those images which are graven in relief on tablets with their noses sawn through into halves. Wherefore let our exhortation unto every man be that he live in the fear of the gods, to the end that we may escape this, and obtain that unto which Love our Captain leadeth us. Him let no man withstand. Whoso is at enmity with the gods withstandeth him; but if we are become friends of God, and are reconciled unto him, then shall we find and meet each one of us his own True Love, which happeneth unto few in our time.

Now I pray Eryximachus not to break a jest upon my discourse, as though Pausanias and Agathon were in my mind; for peradventure they too are of those I speak of, and are both by nature male: but, be that as it may, I speak concerning all men and women, and say that the state of mankind would become blessed if we all fulfilled our love, and each one of us happened upon his own True Love, and so returned unto his original nature.

If this is best of all, it followeth of necessity that that which in our present life cometh nearest thereto is best—this is that each one of us should find the love which is naturally suitable to him; and the God we ought to praise for this is Love, who both at this present time bestoweth on us the greatest benefit, in that he leadeth us unto our own, and for the time to come giveth us promise of that which is best, if we render the observance to godward that is meet, to wit, the promise that he will restore us to our original nature, and heal us of our pain, and make us divinely blessed.

GENERAL OBSERVATIONS ON THE MYTH TOLD BY
ARISTOPHANES

The Myth told by Aristophanes in the *Symposium*[1] differs from all other Platonic Myths in being conceived in a spirit, and told in a manner, reminding one of Rabelais or Swift. It explains the sentiment of love as due to the fact that every human being is a tally:[2] which came about in the following way:—Primitive man was round, and had four hands and four feet, and one head with two faces looking opposite ways. He could walk on his legs if he liked, but he could also roll over and over with great speed like a tumbler; which he did when he wanted to go fast.[3] There were three genders at that time, corresponding to the Sun, the parent of the masculine gender, to the Earth, the parent of the feminine gender, and to the Moon, the parent of the common gender. These round people, children of round parents, being very swift and strong, attacked Zeus and the other gods. Instead of destroying prospective worshippers with thunderbolts, Zeus adopted the plan of doubling the number of the round people by cutting each one of them in two. This not only doubled the number of his prospective worshippers, but humbled them, for they had now to walk on two legs and could not roll; and he threatened, if they gave him any further trouble, to halve them again, and make them merely bas-reliefs, and leave them to hop about on one leg.[4]

[1] 189 D ff.   [2] 191 D.
[3] Mr. A. B. Cook (*Zeus, Jupiter, and the Oak*, in *Class. Rev.* July 1904, p. 326), speaking of the Sicilian *triskeles* as a survival of the Cyclops as primitively conceived—*i.e.* conceived as (1) three-eyed, and (2) as a disc representing the solar orb—remarks that "Plato was probably thinking of the Empedoc-lean uncultivated types (251 K) when he spoke of Janiform beings with four arms and four legs which enabled them to revolve in a circle (*Symp.* 189 E; cf. *Tim.* 44 D)".
[4] In Callaway's *Zulu Nursery Tales*, i. 198-202, the story is told of a woman who is carried away by one-legged people. When they first saw her they said: " 'Oh, it would be a pretty thing—but, oh, the two legs!' They said this because she had two legs and two hands; for they are like as if an ox of the white man is skinned and divided into two halves; the Amadhlung-undhlebe were like one side, there not being another side." In a note *ad loc.* (p. 199) Callaway refers to Pliny (*H.N.* vii. 2) for a nation of one-legged men— "a race of men who should be called one-eyed, single-legged, with wonderful agility in the dance"; and to Lane's notes to the Introduction to the *Arabian Nights*, p. 33—"The Shikk is another demoniacal creature, having the form of half a human being, like a man divided longitudinally."

Now Love is the remembrance of the original undivided state: it is the longing which one half has to be again united to its other half, so that the original Whole may be restored: every human being is a tally.

It is difficult to think of this story[1] as a Platonic Myth in the ordinary sense. Does it deduce any Category, or set forth any Regulative Principle? If it does, it is only as a satirical parody of the impressive Aetiological Myth. Love is a mysterious principle, Plato seems to say; but here is a Comic History of it which may help to make it less mysterious! And yet, after all, does the circumstance that one Aetiological Myth is comic, and another is serious and impressive, constitute a real difference? We have to remember, with regard to these comic or grotesque histories, that at one end of the list of them there are some of the earliest attempts at Myth or Story-telling made by the human race, and at the other end, some of the most effective expressions of the scorn and zeal and pity of civilised man. *The Life of Gargantua and Pantagruel* and *Gulliver's Travels* show us how the comic or grotesque history, as well as the solemn Myth— Myth of Er or *Purgatorio*—may set forth the Universal.

The place held in such a deeply religious system as the Orphic by a savage grotesque like the story of Zagreus enables us to understand how Plato—if only in a spirit of parody—could insert a story like that of the round people in a serious discussion of the nature of Love.

Zagreus[2] was the son of Zeus and Persephone, and his father's darling. But Hera was jealous, and incited the

---

[1] Perhaps suggested by the "many were born with a face before and behind, and double-breasted, the progeny of an ox", of Empedocles. Professor Burnet's illuminating account of the theory of "organic combinations" advanced by Empedocles is full of suggestion for the reader of the Myth told by Aristophanes in the *Symposium*: see especially section 94 of *Early Greek Philosophy*, First Ed.

[2] For the story of Zagreus and its place in religious doctrine and practice, see Lobeck, *Aglaoph.* pp. 547 ff., Gardner's *New Chapters in Greek History*, p. 396, and Jevons' *Introduction to the History of Religion*, p. 355. Dr. Jevons sums up as follows: The Zagreus Myth, before Pythagoreanism affected the Orphic cult, had driven out all others, and was accepted as *the* orthodox explanation of the new worship, by which it was reconciled with the old customary religion. Pythagoreanism afterwards allegorised this Myth in the interest not of religion, but of a philosophical system. See also Olympiodorus ad Plat. *Phaedonem*, 70 c, Grote's *Hist. of Greece*, part i. ch. i. (vol. i. p. 17, n. 1, ed. 1862), and Miss Harrison's *Prolegomena to the Study of Greek Religion*, Introduction, p. xi.

z

Titans to slay the child. They surprised him among his toys, while he was wondering at the image of his own face in a mirror, and tore him to pieces and ate him, all save his heart, which Athena brought to Zeus, who gave it to Semele, and from her Zagreus was born again as Dionysus. The Titans Zeus in anger consumed with his lightning, and out of their ashes arose Man, whose nature thus unites in its composition an evil element—the flesh of the Titans—and a good element—the flesh of Zagreus which they had eaten.

Much was made of this Myth by Orphic and Neo-Platonic interpreters. The dismemberment of Zagreus was symbolic of the resolution of the One unto the Many; his birth again as Dionysus, of the return from the Many to the One; while the moral of all was that by ceremonial rites and ecstasy we may overcome the Titanic element in us.[1]

That Zagreus, the Horned Child, as he is called, repre-sented the bull which was torn to pieces and eaten in a savage rite, and that the Greek story which I have sketched was an Aetiological Myth to explain the rite, it is impossible to doubt. Out of this savage material were evolved the highly philosophical and moral results which I have indi-cated. This parallel I have brought in the hope of making Plato's introduction of the Round People into his Philosophy of Love more intelligible.

I said that the story of the Round People, told by Aristophanes, stands alone among the Platonic Myths in being conceived in a spirit and related in a manner which remind one of Rabelais or Swift. Let me cap it from Rabelais (iv. 57-61):—

Pantagruel[2] went ashore in an island, which, for situation and governor, may be said not to have its fellow. When you just come into it, you find it rugged, craggy, and barren, unpleasant to the eye, painful to the feet, and almost as inaccessible as the mountain of Dauphiné, which is some-what like a toad-stool, and was never climbed, as any can remember, by any but Doyac, who had charge of King Charles the Eighth's train of artillery. This same Doyac, with strange tools and engines, gained the mountain's top,

---

[1] See Rohde, *Psyche*, ii. 117 ff.; Lobeck, *Aglaoph.* 710 ff.
[2] I avail myself of the version of Urquhart and Motteux.

and there he found an old ram. It puzzled many a wise head to guess how it got thither. Some said that some eagle, or great horn-coot, having carried it thither while it was yet a lambkin, it had got away, and saved itself among the bushes.

As for us, having with much toil and sweat overcome the difficult ways at the entrance, we found the top of the mountain so fertile, healthful, and pleasant, that I thought I was then in the true Garden of Eden, or earthly Paradise, about whose situation our good theologues are in such a quandary, and keep such a pother.

As for Pantagruel, he said that here was the seat of Areté—that is as much as to say, Virtue—described by Hesiod. This, however, with submission to better judgments. The ruler of this place was one Master Gaster, the first master of arts in the world. For, if you believe that fire is the great master of arts, as Tully writes, you very much wrong him and yourself: alas, Tully never believed this. On the other side, if you fancy Mercury to be the first inventor of arts, as our ancient Druids believed of old, you are mightily beside the mark. The satirist's[1] sentence that affirms Master Gaster to be the master of all arts is true. With him peacefully resided old Goody Penia, alias Poverty, the mother of the ninety-nine Muses, on whom Porus, the lord of Plenty, formerly begot Love, that noble child, the mediator of heaven and earth, as Plato affirms in the *Symposium*. We were all obliged to pay our homage, and swear allegiance to that mighty sovereign; for he is imperious, severe, blunt, hard, uneasy, inflexible; you cannot make him believe, represent to him, or persuade him anything. He does not hear. . . . He only speaks by signs. . . . What company soever he is in, none dispute with him for precedence or superiority. . . . He held the first place at the Council of Basle; though some will tell you that the Council was tumultuous, by the contention and ambition of many for priority. Every one is busied, and labours to serve him; and, indeed, to make amends for this, he does this good to mankind, as to invent for them all arts, machines, trades, engines, and crafts; he even instructs brutes in arts which are against their nature, making poets of ravens, jackdaws, chattering jays, parrots, and starlings, and poetesses of magpies, teaching them to utter human language, speak, and sing. . . . At the court of that great master of ingenuity, Pantagruel observed two sorts of troublesome and too officious apparitors, whom he very much detested. The first were called Engastrimythes;

[1] Persius, *Prologus*—

       Belly, Master of art, Bestower of talent.

the others Gastrolaters. . . . The first were soothsayers, enchanters, cheats, who gulled the mob, and seemed not to speak and give answers from the mouth, but from the belly. . . . In the holy decrees, 26, qu. 3, they are styled Ventriloqui; and the same name is given them in Ionian by Hippocrates, in his fifth book of *Epid.*, as men who spoke from the belly. Sophocles calls them Sternomantes. . . . As for the Gastrolaters, they stuck close to one another in knots and gangs. Some of them merry, wanton . . . others louring, grim, dogged, demure, and crabbed; all idle, mortal foes to business, spending half their time in sleeping, and the rest in doing nothing, a rent-charge and dead unnecessary weight on the earth, as Hesiod saith; afraid, as we judged, of offending or lessening their paunch. . . . Coming near the Gastrolaters, I saw they were followed by a great number of fat waiters and tenders, laden with baskets, dossers, hampers, dishes, wallets, pots, and kettles. . . .

Those gastrolatrous hobgoblins being withdrawn, Pantagruel carefully minded the famous master of arts, Gaster. . . . From the beginning he invented the smith's art, and husbandry to manure the ground, that it might yield him corn; he invented arms, and the art of war, to defend corn; physic and astronomy, with other parts of mathematics, which might be useful to keep corn a great number of years in safety from the injuries of the air, beasts, robbers, and purloiners; he invented water, wind, and hand-mills, and a thousand other engines to grind corn, and to turn it into meal; leaven to make the dough ferment, and the use of salt to give it a savour, for he knew that nothing bred more diseases than heavy, unleavened, unsavoury bread. He found a way to get fire to bake it; hourglasses, dials, and clocks to mark the time of its baking; and as some countries wanted corn, he contrived means to convey it out of one country into another. . . . He invented mules. . . . He invented carts and waggons. . . . He devised boats, gallies, and ships. . . . Besides, seeing that, when he tilled the ground, some years the corn perished in it for want of rain in due season, in others rotted, or was drowned by its excess, . . . he found out a way to conjure the rain down from heaven only with cutting a certain grass. . . . I took it to be the same as the plant, one of whose boughs being dipped by Jove's priest in the Agrian fountain, on the Lycian mountain in Arcadia, in time of drought, raised vapours which gathered into clouds, and then dissolved into rain, that kindly moistened the whole country. Our master of arts was also said to have found a way to keep the rain up in the air, and make it fall into the sea. . . .

And as in the fields, thieves and plunderers sometimes stole, and took by force the corn and bread which others had toiled to get, he invented the art of building towns, forts, and castles to hoard and secure that staff of life. On the other hand, finding none in the fields, and hearing that it was hoarded up and secured in towns, forts, and castles, and watched with more care than ever were the golden pippins of the Hesperides, he turned engineer, and found ways to beat, storm, and demolish forts and castles, with machines and warlike thunderbolts, battering-rams, ballistas, and catapults, whose shapes were shown us, not overwell understood by our engineers, architects, and other disciples of Vitruvius.

Symposium 202 D—212 A. THE DISCOURSE OF DIOTIMA

What then is Eros?—is he Mortal? Nay, Mortal he verily is not. What then is he? Betwixt Mortal and Immortal, she answered. What sayest thou, Diotima? He is a great Daemon, Socrates: for the whole tribe of Daemons is betwixt God and Mortal. And what is their office? said I. They are Interpreters, and carry up to the Gods the things which come from men, and unto men the things which come from the Gods—our prayers and burnt-offerings, and their commands and the recompenses of our burnt-offerings. The tribe of Daemons being in the midst betwixt these twain—the Godhead and Mankind—filleth up that distance, so that the Universe is held together in the bond of unity. Through the intermediation of these cometh all divination; the art of priests cometh also through them, and of them that have to do with burnt-offerings and initiations and enchantments and every sort of soothsaying and witchery. The Godhead mingleth not with Mankind; but it is through the Daemons only that Gods converse with men, both when we are awake and when we are asleep: and he who hath the wisdom whereby he understandeth this work of the Daemons is a man inspired, and he who hath any other wisdom whereby he excelleth in some art or craft is a mechanic. Now these Daemons are many and of all sorts: and one of them is Eros. And who is his Father, I said, and who is his Mother? That is a longer story, she said, but I will tell it unto thee.

On the day that Aphrodite was born, the Gods made a feast, and with them sat Abundance the son of Prudence. When they had eaten, Poverty, perceiving that there was good cheer, came for to beg, and she stood at the door. Now Abundance, having made himself drunken with nectar—for there was no wine then—entered into the Garden of Zeus, and being heavy with drink, slept; and Poverty, being minded by reason of her helplessness to have a child by Abundance, lay with him, and she conceived and bore Eros. Wherefore Eros became the companion and servant of Aphrodite; for he was begotten on her birthday, and is, moreover, by nature a lover of Beauty and of Aphrodite the Beautiful.

Inasmuch, then, as Eros is the son of Abundance and Poverty, his case standeth thus:—First, he is poor alway; and so far is he from being tender and fair, as most do opine, that he is rough and squalid, and he goeth barefoot and hath no house to dwell in, but lieth alway on the bare earth at doors and on the highways, sleeping under the open sky; for his mother's nature he hath, and he dwelleth alway in company with want. But he hath also his Father's nature, and ever plotteth against the fair and good; being a bold lad, and ever ready with bow strung, a mighty hunter, alway weaving devices, eagerly desiring knowledge, full of inventions, playing the philosopher all his life, a mighty charlatan and master of enchantments and subtle reasons. Inasmuch, then, as he hath the nature neither of Immortal nor of Mortal, he bloometh and liveth when that aboundeth unto him which his heart desireth, and, anon, the very same day he dieth; and then he cometh to life again, because of his Father's nature: that which is continually supplied unto him in abundance runneth away continually, so that he is neither poor nor rich. Moreover, he standeth in the midst betwixt Wisdom and Ignorance; for the matter standeth thus—No God is a Philosopher, to wit, one who desireth to become wise, for a God is already wise; and if there be any man who is wise, neither is he a Philosopher. Nor are the ignorant Philosophers; they desire not to become wise; for herein lieth the evil of Ignorance, that when a man is without Virtue and Wisdom, he nevertheless thinketh that he is sufficiently furnished therewith, and no man desireth that which he thinketh he lacketh not.

Who, then, Diotima, said I, are the Philosophers, if neither the wise nor the ignorant are Philosophers?

A child could answer that, she said: They that are betwixt the two sorts, even as Eros himself is. For Wisdom indeed is of the number of those things which are the most beautiful; and Eros is desire that fluttereth about the Beautiful; wherefore it followeth that Eros is a Lover of Wisdom, a Philosopher, being betwixt the wise and the ignorant. Whereof his parentage is the cause also; for his

Father is wise and rich, and his Mother is not wise and poor. This, my dear Socrates, is the nature of the Daemon Eros; and I marvel not that thou thoughtest another was Eros—for thou thoughtest, as I judge from what thou sayest, that the Beloved, not That which Loveth, is Eros. For this cause, methinks, Eros seemed all beautiful in thine eyes, for 'tis the Beloved that is indeed fair and delicate and perfect, and worthy to be accounted happy; but as for That which Loveth, it is of another kind, such as I have declared.

    *   *   *   *   *   *

The sum of the whole matter, she said, is this: That Love which is Eros is the desire of having the Good alway for his own. Most true, I said. Since this is what Love ever desireth, she said, how shall a man follow after this, and what shall he do that his diligence and endeavour in following after it may be rightly called Love? What is the very thing which he must bring to pass? Canst thou tell it? I cannot tell it, I said, else should I not be here drawn by thy wisdom, thy disciple come unto thee to learn this very thing.

Then I will tell it unto thee, she said:—The bringing of somewhat to timely birth in Beauty, both according to the flesh and according to the spirit—that is the Work of Love. Thy meaning needeth a prophet for the interpretation thereof, I said: I understand it not. Well, I will make it plain, she said.

All mankind, Socrates, do conceive according to the flesh and according to the spirit; and when we are come to the proper time of life, our nature desireth to bring forth: but it cannot bring forth in that which is deformed, only in that which is beautiful: and this work which it doeth when it conceiveth and begetteth is divine: this work is that which in the life of the mortal creature hath immortality; but it cannot be accomplished in aught that is unfit: now, that which is deformed is unfit for the divine; and the beautiful is fit: Beauty, therefore, is the Fate which ruleth nativities and the Divine Midwife. Wherefore, when that which hath conceived cometh nigh unto that which is beautiful, it is filled with soft delight, and being thereby relaxed bringeth forth and begetteth; but when it cometh nigh unto that which is deformed, it is drawn together with frowning and pain, and turneth itself away, and is rolled up, and begetteth not, but holdeth in that which it hath conceived, and is in sore distress. So it cometh to pass that when any one hath conceived, and is already big, he fluttereth alway with vehement desire around that which is beautiful, because the possession thereof easeth him of his sore travail: for, she said, Love is not fulfilled in the Beautiful as thou thinkest, Socrates. Wherein, then? In begetting and bringing forth in the Beautiful. So be it, said I. Yea, she said, it is so; but wherefore in begetting? Because this is that which, in the Mortal, is Immortal from generation unto generation without end. Immortality, together with Good, Love must needs desire, according to our premises, for Love is desire of having Good alway for his own. This, then, followeth further from our argument, that Love aimeth at Immortality.

*   *   *   *   *   *

They who conceive after the flesh, she said, turn them rather to the love of women, by the procreation of children laying up for themselves, as they think, immortality and remembrance and felicity for evermore: but they who conceive after the spirit—for, she said, there are who conceive in their souls more truly than others conceive in their bodies—these, she said, conceive that which is meet for the soul to conceive and to bear: and what is that? Wisdom and all Virtue; whereof all the poets are begetters, and every workman of whom we say that he is a cunning inventor: but the greatest by far, she said, and the fairest part of Wisdom is that which hath to do with the ordering of cities and households, which is called by the names of Temperance and Justice. The man who in his youth hath conceived these in his soul, being inspired of God, as soon as the time of life cometh, desireth to bring forth and beget: so he goeth about seeking the Beautiful wherein he may beget; for in the deformed he will never beget: and beautiful bodies rather than deformed he greeteth with welcome, inasmuch as he hath conceived: and if he happen upon a beautiful soul of noble nature and excellent parts, in a beautiful body, he greeteth the twain—beautiful body and beautiful soul—with double welcome; and upon him who hath the twain he straightway, endeavouring to instruct,

poureth out Speech in abundance concerning Virtue and
what the Good Man ought to be and do; for, methinks,
when he possesseth the Beautiful One and converseth with
him, or being absent remembereth him, that is brought to
birth which long-time before was conceived; and that which
is born these two together rear, so that they have a stronger
bond betwixt them than children after the flesh, and a
surer friendship than spouses, inasmuch as they have in
common fairer and more immortal children. Who would
not rather have born unto him such children than children
after the flesh? Who, having considered Homer and Hesiod
and the other great poets, accounteth them not blessed, in
that they have children which, being themselves immortal,
bestow on their parents immortal fame and remembrance
for evermore? as do also, she said, the children which
Lycurgus left behind in Lacedaemon, saviours of Lacedaemon, yea of Greece; and amongst you of Athens, she
said, Solon is held in honour because of the laws which he
begat; and in many other places, both throughout Greece
and amongst the barbarians, are men honoured for the fair
works which they have brought to light, and the diverse
virtues which they have begotten—yea, even worshipped,
because of these their children; but because of children
after the flesh hath no man been worshipped.

Into these Lesser Mysteries of Eros, peradventure,
mightest thou, even thou Socrates, be initiated; but his
Greater Mysteries of the End and the Perfect Vision, for
whose sake, if any man shall pursue after them in the right
way, these Lesser Mysteries are performed, I know not if
thou art able to receive. Nevertheless, she said, I will do
what in me lies to open them unto thee; do thou endeavour
to follow if thou canst.

He who would rightly approach this Initiation whereof I
now speak must begin in his youth, and come near unto
Beautiful Bodies: and first, if his leader lead him aright, he
will be smitten with love of one of these, and will straightway of his love engender Beautiful Discourse. Thereafter
he will perceive of himself without instruction that the
Beauty which belongeth to any Corporeal Body is kin to
the Beauty of another; and that if the Specifick Beauty is

that which must be sought after, 'twould be foolishness to think that the Beauty which belongeth to all Bodies is not one and the same. When he hath comprehended this he must needs become the lover of all Beautiful Bodies, and his vehement love of the one Body he will remit, despising it now and thinking it a small thing. Thereafter cometh the time when he deemeth the Beauty that is in Souls more precious than the Beauty in the Body; so that if any one hath some goodness of Soul, but little comeliness of Body, such an one pleaseth him well, and he loveth him and careth for him, and in companionship with him bringeth to birth, and seeketh after, such Discourse as shall make young men better; seeking after this, he is constrained to survey that Beauty which is in Morals and Laws, and seeth clearly that it is all of one kindred. Apprehending this Beauty, he must needs deem the Beauty of the Body a small thing.

After Morals, behold him next led up to Sciences, that he may see their Beauty; and looking at Beauty now widely extended, may no longer be as a bondman, mean and paltry, enslaved unto the Beauty of one—unto the Beauty of some boy, or man, or custom—but having turned him unto the Great Sea of Beauty, and looking upon it, may bring forth many Arguments fair and high, many Thoughts out of the fulness of Philosophy, until, having been there strengthened and increased, he can discern that One Science which comprehendeth that One Beauty. Now, I beseech thee, she said, hearken, as diligently as thou canst, to my words and understand them.

Whosoever hath been led by his preceptor thus far into the Mysteries of Eros, and hath surveyed beautiful things in the right order, when he cometh at last to the end of his Initiation, on a sudden shall behold a marvel, a Thing of Beauty, That Thing, Socrates, for whose sake all the former labours were endured—That Which Alway Is, without generation or destruction, or increase or decrease; which is not, on this side, or at this time, beautiful, and on that side, or at that time, deformed; in comparison with one thing, beautiful, and with another thing, deformed; in one place beautiful, and in another, deformed; beautiful in the eyes of

one man, and in the eyes of another, deformed. Nor will the
Thing of Beauty appear unto him as a countenance, or as
hands, or as aught which Corporeal Body hath belonging
unto it; nor as any Speech, or Science, nor as that which
is somewhere in some other thing, as in a living creature, or
in earth, or in heaven, or in any other thing; but he shall
see It as That which Is in Itself, with Itself, of one Form,
Eternal; and all the other beautiful things he shall see as
partaking of It after such manner that, while they come
into being and perish, It becometh not a whit greater or
less, nor suffereth any change at all. 'Tis when a man
ascendeth from these beautiful things by the Right Way of
Love, and beginneth to have sight of that Eternal Beauty—
'tis then, methinks, that he toucheth the goal. For this is
the right Way to go into the Mysteries of Eros, or to be
led by another—beginning from the beautiful things here,
to mount up alway unto that Eternal Beauty, using these
things as the steps of a ladder—ascending from one to two,
and from two to all, Beautiful Bodies, and from Beautiful
Bodies to Beautiful Customs, and from Beautiful Customs to
Beautiful Doctrines, and from these till at last, being come
unto that which is the Doctrine of the Eternal Beauty and
of naught else beside, he apprehendeth what Beauty Itself
is. 'Tis then, dear Socrates, said the Woman of Mantinea,
that life is worth living, and then only, when a man cometh
to behold Beauty Itself; the which if thou hast once seen,
thou wilt hold wealth, and fine raiment, and fair companions, as naught in comparison with it—yea, those fair
companions whom thou now lookest upon with amazement,
and art ready—thou and many others of thy like—to pass
your lives with them, gazing upon them, and, if it were
possible, neither eating nor drinking, but only beholding
them and being with them alway. What thinkest thou,
then, she said, if a man could see Beauty Itself, clear, pure,
separate, not gross with human flesh, and tainted with
colours, and decked out with perishing gauds—what
thinkest thou, if he could behold Beauty Itself, divine,
uniform? Thinkest thou, she said, that it would be a paltry
life for a man to live, looking unto that, beholding it with
the faculty meet therefor, and being with it alway? Under-

standest thou not that thus only shall he be able, seeing
with that whereby Beauty is seen, to bring forth, not Images
of Virtue—for 'tis no Image that he layeth hold of—but
Things True—for he layeth hold of That which is True;
and when he hath brought forth True Virtue and nurtured
her, understandest thou not that then he hath become above
all men beloved of God, and himself immortal?

OBSERVATIONS ON THE DISCOURSE OF DIOTIMA

I

The Myth in which Diotima sets forth the parentage and nature of Eros differs in style from the Myth of the Round People told by Aristophanes, as widely as it is possible for one composition to differ from another. If the Myth of the Round People is so barbarously grotesque that one has difficulty in recognising it as a Platonic Myth, Diotima's Myth is equally hard to bring under that designation, on account of the prevalence of philosophical allegory in its style. It is, indeed, in its first part simply a philosophical allegory[1] setting forth pictorially an analysis of Love into elements which are seen to be identical with those given by an analysis of Philosophy. Love is neither Plenty nor Poverty, but the child of these two; philosophy is neither ignorance nor wisdom, but the outcome of both. This point, however, once reached by the way of allegory thinly disguising the results of previous analysis, Diotima's Discourse henceforward assumes the character of true Myth, if not in its matter—for no further narrative is added—yet certainly in its essential form: it becomes an imaginative development of the notion of philosophy: philosophy is set forth as the Desire of Immortality. Philosophy is not merely a System of Knowledge, but a Life, nay, the Life Eternal— the true Life of the immortal Soul.[2] Diotima's Discourse thus ends in the character of a true Myth, setting forth in impassioned imaginative language the Transcendental Idea of the Soul. It is out of the mood which expresses itself in, and is encouraged by, such impassioned imaginative language that prophetic visions arise, and great Myths about the Soul's creation, wanderings, and goal. Diotima's Discourse in its latter, non-allegorical, part we must regard

[1] Plotinus, *Enn.* iii. 5, may be read for an elaborate interpretation of Diotima's Allegory:—Zeus is Mind, Aphrodite is Soul, Plenty is Reason, Poverty is Matter; and much more to the same effect. Cf. Cudworth, *Intellectual System,* vol. ii. p. 379 (ed. Mosheim and Harrison).

[2] See Zeller's *Plato,* pp. 191-196 (Eng. Tr.), for the connection made, in the *Phaedrus* and *Symposium,* between Eros and Philosophy; and, especially p. 194, n. 66, for the meaning of Diotima's Discourse, and a protest against the Neo-Platonic interpretation of its meaning adopted by Jahn in his *Diss. Plat.* 64 ff. and 249 ff.

as a true Myth—although it has no story, no pictures—
because we feel that it might at any moment break out into
the language of prophetic vision.

Its identification of Love and Philosophy is intended to
bring home to the Imagination the great Platonic doctrine
that Philosophy is Life. The outline, or ideal, presented
here, without articulation, to the Imagination, is articulated,
still for the Imagination, in the astronomical Eschatology of
the *Phaedrus* Myth; and for the Understanding, in the
account given in the *Republic*[1] of the Philosophic Nature and
of the Education which it needs. A vast non-articulated
ideal, like that held up by Diotima in the latter part of her
Discourse, lends itself easily to either kind of articulation—
it may be articulated in an abstract way as a great system
of laws, or pictorially, as a group of symbols making an
Allegory which, because it is so vast, easily assumes the
character of Myth. And Myth may be painted as well as
spoken. As a scheme of education, articulating for the
Imagination the Ideal of "Philosophy is Life", the Spanish
Chapel fresco, which has already[2] been instanced as a
painted Myth, may well be placed beside the scheme set
forth for the Understanding in the *Republic*. The details in
the fresco are the result of minute analysis of the elements
which constitute true education; but they are so presented
to the eye as to reveal to its intuition the spiritual bond which
unites them together in one meaning which transcends the
parts. Faith, Hope, and Charity are hovering in the sky,
and beneath them, also in the sky, are Courage, Temperance, Justice, Prudence. Beneath these are seated in a
row ten Prophets and Apostles, with S. Thomas Aquinas
on a throne in the middle. Beneath these again sit the
Sciences Divine and Natural, fourteen of them; and beneath
each Science sits her greatest earthly Teacher.

The separate figures are symbols, and form groups which

---

[1] 485 B ff. That the scheme of education in the *Republic* articulates for
the Understanding an outline, or ideal, presented to the Imagination is
plainly admitted. The scheme is called a Myth—as 376 E, "Come then,
speaking like story-tellers at leisure, let us teach these men". And 501 E,
The State of which we speak by means of myth: and see Couturat, *de Plat.
Mythis*, p. 50—"The whole of the Republic is, in the opinion of its author
himself, mythical: cf. *Tim.* 26 C, *Rep.* 420 C, 536 B, C, 376 D, 501 E, 443 B, C."

[2] *Supra*, pp. 132 and 250.

may be interpreted as Allegories, but the whole picture which contains them is a Myth.

It is difficult, as I have pointed out before, to distinguish, in the work of a great creative artist, between Allegory and Myth. Allegory, consciously employed as such by a man of genius, always tends to pass into Myth. In dealing with this point I have said that Plato's *Cave*, carefully constructed as it is in all its detail, like the Spanish Chapel fresco, to give a picture of results already in the possession of its author, is, beyond all that, a wonder for the eye of Imagination to be grasped in one impression. Beneath the interpretation of the Allegory we are aware of the enigma of the Myth. Plato, we feel, had seen the whole before he began to articulate the parts. Perhaps, as I ventured to suppose, some weird scene in a Syracusan quarry gave the first suggestion.

I said that, although the former part of Diotima's Discourse is an Allegory, the latter part has the true characteristic of the Myth, setting forth, without narrative or pictures indeed, but in impassioned imaginative language, the Transcendental Idea of the Soul. It is only by accident, we feel, that the Discourse does not break out into the language of prophetic vision.

The Diotima of this Discourse may be taken as a study of the Prophetic Temperament.

Let me try to bring out the essential nature of this temperament by making some passages in Spinoza's *Tractatus Theologico-Politicus* do service as a commentary on Plato's study. To appreciate the nature of the prophetic temperament and the use of prophecy as determined by the great Jewish critic—he was one of the founders of biblical criticism —is, I think, to go far towards appreciating the function of Myth in Plato's Philosophy.

The passages to which I refer are in the first and second chapters of the *Tractatus Theologico-Politicus*. Spinoza begins by distinguishing teachers of natural science from prophets. Although natural science is divine, its teachers cannot be called prophets; for what the teachers of natural science impart as certain, other men receive as certain, and that not merely on authority but of their own knowledge. It is by the faculty of Imagination that prophets are distinguished from teachers of natural science. By Imagination prophets perceive the revelations of God and transcend the limits of the Scientific Understanding. This is why they impart what they perceive almost always in parables, expressing spiritual truths by means of sensible images; for this is the method which their faculty naturally prescribes. Prophets are not endowed with a more perfect Intelligence, but with a more vivid Imagination than other men. Prophecy, as it depends on Imagination, does not *per se* involve certainty: prophets are not made certain of the revelation of God by the revelation itself, but by a sign. Thus Abraham (Genesis xv. 8), on hearing the promise of God, asked for a sign. He, indeed, believed God, and did not ask for a sign in order that he might believe God, but in order that he might know that the thing was actually promised to him by God.[1] Herein prophecy is inferior to natural knowledge, which needs no sign, but has its certainty in itself. The prophet's certainty is not metaphysical but moral. The prophet may be recognised by three marks: (1) he imagines the things revealed as vividly as if they were objects of waking sense, (2) he needs a sign, and (3)—and chiefly—he has a mind inclined to that which is just and good. Though this may seem to show that prophecy and revelation are uncertain, yet they have much that is certain; for God never deceives pious men, "His Elect". He uses them as instruments of His goodness, as he uses the wicked as instruments of His wrath. Now, since the signs are merely to persuade the prophet in a matter where the certainty is not metaphysical but moral, it follows that the signs are suited to the opinions and capacity of the prophet; and the revelation (*i.e.* the thing imagined) varies with the temperament (gay or sad), and the beliefs, of the prophet. The conclusion of all is that prophecy never adds to the knowledge of the prophet or of others, but leaves them in their preconceived opinions; so that, in merely speculative matters, we are not at all bound

---

[1] Similarly, miracles do not make us believe in the existence of God. We must believe in the existence of God before we can believe in the occurrence of miracles.

AA

to believe prophets; but in matters which concern righteousness and moral character we are.[1]

I offer no particular remarks on the foregoing passage, but merely recommend it to the attention of the reader, as defining the use of Prophecy in a manner similar to that in which I think the use of the Platonic Myth ought to be defined.

With Spinoza's view of the end of Prophecy, Henry More's view of the end of Scripture has much in common. The interpretation of the literal text, he explains,[2] must always depend on what we have learned from Philosophy, not from Scripture; but the sole end of the Scripture is the furthering of the Holy Life.

Similarly, John Smith says,[3] "Christ's main scope was to promote an *Holy Life* as the best and most compendious way to a *right Belief*. He hangs all true acquaintance with Divinity upon the doing God's will. If any man will do his will he shall know the doctrine, whether it be of God."

This view of the meaning of Prophecy, and generally of inspired scriptures, held by the Cambridge Platonists in independent agreement with Spinoza, is one which finds much favour at the present day among those critical students of the Bible whose paramount interest is still in religion as a practical concern. Their teaching on the subject of "inspiration" and "divine revelation", in my view, throws much light on the subject of this work. I would summarise my advice to those who wish to realise for themselves the function of the Platonic Myth as follows:—After reading Plato's Myths, each one in its own context, seal the effect of the whole by reading the work of some other great master of Myth—best of all the *Divina Commedia;* then turn to the writings of those modern critics of the Bible whose

---

[1] Prophecy, says Professor P. Gardner (*Jowett Lectures*, 1901, p. 117), "is based on insight, and sees not future events but the tendency of existing forces, and looks beneath the surface of the present and sees its true inwardness. . . . The Jewish prophet dealt far less with the future than with the present. He was first and foremost a teacher of righteousness—one who explained the purposes of God and made his ways bare to man. He was, in fact, a preacher."

[2] *Appendix to the Defence of the Philosophick Cabbala*, ch. xii., especially § 3, pp. 150, 151, ed. 1662.

[3] *Select Discourses* (1660), p. 9 ("The True Way or Method of attaining Divine Knowledge"), and cf. pp. 169 ff. ("Of Prophesie").

paramount interest is still in religion as a practical concern. Were the student to undertake the last-mentioned part of this programme, he would probably find the word "inspiration" a difficulty. He would probably think that the use made of the word by the critics is vague and uncertain. But let him remember that Plato's use of the corresponding Love (especially where Love and Philosophy are identified, as in Diotima's Discourse) is equally vague. Precision is not to be looked for in the description of such a condition or gift. Indeed, Diotima's Philosophy is perhaps even more vague than the "inspiration" of these critics; for the former is the condition of an individual, while the community rather than the individual is the recipient of the latter—"It is not the individual so much as the society or community which is the recipient of divine inspiration," says Professor P. Gardner,[1] interpreting Ritschl. While the "inspiration" of the individual is an abnormal condition, difficult to describe psychologically, and still more difficult to estimate in respect of "value", the "inspiration" received by a community is something which can be definitely reviewed, being the series of ideas of betterment which spring up in the community one after another and actually determine its development. The historian may find it difficult to show how this idea or that arose; but he can generally describe the circumstances in which, having arisen, it "caught on" and became an effective factor in the development of the community. The "idea of emancipating slaves" may serve as an example of what is meant when the "inspiration received by a community" is spoken of; and a prophet is one who can put such an idea before his contemporaries so vividly that it must perforce, sooner or later, realise itself in practice. When we look back over the past life of a nation we see how true it is that the grain of mustard seed becomes the great tree. How the seed came we seldom can tell; it is so small that we should not even have noticed it at all,

---

[1] *Jowett Lectures*, p. 270. Expressing his own view Professor Gardner says: "It may be that in this matter Ritschl goes too far, for, after all, it is only in the consciousness of individuals that divine inspiration can be realised; religious utterances must come from individuals; and the will of individuals must lead society in the right way: nevertheless there is profound and most important truth in the recognition of the divine mission of the society."

unless the tree had grown out of it. We rather infer it from the tree; and if the tree is good we are apt to think of the seed as "divinely implanted" in some special way. What we can trace clearly to antecedents we do not regard with religious feeling; but when we come to some little inexplicable thing, which we recognise, after the event, as source of great things, we say that it comes by divine dispensation.

As the influence of the new biology makes itself more and more felt in the field of historical study, we may expect that the doctrine of "inspiration received by the community" will recommend itself more and more to religious minds, as a solution of the difficulty which few indeed are content to put by wholly—the difficulty of conceiving how the development of beautifully articulated organisms can take place along lines opened up by "accidental variations". This difficulty the new biology has brought home to us thoroughly, by showing us how decisive is the part played in evolution by these "accidental variations" among the factors which maintain the moving equilibrium of life. The objections which stand in the way of accepting the alternative solution—Weismann's theory, which explains "accidental variations" as provided for in the original germ-plasma— seem to be at least as formidable as those which might be brought against the theory of "divine inspiration of which the community or race is the recipient".

II

Excursus on the History of the Doctrine of Daemons

(*Symposium*, 202 e)

The doctrine, here enunciated, of daemons who perform the office of interpreters and mediators between the Gods and Men, played a great part in the History of Religious Belief.

In its original sense daemon is synonymous with God, and means simply "a divine immortal being". But Hesiod's sacred daemons who haunt the earth[1] introduced a specification of the term. These earth-haunting daemons are indeed

---

[1] *Works and Days* 108.

"divine immortal beings", but they are not heavenly, or dwellers on Olympus; they dwell in "the parts about the Earth", and more especially "in the Air". They are, in fact, the disembodied spirits of the men of a long past age— the Golden Age. When these men died, their bodies were buried; but their immortal spirits remained in the neighbourhood of the Earth, and will ever remain there, to be the Guardians and Patrons of mortal men:—

> First of all the undying Gods who inhabit Olympus made a golden race of men endowed with speech, who lived in the age of Cronos, when he reigned in Heaven. They passed their lives like Gods with hearts free from sorrow, apart from toil and grief. Nor was old age a burden, but with feet and hands unfailing they rejoiced in feasts remote from all evil. They died as though overcome with sleep, and possessed all good things; for the soil of its own accord bore them fruit abundantly and ungrudgingly. And they, glad and at peace administered their lands, with many good things, rich in flocks, dear to the blessed Gods. But when the earth had enfolded this generation—these are called sacred Daemons dwelling on the earth, beneficent, protectors from evil, and Guardians of mortal men, bestowers of wealth, and this they have received as a royal privilege.[1]

When the men of the Silver Age died, their spirits went under the Earth. They became "blessed mortals below the earth"[2]—a difficult phrase, on which Rohde may be consulted.[3] They too, although their works on Earth were displeasing to the Gods, receive honour and worship from men—

The third age was that of the Copper Men. They did evil on Earth, and went down nameless to the black pit of Hades.[4]

The fourth age was that of the Heroes—those who fought at Thebes and Troy. Some of them died; some of them were translated in the flesh to the Islands of the Blessed, where they enjoy everlasting felicity:—

> Some the end of death wrapped round, but to others Father Zeus the son of Cronos gave life and an accustomed

---

[1] *o.c.* 109 ff. [2] *o.c.* 125.
[3] *Psyche*, i. 99-102. [4] *o.c.* 137 ff.

seat apart from men, and established them at the world's
end. And they live with hearts untouched by sorrow in the
Islands of the Blest, beside the deep-eddying Ocean, happy
heroes for whom the grain-giving soil bears honey-sweet
fruit ripening three times yearly.[1]

The fifth age is the present—that of the Men of Iron.[2]

No one who reads the *Cratylus*, 397 D ff., where the
etymology of daemons is discussed and Hesiod's verses about
the daemons who haunt the earth are quoted, and the
Laws, iv. 713, and *Politicus*, 272, where the Myth of the
Golden Age of Cronus, when daemons ruled over men, is
told, can fail to see that the Hesiodic account of daemons
has a great hold on Plato's imagination; and it may be
that even the guardians of the *Republic*—men with gold in
their nature (as the auxiliaries have silver, and the
artisans and husbandmen have copper and iron)—are
somehow, in Plato's imagination, parallel to Hesiod's
guardians of mortal men, the spirits of the men of the
Golden Age.[3] But we must not forget that there is a difference
between Plato's daemons of the *Laws* and *Politicus* and of
Diotima's Discourse, and Hesiod's daemons, which is
greater than the obvious resemblance. Hesiod's daemons
who haunt the earth are the spirits of deceased men—as
are Pindar's sacred heroes (*Meno*, 81 c); but the daemons
of the *Laws* and *Politicus*, who rule over men in the Golden
Age, are not spirits of deceased men, but beings of an
entirely different order—Gods, who were created Gods, to
whom provinces on Earth were assigned by the Supreme
God—as they are described in *Politicus*, 272 E; and in
Diotima's Discourse the daemonic, headed by Eros, is
clearly set forth as an order of divine beings essentially
superhuman, not spirits of deceased men. They are, I
take it, of the same rank as, indeed probably identical with,
the God-begotten Gods of the *Timaeus*—created before men,
to be managers of human affairs on behalf of the Supreme

---

[1] *o.c.* 166 ff.   [2] *o.c.* 157 ff.

[3] This parallel is suggested by Mr. Adam in a note on *Republic*, 468 E,
and worked out by Mr. F. M. Cornford in an interesting article on "Plato
and Orpheus" in *The Classical Review*, December 1903.

God.[1] In *Rep.* v. 468 E, on the other hand, Plato's use of the term daemons is strictly Hesiodic—he is speaking not of such Gods at all, but of the spirits of deceased men of the Golden Class. As Mr. Adam, in his note on the passage, says, "Plato compares his 'golden citizens' with the heroes of the Hesiodic golden age. He would fain surround them with some of the romantic and religious sentiment that clung around the golden age of Greek poetry and legend."

The two doctrines of daemons which we find in Plato— that enunciated in the Golden Age Myth and Diotima's Discourse, and that adopted from Hesiod in *Rep.* v. 468 E— were both taken over by the Stoics, and accommodated to the tenets of their "physical science".

According to the Stoics, the Soul is material but its matter is rarer and finer (Chrysippus in Plutarch *de Stoic. Repugn.* 41) than that of the body. The Soul is, in fact, "hot air, or breath".[2]

When Souls leave their earthly bodies they do not immediately perish. According to Cleanthes, they all retain their individuality until the Conflagration: according to Chrysippus, only the Souls of Wise Men.[3] At the Conflagration, however, all Souls perish as individuals—are dissolved back into the one substance, the elemental fire, God, whose sundered parts they were during the term of their individual existence.

---

[1] Chalcidius, in his Commentary on the *Timaeus*, is at pains to show (chap. 135) that the Platonic daemons and the souls of deceased men are of two distinct orders: "Yet many think, following the authority of Plato, that daemons are souls liberated from the functions of the body: that the daemons of worthy men are heavenly, and of evildoers, harmful, and that the same souls after a thousand years take on again an earthly body. Empedocles considers similarly that these souls become long-lived daemons. Pythagoras also, in his Golden Verses:

When with your body laid aside you proceed through the free aether,
You will leave behind your humanity, made a God of the loving sky

with whom Plato seems least to agree, when in the *Republic* he makes the soul of the tyrant tormented after death by Avengers, from which it appears that there is another soul, another daemon; so that what is tortured and what tortures must be separate. And because the Divine Artificer established daemons before he created our souls, he desired that these souls should assist the daemons, and that the latter should offer to be their guardians. Yet these same souls, who needed at least three lives in the body, after they had earned their consecration to airy, even to heavenly mansions, he thought to be necessarily free from incarnation." The whole passage relating to Daemons in the Commentary of Chalcidius (cxxvi.-cxxxv.) is interesting. He compares the Daemons of Plato with the angels of the Hebrews.

[2] Diog. Laert. vii. 157.   [3] *o.c.* vii. 157.

When Souls leave their earthly bodies, they rise into the Air which occupies the space between the Earth and the Moon.[1] That the dissolution of, at any rate, the majority of Souls inhabiting this aerial space takes place before the Conflagration is clearly the view of Marcus Aurelius in a curious passage (*Comment*. iv. 21), in which he meets the difficulty of the Air having room for so many separate beings. Room, he says, is always being made in the Air for new-comers by the progressive dissolution of their predecessors, just as room in the Earth is always made for new bodies by the progressive dissolution of those earlier buried:— "If souls survive, how has the air space enough for those who come from Hades? But how has the earth space enough for the bodies of those buried throughout so long a period? Just as their transformation and dissolution makes way for other dead, so the souls who are assigned to the air, wherever they remain, change and are poured out and suspended, according to the creative Word of the Whole, and in this way leave room for those who come to dwell with them."

It is probably to the Stoic Posidonius, whose astronomy has been mentioned as influential in the development of the theory and practice of Mithras-worship and similar sacramental cults,[2] that the idea of the Air as the habitat of the Souls of the deceased and also of daemons—an order of beings distinct from that of human Souls—is chiefly indebted for its vogue. Posidonius wrote a treatise *On heroes and daemons*, quoted by Macrobius (*Sat*. i. 23),[3] and Cicero (*de Div*. i. 64) quotes him as saying that the Air is full of Souls and Daemons.[4] That belief in Daemons—spirits which have never been incarnate in human bodies—is as consistent with the "materialism" of the Stoics as belief in the continued existence of human Souls in the Air, is insisted upon by Zeller,[4] and, indeed, is obvious.

So much for Stoical belief. But it was exactly the astronomy—Pythagorean and Platonic in its origin— popularised by the Stoic Posidonius, which seems to have suggested a mode of escape from the Stoical doctrine that

---

[1] Posidonius, in Sext. *Phys*. i. 73.
[2] See *supra*, pp. 313 ff.
[3] See Rohde, *Psyche*, ii. 320.
[4] *Stoics, Epicureans, and Sceptics*, p. 333, Engl. Transl.

the Soul, though subsisting for a longer or shorter time after the death of the body, yet is ultimately dissolved. Above the Air—the Stoical habitat of daemons and Souls of deceased men, equally doomed to dissolution, according to the orthodox doctrine of the school—there is the Aether.[1] Into this region Souls purified by Philosophy—or, it may be, by sacramental observances—rise, and there, though united to God, retain their individuality for ever. This is the doctrine of the *Dream of Scipio*—which probably owes its astronomy to Posidonius[2]—and of the *Tusc. Disp.* (i. 17, 18, 19); it is the doctrine to which even the Stoic Seneca (*ad Marc.* 25. 1) seems to incline, and it inspired those sacramental cults, Orphic, Mithraic, and Egyptian, which became so important in the religious life of the first two centuries of the Christian era.[3]

In this doctrine of Aether, the region of the heavenly spheres, as everlasting home of purified Souls, we have, of course, merely the mythology of the *Timaeus* and *Phaedrus*

[1] I use the term "aether" here in its proper sense, as the name of the element which contains the "visible gods", the stars. This element is sometimes, as in the *Epinomis*, 984 (cf. Zeller, *Plato*, p. 615), called fire, while "aether" takes the place of what is properly called fire, in the list "fire, air, water, earth". Bywater (*Journ. of Phil.* vol. i. pp. 37-39, on the *Fragm. of Philolaus*) quotes the *de Coelo*, i. 270 b, and the *Meteor.* 339 b, for "aether" above the four elements, and remarks that "the occurrence of this fifth essence in the Platonic *Epinomis* is one of the many indications of the late origin of that Dialogue".

[2] See Rohde, *Psyche*, ii. 320, and Dieterich, *Eine Mithrasliturgie*, quoted *supra*, p. 313.

[3] The following references to the Commentary of Hierocles (President of the School of Alexandria) on the *Golden Hymn of the Pythagoreans* may be taken to show how the astronomy of the *Timaeus* and *Phaedrus* influenced eschatology even in the fifth century of the Christian era. Hierocles (see Mullach's *Fragm. Phil. Graec.* i. 478 ff.) is commenting on the lines—

But abstain from the foods which we prescribe, and use
judgment in the purifications and the release of thy soul,
and consider each action, establishing the chariot of the mind,
the highest that comes from above,

and, after referring for the chariot to the *Phaedrus* Myth, and remarking that it embodies Pythagorean doctrine, says that, for the purification of the aethereal body we must put away the filth of the terrestial body, and submit ourselves to purificatory observances, which he describes—by means of which we shall rise from the Place of Generation and Corruption, and be translated to "The Elysian Meadow and unbounded Aether". But as the terrestial body must be shed on Earth, its natural connection, *i.e.* the aerial body, must be shed in the aerial region immediately under the Moon (cf. Plut. *de fac. in orbe lunae*, 28, quoted p. 390 *infra*). Then the aethereal or astral body ("the starry, irradiate, light-bearing body, or chariot") which is the *immortal* vehicle of the Soul, is free to ascend, with the Soul, into the Aether:— "Having become after purification what they ever are, some fall into

framed in an astronomical setting somewhat more definite
than that furnished by Plato himself. What it is important,
however, to recognise is that this mythology, so framed,
appeared to Platonists to be a sufficiently "up-to-date"
refutation of the "materialism" of the Stoics. The Soul,
when perfectly purified, rises out of the Air into the Aether,
returning to its original home, and there lives for ever and
ever. Its perfect purification—effected by Philosophy, or
ritual performances, or both—guarantees its immortality;
for its eternal intelligible essence—mind—stripped of
perishing sensible vehicles, terrestrial—body—and aerial—
soul—is alone left. Of this intelligible essence Aether is the
vehicle. The aethereal region is full of "living and conquering flames"[1]—immortal spirits made pure by Philosophy,
and suffering, and holy rites. This Platonist doctrine is set
forth by Plutarch in his *On the daemon of Socrates*, and in his
On the face in the disc of the Moon. In a curious passage in the
latter work (ch. 28) he tells us that reason—mind—has its
home in the Sun. Thither the purified spirit returns, having
shed its corporeal vehicle—body—on Earth, and its aerial—
soul—on the Moon. This is the order of purification. And
the order of generation, he explains, is the contrary of that
of purification:—Of the three parts which make up man,
the Sun supplies mind, the Moon soul, the Earth body.[2]
Death on Earth makes the three two; death on the Moon
makes the two one. Every Soul, whether rational or
irrational,[3] must wander for a time in the region between
the Earth and the Moon. In the lower parts of this region
the unrighteous are punished and corrected, while the
righteous tarry for an appointed time in its highest parts—
in the region of the softest air, which is called the Meadow
of Death;[4] then, being filled, like those initiated, with a

generation according to their nature, others attain knowledge of the whole,
and by that are brought to God. The body that was created with them
needs a locality for its starry state, such as is established for the living. And
it is fitting that the habitation for such a body should be placed in the moon,
as superior to perishing bodies, and moving in the region below the sky, which
the Pythagoreans call the free Aether; the Aetheric being an unsubstantial
and invisible body, free as pure from material suffering. This he who comes
there shall be, or, as they say, he shall be an immortal God, being made like
to them who in the beginning are called immortal Gods by the Poets, but
not by nature an immortal God."

[1] *Par.* x. 64.   [2] Plut. *de fac. in orb. lun.* 28.
[3] *o.c.* 28.   [4] *o.c.* 28.

strange joy, half amazement half hope, they aspire to the Moon. There, now styled daemons by Plutarch,[1] they have their abode, descending sometimes to Earth to help men— to assist at mysteries, to watch and punish crimes, to save in battle and at sea. The good among them (for some of them are wicked and become incarnate again in human bodies) are the Souls of those who lived on Earth in the reign of Cronus, and they are still worshipped in many places. When one of these good Daemons at last loses his power on Earth and fails his worshippers, it is because his lunar death has taken place—his true Self, mind, has at last been separated from the soul, which remains, like a corpse, on the Moon. The separation of mind from soul is effected by the operation in him of Love of the Solar Image— "It answers to love of the image round the Sun, by which it illumines the desirable and holy and blessed, whose whole nature is in some manner or other expanded . . . And the energy of the soul is left behind on the Moon, keeping some vestige of life and dreams . . . The Self of each of us is not passion, nor fear, nor desire, for it is without flesh or moisture, but that by which we think and perceive . . . and of these others the Moon is the element, for they are set free for her, like bodies of the dead for the earth."

Plutarch's other work, mentioned above, the *On the daemon of Socrates*, is so important for the doctrine of Daemons, that it cannot be dismissed in a paragraph like that just devoted to the *On the face in the disc of the moon*. On the whole, I think the best way of laying its contents before the reader is to let it speak for itself in the Myth of Timarchus, which indeed presents all that is essential to Plutarch's daemonology. As in the case of the Aridaeus-Thespesius Myth, I avail myself here again of Philemon Holland's version.

There was one Timarchus of Chaeronea, who died very young, and requested earnestly of Socrates to be buried near unto Lamprocles, Socrates his son, who departed this life but few days before, being a dear friend of his, and of the same age. Now this young gentleman, being very desirous (as he was of a generous disposition, and had

[1] *o.c.* 30.

newly tasted the sweetness of Philosophy) to know what
was the nature and power of Socrates' familiar spirit, when
he had imparted his mind and purpose unto me only and
Cebes, went down into the cave or vault of Trophonius,
after the usual sacrifices and accustomed compliments due
to that oracle performed: where, having remained two
nights and one day, inasmuch as many men were out of all
hope that he ever would come forth again—yea, and his
kinsfolk and friends bewailed the loss of him—one morning
betimes issued forth very glad and jocund. . . . He recounted unto us many wonders strange to be heard and
seen: for he said that being descended into the place of
the oracle, he first met with much darkness, and afterwards,
when he had made his prayers, he lay a long time upon the
ground, not knowing whether he was awake or dreamed.
Howbeit, he thought that he heard a noise which lit upon
his head and smote it, whereby the sutures or seams thereof
were disjoined and opened, by which he yielded forth his
soul; which, being thus separate, was very joyous, seeing
itself mingled with a transparent and pure air. . . When he
looked behind him he could see the Earth no more, but
the Isles all bright and illuminate with a mild and delicate
fire, and those exchanged their places one with another,
and withal, received sundry colours, as it were diverse
tinctures, according as in that variety of change the light
did alter; and they all seemed unto him in number infinite
and in quantity excessive: and albeit they were not of
equal pourprise and extent, yet round they were all alike:
also, by their motion, which was circular, the sky resounded.
. . Amid these Islands there seemed a sea or great lake
diffused and spread, shining with diverse mixed colours
upon a ground of grey or light blue. Moreover, of these
Isles some few sailed, as one would say, and were carried a
direct course down the water beyond the current; but
others, and those in number many, went aside out of the
channel, and were with such a violence drawn back that
they seemed to be swallowed under the waves. . . . And
the same sea hath two mouths or entrances, whereby it
receiveth two rivers of fire breaking into it, opposite one
to the other, in such sort as the blueness thereof became
whitish by reason that the greatest part was repelled and
driven back. And these things he said he beheld with
great delight. But when he came to look downward, he
perceived a mighty huge hole or gulf all round, in manner
of a hollow globe cut through the midst, exceeding deep
and horrible to see to, full of much darkness, and the same
not quiet and still, but turbulent and oftentimes boiling
and walming upward, out of which there might be heard
innumerable roarings and groanings of beasts, cries and

wrawlings of an infinite number of children, with sundry plaints and lamentations of men and women together, besides many noises, tumults, clamours, and outcries of all sorts, and those not clear, but dull and dead, as being sent up from a great depth underneath. . . . One whom he saw not, said unto him: The division of Proserpina, you may see if you will, how it is bounded with Styx. Styx (quoth he) is the way which leadeth unto hell and the kingdom of Pluto, dividing two contrary natures of light and darkness with the head and top thereof; for, as you see, it beginneth from the bottom of hell beneath, which it touches with the one extremity, and reacheth with the other to the light all about, and so limiteth the utmost part of the whole world, divided into four regiments. The first is that of life; the second of moving; the third of generation; and the fourth of corruption. The first is coupled to the second by unity, in that which is not visible; the second to the third, by the mind or intelligence, in the sun; the third to the fourth, by nature, in the moon. And of every one of these copulations there is a Friend, or Destiny, the Daughter of Necessity, that keepeth the key. Of the first, she that is named Atropos, as one would say Inflexible; of the second, Clotho—that is to say, the Spinster; of the third in the moon, Lachesis— that is to say, Lot, about which is the bending of geniture or nativity. As for all the other Isles, they have gods within them; but the Moon, appertaining to the terrestrial Daemons, avoideth the confines of Styx, as being somewhat higher exalted, approaching once only in an hundred seventy seven second measures: and upon the approach of this precinct of Styx, the souls cry out for fear. And why? Hell catcheth and swalloweth many of them, as they glide and slip about it: and others the Moon receiveth and taketh up, swimming from beneath unto her; such, I mean, as upon whom the end of generation fell in good and opportune time, all save those which are impure and polluted: for them, with her fearful flashing and hideous roaring, she suffereth not to come near unto her; who, seeing that they have missed of their intent, bewail their woeful state, and be carried down again, as you see, to another generation and nativity. Why, quoth Timarchus, I see nothing but a number of stars leaping up and down about this huge and deep gulf, some drowned and swallowed up in it, others appearing again from below. These be (quoth he) the daemons that you see, though you know them not. And mark, withal, how this comes about. Every soul is endued with a portion of mind or understanding: but look how much thereof is mingled with flesh and with passions; being altered with pleasures and dolors, it becometh unreasonable. But every soul is not mixed after one sort . . .

for some are wholly plunged within the body . . . others partly are mingled with the flesh, and in part leave out that which is most pure, and not drawn downward by the contagion of the gross part, but remaineth swimming and floating as it were aloft, touching the top or crown only of a man's head, and is in manner of a cord hanging up aloft, just over the soul which is directly and plumb under, to uphold and raise it up, so far forth as it is obeisant thereto, and not over-ruled and swayed with passions and perturbations: for that which is plunged down within the body is called the soul; but that which is entire and uncorrupt the vulgar sort calleth the understanding, supposing it to be within them as in mirrors that which appeareth by way of reflection: but those that judge aright and according to the truth name it Daemon, as being clean without them. These stars, then, which you see as if they were extinct and put out, imagine and take them to be the souls which are totally drowned within bodies; and such as seem to shine out again and to return lightsome from beneath, shaking from them a certain dark and foggy mist, esteem the same to be such souls as after death are retired and escaped out of the bodies; but those which are mounted on high and move to and fro in one uniform course throughout are the Daemons or spirits of men who are said to have intelligence and understanding. Endeavour now therefore and strain yourself to see the connection of each one, whereby it is linked and united to the soul. When I heard this I began to take more heed, and might see stars leaping and floating upon the water, some more, some less, like as we observe pieces of cork shewing in the sea where the fishers' nets have been cast; and some of them turned in manner of spindles or bobbins, as folk spin or twist therewith, yet drawing a troubled and unequal course and not able to direct and compose the motion straight. And the voice said that those which held on a right course and orderly motion were they whose souls were obeisant to the reins of reason . . . but they that eftsoons rise and fall up and down unequally and disorderly are those which strive against the yoke. . . . . Of such as are obedient at the first, and presently from their very nativity hearken unto their proper Daemon, are all of the kind of prophets and diviners who have the gift to foretell things to come, likewise holy and devout men: of which number you have heard how the soul of Hermodorus the Clazomenian was wont to abandon his body quite, and both by day and night to wander into many places; and afterwards to return into it again . . . which it used so long, until his enemies, by the treachery of his wife, surprised his body one time, when the soul was gone out of it, and burnt it in his house. Howbeit, this was not true; for his soul never departed out of his body; but the same being always obedient unto his Daemon, and slacking the bond unto it, gave it means and liberty to run up and down, and to walk to and fro in many places, in such sort, as having seen and heard many things abroad, it would come and report the same unto him. But those that consumed his body as he lay asleep are tormented in Tartarus even at this day for it; which you shall know yourself, good young man, more certainly within these three months (quoth that voice): and for this time see you depart. When this voice had made an end of speaking, Timarchus, as he told the tale himself, turned about to see who it was that spake; but feeling a great pain again in his head, as if it had been violently pressed and crushed, he was deprived of all sense and understanding, and neither knew himself nor anything about him. But within a while after when he was come unto himself, he might see how he lay along at the entry of the foresaid cave of Trophonius, like as he had himself at the beginning. And thus much concerning the fable of Timarchus; who being returned to Athens, in the third month after, just as the voice foretold him, he departed this life.

The Aether, then, according to the Platonist belief which we are examining, is the birthplace of human Souls, and their final abode when they have completed the purification which guarantees immortality to them as Pure Intelligences. But the Air is, none the less, the habitat, and, it would appear, the permanent habitat, of another class of immortal spirits, daemons, who never were incarnate in terrestrial bodies. These immortal daemons occupy the Air, that they may be near to help men on Earth, and mediate between them and God, whose dwelling is in the aethereal region. It is in this interspace between the "visible Gods", the Stars, and the Earth that the author of the *Epinomis*[1] places the daemons, whom he describes as interpreters between men and the Gods. He distinguishes three classes of such daemons: first, those who live in the so-called Aether under the Fire or true Aether, *i.e.* in the higher part of the space between the Earth and the Moon; secondly, those who inhabit the Air round the Earth—these two kinds of

[1] According to Zeller (*Plato*, p. 561, Engl. Transl.), probably Philippus of Opus, one of Plato's pupils.

Daemons are invisible; thirdly, Daemons whose vehicle is watery mist—these are sometimes visible.[1]

It is in the same space between the Earth and the Moon that the Platonist Apuleius, writing in the second century after Christ, places the daemons of Diotima's Discourse, an order of divine mediators between God and men to which he conceives the divine sign of Socrates and the Guardian Angels of all other men as belonging.

"And", he says,[2] "if Plato is right, that God never holds communication with man, then it would be easier for a stone to listen to me, than Jupiter. 'Not so far as that' (for Plato shall answer for his own opinion, in my place) 'not so far as that', he says, 'do I declare the gods to be separated and apart from us, so that in my judgment not even our prayers can reach them. Nor do I consider them to be remote from care for human things, only from contact. There are besides certain divine mediating powers, between the height of heaven and the lowest depths of earth, in that middle space of air, through whom our desires and deserts are communicated to the gods; these the Greeks call by the name of daemons.

"They carry between the dwellers in heaven and earth, from here supplications, from there gifts. They bear hither and thither petitions and succour, as agents and messengers for both. By these same beings, as Plato declares in the *Symposium*, all forewarnings, and the various marvels of the Magi, and all kinds of presentiment are regulated, but of their number those so endowed attend to their separate functions, for which each has his own province assigned, either confirming by dreams, or by dividing the entrails, or watching the flight of birds, or instructing in auguries, or the inspiration of prophets or the lightning stroke, or the movements of clouds, or any other method of discerning the future.

"All these, it must be concluded, are brought about in the will and power and authority of the dwellers in heaven, but by means of the obedience and labour and service of the daemons ... Why, therefore,[3] does so much airy energy lie between the lowest pathway of the moon and the highest peak of Olympus? Why, forsooth? Will it be empty of living creatures, and will that realm of nature be mortal and weak? .... Reason[4] demands that lives appropriate to the air should be recognized. It remains for us to

---

[1] *Epinomis*, 984, 985; cf. Zeller, *Plato* (Engl. Transl.), p. 615.
[2] Apuleius *de Deo Socratis*, vol. ii. p. 116, ed. Bétolaud.
[3] *o.c.* p. 119.   [4] *o.c.* p. 119.

distinguish their nature. For they are by no means earthly, for they differ from earthly beings by their lack of weight.

"Therefore they should be tempered for us by their middle station in nature.

" . . . Let us inwardly create in our minds that type of bodily texture which is neither animal and earthly, nor fine as aether, but in some respect belongs to both kingdoms. . . Because if the clouds,[1] floating on high, whose beginning is from the earth, flow back into the earth, what then do you imagine about the bodies of daemons which are composed of something more subtle? For they are fine clouds, distilled from them, rounded and swelling with vapour, as is the nature of clouds, but drawn together from that purest liquid and serene element of air, and visible to no man by chance, but only if they offer him a form of divinity. Because there is no solid substance in them to hold a point of luminosity which can impinge on our sight, which fortifies itself in solidity, but they possess bodily attachments which are fine and shining and delicate, so that they transmit all the rays of our sight into fineness, and reverberate in reflected light, and frustrate us by subtlety. . . A god[2] has no temporal fulfilment either of enduring hatred or of love, and is therefore to be bound neither by indignation nor pity, nor restricted by limitation; to move with no alacrity but with a mind free from all passion; neither to grieve nor to rejoice, nor hastily to will nor to object to anything.

"But all these qualities, and everything else of a like nature, suit the middle habit of the daemons. For they are between us and the gods; as in the place of their habitation, so in the working of their minds, having in common with those above them, immortality, and with those below, passion. For like us they can suffer all pleasures or excitements of the mind, to be roused by anger and moved by pity, and inveigled by gifts and softened by prayers, and stung by contumely and soothed by honours, and in all other ways they are moved in a similar manner to ourselves. In fact, to sum up: *daemons are animal beings in origin, rational in intellect, passive in mind, aerial in substance, everlasting in time.*"

These Daemons Apuleius distinguishes sharply,[3] as never having been incarnate, from the lower sort of Daemons —Lemures, Lares, Larvae—spirits of deceased men. It is from the number of the Daemons who never were incarnate that the Guardian Spirit attached to each man at his birth comes.

[1] *o.c.* p. 121.   [2] *o.c.* p. 124.   [3] *o.c.* p. 128.

"Out of this higher company of daemons,[1] as Plato declares, each one is attached to a single man as witness and guardian during his lifetime. These, unseen by all, are always present at every decision, not only in action but even in thought. But when life is brought to a close, that being who was assigned to us, bears us away hence, and draws us, in accordance with his guardianship, to judgment, and there assists in pleading our cause. And if there is a crooked argument, he will prove it false, and if the truth is told, he will confirm it. And straightway sentence will be passed on his testimony. So do all of you who hear this divine opinion of Plato, according to my interpretation, thus shape your minds for action or meditation, that you may know that there is nothing human beyond their guardianship, neither in the mind nor outside it, but the daemon carefully participates in everything, beholds everything, understands everything, *lodging in our inmost thoughts in place of conscience.*"[2]

Maximus Tyrius, writing about the same time as Apuleius, has remarks to the same effect in his *Dissertation* (26) on the genius of Socrates, which he describes as one of those immortals of the second rank who are posted between Gods and Men, in the space between Earth and Heaven to to be ministers of the Gods and guardians of men. The number of these mediators between Gods and Men is countless: he quotes Hesiod—

[1] *o.c.* p. 129.
[2] "To a mind carefully formed upon the basis of its natural conscience," says Cardinal Newman (*Grammar of Assent*, ch. v.), "the world, both of nature and of man, does but give back a reflection of those truths about the One Living God which have been familiar to it from childhood. Good and evil meet us daily as we pass through life, and there are those who think it philosophical to act towards the manifestations of each with some sort of impartiality, as if evil had as much right to be there as good, or even better, as having more striking triumphs and a broader jurisdiction. And because the course of things is determined by fixed laws, they consider that those laws preclude the present agency of the Creator in the carrying out of particular issues. It is otherwise with the theology of the religious imagination. It has a living hold on truths which are really to be found in the world, though they are not upon the surface. It is able to pronounce by anticipation, what it takes a long argument to prove—that good is the rule, and evil the exception. It is able to assume that, uniform as are the laws of nature, they are consistent with a particular Providence. It interprets what it sees around it by this previous inward teaching, as the true key of that maze of vast complicated disorder; and thus it gains a more and more consistent and luminous Vision of God from the most unpromising materials. Thus conscience is a connecting principle between the creature and his Creator; and the firmest hold of theological truths is gained by habits of personal religion."

> Thirty thousand immortals are on the all-nourishing earth, as ministers of Zeus.[1]

Some of them heal our diseases, others give counsel in difficulties, others reveal things hidden, others help men at their work or attend them on their journeys; some are with men in the town, others with men in the country; some are near to give aid at sea, others on land; one is at home in Socrates, another in Plato, another in Pythagoras: and the unrighteous Soul is that which has no Guardian Daemon domestic within it.[2]

The doctrine of the individual's Guardian Daemon, set forth in the *Phaedo* Myth and the Myth of Er, and corroborated from the personal experience of Socrates in the *Apology*,[3] *Republic*,[4] and *Theages*,[5] seems, in the works of Apuleius and Maximus Tyrius just now quoted from, to amount very nearly to the identification of that Daemon with Moral Character or Conscience—an identification which, it is interesting to remember, was made even before Plato's time by Heraclitus—"a man's daemon is his character"[6]—and meets us in the teaching of the Stoics, where, indeed, it seems to be only the legitimate consequence of the "naturalism" of the School, and does not surprise us, as it does in the teaching of Platonists: the following passage, for instance, in Arrian's *Dissertationes* (i. 14), giving the words of Epictetus, merely states the doctrine known to moral theology as that of the "authority of conscience":—

> "Zeus establishes for each one a daemon as his ruler, and bestows on him the guardianship over him. He is unsleeping and not to be deceived. To what better and more careful guard has he entrusted every one of us? So whenever you close the doors and make all dark within, remember never to say that you are alone. You are not. But God is within you, and is your own daemon."

To the same effect Marcus Aurelius (*Comment.* v. 27) says:—

---

[1] Works and Days, 252.
[2] This seems to have been the generally accepted view; but Servius on Virg. *Aen.* vi. 743, records another view—that every man at birth has assigned to him two genii, a good and a bad.
[3] 40 A.   [4] 496 c.   [5] 128 D ff.
[6] *Heracliti Eph. Reliquiae*, Bywater, Fr. cxxi.

"He shares the life of the Gods, who unceasingly shows them his own soul content with what has been assigned to it, having done whatever the daemon wished, whom Zeus has given as protector and leader to every man as part of himself. This is his intellect and his reason."

So much for the philosophical outcome of the doctrine of the daemon of each one—that part of the general doctrine of aerial daemons which seems to have been more interesting than any other to Platonists and Stoics alike.

But what, it may be asked, is the ultimate source of this belief in the daemon of each one out of which moral theology, by a rationalising process, has evolved "conscience", or even "noumenal character".[1]

I would suggest that, in order to approach the answer to this question, we first dismiss from our minds those aerial daemons who never were incarnate (although it is to their order, according to Plato, that the daemons attached to individuals belong), and think only of the Hesiodic daemons, the Souls of dead men, inhabiting the Air. The notion of daemons who never were incarnate is subsequent to that of those who are Souls of dead men inhabiting the air, and came in, we may take it, only after the theological doctrine of the transcendence of One Supreme God had established itself. That theological doctrine required mediators between God and men, beings through whom the creative and regulative functions of God are exerted, while He Himself remains from everlasting to everlasting unmoved; and it was only logical to conceive these beings as Powers of the Godhead anterior in time and dignity to the Souls of men.

The primitive doctrine of daemons, with which the later one has less connection than might at first sight appear, is that of the presence on, under, or near the Earth of the Souls of dead ancestors; and it is still a widely spread belief that the company of these Souls is being continually drawn upon to supply infants, as they are born, with Souls. No new Souls come into being; old Souls are always used. I have already adverted to this belief,[2] and return to it here to suggest that it is the source of the doctrine of the Guardian

---

[1] See Rohde, *Psyche*, ii. 317.
[2] See *supra*, pp. 194 ff. and pp. 277 ff.

Spirit of the individual. Every new person born is at once himself and some deceased ancestor. He is essentially double. "In the Niger Delta," says Mr. J. E. King,[1] citing the authority of Miss Kingsley, "we are told that no one's soul remains long below. The soul's return to its own family[2] is ensured by special *ju-jus*. As the new babies arrive, they are shown a selection of small articles belonging to deceased members of the family. The child is identified by the article which first attracts its attention. 'Why, he's Uncle John; see! he knows his own pipe.' "

I would suggest that in "Uncle John" we have the source out of which the notion of the Guardian Genius, the initiator for life,[3] was evolved.

The Jewish doctrine of Angels—on which the reader may consult the *Jewish Encyclopaedia*, article "Angelology"—bears considerable resemblance to the Greek doctrine of daemons as divine beings (not Souls of deceased men) intermediate between God and men. Philo indeed goes the length of identifying the Jewish Angels with the daemons of the Greek philosophers.[4]

The Jewish, like the parallel Greek doctrine, seems to have been largely consequential on the doctrine of the transcendence of One Supreme God.[5]

---

[1] "Infant Burial," *Classical Rev.* Feb. 1903. Mr. King's reference is to Miss Kingsley's *Travels in West Africa*, p. 493.

[2] Cf. Olympiodorus on *Phaedo* 70 c—"that the living and the dead make exchange with one another, on the testimony of the ancient poets, speaking, I say, after Orpheus:

> The fathers themselves, and the sons of their house,
> And chaste wives and cherished daughters.

For everywhere Plato parodies Orpheus."

"Whose opinion," adds Lobeck (*Aglaoph.* p. 797), "seems to be that by a re-migration of souls into bodies it is often brought about, that those who have been united in the bonds of nature and affinity, were in the course of time brought together into the same household, returning to their first condition."

[3] To every man he assigns a daemon,
From the moment of his birth to be his initiator into life.—MENANDER.

[4] *De Somniis*, i. 22; and also calls them reasons (*o.c.* i. 12-19).

[5] See Hatch, *Hibbert Lectures*, 1888, pp. 246, 247: ideas, reasons, daemons, angels, are conceptions which easily pass into one another—a philosophical basis, he argues, for the theory of a transcendent God was afforded by the Platonic ideas and the Stoical reasons.

J.

GENERAL OBSERVATIONS ON MYTHS

WHICH SET FORTH THE NATION'S, AS DISTINGUISHED FROM THE INDIVIDUAL'S, IDEALS AND CATEGORIES

Hitherto we have seen the Individual's Ideals and Categories set forth in Myth. Let us now conclude our review of the Platonic Myths by looking at two, in one of which—the Atlantis Myth[1]—we have a Nation's Ideal set forth—we assist at the spectacle of a Nation led on by a Vision of its Future; while in the other—the Myth of the Earth-Born, the Foundation-myth of the Beautiful City[2]—we have a Nation's Categories deduced—the life of the "social organism" is exhibited as conditioned by its Past, as determined *a priori* by certain deep-cut characteristics.

The Atlantis Myth is introduced in the *Timaeus* as necessary to complete the ideal of the Beautiful City, or Perfect State, presented in the *Republic*. The *Timaeus*, we must remember, stands in very close artistic and philosophic connection with the *Republic*, and begins with a recapitulation of the first five books of the *Republic*. Having recapitulated, Socrates says that he wishes now to see the Constitution of their yesterday's conversation exhibited *in action;* and it is to meet this wish that Critias tells the story of Atlantis—merely summarised in the *Timaeus*, but afterwards begun on full scale in the *Critias*, unfortunately a fragment.

There are two chief points to be noticed about the following on of the Atlantis Myth to complete the *Republic:*—

(1) It is an imaginary Athens in the Atlantis Myth,

---

[1] *Timaeus*, 19 ff. (where it is sketched), and *Critias* (where it is begun on a large scale, but not finished).
[2] *Republic*, 414 B.

which is the Beautiful City of the *Republic* in action. Much has been said and written about Plato's dislike of Athenian democracy and admiration of Spartan institutions as shown in the *Republic*. The ideal city of the *Republic* has been epigrammatically described as "a Dorian State and a Pythagorean Order". But it is a glorified Athens, not Sparta, which represents Hellas against barbarism in the Myth told by Critias. "Athens, with all thy faults I love thee still," is Plato's deepest sentiment.

(2) The action of the Beautiful City is assumed without question to be *war*. The education of the *Republic* is the education of warriors, and the Myth of Atlantis is the History of a Great War which puts that education to practical test. Of all Utopias, Plato's is the most militant. The Philosophers who rule are recruited from the Army. Only those who have first learnt, as patriotic soldiers, to reverence the ideal of Country one and indivisible, can afterwards comprehend that ideal intellectually in its contour and articulation—can take the "synoptic view" required in the Philosopher-King. Industrial people immersed in private affairs never rise, either as patriots or as statesmen, to the ideal of Country one and indivisible. A "Philosophic Banker", as Grote was called, Plato could not have conceived. Civilisation, as its course is sketched in the Second Book of the *Republic*,[1] begins with the formation of an Army. The little rustic City of Pigs contented with mere comfort, can never become the home of civilisation. It is out of the unrest and lust of the Inflamed City that civilisation is evolved; for in order to satisfy its lust it must go to war, and in order to wage war successfully it must have professional soldiers, who, if they are not to turn upon their fellow-citizens and rend them, must be trained in a certain manner. What, then, is to be the training of these soldiers? They were called into existence solely, it would appear, for the purpose of serving the evil policy of the "Inflamed City". But where is now the "Inflamed City"? It is gone—only its soldiers remain; and, by one of those dream-like transformations which mean so much in Plato's Philosophy, its soldiers are changed into the Guardians of

[1] *Republic*, 372, 373.

the Beautiful City to be; and, without a word of explanation
offered, a beginning is straightway made of their training
for the service of that city. And what does this dream-like
transformation mean? That the highest good is won only
in the struggle against difficulties into which evil passions
have brought us—

> What we call sin
> I could believe a painful opening out
> Of paths for ampler virtue.[1]

The contented life of the "City of Pigs" must be succeeded
by the restless lustful life of the "Inflamed City", in order
that upon the necessity of war the beauty of true civilisation
may be grafted by discipline and education.

The doctrine of the *Republic*, then, is that the leaders of
civilisation are men who have been trained for war, "our
Guardian being both a warrior and a philosopher."[2] Here
Plato seems to me to take hold of a fundamental principle
in biology. Look at the races of living creatures: their
specific beauty and intelligence have been developed on
lines laid down by the necessity of defence and attack:
"the victorious cause was pleasing to the Gods". It does not
astonish the reader of the *Republic*, then, to see the Myth of
the Beautiful City completed by the Atlantis Myth, in which
the Military State, small and disciplined, overthrows the
Commercial State, large and luxurious. The individual Soul
may indeed pass out of the cycle of generation and enter into
peace—"has come from martyrdom to this peace";[3] but the
State has no immortal destiny—it is of this world, and is
always implicated in the struggle of the earthly life. "We fight
in order that we may bring peace," is not in Plato's vein.
Were war to cease in the world, what would become of the
Platonic system of Education? Plato does not expect—and,
more than that, does not wish—to see war cease. His ideal
of earthly life is Hellas in arms against Barbarism. War
began in appetite; then it was waged to satisfy passion for
glory; and we ought to hope that the time will come when
it will be waged only in the cause of reason—to propagate
an idea; but let us remember—this is Plato's message to us,

---

[1] Clough, *Dipsychus*.   [2] *Republic*, 525 B.   [3] *Par.* xv. 148.

as I understand it—that the "idea" we fight for—our "under this sign you conquer"—is a sign which shines only before the eyes of the militant, and would fade from the sky if we laid down our arms.

The Atlantis Myth throws the future back into the past— it reflects, in the form of a History of Invaders coming from the West, Plato's hope and fear as he looks towards the East. The shadow of Persian Invasion still darkened Greece. Plato, in the Beautiful City of the *Republic* and the Atlantis Myth, sets forth his ideal of a glorified Athens which, under the spiritual leadership of the Delphian Apollo,[1] shall undertake the political leadership of a united Hellas, in order to stem the onslaught of the Barbarian, and maintain the Hellenic ideal of "culture" against the barbaric reality of "material civilisation". Thus, taken in connection with each other, as they certainly ought to be, the *Republic* and the Atlantis Myth set forth a dream of the future which takes rank beside Dante's dream of Empire and Church in the *de Monarchia*.

Plato's dream was soon to come true, though not in the manner which any forecast of his could have anticipated; for even Aristotle writes as if Alexander had not conquered Asia and opened a new epoch for Hellas and the world. "The history of Greece," says Prof. Percy Gardner,[2] "consists of two parts, in every respect contrasted the one with the other. The first recounts the stories of the Persian and Peloponnesian wars, and ends with the destruction of Thebes and the subjugation of Athens and Sparta. The Hellas of which it speaks is a cluster of autonomous cities in the Peloponnesus, the Islands, and Northern Greece, to-gether with their colonies scattered over the coasts of Italy, Sicily, Thrace, the Black Sea, Asia Minor, and Africa. These cities care only to be independent, or, at most, to lord it over one another. Their political institutions, their religious ceremonies, their customs, are civic and local. Language, commerce, a common Pantheon, and a common art and poetry are the ties that bind them together. In its second phase, Greek history begins with the expedition of

---

[1] *Republic*, 427 B, C.
[2] *New Chapters in Greek History*, pp. 416-417.

Alexander. It reveals to us the Greek as everywhere lord of the barbarian, as founding kingdoms and federal systems, as the instructor of all mankind in art and science, and the spreader of civil and civilised life over the known world. In the first period of her history Greece is forming herself, in her second she is educating the world. We will venture to borrow from the Germans a convenient expression, and call the history of independent Greece the history of Hellas—that of imperial Greece the history of Hellenism."

The ideal, adumbrated in the *Republic* and the Atlantis Myth, of a Hellenic Empire, created and maintained by the joint forces of Athens and Delphi, is one between which and the ideal of personal salvation through union with God there is a very real opposition. The more men live for the ideal of national greatness the less does the ideal of personal salvation concern them. Plato's chief interest undoubtedly was in the ideal of personal salvation, which he derived mainly from the Orphic religion; and it was exactly this Orphic element in Platonism which constituted by far the most important part of its influence on subsequent philosophy, and, more especially, on the development of Christian doctrine and practice. The Heaven and Hell and Purgatory of Christian eschatology come not, to any large extent, from Jewish sources, or from the teaching of the Gospels and Epistles, but mainly from the Apocalypses, which are thoroughly Orphic in matter and spirit.[1] It is not to be supposed, of course, that the Apocalypses got their Orphism or "Sacramentalism"—to use a term which covers the ground better—from Plato. They got it from the teaching of the Orphic and similar sacramental societies which existed throughout the world. But the direction given, at the beginning, to Christian thought and feeling, and, it is safe to add, to Christian practice, by the influence of these societies, produced a condition of religious belief which afterwards lent itself easily to the influence of the refined Orphism of the Platonists.

Just as the ideal of national greatness on Earth, though we see it in the *Republic* and Atlantis Myth swimming into

[1] See Gardner's *Exploratio Evangelica*, p. 270, with reference to Dieterich's analysis of the *Apocalypse of Peter*.

Plato's ken, was of little account to him, and to those whom he influenced, beside the ideal of personal salvation through union with God—so, in the development of Christianity, to which Platonism contributed so much, the materialistic Jewish conception of a reign of the Messiah on Earth, over a chosen people raised in their earthly bodies from the dead, gave place to the spiritual ideal of union with the Heavenly Christ beginning for each man now in this present life and continuing for ever—the ideal which St. Paul came at last to cherish, "having a desire to depart and to be with Christ, which is far better."[1]

---

[1] *Phil.* i. 23; and see Gardner's *Exp. Ev.* pp. 435-438.

THE ATLANTIS MYTH

Critias begins by saying[1] that he heard the story, when he was a boy, from his grandfather Critias, who had heard it from his father Dropides, who got it from Solon. Solon brought it from Egypt, having got it from a priest of Neith— that is, of Athena—at Sais. Solon had been telling the priests of Neith some of the old Greek stories, especially that about the Flood which Deucalion and Pyrrha survived, when a very aged priest exclaimed, "You Greeks are always children; there is not an old man among you!" meaning that the oldest Greek stories were but of yesterday. Deucalion's Flood was not the only one; there were many Floods and other catastrophes before it, by which civilisations both in Greece and in other parts of the world were destroyed. But Egypt had been exempt from catastrophes, and her priests had made records, which were still preserved in continuous series, of all that had happened, not only in Egypt, but in other parts of the world, during the successive periods terminated by the various Floods and other catastrophes. Among these records was one relating to the Athens which flourished before the greatest of the Floods. This Athens, the aged priest told Solon, Athena founded nine thousand years before his time—one thousand years before she founded Sais; and the constitution of the antediluvian Athens was similar to that which the sister city of Sais still preserved, especially in the separation of the class of priests and the class of warriors from a third class, including the castes of artisans, shepherds, huntsmen, and husbandmen. He then went on to give the History of the Great War in which Athens, so constituted, was engaged

[1] *Timaeus*, 20 E.

with the people of the Island of Atlantis, explaining that this island, which was larger than Libya and Asia together, lay in the Ocean outside, off the straits now called the Pillars of Hercules. Beyond this island there were other islands in the Atlantic Ocean, by means of which it was possible to pass to the Continent on the farther side of that Ocean. In the Island of Atlantis itself there was a mighty dynasty of Kings who ruled over that island, over many of the adjacent islands, over parts of the Transatlantic Continent, and over Libya as far as Egypt, and, on the other side of the Mediterranean Sea, as far as Etruria. This mighty Power, collecting all its forces, was moving eastwards to add to its empire the remaining Mediterranean countries, Greece and Egypt, when Athens stood forth as their champion; and, now leading the other Greek States, now deserted by them, waged a glorious war against the invaders, and conquered them, and not only saved Greece and Egypt, but liberated the Western Mediterranean countries which had been enslaved. Then, sometime after, came the Deluge. Athens was overwhelmed, in a day and a night, by flood and earthquake; and the Island of Atlantis sank under the sea, leaving shoals which still render the navigation of the Ocean difficult in these parts.

This is the Atlantis Myth as sketched by Critias in the *Timaeus*.[1]

He then proposes to enter fully into its details, on the understanding that the citizens of the Ideal State constructed in the *Republic* are identified with the citizens of the antediluvian Athens; but first, Timaeus must give his promised account of the creation of the world and of man, so that, when all is said, we may have the full history of man—created in the *Timaeus*, educated in the *Republic*, and acquitting himself nobly in the *Atlantis Myth*.

The *Critias*, in which the Atlantis Myth was to have been told fully, is a fragment—a fragment, however, of considerable bulk; and I do not propose to translate it *verbatim* or to print the Greek text. A detailed account of its contents will serve our purpose sufficiently.

The fragment begins by saying that, in the old time, the

[1] 21 A-25 D.

Earth was divided into provinces, each of which was directly governed by a God, or Gods.[1] Thus Athens was assigned to Hephaestus and Athena, brother and sister, and the Island of Atlantis to Poseidon.

The Athens of Athena and Hephaestus was constituted according to the model set forth in the *Republic*. There were artisans and husbandmen, and a class of warriors originally set apart by certain "divine men". The warriors dwelt together, and had all things in common, being supported by the labour of the other citizens. Men and women alike practised the art of warfare. The territory of the city, co-extensive with Attica as it now is, was the most fertile in the world. What is now a mere skeleton of mountains and rocks was then filled in with rich soil, so that what are now mountains were then only hills; and Pnyx, Acropolis, and Lycabettus formed one almost level ridge of loam. On the top of this ridge, where the Acropolis now is, the warriors lived round the Temple of Athena and Hephaestus, their winter quarters towards the north, and their summer quarters towards the south. The number of these warriors, men and women, was always about twenty thousand. They were the guardians of their own citizens, and the leaders of the other Greeks their willing followers. Such were the ancient Athenians; and they were famous throughout Europe and Asia for the beauty of their bodies and the various virtues of their souls.

To Poseidon the Island of Atlantis was allotted. Near the centre of the island there was a fertile plain, and near it a mountain. In this mountain dwelt the earth-born Evenor, who had a daughter Cleito. Her Poseidon loved, and enclosed the mountain in which she lived with concentric rings of sea and land, three of sea and two of land, so that it could not be approached, for at that time there were no ships. Being a god, he easily brought subterranean streams of water, one cold and the other hot, to this island-mountain, and made it fruitful. Here he begat ten sons; and he divided the whole island of Atlantis among them into ten parts. To the first-born, who was named Atlas, he gave the island-mountain and surrounding territory, and also made him

---

[1] Cf. *Politicus*, 271 D, and *Laws*, iv. 712 E ff.

King of the whole of Atlantis, his nine brethren being
governors under him in their several provinces. From Atlas
were descended the Kings of Atlantis in long and unbroken line; and under them the island prospered greatly,
receiving much through foreign trade, and itself producing
much—metals, timber, spices, and all manner of food for
man, and pasture for the elephants and other animals which
abounded.   Great works were also carried out by these
Kings. . . . First they made a bridge across the rings of sea
which enclosed the ancient metropolis, and began to build
a palace on the island-mountain, to the size and adornment
of which each generation added till it became a wonder.
Then they dug a canal 50 stadia long, 300 feet broad, and
100 feet deep, making a waterway for the largest ships from
the ocean to their metropolis, which thus became a seaport.
They also cut passages for ships through the two rings of
land, and spanned the passages by bridges under which
ships could go.   The first ring of land, like the outermost
ring of sea, was three stadia broad; the second ring of land,
like the ring of sea which enclosed it, was two stadia broad;
while the ring of water which immediately surrounded the
island-mountain was one stade wide; the island-mountain
itself being five stadia across.   The island-mountain and its
palace they surrounded with a wall; and another wall they
built round the circuit of the mid ring of land; and a third
wall round the circuit of the outer ring of land; and also a
wall on either side of the great bridge leading from the
country without to that ring; and towers and gates they
placed at the bridges which spanned the passages cut in
both rings of land.   The stone for the walls they quarried
from the foot of the island-mountain and from both sides of
the two rings of land, thus at the same time making cavities
in the rock which served as covered docks.   The stone was
of three kinds—white, black, and red; and these three
kinds, pieced together in one building, made it beautiful
to behold.   The outermost wall was coated with brass, laid
on like ointment; the middle wall with tin, and the wall of
the Acropolis itself with orichalcum glancing red like fire.
Within the enclosure of the Acropolis was first the holy
place of Cleito and Poseidon, in which no man might set

foot—the spot where the ten sons were begotten. It was surrounded with a golden fence. Thither they brought the seasonable fruits of the earth, from each of the ten provinces, as offerings to each of the ten sons. Then there was the Temple of Poseidon himself, in length a stade, in breadth three plethra, and of proportionate height, on the outside coated all over with silver except the pinnacles, which were coated with gold—a spectacle of barbaric splendour; and within, the roof of ivory inlaid with gold and silver and orichalcum, and all other parts—walls, pillars, and floor—covered over with orichalcum—and images all golden; the God himself mounted on a chariot driving six winged horses, his head towering up to the roof of the temple, and round him in a ring a hundred Nereids riding on dolphins; and there were other images too, which had been put up by private persons within the temple; and outside, golden statues of the Kings and their wives, and many other statues presented by persons at home and in foreign countries belonging to the Atlantic Empire. There was also an altar in keeping with the temple, and there were magnificent palaces hard by.

The numerous fountains of cold and hot water which Poseidon had caused to spring in his island-mountain were housed and made to serve as baths for the Kings, for private persons, for women, and for horses and other beasts of burden; and the water not used in this way was conducted, some of it to the beautiful grove of Poseidon in the island-mountain, some of it by aqueducts across the bridges to the two rings of land, where also there were temples and gardens and gymnasia and race-courses for horses—especially in the outermost of the two rings, where there was a race-course a stade wide running right round the ring. Along this grand course were the quarters of the main body of the troops; a smaller number of trusted troops was quartered in the inner ring of land, and the most trusted of all in the Acropolis itself as bodyguard to the Kings.

The docks close under the island-mountain and the two rings of land were full of war-ships and stores; and when you crossed these two rings and came to the outermost ring of sea, or harbour, you found it and the canal leading to the ocean full of merchant shipping. At the ocean-mouth of this canal the two semicircles met of a wall which ran always at a distance of fifty stades from the outermost ring of sea, and enclosed a densely-populated area.

So much for the royal city. Atlantis itself was a mountainous island, save for the plain in which the royal city stood. This plain was oblong, extending 3000 stades in one direction, and 2000 inland through the centre of the island. The mountains which enclosed it were great and beautiful, and sheltered it from the north wind. A fosse 10,000 stades long, one stade broad, and a hundred feet deep—a work, it may be thought, of superhuman magnitude—was carried round the whole oblong of the plain. The streams from the mountains poured into it, and it had an outlet into the ocean. From the furthest inland part of it parallel canals were cut through the plain at intervals of one hundred stades, and these were connected by cross canals. By means of this system of canals, timber and fruits were brought down to the city. There were two harvests, one after the winter rains, the other in summer, raised by irrigation from the canals. The plain was divided into 60,000 lots, each lot being a square with sides measuring ten stades. Over those fit for military service in each lot was set a Leader; and there were likewise Leaders of those who dwelt in the mountains and other parts of the country—a vast population—according to their settlements and villages. Each Leader was bound to supply a sixth part of the cost of a chariot of war—in this way 10,000 chariots were furnished; he was also bound to supply two horses with riders, and a light chariot for a pair of horses, with a shield-bearer to go on foot with it, and a driver to ride in it and drive the horses; each Leader was also bound to supply two heavy-armed soldiers, two archers, two slingers, and, as skirmishers, three stone-throwers and three men armed with javelins, also four sailors to help to man the fleet of 1200 war-ships. Such was the armament of the capital; and the nine provinces had also their own different armaments, but it would be tedious to describe these.

In each of the nine provinces, as well as in the capital, its own King was supreme over the lives of the citizens and the administration of the laws; but the dealings of the ten governments with one another were determined by the Commandments of Poseidon, which were engraved by the first men on a Table of orichalcum, which was preserved in the Temple of Poseidon on the island-mountain. There, every fifth year and every sixth year alternately, a meeting was held for the discussion of affairs and the judgment of transgressions; and this is how they conducted their business:— There were sacred bulls, which were kept within the precincts of Poseidon. The Ten, who were left alone in the precincts, after they had prayed to the god that they might take that bull which should be an acceptable sacrifice to him, began to hunt the bulls, without weapons of iron, with staves and nooses; and when they had taken one of them they brought him to the Table of the Commandments, and there struck him on the head and shed his blood over the writing, and afterwards burnt his members, and mingled a bowl, casting into it clots of his blood, one clot for each of the Ten. Then they drew from the bowl in golden vials, and poured a libation on the fire, and swore that they would give judgments, and do all things, according to the Commandments of their Father Poseidon written on the Table. When they had drunken of the vials, and dedicated them in the Temple, they supped; and after supper, when it was dark and the sacrificial fire had died down, they put on azure robes exceeding beautiful, and sat down on the ground about the embers, all the lights in the Temple having been extinguished, and there, in the darkness of night, judged and were judged; and when day dawned they wrote the judgments on a golden tablet, and laid it by, along with their robes, for a memorial.

There were laws also regulating the behaviour of the Ten Kings towards one another. They were not to make war against one another; they were to aid any one of their number if his subjects rose against him in rebellion and tried to overthrow his dynasty; they were to take counsel together about war and other matters, always recognising the suzerainty of the line of Atlas; and a majority of the Ten must agree before a King could put to death one of his kinsmen.

For a long while the people of Atlantis preserved the divine nature that was in them, and obeyed the laws and loved the Gods, honouring virtue above gold and all other possessions, and using their wealth in temperance and brotherly love. But in course of time their divine nature, from admixture with human nature, became feeble, and they were corrupted by their prosperity, so that, in the end, their life, at the very time when it seemed most glorious, was indeed most debased, being filled with lust of wealth and power. Then Zeus, God of Gods, whose kingship is the rule of law, perceiving that a noble nation was in a wretched plight, and wishing to punish them that they might be reformed by chastisement, summoned all the Gods to an assembly in his most holy mansion, which, being situate in the centre of the Cosmos, beholds all things which partake of generation; and, when the Gods were assembled, spake unto them thus:—

*   *   *   *   *   *

OBSERVATIONS ON THE GEOLOGY AND GEOGRAPHY OF THE ATLANTIS MYTH

Enough, I hope, has been said to indicate the importance of the Atlantis Myth as setting forth the ideal of Imperial Hellas; and now a few remarks may be added on the interesting, though comparatively unimportant, topics of its Geology and Geography.

Mr. Arthur Platt, in a very instructive article on "Plato and Geology",[1] after quoting from the *Critias* (110 E) Plato's account of the antediluvian Attica as a rolling champaign very different from the broken rocky country of the present epoch, says: "To put this into the language of modern geology we should say, 'The whole of Attica has suffered great denudation, withstood by the underlying hard rocks, which now accordingly stand out like the skeleton of the country'." Mr. Platt does well in claiming for Plato, on the strength of the *Critias*, rank as an "original geologist". "Sir Charles Lyell," he says, "in his history of the progress of geology,[2] has entirely omitted the name of Plato as an original geologist, and I am not aware that this omission has ever been corrected. Yet it is in reality a serious one. . . . This statement of denudation by Plato is, I believe, the first ever made, certainly the first upon so grand a scale. It is true that Herodotus (ii. 10 ff.), when he speaks of the formation of the Delta in Egypt, implies denudation of those districts which furnish the alluvium . . . but he does not call attention to this necessary denudation, and does not seem to have appreciated its consequences, his mind being fixed solely on the formation of the new deposit. Plato therefore must have the credit of the first distinct enunciation of a most important geological doctrine." "The next question," Mr. Platt proceeds, "is: Is this doctrine, however true in general, true of Attica in particular?" and he quotes Lyell's authority for an affirmative answer: " 'The whole fauna,' says Lyell, speaking of the remains of Miocene age discovered by Gaudry in Attica, 'attests the former

[1] *Journal of Philology*, vol. xviii. pp. 134-139 (1889).
[2] *Principles of Geology*, chap. ii.

extension of a vast expanse of grassy plains, where we have now the broken and mountainous country of Greece—plains which were probably united with Asia Minor, spreading over the area where the deep Egean Sea and its numerous islands are now situated.' " Mr. Platt concludes his article with a quotation from Gaudry (*Animaux Fossiles et Géologie de l'Attique*, 1862),[1] in which that geologist gives his own personal experience of the effect of short downpours of rain, in Attica and other parts of Greece, in carrying away vast quantities of soil. "A man accustomed to such débâcles," remarks Mr. Platt, "might more easily talk of 'one night's rainfall' carrying off the whole surface of the Acropolis than could a dweller in our climate." In "compelling nature to do all her work in a single night" Plato was doubtless wrong, as Mr. Platt insists, from the point of view of geology as reformed by Lyell; at the same time, I would have the reader of the *Critias* bear in mind that the geology of that work is, after all, the geology of the Aetiological Myth, in which a result, which Plato, as scientific observer, may well have conceived as due to a secular process, was bound to be attributed to a "catastrophe".

A few words now on the Geography of the Myth. I do not think that it is necessary to suppose, or that it is even likely, that Plato had any sailors' stories of a great land beyond the Western Ocean on which to found his Myth. Nor can the ostensible source of the Myth—Egypt—have been the real source. Egyptologists know nothing of a lost Atlantis.[2] As for the interesting circumstance that recent Physical Geography assumes the former existence of a so-called "Atlantis",[3] that, of course, is without bearing on the question of the source of Plato's Myth.

Atlantis, I take it, is a creation of Plato's own imagination[4]—a creation which he knows how to give verisimilitude to by connecting with the accepted "scientific" doctrine of

---

[1] Pages 450, 451.
[2] So Sander, *Atlantis*, p. 11, on the authority of Brugsch.
[3] See H. J. Mackinder's *Britain and the British Seas*, p. 98—"a continental 'Atlantis' of which Greenland and the Scoto-Icelandic rise may be remnants"; and see also pp. 100, 103, 140, 177, 179, 354, 355, 357.
[4] This, the only reasonable view, as it seems to me, is that of Jowett (Introduction to the *Critias*), Bunbury (*History of Ancient Geography*, i. 402), and Sander, *Atlantis*.

terrestrial catastrophes (which we have already seen presented in the *Politicus* Myth), and also with what was believed, in his day, to be a fact—the shallow muddy nature of the ocean outside the Pillars of Hercules. This supposed fact is recorded by Scylax, whose *Circumnavigation* was written some time before the accession of Philip.[1] Scylax speaks of "many trading stations of the Carthaginians, and much mud, and high tides, and open seas, outside the Pillars of Hercules" (*Perip.* § 1). "It is evident," says Bunbury, commenting on this passage,[2] "that these seas were never at this time visited by Greek traders, while the confused notions of the obstacles to their navigation, purposely diffused by the Carthaginians, were all that had reached our author's ears." Similarly, in the Aristotelian *Meteorologica*, ii. 1. 354 a 22, we are told that the sea outside the Pillars is shallow and muddy, *and windless*, which again shows, Bunbury remarks,[3] "how little it was known to the Greek mariners".[4]

The Island of Atlantis, then, is a creation of Plato's imagination, rendered "probable" by the confirmation of "science" and "observed facts"—a creation intended to contrast with the Beautiful City, the creation of the *Republic*—intended to stand as "the negative", as Sander puts it,[5] of the antediluvian Athens. The People of Poseidon (commerce) must yield to the People of Athena (wisdom) and Hephaestus (handicraft). Carthage, of course, may well have helped Plato to seize the type described in this selfish Commercial Atlantis, greedy of Empire —like England, as she appears to her rivals.

While the attempt to trace Plato's Atlantis to the tales of Phoenician or other navigators who had visited the American islands or continent is, I feel sure, as mistaken on the one side as the Neo-Platonic exegesis is on the other side, which interprets the Myth as an allegory of the struggle of matter against form,[6] yet it must be noted that the Platonic creation

---

[1] Bunbury, *o.c.* i. 385-386.   [2] *o.c.* i. p. 386.   [3] *o.c.* i. 398.
[4] The pseudo-Aristotelian *de Mundo* (see Rose *de Ar. lib. ord. et auct.* pp. 90-100) "bears," says Bunbury (i. 398), "the unquestionable stamp of a much more advanced stage of geographical knowledge than that of the age of Aristotle." See also Grote's *Hist. of Greece*, ii. 462 (ed. 1862).
[5] F. Sander, *Atlantis*, p. 6.
[6] See Sander, *o.c.* p. 17.

was not without practical influence on the age which produced Columbus. Plato was then for the first time being read in Greek by Western scholars,[1] and his wonderful land across the ocean, so circumstantially described in the *Critias*, came to be talked about as a *possibility* at least. Maritime discovery soon converted the possibility into a reality; and Plato was very naturally credited with knowledge which a more critical scholarship than that of the Renaissance now sees that he could not have possessed.

Before closing these observations I must notice a scholium on the opening sentences of the *Republic* which might be taken to imply that the war between Athens and Atlantis was a stock Athenian Myth. The scholium says that at the Little Panathenaea a peplus was woven, and embroidered with the War of Athens and Atlantis.[2] Of course, it might be argued that this custom was subsequent to Plato's time, and that the Myth on the peplus was taken from Plato; for Critias introduces his story as unheard before. This, however, is very unlikely. A popular ceremony can hardly have originated in that way. If the scholiast is right, it is pretty plain that the story of the War of Athens and Atlantis (in spite of what Callias says about its being hitherto unknown) was known at Athens long before Plato's

---

[1] The Atlantis Myth as it appears in the *Critias* was then being read in the West for the first time; but the *Timaeus*, to 53 C, was already known in the Latin version of Chalcidius (*circ.* Cent. V.). It is strange that Dante, who knew the *Timaeus* in this version (either directly, or as Mr. Toynbee, *Dante Dict.* art. "Timeo 2", thinks more probable, through Albertus Magnus and S. Thomas Aquinas), nowhere mentions or refers to Atlantis. The land which Ulysses sights (*Inf.* xxvi.) is the Mount of Purgatory in the Southern Hemisphere, not Fortunate Islands or an Atlantis in the Western Ocean. The commentary of Chalcidius does not touch the introductory part of the *Timaeus*, which is, however, contained in the version; and Dante's references to the *Timaeus* (the only work of Plato of which he shows any special knowledge) are limited to topics occurring in the Discourse of the chief speaker, with which alone the commentary of Chalcidius deals. This seems to make for the view that Dante knew the *Timaeus* only through his own study of the commentary, or through the references of other writers to it and the corresponding part of the version, and that he had no first-hand acquaintance with the version itself as a whole. If he had read the first part of the version, it is difficult to understand his not having been struck by the Destruction of Atlantis, and his not having made use of an event so suitable for poetic treatment.

[2] "They celebrated the Lesser Panathenaea at the Peiraeus. In this another peplos was set up for the Goddess, on which were to be seen the Athenians, her nurslings, conquering the Atlanteans in battle."—Schol. on *Republ.* 327 A.

time. But the scholiast is not right. His note is founded on a stupid misunderstanding of a passage in the commentary of Proclus on the *Timaeus*, where the remark is made that Callias has woven a Myth worthy of Athena. Proclus is evidently speaking metaphorically. There is no question of the Atlantis Myth being actually represented on a peplus.[1]

So far as the *Republic* scholiast is concerned, then, we may adhere to our view that the Atlantis Myth is the product of Plato's own imagination.

---

[1] See Sander, *Atlantis*, p. 13.

THE MYTH OF THE EARTH-BORN

Republic 414 B—415 B

We must try, says Socrates, to invent a Noble Fiction for the good of the People which we have distributed into the three classes of Rulers, Soldiers, and Workmen—a Fiction which, if possible, we must get the Rulers themselves to believe, but, failing that, the other citizens. And let our Fiction eschew novelty: let it be framed after the pattern of those Foundation-Myths which the Poets have made familiar. I hardly know how to recommend my story to the belief, first of the Rulers, then of the Soldiers, and then of the other citizens—it will be difficult, indeed, to get them to believe it; yet, let me make the venture—and tell them that "All the things which they deemed were done unto them and came to pass in their life, when we were bringing them up and instructing them, were dreams, so to speak: all the while, in truth, 'twas under the Earth, in her womb, that they were being fashioned and nourished, and their arms and all their accoutrement wrought. Then, when the making of them was fully accomplished, the Earth, which is their Mother, sent them forth; and now must they take good counsel concerning the Land wherein they are as concerning a Mother and Nurse, and must themselves defend her, if any come against her, and also have regard unto all their fellow-citizens, as unto brethren—children, along with themselves, of one Mother, even of Earth."

We shall further say to them in pursuance of our Myth:—

"All ye of this City are brethren: but God, when He fashioned you, mingled gold in the nature of those of you who were Able to Rule; wherefore are they the most precious: and silver in the nature of the Soldiers: and iron and copper in the Husbandmen and Craftsmen. Now, albeit that, for the most part, ye will engender children like unto their parents, yet, inasmuch as ye are all of one kindred, it will sometimes come to pass that from gold silver will be brought forth, and from silver, golden offspring —yea, from any sort, any other. And this is the first and chiefest commandment which God giveth unto the Rulers, that they be Watchmen indeed, and watch naught else so diligently as the issue of children, to see which of these metals is mingled in their Souls: and if a child of theirs have aught of copper or iron in him, they shall in no wise have pity upon him, but shall award unto him the place meet for his nature, and thrust him forth unto the Craftsmen or Husbandmen; whereas, if there be any one born among these with gold or silver in him, they shall take account of this, and lead him up unto the place of the Watchmen, or unto the place of the Soldiers; for hath not the Oracle declared that the City will be destroyed in the day that Iron or Copper shall keep watch?"

This is the Myth. How are we to get them to believe it? The generation to whom it is first told cannot possibly believe it; but the next may, and the generations after. Thus the Public Good may be served, after all, by our Noble Fiction.

Note on the Myth of the Earth-born

The three metals of this Myth must be taken in connection with the doctrine of Hesiod (*O.D.* 97 ff.); for which the reader is referred to the section on *Daemones* among the Observations on the Discourse of Diotima.[1]

With regard to the fancy which inspires the Myth—the fancy that "our youth was a dream"—I would only remark that Plato seems to me here to appeal to an experience which is by no means uncommon in childhood—to the feeling that the things here are doubles of things elsewhere. The production of this feeling in his adult patient has been dwelt on[2] as one of the chief means by which the Poet effects the purpose of his art.

---

[1] Pages 384 ff. *supra*.   [2] Pages 58, 346 ff. *supra*.

THE MYTHOLOGY AND METAPHYSICS OF THE CAMBRIDGE PLATONISTS

The purpose of this Concluding Part is to show that Alexandrine Platonism, indebted for its chief tenets to the mythology of the *Timaeus*, *Phaedrus* Myth, and Discourse of Diotima, has been, and still is, an important influence in Modern Philosophy.

Our chief concern will be with the "Cambridge Platonists" of the seventeenth century; but we shall keep a watchful eye throughout upon their successors, the English Idealists of the present day.

Before we consider the central doctrine of the Cambridge Platonists and compare it with that of the English Idealists of the present day, we must try to realise the environment of the former. It was, in one word, "academic". That, in the seventeenth century, meant "theological". Their paramount interest was in Theology. They brought to the cultivation of Theology, first, classical, patristic, and rabbinical learning, and secondly, physical science, Cartesian —and Newtonian, if I may be allowed so to call the re-formed science which was already all but ripe for Newton's great discovery.

With regard to their Learning:—It was that of the Renaissance, *i.e.* Platonic, not Aristotelian. The learning of the medieval Church had been Aristotelian; and the great Myth of that Church, the *Divina Commedia*, sprang into life out of the ashes of Aristotelianism. Antagonism to the Roman Church had, doubtless, much to do with the Platonic revival, which spread from Italy. Ficino, the great Florentine Platonist, took the place of Thomas Aquinas, and is the authority the Cambridge Platonists are always found appealing to. Their Platonism, moreover, was that of Plato the mythologist, not that of Plato the dialectician; that is, it was Alexandrine Platonism which attracted them, especially as its doctrine had been used by Philo to interpret the Old Testament, and by Origen and other Fathers to set forth the philosophy of the Christian mysteries, on lines common to them with Plotinus.

Philo, whose method of exegesis has been referred to in the section on Allegory,[1] never thought of doubting that Platonism and the Jewish Scriptures had real affinity to each other, and hardly perhaps asked himself how the affinity was to be accounted for; but the English Platonists, imitators of his exegetical method, felt themselves obliged to satisfy doubts and answer questions. To make good the applicability of the Platonic philosophy to the exegesis of the Holy Scriptures, they felt, with Aristobulus and Numenius,[2] that it was important to be able to show that Plato was *the Attic Moses*. In the Preface to his *Conjectura Cabbalistica, or a Conjectural Essay of interpreting the mind of Moses in the three first Chapters of Genesis, according to a threefold Cabbala, viz., literal, philosophical, mystical, or divinely moral* (1662), Dr. Henry More writes (p. 3):—

> Moses seems to have been aforehand, and prevented the subtilest and abstrusest inventions of the choicest philosophers that ever appeared after him to this very day. And further presumption of the truth of this *Philosophical Cabbala* is that the grand mysteries therein contained are most-what the same that those two eximious philosophers, Pythagoras and Plato, brought out of Egypt, and the parts of Asia, into Europe, and it is generally acknowledged by Christians that they both had their philosophy from Moses. And Numenius the Platonist speaks out plainly concerning his master: What is Plato but the Attic Moses? And for Pythagoras, it is a thing incredible that he and his followers should make such a deal of doe with the mystery of Numbers, had he not been favoured with a sight of Moses his creation of the world in six days, and had the Philosophick Cabbala thereof communicated to him, which mainly consists in Numbers.

---

[1] Pages 230 ff. *supra*.
[2] Aristobulus asserted the existence of a much older translation of the Law from which Plato and the Greeks stole their philosophy. Numenius is the author of the phrase "Atticizing Moses": see Dr. Bigg's *Christian Platonists of Alexandria*, p. 6.

Again in the same work (ch. iii. § 3, p. 100) he writes:—

> That Pythagoras was acquainted with the Mosaical or
> Jewish Philosophy, there is ample testimony of it in writers;
> as of Aristobulus an Egyptian Jew in Clemens Alexandrinus,
> and Josephus against Appion. S. Ambrose adds that he was
> a Jew himself.   Clemens calls him *the Hebrew Philosopher*.
> I might cast hither the suffrages of Justin Martyr, Johannes
> Philoponus, Theodoret, Hermippus in *Origen against Celsus*,
> Porphyrius, and Clemens again, who writes that it was a
> common fame that Pythagoras was a disciple of the Prophet
> Ezekiel.   And though he gives no belief to the report, yet
> that learned antiquary Mr. Selden seems inclinable enough
> to think it true. . . . Besides all these, Iamblichus also
> affirms that he lived at Sidon his native country, where he
> fell acquainted with the Prophets and Successors of one
> Mochus the Physiologer or Natural Philosopher . . . where-
> fore it is very plain that Pythagoras had his Philosophy
> from Moses . . . and now I have said this much of Pythagoras,
> there will be less need to insist upon Plato and Plotinus,
> their Philosophy being the same that Pythagoras's was, and
> so alike applicable to Moses his text.

So much, by way of specimen, to indicate the kind of
evidence by which Plato is proved to be *the Attic Moses*. The
proof, as managed by both More and Cudworth, calls into
requisition a vast amount of uncritical learning. One has
to read these learned lucubrations to estimate the revolution
wrought by Bentley.

One of the oddest results of the desire of the Cambridge
Platonists to show the derivation of Pythagoreanism and
Platonism from the Mosaic philosophy was the thesis maintained by them that the Mosaic philosophy was an atomistic
system—a system which Pythagoras and Plato borrowed and
kept in comparative purity, but which Democritus (the
Hobbes of antiquity—see Cudworth, *Intellectual System*, vol. i.
p. 276, ed. Mosheim and Harrison) corrupted into atheism.
The true Mosaic atomism, or physical science, was of such
a nature as to make it necessary to postulate God as source
of motion; whereas Democritus and modern materialists
explain *everything* by blind mechanical principles. But why
this desire to make out the true philosophy—that of Moses
and the Greeks who retained the Mosaic tradition—
atomistic? Because the Cartesian natural philosophy was

"atomistic", *i.e.* mathematical and mechanical. This was the natural philosophy in vogue—the natural philosophy which was reforming Physics and Astronomy, and was about to bring forth Newton. It need not surprise us, then, if we look at the matter attentively, that these alumni of Cambridge wished to show that Moses taught— allegorically, it is true—the Cartesian or mechanical philosophy. It was as if theologians of our own day were anxious to show that the account of the Creation in *Genesis*, or, if that would be too paradoxical, belief in a Special Providence, is compatible with Darwinism. It is true that More and Cudworth, especially the latter, are not entirely satisfied with the Cartesian theology, although they accept the Cartesian mathematical physics as giving a correct explanation of natural phenomena. It was indeed "atomism" in its genuine Mosaic form which Descartes revived, not the atheistic Democritean atomism; for he posits an "Immaterial Substance"; but he leaves this Substance, as First Principle, too little to do. While recognising immaterial cogitative substance as distinct from extended material substance, he falls into the error of identifying cogitative substance entirely with consciousness, and for the "plastic soul"—a spiritual or immaterial, though non-conscious, principle in Nature—he substitutes blind "mechanism", thus depriving theology of the argument from design. This is the gist of a remarkable criticism of Descartes which occurs in Cudworth's *Intellectual System*, vol. i. pp. 275, 276. It is well worth reading in connection with criticism of the same tendency to be met with in such modern books as Professor Ward's *Naturalism and Agnosticism*.

More, in a notable passage in the *Preface General* to his *Collected Works* (1662), speaks of Platonism as the soul, and Cartesianism as the body, of the philosophy which he applies to the interpretation of the Text of Moses. This philosophy is the old Jewish-Pythagorean Cabbala, which teaches the motion of the Earth and the Pre-existence of the Soul. The motion of the Earth as Mosaic doctrine he discusses in the sixth chapter of his *Appendix to the Defence of the Philosophick Cabbala* (p. 126), and the passage in which he deals with an objection against ascribing the doctrine to Moses may be noted as an instructive specimen of the method of these Cambridge Platonists. The objection—a sufficiently formidable one on the face of it—is that the doctrine does not appear in the Mosaic writings. More takes up the bold position that, although the doctrine of "the motion of the Earth has been lost and appears not in the remains of the Jewish Cabbala, this can be no argument against its once having been a part thereof."

> Though the fame of this part of the Cabbala (he says) be in a manner extinct among the Jews, yet that it was once the hidden doctrine of the learned of that nation seems to me sufficiently credible from what Plutarch writes of Numa Pompilius. For his so strictly prohibiting the use of images in divine worship is very apparently Mosaical . . . and Numa's instructor is said to be not a Grecian but some Barbarian greater and better than Pythagoras himself; and where, I pray you, was such an one to be found, unless descended from the Jews? . . . It seems exceedingly probable from all these circumstances that Numa was both descended from the Jews and imbued with the Jewish religion and learning. What's this to the purpose? or how does it prove the motion of the Earth once to have been part of the Judaical Tradition or Cabbala? Only thus much: that Numa . . . knowing there was no such august temple of God as the Universe itself, and that to all the inhabitants thereof it cannot but appear round from every prospect, and that in the midst there must be an ever-shining Fire, I mean the Sun; in imitation hereof he built a round temple, which was called the temple of Vesta, concerning which Plutarch speaks plainly and apertly, "That Numa is reported to have built a round temple of Vesta for the custody of a fire in the midst thereof that was never to go out: not imitating herein the figure of the Earth, as if she was the Vesta, but of the Universe; in the midst whereof the Pythagoreans placed the Fire, and called it Vesta or Monas, and reckoned the Earth neither immovable, nor in the midst of the Mundane Compasse, but that it is carried about the Fire or Sun, and is none of the first and chief elements of the World." What can be more plain than these testimonies?

The learning of the Cambridge Platonists, of which the above passage enables us to take the measure, is expended in two main directions, pointed out by Philo and by Plotinus respectively. Philo was their master in Scriptural exegesis— the exegesis by which *dogma* was established (although

Plotinus, too, helped them here, especially with regard to the doctrine of the Trinity); but Plotinus was especially their master in what concerned *devotional religion*. It would be tedious to quote passages in which they employ Philo's exegetical method (already illustrated in another part of this work) in order to establish *dogma:* it will be sufficient merely to mention More's *Philosophick Cabbala,* ch. 1, his *Defence of the Philosophick Cabbala,* ch. 1, Cudworth's *Intellectual System of the Universe,* vol. ii. p. 366 and p. 406 (ed. Mosheim and Harrison), and Norris's *Reason and Religion* (1689), pp. 133, 134; but a few words respecting the *aids to devotion* which they derived from their *Cabbala* may not be out of place here.

First, it is to be observed that *ecstasy* was the general form in which they tended to envisage religious devotion; and here, doubtless, Plotinus was their model. The ecstasy of Plotinus is an obscure phenomenon, probably deserving the attention of the physiologist as well as of the theologian;[1] it will be enough, by way of indicating its nature, to refer to Cudworth, who quotes[2] a well-known passage in Porphyry's *Life of* his friend and master *Plotinus:*—

> And that we may here give a taste of the mystical theology and enthusiasm of these Platonists too, Porphyrius in his Life of Plotinus affirmeth, that both Plotinus and himself had sometimes experience of a kind of ecstatic union with the first of these three gods [Cudworth here refers to the Platonic Trinity], that which is above mind and understanding: "Plotinus often endeavouring to raise up his mind to the first and highest God, that God sometimes appeared to him, who hath neither form nor idea, but is placed above intellect, and all that is intelligible; to whom I Porphyrius affirm myself to have been once united in the sixty-eighth year of my age." And again afterwards: "Plotinus' chief aim and scope was to be united to and conjoined with the Supreme God, who is above all; which scope he attained unto four several times, whilst myself was with him, by a certain ineffable energy." That is, Plotinus aimed at such a kind of rapturous and ecstatic union with the One and the Good, "the first of the three highest gods" (called the One and the Good), as by himself

---

[1] For modern cases I would refer to Professor James's *Varieties of Religious Experience* (1902).

[2] *Intell. System,* ii. 315, 316.

is described towards the latter end of this last book (*Enn.* vi. 9), where he calls it "a kind of tactual union", and "a certain presence better than knowledge", and "the joining of our own centre, as it were, with the centre of the universe".

This doctrine, or rather practice, of ecstasy, especially identified with the name of Plotinus, appeals strongly to the English Platonists, who understand it, however, not as a mysterious trance, but as a "Holy Life", ecstatic in the sense of being dead to the flesh and the vanities of the world. Death to the flesh and the world is secured by—nay consists in,[1] Contemplation of the glorious and lovable nature of God. "The highest and last term of Contemplation," says Norris,[2] "is the Divine Essence. Whence it follows necessarily that the mind which sees the Divine Essence must be totally and thoroughly absolved from all commerce with the corporeal senses, either by *Death* or some *ecstatical* and *rapturous Abstraction.* So true is that which God said to Moses, Thou canst not see my face, for there shall no man see me, and live." Similarly, John Smith, in his Discourse on "The true way or method of attaining Divine knowledge", speaks of a good Life as the Fundamental Principle of Divine Science: "If any man will do his will, he shall know the doctrine, whether it be of God."

"Were I indeed to define *Divinity,* I should rather call it a *Divine Life,* than a *Divine Science;* it being something rather to be understood by a *Spiritual Sensation,* than by any verbal description."[3] . . . "Divinity is not so well perceived by a subtle wit, as by a purified sense, as Plotinus phraseth it."[4] . . . "The Platonists . . . thought the minds of men could never be purged enough from those earthly dregs of Sense and Passion, in which they were so much steeped, before they could be capable of their divine *metaphysics;* and therefore they so much solicit a separation from the Body, in all those who would sincerely understand Divine Truth; for that was the scope of their Philosophy. This was also intimated by them in defining Philosophy to be a meditation of Death; aiming herein at only a

---

[1] *Cf.* Aristotle, *E. N.* x. 8. 8. 1178 b 32.

[2] *Reasons and Religion* (1689), p. 3. It is a book "of a devotional nature written for the use and benefit of the *Learned Reader*", "whose Heart may want as much to be inflamed as the other's Head [*i.e.* the head of the unlearned person for whose use devotional books are mostly written] does to be instructed."

[3] Smith's *Select Discourses* (1660), p. 2.   [4] *o.c.* p. 10.

moral way of dying, by loosening the Soul from the Body and this Sensitive life . . . and therefore, besides those purifying virtues by which the Souls of men were to be separated from Sensuality . . . they devised a further way of separation . . . which was their *Mathemata*, or mathematical contemplations . . . besides many other ways they had, whereby to rise out of this dark body; several steps and ascents out of this miry cave of mortality, before they could set any sure footing with their intellectual part in the Land of Light and Immortal Being."[1] "The Priests of Mercury, as Plutarch tells us, in the eating of their holy things, were wont to cry out, Sweet is Truth. But how sweet and delicious that Truth is which holy and heaven-born Souls feed upon in their mysterious converses with the Deity, who can tell but they that taste it? When *Reason* once is raised by the mighty force of the Divine Spirit into a converse with God, it is turned into *Sense:* that which before was only *Faith* well built upon sure principles (for such our *Science* may be) now becomes *Vision*. We shall then converse with God with our Intellect, whereas before we conversed with him only with our Discursive faculty, as the Platonists were wont to distinguish. Before we laid hold on him only with a struggling, agonistical, and contentious Reason, hotly combating with difficulties and sharp contests of diverse opinions, and labouring in it self in its deductions of one thing from another; we shall then fasten our minds upon him, with such a serene understanding, such an intellectual calmness and serenity as will present us with a blissful, steady, and invariable sight of him."[2]

It may perhaps be thought that in the foregoing passage Smith oversteps a little the line which divides "ecstasy" as "Holy Life" from "ecstasy" as temporary state of exalted religious feeling; and perhaps in the following passage too, from his *Discourse of the Immortality of the Soul*, he may be thought to commit the same fault; yet the passage seems to me to contain what is so valuable for our understanding of the influence of Platonism—as mythological, rather than logical system—on present-day religious thought, that I venture to transcribe it, together with the notable quotation from Plotinus included in it:—

Though in our contentious pursuits after science, we

---

[1] *o.c.* pp. 10, 11.
[2] *o.c.* pp. 16, 17. This and the foregoing quotations are all from the *Discourse concerning the True Way or Method of attaining to Divine Knowledge.*

cast *Wisdom, Power, Eternity, Goodness,* and the like into several formalities, so that we may trace down Science in a constant chain of Deductions; yet in our naked Intuitions and Visions of them, we clearly discern that *Goodness* and *Wisdom* lodge together, *Justice* and *Mercy* kiss each other: and all these and whatsoever pieces else the cracked glasses of our Reasons may sometime break Divine and Intelligible Being into, are fast knit up together in the invincible bonds of *Eternity.* And in this sense is that notion of Proclus descanting upon Plato's riddle of the Soul, *as if it were generated and yet not generated,* to be understood; the Soul partaking of Time in its broken and particular conceptions and apprehensions, and of Eternity in its Comprehensive and Stable Contemplations. I need not say that when the Soul is once got up to the top of this bright Olympus, it will then no more doubt of its own Immortality, or fear any Dissipation, or doubt whether any drowsy sleep shall hereafter seize upon it: no, it will then feel itself grasping fast and safely its own Immortality, and view itself in the Horizon of Eternity. In such sober kind of ecstasies did Plotinus find his own Soul separated from his body . . . "I being often awakened into a sense of my self, and being sequestered from my body, and betaking myself from all things else into my self; what admirable beauty did I then behold." . . . But here we must use some caution, lest we should arrogate too much to the power of our own Souls, which indeed cannot raise up themselves into that pure and steady contemplation of true Being; but will rather act with some *multiplicity* or *otherness* (as they speak) attending it. But thus much of its high original may appear to us, that it can *correct* itself for *dividing* and *disjoining* therein, as knowing all to be every way *one* most *entire* and *simple.* . . . We shall add but this one thing further to clear the Soul's Immortality, and it is indeed that which breeds a true sense of it—viz., *True and real goodness.* Our *highest speculations* of the Soul may beget a sufficient conviction thereof within us, but yet it is only True Goodness and Virtue in the Souls of men that can make them both *know* and *love, believe* and *delight* themselves in their *own Immortality.* Though every good man is not so logically subtile as to be able by fit *mediums* to demonstrate his own Immortality, yet he sees it in a higher light: his Soul being purged and enlightened by true Sanctity is more capable of those divine irradiations, whereby it feels itself in conjunction with God, and by a union of rays (as the Greeks speak), the Light of divine goodness mixing itself with the light of its own Reason, sees more clearly not only that it may, if it please the Supreme Deity, of its own nature exist eternally, but also that it shall do so. . . . It is indeed nothing else that makes

men question the Immortality of their Souls, so much as
their own base and earthly loves, which first makes them
wish their Souls were not immortal, and then *think* they
are not; which Plotinus hath well observed and accordingly
hath soberly pursued this argument: . . . "Let us now
(saith he, *Enn.* iv. 7. 10) consider a Soul, not such a one as
is immersed into the Body . . . but such a one as hath cast
away Concupiscence and Anger and other Passions. . . .
Such a one as this will sufficiently manifest that all Vice
is unnatural to the Soul, and something acquired only from
abroad, and that the best Wisdom and all other Virtues
lodge in a purged Soul, as being allied to it. If, therefore,
such a Soul shall reflect upon itself, how shall it not appear
to itself to be of such a kind of nature as Divine and Eternal
Essences are? For Wisdom and true Virtue being Divine
Effluxes can never enter into any unhallowed and mortal
thing: it must, therefore, needs be Divine, seeing it is filled
with a Divine nature by its kindred and consanguinity
therewith. . . . Contemplate, therefore, the Soul of man,
denuding it of all that which itself is not, or let him that
does this, view his own Soul; then he will believe it to be
immortal, when he shall behold it, fixed in an Intelligible
and pure nature; he shall then behold his own intellect
contemplating not any sensible thing, but eternal things,
with that which is eternal, that is, with itself, looking into
the intellectual world, being itself made all lucid, intellectual,
and shining with Sun-beams of eternal Truth, borrowed
from the First Good, which perpetually rayeth forth his
Truth upon all intellectual beings. One thus qualified may
seem without any arrogance to take up that saying of
Empedocles—Farewell all earthly allies, I am henceforth
no mortal wight, but an immortal angel, ascending up into
Divinity, and reflecting upon that likeness of it which I
find in myself. When true Sanctity and Purity shall ground
him in the knowledge of divine things, then shall the inward
sciences that arise from the bottom of his own Soul display
themselves; which, indeed, are the only true sciences; for
the Soul runs not out of itself to behold Temperance and
Justice abroad, but its own light sees them in the contemplation of its own being and that divine essence which was
before enshrined within itself."[1]

So much for Smith's presentation of the "Idea of Soul";
it owes its main features to the doctrine of Love and Recollection set forth in the *Phaedrus* Myth; and the "regulative"
value of the "Idea" is finely appreciated. The regulative

[1] *o.c.* pp. 99-105.

value of the "Idea of God" is as finely appreciated in the
Discourse of the Existence and Nature of God, where he says,[1]
"God is not better defined to us by our *understandings* than
by our *wills and affections*," and notes[2] the pre-eminence, in
Platonism, of the Good, which begets in us the
emotion of Love. Similarly, in his *Discourse of the
Jewish Notion of a Legal Righteousness*, he contrasts the
doctrine of Works set forth by the rabbinical writers
with the Christian doctrine of Faith, and shows that the
latter amounts to a doctrine of "divine grace and bounty
as the only source of righteousness and happiness". St.
Paul's doctrine of "Justification by Faith" is to be explained
platonically as "likeness to God". It is the justification of a
sanctified nature—a nature which, by the grace of God, has
been made a partaker of His life and strength. In Faith
there is a true conjunction and union of the Souls of men
with God, whereby they are made capable of true blessedness. "The Law is merely an external thing consisting in
precepts which have only an outward administration"—it is
the service of the letter and of death: but "the administration of the Gospel is intrinsical and vital in living impressions
upon the Souls of men"—it is the service of the spirit.[3] "By
which," he argues in a significant passage,[4] "the Apostle
(2 Cor. iii. 6, 7) cannot mean the *History* of the Gospel, or
those *credenda* propounded to us to believe; for this would
make the Gospel itself as much an external thing as the
Law was, and according to the external administration as
much a killing or dead letter as the Law was. . . . But,
indeed, he means a *vital efflux* from God upon the Souls of
men, whereby they are made partakers of Life and Strength
from Him."

> I doubt we are too nice Logicians sometimes in dis-
> tinguishing between the *Glory of God* and *our own Salvation*.
> We cannot in a true sense seek our own Salvation more
> than the Glory of God, which triumphs most and discovers
> itself most effectually in the salvation of Souls; for indeed
> this salvation is nothing else but a true participation of the
> Divine Nature. Heaven is not a thing without us, nor is
> Happiness anything distinct from a true conjunction of the
> mind with God in a secret feeling of his goodness and

[1] *o.c.* p. 137. [2] *o.c.* p. 139. [3] *o.c.* p. 311. [4] *o.c.* p. 312.

reciprocation of affection to him, wherein the Divine Glory most unfolds itself. . . . To love God *above ourselves* is not indeed so properly to love him *above the salvation of our Souls*, as if these were distinct things; but it is to love him *above all our own sinful affections*, and *above our particular Beings*. . . . We cannot be completely blessed till the Idea of the Good, or the Good itself, which is God, exercise its sovereignty over all the faculties of our Souls, rendering them as like to itself as may consist with their proper capacity.[1]

I have quoted Smith at considerable length, that the reader may appreciate the place of the Platonist doctrine, or rather discipline, of "ecstasy" in the Life and Philosophy of the Cambridge school. It would be easy to quote similar passages from Cudworth, More, and Norris; but Smith seems to me to "keep his head" better than the others in the intoxicating Neo-Platonic atmosphere, and, moreover, to present "ecstasy" in a form which can be more easily recognised as connecting link between the doctrine of Love and Recollection set forth in the *Phaedrus* Myth and the doctrine of the "Presence of the Eternal Consciousness in my Consciousness", which meets us in the Epistemology and Ethics of T. H. Green and his school.

Leaving the *learning* of the Cambridge Platonists, let us now look at their *science*. Their science was *Cartesian*—that is, it was physics and astronomy treated mathematically, according to mechanical principles, the application of which by Copernicus and Galileo, in the latter branch, had already overthrown the Aristotelian tradition, and produced an intellectual revolution, which can be compared only with that which Darwinism has produced in our own day. Natural science has always been influential in England in giving impulse to Philosophy, and even to Theology. Locke's *Essay* was occasioned and inspired by the activity of the Royal Society; Berkeley's Idealism found expression in a monograph on the physiology of vision; and it was not by mere accident that the University of Newton was the *alma mater* of the English Platonists.

They received the new astronomy with enthusiasm. They were inspired by it. Like Xenophanes, they looked up

---

[1] *o.c.* pp. 410, 411, from "Discourse of the Excellency and Nobleness of True Religion".

at the Heavens and said, "The One is God."[1] "One great
Order" and "Infinite Space" are the scientific ideas which
dominate Cudworth and his friends, and bring conviction
to their belief—otherwise established by the authority of
revelation and Platonic philosophy—in a "Governor of the
Universe", a "Perfect and Infinite Being", a God who, in
Plato's moral phrase, is "The Good", and yet, in scientific
sense, may not unfitly be conceived spatially—as by Cudworth, in a strange passage:[2]—

> It is certain that there can be no mode, accident, or
> affection of Nothing; and consequently, that nothing cannot
> be extended nor measurable. But if space be neither the
> extension of body, nor yet of substance incorporeal, then
> must it of necessity be the extension of nothing, and the
> affection of nothing; and nothing must be measurable by
> yards and poles. We conclude, therefore, that from this
> very hypothesis of the Democritic and Epicurean Atheists,
> that space is a nature distinct from body, and positively
> infinite, it follows undeniably that there must be some
> incorporeal substance whose affection its extension is, and
> because there can be nothing infinite but only the Deity,
> that it is the infinite extension of an incorporeal Deity.

To this strange passage let me append some stanzas from
More's *Philosophickall Poems*, which show how the Copernican
astronomy impressed his imagination—how the centrality of
the Platonic Good in the intelligible world seemed to him to
be imaged by the centrality of the Sun in the visible world.
He has been speaking of the "stiff standers for ag'd
Ptolemee", and proceeds:[3]—

> But let them bark like band-dogs at the moon
> That mindless passeth on in silencie;
> I'll take my flight above this outward Sunne,
> Regardless of such fond malignitie,
> Lift my self up in the Theologie
> Of heavenly Plato. There I'll contemplate
> The *Arch type* of this Sunne, that bright *Idee*
> Of *steddie Good*, that doth his beams dilate
> Through all the worlds, all lives and beings propagate.

---

[1] Arist. *Met.* I. 5. 986 b 24, "Having contemplated the whole heaven,
he declares the One to be God".
[2] *Intellectual System*, vol. iii. p. 232 (ed. Mosheim and Harrison).
[3] *Psychozoia, or Life of the Soul*, pp. 157 ff.

One steddy Good, centre of Essences,
Unmovèd Monad, that *Apollo* hight,
The *Intellectual* Sunne whose energies
Are all things that appear in vital light,
Whose brightness passeth every creature's sight.
Yet round about him, stird with gentle fire,
All things do dance; their being, action, might,
They thither do direct with strong desire,
To embosom him with close embracements they aspire.

Unseen, incomprehensible, He moves
About himself each seeking entity
That never yet shall find that which it loves.
No finite thing shall reach infinity,
No thing dispers'd comprehend that Unity;
Yet in their ranks they seemly foot it round,
Trip it with joy at the world's harmony,
Struck with the pleasure of an amorous stound,
So dance they with fair flowers from unknown root y-crowned.

Still falling short they never fail to seek,
Nor find they nothing by their diligence;
They find repast, their lively longings eek
Rekindled still, by timely influence.
Thus all things in distinct *circumference*
Move about Him that satisfies them all;
Nor be they thus stird up by wary sense
Or foresight, or election rationall,
But blindly reel about the Heart of Lives *centrall*.

So doth the Earth, one of the erring seven,
Wheel round the fixèd Sunne, that is the shade
Of steddy Good, shining in this *Out-heaven*
With the rest of those starres that God hath made
Of baser matter, all which he array'd
With his far-shining light. They sing for joy,
They frisque about in circulings unstay'd,
Dance through the liquid air, and nimbly toy,
While Sol keeps clear the sprite, consumes what may accloy.

The centre of each severall World's a Sunne
With shining beams and kindly warming heat,
About whose radiant crown the Planets runne,
Like reeling moths around a candle light.
These all together one World I conceit.
And that even infinite such worlds there be,
That unexhausted Good that God is hight
A full sufficient reason is to me,
Who simple Goodnesse make the highest Deity.

The mathematical physics of Descartes and the Copernican astronomy were welcomed with joy by the Cambridge Platonists, as affording a far better "Argument from Design" for the existence of God than had been afforded by the Ptolemaic System, which, with its cumbrous commentary of Epicýcles, called the mind away from the wisdom of the Creator to the ingenuity of man. The Copernican astronomy, by taking the fixed stars out of the solid sphere in which the Ptolemaic astronomy held them fast, and showing them to be central suns round which, as round the sun of our system, planets revolve in liquid aether, forces on us the thought that there is an infinity of such solar systems, or worlds, not a rounded-off universe, beyond whose flaming ramparts there is mere nothingness. "The infinity of worlds" was accepted as proof of the existence of an infinite, omnipresent Deity, an Incorporeal Principle—a circle "whose centre is everywhere, and circumference nowhere".[1] A "finite universe" would be an argument for a "Corporeal Deity". This is why the Cambridge Platonists are so anxious to show that the Pythagoreans and Platonists held, with Moses, the doctrine of the motion of the Earth. "Modern Science" had convinced them that this was the only doctrine consistent with a spiritual philosophy.

The profound theological influence which the vast prospect opened up by the reformed astronomy exercised over the minds of men in the seventeenth century cannot be better brought home to us than by a passage in which Newton himself puts his own theological belief on record:[2]—

> The six Primary Planets revolve round the Sun in circles concentrical to the Sun, with the same direction of their motion, and very nearly in the same Plane. The moons (or secondary planets) revolve round the Earth, Jupiter, and Saturn, with the same direction of their motion, and very nearly in the plane of the orbs of the planets. And all these regular motions have not their rise from mechanical causes, seeing the comets are carried in orbs very eccentrical, and that very freely through all parts of the Heavens. . . . This most elegant system of planets and comets could not be produced but by and under the Contrivance and Dominion

[1] More's *Philosophickall Poems*, notes, p. 409.
[2] *Scholium generale* at the end of the *Principia*. I avail myself of Maxwell's translation in his edition of Cumberland's *Laws of Nature*.

of an Intelligent and powerful Being. And, if the fixed stars are the centres of such other systems, all these, being framed by the like counsel, will be subject to the dominion of *One;* especially seeing the Light of the fixed stars is of the same nature with that of the Sun, and the Light of all these systems passes mutually from one to another. And He has placed the systems of the fixed stars at immense distances from one another, lest they should mutually rush upon one another by their gravity. He governs all things, not as the *Soul of the World*, but as the *Lord of the Universe;* and because of His dominion, He is wont to be called *Universal Emperor*. For *God* is a relative word, and hath a relation to servants; and the Deity is the Empire of God, not over His own Body, as is the opinion of those who make Him the Soul of the World, but over His servants. The Supreme God is a Being, Eternal, Infinite, Absolutely Perfect; but a Being, however Perfect, without Dominion, is not Lord God. . . . He governs all things, and knows all things which are done, or which can be done. He is not Eternity and Infinity, but He is Eternal and Infinite; He is not Duration and Space, but He endures and is present: He endures always, and is present everywhere; and by existing always and everywhere, He constitutes Duration and Space, Eternity and Infinity. Whereas every particle of Space is *always*, and every indivisible moment of Duration is *everywhere*, certainly the Framer and Lord of the Universe shall not be *never, nowhere*. . . . We have not any notion of the Substance of God. We know Him only by His properties and attributes, and by the most wise and excellent structure of Things, and by Final Causes; but we adore and worship Him on account of His Dominion. For we worship Him as His servants; and God without Dominion, Providence, and Final Causes, is nothing else but Fate and Nature. There arises no Variety in Things from blind metaphysical necessity, which is always and everywhere the same. All diversity in the Creatures could arise only from the Ideas and Will of a necessarily-existent Being. We speak, however, allegorically when we say that God sees, hears, speaks, laughs, loves, hates, despises, gives, receives, rejoices, is angry, fights, fabricates, builds, composes. For all speech concerning God is borrowed, by Analogy or some Resemblance, from human affairs. . . . So much concerning *God*, of Whom the Discourse from Phenomena belongs to Experimental Philosophy. . . . The main business of Natural Philosophy is to argue from Phenomena without feigning Hypotheses, and to deduce Causes from Effects, till we come to the very First Cause, which certainly is not mechanical.

Besides the better Argument from Design which the reformed astronomy seemed to offer, there was also the famous Cartesian argument from our Idea of a Perfect Being to his Existence. Cudworth[1] seems to feel the difficulties connected with this argument, but is unwilling to declare himself against it. More,[2] however, who is less critical, accepts it thankfully. I have already alluded to one serious objection which Cudworth has to offer to the Cartesian system—viz., that by substituting "mechanism" for the "plastick soul", it leaves the immaterial substance, theoretically retained, little, if anything, to do, and weakens immensely the value of the argument from Design in Nature.[3] However, the general tendency of Cartesianism being favourable to religion, and opposed to Hobbes, Cudworth is satisfied with merely warning his readers against this particular flaw in the system. Holding as he does a brief for Descartes, he argues that "mechanism", in the Cartesian system, is so conceived as to necessitate the assumption of the existence of an immaterial substance as beginning of movement. He evidently attaches more value to this merit in Cartesianism than to its proof of the Existence of God from our Idea of him; and yet it is plainly not a very great merit after all, if we are left with data from which we are, indeed, compelled to infer an Immaterial Power or Force beyond dead matter, but cannot infer Wisdom controlling that Power or Force. We are not surprised, then, to find that Cudworth and his school, Cartesians though they profess to be, are very strenuous in maintaining the contrary of the Cartesian doctrine which makes True and False, Right and Wrong, depend entirely on the Will of God, and not rather on an "Eternal Nature of Things", or "Law of the Ideal World", logically distinct from, and prior to, the Will of God, in accordance with which, however, the Will of God is always exercised. Smith, indeed, the clearest head, I think, among the English Platonists, is so well aware of the difficulty of combining Cartesianism with Platonism that he touches but lightly on the arguments for the existence of God supplied by the

[1] *Intellectual System*, vol. iii. pp. 38 ff.
[2] *An Antidote against Atheism*, Book i. chaps. 7 and 8, pp. 20 ff.
[3] See p. 426 *supra*.

former system, and dwells mainly on the evidence furnished by man's moral nature and sanctified heart. *"A Holy Life,"* he says,[1] "is the best and most compendious way to *Right Belief."* Of the two witnesses spoken of by Kant—"The starry Heaven above, and the Moral Law within"—Smith chose the latter to found his theological belief upon—in this, perhaps, more philosophical than Cudworth and More, the greater lights of the school, who, without ignoring the "argument from the heart", are inclined rather to look to "science"—to "design in nature", and to "epistemology"— for proof of the existence of God.

For the Immortality of the Soul, the other cardinal doctrine of Theology and Morals, Cudworth and More are very busy in producing "scientific" evidence, and, on the whole, find it easy to press the science of their day into the service of the doctrine.

The starting-point of their scientific argument is, that the Soul is an "incorporeal substance". Systems of Philosophy, both ancient and modern, are distinguished as "theistic" and "atheistic", according as they profess or deny the doctrine of "incorporeal substance". The saving merit of Descartes, as we have seen, is that, after all, he recognises "incorporeal substance". On the other hand, Hobbes denies it. In the ninth chapter of the First Book of *The Immortality of the Soul,* More examines Hobbes' disproof of Spirit or incorporeal substance. Hobbes' argument is, "Every substance has dimensions; but a Spirit has no dimensions; therefore there is no spiritual substance". "Here," writes More,[2] "I confidently deny the assumption. For it is not the characteristikall of a *Body* to have dimensions, but to be *impenetrable.* All Substance has *dimensions*— that is, Length, Breadth, and Depth; but all has not *impenetrability.* See my letters to Monsieur Des Cartes." This refutation of Hobbes falls back on the definitions of Spirit and of Body which More has given in an earlier part of the same treatise[3]—Spirit is defined as "a Substance penetrable and indiscerpible"; Body, as "a Substance impenetrable and discerpible". This definition he amends in the chapter

---

[1] *The True Way or Method of attaining to Divine Knowledge,* p. 9.
[2] Page 41. [3] Page 21.

against Hobbes, putting it thus:—Spirit or Incorporeal is "Extended Substance, with *activity* and *indiscerpibility*, leaving out *impenetrability*". More thus plainly ranges himself with those who assumed an extended incorporeal substance; but, of course, there were many incorporealists, among whom was Plotinus,[1] who regarded Spirit as unextended. Cudworth compares the opposite views of these two classes of incorporealists at great length, and ends[2] by leaving the question open, although one might gather that he inclines to the view favoured by More from his speaking of Space as incorporeal *substance*, with the attribute of extension, and infinite; and therefore as equivalent to God, who is the only infinite substance.[3]

But the "incorporeal substance" of Descartes, though a good enough "scientific" beginning for a doctrine of the Immortality of the Soul, is only a beginning; just as it is only a beginning for a "scientific" proof of the existence of God. Cartesianism falls short, according to the Cambridge School, as we have seen, in ignoring the "plastic principle", or "soul of nature". It leaves us between the horns of a dilemma: either mere mechanism, once started by God, produces effects blindly; or God interferes personally in the smallest details. The plastic principle releases us from this dilemma. It may be described as an incorporeal substance, or principle, which, like Aristotle's Nature, works of its own accord without consciousness. To it God, who is Selfconscious Goodness and Wisdom, delegates, as it were, the task of carrying on the operations of nature: these operations are therefore God's operations, and His goodness and wisdom may be inferred from them; but we are not obliged to hold the ridiculous opinion that He produces them by immediate intervention. It is the plastic principle which, in the inorganic world, immediately determines, *e.g.*, the distances of the fixed stars from one another and the paths of their planets, and, in the organic world, appears as that "vegetative part of the Soul" which builds up the body terrestrial, aerial or aethereal, without which, as "vehicle", consciousness would be impossible in the case of finite

---

[1] See Cudworth, *Intell. System*, vol. iii. p. 386.
[2] *o.c.* iii. 398.   [3] *o.c.* iii. 232.

spirits:[1] without this plastic, vehicle-building, principle there could be no "reproduction", to use T. H. Green's terms, of the "Eternal Consciousness". I have already, in an early part of this work,[2] had occasion to describe the use which More makes of the plastic principle in his account of the future existence of the Soul, and would only add here that Cudworth treats of the principle in his *Intellectual System*, vol. i. pp. 235-252 (ed. Mosheim and Harrison)—in a passage well worth the attention of any one interested in the point at issue between the "teleological" and the "mechanical" explanation of the world. The English Platonist of the seventeenth century, with his "plastic soul", makes out, I venture to think, as plausible a case for "teleology" as his successor, the English Idealist of the nineteenth or twentieth century, manages to do with his "spiritual principle". The chief difference between the two advocates is that the former tells us frankly that his plastic soul is "unconscious", while the latter leaves us in doubt whether his "spiritual principle" is "conscious" or "unconscious".

Having attempted to describe—in mere outline—the *learning* and the *science* of the Cambridge Platonists, I now go on to compare their central doctrine with that of the English Idealists of the present day—the school of which T. H. Green may be taken as representative. The comparison will show, I think, that the central doctrine of these English Idealists, equally with that of the Cambridge Platonists, is to be traced to Plato—and to Plato the mythologist, rather than to Plato the dialectician.

The central doctrine of the Cambridge Platonists is the Doctrine of Ideas as presented in the *Phaedrus* Myth—that is, presented to religious feeling as theory of the union of man with God in knowledge and conduct. In the Doctrine of Ideas, as it is presented to the scientific understanding in such contributions to Logic as *Republic*, 509 D ff., the Cambridge Platonists, like their Alexandrine predecessors, seem to take little interest.

The Doctrine of Ideas as adopted by the Cambridge

---

[1] Cudworth thinks it "probable" that no spirit except God can exist without a body of some kind (*Intell. System*, vol. iii. p. 368).
[2] Pages 113 ff.

Platonists may be stated as follows:—Sensible things, which come into existence and perish, are but reflections, images, ectypes, of Eternal Essences, Archetypal Forms, or Ideas. These Ideas are the "Thoughts" of God—the elements which constitute his Eternal Wisdom. The Wisdom of God is that World of Ideas, that *mundus archetypus*, according to the conception of which he created this visible world. Man attains to knowledge only in so far as he apprehends these Eternal Thoughts of the Divine Wisdom—only in so far as, spurred to reflection by the stimuli of sense, he enters into communion with the Mind of God, "sees things in God". This communion is possible only because man's spirit is of one kind with the spirit of God. "All minds partake of one original mind,"[1] are "reproductions of the Eternal Consciousness"[2]—find that its eternal Ideas are theirs too. Thus epistemology involves theology. The theory of knowledge involves the supposition of a "universal consciousness", or "Wisdom of God", as Eternal Subject of those "forms", without the constructive activity of which in the mind of man his sensations would be "blind".

From this sketch it may be seen that the doctrine of archetypal Ideas amounts, in the English Intellectualists, to a Theory of Knowledge, in which the *a priori* element is recognised, as in the Kantian philosophy. Let me fill in my sketch by quoting some passages from More, Cudworth, Smith, Norris, and Berkeley.

In his *antidote against Atheism*,[3] More speaks of "relative notions or ideas"—Cause and Effect, Whole and Part, Like and Unlike—in much the same way as Kant speaks of his "Categories of the Understanding". These "relative ideas", he says, "are no external Impresses upon the senses, but the Soul's own active manner of conceiving those things which are discovered by the outward senses." Again, in the *Cabbala*,[4] in a passage which carries us out of the "Critique of Pure Reason" into the "Metaphysic of Morals", he says: "The Soul of man is not merely passive as a piece of wood or stone, but is forthwith made active by being acted upon; and therefore if God in us rules, we rule with him; if he

---

[1] Cudworth, *Int. System*, iii. 62.
[2] Green, *Prolegomena to Ethics*.
[3] Page 18, bk. i. ch. 6.
[4] Page 154.

contend against sin in us, we also contend together with
him against the same; if he see in us what is good or evil,
we, *ipso facto*, see by him—*In his light we see light;* and so in
the rest." Again, in his *Philosophickall Poems,*[1] the following
curious passage occurs—a passage, I venture to think, of
considerable philosophic import, on account of the wide.
view taken of *innate ideas,* or *a priori forms:* bodies, it is
suggested, are shaped, as well as conscious experience
organised, according to *a priori,* constitutional forms:—

> If plantall souls in their own selves contain
> That vital formative fecundity,
> That they a tree with different colours stain,
> And diverse shapes, smoothnesse, asperity,
> Straightnesse, acutenesse, and rotoundity,
> A golden yellow, or a crimson red,
> A varnish'd green with such like gallantry;
> How dull then is the sensitive? how dead,
> If forms from its own centre it can never spread?

> Again, an universal notion,
> What object ever did that form impresse
> Upon the soul? What makes us venture on
> So rash a matter, as e'er to confesse
> Ought generally true? when neverthelesse
> We cannot e'er runne through all singulars.
> Wherefore in our own souls we do possesse
> Free forms and immateriall characters,
> Hence 'tis the soul so boldly generall truth declares.

> *　　*　　*　　*　　*　　*

> What body ever yet could figure show
> Perfectly, perfect, as rotundity,
> Exactly round, or blamelesse angularity?
> Yet doth the soul of such like forms discourse,
> And finden fault at this deficiency,
> And rightly term this better and that worse;
> Wherefore the measure is our own *Idee,*
> Which th' humane Soul in her own self doth see.
> And sooth to sayen whenever she doth strive
> To find pure truth, her own profundity
> She enters, in her self doth deeply dive;
> From thence attempts each essence rightly to descrive.

The lines with which the last stanza ends find their
commentary in a passage in Smith's *Discourse of the Im-*

[1] Page 238.

mortality of the Soul,[1] in which the movement of a flock of sheep and the cyclic movement of the Soul are distinguished. By the former she goes forth and deals with material things; by the latter she reflects upon herself. What she finds by "reflection" he sets forth in his *Discourse concerning the Existence and Nature of God*.[2]

> Plotinus hath well taught us, *He which reflects upon himself, reflects upon his own Originall*, and finds the clearest Impression of some Eternall Nature and Perfect Being stamp'd upon his own Soul. And therefore Plato seems sometimes to reprove the ruder sort of men in his times for their contrivance of Pictures and Images to put themselves in mind of the Divinities or Angelicall Beings, and exhorts them to look into their own Souls, which are the fairest Images, not onely of the lower Divine Natures, but of the Deity itself; God having so copied forth himself into the whole life and energy of man's Soul, as that the lovely Characters of Divinity may be most easily seen and read of all men within themselves; as they say Phidias the famous statuary, after he made the statue of Minerva with the greatest exquisiteness of art to be set up in the Acropolis at Athens, afterwards impressed his own Image so deeply in her buckler, "that no-one could destroy or remove it, without threatening the whole statue." And if we would know what the Impresse of Souls is, it is nothing but God himself, who could not write his own name so as that it might be read but onely in Rationall Natures. Neither could he make such without imparting such an Imitation of his own Eternall Understanding to them as might be a perpetual Memorial of himself within them. And whenever we look upon our own Soul in a right manner, we shall find an *Urim* and *Thummim* there, by which we may ask counsel of God himself, who will have this alway born upon its breastplate.

The passage which I shall quote from Cudworth is a criticism of Hobbes' "atheistical" doctrine that "knowledge and understanding being in us nothing else but a tumult in the mind raised by external things that press the organical parts of a man's body, there is no such thing in God, nor can they be attributed to him, they being things which depend upon natural causes."[3] To this Cudworth replies:—

> There comes nothing to us from bodies without us but only local motion and pressure. Neither is sense itself the

[1] Pages 65, 66.   [2] Pages 123, 124.   [3] *Intell. System*, iii, p. 60.

mere passion of those motions, but the perception of their
passions in a way of fancy. But sensible things themselves
(as, for example, light and colours) are not known or understood either by the passion or the fancy of sense, nor by
anything merely foreign and adventitious, but by intelligible
ideas exerted from the mind itself—that is, by something
native and domestic to it. . . . Wherefore, besides the
phantasms of singular bodies, or of sensible things existing
without us (which are not mere passions neither), it is
plain that our human mind hath other cogitations or conceptions in it—namely, the ideas of the intelligible natures
and essences of things, which are universal, and by and
under which it understands singulars . . . which universal
objects of our mind, though they exist not as such anywhere
without it, yet are they not therefore nothing, but have an
intelligible entity for this very reason, because they are
conceivable. . . . If, therefore, there be eternal intelligibles
or ideas, and eternal truths and necessary existence do
belong to them, then must there be an eternal mind necessarily existing, since these truths and intelligible essences of
things cannot possibly be anywhere but in a mind. . . .
There must be a mind senior to the world, and all sensible
things, and such as at once comprehends in it the ideas of
all intelligibles, their necessary scheses and relations to one
another, and all their immutable truths; a mind which doth
not (as Aristotle writeth it), sometimes understand, and
sometimes not understand. . . . but such a mind as is
essentially act and energy, and hath no defect in it. . . .
Hence it is evident that there can be but one only original
mind . . . all other minds whatsoever partaking of one
original mind, and being, as it were, stamped with the
impression or signature of one and the same seal. From
whence it cometh to pass that all minds, in the several
places and ages of the world, have ideas or notions of
things exactly alike, and truths indivisibly the same. Truths
are not multiplied by the diversity of minds that apprehend
them, because they are all but ectypal participations of
one and the same original or archetypal mind and truth.
As the same face may be reflected in several glasses, and
the image of the same sun may be in a thousand eyes at
once beholding it, and one and the same voice may be in a
thousand ears listening to it, so when innumerable created
minds have the same ideas of things, and understand the
same truths, it is but one and the same eternal light that is
reflected in them all (that light which enlighteneth every
.man that cometh into the world), or the same voice of
that one everlasting Word, that is never silent, re-echoed
by them. . . . We conclude, therefore, that from the nature
of mind and knowledge it is demonstrable that there can

be but one original and self-existent Mind, or understanding Being, from which all other minds were derived.[1]

This is a passage, I venture to think, of first-rate historical importance. It furnishes the link which connects the Epistemological Theism which we find in the writings of T. H. Green with the Mythology of the *Timaeus* and *Phaedrus*.

Norris's discussion of the *a priori* in knowledge has some points of special interest. Having shown, in the ordinary way, that there are eternal and necessary Truths, *i.e.* eternal and necessary Propositions, he dwells on the point that the simple essences, the mutual relations or habitudes of which are set forth in these propositions, must be themselves eternal and necessary. "There can be no mutual habitudes or relations of things as to affirmation or negation," he says,[2] "without the reality of the things themselves." The point here insisted on by Norris is one which the modern *dictum*, "Things are nothing except as determined by Relations," is apt to make us lose sight of; and his remarks following seem to me to be worth attention:—

> *Two circles touching one another inwardly cannot have the same common centre.* This is a true Proposition. But I here demand, How can it possibly have this certain habitude of division or negation unless there be two such distinct simple Essences as Circle and Centre. Certainly there can be no reference or relation where there is nothing to support it. . . . If there can be no connexion or relation between things that are not, then also there can be no *eternal* connexion or relation between things that have not an *eternal* existence. . . . But there are such eternal habitudes and relations, therefore the simple Essences of things are also eternal. . . . I know very well this is not according to the Decrees of the Peripatetic School, which has long since condemned it as Heretical Doctrine, to say that the Essences of things do exist from eternity. . . . They tell us that the habitudes are not attributed *absolutely* to the simple Essences as in actual being, but only *hypothetically*—that whensoever they shall exist, they shall also carry such relations to one another. There is, says the Peripatetic, only a *conditional* connexion between the subject and the predicate, not an *absolute* position of either. This goes smoothly down with the young scholar at his Logic Lecture, and the Tutor applauds

[1] *Intell. System*, iii. pp. 62-72.
[2] *Reason and Religion*, p. 73.

his distinction, and thinks he has thereby quitted his hands of a very dangerous heresie. But now to this I return answer . . . that these habitudes are not (as is supposed) only by way of hypothesis, but absolutely attributed to the simple Essences, as actually existing. For when I say, for instance, that every part of a circle is equally distant from the centre, this proposition does not hang in suspense, then to be actually verified when the things shall exist in *Nature*, but is at *present* actually true, as actually true as ever it will or can be; and consequently I may thence infer that the things themselves already are. There is no necessity, I confess, they should exist in *Nature*, which is *all* that the objection proves, but *exist* they must. For of nothing there can be no affection. . . . Having cleared our way by making it evident that the simple Essences of things are eternal, the next thing that I consider is, that since they are not eternal in their *natural subsistencies*, they must be eternal in some other way of subsisting. And that must be in some understanding, or by way of *ideal subsistence*.[1] For there are but two conceivable ways how anything may exist, either *out* of all understanding, or *within* some understanding. If, therefore, the simple Essences of things are eternal, but not *out* of all understanding, it remains they must have an eternal existence in some understanding. Which is what I call an *ideal subsistence*. There is, therefore, another way of existing besides that in the Natural World, namely, in the Ideal World, where all the simple Essences of things, have an eternal and immutable existence, before ever they enter upon the Stage of Nature. I further consider, that this understanding wherein the simple Essences of things have an eternal existence must be an eternal understanding. For an Essence can no more eternally exist in a temporary understanding than a body can be infinitely extended in a finite space. Now, this Eternal Understanding can be no other than the Understanding of God. The simple Essences of things, therefore, do eternally exist in the Understanding of God.[2]

God, Norris goes on to argue, is a simple and uncompounded Being, and there is nothing in Him which is not Himself; accordingly, these Eternal Ideas, or Simple Essences of Things; are but the Divine Essence itself, considered "as variously exhibitive of things, and as variously

---

[1] Norris here (*Reason and Religion*, p. 80) draws the distinction of which Lotze makes so much in his *Logic* (Book iii. ch. 2, *The World of Ideas*, pp. 433 ff., English Transl.), between the Reality of Existence and the Reality of Validity.

[2] *Reason and Religion*, pp. 74-81.

imitable or participable by them".[1] "This Ideal World, this Essence of God considered as variously exhibitive and representative of things, is no other than the Divine Logos, the Second Person of the ever Blessed Trinity."[2] Descartes, it is argued,[3] makes God, as *conceptive*, the cause of Truth— *i.e.* as pleased to conceive—*e.g.* a Triangle so and so—not as *exhibitive* of the Eternal Ideas. Here Descartes "blunders horribly". "I am for the dependence of Truth upon the Divine Intellect as well as he, but not so as to make it *arbitrary* and *contingent*, and consequently not upon the Divine Intellect as *conceptive*, but only as *exhibitive*. That is, that things are therefore true inasmuch as they are conformable to those *standing* and *immutable Ideas* which are in the mind of God as Exhibitive and representative of the whole Possibility of Being." God is omniscient, as "comprehending within himself all the Ideas and Essences of things with all their possible references and respects, that is, *all Truth*"[4]—a doctrine which seems to me to be exactly equivalent to T. H. Green's doctrine of "the Eternal Consciousness as subject of all Relations". "We see and know all things in God."[5] This doctrine, Norris tells us, he thought out for himself, and afterwards found in Plotinus, Proclus, St. Augustine, Marsilius Ficinus, and especially in Malebranche, whose doctrine he then proceeds to state:[6]—We know objects by the mediation of "Ideas". The "Ideas" of things are in God. "God by his presence is intimately united to our minds, so that God may be said to be the *Place of Spirits*, as Space is the *Place of Bodies*." Thus "we see all things in God".[7] This is the doctrine of Malebranche, accepted by Norris—a doctrine which labours under the ambiguity attaching to its use of the term "Idea", which means both a mental image derived from a sensible object, and an eternal idea in the Platonic acceptation. But we need not go into this difficulty in Malebranche's doctrine; it is enough here to notice that Norris understands the doctrine as genuinely Platonic. Plato's definition of knowledge as a "Participation of Ideas" amounts, he says,[8] to "seeing all things in God".

---

[1] *o.c.* pp. 81, 82.   [2] *o.c.* p. 85.   [3] *o.c.* pp. 92, 93.
[4] *o.c.* p. 101.   [5] *o.c.* p. 185.   [6] *o.c.* pp. 187-194.
[7] *o.c.* p. 202.   [8] *o.c.* p. 207.

"If we did not some way or other *see God*, we should *see nothing* at all; even as if we did not *love God*, that is, if God did not continually impress upon us the love of good in general, we should *love nothing* at all: for since this Love is the same with our Will, we cannot love or will anything without him, since we cannot love particular goods but by determining towards those goods that motion of Love which God gives us towards himself."[1] "All our Illumination proceeds from the Divine Logos, the substantial Wisdom of God. But St. John speaks more plainly: *This is the true light which enlightens every man that comes into the world.* Now, *true* Light is here the same as *only* Light, and implies that all other pretended lights are false ones. Again, says our Lord, *I am the Light of the World.* And, *I am the way, the truth, and the life.* And again says our Lord in his Prayer, *Sanctifie them through thy truth; thy word is truth:* which is not meant of the written word, but of the Substantial and Eternal Word, as appears from the context. Lastly, the Apostle says expressly of this Divine Word, that *he is made unto us Wisdom.* Which is exactly according to our hypothesis that we see all things in the Ideal World, or Divine Logos. . . . All our Light and Illumination proceeds wholly from him who at first said *let there be light.* We see so much of *Truth* as we see of *God.* The Ideas which are in God are the very Ideas which we see. The Divine Logos is *our Wisdom,* as well as the *Wisdom of his Father.* So absolutely necessary is the *Doctrine of Ideas,* when rightly stated, to the explaining the Mode both of *Divine* and *Human* knowledge; without which I shall venture to affirm that they can neither of them be *explained or understood.*"[2]

The Lord is my Light: "The Platonic Philosophers do wonderfully refine upon Light, and soar very high," as Berkeley writes in *Siris*[3]—himself, at last, a professed adherent of the school of Cudworth:—

As understanding perceiveth not, that is, doth not hear, or see, or feel, so sense knoweth not; and although the mind may use both sense and fancy as means whereby to arrive at knowledge, yet sense or soul, so far forth as sensitive, knoweth nothing. For as it is rightly observed in the *Theaetetus* of Plato, science consists not in the passive perceptions, but in the reasoning upon them.[4]

So much for the epistemology, strictly so called, of the

[1] *o.c.* p. 200.
[3] § 210.
[2] *o.c.* pp. 222-224.
[4] *Siris,* § 305.

Cambridge Platonists. It is a theory of the communion of man with God, derived from the doctrine of ideas as set forth "mythologically" in the *Timaeus*, *Phaedrus*, and *Symposium*.

It is easy to see how this epistemology explains the function ascribed by the school to Reason, as Moral Faculty —as recognising and imposing Obligation. Morality is the Rational Life—the Life regulated by the consciousness of Self, not as passive in the midst of the flux of vanishing sensibles, but as actively displaying its own spiritual nature and kinship with God by communicating in His eternal and immutable nature. Its rational communion in his nature is not an outward act, like looking at a picture which one may turn away from when one pleases: it is an inward act of reflection—cyclic motion—revealing *one's own* permanent nature—permanent, in that it "mirrors" or "reproduces" God's nature; it is an inward act revealing *one's own* permanent nature, which one cannot—even when it would please one to do so—turn one's back upon. The object of Reason, with which Reason is itself identical, is *the whole man*, regarded from the viewpoint of eternity, seen in God, seen in his own proper place in the Cosmos. This object cannot be set aside, as the object of a passing inclination may be set aside. This is how "Reason imposes Obligation". Nor does the physical organism of plant or animal differ in this respect from the moral nature, if we consider the matter philosophically. It *obliges* those functions and acts which are in accordance with its particular Type, its particular Type being a "mode" of the Universe.

"Reason," then, as it is understood by the Platonists, being the consciousness of Self as creature made after the image of God—as mirror of the eternal reasons of things which constitute the Divine Wisdom—"Reason," being this, needs not to have its dictates enforced by any alien power: in being promulgated they are carried out. The moral life is, on its plane, as inevitable as the physical life. All living creatures strive after that good which is competent to their several types in the places which they hold in the great system of the Universe. "There is nothing," says Norris,[1] "in nature more necessary—no, nor *so* necessary

---

[1] *Reason and Religion*, pp. 237, 238.

and invincible, as that motion whereby we are carried forth
to good in general. Here the Soul must not pretend to the
least shadow of Liberty, having no more command over this
motion than she has over the motion of the Sun." "God is
that which we directly and properly love (or desire), and
created goods, or particular goods, are only so far loved as
they resemble and participate of the nature of that universal
good." "If we did not love God . . . we should love nothing
at all. . . . This Love is the same with our Will."[1] We are
reminded of Aristotle's "the divine in us", that answering
nisus or love in us, and in all living creatures, which is
awakened by God, who, himself unmoved, moves all things
by the attraction of loveliness—a doctrine glossed by
Plotinus, where he says that the Principle of Organic Life
is Love contemplating the Ideal Forms, and, by its mere
act of silent contemplation, producing embodiments of them.[2]

That "Reason", in the epistemology and moral theology
of our Platonists, is consciousness of the Whole—of God-in-
Man and Man-in-God—is a point which it is important to
keep steadily in view, not only if we would understand what
is meant by "obligation", but also if we would get behind
phrases to real meaning, when we are told that the "Truths
apprehended by Reason" are "eternal and immutable",
that is, "necessary," being at once the contents of the
Divine Wisdom and the conditions of human knowledge.
No "Truth", taken by itself, can be apprehended as
"necessary"; it can only be accepted as a hypothesis. The
"necessity" of a "Truth" is apparent only to a synoptic
gaze, which takes in the whole order of which the "Truth"
is a part. The whole is first acquiesced in as self-evident
principle, and then we see that its parts severally "cannot
be otherwise". This is the gist of the passage at the end of
the Sixth Book of the *Republic*, where the function of Reason
in Dialectic is set forth. A "Truth" is seen to be "necessary"
when it is seen to be involved in the "whole"; and the
progress of knowledge is a process of integration by which
scattered limbs of experience are pieced together into a
consistent whole, and their natures seen to be such as "cannot
be otherwise". But this process would be impossible unless

---

[1] *o.c.* p. 200.   [2] *Enn.* iii. 8. 7.

the Rational Soul came to her task of integration with a native idea of the "whole". This native idea is not something which is a mere *part* of her. It is herself—the unity of her selfhood of which she is conscious. As her knowledge advances—that is, as she brings more and more data into clearly-seen relation with her own "self-centrality", as More phrases it, she herself spreads from her centre, becoming more and more "adequate" to the objective world, more and more assimilated to God. This growth of the Rational Soul in "Likeness to God"—in "correspondence with environment"—expresses the law of her inmost being, commanding categorically: *Live thy Life.*

"Reason," then, according to the Platonic school, is "organism". How shallow the criticism which finds fault with them for giving us, in Reason, a principle which is not a principle of action, and carries with it no consciousness of obligation! As if organism, with its invincible will to live, did not move, and oblige, to action!

The central doctrine of the English Platonists, which I am trying to set forth, gives an important place to the discussion of the relation of God's "Will" to his "Wisdom and Goodness". By the "Wisdom and Goodness" of God they understand the perfect order of that archetypal world, or system of ideas, or concepts, dwelling from all eternity in the Divine Intellect; by the "Will" of God, the going forth of his Power in the production and preservation of this visible world and all that is in it. They maintain, against Descartes and others, that God's "Will" did not make, and cannot alter, the contents of the intelligible world, which have natures "essential", not "arbitrary". God's "Will" is ruled by his "Wisdom and Goodness"—that is, his "Will" expresses his essential nature. He cannot make right wrong, or true false, by arbitrary act of Will.

> If God do all things simply at his pleasure[1]
> Because he will, and not because it's good,
> So that his actions will have no set measure;
> Is 't possible it should be understood
> What he intends? I feel that he is loved

[1] More, *Phil. Poems*, p. 179.

Of my dear soul, and know that I have borne
Much for his sake; yet is it not hence proved
That I shall live, though I do sigh and mourn
To find his face; his creature's wish he'll slight and scorn.

Nor of well-being, nor subsistency
Of our poor souls, when they do hence depart,
Can any be assured, if liberty
We give to such odde thoughts, that thus pervert
The laws of God, and rashly do assert
That Will rules God, but *Good* rules not God's Will.
What e'er from right, love, equity, doth start,
For ought we know then God may act that ill,
Only to show his might, and his free mind fulfill.

To the same effect, Cudworth:[1]—

Plotinus writeth, "The Deity acteth according to its own nature and essence; and its nature and essence displayeth goodness and justice: for if these things be not there, where should they else be found?" And again, elsewhere: "God is essentially that which ought to be: and therefore he did not happen to be such as he is: and this first *ought to be* is the principle of all things whatsoever that ought to be." Wherefore the Deity is not to be conceived as mere arbitrariness, humour, or irrational will and appetite omnipotent (which would, indeed, be but omnipotent chance), but as an overflowing fountain of love and goodness, justly and wisely dispensing itself, and omnipotently reaching all things. The will of God is goodness, justice, and wisdom; or decorousness, and ought itself, willing; so that that which is absolutely the best, is "an indispensable law to it, because its very essence." God is an "impartial balance" lying even, equal, and indifferent, to all things, and weighing out heaven and earth, and all the things therein, in the most just and exact proportions, and not a grain too much or too little of anything. Nor is the Deity therefore bound or obliged to do the best, in any way of servility (as men fondly imagine this to be contrary to his liberty), much less by the law and command of any superior (which is a contradiction), but only by the perfection of its own nature, which it cannot possibly deviate from, no more than ungod itself.

Now, we must not regard this question of the relation of the "Will" to the "Wisdom and Goodness" of God as one of those bygone questions of scholasticism with which we need

[1] *Intell. System*, iii. 463, 464.

no longer, in our day, trouble ourselves. It is a present-day question—indeed, a perennial question. It raises the whole issue of Pessimism against Optimism.

Pessimism will never infect the bulk of mankind—those who do not reflect, but push their way on, and lead ambitious, industrious lives; but reflective idle people—a growing number in the modern world—it is likely to infect more and more. It is likely to get hold of literature, and even of philosophy, to a greater extent. The number is steadily growing of those who are educated in book-learning, and can make a living by supplying idle readers with reflections on life embodied in the novel and other forms of "light reading". Pessimism suits well with the mood which such writers have to cater for—the mood of habitual lookers-on at life; but those whose energetic temperament moves them to put their hand to things and try to get them done are not troubled with the suspicion that all their work is vanity.

It was a profound insight which caused Plato to debar from philosophy all those who were not likely to have an opportunity of taking an active part in affairs.[1] It is Plato, of all the Greeks the most enthusiastically possessed by the idea of Greek civilisation as an influence to be propagated in the world—it is Plato, with his firm practical hold of the belief that Life is worth living—who stands out, in the History of Philosophy, as the opponent of individualism, whether hedonistic or pessimistic. The individualists of his day, the Sophists, whom he opposes expressly or by implication throughout the whole range of his writings, were men for the most part without close political ties, aliens in the cities where they taught, who cultivated philosophy without patriotism and religion. It was from them that the doctrine "Righteousness does not come by nature, but by law alone," came—a doctrine which answers to the view combated by the Cambridge Platonists, that Right and Wrong, True and False, are creatures of God's arbitrary Will. If this is true, the "virtuously happy, or holy, life" is not worth pursuing; chance is lord of all, and strenuous effort on our part is labour lost. This was how the Cambridge Platonists argued. In our own day, Pessimism is most often disappointed

---

[1] *Republic*, 473 D.

Hedonism. But it may well come from any cause which damps the energies of men: thus, the doctrine of Determinism may produce it by persuading us that our actions are all determined beforehand by the destiny of the Universe, and that we are but the passive spectators even of our own actions. Without denying that destiny, in the sense of law universal, determines our actions, I would submit that the doctrine is too abstract to be of practical consequence. It takes us back to the chief general assumption—the Universe— and omits the immediate antecedent—the concrete character of the individual who performs the actions. It is this immediate antecedent, however, which one who wishes to take a scientific view of the actions must chiefly consider—the Universe, or chain of remote antecedents, may "go without saying"; and, above all, it is this immediate antecedent on which the agent himself must fix his attention; he must "look to *himself*", as the phrase is, not to "the Universe", if he is to do anything worth doing. The abstract doctrine of Determinism, by calling attention away too much from the immediate antecedent of actions—the concrete agent himself— is at once unscientific and practically harmful, tending to paralyse the energy of the agent whose actions it seeks to account for. The agent must "believe in *himself*" if actions are to be done; and he cannot believe in *himself* unless he believes in a system of things which is suitable to him, in which he can get on—a friendly, not an alien world. These two beliefs go together—belief in Self, and belief in a Friendly World. They are the two faces of the same coin. And this is the great truth signified by the doctrine of *Reflection*—circular movement—set forth by the Cambridge Platonists—their doctrine that the Soul's *reflection upon herself* reveals to her that system of Eternal Truths which are at once the principles of human knowledge and conduct, and the Thoughts of God in accordance with which his Will is determined to do everything for the Best. The only sovereign antidote against Pessimism is a belief (tacit, or expressed—better, perhaps, tacit) of this sort. But such belief, it must be remembered, rests not on speculative grounds, but is the birth of conduct. It is the possession of those only who are *in earnest about* the practical life. The issue between "Mechanism" and "Teleology"—for that, again, is the issue involved in the question about the relation of God's "Will" to his "Wisdom and Goodness"—is not one to be settled by logical thinkers, but by moral agents. Logical thinkers, it seems to me, must decide in favour of "Mechanism"; moral agents will always decide in favour of "Teleology". And they are right, because "Teleology" is the working hypothesis of Life, whereas the doctrine of "Mechanism" damps the vital energy on which Life, including the logical understanding itself, depends for its continuance.

The central doctrine of the Cambridge Platonists receives considerable illumination from their treatment of the famous maxim, identified chiefly with the name of Descartes, "Clear and distinct ideas must be true". The maxim, of course, can be traced back to Plato himself, who, at the end of the Sixth Book of the *Republic*, makes clarity the test of truth. It is a maxim which undoubtedly lends itself to abuse, if not limited, as it is carefully limited by Plato in the passage just mentioned, as referring only to "ideas" in the sense of "categories" or "notions"—*organic conditions* of experience— and not also to "ideas" in the more ordinary sense—of "impressions", or *data* of experience. Kant's final proof of the apriority of his Categories of the Understanding is that "we cannot think them away"—their opposites are in- conceivable—they belong to the structure of the mind—are not data received by it. Similarly, the Cambridge Platonists accept as principles of knowledge and conduct those Ideas which the circular motion, or Reflection of the Soul upon herself as mirror of the Divine Wisdom, sees clearly and distinctly. Such are the "relative ideas" (as More calls them), Cause and Effect, Whole and Part, etc., and the Ideas of God and of Immortality. The truth of such "Ideas" is simply "their clear intelligibility". Their truth needs no other witness. It is in order to maintain this view of the self-evident truth of these "Ideas" or "Categories" that Cudworth submits to a searching criticism Descartes' doctrine, that we fall back upon the supposition of the "Veracity of God" as ground of our belief that our clear and distinct ideas do not deceive us. Against this doctrine he argues that not even God could make clear and distinct "Ideas", in the sense of Categories, or principles of knowledge, false: they are essentially true; and their clear intelligibility is alone sufficient warrant of their truth, or objective validity. Our very "Idea" of a Perfect, and therefore Veracious, God is itself one of these categories the truth of which is warranted by their "clear intelligibility". The passage[1] in which Cudworth makes this point against Descartes is, indeed, a notable passage in the History of the "Theory of Knowledge", and merits close comparison with Kant's *Transcendental Analytic* :—

> It hath been asserted by a late eminent philosopher that there is no possible certainty to be had of anything, before we be certain of the existence of a God essentially good; because we can never otherwise free our minds from the importunity of that suspicion which with irresistible force may assault them; that ourselves might possibly be so made, either by chance or fate, or by the pleasure of some evil demon, or at least of an arbitrary omnipotent Deity, as that we should be deceived in all our most clear and evident perceptions, and, therefore, in geometrical theorems themselves, and even in our common notions. But when we are once assured of the existence of such a God as is essentially good—who, therefore, neither will nor can deceive—then, and not before, will this suspicion utterly vanish, and ourselves become certain that our faculties of reason and understanding are not false and imposturous, but rightly made. . . . Now, though there be a plausibility of piety in this doctrine . . . yet does that very supposition that our understanding faculties might possibly be so made as to deceive us in all our clearest perceptions, render it utterly impossible ever to arrive to any certainty concerning the existence of a God essentially good; forasmuch as this cannot be any otherwise proved than by the use of our faculties of understanding, reason, and discourse. For to say that the truth of our understanding faculties is put out of all doubt and question as soon as ever we are assured of the existence of a God essentially good, who therefore cannot deceive; whilst the existence of a God is in the meantime itself no otherwise proved than by our understanding faculties; that is at once to prove the truth of God's existence from our faculties of reason and understanding, and again to prove the truth of those faculties from the existence of a God essentially good: this, I say, is plainly to move round

[1] *Intell. System*, iii. 31-35.

in a circle, and to prove nothing at all . . . so that if we will
pretend to any certainty at all concerning the existence of a
God, we must of necessity explode this new-supplied hypothesis of the possibility of our understandings being so
made as to deceive us in all our clearest perceptions. . . .
In the first place, therefore, we affirm that no power, how
great soever, and therefore not omnipotence itself, can make
anything to be indifferently either true or false. . . . Truth
is not factitious; it is a thing which cannot be arbitrarily
made, but *is*. The divine will and omnipotence itself hath
no imperium upon the divine understanding; for if God
understood only by will, he could not understand at all.
In the next place, we add that, though the truth of singular
contingent propositions depends upon the things themselves
existing without, as the measure and archetype thereof, yet
as to the universal and abstract theorems of science, the
terms whereof are those reasons of things which exist nowhere but only in the mind itself (whose noemata and
ideas they are), the measure and rule of truth concerning
them can be no foreign or extraneous thing without the
mind, but must be native and domestic to it, or contained
within the mind itself, and therefore can be nothing but its
clear and distinct perception. In these intelligible ideas of
the mind whatsoever is clearly perceived to be is; or, which is
all one, is true. . . . The very essence of truth here is this clear
perceptibility, or intelligibility. . . . The upshot of all this
is, that since no power, how great soever, can make anything indifferently to be true, and since the essence of truth
in universal abstract things is nothing but clear perceptibility, it follows that omnipotence cannot make anything
that is false to be clearly perceived to be, or create such
minds and understanding faculties as shall have as clear
conception of falsehoods—that is, of nonentities—as they
have of truths or entities. For example, no rational understanding being that knows what a part is, and what a
whole, what a cause, and what an effect, could possibly
be so made as clearly to conceive the part to be greater
than the whole, or the effect to be before the cause, or the
like. . . . Conception and knowledge are hereby made to
be the measure of all power, even omnipotence or infinite
power being determined thereby; from whence it follows
that power hath no dominion over understanding, truth,
and knowledge.[1]

[1] Compare Spinoza, *Eth.* ii. 43. schol.: "To have the true idea, nothing
else is of importance but perfectly and best to understand the thing; nor can
anyone be in reasonable doubt about the thing, unless he thinks the idea
to be something dumb as if on the canvas of a painting, and to be not the
mode of understanding, but, forsooth, the understanding itself . . . This
can be more clearly and certainly given by the true idea, because truth is

We see, then, that the Epistemology of the Cambridge Platonists involves a Theory of God, according to which the Divine Will is subordinate to the Divine Wisdom and Goodness. A God merely all-powerful would be one of whom, and of whose world, knowledge would be impossible. We have a "clear and distinct idea" of a wise and good God, and in the light of this "idea" see the truth and do the right.

This Platonic doctrine seems to me to contain all that is important in Kant's doctrine of the regulative value of the Idea of God. The Idea of God, Kant tells us, has no object in a possible experience. It lies deeper in human nature than the scientific understanding. Together with the Idea of Soul and the Idea of Cosmos, it has its seat in Reason; which must not be regarded as a "faculty" co-ordinate with other "faculties", but as the whole man—the indivisible organism in which "faculties" inhere. The Idea of God, then, having its seat in Reason, is an attitude of the whole man. An "Idea" which has no object in a possible experience, if expressed in language at all, must be expressed in figurative language; so, I need not apologise for using a figure here to help me, and least of all for using the figure of *Light*, on which "the Platonists do wonderfully refine, and soar very high". The "Idea of God" is like the influence of Light, which draws living creatures out of the prison of darkness into the freedom of its borders. It is not a particular impression, nor yet one of the Categories in which impressions are received, but the Good Hope which urges on the living creature to go forth and meet the impressions of experience and organise his life in the world which they constitute.

It is in feeling the stimulus of this Good Hope that man feels the obligation of the "Categorical Imperative". When I say that the doctrine of the "Categorical Imperative" is deeply embedded in the philosophy of the Cambridge

its touchstone. Truly, as light shows up both itself and darkness, so truth is the touchstone of what is itself and what is false." And again (De intellectus Emendatione VI. 33): "The manner in which we sense formal being is itself certitude. It is clear therefore, that to have a certainty of truth, there is need for nothing else than to have the true idea." And (*op. cit.* IX. 71): "The form of true knowledge ought to be situated in recognition itself, without relation to anything else. It does not recognise an object as a cause, but the power and nature of the intellect should depend on it."

Platonists, I am not trying to get them credit for great originality in their anticipation of a doctrine which has been too much identified with the name of Kant. Every system of Ethics, worthy to be called a system at all, takes us down to the bed-rock of the "Categorical Imperative". But what I do wish to claim for the Cambridge Platonists is that they lay the bed-rock very bare.

The first original obligation (says Cudworth)[1] is not from will, but nature. Did obligation to the things of natural justice, as many suppose, arise from the will and positive command of God, only by reason of punishments threatened and rewards promised, the consequence of this would be that no man was good and just but only by accident, and for the sake of something else; whereas the goodness of justice or righteousness is intrinsical to the thing itself, and this is that which obligeth (and not anything foreign to it), it being a different species of good from that of appetite or private utility, which every man may dispense withal.

Again, in Smith's *Discourse of Legal Righteousness and of the Righteousness of Faith*, the Gospel, as distinguished from the Law, is presented as involving the obligation of a "Categorical Imperative":—

The Righteousness of the Gospel transcends that of the Law in that it hath indeed *a true command over the inward man*, which it acts and informs; whereas the Law by its menaces and punishments could only compel men to *an external observance of it in the outward man;* as the Schoolmen have well observed, "the old Law binds the hand, the new Law binds the mind".

Again, Maxwell,[2] criticising the view which he ascribes (erroneously) to Cumberland, that the obligation of the Law of Nature is not in itself, but in its external sanction, says:—

Although Sin and Punishment are closely connected, yet the obligation of *it may not be done* is distinct from the obligation of *not with impunity*, as Sin and Punishment are of distinct consideration. But a man is *bound*, both when he cannot do a thing *without sin*, and when he cannot do a

---

[1] *Intell. System*, iii. 512.
[2] In his edition of Cumberland's *Laws of Nature*, Appendix, p. 56 (1727).

thing *without punishment*. But because the obligation of "it may not be done" is antecedent to the obligation of "not with impunity", the Precept to the Sanction, and the Sin is made by the Law, the Law hath so much obligation as to make the Sin, before the Penalty is enacted; therefore the Law has an obligation antecedently to the Sanction of it.

Maxwell's view of Cumberland—that he leaves the Law of Nature with no obligation save that derived from self-interest—I consider entirely mistaken; Cumberland is really at one with Maxwell and the whole Platonist school in holding that the moral agent, the subject of obligation, is conscious of obligation in being conscious of the identity of the Law of Righteousness in himself with the Law which rules the Divine Nature. The moral agent is obliged, not because God arbitrarily commands him, and will punish disobedience, but because he is conscious of a Law so august that even God is ruled by it. In Kant this consciousness which the moral agent has of God ruled by the Law of Righteousness is attenuated down to a consciousness of the "universality" of the Law. Thus the English statement of the doctrine of "obligation" enables us to see the theological basis concealed under Kant's superstructure; but, at the same time, shows us how Kant may be successfully defended against the criticism of which Schopenhauer's attack, in the *Basis of Ethics*,[1] may be taken as a specimen—the criticism which urges that the Imperative is, after all, not "categorical", but "hypothetical"—has an external sanction, the penalty which attaches to disobeying God's command. The Platonic doctrine of the relation between the Divine Will and the Divine Wisdom and Goodness, and of man's participation in the archetypal world constituted by that Wisdom and Goodness—the doctrine of the "presence of the Eternal Consciousness in man's consciousness"—explains and justifies Kant's use of the epithet "categorical", and turns the edge of Schopenhauer's criticism, which proceeds on the assumption that the Deity, who undoubtedly stands behind the Kantian moral Imperative, is effective as mere Power threatening punishment, not rather as Wisdom-and-Goodness drawing

[1] Pages 120 ff.

the minds and hearts of all men unto it. In an amusing passage,[1] Schopenhauer compares Kant to a man who dances the whole evening, at a ball, with a masked lady, who turns out, in the end, to be his own wife. That lady is Theology. But Schopenhauer takes for granted that she is the juridical theology modelled after the Roman Civil Law; whereas, if we compare Kant with his next of kin, the English Platonists, we see that his masked theology is the theology of Platonism—a theology as different from the other as the Hellenic genius is different from the Roman. I submit that the "Categorical Imperative" is best understood in close connection with the Greek moral notions of the good and the beautiful. Moral obligation is not essentially pressure brought to bear on the unwilling, but is rather the nisus of a nature eagerly seeking its appointed place in the Cosmos, and, in its efforts, experiencing, by anticipation, the joy of success. Virtue grows up like a flower to the light, joyfully realising its own nature as part of universal nature. This is, indeed, the way in which Maxwell wishes us to understand "obligation"—not juridically, but, if I may foist the term on him, *biologically*. Having quoted Shaftesbury at length, as holding the doctrine of the intrinsic obligation of the Law of Virtue—"That the excellence of the Object, not the Reward or Punishment, should be our motive,"—he states his own view thus:[2] "The Good in Morality, the Good of Virtue, is the Beauteous-Beneficial Life and Practice." This Greek standard he afterwards explains, in a way which reminds one of Kant, as "impartiality between man and man". "We should do all things," he says,[3] "no otherwise than as if Justice itself did them." Maxwell's criticism of Cumberland—that he makes the ultimate motive the self-interest secured by obedience to the Law of Nature—is, as I have said, mistaken; but it is interesting on account of its similarity to the criticism which Schopenhauer brings against Kant. Both critics are, I think, misled by the supposition that their respective authors are juridical and not Platonist theologians. That juridical theology influenced both Cumberland and

---

[1] *o.c.* p. 169.
[2] Maxwell's *Obligation of the Law of Nature*, p. 68 (Appendix to his edition of Cumberland). [3] *o.c.* p. 85.

Kant is, of course, indisputable; but it is a grave error, on the part of the critics, to mistake an influence, which made itself felt in the details of the superstructure, for the theological foundation of the building.   We may grant to Schopenhauer that theology stands masked behind Kant's doctrine of the Categorical Imperative.   But our study of the English Intellectualists—Kant's next of kin—enables us to recognise that theology as the Platonist theology of the communion of man's mind with God's mind rather than that of obedience to God as a superior who issues commands armed with sanctions—the theology of the Freedom of the Gospel, as Smith puts it, rather than that of the Bondage of the Law.

I think I have now said enough to explain the central doctrine of Cudworth and his school in its relationship to the "mythology" of Plato on the one side and to the "formalism" of Kant and of T. H. Green on the other side.   Let me add the observation that Cudworth and his school can hardly be said to make the Theory of Morals an independent subject. They make it merely an illustration of their Theory of Knowledge.   Moral good is simply an *intelligibile*, on the same footing as the other ideas, or Eternal Reasons, required by the epistemology of the school.   Cudworth's *Eternal and Immutable Morality* has much more to say about mathematical Truth than about Right and Wrong.   "Obligation" is treated merely as a case of "clear intelligibility", and the perception of it assimilated to the self-evidence of mathematical principles.   Duty is clearly perceived by Reflection, just as Triangularity is.   This characteristic of the System of Cudworth and his associates—that their Theory of Morals is but a corollary—and is carefully kept in the subordinate position of a mere corollary—of the Theory of Knowledge, is also a characteristic of the English System which, in our own day, represents that of the Cambridge Platonists. T. H. Green's Moral Theory is closely bound up with, and indeed, except so far as "contaminated" by utilitarianism, identical with, his epistemology—an epistemology which, as I have tried to indicate, has close affinity with that of Cudworth and his associates, inasmuch as it includes, as theirs does, a proof of the existence of God—is theology, or epistemology, indifferently. Green's *Prolegomena* and Cudworth's *Eternal and Immutable Morality* are books which should be read in connection; and, in reading them together, let the reader take as his guide the thought that the theology of Green, as well as that of Cudworth, is ecstatic, not juridical. The critic's problem in interpreting the Philosophy of Green is that of interpreting a product of the Renaissance —of the revival of Christian Platonism—I had almost said a late-born product of the Renaissance; but the Renaissance, after all, is not circumscribed by dates—it is always with us as a renovating principle, as a vivid spirit craving for the freedom of personal experience.

Platonism is a temper as well as a doctrine; and in Cudworth and his associates, as in their Alexandrine predecessors, it is even more a temper than a doctrine—an enthusiastic mystical temper, always longing passionately for intuition, always ready to accept the clearness of passionate intuition as Standard of Truth in Divine Things: "Nature itself plainly intimates to us," says Cudworth,[1] that there is some such absolutely perfect Being, which, though not inconceivable, yet is incomprehensible to our finite understandings, by certain passions which it hath implanted in us, that otherwise would want an object to display themselves upon; namely, those of devout veneration, adoration, and admiration, together with a kind of ecstasy and pleasing horror; which, in the silent language of nature, seem to speak thus much to us that there is some object in the world, so much bigger and vaster than our mind and thoughts, that it is the very same to them that the ocean is to narrow vessels; so that when they have taken into themselves as much as they can by contemplation, and filled up all their capacity, there is still an immensity of it left without which cannot enter in for want of room to receive it, and therefore must be apprehended after some other strange and more mysterious manner, namely, by their being, as it were, plunged into it, and swallowed up or lost in it." Similarly, More appeals[2] to the natural remorse of conscience, to good hope, and to reverence and

---

[1] *Intell. System*, ii. p. 519.
[2] *Antidote against Atheism*, book i. ch. 10. p. 29.

worship, as proofs of the existence of God; presenting the faculty of "Divine Sagacity"—the birth of a "Holy Life"— as "antecedaneous to Reason"—Simplify thyself, he says,[1] and walk by the "easie Sagacity", "the simple light of the Divine Love"; while Norris lays it down[2] that "the mind which sees the Divine Essence must be totally and thoroughly absolved from all commerce with the corporeal senses, either by Death, or some ecstatical and rapturous abstraction"; and Smith rests his belief in God and Immortality far more on the certitude of the Heart than of the Head. To these devout Platonists God and Immortality are simply *wants*— wants of the practical volitional part of us, for the sake of which, after all, the thinking part thinks. A God fashioned logically, in such a way as to satisfy the thinking part alone— that is, fashioned by the thinking part making its own satisfaction its end—will be a God who does not satisfy the volitional part, and consequently cannot, in the long run, be maintained. We have much to learn from the Platonists who, by laying stress on the mere want of a God, suggest that the logical faculty ought not to be allowed to have the last word in theology.[3]

That Platonism is a temper is brought home to us by nothing in the History of Philosophy more clearly than by the development of Berkeley's mind. His early thought moved on lines laid down by Locke. In the *New Theory of Vision* (1709) and *Principles of Human Knowledge* (1710), works of his early manhood, he appears as the mid-link between Locke and Hume in the sensationalistic succession. His interest, at this period, is mainly scientific, although there is a theological reference even in this early work which distinguishes it from the work of either Locke or Hume. Experience, though interpreted according to the principles of the Lockian Critique, is yet "the Language of God"— Malebranche's doctrine of "seeing all things in God" doubt-less influences him. In *The New Theory* and *The Principles* Berkeley may be said to adopt sensationalistic doctrine like

[1] *Defence of the Moral Cabbala*, ch. 1, p. 155.
[2] *Reason and Religion*, p. 3.
[3] I would refer, in this connection, to a remarkable Essay on "Reflex Action and Theism", by Professor W. James, in his volume, *The Will to Believe*.

a Platonist. But see how this Platonist temper, showing itself even in works written chiefly under the influence of Locke, hurries the man away from science into action, rouses him into sympathy—always, be it noted, practical and statesmanlike—with the miseries of the Irish people, carries him across the Atlantic on his enthusiastic mission to found a college which should be the centre of evangelical work among the American aborigines. The scheme failed; he returned, disappointed, but not disillusioned, to devote the remainder of his life to the advocacy of philanthropic schemes—and to write that wonderful *Siris, a Chain of Philosophical Reflections and Inquiries concerning the Virtues of Tar-water*, in which the practical Platonism of his nature, pent up, as age and a fatal disorder condemned him to greater retirement, found natural relief in dogmatic expression. It is in *Siris* that Berkeley appears as the latest adherent of the school of Cudworth and More. But what, it may be well asked, is the connection between Tar-water (which Berkeley recommends as a panacea) and Platonism? The answer is, that tar, the exudation of the pine, is the purest vehicle of that "invisible fire or Spirit of the universe" by the agency of which all things live: the introduction of an additional amount of this vital cosmic principle into the human system by means of a decoction of tar has the effect of heightening the bodily powers and expelling all diseases. That there is such a vital principle of the Universe is shown to be the only hypothesis consistent with that Platonism which—to adopt More's phrase with a slight alteration—is "the soul of the Philosophy of which 'modern science' is the body".

Let me close this work with two quotations from *Siris*—eloquent utterances of the Platonist temper:—

It might very well be thought serious trifling to tell my readers, that the greatest men had ever a high esteem for Plato; whose writings are the touchstone of a hasty and shallow mind; whose philosophy has been the admiration of ages; which supplied patriots, magistrates, and lawgivers, to the most flourishing states, as well as fathers to the Church, and doctors to the schools. Albeit in these days, the depths of that old learning are rarely fathomed, and yet it were happy for these lands, if our young nobility and gentry, instead of modern maxims, would imbibe the notions of the great men of antiquity. . . . It may be modestly presumed there are not many among us, even of those who are called the better sort, who have more sense, virtue, and love of their country than Cicero, who, in a letter to Atticus, could not forbear exclaiming, "O Socrates and Socratic men, never can I sufficiently render you thanks!" Would to God many of our countrymen had the same obligations to those Socratic writers! Certainly where the people are well educated, the art of piloting a state is best learnt from the writings of Plato. . . . Proclus, in the first book of his commentary on the Theology of Plato, observes that, as in the mysteries, those who are initiated, at first meet with manifold and multiform gods, but being entered and thoroughly initiated, they receive the divine illumination, and participate in the very Deity; in like manner, if the Soul looks abroad, she beholds the shadows and images of things; but returning into herself she unravels and beholds her own essence: at first she seemeth only to behold herself, but having penetrated further she discovers the mind. And again, still further advancing into the innermost Sanctuary of the Soul she contemplates the race of the Gods. And this, he saith, is the most excellent of all human acts, in the silence and repose of the faculties of the Soul to tend upwards to the very Divinity; to approach and be clearly joined with that which is ineffable and superior to all beings. When come so high as the first principle she ends her journey and rests.[1]

*   *   *   *   *   *

Whatever the world thinks, he who hath not much meditated upon God, the Human Mind, and the Highest Good, may possibly make a thriving earthworm, but will most indubitably make a sorry patriot and a sorry statesman.[2]

[1] *Siris*, §§ 332, 333.   [2] *o.c.* § 350.

INDEX

Adam, Mr., on Plato's attitude to doctrine of Immortality of the Soul, 96
on circle of the Same and the Other, 151
on the position of the Throne of Necessity in the Myth of Er, 172, 173
on the Pillar of Light in the Myth of Er, 174 f.
on the astronomy of the *Politicus* Myth, and the Great Year, 194
on untimely births, 196
on allegorization of Homer, 226
on the Guardians of the *Republic* and the Hesiodic Daemons, 386-7
Adam Smith, Dr. G., on allegorical interpretation, 229
Aeschylus, attitude of, to doctrine of Immortality of the Soul, 89
Aesop's Fables, at once African Beast-tales and Parables, 40
Aether, in *Epinomis, de Coelo, Meteorol.,* 389 f.
Agyrtae (mystery-mongers), 96
Albertus, on the Earthly Paradise, 123
Alfraganus, Dante's use of, 326
Allegorical intepretation, Dr. G. Adam Smith on, 229
Dr. Bigg on, 229
Hatch on, 229
of Myths by Plotinus and Neo-Platonists, 230 ff.
St. Paul authorizes, 229
Chrysostom's opinion of, 229
of Myths, Plato's judgment on, 44 ff., 235
of Myths, Grote on, 225, 226, 235
Neo-Platonic, Zeller's opinion of, 235
Dante's, 237
Allegorical tales deliberately made, 40
Allegorization of Homer, 223
by the Stoics, 225
Plutarch on, 224-5

Allegorization by Stoics, Cicero on, 225
Mr. Adam on, 229
of Old Testament, Philo's, 226 ff.
by Christian Fathers, 229
Allegory of *Castle of Medina*, Spenser's, 250
in *Purgatorio*, xxix, 250
of the *Cave*, Plato's, 243 ff.
of the *Disorderly Crew*, Plato's, 246 ff.
Angels, Jewish doctrine of, and Greek doctrine of Daemons, 401
Apocalypse of Paul, Dr. M. R. James on, 326
Apocalypse, the astronomical, 323
relation of, to Sacramental Cults, 326-9
Apuleius, his interpretation of the Ulysses Myth, 234
demonology of, 396 ff.
Aquinas, St. Thomas, on the Earthly Paradise, 123
Archer-Hind, Mr., his *Timaeus* quoted, 257
Aristippus, Henricus, translated *Phaedo* and *Meno* in 1156, 120
Aristotle and Eudemus echo *Timaeus* 90 c, 270
Aristotle misapprehends the *Timaeus*, 257
his God, 316
poetised astronomy, 169, 170
his poetised astronomy, influence of, on Dante, 169, 170
Plato's Beautiful City misunderstood by, 84
his supposed tomb near Chalcis, 159
gives up ideas of a Personal God and of Personal Immortality of the Soul, 78
Aristotelian astronomy, 316
Ascent takes the place of Descent in eschatology, 313, 314, 328
Stoical doctrine of the levity of the Soul contributed to, 397

Astronomy, part played by, in Poetry, 169
Atlantis Myth and maritime discovery, 417, 418
Attic Moses, Plato as, 424
Axiochus, the, date and characteristics of, 128, 129
  places the world of the departed in the southern hemisphere of the earth, 129
  singular in its localisation of the Meadow of Truth, 319

Bacon, his allegorical interpretation of Myths, 234
  his definition of Poetry, 349
Bacon, Roger, on the Earthly Paradise, 123
Beautiful City, Plato's, not an isolated municipality, but an Empire-city, 84
Berkeley, his Siris characterised and quoted, 467, 468
  as Platonist, 466
Bernard, his translation of Kant's Critique of the aesthetic faculties quoted, 214
Bhagavad Gita, symbolic soul-chariot in, 11
  downward-growing tree as symbol of man on earth, 11
Bigg, Dr., on allegorization of Homer by the Stoics, 226
  on allegorical interpretation, 229
  on Myth of Cupid and Psyche, 238
Boeckh, referred to for Plato's astronomy, 315
Book of the Dead, Egyptian, 9 f., 92, 143
  Tibetan, 9, 15
Bosanquet, Prof. B., on "present" as "extended time", 81
Bran, the Voyage of, referred to for connection between notions of metempsychosis, metamorphosis, and pregnancy without male intervention, 279
Brownell, C. L., quoted for Japanese story of origin of tea, 37
Brunetto Latini, on the infernal rivers, 121
Buddhism, attitude of, to belief in Immortality, 276
  unwritten teaching, 6
  and allegory of the Cave, 15
Budge, Dr., on (Egyptian) Book of the Dead, 92
  on a prehistoric form of burial in Egypt, 340
Bunbury, on the geography of the Atlantis Myth, 417 ff.

Bunyan's Pilgrim's Progress, an allegory and also a Myth, 239 ff.
Burnet, Prof., on the sphonduloi (whorls) of the orrery in Myth of Er., 170
  referred to on Plato's astronomy, 315
  on the Poem of Parmenides, 312
  on the monsters and "organic combinations" of Empedocles, 365
Bury, on spread of Orphic cult, 92
Butcher, Prof., his Aristotle's Theory of Fine Art referred to, 353
Butler, on Necessity and Freedom, 177
Bywater, Prof., on the Epinomis, 389

Caird, Dr. E., on Kant's Ideas of Reason, quoted, 73, 74
Callaway, Nursery Tales of the Zulus, quoted, 31-33
  on one-legged people; cf. Myth told by Aristophanes in Symposium, 364
Cambridge Platonists, their learning, 423 ff.
  influenced in two directions, by Philo and by Plotinus respectively 427 ff.
  maintain that Moses taught the motion of the Earth, 426, 437
  their enthusiasm for the new astronomy, 437 ff.
  their science, 437 ff.
  their central doctrine, the Doctrine of Ideas, as theory of union of man with God, in knowledge and conduct, 442, 443
  go back to Plato the mythologist rather than to Plato the dialectician, 442
  their epistemology, 450
  their epistemology, derived from the doctrine of Ideas "mythologically" set forth, explains their theory of Reason as Moral Faculty, 451
  their discussion of the relation of God's "Will" to his "Wisdom" and "Goodness", 453 ff.
  their doctrine of Categorical Imperative, 460 ff.
  enable us to connect the "formalism" of Kant and Green with the "mythology" of the Phaedrus and Symposium, 463, 464
Campbell, Prof., on Protagoras Myth, 213
Carus, his Gesch. d. Zoologie referred to, 40
Catastrophes, doctrine of, in Plato and the Peripatetics, 192, 193

Categorical Imperative, doctrine of, in Cambridge Platonists, 460
Kant's doctrine of, criticised by Schopenhauer, 463
Categories of the Understanding, mythological deduction of, 298
the Forms seen in the Super-celestial Place explained as, 300
Cave, Plato's Allegory of, 243
importance of, 14, 15
an allegory and also a myth, 40
its meaning, 81
Schwanitz on, 245
Couturat on, 245
Cebetis Tabula, 238
Chalcidius, translated the Timaeus, 120
quoted on Daemons, 387
his version of the Timaeus, how far used by Dante, 419
Charles, Prof. R. H., his editions of Secrets of Enoch and Ascension of Isaiah referred to, 323
Choice of Hercules, 25, 238
Church, Dean, on The Letter to Kan Grande, 42
Cicero, eschatology of his Dream of Scipio and Tusc. Disp., 314
Circe and Calypso Myths, Neo-Platonic interpretation of, 233 ff.
Claudian, on the Earthly Paradise, 123
"Clear and Distinct Ideas", 457
Clough, quoted to illustrate doctrine of Correction and Purification in the Gorgias, 139
Coelo, de, influence of, in the Paradiso, 314
Coleridge, on "poetic faith", 30
on deep sky akin to feeling, 45
quoted for the statement that a poem ought not to be all poetry, 59
on Plato's doctrine of the pre-existence of the Soul, 86
on Wordsworth's Ode on Intimations of Immortality, 86
his Anima Poetae quoted, 251
on Dante's Canzone xx, 251
regards the Platonic doctrine of Pre-existence as mythical, 305, 306
holds that poetry may exist without metre, 352
Comparetti, on gold tablets of Thurii and Petelia, 143, 161
on the Kalewala, 200
Conscience, Cardinal Newman on, as connecting principle between creature and Creator, 398
Guardian Daemon as, 398

Conybeare, Mr., his Philo on the Contemplative Life referred to, 226, 227
Cook, Mr. A. B., on the Sicilian triskeles, and the Myth told by Aristophanes in Symposium, 364
Cornford, Mr. F. M., on the Guardians of the Republic and the Hesiodic Daemons, 386
Courthope, Mr., his definition of Poetry quoted, 61
Couturat, on doctrine of Immortality of the Soul as held by Plato, 95
"the Timaeus is wholly mythical", 193
on the Cave, 245
holds that the whole doctrine of Ideas is mythical, 308
Cratylus, the, on the Philosopher Death, 140, 141
on the Sirens, 141
Creuzer, Plotinus on Beauty quoted, 232, 233
Cudworth, his criticism of Descartes compared with criticism of the same tendency in Prof. Ward's Naturalism and Agnosticism, 426
conceives God spatially, 435
supplies the link between the epistemological theism of Green and the mythology of the Timaeus and the Phaedrus, 447
his criticism of the sensationalism of Hobbes, 445-447
his criticism of Descartes, 457 ff.
Cultus Myth, a variety of the Aetiological story, illustrated, 36
Cumberland, criticized by Maxwell, 462
Cumont, his Mystères de Mithra, 326
his criticism of Dieterich's Mithrasliturgie, 327
Cupid and Psyche, Myth of, Mr. A. Lang on, 238
Dr. Bigg on, 238

Daemon, Guardian, doctrine of, connected with belief in re-incarnation of Souls of ancestors, 399, 400
as Conscience, 398, 399
Daemon, the, of Socrates, 396, 399; cf. 25, 26
Daemons, doctrine of, 384 ff.
two kinds of, recognized by Plato, 386 ff.
Dante, Letter to Kan Grande quoted for distinction between literal and allegorical truth, 42, 43
Convivio quoted for literal, allegoric, moral and anagogic interpretation, his "personal religion", 43, 44

Dante expresses Transcendental Feeling in last canto of *Par.* and 25th sonnet of *V.N.*, 46, 47

V.N. sonnet 24 quoted for effect produced, similar to that produced by Plato's Eschatological Myths, 50

V.N. sonnet 11 quoted to illustrate the magic of certain kinds of Poetry, 63

Hell, Mount of Purgatory, and Earthly Paradise, compared with the Tartarus and True Surface of the Earth in the *Phaedo*, 119 ff.

Research on Water and Land, 121

the tears of this world flow in the rivers of his Hell, 121

singular in locating Purgatory on the slopes of the Mountain of the Earthly Paradise, 122

Mount of Purgatory sighted by Ulysses, 122

his use of the teleological geography of Orosius, 123, 124

his mythological explanation of the distribution of plants, 125

the human race created to make good the loss of the fallen angels, 124

"the seven P's", 143

the three parts of his *D. C.* correspond to the "Three Ways", 145

Lethe and Eunoè, 160 ff.

Earthly Paradise, 160 ff.

his mythology of Lethe and Eunoè compared with the Platonic Recollection, 163

purification by gradual ascent of Mount of Purgatory takes the place of purification by metempsychosis, 164

appearance of Saints in the moving Spheres, 170

and the *Timaeus*, 207

his allegorization of the story of the Three Marys, 237

Inferno iv, 46-63, and Plato's *Cave*, 246

Coleridge on, 251

"suppressed" symbolism in, 251

Procession in *Purg. xxix* ff., 300

on relation of Philosophy to Science, 303

compares the Platonic Ideas to Gods, 308

on the number of Beatrice, 311

Paradiso, latest example of the astronomical apocalypse, 314

Convivio, quoted for his astronomical system, 169, 314 ff.

Dante, on influence of Planets in producing temperaments, 319, 320

regards his vision of *Paradiso* as having sacramental value, 325, 326

theory in the *de Monarchia* compared with that of the *Republic* and Atlantis Myth, 405

his knowledge of the *Timaeus* through the version and commentary of Chalcidius, 419

Darwin, on the feebleness of imagination in the lower animals, 27

his *Expression of the Emotions in Man and Animals* referred to, 303, 304

Dead, Book of the, Egyptian, 9 f., 92, 143

Tibetan, 9, 15

Delphi, place assigned to, by the side of the Platonic State, 80, 81

Descartes, criticised by Cambridge Platonists, as ignoring the "plastic principle", 426, 441

criticised by Cudworth, 426, 439, 441, 457 ff.

Descent to Hades, Dieterich on, 92

Rohde on, 92

Lobeck on, 245

the, eschatology of, 312, 313

Dialogue, the Platonic, two elements in—Argumentative Conversation and Myth, 24

Dieterich, on Orphic *Descent into Hades*, 92, 159

on cooling (*refrigerium*), 166, 167

on Mithraic seven-gated ascent, 167

his *Mithrasliturgie* referred to for influence of Posidonius, 313

his *Mithrasliturgie*, 326 ff.

Dill, Professor, referred to for mixture of Science and Myth in Macrobius, 119

on Plutarch's allegorization of Egyptian Myths, 224

quoted on Macrobius' Commentary on the *Dream of Scipio*, 320, 321

Disorderly Crew, Plato's Allegory of, 246 ff.

Dramatists, the Athenian, their attitude to the doctrine of the Immortality of the Soul, 88 ff.

take the Family, rather than the Individual, as the moral unit, 88 ff.

Dream of Scipio, probably owes its astronomy to Posidonius, 389

astronomical eschatology of, 314

Dream-consciousness, induced by Poetry, 344 ff.

"Dream-thing", the, illustrated from Wordsworth's *Prelude*, 158

Dream-world, the, of the primitive story-teller characterized, 28

Düring, holds that the *Phaedrus* Myth is a "Programme", 299

Earth, rotundity of, recognized by Plato in *Phaedo*, 112
central position of, in *Phaedo*, 112

Earthly Paradise, the, 120 ff.
of Dante and medieval belief, 122 ff.
Dante's, 160 ff.

Earthquake and thunder accompany new birth in Myth of Er and Dante, *Purgatorio xxi*, 165

Ecstasy, Plotinus quoted on, 347-8
as understood by Cambridge Platonists, 428 ff.

"Empirical" distinguished from "Transcendental" Feeling, 351

Enoch, Secrets of, referred to, 323 ff.

Eothen, Kinglake's, quoted to illustrate allegory of *Disorderly Crew*, 246 ff.

Epictetus on Guardian Daemon as Conscience, 399

Epimetheus, contrasted with Prometheus, 216 ff.

Epinomis, demonology of, 395

Er, Myth of, in the *Republic*, 90, 98, 99
great philosophical question raised in, 175 ff.

Evil, origin of, mythically explained in *Politicus* Myth, 193, 194
presence of, in Heaven, 328

Exeter Book, the, on the Earthly Paradise, 123

Expression, importance attached by Plato to, as reacting on that which is expressed, 131, 132
reaction of, on that which is expressed, 303

Eyes, the final cause of, 317, 318

Fairbanks, Mr. A., on cremation and ascent, 341

Fall, the, of Souls as conceived by the Neo-Platonists, 321

Ficino, on the Narcissus Myth, 233

Flinders Petrie, Prof., on *Egyptian Book of the Dead*, 92, 143
referred to for *Egyptian Book of the Dead*, 143

Frutiger, Perceval, his *Mythes de Platon*, quoted, 8, 9, 10

Galton, Mr. F., on power of visualization, 343

Gardner, Prof. P., on *thiasi*, 97
on the story of Zagreus, 365
on Prophecy, 383

Gardner, Prof. P., on new epoch opened for Hellas by Alexander, 405
on Apocalypses, 406

Gebhart (*l'Italie Mystique*) on Dante's "personal religion", 43

Gems, mythological theory of origin of, in *Phaedo*, 112, 113
Dante on origin of virtues of, 113

Geology of Attica in Atlantis Myth, 416 ff.

Gfrörer (*Early Christianity*), on Philo's allegorical method, 227 ff.

Ghosts, H. More on, 114 f.

Gildersleeve, Prof., on Pindar, *Ol.* ii, 93

Glaucon in *Rep.* 608 D, attitude of, to doctrine of Immortality, 90

Goblet d'Alviella, on connection between Egyptian and Greek guidebooks for the use of the dead, 92
on Initiation as Death and Rebirth, 339 ff.

God, a Personal, is a Part, not the whole, 78

God of Lovingkindness in Mithraic doctrine, 167

Goethe, quoted to illustrate the "magic" of certain kinds of poetry, 62

Gollancz, his edition of the *Exeter Book*, 123

Good, the, not one of the objects of Knowledge, but its condition, 85, cf. 69

Gray, Sir George, his version of Maori story of Children of Heaven and Earth, quoted, 34-36

Green, T. H., his doctrine of "the Presence of the Eternal Consciousness in my Consciousness", its Platonic provenance, 434, 442
his Eternal Consciousness compared with the Ideal World of Cambridge Platonists, 449
his Philosophy a revival of Christian Platonism, 464, 465

Grote, on the Cultus Myth, 36, 37
on doctrine of Immortality of the Soul as held by Plato, 86
on *thiasi*, 97
on the general characteristics of the *Politicus* Myth, 192
on the *Protagoras* Myth, 212, 213
on allegorical interpretation, 235-6
on the story of Zagreus, 363

Gummere, Prof., makes metrical form essential to Poetry, 353

Hades, Voyage of Odysseus to, of Orphic origin, 92

Harrison, Miss, on the Cultus Myth, 37

Harrison, Miss, on the Sirens, 140-1
her *Prolegomena to the Study of Greek Religion* referred to, 160
on Dante's Eunoè, 167
on the story of Zagreus, 365
Letter quoted on Stewart's *Doctrine of Ideas*, 4
Hatch, on allegorical interpretation, 229
on Angels and Daemons, 401
Heavens, motion of, determines sublunary events, 192-3
motion of, in the *Politicus* Myth and in the accepted astronomy, 194
Hegel, his view of the divine sign of Socrates, 26
on doctrine of Immortality of the Soul as held by Plato, 86
on the Soul as Universal, 220
Helbig, on Prometheus sarcophagus in Capitol, 221
Heraclitus, his *Dry Soul* as understood by the Neo-Platonists, 232, 322
Hesiod on the Five Ages, 384 ff.
his Daemons, 384, 385
Hierocles, on bodies terrestrial, aerial and astral, 389
Hobbes, his Social Covenant a "foundation-myth", 177
his disproof of Spirit or Incorporeal Substance criticised by More, 440-1
his sensationalism criticised by Cudworth, 445-6
Holland, Philemon, his version of Plutarch's *Moralia*, 330 ff., 391 ff.
Homoiosis (assimilation with God), 11

Idealists, modern English, go back to Plato the mythologist rather than to Plato the dialectician, 442-3
their central doctrine that of the Cambridge Platonists—the Doctrine of Ideas as theory of union of Man with God in knowledge and conduct, 443
Ideas, Doctrine of, how far mythical? 308 ff.
as adopted by Cambridge Platonists and modern English Idealists, 442
Ideas, The Doctrine of, Stewart's book, quoted, 4, 17
"Ideas of Reason", Soul, Cosmos, and God, set forth by Plato in Myth, not scientifically, 74
mythological representation of, 298 ff.
Imagination, rather than Reason, distinguishes man from brute, 27
part played by, in the development of human thought, 27-29

Immisch referred to for medieval translation of the *Phaedo*, 120
Immortality of the Soul, attitude of Simonides, Tyrtaeus, Attic Orators, Dramatists, Aristotle, the Athenian public, to doctrine of, 87 ff.
Plato's doctrine of, according to Hegel, Zeller, Grote, Coleridge, Thiemann, Couturat, Jowett, Adam, 87, 88, 95, 96
personal, presented by Plato in Myth, 78
agnosticism regarding, in the Athens of Plato's day, 87 ff.
conceived by Plato *eminently* in Myth, 87, 98, 99
Plato's doctrine of, according to Jowett, 96
three sorts of, distinguished, 275 ff.
attitude of Buddhism to belief in, 276
"Imperial Hellas", ideal of, in Plato, 405
ideal of, how far it competes with that of personal salvation in Plato, 406-7
Initiation, as ceremonial Death and Rebirth, 329, 339 ff.
Ion, Plato's, a study of "Poetic Inspiration", 344
Isaiah, Ascension of, 323
Islands of the Blessed, 126 ff.
in the Platonic Myths, 127-8
in Greek and Celtic Mythology, 126
in *Gorgias*, identical with "True Surface of the Earth" in *Phaedo*, and "Heaven" in Myth of Er, 126 ff.

Jackson, Dr. H., on the divine sign of Socrates, 26
James, Dr. M. R., on *Apocalypse of Paul*, 326
James, Prof. W., on teleology, 77
his *Varieties of Religious Experience* referred to, 428
his essay on "Reflex Action and Theism" referred to, 466
Jevons, Dr., on *thiasi*, 97
on the story of Zagreus, 365
Johnstone, Mr. P. de L., his *Muhammad and his Power* quoted, 324-5
Jowett, on Imagination and Reason, 27
on Plato's attitude to doctrine of Immortality of the Soul, 96
on the general characteristics of the *Politicus* Myth, 92

Kaibel, on gold tablets found at Thurii and Petelia, 161, 199, 200

Kalewala, the, described, 199, 200
story of the Birth of Iron in the, 200 ff.
German version of, by H. Paul, 200
Kant, his distinction between Categories of the Understanding and Ideas of Reason not explicit in Plato's mind, but sometimes implicitly recognized by him, 70, 71
his distinction between Categories of the Understanding and Ideas of Reason explained, 70 ff.
in charging Plato with "transcendental use, or rather mis-use, of the Categories of the Understanding", ignores the function of Myth in the Platonic philosophy, 97
his *Critique of Judgment* quoted, 214
on distinction between Teleological and the Mechanical explanations of the world, 214
his theology, that of the Platonist, 462 ff.
King, Mr. J. E., on infant burial, 196, 401
Kingsley, Miss, on reincarnation of souls of deceased relatives, 401
Knowledge, Theory of, common to Cambridge Platonists and modern English Idealists, 442, 443
Kühner, on the divine sign of Socrates, 26

Land, Prof. J. P. N., on *Physiologus*, 40
Lang, Mr. A., on Myth of Uranus and Cronus, 34
on Myth of Cupid and Psyche, 238
on savage analogies for Greek mysteries, 340 and 341
Leibniz, his "Pre-established Harmony" and "Prenatal Choice" in Myth of Er compared, 176
describes his doctrines of recollection as mythical, 305, 306
Lelewel, referred to for position of Earthly Paradise, 123
Lélut, on the divine sign of Socrates, 26
Lethe, the River of, its location discussed, 160 ff.
Thiemann on locality of, 159
not one of the infernal rivers, 159, 174
its locality in the *Aeneid*, 159, 160
and Mnemosyne in the Orphic cult, 161 ff.
topography of, in Myth of Er and Petelia Tablet compared, 162
drinking of, precedes re-incarnation, 162

Lethe and Mnemosyne at Oracle of Trophonius, 166
Roscher on reference to, 174
Liddell, Prof. Mark H., makes metrical form essential to Poetry, 353, 354
Lie, the, in the Soul, what? 76
Lobeck, *Aglaophamus* on the "Cycle of Incarnations", 161
on the allegorization of Homer, 223
on story of Zagreus, 365
on reincarnation of souls of deceased relatives, 401
Lotze, his distinction between the Reality of Existence and the Reality of Validity, appears in Norris, 448
Love song, the "magic" of, 62
Lucian on the Stoic "Steep Hill" of virtue, 122
Lucifer, the Fall of, how made use of by Dante, 124

Mackinder, Mr. H. J., on "Atlantis", 417
Macrobius, on the Bowl of Dionysus, 231
his Commentary on the *Dream of Scipio* compared with the *Phaedrus* Myth, 321
on influence of Planets in producing temperaments, 320, 321
Madness, four kinds of, distinguished in *Phaedrus*, 281, 300
"Magic" of certain kinds of Poetry discussed and illustrated, 61 ff.
Mahomed, Vision of, quoted, 324-5
Malebranche, his doctrine of "seeing all things in God" adopted by Norris, 449
Make-believe and belief, 30, 31
Mann, Max Friedr., his *Bestiaire Divin* referred to, 40 ff.
Maoris, their Story of the Children of Heaven and Earth quoted, 34 ff.
Marcus Aurelius on the aerial habitat of souls, 388
on Guardian Daemon as Conscience, 399, 400
Masson, Professor, on Milton's *Concerning the Platonic Idea*, 309
Maximus Tyrius, demonology of, 398, 399
Maxwell, his criticism of Cumberland, 462 ff.
his theory of obligation, 463
Meadow, the, of the Judgment-Seat, position of, 157
Mechanism and Teleology, 457

Metempsychosis and Resurrection, 194
  not necessarily connected with notions of Retribution and Purification, 277
  relation of, to metamorphosis, and to conception without male intervention, 278 ff.
Meteorologica, geography of, 418
Methexis (sharing), 15
Metre and Representation, the place of each in Poetry, 350 ff.
Milindapanha, 11
Millennium, the, H. More on, 115
Millet's "sower", 243
Milton, adheres to old astronomy in Paradise Lost, 168
  his Poem on the Platonic Idea as Aristotle understood it, quoted, 309
Mirror and Bowl of Dionysus, Neo-Platonic interpretation of, 231 ff.
Mitchell, Mrs., on Prometheus sarcophagus in Capitol, 221
Mithras Cult, the seven-gated ladder of ascent, 167
Mithrasliturgie, Dietrich's, 326 ff.
Mnemosyne, drinking of, precedes final disembodiment of purified soul, 162
Models, astronomical, in antiquity, 170
Moore, Dr. E., on authenticity of Research on Water and Land, 120
  on the geography of Orosius, 123, 124
  on references in Paradiso to Revelation of St. John, 322
More, H., on the Plastic Principle in Nature, 322 ff.
  on vehicles, terrestrial, aerial, and aethereal, 114
  on the Millennium, 115
  a soul must have a vehicle of some kind, 115
  on the effect upon terrestrial and aerial bodies of the Fire of the Last Day, 115, 116
  on sunspots 115, 116
  one of his "Myths" quoted, 116 ff.
  indebtedness of his mythology of aerial daemons to that of the Platonists and Stoics, 117
  his belief in witchcraft, 118
  on the number 729, 310
  his view of the end of the Scripture, 382
  his Philosophical Poems quoted, 435, 444, 453, 454
  criticises Hobbes' disproof of incorporeal substance, 440-1

Morfill, Professor, his translation of Secrets of Enoch referred to, 323
Moses Atticus ("the Attic Moses"), 424
Mundo, de (on the Universe) astronomy of, 314
  geography of, 418
Murray, Mr. G. G. A., on Brit. Mus. Gold Tablets, 161
Myer and Nutt's Voyage of Bran, on conception without male intervention, 195
Myers, F. W. H., on the divine sign of Socrates, 26
  makes changes in tension of muscles of the throat essential part of poetic excitation, 355
Mysteries, stronghold in Greece of doctrine of Immortality, 90
Mysticism, Goethe's definition of, 95
Myth, the eschatological, characterized, 38
  interpretation of, must be psychological, 39
  the vehicle of exposition chosen by Plato, when he deals with a priori conditions of conduct and science, 74
  education of children to begin with, according to Plato, 79 ff.
  Plato brings, into conformity with science as far as possible, 112
  not to be take literally, according to Plato, but to be "sung over to oneself" till the charm of it touches the heart, 131, 132
  aetiological, value attached to, by Plato, 196 ff.
  aetiological, in the Kalewala, 199, 200
  its two meanings, 236
  the Phaedo, motif of, Moral Responsibility, 132
  the Gorgias, Moral Responsibility the motif of, 139
  the Gorgias, its theory of Correction and Purification—of Punishment and Pardon, 139, 140
  the Gorgias, its rendering of the wonder and reverence with which man regards Death, 140, 141
  the Gorgias, on the infinite difference between vice with large and vice with small opportunity, 142
  distinguished from Allegory and Parable, 39
Myth and Allegory, Westcott on, 236
  difference between, illustrated from Spanish Chapel fresco, 379
Myth and Ritual compared, 84

Myths, introduction of, perhaps suggested to Plato by certain passages in the conversation of Socrates, 25

Plato's, appeal to that part of the soul which expresses itself, not in theoretic, but in value-judgments, or rather value-feelings, 44, 45

Plato's, effect produced by, compared with that produced by Poetry generally, 46 ff.

Plato's, effect produced by, compared with that produced by contemplation of Nature, 46

Plato's, described as Dreams expressive of Transcendental Feeling, 67 f.

as an organic system, 13 ff.

allegorical interpretation of, Plato's judgment on, 235

allegorical interpretation of, Bacon's, 234

Narcissus Myth, Neo-Platonic allegorization of, 231 ff.

"Necessary" Truth, what? 452

Necessity, the throne of, in the Myth of Er, where? 158, 170 ff.

Nettleship, R. L., on the lack of organic connection in the latter half of *Rep. x*, 99

on the "back of the sky", 170

Newman, Cardinal, on Conscience as connecting principle between creature and Creator, 398

Newton, his *Principia* quoted for his theological belief, 437 ff.

Norris, his Reason and Religion referred to, 429, 430, 447 ff.

on ecstasy and the holy life, 430

on the *a priori* in knowledge, 448

distinguishes, as Lotze does, between Reality and Existence of of Validity, 448

his Ideal World compared with T. H. Green's Eternal Consciousness, 449

adopts Malebranche's doctrine of "Seeing all things in God", 449

on moral obligation, 451

Number 729, 310-311

7, instances given of its importance, 321

Obligation, how Reason imposes, according to Platonism, 451

Old Testament, Philo's allegorization of, 226 ff.

Olympiodorus on the infernal rivers, 174

Optimism and Pessimism, 455 ff.

Orators, Attic, their attitude to the doctrine of the Immortality of the Soul, 87 ff.

Orosius and the doctrine of one continuous inhabited region, 124

Orphic Cult, spread of, 90 ff.

Plato's attitude to, 91

Philosophy described by Plato in terms of, 93

Lethe and Mnemosyne in, 161 ff.

Orphic *Descent into Hades*, 92 ff.

Orphic Priests, as distinguished from Orphic doctrine, Plato's attitude to, 96

Orrery, the, in the Myth of Er, 170

Pandora Myth, in Hesiod, 231

Parable, Reville on, 243

Parables, the, of the New Testament, 243

Paradiso, the, latest example of the "Astronomical Apocalypse", 325

Parmenides, the celestial eschatology of the opening lines of his Poem, 312

Paul, H., his version of the *Kalewala*, 200

Pausanias on Lethe and Mnemosyne at the oracle of Trophonius, 166

Personal God, idea of, presented by Plato in Myth, 78

Pessimism and Optimism, 455 ff.

Phaedo, hydrostatics of, criticised by Aristotle, 120, 121

medieval translation of, 120

Phaedrus Myth, the, celestial or astronomical *mise en scène* of its eschatology, 311 ff.

Philo, his allegorical interpretation of the Old Testament, 227 ff.

on the number 729, 310, 311

on Jewish Angels and Greek Daemons, 401

influence of, on Cambridge Platonists, 428

Philosophy as Life and Immortality, 378, 379

Physiologus, described and quoted, 40 ff.

Pilgrim's Progress at once an Allegory and a Myth, 239

quoted, 239 ff.

Pillar of Light, the, in the Myth of Er, discussed, 157, 172 ff.

Pindar, his eschatology, 92

Plato's Debt to, 94

Pitra on *Physiologus*, referred to, 40

Plain of Truth, the, 316

Plotinus on, 318

Plutarch on, 318, 319

the *Axiochus* on, 319

Planets, influence of, in producing temperaments, 320 ff.

Plastic Principle, the, ignored by Descartes, 426, 441
explains, for Cambridge Platonists, the existence of "vehicles" without which the "Eternal Consciousness" could not reproduce itself, 442
of Cambridge Platonists compared with the "Spiritual Principle" of modern English Idealists, 442

Plato, as the "Attic Moses", 207
his attitude to teleology, 216
his attitude to the allegorization of Myths, 223
his astronomy, 315

Platonism as temper, illustrated by Berkeley's life, 466

Platt, Mr. A., on Plato and Geology, 416

Pliny, on Lethe and Mnemosyne at oracle of Trophonius, 166

Plotinus, attitude of to the "Problem of the Universe", 70
his allegorization of the Myth of Prometheus and Pandora, 230 ff.
his allegorization of the Narcissus Myth, 231 f.
quoted on mirror and bowl of Dionysus, 321 ff.
his interpretation of Diotima's allegory, 378
influence of, on Cambridge Platonists, 428 ff.
on Contemplation and Love (directed to Ideas) as constituting the Principle of Life, 452

Plutarch, on the justice of punishing children for sins of fathers, 88
on allegorization of Homer, 224, 225
his Aridaeus-Thespesius Myth given, and commented on, 329 ff.
his power of colour-visualization, 343
on Mind, Soul and Body supplied by Sun, Moon and Earth respectively, 390, 391
his daemonology, 391 ff.
his Timarchus Myth given, 391 ff.

"Poetic Truth", what? 346

Poetry, chief end of, production and regulation of Transcendental Feeling, 57 ff.
its effect identical with that produced by other Five Arts, and sometimes even with that produced by contemplation of Nature and Human Life, and by the

memories of Childhood and Youth, 60
a Theory of, 344 ff.

Posidonius, influence of, on development of astronomical eschatology, 313 f.
on aerial daemons, 388

Postgate, Mr. J. P., on the Sirens, 141

Pre-existence and Recollection, Zeller on, 304 ff.

Pringle-Patterson, Prof. A. S., referred to, 77
on Categories in Things, 301 f.

Problem of the Universe, relation of Thought and Transcendental Feeling respectively to, 69, 70
attitude of Plotinus, 70

Prometheus, contrasted with Epimetheus, 217 ff.

Prometheus Myth, on Capitoline Sarcophagus, 221 f.
various versions of, 222
lends itself easily to allegorization, 222
allegorized by Plotinus, 230, 231

Prophecy, Prof. P. Gardner on, 382, 383

Prophetic Temperament, the, Diotima a study of, 380 ff.
Spinoza on, 380 ff.

Purgatory, Dante's Mount of, and the Stoic "Steep hill of Virtue" compared, 164, 165

Purification, 355

Rabelais, quoted in comparison with the Myth told by Aristophanes in Symposium, 366 ff.

Rashdall, Dr., referred to for medieval translation of the Phaedo, 120

Recollection, doctrine of, 303 ff.

Recollection, Love, Philosophy, 302

Recollection, Platonic, Dieterich on, 163, 164
compared with Dante's Mythology of Lethe and Eunoè, 163

Refrigerium (Cooling), doctrine of, taken in connection with Dante's Eunoè, 166, 167

Religious Consciousness, the, demands a Personal God, 76
how opposed to the Scientific Understanding, 77 ff.

Renan, on Spanish Chapel fresco, 132

Representation and Metre, the place of each in poetry, 350 ff.

Resurrection, doctrine of, 194

Revelation of St. John, not an "Astronomical Apocalypse", 323
Dante little indebted to, 322

Reville, on the profound philosophy of Myths, 39
  on Rite and Myth, 83
  on Ritual, 249
Ritschl, his view of Inspiration, 383
Ritual, compared with Myth, 83
  with Myth and Allegory, 249 ff.
Robertson Smith, on Relation of Myth to Ritual, 37
Rohde, on Greek agnosticism regarding Immortality of the Soul, 87
  on Orphic Rites, 90 f.
  on Pindar's Eschatology, 92, 93
  on *Descent to Hades*, 159
  on "Cooling", 166, 167
  on untimely births, 196
Rosche, on Lethe, 174
Roth, Leon, letter quoted, 16
Round people, the, of Aristophanes, compared with the Sicilian *triskeles*, 364
  compared with Zulu and Arabian one-legged people, 364
  compared with the monsters of Empedocles, 364, 365
Rouse, Mr., on votive figures, 158, 159
Ruskin, on Spanish Chapel fresco, 132, 250

Sander, on Geography of Atlantis Myth, 417
Scartazzini, on Dante's Purgatory and Earthly Paradise, 122
Schmidt, on Dante's *Research into Water and Earth*, 122
Schopenhauer, his Freedom in Being, compared with Prenatal Choice in Myth of Er, 176, 177
  his definition of Poetry, 349
  his criticism of Kant's Categorical Imperative, 463
Schwanitz, on Allegory of the Cave, 245
Scylax, his *Voyage* referred to, 418
Seneca's *Letter to Marcia*, eschatology of, 314
Sensitive Soul, supervenes upon the Vegetative, 65
Shelley, *Adonais* quoted for effect produced similar to that produced by Plato's Eschatological Myths, 51 ff.
  on distinction between poetry and prose, 353
  his Poem, *The Recollection*, quoted, 357
Simonides, his attitude to doctrine of Immortality of the Soul, 84, 85

Sirens, the, associated with Death, 140, 141
  Miss Harrison on, 140, 141
  Mr. J. P. Postgate on, 141
Smith, John, his view of the relation between a *Holy Life* and a *Right Belief*, 382
  on ecstasy and the Holy Life, 429, 430
  differs from Cudworth and More in relying less on "Science" than on "moral feeling" for proof of the existence of God, 439, 440
  distinguishes movement of sheep and cyclic movement, 444, 445
Socrates, his "mesmeric" influence, 26, 27
  his Daemon, 26
Sophists, the—their use of Allegories or Illustrative Fables, 25
Soul, the Idea of, as represented in Plato's Eschatological Myths, 85 ff.
Soul-stuff, in *Timaeus*, 279 f.
Souls, number of, fixed, 194, 195
Spanish Chapel, fresco referred to, 132
  referred to, to illustrate difference between Myth and Allegory, 379
Spencer and Gillen on souls of ancestors entering into women, 195
Spenser, the human race created to make good the loss of fallen angels, 124
  his allegory of Castle of Medina, 250
Spinoza, his view that religion is a matter of piety rather than of dogmatic truth, 84, 85
  on the Prophetic Temperament, 380, 381
Springs, hot and cold, origin of, in *Phaedo*, 112
Stallbaum, on the general characteristics of the *Politicus* Myth, 192
  on the *Protagoras* Myth, 213
  on Myth and Dialectic, 235
Stevenson, R. L., his *Woodman* quoted, 65
Stoics, the, their doctrine of Assent, 89
  their allegorization of Homer, 225
  their doctrine of the aerial habitat of daemons and souls of the dead, 388 ff.
Story-telling, love of, importance of for the development of man, 28, 29
  always "about people and animals", 29
Stories, distinguished as simply Anthropological and Zoological, Aetiological and Eschatological, 28 ff.

Stories, Simply Anthropological and Zoological, illustrated, 31
Aetiological, illustrated, 34 f.
and magic, 34
various classes of, 34
Cosmological, a variety of the aetiological story, 34-37
Sun, Western rising of, in Atreus Myth, 193
rising where now he sets, and setting where now he rises, in Egyptian story, 193
Symbolism, "suppressed", illustrated from Dante, 251

Tablets, attached to Souls by Judges of the Dead, 143
gold, of Thurii and Petelia, 143, 161 ff.
Tablet, Petelia, quoted, 162
Tannery, on Orphic rites, 91
Tartarus, has entrance and exit separate in Phaedo and Myth of Er, 130
Teleology, attitude of the religious consciousness and the scientific understanding respectively to, 77 f.
Plato's attitude to, 216 ff.
and Mechanism, 457
Teleological and Mechanical explanations of the World, distinction between, set forth in Protagoras Myth, 214 ff.
Theodore of Mopsuestia, his exegesis, 229
Thiasi and personal, as distinguished from official, religion, 97
Thiemann, on doctrine of Immortality of the Soul as held by Plato, 86
on locality of Lethe, 159
Thomas the Rhymer, Ballad of, quoted for rivers of blood in Elf-land, 121
referred to for the "Three Ways", 144
Thompson, regards the Phaedrus Myth as a Rhetorical Paradigm, 297
regards the Phaedrus Myth as an Allegory, 297, 300
Three Ways, the, Ballad of Thomas the Rhymer referred to for, 144
the three parts of Dante's D.C. correspond to, 145
Tides of Atlantic Ocean, origin of, in Phaedo, 112
Timaeus, the only work of Plato which Dante knew directly, 120
reputation of, in Antiquity and the Middle Age, 206
one of a Trilogy, 252, 274
Toynbee, Dr., on Dante's acquaintance with Claudian, 123

Toynbee, Dr., on Dante's acquaintance with Pliny, 166
referred to for Dante's knowledge of Macrobius, 322
on Dante's knowledge of the version of Timaeus made by Chalcidius, 419
Tozer, Mr., quoted for Dante's knowledge of The Dream of Scipio, 322
on Par. xxxi, 79 ff., 329
Transcendental Feeling, production and regulation of, the end of Poetry, 46, 57, 58
expressed by Dante, last Canto of Par., and V. N., Sonnet xxv, 47, 63, 64
Poets quoted to illustrate means employed for production of, 47-57
means employed by Poetry to produce the Dream-consciousness in which it arises, 58 ff.
in a nascent form accounts for the "magic" of certain kinds of Poetry, 61
explained genetically, 64 ff.
two phases of, 66
Imagination the interpreter of, 67
Its relation to Sense and Understanding, 67
Consciousness awareness of "The Good" in, 69, cf. 85
the beginning and end of Metaphysics, 69
Consciousness comes nearest to the object of Metaphysics, Ultimate Reality, in, 69 f.
"Transcendental" as distinguished from "Empirical" Feeling, 351
Tylor, Prof., on the state of the imagination among ancient and savage peoples, 30

Universal, the, of Poetry, 346 ff.

"Vegetative Part of the Soul" fundamental, and source of that implicit Faith in the Value of Life, on which Conduct and Science rest, 64
and "Universal of Poetry", 348 f.
Vehicles, terrestrial, aerial and aethereal, H. More on, 114
aerial, of Souls in Purgatory, Dante on, 115
Vernon, on Lethe and Eunoè, 160
Virgil, where does he localize the River of Lethe? 161
Visualization, colour and form, power of, possessed by Plato, Plutarch and Dante, 342, 343

Volcanic action, explained in *Phaedo*, 112

Volquardsen, his view of the divine sign of Socrates, 26

Votive figures and the Patterns of Lives in the Myth of Er, 158, 159

Wallace, W., on Kant's Ideas of Reason, quoted, 71

Walt Whitman's *Memories of President Lincoln*, quoted for effect produced similar to that produced in Plato's Eschatological Myths, 54 ff.

War, Plato's view of, 403, 404

Ward, Prof., his *Naturalism and Agnosticism* referred to, 426

Weismann, Prof., referred to, 426

Westcott, Bishop, on Aeschylus' view of the Condition of the Dead, 89

Wilamowitz-Möllendorff, on Voyage of Odysseus to Hades, as Orphic episode in *Odyssey*, 92

Witchcraft, Cudworth's and Smith's belief in, 118

Witchcraft, H. More's belief in, 118

Wordsworth, his lines beginning "There was a boy" quoted to illustrate the nature of "poetic effect", 60

on relation of Poetry to Science, 303

on place of metre in Poetry, 352

Yeats, Mr. W. B., referred to for the idea of "poems spoken to a harp", 355

Zagreus Myth, 232

compared with that told by Aristophanes in the *Symposium*, 365 ff.

Zeller, on the divine sign of Socrates, 26

on doctrine of Immortality of the Soul as held by Plato, 86, 96

on allegorization of Homer by the Stoics, 225

on Neo-Platonic allegorization, 235

on Pre-existence and Recollection, 304